Social Insurance, Informality, and Labor Markets

IDB IZA THE WORLD BANK

Social Insurance, Informality, and Labor Markets

How to Protect Workers While Creating Good Jobs

Edited by
Markus Frölich
David Kaplan
Carmen Pagés
Jamele Rigolini
David Robalino

OXFORD
UNIVERSITY PRESS

OXFORD
UNIVERSITY PRESS

Great Clarendon Street, Oxford, OX2 6DP,
United Kingdom

Oxford University Press is a department of the University of Oxford.
It furthers the University's objective of excellence in research, scholarship,
and education by publishing worldwide. Oxford is a registered trade mark of
Oxford University Press in the UK and in certain other countries

First Edition published in 2014

Impression: 1

Published in the United States of America by Oxford University Press
198 Madison Avenue, New York, NY 10016, United States of America

British Library Cataloguing in Publication Data
Data available

Library of Congress Control Number: 2014949667

ISBN 978–0–19–968523–3

Printed and bound by
CPI Group (UK) Ltd, Croydon, CR0 4YY

Contents

Part II Setting the Mandate of the Insurance Programs and Designing Redistributive Arrangements

Part III Financing Social Insurance Programs

List of Figures

List of Tables

Preface*

The performance of Bismarckian contributory social insurance programs around the developing world has been somewhat disappointing. Old-age pensions, health insurance, or unemployment benefits cover only a minority of workers, generally those in large formal firms and the public sector. Workers in small informal enterprises or those who are self-employed or farmers are not part of the insurance programs, leaving a large fraction of the population without insurance. In addition, there are concerns that the design of the systems themselves can have negative effects on labor markets, possibly incentivizing informal employment.

This book reviews the evidence regarding the effects of social insurance programs on labor market outcomes and discusses options to improve their design and implementation with the aim of achieving universal coverage, while simultaneously creating good jobs. It brings together a collection of 15 chapters several of which were presented at the joint conference of the World Bank (WB), the Institute for the Study of Labor (IZA), and the Inter-American Development Bank (IDB) on *Employment and Development* that took place in Mexico City on May 30th – June 1st, 2011. This high-ranking expert meeting was part of a conference series initiated in 2006 in order to stimulate research and knowledge exchange on the topic of development economics.

The World Bank, IZA and the Inter-American Development Bank share a common mission in promoting rigorous research and evidence-based policy analysis to support countries with the design and

* The editors would like to thank all contributing authors and Oxford University Press for effective cooperation during the work on the book. IZA prepared the complete typesetting and index. Mainly, Benedikt Kliche did a perfect job in bringing the volume into shape.

implementation of labor policies to create and provide access to jobs. As an independent think tank concentrating on international labor economics and operating the world's largest network of labor economists, IZA serves as a close partner to both Bank's activities in this field.

The chapters in this book focus particularly on Latin America, partly because of the richness of the available data and because of the relevance of the topic for this region. Yet, many of the findings and policy recommendations apply to other emerging countries with large informal sectors as well. The book starts with an overview that conceptualizes the links between the social insurance system and labor markets, and summarizes the main conclusions and messages from the various chapters. The main message is that social insurance programs can affect both the behaviors of workers and employers through the taxes and subsidies that they generate. These taxes and subsidies can be explicit or implicit. Payroll taxes, for instance, are an explicit tax on employers that can discourage the creation of formal jobs. Small and low productivity firms in particular might not be able to afford these taxes. Non-contributory health insurance or social pensions, on the other hand, are explicit subsidies often targeted to informal sector workers. These explicit subsidies can act as a tax on formal employment (i.e., somebody taking a formal jobs loses the subsidy) and therefore have the potential to promote informality or at least reduce the contribution densities to social security.

But there are also implicit taxes and subsidies that emerge because, in many programs, contributions are not linked to benefits. Some individuals contribute more than the value of the benefits they receive (a tax), while others contribute less (a subsidy). These implicit taxes and subsides are therefore not allocated based on means or where individuals work, but depend on their preferences and behaviors: how much they value the bundle of social benefits, how often they use health services, how long they remain unemployed, how long they contribute to the social security, or when they retire. Workers are likely to change these behaviors in ways that reduce the implicit taxes while increasing the subsidies. They can, for instance, evade the social security, stay unemployed for longer or retire early.

The first chapter of this volume thoroughly discusses the manifold interactions of social insurance, informality, and labor markets in order to set the floor for the 14 topical chapters to follow. The reminder of the book is structured into three different parts: Assessing the Effects of Social Insurance on Labor Markets (Part I), Setting the Mandate of the

Insurance Programs and Designing Redistributive Arrangements (Part II) and Financing Social Insurance Programs (Part III).

Assessing the Effects of Social Insurance on Labor Markets

This part of the book starts with a historic overview of social protection systems in Latin America that shows how social insurance programs were linked to formal labor contracts (Chapter 2). It should be expected therefore that changes in the design of these programs, as well as in the programs targeted to workers without formal contracts, would affect the behaviors of workers and employers. The next four chapters look at these potential effects in the case of pensions, health, unemployment and welfare transfers. Their findings show that these effects can be sufficiently important to deserve consideration when designing or reforming programs.

For instance, the evaluation of a health reform in Uruguay shows that when the bundle of social programs includes benefits that are not valued by all workers fewer will take jobs with a formal contract (Chapter 3). There is also evidence from Mexico's *Seguro Popular* indicating that non-contributory programs can provide incentives for informality (Chapter 4). Regarding unemployment benefits, analytical work in Malaysia suggests that classic unemployment insurance where redistribution is implicit can reduce formal employment (Chapter 5). Finally, the most recent pension reform in Chile and cross-country studies for countries in Eastern Europe and Central Asia indicate that the subsidies and taxes that emerge from social insurance (and assistance programs) can provide incentives to drop out of the labor force or reduce contributions to the social insurance (Chapter 6).

Setting the Mandate of the Insurance Programs and Designing Redistributive Arrangements

The chapters in this part of the book show that more flexibility in the choice of the bundle of programs and more transparency in the design of various subsidies can improve the incentives to enroll and help to increase equity.

An analysis of the literature on behavioral economics suggests that because of the lack of skills, knowledge, and psychological biases many individuals are unlikely to save enough or purchase sufficient insurance to manage various risks (Chapter 7). Governments therefore have a role in developing and promoting social insurance programs and, probably, developing financial literacy programs. However, because different individuals have different preferences and budget constraints, having a single universal mandate or bundle of benefits for all is not efficient. The analytical work on savings for old-age pensions in Chile shows, for instance, that optimal levels of savings and the portfolio of investments vary considerably among individuals based on age, education levels, and, very important, the level and dynamics of labor income (Chapter 8).

Regarding redistribution, there is a general recognition of the importance of various types of subsidies to achieve broader coverage, since many individuals simply cannot afford to save or participate. The problem with many social insurance programs, however, is that redistribution is implicit and can be regressive. This happens when contributions are not linked to benefits and the subsidies the individuals receive are more related to their behaviors than their means. The studies of pensions and unemployment benefits in Argentina, Brazil, Chile, Uruguay, and Mexico show that, contrary to what many might assume, the Chilean pension system in which contributions are linked to benefits and subsidies are targeted to lower income workers, is the most equitable (Chapters 9 and 10). There is also evidence that, with a fixed budget constraint, targeted subsidies can be more effective in reducing poverty than universal transfers (Chapter 11). Indeed the latter risk spreading resources too thin across the entire population, of which a large fraction might not necessarily need such transfers. The downside is that targeting is costly and it may lead to poverty traps if beyond a certain level small increases in earnings imply an abrupt reduction in benefits.

Financing a Universal Social Insurance System

The chapters in the last part of the book point to the need for rethinking financing arrangements, aiming to reduce perceived tax-wedges and provide incentives to create and take formal jobs.

Evidence from Eastern and Central Europe as well as from Latin America shows that a higher tax-wedge is indeed associated with a higher level of informality (Chapter 12). And although the empirical evidence is thin, theory suggests that consumption taxes can mobilize the same amount of revenues as payroll taxes with a lower distortion in labor markets (Chapter 13). Simulations in the case of Mexico using a General Equilibrium Model illustrate how universal pension and health insurance could be financed via a value-added-tax, while payroll taxes are eliminated (Chapter 14).

The discussion of social insurance financing arrangements in the case of Latin America, however, also points to the need not to consider all social security contributions as taxes. Many workers are likely to value at least part of the benefits they receive from the social security. The proper definition of the tax-wedge therefore should be the difference between the total costs of labor and take home pay augmented by the value of the bundle of social insurance benefits (Chapter 15).

Conclusions

Clearly, the various contributions in the book present only a partial assessment of the links between social insurance programs and labor markets and it is not possible therefore to reach definite conclusions and policy recommendations. Much more research and policy analysis is still required. There are nonetheless some general principles that countries can consider in order to expand the coverage of current programs while reducing potential distortions on labor markets:

Have more Flexibility When Setting the Mandate, or Bundle of Benefits, of Social Insurance Programs

Simply because individuals have different preferences and needs, offering to all the same bundle of benefits is likely to create groups that do not value part of what they get or who do not get what they need. Countries instead could focus on only offering a basic and universal level of benefits for core risks (pensions, health insurance, invalidity, and unemployment benefits). Individuals would then be encouraged to add benefits and/or opt for different investments portfolios (in the case of savings schemes).

Make Redistributive Arrangements Transparent and Explicit

To be able to expand the coverage of insurance programs to all workers there is a need for subsidies to either match contributions or finance all or part of the cost of benefits. It seems important, however, to make these subsidies explicit and, depending on fiscal space and different demands for limited public resources, targeted to those who need them the most. To this end, contributory systems would need to link contributions to benefits. In this regard, situations should be avoided in which formal workers are asked to pay for benefits that they would receive for free in the informal sector. In other words, given the cost of a bundle of social insurance benefits, a decision would be made about which part to be financed by individuals (and their employers when available) and which part to be financed through subsidies.

Reduce Tax-wedges

The evidence regarding the effect of tax-wedges on formal employment is strong. It is not only that as the cost of labor increases firms are likely to hire fewer workers and use more capital. Among small and low productivity firms, high tax-wedges might simply not be affordable. Reducing the mandate of the programs and giving more choice to individuals is one way to reduce the perceived tax-wedge. In addition, countries should consider financing all redistributive arrangements from general revenues and not via payroll taxes.

These general principles can lead to different policies in different countries, based on economic, institutional, and political conditions. For instance, where institutional capacity is limited having insurance programs with varying levels of benefits for different workers might not be an option. Similarly, reducing tax-wedges in countries with a high tax-burden and no fiscal space can simply be infeasible. On the other hand, countries that are reforming wasteful subsidies or food subsidies could use part of the savings to reduce payroll taxes. Local conditions will also dictate the extent of redistributive arrangements. Resource rich countries might be able to afford offering a bundle of social insurance to all workers, regardless of their income, and eliminate contributory programs. Others, on the other hand, might want to focus subsidies on those individuals that need them the most, while taking care not to generated undesirable incentives in the labor market.

In all cases, these policy choices will have to be driven by informed discussions among the various stakeholders and social partners. We hope that this book will be useful in these discussions by flagging some of the problems that can arise when designing and implementing social insurance programs.

March 2014

Markus Frölich, David Kaplan, Carmen Pagés,
Jamele Rigolini, David Robalino

1

Social Insurance, Informality, and Labor Markets: How to Protect Workers While Creating Good Jobs

Carmen Pagés
Jamele Rigolini
David Robalino

1.1. Introduction

Most countries implement mandatory insurance and savings programs to help individuals manage risks such as unemployment, disability, illness, longevity, or death. These schemes are often based on a "Bismarckian" model, where benefits are financed by mandatory contributions levied on salaried employment. This type of model faces severe coverage challenges in low and middle income countries, where a substantial part of the labor force, often the majority, is self-employed, or works in subsistence agriculture. In addition, in these countries, a large proportion of salaried employment does not contribute to mandatory insurance programs. There are various reasons for this: small-, low-productivity firms might not be able to afford the necessary contributions, others are exempted from the mandate, and others, in the presence of low enforcement capacity, simply choose to evade. To cope with these challenges, in recent years, many countries have created non-contributory schemes to cover individuals with low or limited capacity to contribute who are working in the informal sector (see Chapter 2 by Kaplan and Levy). Still, in most countries coverage remains far from universal.

Although most of the policy discussions on social insurance have focused on issues related to equity, coverage, and financial sustainability, more recently, concerns have been raised about the effects that poorly designed insurance programs can have on labor markets. The empirical evidence is scant, but at least, theoretically, distortions may be generated from both the supply and demand sides. From the supply side, for instance, non-contributory programs targeted to informal workers can provide incentives to take informal jobs.[1] Social insurance may also reduce incentives to switch jobs if benefits are not portable; provide incentives to withdraw early from the labor force if there are generous early retirement provisions; or reduce incentives to search for jobs when there are generous unemployment benefits. From the demand side, payroll taxes used to finance many programs can provide incentives to operate informally, or to offer informal contracts to workers, particularly when productivity levels are low.

This book aims to shed light on the question of how relevant these distortions are and what can be done to reduce them while providing adequate protection to workers. In this overview we conceptualize the linkages between the social insurance system of a country and the labor market and summarize the main findings and policy recommendations from the different chapters. The overall message is that social insurance programs can affect the level and structure of employment of a country and that these effects can be important enough to deserve consideration. In part, they are explained by a series of explicit and implicit taxes and subsidies that emerge as part of the design of the programs. Going forward, there are a few general principles that countries can follow to expand coverage while reducing potential distortions in labor markets. First, giving more flexibility to individuals in the choice of the bundle of programs, the level of benefits, and the portfolio of investments (in the case of savings programs), while providing better information and incentives to enroll. Second, relying on explicit, integrated, in some circumstances means-targeted redistributive arrangements in order to better contribute to reduce poverty and inequality. Finally, from the point of view of labor markets, countries should aim to reduce perceived tax-wedges. This could be done by better linking contributions to benefits, improving the quality of services, and financing redistributive arrangements through general revenues.

1.2. Conceptualizing the Links Between Social Insurance and the Labor Market

When social insurance programs are linked to the labor market status of workers, both in terms of eligibility for benefits and in terms of financing, they can affect labor supply and labor demand decisions. As described by Kaplan and Levy in this volume (Chapter 2), the tight link between social insurance and labor market status in Latin America (as in many other emerging countriewie ss) is in part due to a series of historical and financial considerations. When social-security institutes were founded in Latin America in the 1940s and 1950s, most countries lacked the ability to collect general taxes from sources such as income or value-added taxes. Given the inability to finance some form of universal social insurance with general taxation, most countries implemented contributory (Bismarckian) social security systems financed with payroll contributions paid for, and for the exclusive benefit, of formal salaried workers.

In a Bismarckian system, the demand side of the labor market can be affected through payroll taxes (paid by employers) and social security contributions (paid by employees) that are often used to finance social insurance programs. These taxes/contributions increase the wedge between the cost of labor and take-home pay and can contribute to reduce formal employment, especially in low and middle income countries with low enforcement capacity. However, as discussed by Gillingham and Jousten at the end of the book (Chapter 15), it is important to note that not all contributions (by the employer and employee) to social security should be considered a tax. Instead, the focus should be on the perceived gap or wedge between the value of social insurance benefits to workers (measured by their willingness to pay) and actual social security contributions.

A number of factors may influence the perceived gap or "tax" component of social insurance. Perceived tax-wedges can emerge if individuals do not value the benefits offered and, given the choice, would either prefer not to purchase them or purchase less of them. As discussed in the second part of the book, how much workers value benefits is not always however the result of a rational and fully informed process - myopia, for instance, can lead workers left to their own devices to choose to buy less insurance and/or have lower savings rates. Another factor are risk-pooling arrangements, which often include an element of systematic, and often implicit, redistribution (e.g., from young to old workers in the case of health) that not all workers value.

In general, however, there are common design problems that may increase the gap between the actual costs of participating in the mandatory system and the perceived benefits. These may include, among others, poor quality of services, excessive "bundling" of benefits that are not universally valued, and contributions that are not linked to expected benefits (and therefore some individuals pay more than what they receive, with the surcharge financing the benefits of others). One example is when the benefit from a social insurance program does not vary across workers, while the contribution increases with wages, creating potentially large perceived tax-wedges for high-income workers. This problem is most obvious in the case of health insurance. Another example is when the social insurance program includes a benefit that is of value to only a subset of the participants, such as maternity benefits, which are of much greater value to workers who are of child-bearing age and want to have a family. In pensions, a gap may also subsist when the implicit rate of return on contributions is perceived by the worker to be too low. In essence, while employees may value some of the benefits that are provided by social security, and may be willing to pay for them, a real or perceived tax-wedge can remain.

This tax-wedge can provide incentives for employers to operate "informally," because it becomes more difficult to transfer the cost of insurance to workers in the form of lower wages. In that case, social insurance implies an increase in labor costs which may induce firms to offer informal contracts to some of their employees (particularly low-skilled workers), or simply hire fewer workers. It has been observed, for instance, that in some countries, firms tend to maintain a size and organizational structure that legally exempt them from the mandate of the social security or other labor regulations (Garicano, Lelarge, and Van Reenen 2012). Other firms simply might not have the level of productivity needed to afford labor and social insurance costs and therefore they self-select in the informal sector. Transfers to the unemployed that take the form of severance pay can also constrain decisions to dismiss workers and, as a result, can reduce incentives to hire formally.

The social insurance system can also affect labor supply. Tax-wedges, real or perceived, can provide incentives to workers for taking informal jobs or becoming self-employed (see Levy 2008). In addition, tax-wedges can interact with subsidies offered by social insurance programs, which can be of two types. First, *explicit* subsidies given to workers in the informal sector by means of "non-contributory" social insurance programs (e.g., health or pensions), which provide benefits to the uninsured and operate in parallel to contributory systems. Because formal workers pay for their benefits while informal workers get them free of costs, non-contributory programs can act as an additional tax on formal employment and provide incentives to enter the informal sector as wage employees or self-employed (see Levy 2008). The second are *implicit* subsidies *within* the contributory social insurance system. These take various forms, including "above market" rates of return on contributions, minimum pension guarantees, minimum unemployment benefits, or provisions for early retirement which are not actuarially fair (i.e., they do not take into account the full cost related to paying pensions for longer). These subsidies can also distort incentives and encourage early retirement, shorter enrollment periods in the social security, or reduce job-search efforts, leading to longer unemployment spells.

To date, however, many of these arguments remain working hypotheses. While the expected sign of the effects is often clear, their magnitude is uncertain. There has not been enough effort to document how different design features of the social insurance system affect the behaviors of firms and workers. This is particularly true when it comes to the effects of benefit payments on informality, inactivity and unemployment. The first part of this book aims to improve our understanding of these effects.

1.3. Assessing the Effects of Social Insurance on Labor Markets

Estimating the effects of insurance on behavior and outcomes is not trivial. Several of the chapters in this volume, however, take advantage of episodes of reform in social insurance to assess the impact of changes in the design and parameters of alternative programs on workers' and firms' behavior. The focus is on the effects that health insurance, pension, and unemployment benefits can have on formal and informal employment, unemployment, and inactivity. One of the chapters also analyzes the effects of payroll taxes on total employment levels.

The tight link between social insurance and the formal labor market makes the decision of whether to work or operate in the formal or informal sector one of the key margins of possible adjustment by workers and firms. There is an ongoing discussion in the literature on whether informal employment can be better explained as a situation of exclusion (informal workers would like to work in the formal sector but they cannot find formal sector jobs) or voluntary exit (informal workers escape the formal ector in order to avoid paying for social insurance benefits to which they assign little value). A parallel discussion frames these alternatives in terms of whether labor markets are segmented or not.

Two chapters identify effects that corroborate the predictions of models where (at least some) workers choose between formal and informal jobs. Bérgolo and Cruces (Chapter 3) find that an increase in workers' valuation of social security benefits increases the probability of formal employment, defined as being registered in the social security. The authors take advantage of a health reform enacted in Uruguay in 2007, which extended health care coverage to the children under 18 of insured workers. To pay for such benefits, contributions increased for all workers, with higher premia for workers with children under 18 years old. The authors compare the probability of not being registered in social security for individuals with and without children under 18 years old before and after the reform. As it could be expected, the authors find that the health care reform significantly reduced private sector informal salaried employment for workers with at least one child (the group affected by the reform) relative to those with no children (the group not affected by the reform) by 5 percentage points. Interestingly, the effects were more important among women than among men, perhaps because they value more the benefits for their children. The effects were also larger among workers with secondary or tertiary education and for workers employed in smaller firms. The results hold when the authors take into account that household members may make joint decisions, and thus defining the household as the unit of observation. They find that the reform reduced the probability that both spouses were working informally, relative to households where at least one spouse worked formally.

Chapter 4 by Bosch, Cobacho, and Pagés looks at the other side of the coin, that is, whether providing benefits free of charge to those who work in the informal sector increases informality. The authors summarize evidence examining the effects of the introduction of *Se-*

guro Popular in Mexico, a far reaching and ambitious program intended to provide health insurance to all workers not affiliated to social security. The program covers a pre-determined set of procedures and treatments, which have increased over time. While social security provides more and better coverage, the difference in benefits between the two types of programs has narrowed over time. Originally, the program intended to charge copayments to beneficiaries depending on income. In practice however, copayments have not taken place and the program is virtually free of charge. The analysis of the effects of *Seguro Popular* is interesting because of the program size, and also because it is representative of a wider trend: the expansion of non-contributory programs intended to cover the informal sector coexisting with similar social security programs paid for, at least partly, with the contributions of the affiliates.

Most of the studies measuring the impact of *Seguro Popular* take advantage of the gradual introduction of the program across Mexican states. In that way, studies compare formality shares at the individual, household and municipality level, in municipalities that already benefit from *Seguro Popular* relative to municipalities that do not. Overall, there is strong evidence that the program has been very effective at increasing health care coverage and reducing health expenditures for Mexican families. There is no evidence yet of statistically significant impacts on health outcomes, but those are likely to materialize in the future. At the same time, however, the establishment of a parallel non-contributory health system has so far generated an increase in the share of informal employment between 0.4 and 1 percentage points, or equivalently between 160,000 and 400,000 jobs over the 2002-10 period. That is equivalent to 8-20% of net formal job creation during the same period.

Bosch, Cobacho, and Pagés also provide evidence of the effects of similar non-contributory health programs in Mexico City and in Colombia. In Mexico City, a large negative impact on social security affiliation of least educated women was registered after the introduction of the program. In particular, the probability that low skilled women (high school education or less) worked in the formal sector was reduced between 4 to 9.7 percentage points after the policy change. Similar results have also been found in Colombia after the introduction of a non-contributory health program for informal workers. Such program increased informality between 2 and 4 percentage points, an effect larger than in Mexico.

In addition, the chapter shows that programs such as *Seguro Popular* can further affect workers' incentives in other relevant dimensions. They show, for instance, that the rollout of *Seguro Popular* was associated with an increase of flows from work to inactivity, and a decline of flows out of unemployment. These findings suggest that *Seguro Popular* made, for some, inactivity and unemployment more attractive.

Transfers through the pension system can also affect labor markets. In a companion paper to their contribution to this volume, Attanasio, Meghir, and Otero (2012) describe the effects that an ambitious reform in Chile, which aimed at providing a minimum level of pensions to those who did not contribute enough during their active life, had on labor market participation and formal/informal work choices. In addition to a basic social pension, the reform instituted a pension subsidy to women designed to compensate for the fact that women tend to leave the labor market (and therefore interrupt their pension contributions) after having children. The reform also strengthened the contributory component of the system by subsidizing contributions for young workers, as well as offering tax incentives aimed at increasing the contributions of the self-employed. The authors find that the introduction of a basic social pension for workers with insufficient contributions had a negative effect on labor market formality: the reform led to a reduction in informal employment of 4.1 percent for workers older than 40 years old. The reform also increased the propensity for women with children to drop out of the labor market due to the income effect associated with the pension subsidy for each child.

Unemployment benefits is another social insurance program that is becoming increasingly popular in middle income countries. On the one hand, the fact that unemployment insurance conditions a monetary payment on unemployment status makes one suspect that the scheme might generate incentives against finding or keeping a job. On the other hand, unemployment insurance may have positive effects on the labor market if they help workers find better jobs. Indeed, to the extent that unemployed workers face liquidity constraints, unemployment subsidies might permit workers to engage in more efficient search and find jobs that better match their skills and/or offer higher and more stable salaries. But how large are these effects?

Chapter 5 by Margolis, Navarro, and Robalino uses a Diamond-Mortensen-Pissarides labor market model of job search to assess the magnitude of labor market distortions associated with unemployment insurance in middle income countries. The authors consider four possible states for active workers: unemployment, self-employment, formal salaried work, and informal salaried work, and calibrate the parameters of the model to match the characteristics of the Malaysian labor market, which currently has no unemployment insurance. They find that, for replacement rates below 50 percent, the effects of unemployment insurance on the labor market are modest: unemployment insurance would only marginally increase the unemployment rate, although it would lead some unskilled workers to transit to self-employment. A larger replacement rate, however, would have a larger impact on the unemployment rate and would also induce higher-skilled workers to transit to self-employment. Part of the reason is that unemployment insurance induces more workers to wait for the "right" job. This increases the tightness of the labor market (i.e., the ratio between job seekers and vacancies) and reduces the probability of being offered formal and informal jobs. Individuals who wait too long might then end up having to take self-employment opportunities. The non-linear relationship between the generosity of benefits and the types of workers drawn to self-employment illustrates the complex nature of unemployment insurance in a labor market.

In Chapter 6, Koettl and Weber address the question of whether it is worthwhile for the working age population to engage in formal employment in New Eastern European Member States of the European Union. They calculate a formalization tax rate that is linked to the level of the tax-wedge and forgone social assistance (i.e. transfers that would be forgone when formal jobs are taken). The main finding of the descriptive analysis is that the disincentives for formal work – when measured through the formalization tax rate – are especially high for low-wage earners. This suggests that formal work might not pay in this segment of the labor market, in particular for the so-called mini-jobs and midi-jobs (low paying part-time work). In the empirical analysis the authors further find a significant positive correlation between the formalization tax rate and the incidence of being informal. Controlling for individual and job characteristics, the higher the formalization tax rate or the marginal effective tax rates (METR) that individuals are facing is – that is, the higher disincentives for formal work – the higher the likelihood to work informally. The main driver of the disincentives in the case of the New Eastern European Member States seem to be forgone transfers.

All in all, this new wave of studies shows that the design of social insurance can affect economic behavior, notably in one crucial aspect for labor markets in developing countries: the formal/informal work margin. The magnitude of the measured distortions will likely depend on the characteristics of the programs and the context where they operate. But the effects seem to be large enough to deserve attention, and call for improvements in program design in order to reduce distortions while providing adequate protection to workers. This does not imply that the objective of policy should be to eliminate all labor market distortions. As stated by Barr and Diamond (2006), there is no way of designing social insurance and protecting workers without altering economic incentives. But the potentially distortive effects of social insurance must be taken into account as part of any reform endeavor, and must be weighed against the objectives achieved by social insurance. The next part of the book offers some lessons on how to move forward in this balancing act.

1.4. Setting the Mandate of the Insurance Programs

The effectiveness of social insurance systems in helping individuals manage social risks depends, to a large extent, on the bundle of benefits offered, and the redistributive arrangements used to reach individuals with no or limited contributory capacity. This part first discusses issues in defining the bundle and level of benefits, taking into account the heterogeneity of beneficiaries in terms of their risk profiles, preferences, and ability to save or afford insurance. Second, it looks at how to implement redistributive arrangements that are progressive, fiscally sustainable, and that minimize some of the labor market distortions discussed above.

1.4.1. Defining the Mandate of the Social Insurance System

A first policy question is whether social insurance programs should be mandatory. Mandatory programs are often justified based on imperfections in insurance markets that lead to adverse selection, and on the obscure term of "myopia," i.e. the inability or unwillingness of individuals to plan for the future and make proper strategic choices about savings and insurance over their lifetime.[2]

Chapter 7 by Robert Holzmann focuses on the issue of "myopia." The author shows that the concept embodies three very different aspects that call for different types of policy interventions: (i) lack of knowledge about financial concepts and products; (ii) limited cognitive abilities to solve complex inter-temporal problems regarding savings, investments, and insurance; and (iii) psychological factors that distort individual perceptions about risks and the future and that make it difficult to commit to save enough or purchase sufficient insurance. The chapter reviews countries' efforts to address these problems through programs aiming to improve financial literacy and to raise awareness about the importance of savings and insurance. It also discusses initiatives, mostly coming from the private sector and inspired by the work of behavioral economists and psychologists, to try to "nudge" individuals to save more or purchase more insurance.

Regarding interventions to improve financial literacy, Holzmann identifies two approaches that have been piloted. The first is a cognitive approach where the focus is on providing general knowledge about financial concepts and products, augmented by skills to apply this knowledge to achieve "good" financial behavior. The second is an outcomes-based approach that aims to directly influence behaviors that are considered important for "good" financial outcomes. These include, for instance, managing money (i.e., living within one's means and tracking one's expenditures); planning ahead; making choices based on an understanding of the options available; and knowing when and how to get help. A review of the limited number of evaluations of these two types of interventions however shows mixed results. For example, training programs in school or in the workplace (e.g., retirement seminars) have not shown to increase participation on voluntary savings or insurance plans, even less in mandatory plans. The author argues that this is to be expected because, while improving knowledge, these programs do not deal with the non-cognitive and psychological factors that affect how individuals use their new knowledge and skills.

In terms of interventions that aim to "nudge" certain behaviors, Holzmann describes some success stories. Financial incentives to promote participation in the 401 K retirement saving plan in the United States is one example. Another intervention is to ask individuals to commit to save future increases in earnings. Little is known, however, about how these incentives could work in the case of public programs. For instance, there have been several proposals to match the contributions of informal sector workers to promote their participation in public pension programs (matching contributions, as opposed to tax breaks, make more sense in environments where a majority of workers do not declare their incomes). But there are no evaluations to date offering evidence of the impact of these programs on take-up rates.

The results of the review suggest that governments cannot relinquish mandatory programs. The second question is then, how to define the mandate of these programs, that is, the set and level of benefits offered to individuals at different income levels.

Two chapters of the book point to an issue which is often overlooked: the difficulty in defining a benefit bundle that "fits all sizes." As discussed above, Chapter 3 by Bérgolo and Cruces shows how different individuals (and households) derive different value from the bundle of social insurance benefits. A bundle that provides insurance to children, for instance, is unnecessarily expensive for childless families. Therefore, a universal bundle of social insurance benefits may fail to address the needs of many, reducing their incentives to pay for it under a payroll-based system.

Similarly, Chapter 8 by Sánchez Martín, Jiménez Martín, Robalino, and Todeschini discusses the challenges involved in setting common contribution rates and investment portfolios in mandatory pension programs. The authors show that in an optimal life-cycle context, savings paths, and the composition of the optimal portfolio, depend on observable individual characteristics that affect labor income. They also depend on unobservable, individual preferences. In this environment, a common savings mandate and a single investment portfolio for all workers can be welfare decreasing, particularly if individuals cannot borrow. The chapter analyses initiatives by countries like Chile to offer default portfolios (often adjusted by age) that individuals can then tailor to their needs. Because, as is well known, only few people switch to other portfolios, so it is important to get these defaults right. Yet the chapter suggests that default portfolios tend to systematically deviate from optimal portfolios because they do not take into account variables such as individuals' level of education and their occupation that affect the mean and variance of labor income. Thus, while it might be that myopic individuals make bad investment decisions, the alternatives proposed by governments may not always score better.

The study for Chile also shows that an important design feature that would deserve more analysis in countries with "multi-pillar" systems is what share of the contribution rate should be invested in pay-as-you-go vs. financial assets. This share is usually decided as part of the political process driving pension reform and, as suggested by the chapter, it is unlikely to be the optimal share for many. These types of misallocation of savings may reduce incentives to enroll among certain categories of workers, in particular when enforcement capacity is low.

Both chapters do not question the need for mandatory social insurance, but show a need to have more flexibility in the way the mandate of various programs is defined. More emphasis could be placed on creating awareness among individuals about the risks they face, and on nudging them to enroll in insurance and/or savings programs (which could be public or private) through, for instance, financial incentives. As mentioned before, there have been some positive experiences, in particular in the private sector, and variants for the public sector could be piloted and evaluated.

It is also important to reconsider the bundles of social insurance benefits that are offered, both in terms of composition and level of benefits. One possibility would be to limit the bundle of mandatory social insurance programs to those covering key risks – health, disability, longevity, death, and unemployment. It also seems worth exploring how to give more options to individuals. Governments, for instance, could offer as a default a basic level of benefits for the various programs, but may encourage individuals to opt for more, if needed, by providing information and training. Similarly, individuals could be given more choice in the composition of savings portfolios – including whether to invest in pay-as-you-go or financial assets – and more information to guide them. Clearly, too many choices can be overwhelming for individuals and managing multiple portfolios is administratively complex and costly. The right balance will depend on the institutional capacity of the social security institutions and country characteristics.

1.4.2. Designing Redistributive Arrangements

Redistribution is essential within the social insurance system to cover segments of society that may not be able to afford to participate in risk-pooling or savings programs. Most redistribution that takes place in social insurance systems in Latin America and elsewhere is, however, of the *implicit* type: it takes place because countries often rely on systems that do not link contributions to benefits and some individuals, not necessarily the poorest, *systematically* "get more" than what they put in, while others "get less." These implicit taxes or subsidies are often not related to people's means but to people's behaviors, including enrollment and retirement decisions, the decision to take formal vs. informal sector jobs, and job-search activity.

Part of the reason for the poor performance of implicit redistributive arrangements, especially in pension programs, is that low-income workers may be less likely to access the benefits provided by the social insurance program due to low contribution densities. But eliminating the requirements for minimum vesting periods would render many programs unsustainable, unless benefits are adjusted accordingly. At the same time, implicit redistributive arrangements within the social insurance system can also reduce the willingness to contribute among those who systematically pay more than they receive. To the extent possible, countries would therefore need to rely more on *explicit* redistributive arrangements, ideally financed out of general revenues. But how these arrangements are designed matters. As discussed above, non-contributory programs that operate in parallel to contributory programs can act as a tax on formal employment, and if transfers are too high there can be negative effects on labor supply. The alternative would be to move to an integrated system of subsidies probably allocated on the basis of means, rather than on the basis of where individuals work. The subsidies, for instance, could take the form of *ex-ante* transfers to top-up the contributions of plan members, or *ex-post* transfers to complement the benefits. These two types of designs are likely to have different effects on behaviors and the finances of the system. For example, in the case of pensions, matching contributions could in principle provide incentives to contribute and therefore reduce the need for *ex-post* transfers.

A key policy decision in designing these explicit transfers is whether and how to target. Should redistributive transfers be universal, or concentrated in low income individuals with limited savings capacity? Universal transfers are less distortive because they only create an income effect, and are unlikely to change much labor supply decisions. At the same time, as shown in Chapter 11 by Acosta, Leite, and Rigolini, universal programs can be significantly more expensive and are thus less effective in reducing poverty and inequality: with limited budgets, a universal transfer can end up "spreading resources too thin," in particular in middle income countries where only a minority may need such transfers (in low income settings or areas with widespread poverty, it can however make more sense to consider universal transfers).

When subsidies are means-tested, attention needs to be given to the implicit marginal tax rates that are created. Classic minimum pension guarantees, for instance, impose a 100 percent marginal tax on contributions: for each unit increase in the contributory pension, the minimum pension guarantee is also reduced by one unit. This may reduce incentives to contribute, particularly among low-income workers who know that, regardless of contributions densities, they will end-up retiring with the minimum. These marginal tax rates can be reduced, for instance, by reducing the subsidy gradually as pension income increases: the Chilean pension system is a good example of how this can be done, although a transfer that is too high may also affect labor supply through its income effect. In principle, minimum unemployment benefits could also be set at their maximum at the bottom of the income distribution and then decline gradually becoming zero after a given level of income.

Things can be more difficult in the case of *ex-ante* transfers – matching contributions – because of the need to be able to assess earnings, particularly outside of the formal sector. Proxy-means tests have proven successful in targeting transfers to the poor, but it is unclear that they can do the same in the middle of the income distribution (see Ribe et al. 2012). Moreover, given the sophistication of some of these schemes, attention should also be devoted to assess countries' capacity to implement them.

1.5. Financing a Universal Social Insurance System

A majority of countries in Latin America, as well as in other regions, finance social insurance programs through payroll taxes (paid by the employer) and individual contributions (paid by the employee). While, historically, it may have been the only way to develop social insurance programs, this type of financing now faces two major problems. First, payroll-based programs have failed to include a large number of self-employed, low-income wage employees, and agricultural workers. Second, payroll taxes may drive low-productivity firms to operate in the informal sector or offer informal work to some of their workers, also reducing coverage and possibly overall productivity (see Levy 2008; Ribe et al. 2012).

Chapter 12 by Lehmann and Muravyev presents a cross-country analysis for Eastern and Central Europe and Latin America, of the effects of employment protection legislation and the tax-wedge on a broad measure of informality – unreported income from the production of legal goods and services. The authors find evidence that a higher tax-wedge is associated with a higher level of informality. On average, a 1 percentage point increase in the tax-wedge is associated with a 0.13 percentage points increase in informality. Other studies have found that a one percentage point increase in the tax-wedge can reduce formal employment by between 0.1 and 0.5 percentage points (see World Bank 2013) and the most affected are likely to be unskilled workers.

These effects, of course, are country specific and will depend on various economic and institutional factors. Still, an important policy question is whether alternative financing mechanisms can be considered in order to reduce or eliminate payroll taxes and individual contributions. Reducing payroll taxes and individual contributions would imply relying more on general revenues. In essence, part of the cost of the bundle of social insurance benefits would be financed by general revenues (a same level for all or different levels based on means), while the difference is financed by individual and employer contributions linked to benefits. All in all, depending on the wiggle room that countries have to reallocate public expenditures towards insurance programs, more reliance on general revenues implies, however, finding ways to raise revenues from non-payroll taxes.

There are many taxes that could be considered and discussing their economic implications is outside the scope of the book. One option that has been proposed, and that is analyzed in Chapter 13 by Bird and Smart, is a consumption tax. The chapter looks at the pros and cons of moving from payroll taxation to value-added tax (VAT) financing in a context of high informal activity (measured, in this case, as firms evading taxes). The authors look at which form of financing minimizes labor market distortions and informal activity for a given level of revenues. They show that, to the extent that firms, in addition to workers, also choose whether to operate formally or informally, differences between labor (i.e. payroll) taxation and VAT are subtle. Either tax (or any tax, for that matter) creates incentives for tax evasion and informality. The nature and magnitude of these incentives differ nonetheless under VAT and payroll taxation, in part, by virtue of their different legal and economic structures. The authors argue that in principle, VAT has enforcement advantages over payroll taxation, because invoices may be checked, but although there is some evidence supporting this conclusion, the importance of this difference in practice seems to remain an open question. But using a simple model of a small open economy with heterogeneous firms, the authors also show that when there is an informal sector, a payroll tax can be more distortive than a consumption tax. In other words, for a given payroll tax τ, there is a value-added tax τ' that delivers the same real wage, the same level of economic activity, and the same shares of formal and informal employment, but *higher* tax revenues paid to the government. While these implications remain to be tested empirically, overall their analysis suggests that moving towards VAT taxation, in addition to its main advantage of de-linking, at least part of, social benefits from an individual's labor market status, may deliver positive impacts on revenues and informal activity.

Bird and Smart, however, do not address the fiscal implications of reaching universal coverage. Even if financing, at least in part, social insurance through general taxation can reduce labor market distortions and help in achieving universal coverage, the question of fiscal sustainability remains. In Chapter 14 of this volume, Arturo Antón and Fausto Hernández, analyze the feasibility and financial sustainability of a proposal first put forward by Levy (2008) for Mexico to finance universal pensions and health insurance by eliminating payroll taxes and increasing the VAT.

The authors address the question by means of a structural general equilibrium model with tax evasion that they calibrate to reflect the Mexican economy. In their model, there are three types of workers: employees formally registered to the social security systems, unregistered employees, and the self-employed who produce a similar good, albeit less efficiently. The authors consider then three different taxes on firms: value-added taxes, income taxes, and social security contributions, with incentives to evade taxation varying with the type of tax. They find that a move toward VAT financing of social security to achieve universal coverage is not only financially sustainable, but may also reduce labor market distortions (though this latter finding depends, among others, on their assumption of an inelastic labor supply). Specifically, reducing VAT exemptions, and moving towards a uniform VAT rate of 16 percent would allow financing a universal social insurance program that provides similar health and pension benefits than the ones offered now by social security, but to everybody. Moreover, the scheme would be financially viable even after taking into account a transfer to poor households to compensate them for the VAT increase.

1.6. Concluding Remarks

The evidence collected in this book shows that the social insurance system interacts with labor markets in a number of margins. When designing new programs or reforming current ones, policymakers should therefore carefully study how workers and firms would react. Perceived tax-wedges (driven by payroll taxes and the gap between the value of social insurance benefits and what individuals pay) can reduce formal employment; parallel non-contributory programs targeted to the informal sector can promote informality; general transfers, through their income effect, can reduce labor supply; and unemployment insurance can alter choices between unemployment, and formal, informal, and self-employment. The magnitude of these effects ultimately depend on context and the level of the explicit and implicit taxes and subsidies.

The chapters in the volume suggest three types of design enhancements that may improve workers' protection while reducing distortions in labor markets.

First, countries could introduce more flexibility when setting the mandate of social insurance programs. Although difficult to enforce in the presence of large informal sectors, mandatory programs still have a role to play to deal with issues of adverse selection and individuals' myopia. But individual preferences and characteristics could play a larger role in defining the bundle and level of benefits, as well as the portfolio of investments in the case of savings schemes. This could help reduce perceived tax-wedges and improve incentives to enroll. A possible avenue, for further analysis, could be to limit the bundle of social insurance benefits to core risks (very old-age, sickness, disability, long-term unemployment, and death) and providing a basic level of benefits – sufficient not only to prevent poverty but also to smooth consumption. In the case of pensions, for instance, the ILO standard of a 40 percent replacement could be the starting point. Individuals could then be "nudged" into saving more or purchasing additional insurance more specific to their needs within or outside the public system. Individuals could also be offered default investments portfolios that take into account characteristics such age, gender, education, and occupation, and then be given information and guidance to make adjustments that better tailor their needs. In the case of pension systems, for instance, individuals could be given the possibility to decide what share of their contributions is invested in pay-as-you-go assets and what into financial assets.

Second, while redistribution remains a fundamental instrument for protecting the neediest and reducing inequality, there are reasons to prefer explicit redistributive arrangements, possibly, especially if resources are scare, targeted based on means and not on where individuals work.[3] This would allow social insurance programs to focus public resources on those who need them the most; better control the unintended effects on behaviors; and reduce reliance on payroll taxes, thus reducing perceived tax-wedges and improving incentives for formal work. To eliminate implicit redistribution, benefits would need to be linked to contributions. Explicit and integrated subsidies can then be used to top-up the contributions and/or benefits of individuals with low or limited savings capacity regardless of where they work.

Finally, there is a need to rethink financing mechanisms. In contributory systems, perceived tax-wedges can be reduced by better linking contributions to benefits; financing redistribution from general revenues; and giving individuals more choice in defining their bundle of social insurance benefits. But systems purely based on payroll taxes will not achieve universal coverage, in particular in low-enforcement settings common to most low and middle income countries. It is thus worth exploring ways to mobilize additional funds – in the form of individual contributions and other taxes – to finance a basic bundle of benefits for all workers.

Two relevant aspects where the book remains silent is the administrative complexity and political economy associated with the implementation and reform of social protection systems. Several of the reforms discussed here (e.g., targeting subsidies, linking contributions to benefits, introducing more individual choice) imply changes in business processes and improvements in management and information systems. And, although there is a good record of countries at all income levels that have been able to introduce some of these changes, for instance in the context of the implementation of social assistance programs (e.g., Pakistan) or defined contribution pension systems (e.g., Bolivia), the demands in terms of institutional capacity should not be underestimated.

Regarding the political economy, the reform of pensions, unemployment or other insurance programs is never easy. Studies suggest that the reforms that countries are able to implement depend on the quality of their policy making process (see Stein and Tommasi, 2008). The policy making process is affected by the number of political actors, their time horizons and the frequency of their interactions, the nature of the arenas in which they interact, the availability of enforcement mechanisms that bind them to their commitments, and the types of political institutions (e.g., the presidential/parliamentary nature of the government, the electoral rules, and the existence of an independent judiciary). Two challenges in the case of social insurance reforms are *timing* and the *representativeness* of different population groups. The benefits of the reforms are usually long-term, and uncertain, while the costs (e.g., rationalizing benefits) can be short term. Furthermore, those who would benefit the most from the reforms, for example informal sector workers and future generations, are often not well represented in the political process. It could be, however, that by making redistributive and financing arrangements explicit – one of the main ingredients of the reforms discussed above – the tradeoffs between different types of social expenditures become more transparent and that this in turn facilitates political consensus.

A final note is that the chapters in this book have not presented exhaustive evidence on how social insurance programs affect labor markets in general. The impacts discussed in the book depend on countries' enforcement capacities, the specifics of the labor market, workers, human capital and preferences, and overall local conditions. Some distortions that may seem minor under a given setting may become important under different ones, and vice-versa. More research is needed to better understand these effects and to assess the impact of some of the reform proposals discussed here.

Notes

1 Given that there are various alternative definitions of informality routinely used in the literature, it is necessary to clarify what we mean by this term. Throughout this chapter, we refer to informal workers as those not covered by social security, either because they are not mandated to contribute (as it is the case with self-employed workers in some countries) or because their employers evade the mandate.

2 Other justifications such as imperfections in capital markets that preclude access to savings instruments or liquidity constraints, do not necessarily call for mandatory systems.

3 The argument, of course, does not apply to *ex post* redistribution motivated by risk-pooling arguments.

References

Levy, S. (2008). Good Intentions, Bad Outcomes: Social Policy, Informality and Economic Growth in Mexico, Washington, DC: Brookings Institution Press.

Barr, N., Diamond, P. (2006). The Economics of Pensions, in: Oxford Review of Economic Policy, 22(1): 15-39.

Camacho, A., Conover, E., Hoyos, A. (2009). Effects of Colombia's Social Protection System on Workers' Choice between Formal and Informal Employment, Documentos CEDE No. 006003.

Garicano, L., Lelarge, C., Van Reenen, J. (2012). Firm Size Distortions and the Productivity Distribution: Evidence from France, mimeo.

Juárez, L. (2009). Are Informal Workers Compensated for the Lack of Fringe Benefits? Free Health Care as an Instrument for Formality, Centro de Investigación Económica, ITAM Working Papers No. 0804.

Ribe, H., Robalino, D., Walker, I. (2010). From Right to Reality. Incentives, Labor Markets, and Challenges of Universal Coverage in Latin America, Latin American Development Forum Series.

Stein, E., Tommasi, M. (2008). Policymaking in Latin America: How Politics Shapes Policies, Washington, DC: Inter-American Development Bank.

Part I

Assessing the Effects of Social Insurance on Labor Markets

2

The Evolution of Social Security Systems in Latin America*

David S. Kaplan
Santiago Levy

2.1. Introduction

Social security systems in Latin America are characterized by extreme levels of truncation. Some workers are affiliated to contributory (or Bismarckian) pillars in which access is restricted to those who make social security contributions while other workers are left uncovered. Increasingly, some measure of social security protection is being extended to those who fall outside of these contributory systems through non-contributory pillars that are financed out of general revenue.

In this chapter, we review the historical development of this fragmented model of social security. In the first half of the 20th century, contributory social security systems were implemented throughout the region despite the fact that, due to the nature of labor markets, their coverage ended up being restricted to those who chose to comply, or could be forced to comply, with the legal obligation to contribute to social security. In fact, by and large, the incentives generated by the social security systems of the region have increased the share of workers and firms that choose activities that are outside the reach of contributory systems.

We argue that this model was adopted for three reasons. First, the model proved to be successful in European countries. Second, given

* *The views expressed here are the authors' and do not necessarily coincide with those of the Inter-American Development Bank (IDB). We thank Ana Paula Sanchez for very helpful comments.*

the limitations of governments both in terms of their abilities to provide widespread benefits and in terms of tax collection, a model that would have offered wider coverage was infeasible at the time. Third, it was hoped that social security benefits would play a redistributive role in transferring resources from the owners of firms to their workers.

Although the problem of limited coverage of contributory social security was clear – workers in the informal sector would not be covered – the hope was that the coverage problem would resolve itself over time. As a consequence of continued economic development, it was thought that the informal sector would gradually disappear as workers shifted from more "traditional" to more "modern" sectors of the economy. Unfortunately, however, the problem of informality proved to be surprisingly persistent, and indeed potentially made worse by the design of social security systems, leading to the realization that reforms were necessary in order to offer social security coverage to informal workers.

With the basic contributory or Bismarckian system firmly in place, the only way to extend coverage, short of redesigning the entire underlying architecture, was to implement parallel non-contributory pillars to offer coverage to those who fell outside of the contributory pillar. Although the gains in terms of coverage were important, these non-contributory pillars act as a further disincentive for the participation in the contributory pillars.

The fragmented social security systems in which a contributory pillar is complemented by a non-contributory pillar forces the governments of the region to make extremely difficult choices. On the one hand, improving the quality of the non-contributory systems offers protection to those who undoubtedly need it, but also aggravates labor market distortions that generate informality since workers and firms in the formal sector are asked to make social security contributions in return for benefits that are increasingly similar to those obtained for free in the informal sector. The costs to an economy in terms of productivity associated with these distortions may be large. On the other hand, not providing important benefits such as pensions and health care to informal workers, worsens the already unacceptable levels of absence of protection against risks observed in the region.

We argue that, although the region has grown accustomed to a system in which contributory pillars are complemented by non-contributory ones, a system of universal benefits financed out of general revenues may be a more attractive option both in terms of the social protection provided and in terms of the implications for productivity. In order to achieve these benefits, however, the region would have to undertake reforms that change the underlying architecture of the social security system instead of simply adding additional pillars to a social security structure that we believe is ill-suited for the region.

The organization of the rest of the chapter is as follows. We begin by describing Otto von Bismarck's vision for social security, which we argue has formed the basis for the social security systems observed in the region to this day. We then go through the events leading up to the adoption of this model for social security, focusing both on when the model was adopted and why this model was chosen despite its limitations, namely the exclusion of informal sector workers from social security coverage. In an effort to establish the fact that a contributory or Bismarckian system is not the only feasible way to provide social benefits, we contrast this model both with the way that public education is provided and with the vision for social security advanced by Sir William Beveridge in 1942 in Great Britain.

We then discuss the disappointing fact that coverage of contributory social security systems has not been expanding in the region. Although many believed that informal labor markets would gradually disappear as Latin America continued its path of economic development, we then explain how the stubborn persistence of labor informality forced economists to change their views about informality and forced policymakers to design policies that would offer coverage to the informal sector. Despite the fact that each incremental effort to extend coverage had a clear logic and justification, we argue that the legacies of the incremental reform processes observed in Latin America are social security systems with important design flaws when analyzed in their entirety rather than on a component by component basis.

2.2. The Bismarckian Vision of Social Security

The contributory model of social security observed in most countries in Latin America, in which salaried workers are provided benefits financed through social security contributions that are proportional to the wage, is often attributed to Otto von Bismarck. Bismarck's vision for social security, which formed the basis for ambitious reform endeavors such as the Law Concerning Health Insurance for Workers (1883), the Accident Insurance Act (1884), and the Law on Invalidity and Old Age Insurance for Workers, Journeymen and Apprentices (1889). This vision can be summed up by the following famous quote:

> The real grievance of the worker is the insecurity of his existence; he is not sure that he will always have work, he is not sure that he will always be healthy, and he foresees that he will one day be old and unfit to work. If he falls into poverty, even if only through a prolonged illness, he is then completely helpless, left to his own devices, and society does not currently recognize any real obligation towards him beyond the usual help for the poor, even if he has been working all the time ever so faithfully and diligently. The usual help for the poor, however, leaves a lot to be desired, especially in large cities, where it is very much worse than in the country.[1]

This quote reveals the defining feature of the contributory social security systems. Social security benefits are not merely aimed at poverty alleviation, but rather constitute additional benefits that have been earned by workers as a result of their diligent and faithful work. In this sense, Bismarckian social security combines two essential elements: the need for social insurance and the fact the access to this social insurance needs to be earned. Those who have engaged in salaried work and have contributed to the system (or have had contributions made on their behalf) are entitled to social protection beyond what is offered to the population at large when in poverty. This vision that social security rights should be earned is perhaps better exemplified in the following statement from President Harry Truman given on the 10th anniversary of the Social Security Act in the United States:

> A sound system of social security requires careful consideration and preparation. Social security worthy of the name is not a dole or a device for giving everybody something for nothing. True social security must consist of rights which are earned rights – guaranteed by the law of the land. Only that kind of social security is worthy of the men and women who have fought and are now fighting to preserve the heritage and the future of America.[2]

Although the wording of the above quote is much stronger than what would be used by policymakers in Latin America, it is also true access to health care and pensions in Latin America for a long time was conditioned to having "earned" these benefits by making social security contributions. Prior to the rise of parallel non-contributory systems, those who were unable or unwilling to make social security contributions were essentially not covered by the social insurance system.

The central thesis of this chapter is that an important legacy of this Bismarckian vision of social security is the truncation of the welfare states of the Latin America. Either as a result of legal exemptions or as a result of enormous problems of enforcement, independent workers are nearly entirely excluded from social security systems of the region, as are all other workers who are not in a salaried relation with a firm. Furthermore, high percentages of salaried workers choose not to contribute (or are illegally excluded from social security by their employers), which is clear evidence of the fact that the value workers assign to the benefits is often below what they are asked to contribute. As a result of all of these problems, social security coverage rates in Latin America tend to be quite low.

2.3. When Did Latin America Adopt the Bismarckian Model?

Liu (2001) analyzed social security initiatives in the world prior to the 1935 adoption of the U.S. Social Security Act. In this report, Chile was the only country in Latin America classified as having a contributory social security system with "general coverage" before 1935. The Chilean program consisted of old-age, disability, and health benefits. Argentina, Brazil, Cuba, Ecuador, and Uruguay were classified as having contributory social security systems with "coverage not available to major sectors of industry and commerce, limited to selected population groups, such as railroad, bank, public utilities employees, and the like." For the most part, social security simply did not exist in the region prior to 1935.

In January of 1936, however, the International Labour Organization (ILO) held its First Labour Conference of American Member States in Santiago Chile. Among the resolutions adopted was the "Resolution concerning the fundamental principles of social insurance." This resolution, which was later ratified and expanded at the second conference in 1939 in Havana, Cuba, established the Bismarckian model as the standard for the region. In particular, the resolution specifically mentions the salaried worker as the desired target of social insurance scheme by saying:

> Wage earners obtain the means of livelihood for themselves and their families by the regular exercise of a trade in the service of an employer, and any cessation or interruption in their work, whether resulting from industrial accident, sickness, old age, invalidity, premature death or involuntary unemployment, destroys the economic basis of the wage-earning family and causes hardship and privation for the worker and his dependents.[3]

The set of social security benefits agreed upon in the resolutions is for the most part what is observed today in most social security systems in the region. The package of benefits includes financial support in case of temporary or permanent disability, medical insurance, an old age pension, a disability pension, a widower's pension, and coverage in the case of workplace accidents. As far as the financing of such a scheme is concerned, the resolution states:

> Insured persons and their employers should share in providing the financial resources of the insurance scheme, the payment of the joint contribution being effected by the employer, who deducts the insured person's share from his wages.[4]

We therefore see that basic architecture for Latin American social security schemes was essentially agreed upon in 1936. Wage earners would be the target of social security schemes. Furthermore, wage earners would become eligible as beneficiaries due to a combination of payroll deductions and employer contributions made on the employee's behalf.[5]

Under this architecture social security institutes were established throughout the region, all of course under a Bismarckian scheme in which access to social security benefits is linked to the contributions of wage earners. In Ecuador, for example, a social security institute was established in 1935 with a series of expansions of coverage through 1940. Peru established a social security institute in 1936. Numerous countries established social security institutes in the 1940s including Argentina (1946), Colombia (1945), Costa Rica (1941), El Salvador (1949), Guatemala (1946), Mexico (1943), Panama (1941), Paraguay (1943), Uruguay (1943), and Venezuela (1946). This regional trend continued into the 1950s with social security institutes being established in Bolivia (1956), Honduras (1957), and Nicaragua (1956).

It is interesting to note that the participants in the 1936 ILO conference seemed to be aware of the fact that the design of a social security system could have important effects on the labor market decisions of workers. In referring to the qualifying conditions necessary to receive a pension, the resolution states:

> The duration of the qualifying period should not be longer than is strictly necessary to preclude persons from entering insurance with intent to take undue advantage of it and to ensure some consideration for the benefits afforded.[6]

In today's terminology, we would say that the authors of the resolution understood that the decision to participate in the social security system – the decision to work in the formal sector – is to some extent a choice made by the worker. These decisions are at least partially the result of weighing the benefits of affiliation against the costs of making social security contributions. Nevertheless, for reasons that will be explored later in the chapter, this Bismarckian framework was viewed as the most viable option for the region at the time.

2.4. A Comparison Between Social Security Policy and Education Policy

The social security architecture of Latin America is so familiar to many of us that we might forget that most other social programs are provided and financed in an entirely different manner. As an example, we consider the provision of public education in the region. To our knowledge, there are no "contributory" education systems that only cover the children of formal-sector workers. There are of course private schools for those who choose not to send their children to public schools, just like there are options for private health insurance and private plans for investing for retirement, but there are no public-education systems in which access is linked to the labor status of the parents.

We believe that it is worthwhile to reflect upon the difference in society's views on publically-provided health care versus publically provided education. Consider, for example, the 1948 Universal Declaration of Human Rights of the United Nations. Many components of social security such as health care, income support in old age, and support during unemployment spells, are considered to be fundamental and universal rights. The declaration states:

> Everyone has the right to a standard of living adequate for the health and well-being of himself and of his family, including food, clothing, housing and medical care and necessary social services, and the right to security in the event of unemployment, sickness, disability, widowhood, old age or other lack of livelihood in circumstances beyond his control.[7]

In the case of education, however, special emphasis is placed on the fact that access to primary education should be free. Specifically, the resolution states "Everyone has the right to education. Education shall be free, at least in the elementary and fundamental stages. Elementary education shall be compulsory."[8]

It is worth emphasizing that the resolution does not state that education shall be free only for people who are sufficiently poor, which would suggest redistribution as a motive. The resolution also does not condition access to education to taxes that are deducted from wage income, which would suggest that access to free education is earned as a result of labor market status. According to the UN declaration, even wealthy families have the right to send their children to a public school free of charge. On the other hand, there is no such clear language with regard to health care. Since health care is judged to be a universal right, its access must be free for people who are unable to pay, justifying the non-contributory health programs that have arisen recently in the region. However, there is no prohibition to conditioning access to free health care to those who are below some poverty threshold, or to those who have made social security contributions.

The above difference in visions between education and health policies is exactly what we observe in the region. Although it is true that higher income families in Latin America tend to send their children to private schools, all families have the right to send their children to public school free of charge if they choose to. Wealthier families, however, typically are excluded from non-contributory health care programs, either because they would fail a proxy-means test or because they are affiliated to contributory programs.

The idea that access to education should be free substantially predates the 1948 Universal Declaration of Human Rights. Free access to primary school education, for example, was guaranteed by the 1839 Peruvian constitution, the 1844 Constitution in the Dominican Republic, and the 1860 Chilean Constitution. In 1870, a decree by Venezuelan President Guzman Blanco also guaranteed the right to free access to primary school education. The 1884 Argentinean education law did the same. The 1949 Costa Rican Constitution, in addition to stating that primary school education should be free of cost, specifically states that it should be "paid for by the Nation," that is, financed out of general revenue.

One of our arguments in this chapter is that, at least for certain components of benefits usually associated with social security, there is no good reason to condition access to labor market status in a way that would seem entirely inappropriate in the case of education. In particular, risks that are common to all workers (such as longevity, disability, death, or ill health) should be funded from a common source of revenue. Risks that are specifically related to salaried workers, such as the risk of being laid off from one's job, should be funded from taxes on salaried workers' wages. We argue that our willingness to condition access to all social security benefits to labor market status is partly the result of a historical process through which we have gotten used to the idea that health care or pensions should be linked to labor market status despite the fact these requirements lead to erratic coverage and perverse labor market incentives.

2.5. The Beveridge Model of Social Security

In addition to reflecting upon the fact that certain elements of social policy, for example access to education, do not have any contributory element, it is also worth noting that, even for elements of social policy that we generally consider to be part of social security such as health care and pensions, there exist alternatives to the Bismarckian contributory model. In November of 1942, nearly six years after the ILO's first Labour Conference of American Member States in Santiago, Chile, Sir William Beveridge presented his report to the United Kingdom parliament putting forth a model for social security that was quite different from the Bismarckian model. For example, the Beveridge model specifies that benefits should be "comprehensive." Specifically, the report states:

> ... social insurance should be comprehensive, in respect both of the persons covered and of their needs. It should not leave either to national assistance or to voluntary insurance any risk so general or so uniform that social insurance can be justified.[9]

Although the report recognizes that salaried workers have a special need for certain benefits such as unemployment insurance, the report specifies that many benefits, such as health and pensions, should have universal coverage. In particular, the report proposes "to introduce for all citizens adequate pensions without means test." With regards to healt hcare, the report states:

> Medical treatment covering all requirements will be provided for all citizens by a national health service organised under the health

> departments and post-medical rehabilitation treatment will be provided for all persons capable of profiting by it.[10]

The Beveridge report also differed substantially from the Bismarckian model insofar as the Beveridge proposal contemplated that benefits would not be linked to contributions, and therefore that the benefits would be delinked from labor market status. Specifically, the report states:

> All insured persons, rich or poor pay the same contributions for the same security; those with larger means will pay more only to the extent that as tax-payers they pay more to the national Exchequer and so to the State share of the Social Insurance Fund.[11]

It is also interesting to note that the potentially distortionary effects of social policy appear to have been taken into account by Beveridge in the elaboration of his proposal. In particular, the report cites the practice of means testing of benefits as a potential disincentive to savings. That is, the potentially distortionary effects of means testing are used as one of the justifications for universal coverage of social security benefits.

We therefore see that, when the Bismarckian model for social security was being established in Latin America, another model for social security was emerging. If this vision for social security, in which the link between labor market status and social security benefits is much less important, had exhibited a stronger influence in Latin America during the first half of the 20th century, the entire architecture of the welfare state might be fundamentally different in the present.

2.6. Why Did Latin America Adopt the Bismarckian Model?

Although the question of why the Bismarckian model was chosen is more difficult to answer than the question of when the model was adopted, one can gain some insights from some of the language used in the resolution that was adopted at the 1936 ILO conference. Specifically, the resolution states:

> The establishment of compulsory social insurance, as fifty years of experience have shown, is at once the most rational and the most effective means of affording to the workers the security to which they are entitled.[12]

One aspect of the above quote that merits reflection is the phrase "fifty years of experience." From what countries did these fifty years of experience arise? Since, as we argued earlier, compulsory social security systems for the most part did not exist in Latin America, it seems likely that these fifty years of experience were generated in mainly upper income European economies with labor markets that were (and still are) quite distinct from the labor markets on which this architecture would be imposed in Latin America. In this sense, one might argue that an architecture for social security that had proven to be successful in some contexts was transplanted to a region in which the underlying conditions made the chances of successful implementation substantially lower.

Any analysis of why the Bismarckian model, which necessarily implies a fragmentation of the welfare state in which salaried workers receive the benefits of social security but also face the burden of financing this coverage, must also consider the feasible alternatives of the time. In 1936, when the basic architecture was agreed upon at the ILO's First Labour Conference of American Member States, Latin America probably lacked both the tax base and the administrative capacity to finance and implement a system with more general coverage.

The historian Leslie Bethel, for example, describes the period from the late 1920s to the late 1950s as one in which the "oligarchic" states of Latin America were transformed into "modernizing" states. In further describing this period he states

> ... there was a quantum leap in administrative responsibilities (and sometimes, although this was less certain, in capabilities as well), with much more extensive provision of education, health (mortality rates fell dramatically in the thirties and forties) and urban services. The material basis for all this were a considerable expansion of the tax base, of official powers of economic regulation, and even of the entrepreneurial responsibilities directly assumed by the state, ...[13]

We therefore see that, at the time when Bismarckian social security systems were being implemented in Latin America, the goal of providing universal access to many of the benefits normally associated with social security would have been infeasible. For this reason, a more limited scheme for formal salaried workers was likely the only option.

A key reason why social security schemes with universal access were likely infeasible when the Bismarckian systems were introduced in Latin America is the tax base was insufficient to fund them out of general revenue. Since those times, however, the tax base of Latin-American countries has expanded considerably, particularly with the introduction of the value-added tax (VAT). The first countries to adopt this tax scheme were Brazil (1967) and Uruguay (1968). By

1977, the VAT had also been adopted in Argentina, Bolivia, Chile, Colombia, Costa Rica, Honduras, Nicaragua, Panama, and Peru.[14] The VAT has now been adopted throughout Latin America and, in several countries, collects revenues as a share of GDP that are comparable or even higher than what is observed in advanced economies.

We therefore see that, even if the countries of Latin America would have wanted to adopt a system of social insurance with universal coverage (as in the Beveridge model of social security discussed earlier), they probably lacked both the ability to raise sufficient tax revenue and the administrative ability to provide general coverage. These institutional restrictions, however, do not seem to be binding impediments in the present day.

Still another reason why Latin America adopted the Bismarckian model of social security was the perception that this model would play an important role in improving the distribution of wealth. Mesa-Lago (1978) makes this point clearly by stating that "social security is also seen as a mechanism for income redistribution – to help the needy in society by taxing the wealthy" (p. 6). The author then describes the experiences of Argentina, Chile, Peru, and Uruguay and notes that the social security programs of the region have not achieved this goal. In particular, Mesa-Lago concludes that the wealthiest in Latin-American society disproportionately receive the benefits of social security. This result is consistent with those of much more recent studies such as Forteza and Ourens (2012) that demonstrate that the internal rate-of-return for pension contributions for low-wage workers is substantially lower than for high-wage workers. Equally important, the argument that Bismarckian social security can be used to redistribute income from firms to workers fails to take into account that the real incidence of contributions made to social security is different from the statutory incidence, and many studies show that the real incidence falls mainly on the workers.

In summary, there are at least three complementary explanations for why the Bismarckian model of social security was adopted in Latin America. First, a model that proved to be successful in countries with very different characteristics (such as, greater ability to enforce regulations and lower levels of labor informality) was transplanted to Latin America, in spite of the fact that the functioning of these systems would be complicated by the different economic conditions present in Latin America. Second, Latin American governments lacked both the administrative capability of providing benefits with wider coverage and the tax base to finance this expanded coverage and therefore chose the Bismarckian model as the only viable option at the time. Third, it was hoped that social security systems would achieve the goal of transferring wealth from firm owners to their employees.

Regardless of the underlying explanation for the adoption of the Bismarckian model of social security in Latin America, it seems clear that the decisions taken in the late 1930s, which were then implemented over the next 20 years, put in place the basic structure and institutions that form the basis for the social security systems observed throughout the region today. Therefore, it may be worthwhile to evaluate whether this basic architecture has served the region well and, given the advances in tax collection and benefits provision that have been observed in the region, whether an alternative design might be both viable and desirable.

2.7. The Expected Expansion of Coverage Never Materialized

At the time when the Bismarckian system of social security was being implemented in Latin America, policymakers expected that the coverage problem due to high rates of informality would be solved over time as a natural consequence of economic development. The Lewis (1954) dual sector model of economic growth represented the prevailing views on formal versus informal employment for many years. In this model, labor is segregated into two sectors: the first is the modern or formal sector in which wages are high, and the second is the subsistence or informal sector in which wages are low. Wages are higher in the formal sector in order to entice workers to leave the informal sector. Lewis further assumes that wages in the subsistence or informal sector do not rise with economic development.

The Lewis model predicts two phases of economic growth. In the first stage, while an informal sector continues to exist, economic growth involves a shifting of workers from the informal to the formal sector. During this stage of economic development, however, wages in the formal sector do not rise with economic growth because new formal workers can be hired from the pool of subsistence workers. Once the informal sector disappears, however, the more "standard" effects of increased labor demand take over and economic growth is now characterized by rising real wages.

The growth paths of several (not Latin-American) countries appeared to lend credibility to the Lewis model. As pointed out in Fields (2004), for example, the growth path of Taiwan from the 1950s onward seems to match the predictions of the Lewis model quite well. From 1955-70, high growth was not particularly associated with real wage growth. After 1970, however, real wages seemed to take off. Chen and others (2002) cite the post World War II experiences of Japan and Europe as lending support to the Lewis model. The Lewis model, along with the prediction that informality would disappear over time as a result of the natural course of economic development, therefore seemed to be a good predictor of what would occur in Latin America.

The link between the two sectors of the Lewis model and a Bismarckian social security system is clear. Workers in the modern or formal sector would likely be participating in the contributory social security scheme. Workers in the subsistence or informal sector would not. Based on the theoretical predictions of the Lewis model as well as the growth experiences of Asian and European countries, policymakers in Latin America could reasonably have expected that a natural consequence of economic growth would be for the informal sector to gradually shrink and eventually disappear entirely. The apparent weakness of a Bismarckian social security system to offer coverage to all workers would therefore be expected to resolve itself over time as the disfavored sector simply disappeared. In other words, policymakers in the period when social security was taking hold in Latin America could have reasonably expected social security systems to approach universal coverage over time without the need for important structural reforms.

One of the earliest analyses in which the persistence of the informal labor market was recognized was ILO (1972). This report, which analyzed the labor market in Kenya, asserted that "the informal sector in urban areas will expand in the next 20 years regardless of policies followed." Informality has indeed proven to be quite persistent in the developing world and, unfortunately, Latin America has not been the exception. As noted in a recent flagship publication of the LAC region of the World Bank titled "Informality: Exit and Exclusion" (Perry et al. 2007), informality in fact generally increased in the 1990s in Latin America. Using more recent data, Figure 2.1 shows that more than 50% of workers are informal in the majority of countries in the region. Although informality is higher for lower-income workers, Figure 2.1 shows that in many countries informality is quite high even in the highest quintile of the income distribution. That is, the Bismarckian social security system in many countries is failing even at the highest income levels. Given that the Bismarckian social security system was implemented in most countries some sixty or seventy years ago, the fact that large segments of workers continue to lack coverage is extremely troubling.

Figure 2.1

Coverage of Contributory Social Insurance, by Country and Income Quintile

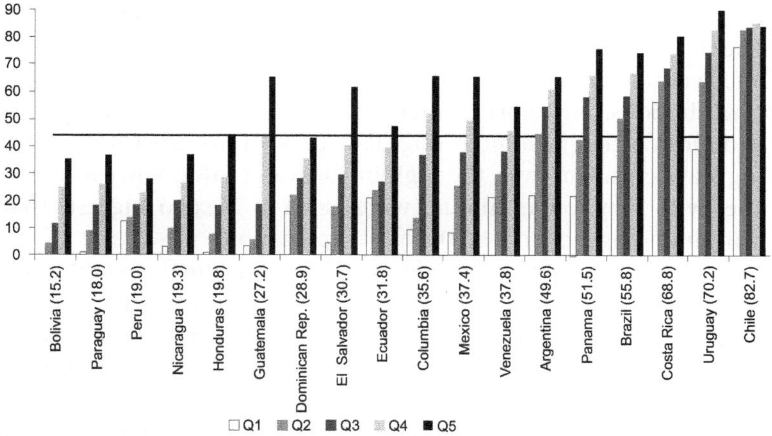

Note: Each bar represents the percentage of employed workers aged 20 and older who are currently contributing to social security; the number in parenthesis after the country name is the average coverage in that country (in percent). The thick horizontal line corresponds to the population-weighted Latin American average.

Source: Levy and Schady (2013) based on data from Rofman and Oliveri (2012).

2.8. Why Has Informality Been So Persistent?

The reason why informality has been so persistent is likely related to a literature that has emerged in the past decade or so that shows that the informal sector is much more complex than the idea from Lewis (1954). In the Lewis model, the informal sector is nothing more than a subsistence sector in which those that cannot find a job in the modern sector work because they have no other alternative. Recent evidence, however, shows that many informal workers are not queuing up for jobs in the formal sector, contrary to the predictions of the

Lewis model. Furthermore, many policy variables such as taxes and social benefits will affect the choices that workers make.

One of the early papers to make this point was Johnson and others (1998), who argue that firms in the unofficial (or informal) sector escape most taxation, which may result in a strong incentive for informality. The informal sector may be particularly attractive to firms when public goods, such as contract enforcement and effective regulation, provided to the formal sector are of low quality.

A more basic question, however, is why workers and firms would have incentives to evade social security taxes. As we mentioned earlier, to the extent that the workers value social security benefits, they ought to be willing to pay their share of social security contributions and accept lower wages to compensate the firm for its share of these contributions. One explanation for the evasion of social security contributions is that minimum-wage laws prevent workers from accepting wage cuts. However, the high incidence of informality in countries with very low minimum wages such as Mexico suggests that minimum wages cannot be the only explanation.

Levy (2008) advances two additional reasons why firms and workers might wish to avoid social security contributions. First, workers might not place a high value on the bundled package of social security benefits that they would receive in exchange for social security contributions. In this case, social security contributions would effectively be a tax on formal work. Second, to the extent that workers value the non-contributive benefits offered to those who are not contributing to social security, the existence of non-contributory programs would constitute a subsidy to informality. The combination of taxing formal work and subsidizing informal work is a clear recipe for high levels of informality.

In general, it is difficult to ascertain workers' valuations of benefits. Given the tendency towards offering more generous benefits in the parallel non-contributory systems, however, it seems likely that the valuation of the benefits afforded to social security contributors has been decreasing over time. One attempt to estimate the valuation of social security benefits by Mexican workers can be found in Levy (2008), who estimates that low-wage formal workers value the non-wage benefits attached to formal sector work at no more than 50% of the non-wage costs attached to formal work and goes a long way towards explaining the observed evasion of social security contributions.

Maloney (2004) focuses more on workers' decisions (particularly, the decision to choose self-employment) and focuses on Latin America to challenge the view of the informal sector as the disadvantaged segment of the labor force. Maloney cites several statistics that suggest the self-employed, who represent a large share of those not covered by social security systems, are generally quite content with their status compared to other reasonable alternatives. He cites survey evidence from the province of Jujuy in Argentina, for example, in which 80% of the self-employed had no desire to change jobs. He also cites data from Paraguay suggesting that only 28% of those in the informal sector expressed a desire to change occupations.

The idea that the informal sector may be an attractive option for many workers, instead of being their last resort also explains the active flows in and out of informality. Bosch and Maloney (2010), for example, examine labor market flows in Brazil and Mexico and find anything but a segmented labor market in which the informal sector is composed of those who are waiting for an opportunity to enter the formal (privileged) sector. In particular, flows from formality into informality are not counter-cyclical, but, if anything, pro-cyclical. In other words, when economic conditions are favorable, many workers appear to choose informality as their preferred labor market status.

This view of a dynamic labor market where individuals evaluate the advantages and disadvantages of formal employment prior to deciding the sector in which they want to work, also coincides well with the growing evidence that the choice of formality of informality is partially affected by policy-induced incentives in the labor market. Bérgolo and Cruces (2011 and Chapter 3 in this volume), for example, find that the extension of health benefits to spouses of formal-sector workers increased the probability that a married person will work in the formal sector compared to a single person. That is, increasing formal sector benefits for married workers compared to single workers increased the formal sector participation of married workers compared to single workers.

While Bérgolo and Cruces (2011 and Chapter 3 in this volume) studied the effects of a reform that increased the attractiveness of the formal sector, several other studies investigated the effects of reforms that decreased the attractiveness of formal sector work. For instance, Amarante and others (2011) studied the effects of a conditional cash transfer program in Uruguay in which a person would lose benefits once formal sector earnings exceeded a certain amount. They find that those who were eligible for this program on the basis of their score on a proxy means test had significantly lower formal sector earnings. Aterido and others (2011) and Bosch and Campos-Vasquez (2011) both found that the introduction and expansion of a non-contributory health program in Mexico made informality a more attractive option and therefore reduced formal sector employment.

There also exist studies relating changes in payroll taxes to labor markets. Using data from Colombia, Kugler and Kugler (2009) find that a 10% increase in payroll taxes reduces wages by between 1.4% and 2.3% and in employment by between 4% and 5%. Aguilar and Rendon (2010) find that non-wage labor costs in Peru reduce formal-sector employment by 17% for white-collar workers and by 53% for blue-collar workers. The importance of these studies is that they show that the taxes used to finance a Bismarckian contributory social security system reduce the size of the formal sector.

Of course, the decisions of firms will also likely be affected by the social security system. Firms may be willing to pay workers a higher net wage in exchange for not registering them with social security as a way to avoid contributions. Additionally, Antón and others (2012) find that the fact that smaller firms are less likely to be audited generates an implicit wage subsidy for small, less-productive firms that can avoid higher percentages of social security obligations and as an implicit wage tax on larger, more-productive firms that face more-stringent monitoring.

In summary, policymakers around the time when the Bismarckian social security model was being adopted in Latin America probably expected the problem of informality to resolve itself as economic development continued. The persistence of informality can probably be explained by the fact that the informal sector is not simply a disadvantaged subsistence sector from which all workers are hoping to escape. We have learned that the informal sector is to a large extent comprised of workers who are responding to distortionary incentives such as high labor taxes and low valuations of the benefits afforded to formal-sector workers. As we will argue in the next section, the trends in the region show that there have been increasing distortions associated with formal-sector work, therefore increasing the burden on social security systems based on mandatory contributions from salaried workers.

2.9. The Movement Towards Parallel Non-Contributory Programs

In light of the failure to incorporate sufficiently high percentages of workers into the Bismarckian contributory social security systems, many countries began to implement parallel non-contributory programs. In Brazil, for example, a non-contributory pension for rural workers was implemented in 1967 and greatly expanded in the 1990s. In Chile, a non-contributory pension program was adopted as a part of the 1981 pension reform. More recently, the Chilean pension reform of 2007 implemented a "solidarity pillar" that provided a basic pension on a means-tested basis to those who have not participated in the contributory system. The benefits of the solidarity pillar are gradually reduced as a function of the resources the worker has accumulated in the contributory program. Non-contributory pension systems were also introduced in Argentina (1993), Bolivia (1993), Costa Rica (1995), and Uruguay (1995), and more recently, Mexico (2006).

The region has also seen the introduction of numerous non-contributory health care systems. In 1993, Colombia instituted its "subsidized regime," offering health care to those who fall below a certain poverty threshold, unless they are affiliated to the contributory regime. In 2002, Mexico began to implement a non-contributory health program titled "Seguro Popular" and expanding its scope rapidly over time, both in terms of the number of people covered and in terms of the medical procedures offered.[15]

It is also worth mentioning that conditional cash transfers (CCTs) have become prolific in the region and most have a health component. Perhaps more importantly, however, is that the targeting mechanism for program eligibilty is partly affected by the social security status of the individual. Specifically, according to table 8.2 of IDB (2010), a person's status as a contributor to the social security may be used to deny access to the benefits of a CCT in Argentina, Chile, Colombia, Ecuador, Mexico, Paraguay, and Uruguay. We therefore see that, in addition to the fact that formal-sector work is taxed and that the existence of non-contributory systems implies that informal work is subsidized, some workers risk losing direct transfers from the government as a result of joining the formal sector. It is no wonder that the expansion of coverage of contributory social security schemes has been disappointing.

The motivation for implementing these parallel non-contributory social security programs is clear. If the existence of the contributory pillar of social security is taken as given, the only way to offer important measures of social protection such as health care and pensions to informal workers is to add non-contributory pillars on top of the contributory pillars. Nevertheless, we argue that it would be beneficial for the region to consider a more comprehensive reform agenda that would involve redesigning the entire social security architecture rather than adding additional programs to cover the gaps left by the Bismarckian contributory system.

2.10. The Result of a Long Historical Process is a Poorly Designed Patchwork System of Social Security

What has been the result of this long process in which contributory social security systems were implemented, with limited coverage, and later complemented by non-contributory parallel systems? In this section, we argue that the end result is a poorly-designed system that neither serves the goal of promoting labor market efficiency nor the goal of providing effective social protection. In particular, the contributory component of social security in the region is quite costly for workers and firms. This distortionary system, in addition to negatively affecting productivity, makes tax collection more difficult, thereby making the financing of social protection more challenging.

How costly is the contributory system to workers and firms? Figure 2.2 uses data from IDB (2010) to show the non-wage labor costs associated with formal employment. Social security contributions are typically a large component of these non-wage costs, as are dismissal costs and other elements related to labor regulation. The average value for non-wage labor costs as a percentage of the wage for the 16 countries in the figure is over 36%.

It is clear that the distortionary effects of contributory social security can have important negative effects on productivity. Workers may, for example, choose self-employment as a way to avoid social security taxes even if their productivity would be higher as a salaried employee in a large firm. However, these labor market distortions also have important effects on the governments' public finances, which in turn affect their ability to finance social expenditures.

Figure 2.2

Non-Wage Labor Costs in Latin America and the Caribbean

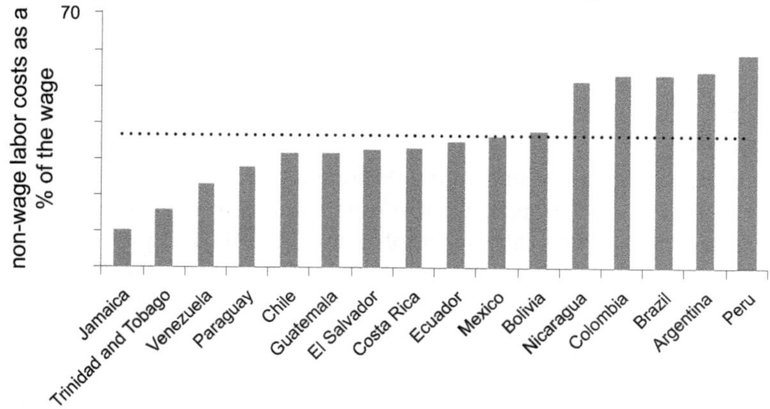

Source: Table 8.1 from Pagés (2010).

Anton and others (2012), for example, study the effects of increasing benefits provided to the non-contributory pillar in Mexico. Since each peso spent on benefits to the non-contributory pillar makes the formal sector less attractive, increased benefits for informal workers lead to a decrease in formality, and therefore an increase in tax evasion. Specifically, each additional peso spent on benefits for informal workers causes a reduction of four cents in tax revenue, making the real fiscal cost 1.04 pesos for each peso spent on benefits for informal workers.

We therefore see that the truncated welfare state that is generated by imposing non-contributory social security on top of a system of Bismarckian contributory social insurance increases the costs of providing social benefits. Given the very limited fiscal space that characterizes the public finances of the region, this concern adds to the inefficacy of protections against risks and to the productivity costs of Bismarckian social security, and further justifies a complete redesign of the social security architecture upon which the region's welfare states are constructed.

2.11. An Alternative Social Security Model Can Be Implemented

Latin America has adopted the Bismarckian model of social security for historical reasons that were detailed earlier in this chapter. There is no need for the region, however, to remain tied to these historical shackles when better alternatives exist and are feasible to implement.

Recall that Sir William Beveridge offered an alternative model for social security in which access to many types of benefits such as health care and pensions is universal, that is, not linked to the employment status of the individual. However, one might be tempted to think that universal access to government-provided health care, despite being feasible for upper income countries such as Great Britain, might not be realistic in the context of Latin America. It is worth noting in this regard that Brazil has already implemented a universal public health care system. It is also worth noting that Bolivia has implemented a universal non-contributory pension. We therefore see that the link between benefits and labor market status to which we have grown so accustomed is not a an indispensable feature of policy.

Along these lines, it is worth pointing out that the proposal outlined in Levy (2008), further elaborated in Anton and others (2012), in which many social security benefits are not financed from wage-based social security contributions, but rather financed out of general revenue, is in fact a viable model for at least some countries of the region. This type of ambitious reform agenda, however would require fiscal reforms to collect more revenue from general taxes in order to finance universal benefits (much like what was undertaken in the 2012 Colombian fiscal reform). Given the inability of the contributory systems of the regions to significantly expand coverage over the last 60-70 years, we argue that it may be time to abandon a failed design and to try a new approach that is better suited to the labor markets of the region.

In its essence, the proposal described in Levy (2008) and Anton and others (2012) is quite simple. In the same way that public education is made available to everyone and financed out of general taxes that everyone pays, the proposal is to offer certain social security benefits to all workers. Benefits such as health care and a basic pension, which would appear to cover risks faced by all workers, would be natural candidates for this type of universalization and would be financed out of general tax revenue. This much simpler architecture, which is now quite feasible given the improved abilities of the region to provide benefits and to raise revenue through general taxation, would eliminate some of the most egregious labor market distortions that have impeded productivity growth and, at the same time, deliver social services in a much simpler, more transparent, and fiscally responsible manner.

2.12. Conclusions

The Bismarckian model of contributory social security has been the dominant system in the region for 60-70 years. After such a long time operating under this architecture, one becomes accustomed to the model and treats it as a permanent feature of social policy. We argue that the Bismarckian model, which seems poorly suited to the labor markets of Latin America, was adopted as a result of a long historical process. Despite the fact that the Bismarckian model of contributory social security may appear to be an entrenched feature of social policy in the region, we argue that an alternative model, in which many of the standard social security benefits are provided universally, and financed out of general revenues, is a much more appropriate model for Latin America. This redesign of the social security architecture will allow labor markets to operate more efficiently and, at the same time, simplify and improve the systems for delivering social security benefits.

The creation of social security systems in the region some 60 or 70 years ago represented an enormous challenge to the region. Similarly, a complete redesign of the social security architecture of the region, would be another important challenge for the region. In light of the failure of the contributory systems to effectively expand coverage, and in light of the ever worsening labor market distortions associated with the truncated social security design that currently exists in the region, we argue that it is time to take on this challenge and finally achieve universal coverage in a fair, transparent, and coherent manner.

Notes

1 Hollyday (1970): 65.
2 Harry S. Truman: Statement by the President on the 10th Anniversary of the Social Security Act, August 13, 1945. Online by Gerhard Peters and John T. Woolley, The American Presidency Project, http://www.presidency.ucsb.edu/ws/?pid=10284.
3 ILO (1936): 271.
4 ILO (1936): 276.
5 Over time, several countries such as Chile, Colombia, and Costa Rica have made coverage mandatory for independent workers as well.
6 ILO (1936): 277.
7 Universal Declaration of Human Rights, United Nations, article 25.
8 Universal Declaration of Human Rights, United Nations, article 25.
9 Beveridge (1942): 121-2.
10 Beveridge (1942): 426.
11 Beveridge (1942): 121.
12 ILO (1936): 270.
13 Bethell (1998): 437.
14 Tanzi (2008) shows that the collection of general government revenue in Latin America and the Caribbean has increased significantly since 1990.
15 Interestingly, Brazil implemented its "unified health system" in 1990, delinking the health system from the labor market.

References

Aguilar, G., Rendón, S. (2010). Employment and Deadweight Loss Effects of Observed Nonwage Labor Costs, in: Economic Inquiry, 48(3): 793-809.

Amarante, V., Manacorda, M., Vigorito, A., Zerpa, M. (2011). Social Assistance and Labor Market Outcomes: Evidence from the Uruguayan PANES, mimeo.

Aterido, R., Hallward-Driemeier, M., Pagés, C. (2011). Does Expanding Health Insurance Beyond Formal-Sector Workers Encourage Informality? Measuring the Impact of Mexico's Seguro Popular, IZA Discussion Paper No. 5996.

Antón, A., Hernández, F., Levy, S. (2012). The End of Informality in Mexico? Fiscal Reform for Universal Social Insurance, IDB Discussion Paper No. 209.

Reyes, A., Hallward-Driemeier, M., Pagés, C. (2011). Does Expanding Health Insurance Beyond Formal-Sector Workers Encourage Informality? Measuring the Impact of Mexico's Seguro Popular, World Bank Policy Research Working Paper No. 5785 (also available as IZA Discussion Paper No. 5996).

Bérgolo, M., Cruces, G. (2011). Labor Informality and the Incentive Effects of Social Security: Evidence from a Health Reform in Uruguay, IDB Working Paper No. 62318 [Chapter 3 in this volume].

Bethell, L. (1998). Latin America: Economy and Society Since 1930, Cambrigde, New York, Melbourne: Cambridge University Press.

Beveridge, W. (1942). Social Insurance and Allied Services, Presented to Parliament by Command of His Majesty, Part V, London: HMSO.

Bosch, M., Campos-Vázquez, R. (2010). The Trade-offs of Social Assistance Programs in the Labor Market: The Case of "Seguro Popular" Program in Mexico, Serie documentos de trabajo del Centro de Estudios Económicos Working Paper No. 12.

Bosch, M., Maloney, W. F. (2010). Comparative Analysis of Labor Market Dynamics Using Markov Processes: An Application to Informality, in: Labour Economics, 17(4): 621-31.

Chen, M.A., Jhabvala, R., Lund, F. (2002). Supporting Workers in the Informal Economy: A Policy Framework, ILO Working Paper No. 2002/2.

Fields, Gary S. (2004). Dualism in the Labor Market: A Perspective on the Lewis Model After Half a Century, in: The Manchester School, 72(6): 724-35.
Forteza, A., Guzmán, O. (2012). Redistribution, Insurance and Incentives to Work in Latin-American Pension Programs, in: Journal of Pension Economics and Finance, 11(03): 337-64.
Hollyday, F. B. M. (1970). Bismarck, Englewood Cliffs, NJ: Prentice Hall.
International Labour Office (1972). Incomes, Employment and Equality in Kenya, Geneva: International Labour Office.
International Labour Organization (ILO) (1936). Resolutions Adopted by the Conference, Labour Conference of the American States which are Members of the ILO, Santiago, (Geneva).
Johnson, S., Kaufmann, D., Zoido-Lobatón, P. (1998). Regulatory Discretion and the Unofficial Economy, in: American Economic Review, 88(2): 387–92.
Kugler, A., Kugler, M. (2009). Labor Market Effects of Payroll Taxes in Developing Countries: Evidence from Colombia, in: Economic Development and Cultural Change, 57(2): 335-58.
Levy, S. (2008). Good Intentions, Bad Outcomes: Social Policy, Informality and Economic Growth in Mexico, Washington, DC: Brookings Institution Press.
Levy, S., Schady, N. (2013). Latin America's Social Policy Challenge: Education, Social Insurance, Redistribution, in: Journal of Economic Perspectives, 27(2): 193-218.
Lewis, W. A. (1954). Economic Development with Unlimited Supplies of Labor, in: Manchester School of Economic and Social Studies, 22: 139-91.
Liu, L. (2001). Foreign Social Security Developments Prior to the Passage of the U.S. Social Security Act of 1935, Special Study No. 8: U.S. Social Security Administration.
Maloney, W. (2004). Informality Revisited, in: World Development, 32(7): 1159-78.
Mesa-Lago, C. (1978). Social Security in Latin America: Pressure Groups, Stratification, and Inequality, Pittsburgh, PA: University of Pittsburgh Press.
Pagés, C. (Ed.) (2010). The Age of Productivity: Transforming Economies from the Bottom Up, Washington, DC: Inter-American Development Bank.
Perry, G., Maloney, W. F., Arias, O. S., Fajnzylber, P., Mason, A. D., Saavedra-Chanduvi, J. (2007). Informality: Exit and Exclusion, Washington, DC: The World Bank.
Rofman, R., Oliveri, M.L. (2012). Pension Coverage in Latin America: Trends and Determinants, World Bank Social Protection & Labor Discussion Paper No. 1217.
Tanzi, V. (2008). Tax Systems and Tax Reforms in Latin America, in: Bernardi, L., Barreix, A., Marenzi, A., Profeta, P. (Eds.), Tax Systems and Tax Reforms in Latin America, New York: Routledge, 1-16.

3

Labor Informality and the Incentive Effects of Social Protection Systems: Evidence from a Health Reform in Uruguay*

Marcelo Bérgolo
Guillermo Cruces

3.1. Introduction

Social protection systems have evolved heterogeneously in Latin America, but all the countries in the region have both contributory and non-contributory programs (Bertranou 2004).[1] For historical reasons tied to the emergence of labor movements by industrial sector, most countries have established some variant of a contributory social security. Individuals who did not have access to the system's benefits through wage contributions received some level of non-contributory social services.

Such systems can function adequately for people with coverage, and they were created with the implicit objective of achieving wide coverage. However, the countries in the region are characterized by

* *This chapter was financed as a part of the Regional Dialogue on Social Security organized by the Labor Markets Unit of the Inter-American Development Bank (IDB). It also received partial funding from CEDLAS' IDRC-sponsored project Labour Markets for Inclusive Growth in Latin America (www.labor-al.org). We wish to thank María Laura Alzúa, David Kaplan, and Carmen Pagés for comments on preliminary versions of this chapter, and attendants to the 6th IZA-World Bank Employment and Development conference in Mexico DF (May 2011). The usual disclaimer applies. The views expressed here are those of the authors and do not necessarily reflect those of their institutions or those of the funding agencies.*

high levels of informality, which we define in this chapter as jobs that do not provide access to social security benefits. Given the size of the informal sector in so many countries, in the best of cases the result was an incomplete or two-tiered protection system.[2]

There is an extensive literature on the economic mechanisms explaining formal-informal labor market (see, for example, Fields 1990; Harris and Todaro 1970; Maloney 1999). Some recent studies suggest that the coexistence of partial contributory systems, universal and means-tested benefits generate a complex incentive structure, which could at least partly explain the levels of informality seen in region (Levy 2008). In a world where workers evaluate the package of benefits provided by the social protection system (with some space for the valuation of future benefits – see Summers 1989) and the cost in terms of contributions, while employers impose the "tax" implied by the contributions with the probability of being detected and punished, workers' access to similar social benefits through the contributory and non-contributory systems would reduce the incentives for formal sector employment.[3]

This mechanism is particularly relevant in Latin America, where many countries have expanded or are planning to expand their social protection systems through (conditional and unconditional) income transfer programs and other non-contributory benefits (ECLAC 2006; Rawlings 2004). In this framework, a deep debate is needed on the consequences of the expansion of non-contributory social welfare programs for the Latin American economies, especially in terms of the effects on the interaction of the formal and informal segments of the labor market.

This study contributes to the discussion by analyzing the potential effects on informality of recent extension of health coverage to the dependants of formal workers (i.e., to be registered and contribute to the social security system) in Uruguay as part of a 2008 policy reform. This country has one of the oldest and most developed contribution-based social security systems in Latin America, with the highest coverage among the cluster of countries in the region with relatively low levels of labor informality (Gasparini and Tornarolli 2009). The system is based on employer and employee contributions from formal jobs, and provides the covered workforce with a bundle of benefits, including health coverage, and pensions among others. The 2008 exogenous expansion of the health coverage to dependent children of formal workers provides a policy experiment setting to study the presence and quantitative relevance of the incentives of social security on labor market formality. This study's main outcome of interest is thus the worker's decision to operate formally or informally.

The rest of the chapter is organized as follows. The next section briefly describes the social protection system in Uruguay. Section 3.3 discusses the recent health reform and the resulting incentives on workers' decisions about working in the formal sector. Section 3.4 presents empirical evidence on the effects of the health reform on labor market informality. Finally, Section 3.5 builds on the empirical results to conduct a discussion of the policy issues that emerge from the overlap of contributory and non-contributory programs in the context of informality in the labor market.

3.2. The Social Protection System in Uruguay

The social protection system in Uruguay is structured mainly around a set of contributory programs.[4] The most important institution responsible for social security benefits for the workforce is the public Social Security Bank (*Banco de Previsión Social*, or BPS), which administers services for registered salaried workers employed in the private sector.[5]

Private sector employees and employers are required by law to make contributions to the BPS, which in turn offers workers a set of services – a bundle of social benefits that is essentially provided for salaried workers in the private sector.[6] These benefits have traditionally included post-retirement benefits (retirement and pensions), as well as other benefits during the working stage of the life cycle, including access to certain health care services (health insurance), unemployment insurance, and family allowances for workers with dependents. While the total amount of the contributions is the sum of the different components (mainly employee contributions for health insurance and retirement pensions), the bundle of social benefits is indivisible and is tied to a single contribution that encompasses all these benefits. Consequently, BPS affiliation guarantees the worker access to all the services in the social benefits package.

Workers who are not covered by social security benefits – that is, who are not registered with the BPS or similar institutions – have access to some non-contributory programs, including non-contributory pensions and, more recently, family allowances. These programs generally have stricter requirements, such as being below a specified income threshold. Figure 3.1 illustrates the evolution of the informality rate for salaried workers in the 2001-9 period.

Figure 3.1
Informality in Uruguay, 2001–2009

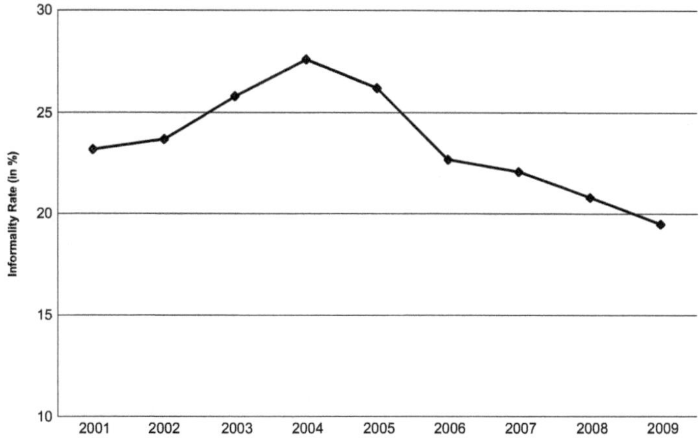

Note: Informal workers are defined as salaried workers who do not have the right to a retirement pension. The informality rate represents the share of adults in informal jobs.
Source: Authors' construction, based on SEDLAC (CEDLAS and World Bank, 2011).

3.3. The Health Reform and its Labor Market Incentive Effects

3.3.1. The 2008 Health Reform

The BPS historically granted health care packages to registered private employees only. Under this contributory scheme, employers and workers paid 5 and 3 percent of taxable wages, respectively, for a total contribution of 8 percent. Contributing workers are eligible to select a health care provider in the private sector, paid for by the BPS. Uninsured individuals can choose to pay for their own private health care package, use the public health care system (subject to a means test), or remain uncovered.

In December of 2007 Uruguay's Parliament approved a bill (number 18, 211/2007) to reform the health care component of the social protection system. This bill created a national health care system (NHS) geared to extending comprehensive care to all residents and guaranteeing equitable and universal coverage through the coordination of the public and private health care sectors.[7] The pivotal component of the reform was the extension of health care coverage to workers' dependents, mainly children and spouses or partners. Because of fiscal restrictions, however, coverage was extended in stages. The first stage began in January 2008, when the NHS incorporated workers' children. To qualify, children must be under 18 years old. Their inclusion is universal and irrespective of previous health coverage arrangements.

The reform also substantially modified the financing of health care services. The new scheme is financed through a public fund called the National Health Fund (*Fondo Nacional de Salud,* FONASA; Law 18, 131/2007), which is managed by the BPS. One noteworthy feature of the reform was the increase in almost all contributions. For example, employee contributions grew from 3 to 6 percent of taxable earnings for individuals with children, while contributions for individuals with no children increased from 3.0 to 4.5 percent. Employer contributions remained unchanged at 5 percent under the new scheme.

The expansion of health care coverage to workers' children following the reform affects both public employees and private sector workers registered with the BPS. However, many public workers were already entitled to this extended coverage by the state, so the extension of coverage was most significant for registered private sector workers, who had to pay for their children's health care (in private sector) directly prior the reform. Even children of formal low-income workers, who previously used public health services, are now eligible for private care since FONASA entitles them to choose an IAMC in the private health sector.

3.3.2. Health Insurance Expansion and Incentives for Formal-Sector Employment

The reform could potentially have a series of effects on workers incentives and subsequent labor market outcomes. Given the non-negligible level of informality in the Uruguayan labor market, the decision to operate formally or informally – that is, as a registered or unregistered worker – should be subject to an important margin of behavioral change.[8] This is especially relevant in cases of workers at the margin of the labor market and for those at the margin between the formal and informal sectors (Maloney 1999; 2004; Heckman and

Pagés 2004; Fields 2005; Gunther and Launov 2012). The decision on formal versus informal employment should be guided by a cost-benefit analysis in which individuals compare the gains from contributing to the BPS, which consist of the bundle of social security benefits described above, with its cost in terms of increased contributions.

If workers value mandated benefits - mainly those immediately available, such as health insurance - then their behavioral labor supply responses must internalize that these are only obtainable through formal employment contributions. In particular, health insurance is a substantial component of the mandated benefits package in Uruguay in terms of both the BPS's total expenditure and the quality and quantity of health care services provided. The expansion of health care coverage to other household members may thus modify the incentives for workers to operate formally. Some workers might decide to move into formal jobs or to negotiate different employment conditions with their employers in order to profit from the expansion, despite the higher cost in terms of contributions (which increased from 3 to 6 percent of taxable labor earnings for those taking advantage of this option). However, the net impact of the health care reform on formality is ambiguous, as it depends on whether the allocation of workers to the formal and informal sectors of the labor market is decided at the individual or household level.

From the perspective of an individual worker, the incentive to become a formal employee stems from the benefit of no longer needing to pay directly for a child's health care once it is covered by the social security contribution. These incentives are substantial: for a worker with an average salary, the direct cost of paying for IAMC coverage for their children is comparable to the total payroll tax of a registered worker, which provides the worker access to the whole bundle of social security benefits (including retirement savings and unemployment insurance).[9] Thus, at the individual level, the reform would potentially increase the incentives of private sector workers to become formal, and this incentive should also result in an increase in the number of children affiliated with the IAMC.

If the decision to operate formally or informally is taken jointly at the household level, the health care reform may have a differential impact for adults within the household depending on the intra-household allocation of employment relations before the policy change. Galiani and Weinschelbaum (2012) analyze this point from a theoretical perspective and also provide empirical results for Latin

America. Their study indicates that secondary workers have a higher probability of operating informally when primary workers are formal. Under the health care reform in Uruguay, if more than one member of the household is formal, the health coverage for children incurs a double contribution, since the law stipulates that payroll taxes are computed at the individual and not the household level. In these cases, the reform may induce some household workers to move toward the informal sector, as children would still receive coverage with only one formal worker in the household. When all workers in the household are informal, the reform may induce some of them to operate formally in order to obtain health coverage for children and spouses. Finally, in households who have members in both sectors, the policy might not induce any changes in their formality status. The incentives also remain unchanged for households with older or no children - in fact, there may even be incentives to leave the formal sector due to the increase in the payroll tax linked to the health insurance component, which rose from 3.0 to 4.5 percent for those without children.

3.4. Data and Identification Strategy

3.4.1. Data

The empirical analysis in this chapter is based on repeated cross sections of household survey microdata from the *Encuesta Continua de Hogares* (ECH) for the years 2001 through 2009. The survey is a nationwide cross-sectional household survey, which is carried out by the Uruguayan National Institute of Statistics (*Instituto Nacional de Estadística*, INE). The ECH is the main source for information on income, employment and socio-economic characteristics of households and individuals

Since 2001, the ECH includes a standard question, which asks respondents whether or not their current job entitles them to a pension or retirement savings. This question allows for quantification of the proportion of workers who are registered in the social security system.[10] Thus, this question is generally used as a proxy to identify a worker's formality status according to the legal definition (see Gasparini and Tornarolli 2009, for a discussion of alternative definitions in Latin America). In what follows, this constitutes the main dependent variable used for the econometric estimates.

The sample analysis is limited to private sector workers ages 19 through 60, who resided in urban areas.[11] The treatment group (those exposed to the policy change) consists of all adult private sector salaried workers who reside in a household with at least one child younger than 18 years old. The control group consists of adult salaried workers in the private sector with no children. The final sample is a multiyear pool of ECH microdata, including the following years: 2001-7 and 2009 (2008, defined as an adjustment period, has been omitted).

3.4.2. *Identification Strategy*

The aim of the estimates presented below is to identify the causal effect of the HR on formality levels, and thus provide evidence on the direction and magnitude of the net incentive effects discussed in the previous section.[12] The empirical strategy exploits the exogenous extension of health care coverage for workers' children due to the HR in 2008 to isolate the impact of this policy on individual formality choices.[13] The econometric approach is based on the difference-in-differences (DD) methodology (Angrist and Krueger 1999; Bertrand, Duflo, and Mullainathan 2004).

This framework compares the results of a treatment group exposed to the policy change with another similar group, which feasibly represents the unobserved counterfactual evolution for the treated group. The estimation strategy compares formality levels among workers with children younger than 18 years and workers with no children before and after the policy change. Finally, the time period used to obtain the estimates is 2001-9, with 2001-7 defined as the pre-policy period and 2009 as the post-policy period, while 2008 is used as the period to capture the behavioral adjustments of workers.

3.5. Empirical Results: Incentive Effects and the Health Reform in Uruguay

3.5.1. *Effects at the Individual Level*

This section provides empirical evidence on how the incentives from the social security system affect labor market formality in Uruguay and the extent to which workers respond to the policy incentives discussed above when they are making decisions about formal and informal status. Table 3.1 and 3.2 show the results discussed in the next paragraphs.

Results in Table 3.1 show the health care reform significantly induced private sector salaried workers with at least one child (the group affected by the reform) to switch to formal employment, with a change in the informality rate of about 1.1 and 1.3 percentage points, on average, relative to those without children (the group that was not affected by the reform). In terms of the pre-intervention average, this effect represents a 5 percent decrease in the probability to operate informally.

The analysis also explores heterogenous effects of health care reform on labor informality for different socioeconomic groups, defined by gender, age, educational level, and firm size. Table 3.2 reports the estimates by gender and firm size. In terms of gender, the effect for men is not significant and very close to zero (less than 0.3 percentage points). Most of the effects arise from the reform's impact on female salaried workers – the effect is around 2.6 percentage points, and it is statistically significant at the 1 percent level (column 3). This represents a decrease of 7 percent from the pre-policy average for women. These results are qualitatively similar to those found by Juárez (2009) and Bosch and Campos-Vázquez (2010) for the Mexican programs *Programa de Servicios Médicos y Medicamentos Gratuitos* (PSMMG) and *Seguro Popular*, respectively.

Table 3.2 also reports the estimated effect of the health care reform by firm size (columns 3–6). The results demonstrate negative and statistically significant effects at the usual levels for those employed in small firms (one employee) and large firms (more than 50 employees).[14] Among salaried workers employed in small firms, the reform produced a 4.6 percentage point decrease in the likelihood of working without contributing to social security, compared with a 0.8 percentage point decrease for those employed in larger firms. These findings are consistent with the fact that in smaller firms, workers may have more room to negotiate employment conditions with their employers.

Although not reported in Table 3.2, the impact of the health care reform also varies by age group and educational level (see Bérgolo and Cruces 2011). While the effect of the reform is negative and statistically significant across all age groups considered in the analysis, the impact is stronger for older workers than for younger workers both in absolute terms and relative to the pre-policy average informality rate. For the youngest group (aged 19–29), the likelihood of working without contributing to social security falls by 1.0 percentage point (a decline of 3

Table 3.1

Effect of Health Reform on Informality

	Sample: salaried workers in private sector	
	(1)	(2)
Effect of Health Reform	−0.0119***	−0.0125***
on informality	[0.0037]	[0.0033]
Socio-economic Covariates	No	Yes
Observations	84109	84109
R^2	0.04	0.31
Percent Informal (average 2001-7)	26.33	

Note: Data are from survey years 2001-7 and 2009 of the *Encuesta Continua de Hogares* (ECH). The dependant variable is informal status, which is equals 1 if the worker is not entitled to retirement savings. The "treatment indicator" equals 1 if the worker has at least one child and the observation is in the post intervention period, the year 2009. Controls include age, age-squared, gender, head of household status, marital status, years of education, years of education-squared, number of children in the household, and a full set of firm size, industry, departments, time dummies and a constant. Robust standard errors in brackets are clustered by year. Regressions are weighted with ECH supplement weights.
* significant at 10%; ** significant at 5%; *** significant at 1%.

Source: Based on Bérgolo and Cruces (2011).

Table 3.2

Heterogeneous Effect of Health Reform in Uruguay on Informal Employment Levels

	By gender		By firm size (number of employees)			
	Male	Female	[1]	[2-4]	[5-49]	[+50]
	(1)	(2)	(3)	(4)	(5)	(6)
Effect of Health Reform	−0.0024	−0.0259***	−0.0469***	0.0055	−0.0057	−0.0078**
on informality	[0.0047]	[0.0037]	[0.0097]	[0.0077]	[0.0068]	[0.0029]
Observations	44171	39938	11453	14088	29755	28813
Percent Informal (avge. 2001-7)	20.1	33.43	69.03	47.54	18.23	4.34

Note: See Table 3.1.
Source: Based on Bérgolo and Cruces (2011).
* significant at 10%; ** significant at 5%; *** significant at 1%.

percent), while for the oldest group (aged 50–60) the estimated impact is a decrease of about 2.1 percentage points, which represents an 8 percent reduction. Regarding educational level, the results show a negative and statistically significant effect of health care reform for workers with secondary and tertiary levels of education and no significant effects on workers in the low educational group. For those with secondary education, labor informality decreases by 2.0 percentage points after the reform, a 0.6 percentage point reduction rate for the tertiary education group. In both groups, this impact represents a decrease of 8 percent relative to the pre-policy period average.

3.5.2. *The Impact of Health Reform on Intra-Household Labor Arrangements*

As discussed above, the direction of the reform's effect on formality probably depends on the existing intra-household allocation of employment relations prior to the reform. Thus, the health care reform may generate changes in labor arrangements within the household, since health coverage for children only requires one adult to be a formal employee. The incentive will be greatest for nuclear households in which both adults operate informally, while for other types of household the decision depends on the valuation of additional social security benefits. To account for these movements in status within the household, the study explores the possible effects of the health care reform on labor informality, taking into consideration the effects of potential joint decision-making by household members.

Table 3.3 reports a second set of estimates uses for the household, as opposed to the individual, as unit of observation. This analysis uses the same difference-in-differences approach as before, although the dependent variable is defined at the household level. Column (1) explores the possible reduction in the probability for households with children in which both spouses have informal jobs. The estimates indicate a decrease in the proportion of households with children in which both spouses are informally employed. The HR results in a 4-percentage point decrease in the probability of both spouses in the same household having an informal job. Column (2) presents a second specification which tests for a re-allocation of households from those in which both spouses were in formal employment to a household in which only one spouse was formally employed. While the sign of the coefficient of interest is negative, the estimate is small and not statistically significant at the standard levels. This result suggests that the possible incentives of the HR on a household in which both spouses are formal workers to become a household with one formal and one informal worker may be attenuated by the unwillingness of the household in the face of one member losing other social security benefits.

As an additional check of the predictions discussed above, Column (3) of Table 3.3 compares households with both spouses operating in the informal sector with those where at least one spouse is formal. In these cases, there should be a (relative) decrease of the first type of households in response to the HR. The estimates confirm this prediction, with a 2 percentage points decrease in the likelihood of both spouses to be informally employed for households with children following the HR. This represents a 20 percent decline relative to the pre-period rates.

In sum, the results indicate that the health care reform had a sizable impact on women, middle-aged and older workers, and workers with secondary and higher education. In addition, the reform's effect seemed to be more relevant for workers employed in small firms. This evidence suggests that the reform increased the incentives for workers to operate formally, either by renegotiating their employment conditions with their employers or by moving to other formal jobs. The evidence also indicated that household members react jointly to the change in the incentive structure implied by the extension of benefits to children.

For the case of Uruguay, these results support the expected theoretical prediction that improving the benefits from a mandated social package provides additional incentives to become a formal worker. They also imply a positive valuation of mandated social security benefits for a subset of the population.

3.6. Conclusions and Policy Discussion

This chapter analyzed the impact of the introduction of a health insurance reform on labor informality in Uruguay – the extension of health coverage to the children of private sector salaried workers which contribute to the social security system. The results indicate that the HR had a sizable impact on women, middle age and older workers, and for workers with secondary and higher education. In

Table 3.3

Effect of Health Reform on Formality Joint Decision of Households. Estimation Results for Dependent Variable

	Dependent variable: formality status of spouses in the household		
	1= Both informal 0 = Exactly one spouse formal	1 = Exactly one informal 0 = Both spouses formal	1 = Both informal 0 = At least one spouse formal
	(1)	(2)	(3)
Effect of Health Reform	-0.0421***	-0.0058	-0.0198***
on informality	[0.0130]	[0.0057]	[0.0041]
Observations	4812	13466	14592
R^2	0.20	0.29	0.22
Percent both Informal (avge. 2001-7)	26.16		9.75
Percent one Informal (avge. 2001-7)		30.49	

Note: See Table 3.1.
* significant at 10%; ** significant at 5%; *** significant at 1%.
Source: Based on Bérgolo and Cruces (2011).

addition, the effect of the HR seemed to be more relevant for workers employed in small firms. This evidence suggests larger incentives for workers to become formal in jobs in which they have greater bargaining power, renegotiating employment conditions with their employers or moving to other formal jobs. The evidence also indicated that household members react jointly to the change in the incentive structure implied by the extension of benefits to children.

The empirical results support the expected theoretical prediction that improving the benefits from a mandated social package provides additional incentives to become a formal worker. Furthermore, these results seem to be robust to different specifications and controlling for additional dimensions. The main finding is that labor informality decreased in Uruguay due to the HR's expansion of health care coverage, and workers and households were able to react to the new incentive structure. The results also imply a positive valuation of social security mandated benefits for a subset of the population.

Evidence that social security systems imply sizeable incentive effects for workers, and that workers react to these incentives, has serious implications for the design of labor market policies and social protection systems in developing countries. This is especially relevant in the context of the expansion of non-contributory elements such as conditional cash transfer programs. Like most countries in Latin America, Uruguay has expanded its social protection system in the past decade. One thing that Uruguay did differently, however, was to base some of the expansion on its contributory programs – the pensions system, health insurance, and unemployment insurance. Furthermore, the extension of the income transfer system to groups that have traditionally been excluded from coverage was accomplished within the existing traditional social welfare framework – namely, through the expansion of the family allowance program. Thus, instead of extending differentiated benefits and services to people who could not make contributions, the new scheme (which was mainly implemented in the second half of the 2000s) represented an original alternative to the new regional paradigms in the area of social welfare (see ECLAC 2006, chap. 5).

The extent to which the changes to these programs are able to satisfy coverage objectives while at the same time improving the willingness of workers to contribute to social security depends, in part, on the workers' valuation of the costs and benefits of social security, the alternatives to these costs and benefits, the magnitude of the changes introduced, and the degree of consistency among the incentives they generate. In some cases, the design of some reforms in Uruguay appears to be consistent with better incentives for workers to contribute to social security and thus to obtain coverage through the bundle of social security benefits. In other cases, the changes may have improved worker coverage at the expense of generating adverse incentives to registering for social security. In still other cases, the changes introduced to the programs have probably generated ambiguous incentives.

The empirical evidence on the effect of these reforms on formality is scarce. With regard to the extension of health insurance to cover the children of registered workers, as showed the evidence suggests that the reform improved workers' willingness to contribute to social security. In principle, the expansion of this contributory program appears to have reconciled the objectives of improving population coverage and providing incentives for workers to operate formally. The pensions system reforms carried out in the last two dacades, however, does not appear to have achieved the same result. In this case, there is no evidence that the penalty in terms of the rate of return for short contribution histories, after the reform in 1995, has changed the contributions profile of workers. Moreover, some studies indicate that a very large share of workers will not reach the minimum years of contributions required to retire from the labor market at the normal retirement age, even after the requirement was lowered from 35 to 30 years in the 2008 reform (Bucheli, Forteza and Rossi 2008).

Some of these reforms appear to have narrowed the coverage gaps, but the gaps are still large, in particular those associated with the contributory social protection system (Arim, Cruces and Vigorito 2009). The strategy of expanding the contributory programs to narrow the coverage gaps and at the same time improve the levels of formality in the economy clearly has limitations. One possible restriction has to do with the difference between the State's and the worker's valuation of contributory benefits and how these benefits are provided to the workers – bundling benefits. The state requires workers to buy a whole set of goods and services, so as to fulfill certain objectives that are considered socially necessary. This bundling requires workers to assess a single set of components that have widely different characteristics – present versus future consumption, collective versus individual needs, monetary versus in-kind receipts, everyday use versus emergencies, and so forth. The imperfect match between the individual needs (or preferences) of workers and the set of benefits in the bundle implies that workers may not want to consume all the benefits, or at least not all at the same time. The impossibility of splitting up the package of benefits lowers the value of social security for workers and thus reduces their willingness to contribute (Levy 2008). After the health care reform in Uruguay, many workers may be willing to contribute 6% of their wages to obtain health insurance coverage for their families, but they do not want to contribute additional resources to gain access to the rest of the benefit bundle. While the expansion of health insurance has increased the formality incentives for a group of workers, the share of individuals with health coverage would probably be greater if they could make contributions for this benefit alone.

In addition, there is a limit to how far coverage can be expanded through the redesign of contributory social welfare programs, given by the current productive and labor market conditions of a developing country like Uruguay. One indication of this restriction is the difficulty of lowering the levels of informality even in periods of strong growth, such as the 2004–10 period in Uruguay.

Given this framework, what are the options for continuing to expand the social protection system in Uruguay? One option is to continue expanding and/or reforming the contributory social welfare scheme so as to generate incentives for workers to make contributions. Given the limitations discussed above, this strategy requires rethinking the criteria for supplying the bundle of social benefits – for example, considering the possibility of breaking up the bundle and having workers voluntarily "buy" the type and quantity of social goods and services desired based on their individual preferences. The workers' valuation will be influenced by the available alternatives and their costs, as well as by the quality of these alternatives (non-contributory benefits and services provided by the market). An alternative that does not alter the compulsory nature or indivisibility of the bundle of social benefits, while still being based on the expansion of the contributory system, would require deep changes in the design of the bundle so as to improve the incentives to contribute or at least eliminate mechanisms that generate counter-incentives. One possibility would be to consider the household, rather than the individual, as the basis for contributions. In Uruguay, as in most countries, each worker must pay for all the benefits in the bundle even when some of the benefits extend to the family, thereby generating situations of overlapping contributions by different family members. The health reform provides an example of this design issue: in nuclear households, both spouses must make contributions to extend their health coverage to their children, but one of the spouses does not "enjoy" the additional benefit implied by the extra contribution (that is, only one contribution is necessary to cover the children). This incentive may become more important in 2011, when health coverage is extended to the spouses of formal workers (as established by the Law).

A second option would be to expand the existing non-contributory programs or to implement new programs that are not tied to the contribution history of the beneficiaries, so as to provide coverage to workers and their families who participate in the labor market without contributing to social security. In this case, the scale would be tipped toward coverage rather than incentives. For example, the extension of the family allowance program in Uruguay has huge benefits, but it undoubtedly removes one of the distinctions between formal and informal employment: under the new system, everyone receives the allowance, but only some "pay" for the benefits implicitly through their contributions. The same situation arises with less immediate benefits like retirement, where less stringent qualifications for the benefits are currently under discussion, or even the expansion of the non-contributory component of pensions. The evidence on the incentive mechanisms affecting formality and informality in the region's labor markets suggests that the coexistence of contributory and non-contributory programs – while providing broader coverage of the population – probably undermines the incentives to contribute to social security.

Finally, at the other extreme, there is the possibility of moving toward a universal system financed through taxes (that is, universal incomes for the elderly and children, universal access to unemployment and health insurance, and so forth). Under certain regulatory conditions, this could be considered the "first best" option in terms of equity, efficiency, and coverage (see Levy 2008). However, these universal social protection systems appear to be difficult to implement in the short and medium terms, since there are so many different interests involved and so many norms and regulations that would need to be modified.

The near future for Uruguay and the rest of the countries in Latin America will probably be sealed by a "second best" scenario, in which the traditional systems live side by side with ever-growing non-contributory programs. The key may lie in conducting a cost-benefit analysis of the programs and then defending those that appear to have a positive balance in net terms.[15] In this case, one potential problem is that the presence of disincentives leads to the rejection of measures with a potential positive net impact.

In the absence of governments with a broad mandate to reform social security and to institute far-reaching transformations, it will be necessary to design policy options that minimize the incentive conflicts (in terms of informal work, labor market participation, and so forth). This is ultimately the objective of the research agenda that is being developed in the region on the interaction between social protection systems and labor markets.

Notes

1 Contributory programs are those in which financing and access to benefits (such as health care, old age pensions, and workers' compensation) are directly related to contributions made by the workers, their employers, and, in some cases, the state. In contrast, non-contributory programs are not tied to the workers' contribution history, and their financing is largely dependent on taxes (Bertranou 2004).
2 See Gasparini and Tornarolli (2009) for a thorough analysis of the evidence for the region.
3 Levy (2008) considers contributions and premiums to be taxes on formality when there is also a non-contributory benefits system.
4 Although, in the past there were also programs that did not depend on the beneficiary's contribution history (Bertranou, 2005; Ferreira-Coimbra, and Forteza 2004).
5 The other institutions give coverage to other groups of workers. In particular, two social security institutions cover to the police and armed forces, respectively. The other three institutions administer services for professionals and for workers in the financial sector. Each of these institutions provides different bundles of benefits, usually broader than those provided to BPS beneficiaries.
6 These benefits are generally also provided to public sector employees when they sign an employment contract.
7 In implementing the health care reform, the government sought to strengthen three areas: health care coverage (focusing on primary care); health management; and health financing.
8 Whether workers have the power to make that decision or whether it all comes down to an employer's cost-benefit analysis is a contentious issue in the literature. Instead of opting for one of the two extremes, we assume that the worker has some degree of influence in this decision (see for instance, Levy 2008).
9 In 2008, the average monthly wage for salaried workers with children was around US$630 (at 2005 purchasing power parity), of which about US$130 corresponded to social security contributions for formal workers. In the same period, the average amount that workers paid to enroll a child in an IAMC was US$60. Since salaried workers have two young children, on average, the total amount paid for private health care would amount to US$120.
10 In addition, starting in 2008 after the implementation of the HR, the ECH also includes a question about whether or not individuals are entitled to health insurance by the NHS.
11 See the working paper version of this chapter (Bérgolo and Cruces 2011) for details about the sample restrictions and summary statistics for treatment and control groups in the pre-policy and post-policy periods.
12 For more details on the empirical strategy see Bérgolo and Cruces (2011).
13 Boyle and Lahey (2010) and Gruber and Madrian (1995) among others, use a similar approach to analyze the effect of health coverage extensions on different outcomes in the US labor market.
14 The information recorded by the ECH does not support a further breakdown of wage earners working in firms of "more than 50 employees."
15 Cruces and Gasparini (2008) discuss these aspects in the context of the universal family allowance in Argentina.

References

Angrist, J., Krueger, A. (1999). Empirical Strategies in Labor Economics, in: Ashenfelter, O. C., Card, D., (Eds.), Handbook of Labor Economics, vol. 3A, Amsterdam: Elsevier, 1277-1366.

Arim, R. , Cruces, G., Vigorito, A. (2009). Programas sociales y transferencias de ingresos en Uruguay: los beneficios no contributivos y las alternativas para su extensión, Serie de Políticas Sociales, 146, Santiago: U.N. Economic Commission for Latin America and the Caribbean, Social Development Division.

Bérgolo, M., Cruces, G. (2011). Labor Informality and the Incentive Effects of Social Security: Evidence from a Health Reform in Uruguay, IDB Working Paper No. 62318.

Bertrand, M., Duflo, E., Mullainathan, S. (2004). How Much Should We Trust Differences-in-Differences Estimates?, in: Quarterly Journal of Economics, 119(1): 249-75.

Bertranou, F. (2004). Protección social y mercado laboral, Geneva: International Labor Organization, Santiago Office.

Bertranou, F. (2005). Protección social, mercado laboral e institucionalidad de seguridad social, in: Empleo y protección social: de la crisis al crecimiento, Geneva: International Labor Organization, Santiago Office.

Bosch, M., Campos-Vázquez, R. (2010). The Trade-offs of Social Assistance Programs in the Labor Market: The Case of "Seguro Popular" Program in Mexico, Serie documentos de trabajo del Centro de Estudios Económicos Working Paper No. 12.

Boyle, M., Lahey, J. N. (2010). Health Insurance and the Labor Supply Decisions of Older Workers: Evidence for a U.S. Department of Veterans Affairs expansion, in: Journal of Public Economics, 94(7-8): 467-78.

Bucheli, M., Forteza, A., Rossi, I. (2008). Work Histories and the Access to Contributory Pensions: The Case of Uruguay, in: Journal of Pension Economics and Finance, 9(3): 369–91.

ECLAC (U.N. Economic Commission for Latin America and the Caribbean) (2006). La protección social de cara al futuro: Acceso, financiamiento y solidaridad, Santiago.

Cruces, G., Gasparini, L. (2008). Programas sociales en Argentina: alternativas para la ampliación de la cobertura, CEDLAS Working Paper No. 0077.

Ferreira-Coimbra, N., Forteza, A. (2004). Protección social en Uruguay: Financiamiento, cobertura y desempeño, 1990–2002, Geneva: International Labor Organization, Santiago Office.

Fields, G. S. (1990). Labour Market Modelling and the Urban Informal Sector: Theory and Evidence, in: Thurnham, D., Salome, B., Schwarz, A. (Eds.), The Informal Sector Revisited, Paris: OECD, 49-69.

Fields, G.S. (2005). A Guide to Multisector Labor Market Models, Paper prepared for the World Bank Labor Market.

Fiszbein, A., Schady, N. (2009). Conditional Cash Transfers: Reducing Present and Future Poverty, Washington, DC: The World Bank.

Galiani, S., Weinschelbaum, F. (2012). Modeling Informality Formally: Households and Firms, in: Economic Inquiry, 50(3): 821–38.

Gasparini, L., Haimovich, F., Olivieri, S. (2007). Labor Informality Effects of a Poverty-Alleviation Program, CEDLAS Working Paper No. 0053.

Gasparini, L., Tornarolli, L. (2009). Labor Informality in Latin America and the Caribbean: Patterns and Trends from Household Survey Microdata, CEDLAS Working Paper No. 46.

Gruber, J., Madrian, B. C. (1995). Health Insurance Availability and the Retirement Decision, in: American Economic Review, 85(4): 938–48.

Gunther, I., Launov, A. (2012). Informal Employment in Developing Countries. Opportunity of Last Resort?, in: Journal of Developing Economics, 97(1): 88-98.

Harris, J., Todaro, M. (1970). Migration, Unemployment, and Development: A Two-Sector Analysis, in: American Economic Review, 60(1): 126–42.

Heckman, J., Pagés, C. (Eds.) (2004). Law and Employment: Lessons from Latin America and the Caribbean, Cambridge, MA: National Bureau of Economic Research.

Juárez, L. (2009). Are Informal Workers Compensated for the Lack of Fringe Benefits? Free Health Care as an Instrument for Formality, Centro de Investigación Económica, ITAM Working Papers No. 0804.
Levy, S. (2008). Good Intentions, Bad Outcomes: Social Policy, Informality and Economic Growth in Mexico, Washington, DC: Brookings Institution Press.
Maloney, W. (1999). Does Informality Imply Segmentation in Urban Labor Markets? Evidence from Sectoral Transitions in Mexico, in: World Bank Economic Review, 13(2): 275–302.
Maloney, W. (2004). Informality Revisited, in: World Development, 32(7): 1159–78.
Rawlings L. (2004). A New Approach to Social Assistance: Latin America's Experience with Conditional Cash Transfer Programmes, in: International Social Security Review, 58(2–3): 133–61.
Summers, L. (1989). Some Simple Economics of Mandated Benefits, in: American Economic Review, 79(2): 177–83.

4

Effects of Non-Contributory Systems on Informality: Taking Stock of Eight Years of Implementation of Mexico's *Seguro Popular*[*]

Mariano Bosch
M. Belén Cobacho
Carmen Pagés

4.1. Introduction

On average, one out of two workers in the Latin American region is informal, meaning that they do not contribute to social security in their job. This fact has traditionally left large segments of the population exposed to financially crippling health shocks and in high risk of old-age poverty due to lack of pension coverage.

However, the provision of social security in the Latin American region is rapidly changing. The last two decades have seen an unprecedented expansion of non-contributory systems, side by side with traditional social security. This is a direct consequence of the inability of social security systems to reach wide levels of coverage, either by design (most social security systems explicitly exclude the self-employed – a large percentage of employment in developing economies) or the inability of states to curb the evasion of social security contributions among a large majority of employers. Given the difficulties associated with reforming social security systems, many countries

* *The authors thank Markus Frölich for his valuable comments at various stages of this chapter.*

are resorting to the creation of parallel non-contributory schemes directly financed with general revenues which become available to those who are not entitled to social security.

While the upside is the rapid progress in coverage that such initiatives have promoted, there are important potential pitfalls that should be considered as well. Since workers have to demonstrate that they are not in social security (i.e. that they are informal) to qualify for the non-contributory benefits, the risk is that those who are contributing to social security stop doing so to benefit from free-of-cost benefits (Levy 2008), a risk particularly high in Latin America where the literature has shown large flows between formal and informal jobs (Bosch and Maloney 2008; Pages and Stampini 2009). To mitigate this risk, benefits provided by non-contributory programs tend to be lower than those provided by social security. However, political and legal pressures may make unfeasible the maintenance of parallel (contributory and non-contributory) systems with different levels of benefits. Further, low willingness or ability to pre-pay for insurance among low-income workers implies that for many, social security acts like a tax to becoming formal, while non-contributory regimes act as a subsidy on informality or inactivity. It is therefore expected that the introduction of such non-contributory regimes will further distort the labor market, fostering informality and reducing labor market participation, with potentially grave impacts on resource allocation and aggregate productivity. In parallel, there are substantial fiscal implications, as non-contributory systems represent large and growing unfunded commitments that governments will have to fulfill in the future.

The *Mexican Seguro Popular* (SP) is one of such programs designed to provide affordable health care to the 50 million uninsured people in Mexico. This chapter summarizes the latest evidence of the major impacts of this far reaching and, to some extent, controversial program. We first review the evidence regarding the impact of SP on health related outcomes and then focus on the consequences of SP on the labor market.

As in many other Latin American countries, access to health care in Mexico is intimately linked to formal work status. Mexico's health care system was born in 1943. Two institutions were created for formal-sector workers – the *Instituto Mexicano de Seguro Social* (IMSS) for registered private employees, and later, the *Instituto de Seguridad y Servicios Sociales de los Trabajadores del Estado* (ISSSTE), for public employees.[1] Workers affiliated to either IMSS or ISSSTE are considered formal-sector workers. They (and their families) have access to a bundle of benefits that include health and pensions.

In parallel to IMSS and ISSSTE, the *Secretaría de Salud y Asistencia* (SSA) was created to serve all individuals outside the formal sector (denominated in this chapter as *the uninsured*). SSA's main role was purely one of "social assistance." However, due to the overwhelming demand for affordable health care for poor families, a number of programs were designed to provide access to health care to the low-income population. By 2000, the inequalities in this system were apparent. Nearly 50% of the Mexican population, amounting to 47 million people, were not insured by either IMSS or ISSSTE and were relying on the SSA or private institutions for their health care. The World Health Organization ranked Mexico 144th out of 191 countries in fairness of health care and the Mexican Ministry of Health estimated that 2 to 4 million families (10 to 20% of the total population) suffered catastrophic and impoverishing health care expenses every year. These families were almost exclusively drawn from the lowest income quintile, and were four times more likely to be uninsured than insured (Knaul and Frenk 2005). The pressure for reform was mounting and in 2003 a new health system was established.

Nine years later, with almost 90% of the uninsured population affiliated to SP in 2010, universalization of the health care protection in Mexico is in principle almost attained. This is an impressive achievement. However, to get here, Mexico took a very different route to that followed by other countries where a state-provided or state-funded health system covers the whole population. The introduction of SP generated an alternative, and arguably competing, health care system to that originally established by social security. By the end of 2010 the number of individuals covered by SP surpassed those covered by IMSS. Reviewing the evidence we highlight three main lessons learnt from the Mexican experience:

First, the expansion of SP coverage has reduced the financial burden imposed by health expenditures, particularly catastrophic ones, to the formerly uninsured households in Mexico.

Second, we have also learned about the difficulties of creating a culture of prepayment. As of 2010, the contributions of the affiliates cover less than 0.5% of SP expenditure. This is an important lesson for other countries which seek to expand the reach of contributory systems with subsidized contributions or matching agreements which imply co-financing between the state and individuals.

Finally, some of the fears that parallel non-contributory systems would directly compete with the contributory one have come true. Offering virtually free health services to workers conditional on being employed in the informal sector constitutes a *de facto* subsidy to informal employment. There is evidence that the implementation of SP has changed incentives to contribute to social security and workers and firms have responded to these changes. The available evidence so far points at a relocation of between 0.4 and 1 percentage points which is equivalent to 160,000 to 400,000 workers. During this same period, around 2 million formal jobs were created suggesting that the increase would have been between 8% and 20% higher in the absence of SP. This reallocation has been more intense among small firms and unskilled workers.

In the rest of this chapter, we first describe the reform and its implementation. Then the evidence on the direct health benefits is reviewed, as well as any indirect effects on the social security system and on the labor market. We finally discuss lessons to be drawn from the Mexican experience.

4.2. The Reform

The 2003 reform establishing the System for Social Protection in Health (*Sistema de Protección Social en Salud*, SSPH) was designed to increase financial protection by offering subsidized, publicly provided access to health insurance to those without social security protection. This reform institutionalized an existing pilot program: *Seguro Popular de Salud* or Popular Health Insurance that had been running in some Mexican states since 2002.[2] It is worth noting that covering the uninsured (those not covered by either IMSS or ISSSTE) was not a new phenomenon. The Mexican government, through the SSA, had provided health care for the uninsured since the advent of the formal social protection institutions. In fact, since the mid-1990s, well before the implementation of SP, there had been a steady increase in health spending for the uninsured population; the share of total health spending for the uninsured increased from 19% in 1990 to 44% in 2010. The innovation behind SP was to create an official entitlement for the uninsured (targeting universal health coverage) as well as the increase in budget allocation.

The transition to universal coverage translated into an annual goal of affiliating 14.3% of the approximately 12 million uninsured families. The law stipulated to focus the affiliation process on the poorest quintile of the population and thus the transition phase had been highly progressive (Knaul et al. 2006). As stated SP operated prior to the reform as a pilot program between 2001 and 2003. Then coverage under SP expanded progressively since 2003, and it achieved close to universal access to all of the uninsured population by 2010. Knaul and Frenk (2005) describe the key innovations and expected benefits of the Mexican health reform, describing encouraging results of the initial stages of implementation. Interestingly, since affiliation to SP is voluntary, some of the uninsured never affiliated. One possibility is that, since SP is not contingent on health status, they do not affiliate until they are exposed to a health shock. A second possibility is perhaps SP facilities are not nearby and hence there is not a large incentive to affiliate.

One of the objectives of the reform was creating and guaranteeing an explicit basic universal package of services to all affiliates. Services covered included a package of essential primary and secondary interventions managed and delivered at the state level, and a package of high-complexity health care interventions financed through a fund for protection against catastrophic health spending administered at the federal level. Only households not covered by social security health services are eligible for the program, and this is the single eligibility criterion (González-Pier 2006). Hence, affiliation is conditional on labor status, not on income level. The number of services covered by SP has been increasing over time (for example the number of covered secondary interventions increased from 91 in 2003 to 275 in 2010), implying that the gap in the quality of service received by the insured vs. the uninsured has been closing.

Another aim of the reform was to promote a "culture of co-payment" (Secretaría de Salud, 2002), so their affiliates were obliged to pay an annual premium in exchange for access to health services. When it was legislated in 2003, it was stipulated that SP would be financed through tripartite contributions from the federal government, the states, and individual contributions. This financing design was aimed at increasing health expenditures as a percentage of GDP, particularly for the uninsured, and at increasing the progressivity of transfers across states. Initially, the size of the payment was set to increase with economic status, while the poorest 20% of the households were declared exempt from all payments.[3]

4.3. Implementation of, and Affiliation to, *Seguro Popular*

After its passage into law in 2003, SP was implemented in stages across states. It is important to note that health services for the informal workers were already available before SP and hence if the provision of such services generated any distortions in the labor market, they were already in place before the implementation of SP. The institutionalization of SP improved those services, potentially strengthening such effects.

SP had begun in five states in 2002 (Colima, Jalisco, Aguascalientes, Tabasco and Campeche). According to Mexican officials, these states were chosen initially due "to the capacity of offering the services, large concentration of urban and semi-urban population and the existence of previous benefit programs from the government" (Secretaría de Salud 2002). In order to start the program in the rest of the 26 states and Mexico City, the federal government needed to sign an agreement of participation with each state. However, during 2002 and 2003, 14 other states (Sinaloa, Tamaulipas, Baja California, San Luis Potosí, Sonora, Coahuila, Guanajuato, Zacatecas, Oaxaca, México, Quintana Roo, Guerrero, Hidalgo, Chiapas, and Morelos) started to implement SP without a formal agreement with the federal government. According to SP officials, this was possible before 2004 if the municipal government agreed to offer the program. This was still considered by the SSA as the pilot phase. Throughout 2003, 2004 and 2005, all states except Mexico City (DF) had signed the official agreement with the federal government. This agreement included not only the required funds to finance the program but also its rules of operation. The rules of operation stated that the program needs to be implemented in localities with high poverty incidence and/or localities with indigenous populations, but the localities also needed to have health facilities in close range. Hence, the decision of which municipalities were affiliated first was a decision based on existence of agreements with state governments and available infrastructure.

The expansion of SP was very fast. By 2010, SP included more than 43 million affiliates (Secretaría de Salud 2010) although this number could be an overestimate. According to the 2010 Population Census there are only 26.2 million affiliates, and according to the 2009 National Employment and Social Security Survey (*Encuesta Nacional de Empleo y Seguridad Social*, ENESS) only 12.7 million. In any case, affiliation seems to have been rapid and intense. This is shown in Figure 4.1, which plots the evolution of the affiliation of individuals and households to SP from 2002 to 2010 according to the SP registry.

Figure 4.1

Number of Individuals and Households Affiliated with SP: 2002-2009

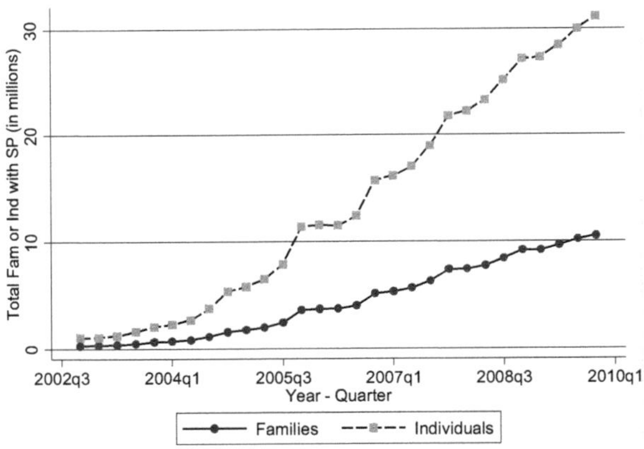

Notes: Number of individuals and households registered with SP according to the administrative records 2002-9, including children and dependants.
Source: Bosch and Campos (2010).

A crucial issue in the impact evaluations of SP is how this roll out across municipalities was undertaken. In principle, although the rule governing the process states that the poorest regions (subject to minimum infrastructure requirements) should have priority, in practice other considerations seem to have played a dominant role. Barros (2009) shows how political and logistical concerns seem to have driven the implementation sequence of SP program across states in Mexico. In particular, he shows that the intensity target, measured as the ratio of the total number of households agreed (by the federal and state governments) to enroll in SP, and the total number of households not covered by social security in the state, is uncorrelated with the initial level of economic development and regional health needs. Some authors have seen a political motivation in the way SP was implemented: Díaz-Cayeros et al. (2006) argue that municipalities in smaller states were given preference to achieve full coverage of SP so the federal government could claim full coverage in the state before the presidential election of July 2006. Furthermore, there seems to be a correlation between the early implementation of SP and the affiliation of the state governor in post pilot municipalities. Bosch and Campos (2010) show that bigger municipalities implemented SP earlier, but variables related to the income, number of uninsured, and industrial structure were not significant in predicting the timing of affiliation of a municipality to SP. Azuara and Marinescu (2011) show that the level of informality in a municipality or state prior to the introduction of SP is not correlated with the moment when SP is introduced. They also examine whether the year of introduction of SP is predicted by observable variables in 2000, at either the municipality or state level. Similarly, Aterido, Hallward-Driemeier and Pagés (2011) show that the growth rate of informality prior to the introduction of SP does not predict the arrival of SP either. All these studies conclude there is no evidence that informality in states or municipalities determined the timing of the expansion of SP, and suggest that the introduction of the program was close to random. Most studies that we review below rely on that variation to obtain results, as a difference-in-differences methodology is used in many of them, based on the fact that in some municipalities SP started earlier while it was available in other municipalities only later.

4.4. Direct Effect of *Seguro Popular* on Health Services Provision and Health Outcomes

As discussed above, the reform increased substantially the affiliation to the *Seguro Popular*. However, affiliation to SP did not immediately imply access to health services since many municipalities did not have the infrastructure or resources to deliver health care. Furthermore, it remained to be seen whether SP had the capability to improve health outcomes of the insured population.

Figure 4.2

Per Capita Expenditure in Insured/Per Capita Expenditure in Uninsured

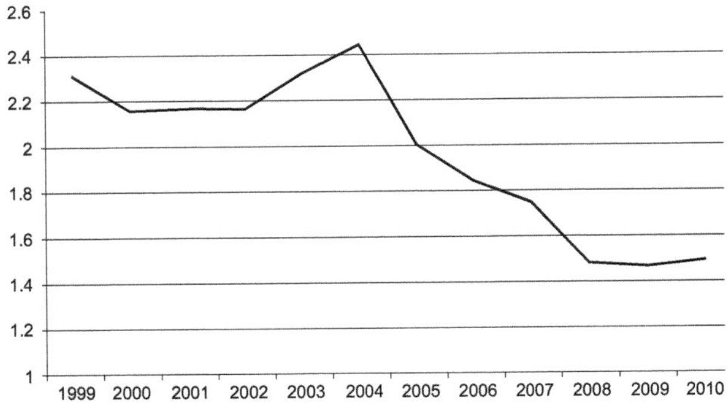

Note: The per capita on the insured is calculated as the health care expenditures executed by IMSS and ISSSTE divided by the total number of affiliates to these programs. Similarly, the per capita expenditure on the uninsured is calculated as the health expenditure executed by the SSA divided by the number of uninsured.

Source: Dirección General de Información en Salud (DGIS). Base de datos de cuentas en salud a nivel federal y estatal, 1990-2007. Sistema Nacional de Información en Salud (SINAIS). [México]: Secretaría de Salud.

During 2006, a series of articles were published in *The Lancet*, under the name of Health System Reform in Mexico (Frenk et al. 2006; González-Pier et al. 2006; Lozano et al. 2006; Knaul et al. 2006; Gakidou et al. 2006; Sepúlveda et al. 2006). Those articles argue that the health system reform in Mexico, and the SP program in particular, has been a complete success. Frenk et al. (2006) state that the reform of the health system allowed for a substantial increase in public investment in health, and it realigned incentives towards a better quality service. The total public health expenditure as a share of GDP increased from 2.6 in 2000 to 3.1 in 2010. Furthermore, the allocation of resources between insured and uninsured population was also altered. Figure 4.2 shows that the relative per capita health expenditure between the insured and the uninsured fell from 2.2 to 1.5 during the 2000-2010 decade, and particularly so after the implementation of SP in 2004.[4]

Yet while the reform increased coverage of health services and per capita expenditures for the uninsured population, and it partially redressed large funding inequities across states, some key goals of the reform could not be accomplished (Lakin 2010). First, the reform introduced a copayment for all families except for the 20% poorest

Table 4.1

Effects of *Seguro Popular* on Health Outcomes

Authors	Data	Methodology	Main results
Knaul et al. (2006)	ENIGH 1992-2004 (every 2 years) ENSANut 2005-05	Descriptive statistics OLS	Negative association between out-of-pocket health spending/catastrophic spending and coverage of SP.
Aguilera and Marrufo (2006)	Hospital discharge data at the state level		No significant effect of SP program on the incidence of low birth weight.
Gakidou et al. (2006)	ENSA 2000 for coverage and responsiveness ENSANut 2005-6 for catastrophic expenditure, coverage, responsiveness, hospital use and functional health status ENED 2002-3 for responsiveness ENIGH 2000 and 2004 for catastrophic expenditure *Census* and *Padrón del SP* 2002-6 for affiliation SAEH 2000-5 for hospital use SICUENTAS and the Health Statistics Bulletin 2000-5 for health expenditure SEED 1995-2005 for mortality rates SINERHIAS for the concentration of doctors and nurses	Descriptive statistics Logistic regression	Affiliation is preferentially reaching the poor and the marginalized communities; Federal non-SS expenditure increased by 38% from 2000 to 2005; proportion of individuals paying for medication among SP affiliates is 41.3%, in uninsured people is 73.8% and in individuals in SS is 30.7%; Equity of public-health expenditure across states improved; SP affiliates used more inpatient and outpatient services than uninsured people; effective coverage of 11 interventions has improved between 2000 and 2005–6; Inequalities in effective coverage across states and wealth deciles have decreased; catastrophic expenditures for SP affiliates are lower than for uninsured people.

Table 4.1. (continued)

Effects of *Seguro Popular* on Health Outcomes

Authors	Data	Methodology	Main results
Scott (2006)	ENIGH 2004	Descriptive statistics	Higher utilization rates of public health services for SP affiliates than for the rest of the uninsured, and higher for higher income groups; household health expenditures lower for SP beneficiaries; incidence of catastrophic health expenditures lower across deciles for SP beneficiaries.
Gallardo-García (2006)	Mexican Family Life Survey 2002	Dynamic discrete choice model	Negligible impact on birth weight.
Esquivel and Ordaz (2008)	ENEU 1995-2004	Propensity score matching	The presence of a member in the family working in the formal sector has a positive effect to work in the formal sector. No evidence of an effect of the social policy in Mexico on informality.
Díaz-Cayeros (2006)	Mexico panel 2006	Propensity score matching	No significant effect of social assistance programs on PAN's (*Partido de Acción Nacional*) victory in 2006 elections.
Sosa-Rubí et al. (2009)	ENSANut 2006	Multinomial probit estimation	Robust, significantly positive impact of SP on pregnant women's access to obstetrical services.
Harris and Sosa-Rubí (2009)	ENSANut 2006	Latent class model	Enrollment in SP is associated with a mean increase in 1.65 prenatal visits during pregnancy; 59% of this treatment effect is the result of increased prenatal care among women who had little or no access to care.
Galárraga et al. (2008)	ENIGH 2006, ENSANut 2006 SP Impact Evaluation Survey	Bivariate probit estimation	Using the ENIGH: No effect on catastrophic health expenditures; statistically significant effect on the reduction of household's expenditures on medicines and outpatient care. Using ENSANut and SP Impact Evaluation Survey: SP reduces the probability of catastrophic health expenditures; reduction of the probability of expenditures on medicines and outpatient care among SP insured families.

Table 4.1. (continued)

Effects of *Seguro Popular* on Health Outcomes

Authors	Data	Methodology	Main results
Hernández-Torres et al. (2008)	SP Impact Evaluation Survey 2002 Campeche and Colima	Probit model	8% of reduction in catastrophic expenditure on health, independent of the economic level or the kind of service.
King (2009)	Experimental design	Experimental Design	23% of reduction from baseline in catastrophic expenditures. The intention-to-treat effect on health spending in poor households was 426 *pesos*; the complier average causal effect was 915 *pesos*; no effects on medication spending, health outcomes, or utilization.
Barros (2009)	ENSA 2000 ENSANut 2006 ENIGH 2000, 2004, 2005, 2006	Differences in differences	SP decreases households' health expenditures: 4.2% of increase in savings of non-health expenditures; reduction of 40% of people not seeking care due to financial constraints; negligible effect on health status.

households (later extended to the 40% poorest), however in practice very few households paid the premium. As previously discussed, fast implementation was partly motivated by political considerations. According to official figures, only 7.2% of affiliates were paying in June 2005, which led to a substantial financing gap (Lakin 2010). As of 2010, the contributions of the affiliates constitute less than 0.5% of SP expenditure. Thus, the reform did not help create a culture of prepayment. Furthermore, the states were supposed to co-pay part of the cost of the implementation of SP but were unable to meet the financing demands and so most of the cost was absorbed by the federal budget with very little copayment from the users or the states.

A second important shortcoming was the inability to guarantee a universal package of benefits. Many clinics and hospitals could not provide some of the services that were part of the universal package. Perhaps because of this, the evidence regarding how much the conditions of the uninsured have improved with SP is still inconclusive. Some authors document increased access to medicines (Garrido-Latorre et al. 2008), an increase in the use of health services by those affiliated to SP (Gakidou et al. 2006; Scott 2006; Sosa-Rubí et al. 2009; Harris and Sosa-Rubí 2009) and a reduction in catastrophic health expenditures (Gakidou et al. 2006; Scott 2006; Knaul et al. 2005; Knaul et al. 2006; Galárraga et al. 2008; Hernández-Torres et al. 2008). However other studies document only small improvements in access to health services for SP affiliates relative to non-affiliates (Urbina 2008). Related to this is the fact that there were important lags in the implementation of SP. Bosch and Campos-Vazquez (2010) show that 3 years after the implementation of SP in a municipality there is a significant increase in medical personnel by not in medical infrastructure, suggesting the sluggish construction of facilities to deliver health care.

A third issue is that so far, studies have found no discernible effects on health outcomes (Aguilera and Marrufo 2006; Gakidou et al. 2006; Scott 2006; Knaul et al. 2006). Table 4.1 summarizes the data and the methodology used, as well as the results found in a large number of studies assessing the effects of SP on health related outcomes.

The two most systematic studies up to date on the effects of SP on health outcomes corroborate some of these findings. King et al. (2009), using an experimental approach, and Barros (2009), using triple differences in differences, show that SP significantly reduced health catastrophic expenditures of Mexican households, but they did not find any significant effects on health outcomes, at least so far.

However, their findings are mixed when it comes to assessing service utilization. While Barros (2009) finds a substantial increase, King et al. (2009) cannot identify any significant changes. We briefly describe these studies.

King et al. (2007, 2009) take advantage of the implementation of SP to introduce an experimental component to evaluate the program. During the early stages of the roll out of SP, King et al. (2007) were able to clearly define treatment and control areas. In particular, the experiment consisted in, first, defining a series of contiguous geographic regions (called health clusters), each one including an actual or future health clinic or facility and the population area around it. Then health clusters were matched in pairs, so that members of each pair were as similar as possible on a range of background characteristics. Then they randomly treated one health cluster from each pair with an active advertisement campaign to encourage individuals to affiliate with SP, along with the health facilities, drugs, and doctors necessary to implement the program effectively. The other health cluster in each pair did not receive any extra treatment. At the time of random assignment, they conducted a baseline survey of the health facility within each health cluster, and a survey of randomly selected households within the pairs of clusters (chosen based on likelihood of compliance with encouragement to affiliate and similarity of the clusters within each pair). This baseline household survey is used to verify that the treated and control groups are similar on a wide range of health characteristics and other variables. Ten months later they conducted follow-up surveys of the health facilities and individuals within each health cluster, which are used to ascertain the short-brun effect of the program. Primarily, the estimates indicated a 23% reduction from baseline in catastrophic health expenditures. Contrary to expectations and previous observational research, they found no effects on medication spending, health outcomes, or utilization. Nevertheless, by the authors' own admission, this experiment could say little about the long term health impacts of the program.

Barros (2009) estimates the impact of the SP program by analyzing differences over three dimensions. The first dimension is the variation in the program intensity target, measured as the ratio of the total number of households agreed (by the federal and state governments) to enroll during a single quarter, and the total number of households not covered by social security in the state (as of 2007). The program intensity quarter is measured at the time of the cross-section (first quarter of

2006). The second dimension is the differences across time before and after the program was initiated in a particular state. Finally, the third dimension is the differences over SP eligibility, comparing individuals with and without social security (people in the informal sector to people in the formal sector). To support this specification, the author tests the assumption that social security coverage among the population in a region is not affected by the regional intensity of SP (households switching from the formal to the informal labor market to become SP-eligible) and finds no correlation. However, as we will see later, there is some evidence against these assumptions. With this caveat in mind, Barros (2009) results show that SP increased by 4.2 percentage points the amount of resources that beneficiaries were able to spend on non-health expenditures, or save, and encourage beneficiary people to seek care. In particular, while SP-eligible households at baseline were 10.4 percentage points more likely than social security households not to seek care due to financial concerns, the effect of SP has been to close this gap by about 40% (4.2 percentage points reduction over the initial 10.4 percentage points difference). However the effect on health status is negligible, and evidence of an impact on labor supply or earnings is not found. This way, the author states that the policy motivation of having a redistributive impact is reached, in the sense that tax revenues come from formal households and go to SP which is applied to informal households suffering from any sickness.

In sum, there seems to be evidence that, as expected, the provision of a universal health insurance service has reduced substantially the catastrophic expenditures that poor Mexican families had to incur in the face of a health shock. However, there is little consensus on whether services have improved substantially for SP beneficiaries relative to non-beneficiaries (who can get services at clinics and hospitals of the Secretary of Health). While so far the evidence has not found significant changes in the health of those affected by this reform, more medium and long-run analysis is needed to establish the health effects of SP.

4.5. Unintended Effects of *Seguro Popular* on the Labor Market

Seguro Popular was designed to provide affordable health care to those workers and their families who were not affiliated with social security. In fact, a pre-requisite to join SP was that the worker was not covered by the formal social protection mechanisms provided by the IMSS or the ISSSTE. Hence, there was concern by policy-makers, and economists, that workers and firms could opt out of IMSS and join SP. This issue is of particular relevance in Mexico because a number of studies provide evidence of the large degree of mobility between formal (the insured) and the informal (the uninsured) labor markets (Maloney 1999; Bosch and Maloney 2008; Pagés and Stampini 2009). Around 25% of formal workers are found in the informal sector or in non-employment a year later. Although the evidence on whether these two markets are integrated is far from being conclusive, the introduction of SP makes informal jobs more attractive. This may motivate some formal workers to seek jobs in the informal sector. However, SP does not necessarily generate incentives to change jobs, but to change labor status, from formal (covered by IMSS) to informal (not covered by IMSS) and so workers might find it optimal (probably in collusion with the employer) to change labor status (i.e to stop contributing to social security) within the same job in the same firm. All this might reduce the number of workers who normally transition from informal to formal jobs and increase the number of workers that transit from formal into informal jobs. In turn this might affect firm's decision to comply with formality. In particular, it might induce firms to cheat more, as the firms might be inclined to appropriate the surpluses generated by SP by offering informal contracts. Finally, the introduction of SP may also affect the decisions of unemployment/non-participation, as those who are searching for a job may stop searching or search less intensively when the SP benefit is made available.

This potential shift towards informal activities or non-employment is worrisome at least for three reasons. First, because the benefits from formal social protection are bundled (Levy 2008), hence, contribution to social security entitles the worker not only to health care but also to other important benefits. Perhaps the most important of those is access to a pension scheme. If workers or firms (or both) choose to avoid social security contributions knowing that SP provides affordable health care, this may trigger the loss of all other benefits as well. This would imply expanding health care coverage at the expense of reducing other social protection mechanisms, in particular, reducing the efficiency of the pension system to prevent old-age poverty. Second, workers choosing informal arrangements in the provision of health care may have implications at the aggregate level, since this "informalization" of firms and workers may lead to a lower scale of production (smaller firms), lower employment rates, lower investment and lower overall productivity with ultimate implications for overall growth. And finally, there are clear fiscal implications as the shift towards informal activities reduces the tax base.

Perhaps because of the larger implications for poverty, productivity and growth, the search for unintended effects of SP in the labor market has been extremely active with a large number of studies using a variety of data sets. However, the results have been mixed, and no real consensus has been reached in the literature. Some early studies do not find any impact of SP on the share of formal workers in the labor market (Gallardo-García 2006; Esquivel and Ordaz 2008; Barros 2009; Campos and Knox 2010; Aguilera 2011).

Others find relatively small increases in the share of informality for particular population groups (Azuara and Marinescu 2011; Duval and Smith 2011). However, a new wave of papers (Aterido, Hallward-Driemeier, and Pagés 2011; Bosch and Campos 2010; Bosch and Cobacho 2011; Pérez-Estrada 2011) is consistently finding systematic reallocation effects of SP in the labor market. Table 4.2 shows the data sources, period of analysis, methodology and main results of this literature. While the identification strategy is relatively similar in most of these studies, the data employed, geographical coverage and time span vary substantially, constituting the most likely source of the discrepancies in the results.

As mentioned before, SP was not randomly implemented across municipalities, but most of the studies rely on the timing of the SP roll out as the main mechanism to identify its effects in the labor market.[5] That is, in one way or another, all studies try to identify employment effects implementing a difference-in-differences approach. Since the implementation of the program was at the municipality level, these geographical divisions have constituted the main unit of analysis, although state level variation has also been used (see Barros 2009). Having said this, there are some differences in the identification strategies due to the particularities of the data that we describe below.

In one of the earliest studies regarding the effects of SP on the labor market, Barros (2009) uses the National Income and Expenditure Survey (*Encuesta Nacional de Ingresos y Gastos de los Hogares*, ENIGH) 2000-6 to show no evidence of any shift towards informal employment after the implementation of SP. He suggests the lower quality of health care

Table 4.2

Effects of *Seguro Popular* on the Labor Market

Authors	Data	Methodology	Main results
Gallardo-García (2006)	Mexican Family Life Survey 2002	Dynamic discrete choice model	No significant impact on informal sector.
Parker and Scott (2008)	2000 Population Census	Differences in differences	Effects in rural but not urban municipalities using MxFLS.
	2005 Conteo de Población		No effects using the Census data.
	Rand´s Mexican Family Life Survey (MxFLS) 2000-2005		
Barros (2009)	ENSA 2000	Triple differences in differences	No evidence of an impact on labor supply or earnings.
	ENSANut 2006	Repeated cross sections	No evidence of any trend towards informal sector.
	ENIGH 2000, 2004, 2005, 2006		
Campos and Knox (2010)	ENE and ENCELURB 2001-4	Differences in differences	No effect of SP on informal sector.
	Oportunidades 2002-4	Repeated cross sections	
	ENOE 2005, 2006		
Azuara and Marinescu (2010)	ENE 1995-24	Differences in differences	A decrease of 0.8 percentage points in the share of formal employment for workers with less than 9 years of schooling; 1 percentage point for married workers with children or over 34 years old.
	ENOE 2005-9	Repeated cross sections	No impact of SP on wage gains for workers moving from one sector to the other.
Bosch and Campos (2010)	IMSS data 2000-9	Differences in differences	Negative impact of SP on the level of formal employment of around 4 percentage points among small and medium firms; strong negative impact on the level of employer registration of employers of around 4 percentage points.

Table 4.2. (continued)

Effects of *Seguro Popular* on the Labor Market

Authors	Data	Methodology	Main results
Aterido et al. (2010)	ENE 2000-2004 ENOE 2005-9	Differences in differences Panel data estimation	0.4%-0.7% of households remain informal due to SP; higher sensitivity among larger households and households headed by individuals with less than secondary completed education. Effects also larger among individuals whose spouses are affiliated to social security. Higher informality associated with reduced transitions from informal to informal jobs. Little effect on transitions from formal to informal sector. Adverse effects also on flows out of unemployment and on participation. Informal workers pay partly for SP benefits through lower wage growth.
Duval and Smith (2011)	ENE 2000-4 ENOE 2005-9	Differences in differences Repeated cross sections	Small effect of SP (larger in rural areas) on reducing the probability of looking for a formal sector job.
Pérez-Estrada (2011)	ENE 2000-4	Differences in differences	Negative effect of SP on the share of formal workers of 1 percentage point.
	ENOE 2005-8	Repeated cross sections	Large effect on the informal wage premium, decreasing average informal wages by 9% and increasing average formal wages by 5%.
Bosch and Cobacho (2011)	ENAMIN 1996, 1998, 2002 and 2008	Differences in differences Repeated cross sections	Negative impact of SP on formal job creation in small firms. 10% of increase in the time of exposure to the SP increases the formality rate of workers between 25-35 and workers with more than 35 years of age (relative to workers between 16-24) in 1.1 p.p. and 2.1 p.p. respectively.

services of SP compared to the social security system as a possible reason. As argued before, the author identifies the effect of SP using the intensity target at the state level. Perhaps this larger level of aggregation (state level) compared to other papers (municipality level) is working against finding an effect. The author also explains that another admissible reason could be that the time frame (the last year of the survey is 2006) is not long enough to analyze the possible effect on informality. This is particularly true for SP since affiliation did not immediately imply access to services and hence, as other authors claim, there can be important lags in the effect of SP on the labor market.

In a similar study, Campos and Knox (2010) try to unveil employment effects of SP using the quarterly National Survey of Employment (*Encuesta Nacional de Empleo*, ENE) and the Urban Household Evaluation Survey (*Encuesta de Evaluación de los Hogares Urbanos*, ENCELURB). These data sets cover over 150 municipalities between 2001 and 2004 – the early years of SP implementation. To study the existence of any effect of the SP program on shifts in employment out of the formal sector, they compare municipalities where workers were given access to the SP program during that period to municipalities which had not yet received the program by that time. They obtain a small negative but not significant effect, so they conclude there is little change in the likelihood of being formally employed in a municipality once it gains access to SP. Males with less than a high school education have the largest negative response to the SP program, with a 1 percentage point decline in the share of formal employment rates after the introduction of SP, although this result is not statistically significant either. They additionally use the two first years of the *Encuesta Nacional de Ocupación y Empleo* (ENOE), and their conclusions remain unchanged.

Both Barros (2009) and Campos and Knox (2010) suggest that the relatively short time span after the implementation of SP could be a factor explaining the lack of significant results. This is partially confirmed by Azuara and Marinescu (2011), who extend the work of Campos and Knox (2010) using the labor force surveys ENE for 1995 to 2004, and ENOE from 2005 to 2010 and find some negative impacts of SP, albeit very imprecisely estimated. Although they find no significant effect of SP when they analyze the whole employed population (they find a non-significant 0.8 percentage points increase in the share of informal employment), they do report a significant decrease in the share of formal employment for less-educated workers (with less than 9 years of schooling). In particular, the implementation of

SP was associated with a 1 percentage point increase in the share of informal employment among less-educated workers. Slightly larger significant increases in informality are found when further restricting the sample to married workers with children or to workers over 34 years old. However, even among these groups, the size of the impact is close to 1 percentage point. They explain this heterogeneity in the impact by the fact that some workers are likely more sensitive to the availability of health insurance when choosing to work formally or informally than others. They also analyze the effect of SP on the probabilities of transition between all the employment statuses: informal employment, formal employment, and non-employment. They do not find any significant effect on any of the probabilities, even restricting to workers with less than 9 years of education. Similarly, they do not find any impact of SP on wage gains for workers moving from the formal to the informal sector, nor for workers moving in the opposite direction, concluding that marginal workers do not value health benefits much.

Other papers have also used the ENE-ENOE data set to unveil effects of SP using slightly different approaches. Aterido, Hallward-Driemeier, and Pagés (2011) analyze the impact of SP on workers' decisions about formal vs. informal jobs, taking advantage of the panel dimension of the data set which allows them to control for decisions at the household level and for unobserved heterogeneity across households. Their analysis also takes into consideration that program coverage depends not only on the individual's employment status, but also on that of other household members. They conclude that the introduction of SP has generated a decrease in the share of formal employment of 0.4-0.7 percentage points, with adjustments largely occurring within a few years of the program's introduction. Furthermore, rather than encouraging exit from the formal sector, SP is associated with a 3.1 percentage point reduction (a 20% decline) in the inflow of workers from informal salaried into formal salaried employment.

Their study also explores the effects on the participation-non participation margin, and finds evidence of significantly decreased flows out of unemployment and lower labor force participation into formal salaried employment of around 1-2 percentage points. They find the impact to be larger for those with lower education attainment, and for individuals in larger households.

Pérez-Estrada (2011), also exploiting the ENE-ENOE 2000-8, confirms earlier studies that SP decreased the share of formal employment by around 1 percentage point. Furthermore, this effect was coupled with a 15% decrease of relative informal wages, suggesting that part of the benefits of SP was translated into lower wages for the uninsured.

Parker and Scott (2008) obtain different results for the early years of the program depending on the data. Using Rand's Mexican Family Life Survey (MxFLS) 2002–5, they find a disincentive effect in rural municipalities: beneficiaries of SP are 13 to 15 percentage points less probable to be formal in rural areas, and about 7 percentage points in urban areas. However, using aggregate data from the 2000 and 2005 Census, they do not find significant effects.

Duval and Smith (2011) analyze the impact of the program on the willingness to search for a job in the formal sector, and the probability of actually getting one. The main contribution of this chapter to the literature is that the authors anchor the discussion with a model that identifies the willingness to apply for a formal sector job. They depart from the traditional sector allocation model by adding an additional equation capturing the hiring decisions of formal sector employers, classifying informal-sector workers depending on whether they are voluntary or involuntary. They use data from ENE from 2002 to 2004, ENOE from 2005 to 2009, and administrative data from the program to estimate the degree of presence of the program at the state level. The results show that SP generated disincentives to look for a formal job in rural areas, although according to the authors this negative effect is small if compared to other determinants of sector allocation decisions.

A slightly different approach is taken by Bosch and Campos-Vazquez (2010) who employ data at the municipality level directly from the IMSS registry for the period 2000-9. The IMSS data is available for a balanced panel of 1395 municipalities that constitute 99% of total employment registered with IMSS. They use a difference-in-differences approach, comparing the evolution of the registration of employers and employees against the timing of the roll out of SP. They find evidence of a negative impact of the program on registration of employees in small and medium firms (up to 250 employees), which according to the Economic Census in 2009, account for 99% of all firms in Mexico. However, as expected, no effect is found for large firms. An interesting finding is that the effects of SP on the labor market occur with substantial lags. In particular, after three years from the initial implementation of SP, the level of employee registration with IMSS is 4% lower than it should have been in firms of less than 250 employees. They conclude that around 300,000 jobs were not registered with IMSS due to the SP. This contrast with the nearly 2 million jobs created during this period. That is, in the absence of SP, the economy should have produced 15% more formal jobs. The authors also show that young and female workers present stronger negative effects after the implementation of SP.

An additional novel result from this study is that registration of employers was also substantially reduced by SP. This is important since SP was aimed at providing health care insurance to a large segment of informal self-employed. Similar to the effects on employees, three years after implementation of SP, the level of employer registration with IMSS was 4% lower than it should have been. This resonates with the fact that according to the Economic Census from 2003 to 2008, 630.000 new firms with up to 5 employees were added to the economy in a time when the growth in the number of registered employers with IMSS in the same type of firms was virtually zero.

Note that this result refers to the *level* of employment and not to the share, since the IMSS data does not contain data on informal or unemployed workers. Hence it is not entirely comparable with previous studies that employ the labor force surveys (ENE-ENOE). A drop in 300.000 formal jobs represents an increase in the share of informal employment of around 0.75 percentage points, quantitatively very much in line with previous estimates but with substantial smaller standard errors due to the expanded sample of municipalities.

One idea that emerges strongly from Bosch and Campos (2010) is that the effects of SP are better observed in small firms. First, because they are in the threshold between formality and informality and hence more likely to react to changes in the incentive structure, and second, because evasion is easier for them. Bosch and Cobacho (2011) use data from the National Microenterprise Survey (ENAMIN) to study the effects of the program in small firms. Their identification strategy builds on two previous results. First, the effects of the SP were stronger in small and medium firms. Second, younger workers seem to have been more affected by the reform (Bosch and Campos 2010). The ENAMIN samples specifically small firms in Mexico, with detailed information about them. Due to the fact that a large number of these firms and municipalities are completely informal, the authors focus only on those firms that have some attachment with formality (either because the employer is registered with IMSS, or there is at least one employee with IMSS). In particular, the authors test whether young workers (relative to older workers) show a higher degree of informality in those municipalities which had been exposed longer to SP. Using a difference-in-differences approach, across age groups in municipalities with different exposures to the program, the authors show strong effects on informalization in those municipalities more exposed to the program. On average, a 10% increase in the time of exposure to SP decreases the share of formal employment of young workers by 1.1 and 2.1 percentage points relative to workers between 25-35 and older than 35, respectively. It is however difficult to compare this result to others since it only corresponds to a very small set of firms.

Finally, in a significant departure of the use of the roll out of SP as the identifying variation, Aguilera (2011) employs the social security administrative database of the pension system (*Sistema de Ahorro para el Retiro*, BDSAR) that contains individual information about all workers that participate or have participated in the formal sector between August 1997 to February 2006. She then matches this database provided by the randomized experiment implemented by King et al. (2007) described above at the zip code level. The results suggest that SP has no impact in the short run on formal employment or the probability of entering or leaving the formal sector. However, by the author's own account, the reduced scale of the experiment (only a few municipalities) and the short time span may work against finding any effects in the labor market.

In all, our understanding of the literature is that while the papers analyzing the early years of SP do not find significant effects of the program in the labor market, there seems to be some agreement that the data covering up to the end of the roll out in 2010 is showing some evidence of a reallocation effect from the formal towards the informal sector.

However, the extent of this reallocation is a matter of debate. On one end, Azuara and Marinescu (2011) claim no effect on the overall share of informality (although they find a positive but insignificant increase in the share of informal employment of around 0.8 percentage points). They do, however, find a significant increase in the share of informal employment for some subgroups, especially the unskilled, of around 1 percentage point (which would imply a 0.6 percentage point over total employment). Other studies using the same data set do report a significant increase in the share of informal employment of the order of 0.4

to 1 percentage point (Aterido, Hallward-Driemeier, and Pagés 2011; Pérez-Estrada 2011). To put these numbers in perspective, as of 2010, Mexico had around 40 million non-public workers. Hence, a 1 percentage point change in the share of formal employment implies a 400.000 workers reallocation from the formal to the informal sector (assuming that there are no overall employment effects). Even in Azuara and Marinescu (2011), a 1 percentage point increase in the share of informal employment among unskilled workers would imply a reallocation of over 240,000 workers. In fact, all these estimates are very much in line with the evidence found by Bosch and Campos-Vazquez (2010) using IMSS data which show a very significant decrease in the level of formal employment among small and medium firms of around 4%, equivalent to 300,000 formal workers.

4.6. Discussion and Conclusions

Nine years after the implementation of SP we have learned a few things about its effects. The expansion of SP coverage has reduced the financial burden imposed by health expenditures, particularly catastrophic ones, to the previously uninsured households in Mexico. The reform has also increased the volume of resources directed to the health sector. These are remarkable achievements likely to bring far reaching welfare gains for many families in Mexico. While studies so far have found little evidence of enhanced health outcomes as a result of SP, such effects may take some time to materialize. Further evaluations should be undertaken in order to assess those effects in years to come.

We have also learned about the difficulties of creating a culture of prepayment. As of 2010, the contributions of the affiliates constitute less than 0.5% of SP expenditure. This is an important lesson for other countries which seek to expand the reach of contributory systems with subsidized contributions or matching agreements which imply co-financing between the state and individuals. The evolution of the Mexican experience suggests a low willingness to pre-pay for health insurance even if *ex post* health expenses may drive families to poverty and destitution.[6] These results should also provide a note of caution to proposals suggesting matching contributions in pensions, as the willingness to pre-pay for pensions may be even lower than the willingness to pre-pay for health. The low willingness to prepay for health and pensions can explain why many workers are in the informal sector in the first place, as neither workers nor firms are willing to cover the *ex ante* costs of such benefits.[7]

In this scenario, offering virtually free health services to workers conditional on being employed in the informal sector further increases the disincentives to work in the formal sector, constituting a *de facto* subsidy to informal employment. There is evidence that the implementation of SP has changed incentives to contribute to social security, and workers and firms have responded to these changes. The available evidence so far points at a relocation of between 0.4 and 1 percentage point which is equivalent to 160,000 to 400,000 workers. During this same period around 2 million formal jobs were created, suggesting that the increase would have been between 8% and 20% higher in the absence of SP. Several studies suggest that this reallocation has been more intense among small firms and unskilled workers; that is, among workers with lower ability to pay for social security and in firms where it is easier to evade contributions.

Importantly, evidence of such adverse effects on formality is not restricted to the experience of the introduction and implementation of SP. A similar health care program implemented in Mexico DF only in 2001, studied in Juárez (2009), shows a very large and negative impact of affiliation of less educated women with social security. In particular, Juarez (2009) shows that women, with at most a high school education, are between 4 to 9.7 percentage points less likely to have a formal job after the policy change, several times higher than SP effects.

Other countries with similar approaches to the universalization of the health care access have also shown negative effects in registration to social security for the uninsured. Camacho et al. (2009) show that the expansion of social programs in the early nineties in Colombia inadvertently created incentives for people to become informal. Their estimated increases in informality are substantially larger than those found for SP, between 2 and 4 percentage points.

In contrast, some experiences in Latin American countries have shown that health coverage can be improved hand in hand with more formal jobs if the right incentives are provided. Bérgolo and Cruces (2011 and Chapter 3 in this volume) study the effects of social security benefits on labor market informality in Uruguay. The reform improved formal social security by extending health benefits to private sector salaried workers' dependants, mainly children and spouses, and thus changed the incentive structure of holding formal jobs within the household. Their findings indicate that after the health reform, the informality rates among workers fell significantly by about 1.3 percentage points (a 5% change) with respect to those not affected by the reform. These effects provide evidence of substantial incentive effects of social security benefits on the type of employment. Similarly, Calderón-Mejía and Marinescu (2011) analyze the effects of unifying health and pension system payments, which required employers to make contributions to these two plans through a unified payment system. Their results suggest that the reform had large positive effects on full formality. However, it also increased full informality, due to some workers (or their employers) who before the reform had chosen to contribute only to the health insurance scheme, and after the reform they chose to not contribute to any scheme through the unified payment system.

All public policies face trade-offs and ultimately policy makers have to balance the benefits of a particular policy against the costs. The larger question from a policy perspective is whether this is the right model to pursue for other countries with similar health coverage problems. This is part of a larger debate in Latin America and in other developing countries about how to extend the reach of health care and old age pensions. The recent trends in the region have been to entitle informal workers (and their families) with a series of non-contributory benefits. The concern is that the expansion of non-contributory entitlement programs currently underway might generate fragmented and unequal social protection systems and alter significantly the incentives to participate in contributory programs.

A reduction in formal employment of a few percentage points may be considered a magnitude countries can live with. However we highlight a number of points that might be relevant in the evaluation of the costs of SP.

First, a point not often made is that these estimates refer to the short to medium-run effects of SP on the labor market since the difference between treatment and control municipalities are at maximum 6 years apart. The findings in Bosch and Cobacho (2011) indicate that the intensity of exposure, measured by the (log of) number of quarters in which a municipality is exposed to the program matters, with longer exposures being associated with larger disincentive effects.

Second, while the package of services and the cost of the benefits offered by social security are larger than that offered by SP, Figure 4.2 clearly shows that the relative volume of resources that goes to insured populations is rapidly declining, while the number of interventions and services that, in principle, are offered to SP affiliates has been progressively increasing. It is therefore expected that as these differences become smaller, free, high quality health care will look increasingly more attractive, particularly for low and middle-income households affiliated to social security. In Colombia where a similar dual system exists, legal pressures have made non-viable the survival of parallel contributory and non-contributory systems. In particular, the Constitutional Court (2008) issued a decision ordering the government to unify the benefits in the two systems, first for children, and then progressively for adults, raising doubts of how to finance and determine eligibility of health benefits. Mexico might face similar problems in the future since improving health services for the uninsured, a good policy objective in itself, might generate further and further distortions in the labor market.

Third, the SP is by no means the only social program in Mexico. A wide variety of programs aimed at the uninsured are present now in Mexico, ranging from housing and day care to non-contributory pensions. In fact, according to Levy (2011), the SP budget represents only 25% of all the programs aimed at protecting the uninsured. Hence, the estimates here could just represent a fraction of the real reallocation effect that social protection for the uninsured is generating in Mexico. This is particularly true in a context where there are large flows between formal and informal jobs and hence workers stay part of their working lives in the informal sector. The "innovation" of the SP with respect to other similar programs is that it offered a reasonable identification strategy for economists to measure its effects (i.e. program implementation was staggered across the country). Hence, whatever effects the literature is finding from SP are estimated on top of a labor market already distorted by numerous non-contributory programs for informal workers.

Fourth, another important aspect to consider is the cost in terms of foregone productivity and output. The results presented here suggest that the combination of taxes to formal jobs and subsidies to informal ones reallocates economic activity towards informal, less productive firms. If that is so, output and productivity declines because a larger share of economic activity takes place in smaller, less productive firms.

Fifth, while non-contributory programs like SP increase health coverage, they also make participation in other mandatory social security programs (such as pensions) less likely. That is, the evidence so far suggests a direct trade-off between promoting health coverage and other benefits. More incentives to access health care through the informal non-contributory system would ultimately mean lower pension coverage, which in turns reinforces the need for implementing non-contributory pension programs, which are already spreading rapidly throughout the region.

All of this does not imply that countries should not purse universalization of health care and pension coverage. On the contrary, this is a goal that we strongly advocate. Again, it is a question of what is the right model to achieve it. We believe that such goal may be more efficiently pursued with an integrated package of services for the whole population with subsidies offered to all workers (formal and informal) based on their earnings capacity, rather than having parallel fragmented systems. This is the thrust of health care systems funded partially or totally with general revenues, and where co-financing, if any, is based on earning ability or fixed copayments, rather than on work status. As indicated above, implementing co-financing may be difficult, other than for high-income families; therefore countries must be prepared to find alternative sources of financing to firms' and individuals' contributions in order to provide access to these services.

Notes

1 These two institutions operate under mutual systems whereby privately and publicly employed workers (and their families) are entitled to a full spectrum of benefits, not only health care, but also other benefits such as pension and disability benefits, housing loans and in the case of dismissal, severance payments. In exchange for these benefits and rights, employees and their employers pay payroll taxes amounting to roughly 25% of their salaries excluding other local and federal taxes. Under this system, the workers and their families are not charged for the use of health services and they have access to a wide range of prescription drugs.

2 The *Seguro Popular* pilot program started in 2002. The new law for the creation of the SSPH was passed by Congress in April, 2003. The law came into effect in January 2004 (González-Pier et al. 2006).

3 By 2010 the poorest 40% of the households were exempt from any payment, and families up to the seventh decile with at least 1 child younger than 4 years of age were also exempt. A detailed description of the contribution system of the program can be found in Frenk et al. (2006).

4 The per capita on the insured is calculated as the health care expenditures executed by IMSS and ISSSTE divided by the total number of affiliates to these programs. Similarly, the per capita expenditure on the uninsured is calculated as the health expenditure executed by the SSA divided by the number of uninsured. Data obtained from the Secretaria de Salud at http://portal.salud.gob.mx/.

5 Perhaps the only exception to this is Aguilera (2011) which takes advantage of King's et al. (2009) experimental design to analyze the effects in the labor market.

6 Interestingly, a survey of social protection conducted by the Inter-American Development Bank shows around 85% of Mexicans consider that either the government or the employers should be ultimately responsible for providing health care for workers.

7 It is possible to argue that health insurance and pensions insurance may well be treated differently. Health shocks are often individual true shocks (unforeseeable random events). The issue with pensions has more to do with savings than with insurance. The only risky elements are longevity (which is easily insurable at a macro level as there are few moral hazard/adverse selection problems, at least if a death register exists) and inflation risk. Given such differences it is unlikely that the same policy institution would be optimal for both aspects.

References

Aguilera, N. (2011). The Short Term Causal Effects of Seguro Popular on Formal Employment, mimeo.

Aguilera, N., Marrufo, G. (2006). New Evidence of the Effects of Publicly Provided Insurance on Health Outcomes: The Case of the Seguro Popular, Presented at LACEA 2006.

Aterido, R., Hallward-Driemeier, M., Pagés, C. (2011). Does Expanding Health Insurance Beyond Formal-Sector Workers Encourage Informality? Measuring the Impact of Mexico's Seguro Popular, IZA Discussion Paper No. 5996.

Azuara, O., Marinescu, I. (2011). Informality and the Expansion of Social Protection Programs. Evidence from Mexico, MPRA Paper No. 35073.

Barros, R. (2009). Wealthier But Not Much Healthier: Effects of a Health Insurance Program for the Poor in Mexico, SIEPR Discussion Paper No. 09-002.

Bérgolo, M., Cruces, G. (2011). Labor Informality and the Incentive Effects of Social Security: Evidence From a Health Reform in Uruguay, IDB Working Paper No. 62318 [Chapter 3 in this volume].

Bosch, M., Campos-Vázquez, R. (2010). The Trade-offs of Social Assistance Programs in the Labor Market: The Case of "Seguro Popular" Program in Mexico, Serie documentos de trabajo del Centro de Estudios Económicos Working Paper No. 12.
Bosch, M., Cobacho, M.B. (2011). Welfare Policies and Informalization: The Effect of Popular Insurance on Semi-formal Firms in Mexico, mimeo.
Bosch, M., Maloney, W.F. (2008). Cyclical Movements in Unemployment and Informality in Developing Countries, IZA Discussion Paper No. 3514.
Calderón-Mejía, V., Marinescu, I. (2011). The Impact of Colombia's Pension and Health Insurance Systems on Informality, IDB Working Paper No. 62338.
Camacho, A., Conover, E., Hoyos, A. (2009). Effects of Colombia's Social Protection System on Workers' Choice between Formal and Informal Employment, Documentos CEDE No. 006003.
Campos-Vázquez, R.M., Knox, M.A. (2010). Social Protection Programs and Employment: The Case of Mexico's Seguro Popular Program, Centro de Estudios Económicos, El Colegio de México, A.C. Working Paper No. 2010-14.
Corte Constitucional de la República de Colombia, Sala Segundo de Revisión (2008). Constitutional Court of Colombia, Sentencia No T-760 de 2008.
Duval, R., Smith, R. (2011). Informality and Seguro Popular under Segmented Labor Markets, mimeo.
Díaz-Cayeros, A., Estévez, F., Magaloni, B. (2006). Buying-off the Poor: Effects of Targeted Benefits in the 2006 Presidential Race, Conference on the Mexico 2006 Panel Study, Boston, MA: Harvard University.
Esquivel, G., Ordaz, J. L. (2008). ¿Es correcto vincular la política social a la informalidad en México? Una prueba simple de las premisas de esta hipótesis, in: CEPAL Serie Estudios y Perspectivas (México), 104.
Frenk, J., González-Pier, E., Gómez-Dantés, O., Ángel Lezana, M., Knaul, F. M. (2006). Comprehensive Reform to Improve Health System Performance in Mexico, in: The Lancet, 368(1): 1524–34.
Gakidou, E., Lozano, R., González-Pier, E., Abbott-Klafter, J., Barofsky, J. T., Bryson-Cahn, C., Feehan, D. M., Lee, D. K., Hernández-Llamas, H., Murray, C. J. (2006). Assessing the Effect of the 2001–06 Mexican Health Reform: An Interim Report Card, in: The Lancet, 368(5): 1920-35.
Galárraga, O., Sosa-Rubí, S. G., Salinas, A., Sesma, S. (2008). The Impact of Universal Health Insurance on Catastrophic and Out-of-pocket Health Expenditures in Mexico: A Model With an Endogeneous Treatment Variable, Health, Econometrics and Data Group, HEDG Working Paper No. 08/12.
Gallardo-García, J. R. (2006). Health Insurance and Pregnancy Outcomes: An Analysis of Fertility, Prenatal Care and Employment in Mexico, Dissertations available from ProQuest, Paper AAI3211073.
Garrido-Latorre, F., Hernández-Llamas, H., Gómez-Dantés, O. (2008). Surtimiento de recetas a los afiliados al Seguro Popular de Salud de México, Salud Pública de México, 84(50): 429-36.
González-Pier, E., Gutiérrez-Delgado, C., Stevens, G., Barraza-Lloréns, M., Porras-Condey, R., Carvalho, N., Loncich, K., Dias, R. H., Kulkarni, S., Casey, A., Murakami, Y., Ezzati, M., Salomon, J. A. (2006). Priority Setting for Health Interventions in Mexico's System of Social Protection in Health, in: The Lancet, 368: 1608-18.
Harris, J. E., Sosa-Rubí, S. G. (2009). Impact of "Seguro Popular" on Prenatal Visits in Mexico, 2002-2005: Latent Class Model of Count Data with a Discrete Endogenous Variable, NBER Working Paper No. 14995.
Hernández-Torres, J., Ávila-Burgos, L., Valencia-Mendoza, A., Poblano-Verástegui, O. (2008). Seguro Popular's Initial Evaluation of Household Catastrophic Health Spending in Mexico, in: Revista de Salud Pública, 10(1): 18-32.
Juárez, L. (2009). Are Informal Workers Compensated for the Lack of Fringe Benefits? Free Health Care as an Instrument for Formality, Centro de Investigación Económica, ITAM Working Paper No. 0804.
King, G., Gakidou, E., Ravishankar, N., Moore, R. T., Lakin, J., Vargas, M., Tellez-Rojo, M. M., Hernandez Avila, J. E., Hernandez Avila, M., Hernandez Llamas, H. (2007). A "Po-

litically Robust" Experimental Design for Public Policy Evaluation, with Application to the Mexican Universal Health Insurance Program, in: Journal of Policy Analysis and Management, 26(3): 479–506.
King, G., Gakidou, E., Imai, K., Lakin, J., Moore, R. T., Nall, C., Ravishankar, N., Vargas, M., Téllez-Rojo, M. M., Hernández Ávila, J. E., Hernández Ávila, M., Hernández Llamas, H. (2009). Public Policy for the Poor? A Randomised Assessment of the Mexican Universal Health Insurance Programme, in: The Lancet, 373: 1447–54.
Knaul, F. M., Arreola-Ornelas,H., Méndez, O., Martínez, A. (2005). Fair Health Financing and Catastrophic Health Expenditures: Potential Impact of the Coverage Extension of the Popular Health Insurance in Mexico, in: Salud Pública de Mexico, 47(1): 54-65.
Knaul, F. M., Arreola-Ornelas, H., Méndez-Carniado, O., Bryson-Cahn, C., Barofsky, J., Maguire, R., Miranda, M., Sesma, S. (2006). Evidence is Good for Your Health System: Policy Reform to Remedy Catastrophic and Impoverishing Health Spending in Mexico, in: The Lancet, 368: 1828-41.
Knaul, F. M., Frenk, J. (2005). Health Insurance in Mexico: Achieving Universal Coverage Through Structural Reform, in: Health Affairs, 24(6): 1467-76.
Lakin, J. M. (2010). The End of Insurance? Mexico's Seguro Popular, 2001-2007, in: Journal of Health Politics, Policy and Law, 35(3): 313-52.
Levy, S. (2008). Good Intentions, Bad Outcomes: Social Policy, Informality and Economic Growth in Mexico, Washington, DC: Brookings Institution Press.
Lozano, R., Soliz, P., Gakidou, E., Abbott-Klafter, J., Feehan, D.M., Vidal, C., Ortiz, J. P., Murray, C. J. (2006). Benchmarking of Performance of Mexican States with Effective Coverage, in: The Lancet, 368: 1729-41.
Maloney, W. F. (1999). Does Informality Imply Segmentation in Urban Labor Markets? Evidence from Sectoral Transitions in Mexico, in: World Bank Economic Review, 13(2): 275-302.
OECD (2005). OECD Reviews of Health Systems - Mexico, OECD Publishing.
Pagés, C., Stampini, M. (2009). No Education, No Good Jobs? Evidence on the Relationship Between Education and Labor Market Segmentation, in: Journal of Comparative Economics, 37: 387–401.
Parker, S., Scott, J. (2008). An Evaluation of the Mexican Seguro Popular Program: Work and Formal Sector Participation, CIDE, mimeo.
Pérez-Estrada, J. (2011). The Employment and Wage Effects of Expanding Health Insurance Coverage: The Case of Mexico, UCLA, mimeo.
Scott, J. (2006). Seguro Popular Incidence Analysis. In Decentralized Service Delivery for the Poor, Washington, DC: World Bank Publications, vol. 2: 147–66.
Secretaria de Salud (2002). Programa nacional de salud, 2001-2006, Mexico City; Secretaria de Salud.
Secretaría de Salud (2010). Sistema de Protección Social en Salud. Informe de Resultados 2010.
Sepúlveda, J., Bustreo, F., Tapia, R., Rivera, J., Lozano, R., Oláiz, G., Partida, V., García-García, L., Valdespino, J. L. (2006). Improvement of Child Survival in Mexico: The Diagonal Approach, in: The Lancet, 368: 2017-27.
Sosa-Rubí, S., Galárraga, O., Harris, J. E. (2009). Heterogeneous Impact of the "Seguro Popular" Program on the Utilization of Obstetrical Services in Mexico, 2001-2006: A Multinomial Probit Model with a Discrete Endogenous Variable, in: Journal of Health Economics, 28(1): 20-34.
Urbina, M. (2008). Sistema de protección social en salud: Seguro Popular en salud: Evaluación y consistencia de resultados 2007, Coneval.

5

Unemployment Insurance, Job Search, and Informal Employment*

David N. Margolis
Lucas Navarro
David Robalino

5.1. Introduction

In developing countries, income protection in the case of unemployment is mainly provided through severance pay, which is regulated by the labor code. These systems cover only a minority of the labor force, are difficult to enforce, and carry considerable risk of default, particularly during times of crisis, given that employers seldom provision for the benefits (Holzmann et al. 2011). Meanwhile, only a few countries have introduced contributory unemployment benefit programs. Part of the reason is the concern that traditional unemployment insurance systems (or providing basic unemployment assistance) can lead to abuse, promote unemployment, and generate large fiscal outlays, particularly in the presence of informal employment and weak institutional capacity to monitor job-search and employment status.

The empirical evidence, mainly coming from high-income countries, is mixed.[1] In general, studies find that there is a positive correlation between the level and duration of benefits and the length of the unemployment spell, which can lead to higher unemployment rates.

* *This chapter was prepared as part of a set of Analytical and Advisory Activities provided to the Government of Malaysia. Access to the data used here was provided under conditions set by Malaysia's Department of Statistics and the Economic Planning Unit; interested individuals are invited to contact the DoS and EPU to arrange access if desired.*

At the same time, evidence from Denmark, France, Germany, Italy, Ireland, and Spain shows that longer unemployment spells can also be associated with "better matches"; workers are able to find better and more stable jobs (Tatsiramos 2009).

Less is known about the effects of unemployment insurance in developing countries. The few studies available would suggest that effects on the duration of unemployment spells and employment levels are modest. Two studies for Brazil find no quantitatively meaningful effect of the UB system on the duration of unemployment spells. The first exploited changes in eligibility conditions and showed that, if anything, unemployment benefits allowed faster transitions into self-employment (Cunningham 2000). A second compared the exit rates from unemployment among formal-sector workers (eligible for unemployment benefits) and informal-sector workers (not eligible for unemployment benefits). It showed that the former had higher exit rates even after controlling for unobserved characteristics that are correlated with work in the formal sector (Margolis 2008). At the other extreme, van Ours and Vodopivec (2008) show that in the case of Slovenia, the shortening of the potential duration of UI benefits substantially reduced the length of the unemployment spell. A more recent paper based on a structural model for Brazil finds the unemployment insurance system mainly reduces transitions into informal jobs (Robalino et al. 2011).

This chapter analyses the potential impacts of introducing an unemployment insurance (UI) system in Malaysia, which currently has no such system. The analysis is based on a structural job search model with unemployment and three employment sectors: formal and informal wage employment, and self-employment. The parameters of the model are estimated to replicate the structure of the labor market in Malaysia in 2009 and the distribution of earnings for informal, formal and self-employed workers. The model is used to simulate the effects of alternative unemployment benefit system designs that depend on the replacement rate, the vesting period for benefits, the duration of benefits, and the contribution rate. We look at changes in the shares of individuals across employment states, the unemployment rate, and average earnings by sector.

The results suggest that an unemployment insurance system in Malaysia would have only a modest negative effect on unemployment if benefits are not overly generous. The system would induce a reallocation of labor from wage into self-employment while increasing average wages in the formal and informal sectors. The effects on the average earnings of the self-employed would depend on the generosity of the system. With a 50% replacement rate, most workers entering self-employment would be low-skilled workers, driving average earnings down. High-skilled workers would change behavior significantly with more generous systems. As they remain unemployed for longer, wage employment offers fall, and a larger share enters self-employment, driving up average earnings among the self-employed. Although the analysis focuses on Malaysia, the results are likely to be relevant for other middle-income countries, particularly in Latin America, which share similar demographic, levels of education and labor market structures.

The remainder of this chapter is structured as follows. Section 5.2 provides a brief description of the Malaysian labor market, while Section 5.3 lays out a 4-state (unemployment, self-employment, formal wage and salary employment, informal wage and salary employment) job search model. Section 5.4 describes the data used for the estimations, Section 5.5 covers the reduced form and simulated pseudo method of moments estimation results, while Section 5.6 presents the microsimulation results. Section 5.7 concludes.

5.2. Overview of Current Malaysian Labor Markets

Over the last decade both employment and labor productivity have been growing in Malaysia (see Figure 5.1). Between 2000 and 2008 the adult population grew by an average of 2.6 percent annually over this period, while employment grew by an average of 2.8 percent per year and labor productivity grew on average by 3.7 percent.

Similar to middle-income countries in Latin America, Malaysia has a young and relatively well educated working-age population. Over 60 percent of the working-age population is under 40 years old, and over 35 percent was under 25 years old.[2] About 57 percent of the workforce has some form of secondary education certification and 14.4 percent of the population has a post-secondary certification, with over 5 percent having a tertiary education degree. However, there are clear regional disparities; for example, the working-age population in East Malaysia, especially the states of Sabah and Labuan, is much less educated than that of Peninsular Malaysia.[3]

Figure 5.1

Working-Age Population, Employment, and Labor Productivity Trends, 2000-2008

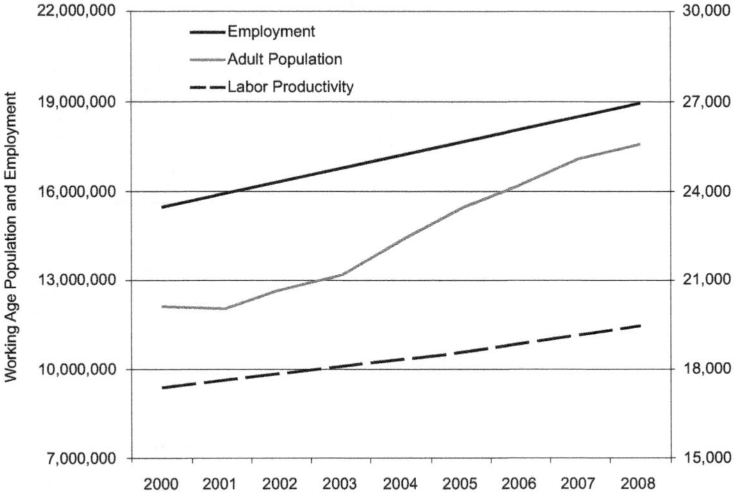

Notes: Labor productivity is measured as GDP per worker in 1990 USD converted at PPP rates.
Source: World Development Indicators.

The differences in compensation, hours worked and formality levels[4] among population groups (sex, region, age, level of education, and sector of activity) are also important (Tables 5.1 and 5.2). Men are more likely to be in formal jobs (55 percent) than women (48) and also earn more – men's base monthly compensation is on average 17 percent higher than women's. Not surprisingly, education is an important determinant of labor market outcomes. Only 25 percent of those with primary education or less are in formal employment against 44 percent for those with secondary education and 68 percent for those with higher education. One explanation consistent with the model developed below is that formal contracts are not for low-productivity workers, who end-up working in low-productivity activities often in small firms in the informal sector or as self-employed. Thus there are large difference in earnings: the average worker with higher education earns five times more than the average worker with primary education or less.

Table 5.1
Working-Age Population

	Peninsular	Sarawak	Sabah and Labuan	Total
General Demographics				
Male	50.3	49.4	50.0	50.2
Malaysian Citizen	95.6	96.5	75.6	93.7
Never Married	46.8	42.7	47.3	46.5
Married	48.9	53.4	48.9	49.3
Widowed	3.3	2.7	2.6	3.2
Divorced / Separated	1.0	1.1	1.2	1.0
Highest certifcate obtained				
Not Applicable	3.6	10.2	13.1	5.1
No Certificate	10.0	12.8	16.0	10.8
UPSR/UPSRA or equivalent	11.5	17.1	17.9	12.6
PMR/SRP/LCE	23.9	24.3	20.8	23.7
SPM/MCE	35.3	27.6	22.5	33.4
STPM/HSC or equivalent	2.9	2.4	2.9	2.9
Certificate	1.5	0.8	0.9	1.4
Diploma	5.4	2.3	2.6	4.8
Degree	5.8	2.6	3.4	5.3
Status in employment				
Not Employed	49.6	46.3	46.7	49.0
Employer	2.0	1.6	1.8	1.9
Government Employee	6.8	6.2	6.0	6.7
Private Employee	29.7	27.0	30.4	29.5
Own Account Worker	9.6	12.0	11.5	10.0
Unpaid Family Worker	2.3	6.8	3.7	2.8
Age				
15-24	37.7	37.2	43.4	38.2
25-39	26.2	25.9	25.8	26.1
40-44	23.3	23.7	21.9	23.2
55-64	12.8	13.1	8.9	12.5

Note: The Labor Force Survey does not sample collective housing. All figures are percentages using LFS sample weights.
Source: Labor Force Survey 2009.

Table 5.2

Compensation, Hours, Employment, and Formality

	Base Monthly Compensation	Total Monthly Compensation	Total Weekly Hours Worked	Total Hourly Compensation	Share of Employment	Share Employer/ Own-Account	Share Formal: All Jobs	Share Formal: Wage & Salary
Women	1,246	1,331	44.0	7.41	36.1%	15.1%	54.9%	68.0%
Men	1,456	1,580	46.0	8.51	63.9%	28.1%	47.7%	61.5%
Peninsular	1,484	1,596	45.1	8.69	80.8%	23.0%	51.8%	64.2%
Sarawak	1,012	1,094	44.9	6.13	9.0%	25.5%	42.3%	62.0%
Sabah and Labuan	821	938	47.2	4.94	10.1%	24.8%	42.6%	62.0%
Age 15-24	790	854	46.1	4.55	19.1%	8.1%	61.9%	67.8%
Age 25-39	1,514	1,635	45.2	8.86	39.4%	16.0%	59.9%	69.7%
Age 40-54	1,705	1,844	44.8	10.14	31.5%	31.0%	41.1%	57.3%
Age 55-64	1,442	1,548	44.5	8.64	10.0%	58.1%	16.7%	35.8%
Completed Primary or Less	802	862	46.1	4.55	29.1%	36.1%	25.1%	43.3%
Completed Lower Secondary	987	1,059	46.0	5.6	14.2%	26.9%	44.1%	58.1%

Table 5.2 (continued)

Compensation, Hours, Employment and Formality

	Base Monthly Compensation	Total Monthly Compensation	Total Weekly Hours Worked	Total Hourly Compensation	Share of Employment	Share Employer/ Own-Account	Share Formal: All Jobs	Share Formal: Wage & Salary
Completed Upper Secondary	1,163	1,274	45.5	6.87	35.4%	17.9%	58.3%	68.8%
Completed Pre-University	1,952	2,125	43.6	11.89	12.5%	13.8%	65.2%	72.2%
Completed Higher Education	4,111	4,358	42.7	24.29	8.7%	11.5%	68.1%	73.4%
Resource-Based Industry	952	1,027	44.7	5.62	6.9%		15.3%	44.1%
Manufacturing	1,355	1,454	44.6	7.93	31.1%		77.8%	84.0%
Services	1,668	1,952	43.7	11.36	62.0%		48.3%	58.6%

Note: Base Monthly Compensation, Total Monthly Compensation, and Total Hourly compensation are expressed in 2010 RM by using the CPI to convert the nominal 2009 figures.

Figures refer only to wages and salaries received and do not include any residual income earned by entrepreneurs. Calculations include private employees and own-account workers for employment share, hours, and compensation.

Source: Labor Force Survey 2009 (compensation, hours, and employment share); Household Income Survey 2007 (Share of formal jobs).

5.3. The Model Framework

Search and matching models have been extensively used for the analysis of the quantitative effects of labor market policy. In this chapter we adapt the Diamond-Mortensen-Pissarides style of dynamic job search model (Pissarides 2000) to fit the situation of labor markets with large informal sectors. In this type of model, unemployed individuals engage in job search activity and the decision to accept a job depends on the value of the job, which is itself a function of the job's stability and the opportunity cost of not being able to search for a better job while employed. This sort of model has been extensively analyzed and some recent extensions of this framework have introduced informal labor markets and self-employment (Albrecht et al. 2009).

This chapter continues in this literature by integrating both an informal sector and self-employment, although it does not solve analytically for the equilibrium labor market tightness and the shares of offers from the formal and informal sector wage employers. Appendix A describes the basic structure of the model.[5] The model defines a set of value functions for different labor market states and a wage determination mechanism. The model is solved numerically in Section 5.5.

5.3.1. Unemployment Value Function

Let $U(y, \tilde{w})$ be the value of unemployment for a worker of type y, which can be written as

$$\begin{aligned} rU(y, \tilde{w}) = b(\tilde{w}) &+ \alpha \max[N_0(y) - U(y, \tilde{w}), 0] + \\ & m(\theta)\psi E\max[N_I(x, y) - U(y), 0] + \\ & m(\theta)(1 - \psi)E\max[N_F(x, y) - U(y, \tilde{w}), 0]. \end{aligned} \tag{1}$$

This worker receives a flow utility of $b(\tilde{w})$, where $\tilde{w}$ is the wage on the previous job, while unemployed.[6,7] At a rate α, the worker meets an opportunity for self-employment and, if it is taken, realizes a capital gain of $N_0(y) - U(y, \tilde{w})$. The matching function $m(\theta) = a\theta^\beta$ determines the probability of an individual meeting a vacancy for a wage and salary job, with θ being the ratio of vacancies to unemployment (i.e. a measure of labor market tightness). Conditional on meeting a vacancy, a worker meets a formal sector vacancy with probability

$1 - \psi$ and an informal-sector vacancy with probability ψ. If the job is taken, the worker realizes a capital gain of $N_j(x, y) - U(y, \tilde{w})$. The employment value functions consider that the initial flow value of the match is given by the sector-specific productivity x, which varies across individuals and sectors (formal and informal).

5.3.2. *Self-Employment Value Function*

Let $N_0(y)$ be the value of self-employment for a worker of type y, which can be written as

$$rN_0(y) = y + \lambda_0(U(y, y) - N_0(y)). \tag{2}$$

This expression shows that the self-employed receives a flow value equivalent to her type y, but at rate λ_0 the opportunity ends in which case there is a (negative) capital gain of $U(y, y) - N_0(y)$.[8]

5.3.3. *Wage and Salary Sector Value Functions*

Let $N_F(x, y)$ and $N_I(x, y)$ be the values of employment in the formal sector and informal salaried sector, respectively, for a worker of type y with a draw x from the sector-specific productivity distribution. The flow values of these jobs can be written as

$$rN_F(x, y) = w_F(x, y) + \lambda_F(U\ (y, w_F(x, y)) - N_F(x, y)) \tag{3}$$

$$rN_I(x, y) = w_I(x, y) + \lambda_I(U(y, w_I(x, y)) - N_I(x, y)), \tag{4}$$

respectively. A worker of type y who has a formal sector job receives a wage $w_F(x, y)$ determined by Nash bargaining. Idiosyncratic shocks that destroy the match and send the individual back to unemployment arrive at rate λ_F. A similar idea applies to the value of employment in the informal wage sector.

5.3.4. *Employer-Side Value Functions*

Let V_j and $J_j(x, y)$ be the value of the expected profit of posting a vacancy and the value of a filled job in sector $i \in \{F, I\}$. The filled job values can be written as

$$rJ_F(x, y) = x - w_F(x, y)\ (1 + \tau\ ) + \lambda_F(V_F - J_F(x, y) - s)$$

$$rJ_I(x, y) = \varepsilon x - w_I(x, y) + \lambda_I(V_I - J_I(x, y)).$$

Regulations affecting the formal sector filled job value are payroll taxes τ and severance payments s. Note that regulations do not affect $J_I(x, y)$ but the flow value of productivity therein is εx, where $\varepsilon < 1$.

The values of formal and informal sector vacancies, V_F and V_I, are defined respectively by

$$rV_I = -c + \frac{m(\theta)}{\theta} \text{Emax}\left[J_I(x, y) - V_I, 0\right] \tag{5}$$
$$rV_F = -c + \frac{m(\theta)}{\theta} \text{Emax}[J_F(x, y) - V_F, 0].$$

The expectation term in (5) reflects the assumption that the firm does not know in advance which type of worker it will meet.

5.3.5. *Wages*

As standard in this literature, a surplus is realized when a match is formed. This surplus is given by the net gain from matching for both the firm and the worker, that is, $N_s(x, y) - U(y) + J_s(x, y) - V_s$.

Wages are determined by rent sharing over the surplus of the match. A wage is a solution to a generalized Nash Bargaining problem with threat points equal to the worker's and the firm's respective continuation values. Given an exogenous share parameter β and the free entry condition ($V_j = 0$), the formal contract wage $w_F(x, y)$ for a worker of type y producing at x solves

$$\max_{w_F(x,y)} \left[N_F(x, y) - U(y)\right]^\beta \left[J_F(x, y) + s\right]^{1-\beta}$$

which implies,

$$w_F(x, y) = \beta\frac{(x + rs)}{1 + \tau} + (1 - \beta)rU(y). \tag{6}$$

Similarly, the informal wage $w_I(x, y)$ solves

$$\max_{w_I(x,y)} \left[N_I(x, y) - U(y)\right]^\beta J_I(X, y)^{1-\beta}$$

and the wage function can be written as

$$w_I(x, y) = \beta \in x + (1 - \beta)rU(y). \tag{7}$$

The wage in sector i is the weighted average of the worker's productivity and the worker's outside options. Of course, regulations affect the formal wage bargaining process.

5.4. The Data

The model is estimated on two separate data sources from Malaysia, the Household Income Survey,[9] or HIS, and the Labor Force Survey with the Wages and Salaries Supplement,[10] or LFS. These data sources are complementary in that neither source is perfectly suited for estimation of the model presented in Section 5.3, but the limits of each source can be compensated by the advantages of the other. Both data sources are thus used to estimate different components of the model, and as both surveys are designed to be representative of the same population (and sample weights are always used), no further correction for sampling is necessary.[11]

5.4.1. The Household Income Survey (2009)

The HIS is a household survey that is representative of the population of Malaysia that does not live in collective housing.[12] It is comprised of 4 components: basic identification, sociodemographic characteristics of the household members, basic information on activity status and sources of income.

The HIS is particularly useful for the purposes of this chapter because it allows for separate measurement of income from paid employment and self-employment income. In terms of income from paid employment, the survey distinguishes between the various components and separately measures employer contributions to social security, pensions, etc. on the worker's behalf.[13] It does not, however, directly measure the amount received in severance payments.[14] In terms of self-employment income, it allows for the separation of total self-employment earnings into own consumption use and income, with the latter being broken into agricultural and non-agricultural self-employment earnings.

There are two main difficulties with using exclusively the HIS for this chapter. First, the information on labor market status does not specifically designate unemployment as a labor market state.

The available categories are:

1. Employer
2. Government employee
3. Private employee
4. Own-account worker
5. Unpaid family worker
6. Housewife / Looking after home
7. Student
8. Child not at school
9. Others (specify)

It is therefore impossible to calculate the share of the workforce in each state as defined by out model, unless one assumes that all codes other than 1-4 are unemployed.

Second, the survey collects data referring to the previous year's values, so the questions on activity status are phrased as

> What did .... (usual member) .... do MOST OF THE TIME during the last twelve (12) months?

and the income questions refer to all income received during the previous year. There is no calendar, so it is impossible to know whether a low amount of earnings is due an individual working part of the year or being poorly paid for a full year of work. Moreover, and more importantly for the estimation of the model in Section 5.3, it is impossible to measure the length of employment and unemployment spells.

5.4.2. The Labor Force Survey with the Wages and Salaries Supplement (2009)

The LFS is a standard labor force survey, focusing on the working-age population that does not live in collective housing. The LFS has 3 components: identification, household member characteristics and labor force particulars. The wages and salaries supplement provides additional information on income for government and private employees only.

The main advantage of the LFS over the HIS is that its "labor force particulars" component is more thorough than that of the HIS. Questions are asked relative to the reference week, ILO-standard unemployment definitions are used, and there is enough information to calculate the distribution of unemployment durations within the stock of unemployed.[15]

Unfortunately, the income component of the LFS is not as rich as the HIS. In particular, there is no information on earnings from any source other than wages, salaries and overtime payments. This implies that the data cannot be used for estimating y directly, as self-employment earnings cannot be seen. Moreover, the wages and salaries supplement measures gross earnings but provides no means of quantifying the value of employer or employee contributions to social insurance, implying that one cannot distinguish formal from informal wage and salary work from this data source.

5.5. Estimation

The structural parameters of the model were estimated by a simulated pseudo-method of moments procedure as follows. A reduced form model was estimated to recover values of y for each individual in the population, as well as the distributions $G_F(x|y)$ and $G_I(x|y)$. With this information, careers were simulated as follows. Starting from unemployment, the individual receives self-employment offers, formal job offers and informal job offers, and accepts or refuses them according the behavior dictated by the value functions in Section 5.3. When self-employed, formally employed or informally employed, job destruction shocks arrive with probabilities λ_0, λ_F and λ_I respectively. Each individual's transitions and wages were repeatedly simulated until the simulations converged to a stable share of the population in each labor market state and stable wage distributions within the formal and informal employment states. The structural parameters of the model were adjusted until the steady state shares in each labor market state and the steady state wage distributions matched those found in the data, at which point the model was considered to have converged.

It is important to stress that the full structural model was not estimated, meaning that the parameters and the distribution of y variables recovered is robust to certain functional form assumptions.[16] The simulations do exploit the functional forms of expressions 1, 2, 3, and 4, and the productivity draws are assumed to come from logistic distributions. However, the steady state version of the model is not solved analytically nor is it structurally estimated.[17] It is also worth noting that the income variables used in the estimation are those drawn from a data source that reflects annual incomes rather than monthly, weekly or hourly earnings. The absence of data on earnings in self-employment prevented us from using the Malaysian LFS for all individuals, and mixing data sources for measurement of a single variable is not good practice.

The remainder of this section describes how each of the steps was performed.

5.5.1. *Direct Recovery of Parameters and Population Moments*

There are several key parameters of the model that can be directly recovered from the data.

- τ, *the payroll tax rate for workers in the formal sector.* As mentioned in Section 5.4.1, the Household Income Survey (HIS) data allows for separate measurement of gross compensation and and employer contributions to social insurance. It is therefore straightforward to calculate
$$\tau = \frac{\text{Total Compensation Cost}}{\text{Gross Compensation}} - 1 = 0.123.$$
- *Share of population in each employment state (Unemployment, Formal Employment, Informal Employment, and Self-Employment).* As mentioned in Section 5.4, the HIS does not allow for the identification of unemployment while the Labor Force Survey (LFS) does not allow one to distinguish formal from informal wage and salaried employment. However, the estimation strategy only requires the shares of the active population in each employment state, not the identification of the employment state for any particular individual. Accordingly, the shares in unemployment (0.0202), self-employment (0.2140) and wage and salary employment (0.76857) were calculated directly from the LFS. The share of wage and salary employment that is in the formal sector (0.6451) was calculated directly from the HIS. This latter share was multiplied by the share in wage and salary employment to obtain the population share in formal employment (0.4940) and the share in informal employment (0.2717).
- Mean and variance of log earnings in the formal, informal, and self-employment sectors. These values were calculated directly from the HIS data, with the following results (Table 5.3).

Table 5.3

Moments of Earnings Distributions, by Sector

Sector	Mean	Standard Deviation
Self Employed	9.436	1.069
Formal	10.001	0.716
Informal	9.640	0.901

Source: HIS (2009) and authors' calculations.

5.5.2. Recovery of y for All Sampled Individuals

According to the model, individuals in self-employment earn the value of their type, y_i. This implies that one can use observed income of those in self-employment to characterize the determinants of an individual's type, and use this estimation to recover an estimate of the (unobserved) type for each person in the rest of the population, namely the unemployed and those in wage and salary employment.

Worker type is assumed to be a function of observed characteristics[18] Z_i, i.e.

$$y_i = Z_i\gamma \tag{8}$$

However, we further assume that there can be idiosyncratic shocks that affect the income an individual draws from her self-employment at a point in time, and these shocks can be written as $\nu \sim N\ (0,\ \sigma_\nu)$. This implies that the income equation from self-employment takes on a standard Mincerian form, namely

$$w_i^{SE} = y_i + \nu_i = Z_i\gamma + \nu_i \tag{9}$$

As suggested by Section 5.3, being observed in employment is the result of an optimization decision conditional on benefits received in unemployment, the income drawn from self-employment, the riskiness of self-employment, the likelihood of getting a formal or informal sector job offer and the wages and job stability associated with those offers. This implies that the set of individuals actually observed in self-employment is a selected sample, so estimation of equation 9 requires a correction for selection bias. The selection into self-employment is thus modeled as a function of observables[19] A, and we adopt the standard Heckman (1979) formulation for estimation of the vector γ. The results of this estimation are found in Table 5.9 in the Appendix. These results are used to estimate the value of of y for all individuals in the sample, including those not observed in self-employment.

5.5.3. Estimation of the Distributions of Sector-Specific Productivity Draws $G_I(x|y)$ and $G_F(x|y)$

The distributions $G_j(x|y)$, with $j \in$ {Formal, Informal} , are assumed to be logistic with mean equal to $y + \widetilde{k}_j$, where $\widetilde{k}_j$ is a form of unobserved individual-specific heterogeneity that shifts the mean of the x distribution. It is assumed that $\widetilde{k}_j$ is a Bernoulli-distributed random variable. Recovering these distributions (one each for formal and informal wage employment) requires four step procedure:

1. Using the same determinants of wages as were used in the recovery of y from the self employed, estimate the part of wages that is not due to y;
2. Recover the part of this residual that is explainable by "unobserved" characteristics, and use this to characterize the distribution of the heterogeneity component $\widetilde{k}_j$;
3. Recover the value of the draw that is added to the mean $y + \widetilde{k}_j$; and
4. Calculate the distribution of these draws.

One first needs to estimate the relation between wages and y.[20] Since wages are not observed for each individual in every sector, recovery of the distributions of x begins with estimation of sector specific Mincer equations.[21] This estimation represents the first step in recovery of the unobserved heterogeneity and x distributions.

The first-stage residuals of these Mincer regressions are decomposed into a component that is explainable by the full set of variables, including the instruments that are considered "unobservables" for the purposes of the wage equation, and an orthogonal second-stage residual component. The expected first-stage residuals are divided into two groups at the median. The average predicted residual for each subgroup is calculated, the mean for the smaller half of the observations is subtracted from the expected wage resulting from the first stage regression (to normalize the support of the k_j distribution to 0 and a positive value) and their difference becomes the estimator of k_j [22], each of which occurs (by construction) with probability 0.5.

The result of these calculations is a distribution (centered around y or $y + k_j$) of means for the draws from the x distribution. Subtracting this mean from the observed wage gives an estimator of the value of the draw from the x distribution.[23] The variance of the estimators for each distribution is calculated and converted into a scale parameter for each sector's distribution of x draws. For the formal sector, this gives 20.726 as the variance of the logistically distributed shock, or a scale parameter for a logistic distribution of $\sqrt{\frac{3\text{var}(x)}{\pi^2}} = 2.510$ and for the informal sector this gives 20.227 as the variance of logistically distributed shock and a scale factor of $\sqrt{\frac{3\text{var}(x)}{\pi^2}} = 2.480$.

5.5.4. *Recovery of the Remaining Parameters by Simulated Pseudo Method of Moments*

The simulation focuses on a sample of 500 individuals drawn from the distributions of y_i and x_i[24] as estimated in the previous section, where i indexes the individual and s the sector (formal, informal, or self-employment). Figure 5.2 describes the distribution of y in the population. At the beginning of the simulation all workers are unemployed and the number of vacancies is equal to the number of unemployed. As noted in Section 5.3.1, the matching function $m(\theta) = a\theta^{\beta}$ determines the probability of an individual meeting a vacancy, with θ being the ratio of vacancies to unemployment (i.e. a measure of labor market tightness). Contracts are only agreed upon when both profits are positive and the flow value of a given job offer is higher than the value of unemployment.

The micro simulation model follows over time (monthly) each of the individuals in the sample, who are characterized by y_i and x_i. Through aggregation, the model generates steady state distributions for variables of interest: the current unemployment rate in Malaysia; the shares of informal, formal, and self-employment; as well as the mean and variance of the log of earnings for each type of job. To conduct policy simulations, we have to estimate 7 parameters in order to match these distributions. The parameters are: job destruction rates (3); the share of informal vacancies; the arrival rate of job opportunities for self-employment; the bargaining power coefficient; and the scale factor in the matching function. The identification of the model parameters is based on the minimization of the following function in the absence of an unemployment benefit system:[25]

$$\sum_{j=1}^{3} (s_j - s_j^*)^2 + (w_j - w_j^*)^2 + (v_j - v_j^*)^2 \tag{10}$$

where s_j is the share of the labor force working in sector j, w_j is the average of log wages across individuals working in the sector, v_j is the variance, $j = 1$: informal, 2:formal, 3:self-employed, and a^* indicates the target values of the variable, estimated from the data.

The values of the recovered parameters,[26] conditional on the sample of individuals drawn, are presented in Table 5.4.[27] The model is able to closely reproduce the employment shares but predicts higher wages for informal sector workers than found in the data, as seen in Table 5.5. We find job destruction rates ranging between 1 and 5% per month, the lowest in formal sector and the highest in the informal sector. The arrival rate of opportunities in self-employment is close to 8% per month whereas the share of informal job offers is close 40%. Finally, for the sample of individuals drawn, workers appear to have a relatively high bargaining power (> 0.7) but below what would be observed in a perfectly competitive market.

Figure 5.2

Distribution of y in the Population

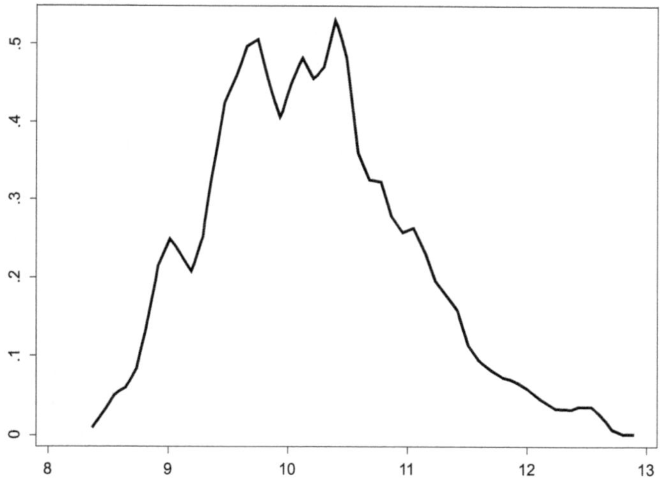

Source: Authors calculations based on estimates derived according to Section 5.5.2.

Table 5.4

Value of Model Parameters Estimated for the Policy Simulations

Parameter	Value	Description
β	0.7646	Bargaining power
a	0.5631	Scale factor in matching function
α	0.0817	Arrival of self-employment opportunities
ψ	0.4	Share of informal job offers
λ_i	0.0477	Job destruction rate in the informal sector
λ_F	0.01	Job destruction rate in the formal sector
λ_I	0.01	Job destruction rate for the self-employed

Table 5.5

Performance of Estimated Model

Population Moment	Estimated Values	Observed Value
Share informal work	0.263	0.281
Share formal work	0.538	0.511
Share self-employment	0.174	0.186
Mean log-wage informal sector	10	9.640048
Std log wage informal	1.2	0.9005742
Mean log-wage formal sector	10.2	10.00101
Std log wage formal	0.7	0.71
Mean log-earnings self-employment	9.7	9.436391
Std log-earnings self-employment	1.5	1.06

5.6. Microsimulations of Policy Experiments

Based on the estimated parameters, several policy experiments were conducted to assess the labor market impact of introducing an unemployment insurance system.

We considered 25 types of unemployment insurance systems based on variations in the values of the following policy parameters: the replacement rate; the contribution rate to the system (assumed to be paid by the employer); the vesting period (i.e., the number of contributions necessary to qualify for benefits); and the duration of unemployment benefits. Although the last two are inconsistent with a literal interpretation of the model in Section 5.3, they are nevertheless closer to situations found in the real world. The implicit assumption here is that workers are myopic and only take into account the availability of unemployment benefits in the next period when deciding whether to take a given job offer. The simulations take as a reference situation a world without unemployment benefits, i.e. where the payroll tax rate, replacement rate, vesting period and benefit duration are all zero.

The ranges considered for each of the parameters are summarized in Table 5.6. The results of the various simulations are presented in Appendix Table 5.11. We also analyze the impact of the unemployment benefit system in the case of a lower value for the bargaining coefficient, chosen to be 0.3.[28] The results of these simulations are presented in Appendix Table 5.12. Table 5.7 summarizes the key results from these tables for employment shares, while Table 5.8 summarizes the key results for average earnings.

Table 5.6

Values of Policy Parameters for Unemployment Benefit Systems

Policy Parameter	Set of Values
Contribution Rate	{0,0.01,0.02,0.03,0.04,0.05}
Replacement rate	{0.5,0.6,0.7,0.8,0.9,1}
Vesting Period (months)	{0,1,2,3,4,5,6}
Duration (months)	{2,4,6,8,10,12,∞}

The results in Table 5.11 suggest that, in general, an unemployment benefit system based on risk-pooling would have modest effects on labor markets, except in the case of very generous replacement rates. The main effects would be a modest increase in the unemployment rate, the reallocation of labor from wage employment into self-employment, and an increase in the average wage in both the formal and informal sectors. The unemployment benefit system increases the flow value of unemployment and the flow value of formal jobs (through an increase in wages and a higher expected income when the labor contract ends), but the first effect dominates for a high value of the bargaining power parameter. Because the flow value of unemployment increases, individuals receiving job offers are less likely to take them, which increases the unemployment rate. In all cases simulated, the increase in the unemployment rate as a result of introducing unemployment insurance is below 1 percentage point and in most cases less than or equal to 0.6 percentage points, which is to be compared to an unemployment share of 2.02 percent in the absence of unemployment insurance. As individuals become less likely to take job offers, unemployment rises and the labor market tightness measure $\left(\theta = \frac{V}{U}\right)$ falls. Other things being equal, individuals are then more likely to enter self-employment. The share of self-employment can increase by up to 3 percentage points in the simulations examined here.

Table 5.7

Effects of Alternative Unemployment Benefit Systems on Employment Shares

Pay Roll Tax	Replace-ment Rate	Vesting Period	Dura-tion	Share Unemployed	Share Informal	Share Formal	Share Self-Employed
			Estimated Bargaining Power (β = 0.7646)				
0	0	0	0	0.0%	0.0%	0.0%	0.0%
0.01	0.5	6	**6**	0.4%	−0.5%	−0.3%	0.3%
0.01	0.5	6	**12**	0.4%	−0.7%	0.0%	0.3%
0.01	0.5	**2**	6	0.5%	−0.5%	−0.3%	0.3%
0.01	0.5	**5**	6	0.4%	−0.5%	−0.3%	0.3%
0.01	**0.7**	6	6	0.6%	−2.6%	−0.6%	2.7%
0.01	**0.9**	6	6	1.0%	−1.2%	0.3%	0.0%
0.02	0.7	6	6	0.6%	−2.6%	−0.6%	2.7%
0.05	0.7	6	6	0.6%	−2.6%	−0.8%	2.7%
0	**0.5**	**0**	**0**	1.8%	−0.1%	−1.7%	0.0%
0	**1**	**0**	**0**	45.9%	−23.0%	−26.6%	3.6%
			Low Bargaining Power (β = 0.3)				
0	0	0	0	0.0%	0.0%	0.0%	0.0%
0.01	0.5	6	**6**	−4.3%	−0.5%	12.1%	−7.3%
0.01	0.5	6	**12**	−4.5%	−0.4%	14.1%	−9.2%
0.01	0.5	**2**	6	−4.4%	−0.4%	12.5%	−7.6%
0.01	0.5	**5**	6	−4.3%	−0.5%	12.1%	−7.3%
0.01	**0.7**	6	6	−1.9%	1.6%	6.6%	−6.3%
0.01	**0.9**	6	6	0.3%	1.5%	−1.4%	−0.4%
0.02	0.7	6	6	−2.0%	1.7%	6.6%	−6.3%
0.05	0.7	6	6	−1.1%	2.1%	6.4%	−7.4%
0	**0.5**	**0**	**0**	−6.5%	4.5%	12.8%	−10.8%
0	**1**	**0**	**0**	38.7%	12.0%	−20.6%	−6.2%

Note: Table presents the difference in steady state values between the simulated and baseline scenarios.

As discussed above, the unemployment benefit system also has a direct impact on wages in the formal sector, increasing the flow value of formal jobs and dampening the negative effect that the increase in the flow value of unemployment has on acceptance rates. In the simulations, the average wage in the formal sector increases by between 3 and 5 percent (more in the case of unemployment assistance). The other important effect is the change in average earnings of self-employed workers. Because earnings in that sector only depend on the level of human capital of the individual, changes provide information about the types of workers who are more likely to move in or out of the sector. The results show that average earnings fall when the replacement rate of the unemployment insurance systems is 50%, indicating that low-skilled workers disproportionately move to this sector. This also explains the increase in the average wage of the informal sector since those leaving are more likely to be low-skilled workers. Moreover, the unemployment benefit system has an additional indirect positive effect on the wages of informal-sector workers in that it increases the flow value of unemployment through the increase in formal sector wages. When the replacement rate is above 50%, however, average earnings for the self-employed increase, indicating an inflow of workers with higher productivity. The interpretation is that as the replacement rate increases, the additional flow value of unemployment makes self-employment attractive even for high-skilled workers - for whom the "opportunity cost of unemployment is higher."

Table 5.8

Effects of Alternative Unemployment Benefit Systems on Average Earnings

Pay Roll Tax	Replace-ment Rate	Vesting Period	Dura-tion	Mean Wage Informal	Mean Wage Formal	Mean Wage Self-Employed
		Estimated Bargaining Power (β = 0.7646)				
0	0	0	0	0.0%	0.0%	0.0%
0.01	0.5	6	**6**	12.3%	4.0%	−4.9%
0.01	0.5	6	**12**	13.4%	3.8%	−4.9%
0.01	0.5	**2**	6	12.3%	4.0%	−4.9%
0.01	0.5	**5**	6	12.3%	4.0%	−4.9%
0.01	**0.7**	6	6	11.3%	4.1%	3.5%
0.01	**0.9**	6	6	22.5%	1.7%	2.0%
0.02	0.7	6	6	11.3%	3.2%	3.5%
0.05	0.7	6	6	11.5%	0.4%	3.5%
0	**0.5**	**0**	**0**	24.2%	8.9%	−7.0%
0	**1**	**0**	**0**	−86.3%	−2.8%	35.8%
		Low Bargaining Power (β = 0.3)				
0	0	0	0	0.0%	0.0%	0.0%
0.01	0.5	6	**6**	0.6%	1.7%	1.2%
0.01	0.5	6	**12**	0.6%	0.9%	1.1%
0.01	0.5	**2**	6	0.6%	1.2%	1.1%
0.01	0.5	**5**	6	0.6%	1.7%	1.2%
0.01	**0.7**	6	6	1.1%	−5.4%	0.7%
0.01	**0.9**	6	6	0.4%	−7.4%	1.2%
0.02	0.7	6	6	1.1%	−5.9%	0.6%
0.05	0.7	6	6	0.4%	−10.3%	0.7%
0	**0.5**	**0**	**0**	0.6%	−18.2%	1.3%
0	**1**	**0**	**0**	−40.0%	109.2%	−1.1%

Note: Table presents the difference in steady state values between the simulated and baseline scenarios.

Overall, the effects of the unemployment benefit system become more important as the replacement rate increases. However, there are no systematic effects from changes in the duration of benefits or the vesting period. This is likely to be an artifact of the current simulations. Indeed, we have run only one set of random shocks that affect individuals over time. Because individuals can be in different states at time t in different policy simulations, the individual specific shock at time t (which is the same for a given individual across simulations) sometimes determines whether a job offer is made and sometimes whether a job is destroyed. For instance, the share of formal employment can change because initial changes in behavior put individuals on a stochastic path where they receive fewer formal job offers.

The contribution rate also appears to have only a marginal impact on the unemployment rate and employment shares, at least when kept below 5 percent. It does, however, considerably dampen the increase in the average formal sector wage. Indeed, the main effect of the contribution rate is to reduce the wage paid for a given skill level, meaning that firms pass at least part of the cost of additional payroll taxes through to the worker in the form of lower wages. Other things being equal, this reduces the likelihood of taking formal sector jobs but not enough to have substantial effects on employment shares.

Lowering the bargaining power of workers, as seen by Table 5.12, changes the results considerably. As indicated above, introducing UI reduces the likelihood of individual accepting informal job offers or opportunities for self-employment. However, those receiving formal job offers are this time more likely to take them, and formal sector wages rise under UI. When the bargaining power of workers (β) falls, formal sector wages also fall. However, introducing a UI system induces a larger increase in formal sector wages when bargaining power is low than when it is high. This is because the bargaining process puts more weight on the flow value of unemployment (relative to the flow value of employment) when bargaining power is low than when it is high, so a given change in the flow value of unemployment leaders to a larger increase in the formal wage, and thereby the value of formal employment, than in the situation with a higher bargaining power for workers. As a result, we see a larger increase in the share of formal employment and a larger reduction in self-employment across the simulations (except in the case of very generous unemployment assistance) when β is lower. This result, although not directly relevant for Malaysia, points to the importance that unemployment benefit systems can have in non-competitive labor markets where employers have more bargaining power relative to workers.

As noted in endnote 7, the model assumes that the state can enforce eligibility rules and ensure that only the unemployed can draw UI benefits. Relaxing this assumption so as to allow those employed in the informal sector (either in wage or self-employment) to draw benefits would have both direct and indirect effects on the model's outcomes. The direct effect of allowing UI receipt while in the informal sector is that the value of informal sector jobs and self-employment has increased since at least with some probability benefits can be drawn while working. The value of unemployment also increases since part of the benefits can continue to be drawn if the individual exits unemployment into an informal sector job. Another indirect effect of relaxing the assumption is that formal sector employment becomes more valuable as the level of unemployment benefits which enters the value function increases. Presumably, therefore, workers would be less likely to remain unemployed and more likely to work in any sector, shortening unemployment durations. Without formally estimating this more complex model, however, it is impossible to quantify how much the share in each employment state would change as enforcement is weakened.

5.7. Conclusion

This chapter has presented a Diamond-Mortensen-Pissarides type of macro labor market model to analyze the effects of introducing unemployment insurance. Although the application focuses in Malaysia, the results are likely to be relevant for other middle-income countries. The model has four labor market states (unemployment, self-employment, informal wage employment and formal wage employment) and was estimated to replicate the structure of the labor market in Malaysia in 2009 and the distribution of earnings for informal, formal and self-employed workers. The model is estimated using direct techniques, OLS regression, selection-corrected regression, and simulated pseudo method of moments estimators on data from Malaysia in 2009.

The model is then used to simulate the effects of alternative unemployment benefit system designs that depend on the replacement rate, the vesting period for benefits, the duration of benefits, and the contribution rate. The results suggest that introducing an unemployment insurance system in Malaysia would have only a modest negative effect on unemployment if benefits are not overly generous. The model suggests that a UI system would induce a reallocation of labor from wage into self-employment while increasing average wages in the formal and informal sectors. The effects on the average earnings of the self-employed would depend on the generosity of the system. With a 50% replacement rate, most workers entering self-employment would be low-skilled workers, driving average earnings down. High-skilled workers would move into self-employment with more generous systems, thereby increasing average earnings.

Although outcomes appear unaffected by variations in the vesting period needed to obtain benefits, and only slightly affected by changes in the duration of benefits, they do vary with the payroll tax rate, the replacement rate and worker bargaining power. The model suggests that these variations are due to workers changing their behavior in response to changes in the flow value of formal employment (both directly – for those coming from the formal sector – and indirectly for the others) and the flow value of unemployment.

Appendix A: Basic Structure of the Model

Our model considers a labor market with salaried and self-employed workers in the spirit of Albrecht et al. (2009). Wage workers can produce with firms offering either a formal or an informal contract. That is, firms can create vacancies in the formal or the informal sector. While formal contracts are subject to labor market regulations like payroll taxes τ , informal contracts are not directly affected by labor market policy. It is also assumed that matches in the informal sector produce a flow value of output which is a fraction $\varepsilon < 1$ of what the same match would yield with a formal contract.[29]

The parameter ε can be interpreted for example as the expected cost of a fine for not complying with regulations. Even though we allow for two types of vacancies for wage jobs, we maintain the assumption that search is random. That is, letting ϕ denote the fraction of informal sector vacancies, the effective contact rate for informal and formal vacancies for the worker are $\phi m(\theta)$ and $(1 - \phi)m(\theta)$, respectively, where $\theta = \frac{\text{Vacancies}}{\text{Unemployment}}$ is a measure of labor market tightness and $m(\cdot)$ is a standard matching function.

Worker participation in the different sectors will be related to, but will not depend exclusively on, the worker's type. We assume an exogenous distribution, $y \sim F(y), \underline{y} \leq y \leq \overline{y}$, of types across workers.

Self-employed workers receive an income y equivalent to their type. Opportunities to work in the self-employment sector arrive to the unemployed at exogenous Poisson rate α, and employment ends at exogenous Poisson rate λ_0.

We allow for *ex post* idiosyncratic initial match productivity in both wage sectors. When a worker of type y meets a prospective employer with a vacancy, she draws a match-specific productivity, $x \sim G_i(x|y)$, $\underline{x} \leq x \leq \overline{x}$, where the subscript $i \in \{F, I\}$ indicates whether the job is in the formal or informal sector. In order to relate x with y, we assume first-order stochastic dominance, i.e., $y' > y \Rightarrow G_i(x|y') < G_i(x|y)$ like in Albrecht et al. (2010). This means that the higher the value of the worker type indicator y, the greater her expected productivity. Once x is realized, the parties decide to produce if the net surplus of the match is positive and continue searching otherwise. The match surplus, and thereby the negotiated wage, depend both on the productivity x and on the worker's type.

As an attractive feature of the model, note that there is not perfect segmentation of large groups of workers across the sectors given that match productivity not only depends on the worker's type but also on match-specific characteristics. It is thus possible to have workers with employment histories in the three sectors as reflected in the data for many developing countries.

Appendix B: Regression Results

Table 5.9

Results From Estimation of y

VARIABLES	log (Self Employment Income)	Selection Into Self Employment
SPM/SPVM	0.368***	−0.221***
	(0.0289)	(0.0204)
STPM/HSC/STA	0.696***	−0.424***
	(0.0648)	(0.0435)
Sijil	0.578***	−0.383***
	(0.0876)	(0.0647)
Diploma	1.096***	−0.509***
	(0.0592)	(0.0358)
Advanced Degree	1.558***	−0.629***
	(0.0694)	(0.0367)
No Degree	−0.343***	0.239***
	(0.0282)	(0.0209)
Female	−0.646***	−0.140***
	(0.0244)	(0.0252)
Age	0.0762***	0.0158***
	(0.00655)	(0.00473)
Age^2	0.0950***	0.0144***
	(0.00697)	(0.00556)
Constant	9.249***	−1.913***
	(0.220)	(0.0992)
atanh (ρ)		−0.783***
		(0.0744)
log (σ)		0.0280
		(0.0311)
Observations	63,817	63,817

Notes: Robust standard errors in parentheses. *** p<0.01, ** p<0.05, * p<0.1. Main and selection models also include controls for 16 states. Selection model includes controls for 10 relations to household head and 5 marital statuses.

Table 5.10

Mincer Regressions for Wage and Salary Sectors

VARIABLES	Formal	Informal
SPM/SPVM	0.263***	0.369***
	(0.01)	(0.0143)
STPM/HSC/STA	0.456***	0.668***
	(0.0175)	(0.0277)
Sijil	0.493***	0.646***
	(0.0203)	(0.0377)
Diploma	0.729***	1.086***
	(0.0124)	(0.0203)
Advanced Degree	1.126***	1.351***
	(0.0123)	(0.0192)
No Degree	0.199***	−0.256***
	(0.0129)	(0.0156)
Female	0.268***	−0.311***
	(0.00618)	(0.0101)
Age	0.0911***	0.122***
	(0.00203)	(0.00271)
Age^2	0.0911***	−0.129***
	(0.00272)	(0.00349)
Constant	7.765***	6.998***
	(0.0379)	(0.0526)
Observations	30,563	20,070
R^2	0.486	0.469

Notes: Standard errors in parentheses. *** p<0.01, ** p<0.05, * p<0.1.
Models also includes controls for 16 states.

Appendix C: Simulation Results

Table 5.11

Effects of Changing System Parameters on Employment Shares and Wages

Pay Roll Tax	Replacement Rate	Vesting Period	Duration	Share Unemployed	Share Informal	Share Formal	Share Self-Employed	Mean Wage Informal	Mean Wage Formal	Mean Wage Self-Employed
0	0	0	0	0.0%	0.0%	0.0%	0.0%	0.0%	0.0%	0.0%
0.01	0.5	6	**2**	0.2%	−1.2%	0.0%	1.0%	7.0%	3.0%	−3.5%
0.01	0.5	6	**4**	0.4%	−0.3%	−0.4%	0.3%	10.6%	3.7%	−4.9%
0.01	0.5	6	**6**	0.4%	−0.5%	−0.3%	0.3%	12.3%	4.0%	−4.9%
0.01	0.5	6	**8**	0.4%	−1.0%	−0.3%	0.9%	12.8%	4.1%	−5.3%
0.01	0.5	6	**10**	0.5%	−0.5%	−0.3%	0.3%	12.5%	4.0%	−4.9%
0.01	0.5	6	**12**	0.4%	−0.7%	0.0%	0.3%	13.4%	3.8%	−4.9%
0.01	0.5	**1**	6	0.5%	−0.5%	−0.3%	0.3%	12.3%	4.0%	−4.9%
0.01	0.5	**2**	6	0.5%	−0.5%	−0.3%	0.3%	12.3%	4.0%	−4.9%
0.01	0.5	**3**	6	0.5%	−0.5%	−0.3%	0.3%	12.3%	4.0%	−4.9%
0.01	0.5	**4**	6	0.5%	−0.5%	−0.3%	0.3%	12.3%	4.0%	−4.9%
0.01	0.5	**5**	6	0.4%	−0.5%	−0.3%	0.3%	12.3%	4.0%	−4.9%
0.01	**0.6**	**6**	6	0.6%	−1.4%	−0.1%	0.9%	12.8%	4.6%	−4.0%

Table 5.11 (continued)

Effects of Changing System Parameters on Employment Shares and Wages

Pay Roll Tax	Replace-ment Rate	Vesting Period	Dura-tion	Share Unemployed	Share Informal	Share Formal	Share Self-Employed	Mean Wage Informal	Mean Wage Formal	Mean Wage Self-Employed
0.01	**0.7**	6	6	0.6%	−2.6%	−0.6%	2.7%	11.3%	4.1%	3.5%
0.01	**0.8**	6	6	0.7%	−2.7%	−0.5%	2.5%	17.0%	1.6%	4.9%
0.01	**0.9**	6	6	1.0%	−1.2%	0.3%	0.0%	22.5%	1.7%	2.0%
0.02	0.7	6	6	0.6%	−2.6%	−0.6%	2.7%	11.3%	3.2%	3.5%
0.03	0.7	6	6	0.6%	−2.6%	−0.6%	2.7%	11.3%	2.2%	3.5%
0.04	0.7	6	6	0.6%	−2.6%	−0.6%	2.7%	11.3%	1.3%	3.5%
0.05	0.7	6	6	0.6%	−2.6%	−0.8%	2.7%	11.5%	0.4%	3.5%
0	**0.5**	**0**	**0**	1.8%	−0.1%	−1.7%	0.0%	24.2%	8.9%	−7.0%
0	**0.6**	**0**	**0**	2.6%	−1.1%	−2.5%	1.1%	23.5%	9.1%	0.2%
0	**0.7**	**0**	**0**	3.2%	1.0%	−4.0%	−0.2%	33.3%	6.7%	−3.4%
0	**0.8**	**0**	**0**	3.5%	0.5%	−4.4%	0.3%	38.9%	3.9%	2.2%
0	**0.9**	**0**	**0**	5.0%	−1.2%	−7.3%	3.5%	43.7%	4.3%	10.5%
0	**1**	**0**	**0**	45.9%	−23.0%	−26.6%	3.6%	−86.3%	−2.8%	35.8%

Note: Table presents the difference in steady state values between the simulated and baseline scenarii. Simulation using parameters from Table 5.6 and using the estimated bargaining power parameter of $\beta = 0.7646$.

Table 5.12

Effects of Changing System Parameters on Employment Shares and Wages (Low Bargaining Power)

Pay Roll Tax	Replace-ment Rate	Vesting Period	Dura-tion	Share Unemployed	Share Informal	Share Formal	Share Self-Employed	Mean Wage Informal	Mean Wage Formal	Mean Wage Self-Employed
0	0	0	0	0.0%	0.0%	0.0%	0.0%	0.0%	0.0%	0.0%
0.01	0.5	6	**2**	-3.7%	-0.2%	10.4%	-6.5%	0.6%	0.0%	1.3%
0.01	0.5	6	**4**	-4.1%	-0.4%	11.8%	-7.3%	0.7%	1.9%	1.2%
0.01	0.5	6	**6**	-4.3%	-0.5%	12.1%	-7.3%	0.6%	1.7%	1.2%
0.01	0.5	6	**8**	-4.5%	-0.4%	14.1%	-9.2%	0.6%	0.9%	1.1%
0.01	0.5	6	**10**	-4.5%	-0.4%	14.1%	-9.2%	0.6%	0.9%	1.1%
0.01	0.5	6	**12**	-4.5%	-0.4%	14.1%	-9.2%	0.6%	0.9%	1.1%
0.01	0.5	**0**	6	-5.9%	5.2%	11.9%	-11.1%	0.7%	20.3%	1.1%
0.01	0.5	**1**	6	-4.4%	-0.4%	12.5%	-7.6%	0.6%	1.2%	1.1%
0.01	0.5	**2**	6	-4.4%	-0.4%	12.5%	-7.6%	0.6%	1.2%	1.1%
0.01	0.5	**3**	6	-4.3%	-0.5%	12.1%	-7.3%	0.6%	1.7%	1.2%
0.01	0.5	**4**	6	-4.3%	-0.5%	12.1%	-7.3%	0.6%	1.7%	1.2%
0.01	0.5	**5**	6	-4.3%	-0.5%	12.1%	-7.3%	0.6%	1.7%	1.2%
0.01	**0.6**	6	6	-3.2%	0.8%	9.2%	-6.7%	0.7%	-3.6%	1.6%

Table 5.12 (continued)

Effects of Changing System Parameters on Employment Shares and Wages (Low Bargaining Power)

Pay Roll Tax	Replace-ment Rate	Vesting Period	Dura-tion	Share Unemployed	Share Informal	Share Formal	Share Self-Employed	Mean Wage Informal	Mean Wage Formal	Mean Wage Self-Employed
0.01	**0.7**	6	6	-1.9%	1.6%	6.6%	-6.3%	1.1%	-5.4%	0.7%
0.01	**0.8**	6	6	-1.0%	2.0%	3.6%	-4.6%	0.6%	-8.2%	0.4%
0.01	**0.9**	6	6	0.3%	1.5%	-1.4%	-0.4%	0.4%	-7.4%	1.2%
0.02	0.7	6	6	-2.0%	1.7%	6.6%	-6.3%	1.1%	-5.9%	0.6%
0.03	0.7	6	6	-1.9%	2.5%	5.5%	-6.2%	0.9%	-9.3%	0.9%
0.04	0.7	6	6	-0.6%	1.5%	4.4%	-5.3%	0.6%	-6.0%	0.5%
0.05	0.7	6	6	-1.1%	2.1%	6.4%	-7.4%	0.4%	10.3%	0.7%
0	**0.5**	**0**	**0**	-6.5%	4.5%	12.8%	-10.8%	0.6%	18.2%	1.3%
0	**0.6**	**0**	**0**	-5.9%	7.6%	10.1%	-11.8%	1.0%	25.7%	1.3%
0	**0.7**	**0**	**0**	-4.8%	6.6%	7.1%	-8.8%	0.4%	22.4%	1.5%
0	**0.8**	**0**	**0**	-4.2%	4.2%	3.0%	-3.1%	0.1%	11.1%	1.0%
0	**0.9**	**0**	**0**	-0.2%	-2.5%	-5.0%	7.7%	0.2%	24.6%	2.0%
0	**1**	**0**	**0**	38.70%	-12.00%	20.60%	-6.20%	-40.00%	109.20%	-1.10%

Note: Table presents the difference in steady state values between the simulated and baseline scenarii. Simulation using parameters from Table 5.6 and using the estimated bargaining power parameter of $\beta = 0.3$.

Notes

1 For reviews see Holmlund (1998), Vodopivec et al. (2005), and Olinto et al. (2007).

2 In the states of Sabah and Labuan, there are over 5 percent more people under the age of 25 and roughly 4 percent fewer people over the age of 55 than in the other regions. The state of Sarawak differentiates itself from Peninsular Malaysia in that its demographic bulge happened earlier, so that there are more people in their thirties and fewer people in their twenties and teens in Sarawak than in Peninsular Malaysia and Sabah/Labuan.

3 Forty percent of the working-age population of Sarawak has at most a primary education, while the number rises to 47 percent for Sabah/Labuan. Conversely, nearly 60 percent of the working-age population in Peninsular Malaysia has a secondary degree (compared with 52 percent in Sarawak and 43.3 percent in Sabah/Labuan) and 15.6 percent have a post-secondary certification (compared with 8.1 percent in Sarawak and nearly 10 percent in Sabah/Labuan).

4 For the purposes of the data work in this report, employment in the "formal sector" is defined as holding a job for which the employer makes Employer's Provident Fund (EPF) or Social Security (SOCSO) contributions. By this definition, self-employed individuals who are not required to contribute are considered to be "informal," and this definition will also classify some teachers or health workers employed by the public sector as informal, since their employer is not required to contribute to EPF and SOCSO on their behalf.

5 See Margolis et al. (2011) for the full structural model with expressions for equilibrium employment rates in each sector and wage distributions.

6 For simplicity of exposition, it is assumed that all ex-workers, including self-employed and informal-sector workers, can draw unemployment benefits, as a function of their earnings prior to unemployment. This assumption is relaxed in the numerical simulations, where the replacement rate for unemployment spells following self-employment or informal wage employment is set to zero.

7 It is assumed that individuals can only receive unemployment benefits when unemployed, i.e. not when self-employed or in informal employment. This implies significant enforcement capacity on behalf of the government, which may not be appropriate. We discuss the implications that relaxing this assumption might have in Section 3.6.

8 As savings are not a component of the model, it is assumed that taking a self-employment opportunity requires no startup capital.

9 The HIS is collected by the Department of Statistics for the Economic Planning Unit.

10 The LFS is collected by the Department of Statistics.

11 It should be noted that some variables needed to be built from both sources. See Section 3.5.1 for details.

12 The exclusion of collective housing is likely to be an issue for some sectors, particularly agriculture where many workers live in collective housing in the middle of plantations.

13 The actual question asked is "How much did .... earn during the last twelve (12) months from paid employment?' for which one earnings category is "Employer's contributions to EPF, SOCSO, etc.".'

14 It should be noted that Malaysia does not have an explicit unemployment insurance system, however it does provide for mandatory severance pay in the case of dismissal or redundancy-based separation from (formal) jobs (Holzmann and Vodopivec 2011).

15 Unemployment durations are measured as: less than 3 months, 3 months - less than 6 months, 6 months - less than 1 year, 1 - 3 years and more than 3 years.

16 This is not meant to imply that the estimation is fully non-parametric; in particular, a Heckman-type selection correction is employed in the estimation of y, implying joint normality between the disturbance term of the expression that determines Y

and that which determines the probability of self-employment; see Section 3.5.2 for details.

17 See Margolis et al. (2011) for the full structural estimation.

18 The explanatory variables included in Z that determine human capital are the highest degree obtained (7 levels), sex, age, age squared, and indicators for the state of residence (16 levels).

19 The variables included in the A vector are limited by the relatively limited set of variables available in the LFS and HIS. Accordingly, the A vector includes the same variables as in Z, plus marital status (5 levels) and relation to household head (10 levels).

20 In the model outlined in Section 3.3, the wage is the result of Nash bargaining over the surplus of the employment relation between the employer and the individual. The surplus is a proportional to x, and the result of the bargaining gives a share of the surplus to the individual in the form a wage that must exceed the individual's outside option. These expressions imply that the relation between the wage and x is linear; see Margolis et al. (2011) for details. Since $w = a + bx$, where a and b are unknown parameters,

$$E(x) = \frac{E(w)}{b} - \frac{a}{b} \text{ and } \operatorname{var}(x) = \frac{\operatorname{var}(w)}{b^2}.$$

Since this paper does not need to provide a structural interpretation to the intercept or slope parameters of the linear relation in order to apply the simulation estimator, one can simply recover the mean and variance of the distribution of w, which will themselves be linear functions of the underlying (and unknown) mean and variance of x, and use these estimated parameters in the simulations.

21 Note that although selection into employment in each sector is an issue, as it was for self-employment, there exist no valid exclusion restrictions for estimating a selection corrected Mincer equation. This is because the wage is the result of bargaining between the worker and employer, whereas in self-employment it was only a function of the individual's type and a shock. The bargaining dimension implies that wage outcomes will depend on the value of the surplus, which itself is a function of all of the same factors that determine selection into one sector or the other. This dependence is modeled as affecting the distribution of $\widetilde{k}_j$, namely $P(\widetilde{k}_j) = 0 = 1 - \Phi(A_i k_j)$ and $P(\widetilde{k}_j = k_j) = \Phi(A_i k_j)$. The estimation of the sector specific Mincer equations can thus be written as $w_i^j = Z_i \gamma^j + v_i^j$. The results of these models are found in Table 5.10 in the appendix.

22 The estimates are $k_F = 3.167 * 10^{-3}$ and $k_I = 1.407 * 10^{-4}$.

23 More precisely, as noted in equations 6 and 7, the wage is a linear transformation of the (rescaled) reservation utility and a draw from the x distribution. As the reservation utility depends on the expected wage, which is a function of $y + k_j$, the draw of x can be approximated by the difference between the observed wage and $y + k_j$. This approximation is best when $\beta = 1$.

24 For consistency in the simulations, the productivity draws x are assumed to be the same across firms within the same sector for a given individual.

25 The estimation uses the ANT algorithm (Miller 1998).

26 The severance pay parameter, s, is set to zero for the purposes of the simulation.

27 Clearly, different samples would lead to different values for the model parameters. In principle, one could bootstrap samples to estimate standard errors for the parameters. In the micro-simulation estimation, however, we keep the sample of individuals constant.

28 Changing the value of the bargaining coefficient, of course, changes the employment shares and the distribution of wages. The impacts of the simulated unemployment benefit systems are analyzed against this new (counterfactual) steady state.

29 A similar assumption is done in Bosch and Esteban-Pretel (2009).

References

Albrecht, J., Navarro, L., Vroman, S. (2009). The Effects of Labour Market Policies in an Economy with an Informal Sector, in: Economic Journal, 119(539): 1105–29.
Albrecht, J., Navarro, L., Vroman, S. (2010). Public Sector Employment in an Equilibrium Search and Matching Model, mimeo.
Bosch, M., Esteban-Pretel, J. (2009). Cyclical Informality and Unemployment, CIRJE F-Series No. CIRJE-F-613, CIRJE University of Tokyo.
Cunningham, W. V. (2000). Unemployment Insurance in Brazil: Unemployment Duration, Wages and Sectoral Choice, Technical Report, Washington, DC: The World Bank.
Heckman, J. J. (1979). Sample Selection Bias as a Specification Error, in: Econometrica, 47(1): 153–61.
Holmlund, B. (1998). Unemployment Insurance in Theory and Practice, in: Scandinavian Journal of Economics, 100(1): 113–41.
Holzmann, R., Vodopivec, M. (Eds.) (2011). Reforming Severance Pay, Washington, DC: The World Bank.
Holzmann, R., Pouget, Y., Vodopivec, M., Weber, M. (2011). Severance Pay Programs around the World: History, Rationale, Status, and Reforms, IZA Discussion Paper No. 5731.
Margolis, D. N. (2008). Unemployment Insurance versus Individual Unemployment Accounts and Transitions to Formal versus Informal Sector Jobs, Paris: Centre d'Economie de la Sorbonne, mimeo.
Margolis, D. N., Navarro, L., Robalino, D. A. (2011). A Structural Model of Informality, Self Employment and Job Search, Washington, DC: The World Bank, mimeo.
Miller, J. H. (1998). Active Nonlinear Tests (ANTs) of Complex Simulation Models, in: Management Science, 44(6): 820–30.
Pissarides, C. A. (2000) Equilibrium Unemployment Theory, 2nd Edition, Vol. 1 of MIT Press Books, Cambridge, MA: The MIT Press.
Robalino, D. A., Zylberstajn, E., Robalino, J. D. (2011). Incentive Effects of Risk Pooling, Redistributive and Savings Arrangements in Unemployment Benefit Systems: Evidence from a Job-Search Model for Brazil, IZA Discussion Paper No. 5476.
Tatsiramos, K. (2009). Geographic Labour Mobility and Unemployment Insurance in Europe, in: Journal of Population Economics, 22(2): 267–83.
van Ours, J. C., Vodopivec, M. (2008). Does Reducing Unemployment Insurance Generosity Reduce Job Match Quality?, in: Journal of Public Economics, 92 (3-4): 684–95.
Vodopivec, M., Wörgötter, A., Raju, D. (2005). Unemployment Benefit Systems in Central and Eastern Europe: A Review of the 1990s, in: Comparative Economic Studies, 47(4): 615–51.

6

Does Formal Work Pay? The Role of Labor Taxation and Social Benefit Design in the New Member States*

Johannes Koettl
Michael Weber

6.1. Introduction

This chapter investigates the question if – given the high levels of informality and inactivity in some European countries – it is actually "worthwhile" for the working-age population to engage in income-generating activities. If so, what are the incentives that employers, the self-employed, and workers have to actually register these activities and pay taxes and contributions on the income generated?

There are a number of reasons why employers, the self-employed, and workers might decide not to register their activities. First, regulations in the product and labor market – like product licensing,

* *The original version of this chapter was published as: Koettl, J. / Weber, M. (2012). Does Formal Work Pay? The Role of Labor Taxation and Social Benefit Design in the New EU Member States, in: Research in Labor Economics, 34: 167-204. © 2012 by Emerald Group Publishing. The chapter is also part of background technical analysis of the 2012 World Bank study "In From the Shadow: Integrating Europe's Informal Labor." The chapter greatly benefited from research support from Isil Oral and Victoria Strokova; comments by Hartmut Lehmann, Truman Packard, Konstantinos Tatsiramos, two anonymous referees, and participants at a joint 2011 IZA/World Bank Workshop on "Institutions and Informal Employment in Emerging and Transition Economies"; and a close cooperation with Claudio Montenegro as well as with Tatiana Goridne, Herwig Immervoll, and Dominique Partout. All errors are those of the authors. The views and opinions expressed in this chapter are solely those of the authors and do not represent the views and opinions of the World Bank, its board of Executive Directors, or the countries they represent.*

employment protection legislation (EPL), and minimum wages - might be too stringent, so in order to circumvent these regulations, people might decide to operate outside the formal economy (Perry et al. 2007; OECD 2004; Schneider and Klinglmair 2004; Terrell and Grindling 2002; Bertola et al. 2001). Second, certain administrative procedures related to paying taxes, accounting, and completing statistical questionnaires might deter people from operating in the formal sector (Bassanini and Duval 2006; Djankov et al. 2002). Third, people and firms might want to avoid paying taxes on revenues, income, profit, or property and social security contributions (Davis and Henrekson 2004; Betcherman and Pagés 2007). Fourth, formal income might lead to a withdrawal of social benefits - like social assistance or unemployment benefits - so that people might prefer informal or no work over formal work (EC 2003; EC 2004; OECD 2004). Fifth, enforcement of existing legislation on regulations and taxation might be lax, therefore the risks of circumventing regulations and avoiding taxes might be low (Schneider and Enste 2000; Hanousek and Palda 2003).

To answer the main question of the chapter whether formal work pays, we focus on the role of labor taxation and social benefit design in explaining the incidence of informal employment. More specifically it investigates what disincentives for formal work might be provided to people in working age so they choose to "exit" into informality (Perry et al. 2007). Since labor taxation and social benefit design only partly explain informality, the analysis presented below highlights how for lower-wage earners the value of formal social security benefits that come with formal employment would at times have to be enormously high to offset the opportunity costs of formalization. The conclusion is that formal (part-time) jobs at low-wage levels - so-called mini-jobs and midi-jobs - are not economically viable for low-wage earners in some countries. This lack of economic viability might exclude a substantial part of the working-age population from formal employment and social security coverage. In this latter sense, informality and inactivity might not only be a deliberate choice of exit, but are also a matter of "exclusion" (Perry et al. 2007).

The analysis starts by examining which incentives or disincentives the informally employed and their employers face when considering formal work. For the informally employed, switching to formality will have a number of implications for both workers and firms. First, it implies that workers and their employers will enter as contributors to social security. This means that both the employer and the worker have to contribute to pension funds, health insurance funds, and unemployment insurance funds. The decision on contributions will strongly be influenced by the value that informal workers attach to being covered by social security. Second, workers will have to pay personal income tax on their formal gross wages. This decision will be influenced by the value informal workers put on public services and social norms about paying taxes (Torgler 2003; Torgler and Schneider 2009). Paying social security contributions and income tax combined will decrease workers' take-home pay when compared to their informal wage. Third, informal workers after formalizing might no longer be eligible to a number of income-tested benefits such as social assistance, family benefits, or housing benefits. Firms, finally, which are formalizing informal workers, will have to generate additional formal revenues by switching informal revenues to formal revenues. This implies paying additional taxes in the product market, like sales or value-added taxes.

In the New Eastern European Member States of the European Union (NMS) informality is high[1] and the demographic transition will considerably increase the need for participation in the formal sector in the future. For the social contract of these countries to survive, more people will need to contribute through taxes and social security contributions. Those who currently do not work and those who work informally will need to be activated and convinced to participate in the formal sector of the labor market. Arguably, one pre-condition for participation in the formal sector is that formal work has to pay. In other words, the incentives for formal work that originate in the tax and benefit system of a country have to be aligned to encourage formal work. Incentives alone, though, might perhaps not be the binding constraint. Labor taxation and benefit design are but two pieces of the puzzle that explain high levels of informality among the working-age population of the NMS. We are not trying to identify which of these potential reasons are the main causes for high levels of informality, but we narrowly focus on the incentives and disincentives for formal employment provided by the labor taxation and benefit system. For a very recent discussion on drivers of informal employment and potential policy options to address them see Lehmann (2010).[2]

One indication that at least taxation in general plays a prominent role in income-generating activities comes from enterprise surveys. For example, the World Bank Enterprise survey for 2009 (World Bank 2011b) reveals that on average, 45 percent of firms in the NMS cite tax rates as a one of the major obstacle for doing business. The question in the survey refers to all types of taxes, and, hence, not specifically to labor taxes. Nevertheless, the results indicate that in the NMS, tax rates are perceived as a greater obstacle to doing business than any other impediment in the ranking, like tax administration (24 percent), competition from informal enterprises (23 percent), licensing (14 percent), labor regulations (14 percent), and trade regulations (8 percent). Therefore, although the results of this enterprise survey are not a direct measurement of obstacles to formal employment, they give an indication that tax rates could be perceived as a constraint for creating new formal jobs.

The contribution of this chapter is twofold: First, we present a detailed descriptive analysis of the tax and benefit systems of the NMS, describing disincentives for formal employment stemming from labor taxation and social benefit design. In doing so, we not only analyze standard measurements of disincentives like the tax-wedge and the marginal effective tax rate (METR), but we also develop a new and innovative measurement of disincentives for formal work, the so-called formalization tax rate (FTR). The FTR goes beyond the usual measurements of the tax-wedge and METR by combining both. It expresses the opportunity costs of formal employment by measuring what share of informal income is being taxed away – in terms of income tax, social security contributions *and* withdrawn benefits – when formalizing, and therefore how much workers have to gain in return for formalization in terms of social security benefits and employment protection. For this exercise, the analysis relies on the Organization of Economic Co-operation and Development (OECD) Tax and Benefit model, which is available for most OECD countries as well as the Baltics, Bosnia and Herzegovina, Bulgaria, Macedonia, Romania, and Serbia (OECD 2011; Immervoll 2007).[3] This descriptive analysis is presented in Section 6.2.

Second, we present an empirical analysis that combines the synthetic measurements of the FTR, the METR, and the tax-wedge with actual informality patterns by using data from the European Union Statistics on Income and Living Conditions (EU-SILC; Eurostat 2008), investigating the question if and how much these disincentives matter for informal employment. To this end, the analysis matches these synthetic measurements to individual observations for six countries in the EU-SILC 2008 data: Bulgaria, Czech Republic, Estonia, Latvia, Poland, and Slovakia. In other words, for each individual in the survey, we define synthetic measurements of disincentives for formal work stemming from the tax and benefit system of his or her country of residence. The empirical analysis then explores the correlation between disincentives for formal work and the incidence of informal employment in these six countries. This analysis is presented in Section 6.3.

The main finding of the descriptive analysis is that the disincentives for formal work – when measured through the FTR – are especially high for low-wage earners. This suggests that formal work might not pay in this segment of the labor market, in particular for the so-called mini-jobs and midi-jobs (low paying part-time work). The empirical analysis finds a significant positive correlation between FTR or METR and the incidence of being informal. Controlling for individual and job characteristics, the higher the FTR or the METR that individuals are facing is – that is, the higher disincentives for formal work – the higher the likelihood to work informally. The tax-wedge, on the other hand, yields a negative correlation, suggesting that the tax-wedge is not sufficiently capturing disincentives for formal work.

6.2. Measurements of Informality and Disincentives for Formal Work

This section offers a descriptive analysis of the tax and benefit systems in the NMS and benchmarks them against other OECD countries. The section starts by discussing various definitions of informal employment. Next, the theoretical foundations of the decision between formal and informal employment are outlined. Finally, three different measurements of work disincentives are introduced and discussed.

6.2.1. Definition of Informal Employment

The definition of informal employment is not straightforward. A comprehensive and widely accepted definition was provided by the

International Labor Organization (ILO) in 2003. It includes: (i) own-account workers and employees employed in their own informal sector enterprises; (ii) unpaid family workers, irrespective of whether they work in formal or informal sector enterprises; (iii) members of informal producers' cooperatives; (iv) own-account workers engaged in the production of goods exclusively for own final use by their household; and finally, (v) employees holding informal jobs in formal sector enterprises, informal sector enterprises, or as paid domestic workers employed by households. In this last category, informal jobs are those not subject to legislation, income taxation, social protection, nor entitlements to codified benefits such as advance notice of dismissal, severance pay, paid annual or sick leave (ILO 2003; Hussmanns 2004).

This comprehensive definition of informality is constrained by data availability. Particular measurement challenges are: (i) measuring the status of self-employed, own-account workers, and employers, as this requires identifying if their enterprise is registered or not; and (ii) measuring the status of employees, as this requires identifying the nature of their employment contract. With regard to the self-employed, if it is not possible to determine the legal status of the enterprise, a variety of alternative measures have been developed. The most widely used is the size of the enterprise, with employers or self-employed of enterprises with less than 5 or 10 employees defined as informal, all others as formal. Another measurement developed by Hazans (2011) qualifies the firm size measurement by combining it with the professional status of self-employed or employers - only *non-professional* employers or self-employed with a small enterprise are defined as informal. With regard to employees, the most common measurement defines those with no written employment contract as informal. Alternatively, informal employment is sometimes also measured as those employees who do not contribute to social security. If neither measurement is available, the firm size is again the most common measurement, defining all employees in firms with less than 5 or 10 employees as informal. Unpaid family workers, finally, are relatively easy to measure directly from surveys.

In this chapter, two related definitions of informal employment are used. For the descriptive analysis of this section, we use the legalistic definition: informally employed are all those who do not report any of their labor income to tax and social security authorities. These are all self-employed, employers, own-account workers, unpaid family workers, and employees who *completely* conceal their labor income and pay neither social security contributions nor personal income taxes. Section 6.2 uses only data from the OECD Tax and Benefit model (OECD 2011) and analyzes synthetic measurements. These synthetic measurements are exclusively derived from legislation – that is, they measure what individuals *should* pay in taxes and what benefits individuals *should* to be entitled to according to the law; it does not measure the actual incidence of tax payments and entitlement consumption.

For the econometric analysis of Section 6.3 survey data from EU-SILC (Eurostat 2011) is used. Data limitations require deviating from the preferred legalistic definition of informal employment with regard to the self-employed. Informal employees, as previously defined, are as those for whom no social security contributions are being paid by their employers. Also, unpaid family workers are identified as informal. However, for the self-employed the definition deviates from the legalistic definition of the descriptive analysis. Due to data restrictions, a less precise "productivity" definition as suggested by Hazans (2011) is applied. Accordingly, all non-professional employers who employ five or fewer workers (including those with no employees) are identified as informal.

Applying this productivity definition to the informal self-employed yields rather high informality rates among the self-employed (see below). This productivity definition could therefore potentially overestimate informality rates for this group. As a robustness check, the analysis is performed restricting the sample to either only the self-employed or only employees. The results do not differ substantially from those for the whole sample. Hence, the behavior of the self-employed, using the productivity definition, corresponds to the behavior of employees with regard to work disincentives and informal employment. This suggests that the productivity definition used to identify informal self-employed does not conflict with the results using the legalistic definition for employees.

6.2.2. The Comparison Between Formal and Informal Employment

This chapter attempts a comparison between two theoretically identical workers, one working formally and one informally. The formal worker faces certain costs for working formally which are measured by the overall and marginal taxes that need to be paid. The informal worker does not have to pay taxes. So, how much the informal worker's theoretical formal twin has to pay in overall taxes (the tax-wedge) or in marginal taxes (the marginal effective tax rate) are important indicators for formal work disincentives. Similarly, the difference in net income of the informal worker and the informal worker's formal twin is a comprehensive indicator for how much income is taxed away through formalization (the formalization tax rate). Each of these three measurements centers on the individual worker. Therefore, the focus of the analysis is primarily on the worker's choice between formal and informal employment. The key question is how to construct two identical workers. That is, what income would an informal worker have in the formal sector, and what income would a formal worker have in the informal sector?

We assume that two workers are identical if they generate the same total labor cost for the employer. This approach has some important implications. In particular, it implies that the entire tax-wedge is born by the formal worker and therefore enters in its entirety as an opportunity cost of formal work. Such an interpretation assumes that the employer has a very strong bargaining position and is able to roll over all taxes to the worker. In other words, the labor supply curve is infinitely inelastic. Empirical evidence suggests that labor supply could indeed be relatively inelastic in the low-wage segment, but not so much in the higher-wage segment (see for example, Betcherman and Pagés 2007). This could suggest that in the higher-wage segment, the empirical analysis might be less adequate.

The suggested methodology might make it difficult to interpret the decision process between formal and informal employment. We model this primarily as the worker's decision, which in turn depends on the financial disincentives provided by the tax and benefit system. In reality, the decision will clearly also build upon preferences – in particular time preferences – about the value of social security benefits, employment protection, and risk. Yet, for the analysis these preferences cannot be measured with the available data, which means that we assume that the marginal product of labor is equal among the two identical workers. This further implies that the decision between formal and informal employment can only take place within the same firm, if one further assumes that the marginal product of labor of the worker is firm-specific. In that sense, the informality decision as modeled in this chapter would only apply to the limited case where workers are formalized within the same firm. If, on the other hand, one assumes that the marginal product of labor is not firm-specific, but tied to the worker's abilities, the informal worker could also move to other firms when formalizing. This position implies a more competitive labor market in which workers are able to move relatively freely between jobs and, therefore, are confronted with an integrated labor market (Maloney 1999; 2004). This assumption also implies that there is no wage gap between the formal and informal sector. Empirical evidence suggests that the latter might not be the case, at least not for employees. Perry et al. (2007) find that there is a considerable wage gap between formal and informal salaried workers in Latin American countries and a considerable segmentation in the labor market.

Despite this imprecision and difficulties in interpretation, we consider the measurement concepts put forward as sufficiently adequate to allow for a meaningful analysis. The central question then is how to measure these opportunity costs or disincentives of formal work. As mentioned above, we investigate three measurements: first, the tax-wedge; second, a new indicator, called the formalization tax rate (FTR); and third, a marginal measurement, the marginal effective tax rate (METR).

6.2.3. Labor Taxation: The Tax-Wedge

Labor taxes in the NMS are high at lower-wage levels. A comparison with other EU, OECD, and neighboring countries shows that the tax-wedge on labor at lower-wage levels (33 percent of a country's average wage) tends to be relatively high (see Figure 6.1).[4] The tax-wedge is a so-called synthetic measurement, meaning it is purely based on legislation and therefore measures what individuals are *supposed* to pay, not what they actually pay, in taxes and social security contributions. It measures the difference between total labor costs and take-home pay as a percentage of total labor costs. This difference consists of personal income tax and social security contributions paid by the worker and the employer. Hence, the tax-wedge t is defined as

$$t = \frac{TLC^E - NI^W}{TLC^E} = \frac{IT^W + SSC^W + SSC^E}{TLC^E}$$

where TLC^E is the total labor costs paid by the employer, NI^W is the net income of the worker, IT^W is the income tax paid by the worker,

Figure 6.1

Labor Taxation Tends to Be Relatively High for Low-Wage Earners (at 33 Percent of Average Wage) in the NMS

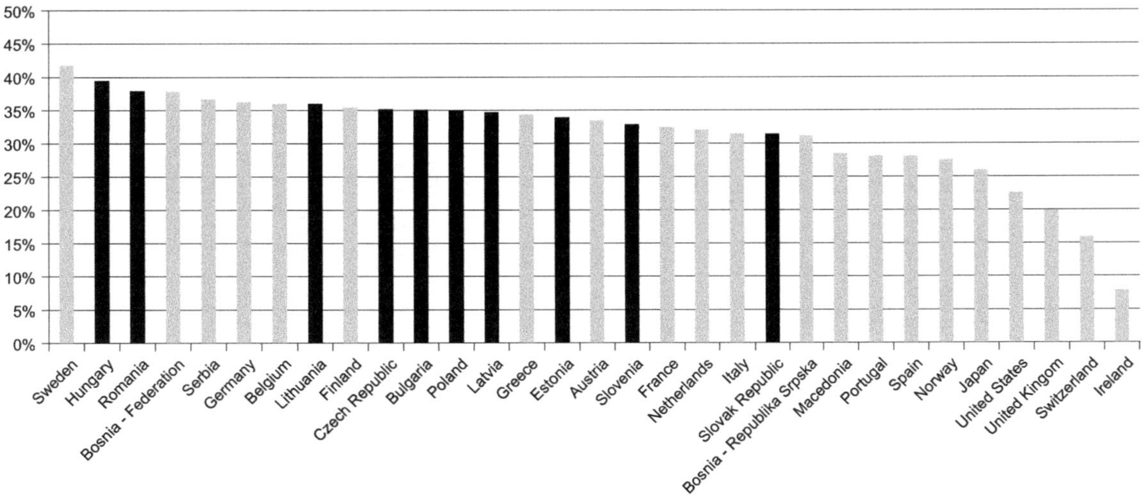

Note: Columns represent the tax-wedge for low-income earners (singles with no children at 33 percent of average wage) in 2008 (for Bosnia, Macedonia, and Serbia, 2009). NMS depicted in black.

Source: Authors' calculation based on OECD Tax and Benefit model (OECD 2011).

SSC^W is the social security contribution paid by the worker, and SSC^E is the social security contribution paid by the employer. It therefore expresses the costs of social security contributions by employers and employees and the personal income tax of employees as a share of total labor costs, or the share of total labor costs that is "taxed away."

In the case of informal employment, neither the worker nor the employer has to pay any taxes or social security contributions so that the worker's net income equals total labor costs and the tax-wedge is zero. The tax-wedge is therefore a good first approximation to measure incentives faced by employers and workers for informal employment. It measures the gains of informal employment. Although it cannot give any information on how these gains can potentially be shared between the worker and the employer, it nevertheless gives valuable information on the incentives that workers and employers face when choosing between formal or informal employment.

The tax-wedge varies depending on family type and wage level. The OECD Tax and Benefit model calculates (i) income tax and social security contributions paid by the employer and the worker, (ii) for 10 different family types, (iii) for individuals earning between 0 and up to 367 percent of average wage, and (iv) for most OECD countries. This data reveals that for single persons with no children receiving a gross wage of 33 percent of the average wage, only a few EU-15 countries – like Sweden, Germany, Belgium, and Finland – charge higher taxes than most of the NMS. Also, labor taxation in the NMS is not very progressive. While in most other countries, labor taxes increase significantly with the wage level in the NMS, labor taxes increase by less than 10 percentage points. For most EU-15 countries, taxes increase by over 10 percentage points between 33 and 100 percent of average wage level. Although countries with a high tax-wedge at lower-wage levels can be expected to display less progressivity, the NMS display especially low levels of progressivity. All NMS except for Hungary and Slovenia are below the trend line in a cross-county comparison (see Figure 6.2).[5] In particular, for single workers without children, Bulgaria stands out with zero progressivity of labor taxes. This is important because low progressivity means that there is some room for lowering the tax-wedge for low-wage earners in a fiscally neutral way by increasing progressivity.

Figure 6.2

In the NMS, Labor Taxation Tends to Be Not Very Progressive

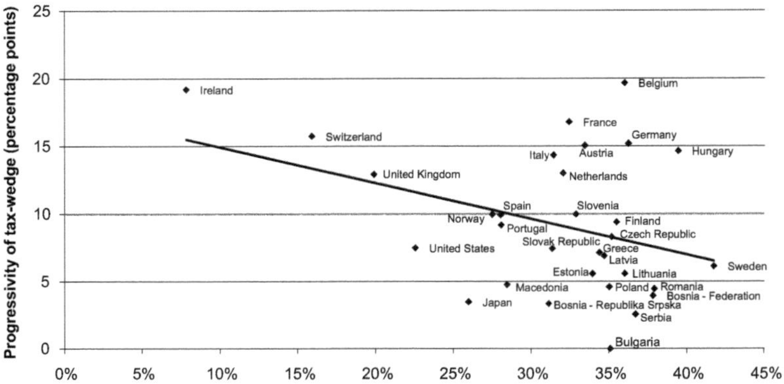

Note: Data points represent the tax-wedge for low-income earners (single person with no children at 33 percent of average wage; x-axis) in relation to a country's progressivity of the tax-wedge (the percentage point increase of the tax-wedge between 33 and 100 percent of average wage; y-axis) in 2008 (for Bosnia, Macedonia, and Serbia, 2009).

Source: Authors' calculation based on OECD Tax and Benefit model (OECD 2011).

Nevertheless, with the exception of Bulgaria in all countries labor taxation displays some degree of progressivity.[6] A typical graph of the tax-wedge over the wage level for the NMS is depicted in Figure 6.3 – in this case, for Estonia and Latvia.[7] As can be seen, the tax-wedge is lower for low-wage earners (around 26 percent for Estonia and Latvia) and starts to significantly increase from a certain wage level onwards (around 20 percent of average wage) to levels of about 40 to 45 percent of total labor costs. What is interesting, though, is that some countries display much lower tax-wedges for low-wage earners, as in the case of Australia and the United Kingdom (see Figure 6.3).[8] Both have a tax-wedge of 0 percent for low-wage earners, and only for wage levels above 20 percent of average wage the tax-wedge is increasing significantly.

A closer look at Figure 6.4 reveals that in the NMS, the tax-wedge tends to be high for a relatively large spectrum of low-wage earners. The wage level from where onwards the tax-wedge starts to increase significantly is also relatively high. In many high-income OECD countries, to the contrary, the tax-wedge is low for the lowest-wage earners, but the tax-wedge also tends to increase across the whole wage spectrum.

Figure 6.3

In Estonia and Latvia, the Tax-Wedge for Low-Wage Earners is Higher than in Australia or the United Kingdom

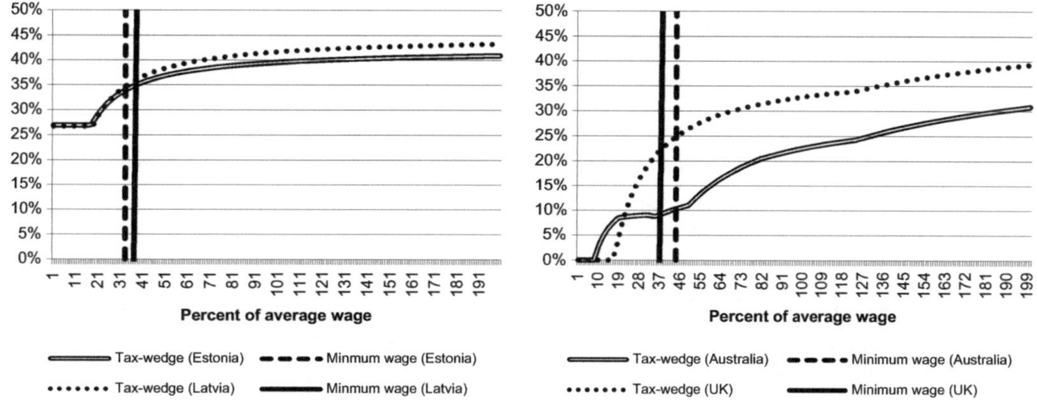

Note: Graphs show the tax-wedge for single person with no children. Countries have been chosen to illustrate contrasting examples.
Source: Authors' calculation based on OECD Tax and Benefit model (OECD 2011).

Figure 6.4

In the NMS, the Tax-Wedge for the Lowest-Wage Earners Tends to be High, and the Wage Level Where the Tax-Wedge Increases Significantly is Relative High

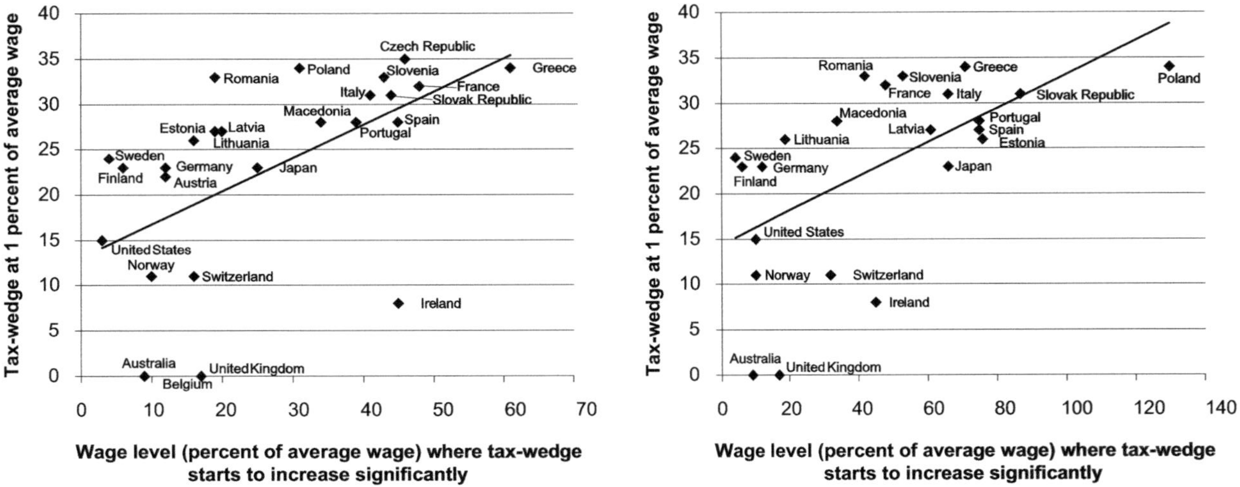

Note: The scatter plot depicts the wage level where the tax-wedge starts to increase (x-axis) versus the tax-wedge at 1 percent of average wages (y-axis). Hungary, the Netherlands, and Serbia feateur falling tax-wedges at low-wage levels and are not depicted, just like Bulgaria which has a flat tax-wedge. Austria, Belgium, and Canada have partly negative tax-wedges at low-wage levels, especially for families, and are also not included in the right scatter plot (Canada also in the left).

Source: Authors' calculation based on OECD Tax and Benefit model (OECD, 2011).

6.2.4. *Social Benefits*

Aside from the tax-wedge, the withdrawal of social benefits is the main contributor to the opportunity costs of taking up formal work for individuals with low skills/earnings potential. Consider an informal worker who earns a certain level of informal wage.[9] If this worker were to work in the formal sector, various implicit opportunity costs occur to the worker and the worker's employer. First, assuming that the marginal labor product does not change because of formalization, total labor costs of the informal worker have to be the same as for the formalized worker. For the informal worker, total labor costs are the informal wage. For the formalized worker, total labor costs are the net wage plus the income tax and both the worker's and the employer's social security contributions. That is, the net wage plus the entire tax-wedge. Comparing the informal wage with the worker's potential formal net wage, the entire tax-wedge enters as an opportunity cost of formal work for the informal worker and the worker's employer. Second, informal workers also face implicit opportunity costs because they might lose parts of certain income-tested benefits – most importantly social assistance, housing benefits, and family benefits – once they have a formal income on record. For example, if an informal worker receives a certain amount of social assistance, this benefit will be decreased or completely withdrawn if the worker formalizes. This amount of the withdrawn benefit also enters as an opportunity cost of formal work.

Therefore, both of these losses – the tax-wedge and withdrawn benefits – have to be taken into account when considering the implicit opportunity costs of formalization. At the same time, though, informal workers gain from formalization: they gain a future right to an old age pension and they gain immediate rights with regard to disability insurance, workers compensation, health insurance, and unemployment insurance.[10]

Arguably, the most important of these potential gains are old age pension and health insurance. With regard to old age pensions, though, one has to keep in mind that especially low-wage earners tend to discount future benefits more because their concerns are focused on short-term income, and in cases of poverty, day-to-day consumption.[11] Also, any means-tested social pensions for the elderly might further discount the value of a vested old age pension. In addition, especially in developing and transition countries, workers might discount the value of pension benefits because of a lack of trust in social security contributions.[12]

Finally, the value attached to the most important benefit, health insurance, could be low because in many countries it can be accessed for free. Nevertheless, there is no reliable concept of measurement available at this point that can properly quantify the value that workers attach to these formal benefits – may it be short-term or long-term social security benefits or other benefits like employment protection. In the analysis presented below, this shortcoming has to be kept in mind.

Regarding the potential role of benefit withdrawal, Table 6.1 and Table 6.2 provide information on the coverage and generosity of the social benefits considered for some of the countries analyzed in Section 6.3. Overall the family benefits seem to be the most important type of benefit, reaching between 21 and 47 percent of the total population. Social assistance and housing benefits seem less important for the population at large but do reach between 6 and 15 percent of the poorest income quintile. For these poorest households, social assistance benefits finance between 10 (Poland) and 40 (Estonia) percent of total household consumption.

Table 6.1

Coverage[a] of Social Benefit Programs (Percent, Various Years)

	Social Assistance		Family Benefits		Housing Benefits	
	Total population	Poorest quintile	Total population	Poorest quintile	Total population	Poorest quintile
Bulgaria 2007	3.8	14.5	20.8	35.3	4.1	13.8
Estonia 2004[b]	2.0	6.7	47.2	57.5	—	—
Latvia 2009[b]	2.7	5.9	43.9	60.7	—	—
Poland 2008	4.4	14.2	21.3	51.2	3.8	9.4

Notes: [a] Coverage indicates the percent of individuals who receive social assistance transfers.
[b] Social assistance includes housing benefit.
Source: World Bank (2011a).

Table 6.2

Generosity[a] of Social Benefit Programs (Percent, Various Years)

	Social Assistance		Family Benefits		Housing Benefits	
	Total population	Poorest quintile	Total population	Poorest quintile	Total population	Poorest quintile
Bulgaria 2007	21.5	33.8	3.6	7.6	5.8	8.0
Estonia 2004[b]	26.3	39.9	7.0	18.0	—	—
Latvia 2009[b]	6.7	12.1	2.5	7.7	—	—
Poland 2008	7.7	9.6	3.1	5.2	3.4	4.4

Notes: [a] Generosity indicates the transfer as a share (percent) of total consumption of beneficiary households.
[b] Social assistance includes housing benefit.
Source: World Bank (2011a).

6.2.5. *The Formalization Tax Rate*

As discussed above, the implicit costs of formalization for informal workers are a measurement of the necessary minimum value of social security benefits and employment protection they receive in return for formalization. The value of rights to pension and unemployment insurance – but also from formal employment protection legislation – they gain from formalization must exceed their implicit opportunity costs from formalization. Figure 6.5 depicts this implicit cost to the informal worker as a share of informal income, the so-called formalization tax rate (FTR). The formalization tax rate measures the difference between informal income (informal wage, social assistance, and family and housing benefits at the level of no formal wage) and formal net income (formal net wage, in-work benefits, social assistance, and family and housing benefits at formal wage level) as a share of informal income.[13] Just like the tax-wedge, it is a synthetic measurement that is based on legislation on taxes and social benefits, measuring the difference in net income between an informal worker (informal wage and social benefits) and the theoretical income of the same informal worker if he or she were to formalize.

More precisely, the FTR $t^F(w)$ is defined as

$$t^F(w) = \frac{NI^I(w) - NI^F(w)}{NI^I(w)}$$

where $NI^I(w)$ is the net income of an informal worker and $NI^F(w)$ is the income of a formal worker at a certain (gross) wage level w. The net income of an informal worker is the wage the worker receives plus any benefits the worker is entitled to. Since the benefit level depends on the level of formal wage, an informal worker can claim benefits at formal wage level $w = 0$, or

$$NI^I(w) = w + B(0)$$

where $B(w)$ is the benefit function. The question that arises is what the net income of a comparable formal worker at the same wage level would look like. Note that an employer will not consider two workers to be equal based on their gross wage, but based on total labor costs, in other words, two workers are equal if their marginal product of labor is equal. Hence, it will be useful to compare an informal worker with a formal worker whose total labor costs (and not gross) wage, equal

Figure 6.5

For Low-Wage Earners, the Opportunity Costs of Formal Work (Formalization Tax Rate, FTR) are Higher in Bulgaria and Latvia than in Australia and the United States

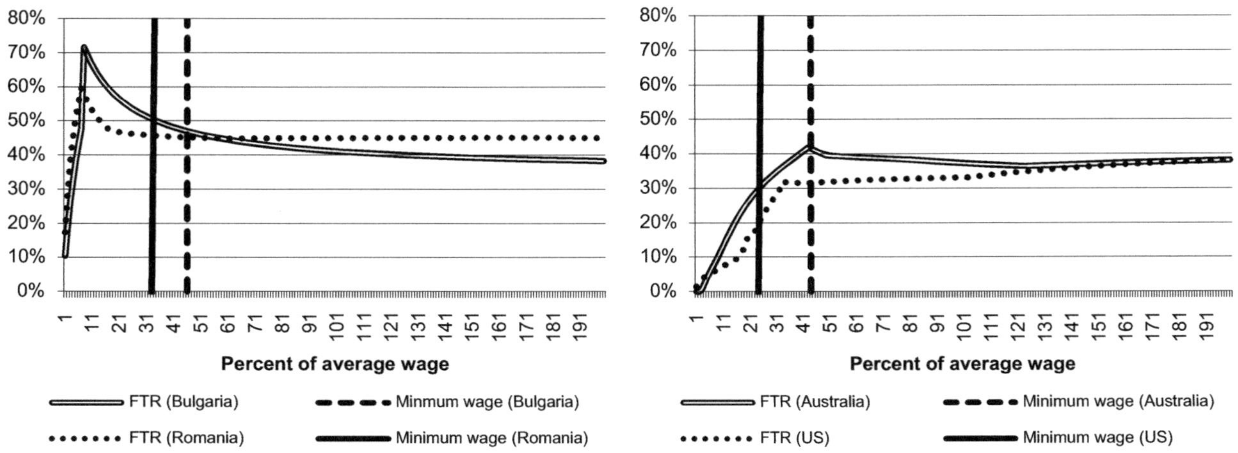

Note: Graphs show the formalization tax rate (FTR) for single person with no children. Countries have been chosen to illustrate contrasting examples.

Source: Authors' calculation based on OECD Tax and Benefit model (OECD 2011).

the informal worker's wage. Therefore, one needs to compare the net income of an informal worker earning w with the net income of a formal worker earning a gross wage of $w^*(w) = w - SSC^E(w)$. That is, the formal worker's gross wage $w^*(w)$ is equal the total labor cost of a comparable informal worker, reduced by the social security contributions paid by the employer $SSC^E(w)$ at that level of total labor costs w. This, in turn, means that the net income of a comparable formal worker is

$$NI^F(w^*) = w^* - IT(w^*) - SSC^W(w^*) + B(w^*)$$

where $IT(w^*)$ is the income tax, $SSC^W(w^*)$ the social security contribution paid by the worker and $B(w^*)$ the benefits claimed by the worker, all at formal gross wage level $w^*(w)$ as defined above.

Comparing these two workers described above leads to the following interpretation. A worker who earns a certain wage in the informal sector is discussing with his or her employer to formalize. Since the worker does not have any formal income, the worker also claims benefits as if he or she had no income. The employer and the worker now consider how much the worker would earn, net of income tax and social security contributions, in the formal sector. They also take into account any changes in benefits the worker could claim given his or her formal wage. The formalization tax rate measures how much of the informal income would be taxed away, through taxes, social security contributions, and changes in benefits if the worker were formalized.

How does the FTR look in different countries? In order to calculate and illustrate the FTR, the OECD Tax and Benefit model also provides all the necessary information on social assistance, housing, family, and in-work benefits. Consider the contrasting examples of Bulgaria and Romania on the one hand and Australia and the United States on the other (see Figure 6.5). For lower wage levels, the FTR in Bulgaria and Romania is higher than in Australia and the United States. In Bulgaria, the FTR for a single person with no children peaks at around 70 percent (around 60 percent for Romania) at a wage level of about 10 percent of average wage. This means that in Bulgaria, a single person with no children who earns less than the minimum wage in the informal sector has to give up between 50 to 70 percent of income to formalize. By contrast, in Australia and the United States, the FTR peaks at a lower value – around 40 percent in Australia and 30 percent in the United States – and at a higher wage level of around 30 to 40 percent (although in the case of the United States, the FTR continuous to increase at higher wage levels, yet at a slow rate).

Figure 6.6

In the NMS, the Opportunity Costs of Formal Work Tend to be Highest at Lower Wage Levels

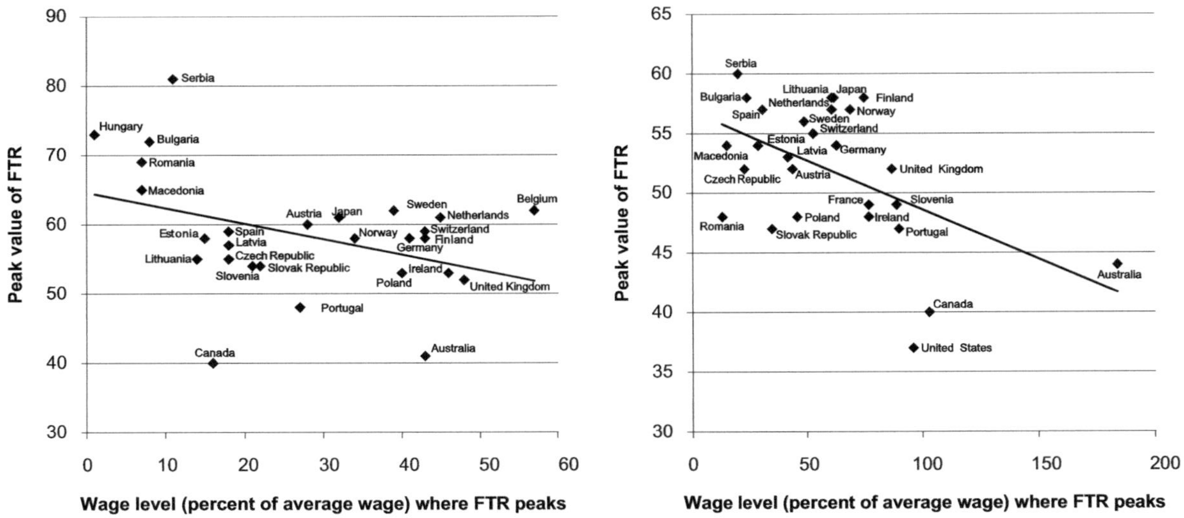

Note: The scatter plot depicts the wage level where the formalization tax rate (FTR) peaks (x-axis) versus the peak value of the FTR (y-axis). Countries with a continuously and significantly increasing FTR were omitted. In countries where the FTR forms a plateau and increases only slightly with the wage level, the lowest wage level at which the FTR stops to increase significantly was chosen as the peak.

Source: Authors' calculation based on OECD Tax and Benefit model (OECD 2011).

A more comprehensive comparison shows that in the NMS the opportunity costs of formal work tend to peak at lower wage levels than in high-income OECD countries. Figure 6.6 reveals that both for single persons and one-earner couples with two children, the costs of formalization in the NMS generally tend to be highest for low-wage earners (less than 30 percent of average wage for singles). In some countries, like Bulgaria, Hungary, and Romania, the FTR for singles is particularly high and peaks at around 70 percent. For families, the FTR tends to be lower and peak at somewhat higher wage levels.

The main reasons for the high opportunity costs of formal work are labor taxation and the sudden withdrawal of social assistance and family benefits at higher wage levels. Labor taxation has already been discussed above as one of the potential obstacles to formal employment at the lower wage levels. The design of income-tested benefits also plays an important role; social assistance is often paid out as a top-up to earned gross income to guarantee a minimum gross income. Any earned household gross income is subtracted from social assistance that is paid out. This means that any formal mini-job at low-wage levels does not pay. Likewise, for higher-paid midi-jobs, the net gain in income might not be very high because of the sudden loss of social assistance. A more phased-in withdrawal of social assistance through (formal) income disregards for all household members could decrease this disincentive. Income-tested family and housing benefits also contribute to the formalization tax rate if the formal income would exceed the threshold for eligibility.

6.2.6. The Marginal Effective Tax Rate

The marginal effective tax rate (METR) also suggests that formal work does not pay at lower wage levels. The METR measures at a given wage level how much of an *additional* dollar earned in formal gross wage is taxed away, either as labor tax or in the form of withdrawn benefits. It is therefore an indication of how much it pays for workers to earn more gross income, either by increasing work hours or receiving higher wages. Just like the tax-wedge and FTR, also the METR is a synthetic measurement of disincentives for formal work, based on legislation – what people ought to pay in taxes and are entitled to – and not on actual income, tax, and benefit consumption data.

In many countries, at low-wage levels (below 10 percent of average wage), every dollar earned is subtracted from entitlements to social assistance; hence a 100 percent of any additional dollar earned is taxed away. For example, in the Czech Republic and Slovenia, every additional dollar earned in formal income is a 100 percent taxed away through withdrawal of social assistance at wage levels below 20 percent of average wage (see Figure 6.7). In other countries, like Portugal and the United States, incentives for formal work are better for low-wage earners in these countries. In Portugal, only 50 percent of every additional earned dollar is taxed away and in the United States it is significantly less. In the United States, this is mainly achieved through so-called in-work benefits and tax credits that subsidize work at low-wage levels.

Overall, the NMS tend to have high METRs – usually at 100 percent – at low-wage levels, although the METR tends to drop at lower wage levels than in high-income OECD countries (Figure 6.8). A notable exception is Poland, which according to the OECD Tax and Benefit model has the lowest METR at low-wage levels of all countries. This is due to an apparent lack of a comprehensive, federally administered social assistance program. Nevertheless, Poland might have a *locally* administered social assistance program. If this is indeed the case, it is unfortunately not captured by the OECD Tax and Benefit model. So, the actual METR could be higher than predicted.[14]

6.3. Do Disincentives for Formal Work Matter?

This section performs an empirical analysis at the individual level that investigates how incentives correlate with informality, controlling for individual and job characteristics.

6.3.1. Data

The analysis is based on the European Survey for Income and Living Conditions (EU-SILC) for the year 2008. The survey covers a wide range of European countries and includes detailed questions on employment, income, taxes, and social security contributions. This allows to apply a comprehensive definition of informal workers and self-employed for a number of countries. In particular, the survey includes a question on the amount of social security contributions paid by the employer on behalf of the worker. This

Figure 6.7

For Low-Wage Earners, the Marginal Effective Tax Rate (METR) is at 100 Percent in the Czech Republic and Slovenia, while it is Much Lower in Portugal and the United States

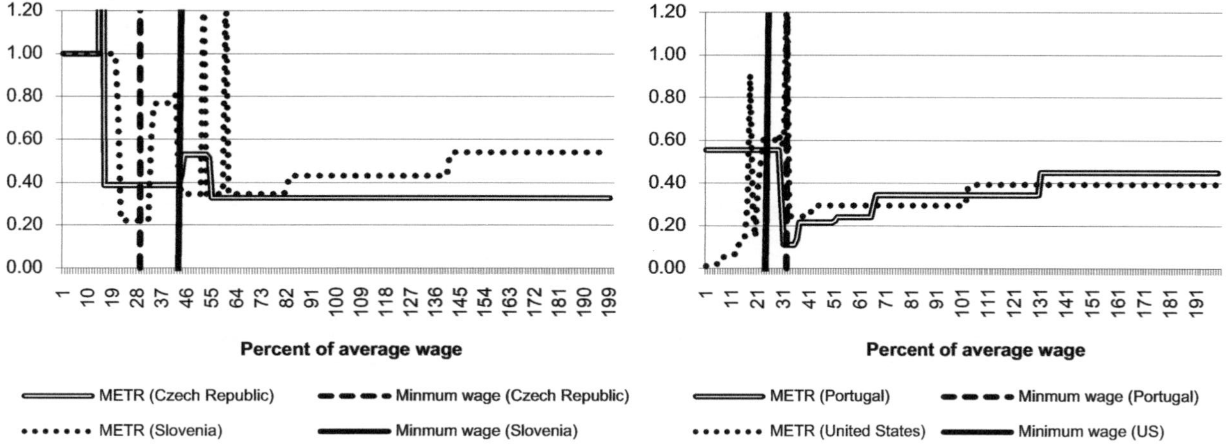

Note: Graphs show the marginal effective tax rate for singles with no children. Countries have been chosen to illustrate contrasting examples.
Source: Authors' calculation based on OECD Tax and Benefit model (OECD 2011).

Figure 6.8

In the NMS, the Marginal Effective Tax Rate (METR) Tends to be High at Low-Wage Levels, but Also Tends to Drop Significantly at Lower Wage Levels than in High-Income OECD Countries

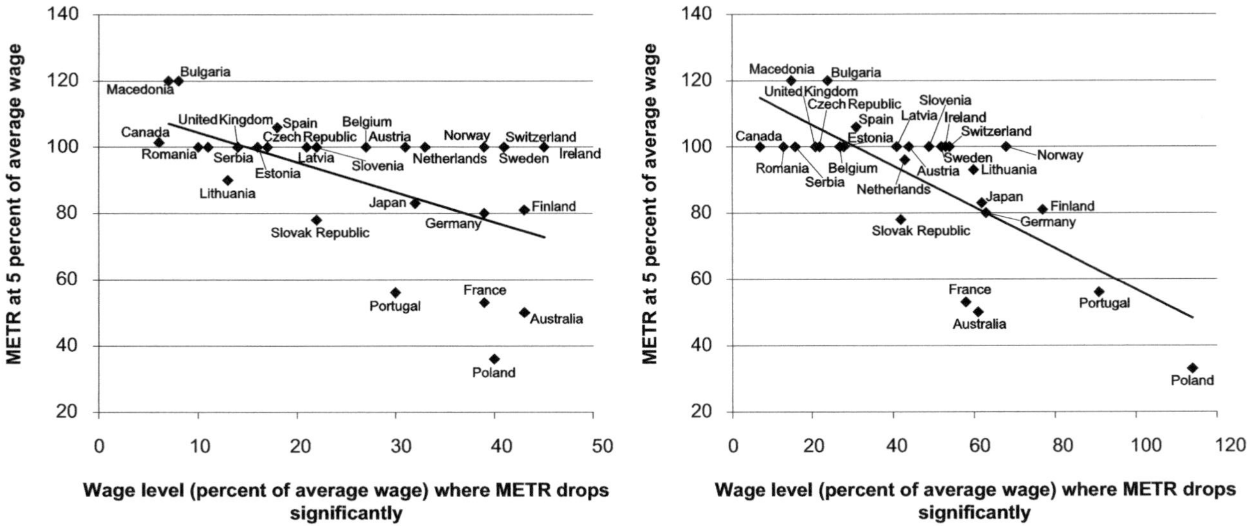

Note: The scatter plot depicts the wage level where the marginal effective tax rate (METR) drops significantly (x-axis) versus the value of the METR at 5 percent of average wage (y-axis). Countries with a METR that increases with the wage level even at lowest wage levels were omitted (Greece, Hungary, Italy, and the United States).

Source: Authors' calculation based on OECD Tax and Benefit model (OECD 2011).

question allows the identification of informal workers as those dependent employees for whom no social security contributions are paid. In addition, unpaid family workers are identified as informal. Finally, non-professional employers who employ five or fewer workers (including those with no employees) are also identified as informal.[15]

The analysis is performed for six NMS: Bulgaria, the Czech Republic, Estonia, Latvia, Poland, and Slovakia, which yields a total sample size of 48,865 employed individuals. The dependent variable is a binary indicator that takes the value of one for informal workers and zero for formal ones.

The independent variables for the regression are age, gender, education, geography (degree of urbanization), employment status of the spouse, citizenship, income, and sector. The age variable is grouped into five categories: age 15 to 24, 25 to 39, 40 to 54, 55 to 64, and 65 or older. Similarly, the education variable is grouped into three categories: high (post-secondary or tertiary education), medium (secondary education), or low (primary or pre-primary education).[16] For geography, the three categories are densely, intermediate, or sparsely populated area. The employment status of the spouse has four categories, namely formally employed, informally employed, inactive, or no spouse. Citizenship can either be the same as the country of residence (local), or of another EU country, or a non-EU country. The sector variable follows the NACE standard.[17]

Income groups are categorized based on income as a percentage of average wage of the country of residence. That is, income (employee and self-employment cash or near cash income) is calculated as a share of the official average wage. The average wage data is taken from OECD (2011). Note that for unpaid family workers, income is 0, while for some self-employed and employers, it can also be negative (in the case of a loss from self-employment or business activities). Income groups are then defined as those earning (i) 0 or less; (ii) more than 0 but less than 25 percent of average wage; (iii) 25 percent or more, but less than 50 percent of average wage; (iv) 50 percent or more, but less than 100 percent of average wage; (v) 100 percent or more, but less than 200 percent of average wage; and (vi) 200 percent of average wage or more.

The main innovation of the analysis stems from the attempt to measure incentives and disincentives for formal work that are being provided by the tax and benefit system at the *individual* level. That is, the FTR, METR, and the tax-wedge are defined for each individual in the sample. This yields a synthetic measurement – purely based on *de jure* tax obligations and entitlements – of incentives and disincentives for formal work at the individual level.

To this end, we use the OECD Tax and Benefit model (OECD 2011) for the year 2008 for the six countries in the sample. The OECD Tax and Benefit model already provides the METR, and the FTR is calculated using the same model and according to the methodology developed by Koettl (2009) and described above. Both FTR and METR depend on three variables: (i) individual income, expressed as percent of average wage; (ii) household type (single or family); and (iii) the income of the spouse, if applicable. First, individual income as percent of average wage is calculated as outlined above, expressing the individual's cash or near cash income from dependent work and self-employment as a percent of average wage. The model is limited to the extent that the OECD Tax and Benefit model only provides calculations up to a certain level of income – for individuals, up to 200 percent of average wage, for certain types of families up to 367 percent of average wage. Since FTR and METR vary mainly at lower wage levels and are fairly constant from a certain income level onwards, we assume that individuals with income above the limitations set by the OECD Tax and Benefit model face the same incentives as those individuals at the boundary.[18]

Second, the OECD Tax and Benefit model is provided for 10 household types, from singles with or without children to one- and two-earner couples with or without children. For the latter type, the model is provided for three different income levels for the spouse.[19] These 10 OECD household types are matched to the household types provided in the EU-SILC data set. Certain assumptions have to be made in doing so. For example, the number of children is not taken into account, all individuals with children are assumed to face the same incentives as those with two children. In households with children, a couple, and additional adults, the children are matched to the couple while the additional adults are assumed to be singles. Finally, in households with children, but not couples, children are matched to those singles in a certain age group (35 to 45).

Third, for individuals with a spouse working in the formal sector, the spouse's income also has to be taken into account. The OECD Tax and Benefit model does so for three income levels of the spouse: 67, 100, and 167 percent of average wage. The spouse's income is then

Table 6.3

Informality Rates Across Different Groups and Countries

	Bulgaria (%)	The Czech Republic (%)	Estonia (%)	Latvia (%)	Poland (%)	Slovakia (%)	Total (%)
By employment status							
Self-employed	71.4	82.8	71.5	70.9	87.1	81.5	83.9
Employees	7.3	0.1	3.3	6.3	27.1	2.2	16.2
By sex							
Male	19.5	17.1	10.8	15.9	42.6	14.2	31.5
Female	12.9	8.9	4.6	8.6	35.5	6.0	23.7
By age							
15–24	19.3	7.8	6.9	11.0	44.6	7.7	30.2
25–39	15.4	12.2	7.4	12.6	35.6	10.2	26.2
40–54	15.7	15.8	7.8	13.4	40.5	11.0	28.8
55–64	17.9	13.2	7.2	9.7	45.2	10.5	28.0
65 or more	34.4	30.8	13.2	11.1	73.7	25.2	48.4
By income group							
0% of AW or less	79.8	100.0	67.8	82.8	92.7	80.5	91.7
1–24% of AW	37.6	23.3	29.1	29.0	66.6	18.5	55.4
25–49% of AW	17.1	14.9	5.9	15.2	40.4	11.8	30.0
50–99% of AW	11.8	10.3	3.0	9.7	29.2	8.0	19.5
100–200% of AW	11.2	13.7	6.9	7.1	29.3	10.9	20.9
200% of AW or more	29.8	27.1	24.2	9.8	25.7	21.6	25.4

Table 6.3 (continued)

Informality Rates Across Different Groups and Countries

	Bulgaria (%)	The Czech Republic (%)	Estonia (%)	Latvia (%)	Poland (%)	Slovakia (%)	Total (%)
By sector							
Health services	3.3	2.1	1.9	2.6	17.8	4.2	11.2
Mining, manufacturing	7.6	7.7	3.9	7.8	27.5	8.3	18.3
Construction	22.6	31.2	14.4	21.1	49.7	27.4	38.2
Trade and repair	24.4	19.0	8.4	10.9	42.9	13.7	32.0
Transport and storage	13.6	9.2	10.3	11.0	40.1	8.1	26.7
Accommodation and food	19.0	19.1	6.8	10.9	49.8	7.6	28.1
ICT	10.0	13.0	9.4	4.5	25.6	6.5	18.0
Financial services	1.3	22.6	7.1	5.1	24.1	15.6	20.1
Professional services	14.1	17.8	5.0	10.8	31.7	12.2	24.4
Public sector	1.6	0.7	1.0	2.5	21.1	2.1	11.5
Education	1.1	2.0	1.1	1.8	15.8	2.7	10.2
Agriculture	54.3	26.9	33.2	46.7	93.2	15.4	80.6
Overall	16.5	13.6	7.7	12.3	39.5	10.4	28.0

Source: Authors' calculations based on EU SILC 2008 and OECD 2011.

matched to 67 percent of average wage for all those earning more than 0 but less than 83.5 percent of average wage; to 100 percent of average wage for all those earning more than 83.5 but less than 133.5 percent of average wage; and to 167 percent of average wage for all those earning more than 133.5 percent of average wage. That is, we assume that all individuals face the same FTR and METR who have a certain income level and whose spouse works in the formal sector within the income brackets of (i) 1 and 83.5 percent of average wage; (ii) 83.5 and 133.5 percent of average wage; and (iii) above 133.5 percent of average wage.

6.3.2. Descriptive Statistics

According to EU-SILC 2008, the sample of around 49,000 is representative for about 27 million workers in Bulgaria, Czech Republic, Estonia, Latvia, Poland, and Slovakia. Of these, 28 percent are engaged in informal work (see Table 6.3). These 28 percent are largely made up of non-contributing workers (13 percent) and non-professional own-account workers (11 percent); the rest are family workers (2 percent) and non-professional employers in small firms (2 percent). The complement of 72 percent formal workers comprises largely of contributing workers (70 percent). Employers (in large firms or professionals in small firms) and professional own-account workers account for only 1 percent of all represented workers each.

Looking at gender, the share of males among informal workers is 63 percent. This is much higher than the corresponding share for formal workers (53 percent). This structural composition can be found in all countries represented in the sample. With respect to age, the group of 40 to 54 year olds holds the highest share (42 percent) among informal workers followed by the 25 to 39 year olds (37 percent). The age groups 15 to 24 and 50 to 64 account for 10 and 9 percent respectively, while the age group of 65 and older comprises only 2 percent of all informal workers. This distribution of workers and age is rather similar across all countries. Only the Czech Republic and Slovakia have slightly lower shares of informal youth (15 to 24 years) which are compensated by higher shares of workers in the age bracket of 40 to 54 years. Comparing the age distribution of informal workers with those of formal workers, no distinctive difference can be found in the sample. The overall informality rate of 28 percent is within a range of +/- 2 percent for all age groups except for those workers that are 65 years and more. The informality rate for this age group that only represents 1 percent of all workers is 48 percent. The informality rate of the young is 30 percent; the rate for the age group of 25-39 year olds is 26 percent, and around 28 percent for the remaining groups.

In addition to these demographic considerations, the composition of the informal workers by sectors and income groups provide further interesting insights. The agricultural sector holds with 26.1 percent the highest share of informal workers, while it represents only 2.4 percent of all formal workers. The informality rate for agriculture is consequently high, it amounts to 80.6 percent.[20] The second highest informality rate can be found in the construction sector. The rate is 38.2 percent and is followed by the rates of the categories "Others" (33 percent), "Trade and Repair" (32 percent), and the "Accommodation and Food Services" (28.1 percent). All other sectors are below the overall informality rate of 28 percent.

By income group, informality rates are highest for the three lowest income groups. These are "0 income of the average wage or less" with 92 percent, "1 to 24 percent of the average wage" with 55 percent, and '25 to 49 percent of the average wage' with an informality rate of 30 percent. The other income groups are below the average informality rate. The highest share of informal workers can be attributed to the groups "50 to 100" and "25 to 49" percent of the average wage. Their shares are 32 and 23 percent respectively, with the latter group covering a lower percentage range. In contrast, the groups "50 to 100" and "25 to 49" percent of the average wage represent 48 percent and 20 percent in the corresponding categories for formal workers. Consequently, the distribution of informal workers across the income groups is distinctively different from the distribution of formal workers with particularly high informality rates for the three lowest income groups.

6.3.3. *Econometric Analysis*

To quantify the effects of the explanatory variables on the dichotomous outcome variable, a generalized linear model with a probit link function was applied. For a binary outcome the probit equation is

$$P(Y_i = 1) = F(X'_i \cdot \beta + \varepsilon_i)$$

with outcome variable Y_i and explanatory variables X_i for respondent i. $F(.)$ stands for the cumulative distribution function of the standard normal (probit model) distribution.[21]

It is important to highlight that characteristics such as preferences for working independently, for flexible working hours and the possibility to receive on-the-job training are not observed, which potentially could cause an omitted variable bias. However, we have made an effort to control for a large number of characteristics to reduce the potential bias as much as possible. In addition, the analysis does not establish a causal relationship, but mere correlations and should be interpreted with some caution. Causal relationships could point in either direction. High work disincentives might cause a high incidence of informal employment or high levels of informal employment might lead to high tax rates on formal labor, thereby increasing disincentives for formal work.

6.3.4. Expected Results

The interpretation and use of the tax-wedge as a measurement of disincentives for formal work suggests that the higher the tax-wedge, the higher the disincentives for formal work and, hence, the higher the incidence for informality. Consequently, one would expect a positive correlation between the tax-wedge and the incidence of informality. However, the descriptive statistics regarding informality rates (Table 6.3) and the tax-wedge (Figure 6.1 to Figure 6.3) point at a negative correlation. The tax-wedge is lowest with low-wage earners and strictly increases with income level (Figure 6.3). At the same time, the incidence of informality is highest among low-wage earners (Table 6.3), which should lead to a negative correlation.

Does this imply that work disincentives do not matter? Not necessarily, since there could be an income effect or the tax-wedge could be an insufficient measurement of disincentives for formal work. With regard to the income effect, low-wage earners might earn so little that they cannot afford to forego any amount of income. So even giving up a relative small amount of income could effectively be a higher disincentive for a low-wage earner than giving up a relatively larger amount of income for a high-wage earner. With regard to insufficient measurement, the tax-wedge does not take any loss of benefits into account, as already discussed. Figure 6.5 and Figure 6.7 show a less straightforward relationship between income on the one hand, and FTR or METR on the other when compared to the tax-wedge.[22] Assuming that FTR and METR address the shortcomings of the tax-wedge, a positive correlation between FTR or METR and the incidence of informality is expected.

Furthermore, the marginal effects of FTR and METR are expected to be higher for low-wage earners than middle- or high-wage earners for two reasons. One is the income effect as described above with forgone income having a higher importance for low-wage earners, resulting in a higher correlation between work disincentives and informality. The second reason is that the marginal effect not only depends on the coefficient but also on the incidence of informality. An estimation with a restricted sample of only low-wage earners should yield higher marginal effects when compared to an estimation with the full sample.

6.3.5. Results

The results of the regression are presented in Table 6.4 for the full sample and Table 6.5 for low-wage earners only. We report marginal effects, computed at the mean characteristics. Controlling for individual and job characteristics (income and sector) there is a significant positive correlation between FTR or METR and the probability of being informal. In particular, a 1 percentage point increase in the FTR (METR) increases the probability of being informal by 1.1 percent (0.8 percent) for the full sample. For the low-wage earners the correlation is stronger for both, FTR and METR. The marginal effects for the restricted sample are more than double compared to the ones for the full sample: 2.5 percent for FTR and 1.6 percent for METR. Estimations with a restricted sample of only high-wage earners (100 percent of average wage or above) confirm that the correlation is less strong, with coefficients either smaller or negative or insignificant. This confirms the expectations as outlined above.

The marginal effect for the tax-wedge is negative for both samples. As discussed above, the tax-wedge increases with income, and because informality rates are lower at higher income levels, the overall correlation turns out to be negative. Therefore it seems that the tax-wedge might not sufficiently capture individual differences in disincentives for formal work. In that sense, the tax-wedge does not seem appropriate as a measure for individual disincentives for formal work. The rest of the discussion will therefore focus on the specifications using FTR and METR.

As for the individual characteristics, the correlation with sex (male being the baseline category) clearly stands out as significant and negative. That is, women are clearly less likely to work informally. For the full sample, being female decreases the probability of being informal

Table 6.4

Probit Regression Results with Informality Dummy as the Dependent Variable, Reporting Average Marginal Effects (Full Sample)

	(i)	(ii)	(iii)
Formalization tax rate	0.011***		
Marginal effective tax rate		0.008***	
Tax-wedge			–0.084***
Country			
Bulgaria[a]			
The Czech Republic	–0.095***	–0.077***	0.846***
Estonia	–0.110***	–0.101***	0.176**
Latvia	–0.086***	–0.113***	0.554***
Poland	0.163***	0.123***	0.404***
Slovakia	–0.028**	–0.071***	0.372***
Age group			
15-24 [a]			
25-39	0.017	0.010	–0.029**
40-54	0.030**	0.027**	–0.012
55-64	0.015	0.020	0.026*
65+	0.120***	0.137***	0.181***
Sex			
Male[a]			
Female	–0.076***	–0.080***	–0.079***
Education level			
High[a]			
Medium	0.053***	0.058***	0.042***
Low	0.111***	0.107***	0.089***
Employment status of spouse			
Formal[a]			
Informal	0.239***	0.272***	0.381***
Inactive	0.002	0.032***	0.144***
No spouse	–0.018*	0.017*	0.365***
Degree of urbanization			
Densely populated[a]			
Intermediate	–0.023	–0.021	0.060
Thinly populated	0.040	0.038	0.066
Citizenship			
Local[a]			
Other EU country	0.051***	0.051***	0.043***
Others	0.037***	0.039***	0.030***

Table 6.4 (continued)

	(i)	(ii)	(iii)
Income group			
0% of AW or less[a]			
1-24% of AW	–0.132***	–0.183***	–0.198***
25-49% of AW	–0.259***	–0.289***	–0.274***
50-99% of AW	–0.389***	–0.393***	–0.417***
100-200% of AW	–0.272***	–0.278***	–0.266***
200% of AW or more	–0.202***	–0.209***	–0.179***
Sector			
Health services[a]			
Mining, manufacturing, utilities	0.055***	0.053***	0.046***
Construction	0.281***	0.282***	0.248***
Trade and repair	0.224***	0.225***	0.205***
Transport and storage	0.150***	0.151***	0.144***
Accommodation and food services	0.231***	0.233***	0.208***
ICT	0.113***	0.116***	0.096***
Financial services	0.142***	0.143***	0.116***
Professional services	0.155***	0.146***	0.140***
Public sector	–0.004	–0.008	0.002
Education	–0.022	–0.020	–0.024
Agriculture	0.502***	0.509***	0.444***
Others	0.298***	0.296***	0.284***
Number of observations =	47,065	47,065	47,065
Wald $chi^2(37)$ =	5,865.19	6,393.39	4,876.38
Prob > chi^2 =	0	0	0
Pseudo R^2 =	0.2642	0.2878	0.5138
Log pseudo–likelihood =	–20,023.73	–19,382.73	–13,231.89
Mean dependent variable	0.2650287	0.2650287	0.2650287

Note: [a] Baseline category. Regressions based on individual data from EU-SILC (Eurostat 2008) with matched data for individual FTR, METR, and tax-wedge from OECD Tax and Benefit model (OECD, 2011). Coefficients are interpreted as follows: In the specification with FTR, an increase of 1 percentage point of the FTR increases the probability of being informal by 1.1 percent; living in the Czech Republic decreases probability of being informal by 9.5 percent when compared to living in Bulgaria; being female decreases probability by 7.6 percent; having low education increases probability by 11.1 percent when compared to someone with high education; and so on.
* Statistically significant at: 10 percent.
** Statistically significant at: 5 percent.
*** Statistically significant at: 1 percent.

Table 6.5

Probit Regression Results with Informality Dummy as the Dependent Variable, Reporting Average Marginal Effects (Low-Wage Earner Sample)

	(i)	(ii)	(iii)
Formalization tax rate	0.025***		
Marginal effective tax rate		0.016***	
Tax-wedge			−0.092***
Country			
Bulgaria[a]			
The Czech Republic	−0.197***	−0.193***	0.687***
Estonia	−0.158***	−0.193***	−0.042
Latvia	−0.109***	−0.234***	0.289**
Poland	0.268***	0.088***	0.422***
Slovakia	−0.003	−0.180***	0.197***
Age group			
15-24 [a]			
25-39	0.029	0.010	−0.038
40-54	0.083***	0.089***	0.167
55-64	0.095***	0.127***	0.056*
65+	0.162***	0.205***	0.127*
Sex			
Male[a]			
Female	−0.088***	−0.091***	−0.120***
Education level			
High[a]			
Medium	0.022	0.017	−0.003
Low	0.036**	0.060	0.054
Employment status of spouse			
Formal[a]			
Informal	0.154***	0.083***	0.426***
Inactive	0.085***	−0.132***	0.212***
No spouse	−0.102***	−0.047***	0.356***
Degree of urbanization			
Densely populated[a]			
Intermediate	0.072***	0.073***	0.080***
Thinly populated	0.046***	0.051***	0.046**
Citizenship			
Local[a]			
Other EU country	−0.096	−0.090	−0.012
Others	−0.009	−0.029	0.177
Income group			
0% of AW or less[a]			
1-24% of AW	−0.158***	−0.320***	−0.380***
25-49% of AW	−0.450***	−0.529***	−0.557***

Table 6.5 (continued)

	(i)	(ii)	(iii)
Sector			
Health services[a]			
Mining, manufacturing, utilities	0.131***	0.127***	0.112***
Construction	0.332***	0.318***	0.273***
Trade and repair	0.224***	0.232***	0.220***
Transport and storage	0.231***	0.209***	0.227***
Accommodation and food services	0.193***	0.184***	0.180***
ICT	0.246***	0.225***	0.197***
Financial services	0.333***	0.332***	0.291***
Professional services	0.197***	0.169***	0.180***
Public sector	−0.039	−0.091	−0.032
Education	−0.011	0.008	−0.012
Agriculture	0.545***	0.558***	0.500***
Others	0.298***	0.308***	0.350***
Number of observations =	14,328	14,328	14,328
Wald $chi^2(34)$ =	2,267.19	2,810.70	4,261.33
Prob > chi^2 =	0	0	0
Pseudo R^2 =	0.3409	0.3976	0.5669
Log pseudo-likelihood =	−6,373.44	−5,824.83	−4,187.99
Mean dependent variable	0.4047872	0.4047872	0.4047872

Note: Baseline category. Regressions based on individual data from EU-SILC (Eurostat, 2008) with matched data for individual FTR, METR, and tax-wedge from OECD Tax and Benefit model (OECD, 2011). Coefficients are interpreted as follows: For low-wage earners, in the specification with FTR, an increase of 1 percentage point of the FTR increases the probability of being informal by 2.5 percent; living in the Czech Republic decreases probability of being informal by 19.7 percent when compared to living in Bulgaria; being female decreases probability by 8.8 percent; having low education increases probability by 3.6 percent when compared to someone with high education; and so on.
* Statistically significant at: 10 percent.
** Statistically significant at: 5 percent.
*** Statistically significant at: 1 percent.

by 7.6 (specification with FTR) and 8 percent (METR). For low-wage earners, the correlation is stronger with 8.8 and 9.1 percent, respectively. This is in contrast to findings in other developing countries. Perry et al. (2007), for example, find that in Latin America, women seem to value informal self-employment because the flexibility of the informal sector allows them to better balance their home and income-earning roles. Accordingly, informality rates in Latin America tend to be higher among women when compared to men. In transition countries, though, this seems not to be the case, as also confirmed by Hazans (2011).

In terms of age, there seems to be no clear correlation between informality and age. The only consistent effect across specifications is observed for the age group 65 and older, which is more likely to be in informal employment compared to the 15 to 24 age group. With regard to education, the low and medium educated are significantly more likely to be informal when compared to the highly educated in the full sample.

The results regarding the employment status of the spouse are somewhat surprising: there is a clear positive correlation between working informally and having an informally working spouse. This suggests that households do not make strategic decisions along the line of one partner working formally (and receiving employment and social protection, including for dependents) while the other one works informally. This result is robust with regard to restricting the sample to various sub groups, the agricultural or non-agricultural sector, low-wage earners, employees, or self-employed. Regarding inactive spouses or being single, the results are more ambiguous.

Other individual characteristics like geography (rural or urban) and citizenship did not yield any clear significant correlations. Although for the sample there seems to be no correlation between informality and geography, for low-wage earners the probability of being informal is higher when living in less densely populated areas. With regard to citizenship, the full sample suggests a highly significant positive relation between foreign citizenship (both EU and non-EU) and being informal, yet this is not the case in the restricted sample.

The income variable confirms the expected relationship between income and informality. Those with no or negative income are clearly most likely to be informal, which is certainly explained by all unpaid family workers falling into this category. For the other income groups, the likelihood of being informal decreases with income and is lowest for the income group earning 50 to 99 percent of average wage. For those earning more than average wage, though, the likelihood of being informal seems to increase again. One possible explanation is that enforcement of tax and contribution collection is highest for those earning around average wage, because they are the largest group of contributors. In other words, tax revenue collection is geared towards the middle class.

Regarding job characteristics, agriculture consistently yields a significant and highly positive relationship with being informal. Other sectors with similar results are construction, trade and repair, transport and storage, and accommodation and food services. Public sector and education do not seem to have a significantly higher probability of being informal, but one has to bear in mind that the baseline category is health services, which by itself is mainly public. This also applies to the education sector.

6.4. Conclusions and Policy Implications

The analysis presented defines three different synthetic measurements of disincentives for formal work: two standard measurements, namely the tax-wedge and the marginal effective tax rate (METR); and a new, innovative measurement called formalization tax rate (FTR). The novelty of the latter is that it measures disincentives stemming not only from labor taxation, but also from benefit withdrawal due to formalization. A descriptive analysis across a large number of OECD and Eastern European countries reveals that the disincentives for formal work - when measured through the FTR - are especially high for low-wage earners. This suggests that formal work might not pay in this segment of the labor market, in particular for the so-called mini-jobs and midi-jobs (low paying part-time work).

Another novelty is the empirical analysis that complements the descriptive analysis. Using EU-SILC 2008 data and OECD Tax and Benefit data for six Eastern European countries, we match disincentives for formal work that depend on income and family type to individual observations in a large data set. More precisely, EU-SILC data is matched with individual synthetic measurements of disincentives for formal work - namely the tax-wedge, METR, and the FTR - coming from the OECD Tax and Benefit model. Applying a probit regression, the analysis finds a significant positive correlation between FTR or METR and the probability of being informal. In other words, controlling for individual and job characteristics, the higher the FTR or the METR is that individuals are facing, the more likely they are to work informally. The tax-wedge, on the other hand, yields a negative correlation, indicating that the tax-wedge is not sufficiently capturing disincentives for formal work. This also suggests that in cross-country analysis in which the tax-wedge is used as an independent variable to explain informality levels, it might be more appropriate to use a tax-wedge that is more representative for low-wage earners, not for average-wage earners. For example, calculating the tax-wedge at 33 percent of the average wage would represent better the actual tax-wedge faced by most informal workers.

These results lead to the question on how formal work can be made more viable for low-wage earners. The two main policy tools to make formal work pay are to decrease labor taxation at the lower wage levels and to reform benefit design for social assistance, housing, and family benefits. On the former, policies linked to wage subsidies, social security contribution credits, in-work or employment-conditional benefits (cash benefits or refundable credits conditional on formal) for low-wage earners could play an important role (Immervoll and Pearson 2009). With regard to reforming the design of social assistance, housing, and family benefits, the key is to keep the marginal effective tax rate in mind when designing benefit withdrawal.

Finally, it should be pointed out that most of the reforms discussed above have fiscal costs. Given fiscal constraints, there might be little fiscal space available to push through these reforms. In particular, reforms that aim at making work pay at the low-wage end – like wage subsidies or tax credits – can considerably reduce tax revenues, including social security contributions, or increase public expenditures. In this regard, though, the NMS are in a favorable position: as shown above, their tax systems are relatively non-progressive. Making the relatively non-progressive tax system more progressive could make any future reforms along these lines fiscally neutral to a large extent.

Notes

1 See, for example, Hazans (2011), as well as descriptive statistics presented further below in this text.
2 Lehmann (2010) establishes that EPL, the tax-wedge, and union density have positive impacts on the level of informal employment in transition countries and quantifies these impacts.
3 The models for the non-OECD countries were developed under a recent research partnership between the OECD and the World Bank.
4 In many countries, full-time work at 33 percent of the average wage is below the legal minimum wage. Nevertheless, the same tax-wedge applies to someone receiving average wage, but working 33 percent part-time, although there can be slight variations in the tax-wedge for part-time workers when compared to full-time workers.
5 The assumed relationship is that tax systems need to raise a certain fixed amount of resources, and those that put higher taxes on lower wages have less need to increase taxes at higher wages and hence display less progressivity.
6 Exceptions are Hungary and the Netherlands, which have a social security contribution floor. Such a floor has to be paid independent of actual wages earned and therefore increases the tax-wedge significantly at lower wage levels.
7 For the sake of illustration, the countries chosen in this and the following graphs are rather contrasting. That is, for the NMS, countries with fairly high disincentives in the low-wage sector have been chosen; for the OECD, countries with rather low disincentives in the low-wage sector have been chosen.
8 The four countries are chosen as illustrating examples, with typical yet contrasting tax-wedges.
9 Only workers who are not registered at all are considered; partially formal workers who underreport their wages are not considered.
10 To the extent that these benefits are also offered to informal workers for free or at low cost, they do not enter as opportunity costs of formal work (Levy 2008).
11 See, for example, Lawrance (1991) on the relationship between time preference and poverty.
12 For an analysis on Bulgaria, see Perotti and Sanchez Puerta (2009).
13 For a more detailed definition and discussion, see Koettl (2009).
14 Koettl and Weber (forthcoming) provide a detailed overview of the tax-wedge, the FTR, and the METR for a large number of OECD and Eastern European countries, including the NMS and some Western Balkan countries. It presents a graphical depiction of these synthetic measurements for disincentives for formal work for two family types across the 0-200 percent of average wage spectrum, country by country. Where available, an estimate of the informality rate - based on EU-SILC 2008 - is included in the graphs.
15 The definition of informality for the self-employed and employers follows Hazans (2011).
16 For the Czech Republic and Slovakia, the employed are categorized only in the first two categories.
17 NACE stands for "Nomenclature generale des activités économiques dans la Communauté européenne" and codes economic activity into various sectors and subsectors.
18 This is obviously a simplifying assumption. Yet, the only variation that could occur at income levels beyond the boundary are higher income tax brackets or ceilings on social security contributions, which could shift both the FTR and METR to some limited extent.
19 More precisely, the OECD Tax and Benefit model is provided for (i) single; (ii) single with two children; (iii) one-earner couple with no children; (iv) one-earner couple with two children; (v) two-earner couple with no children, spouse earning 67 percent of average wage; (vi) two-earner couple with no children, spouse earning

100 percent of average wage; (vii) two-earner couple with no children, spouse earning 167 percent of average wage; (viii) two-earner couple with two children, spouse earning 67 percent of average wage; (ix) two-earner couple with two children, spouse earning 100 percent of average wage; and (x) two-earner couple with two children, spouse earning 167 percent of average wage.

20 In the literature, analysis on informal employment is often restricted to the non-agricultural sector. The analysis presented below focuses on disincentives in general and will therefore include the agricultural sector. Nevertheless, the analysis controls for sectors and therefore takes into particularly high incidence of informal employment in agriculture.

21 A correlation analysis helped to explore pairwise collinearity. Moreover, multicollinearity of the explanatory variables was explored by variance inflation factors (VIFs; Fox and Monette, 1992). None of the variables showed pairwise collinearity or multicollinearity.

22 For a detailed description of the tax-wedge, FTR, and METR across many OECD and transition countries, see Koettl and Weber (forthcoming).

References

Bassanini, A., Duval, R. (2006). Employment Patterns in OECD Countries: Reassessing the Role of Policies and Institutions, OECD Economics Department Working Paper No. 486.

Bertola, G., Jimeno, J. F., Marimon, R., Pissarides, C. (2001). EU Welfare Systems and Labor Markets: Diverse in the Past, Integrated in the Future?, in: Bertola, G., Boeri, T., Nicoletti, G. (Eds.), Welfare and Employment in a United Europe: A Study for the Fondazione Rdolofo Debenedetti, Cambridge, MA: MIT Press, 23-122.

Betcherman, G., Pagés, C. (2007). Estimating the Impact of Labor Taxes on Employment and the Balances of the Social Insurance Funds in Turkey, Washington, DC: The World Bank.

Davis, S. J., Henrekson, M. (2004). Tax Effects on Work Activity, Industry Mix and Shadow Economy Size: Evidence from Rich-Country Comparisons, NBER Working Paper No. 10509.

Djankov, S., Lieberman, I., Mukherjee, J., Nenova, T. (2002). Going Informal: Benefits and Costs, Washington, DC: The World Bank, mimeo.

European Commission (EC) (2003). European Employment Strategy: 2003 National Action Plans, Brussels: EC.

European Commission (EC) (2004). Undeclared Work in an Enlarged Union: An Analysis of Undeclared Work: An In-Depth Study of Specific Items, Brussels: EC.

Eurostat (2008). EU-SILC – European Union Statistics on Income and Living Conditions, Luxembourg: Eurostat.

Fox, J., Monette, G. (1992). Generalized Collinearity Diagnostics, in: Journal of the American Statistical Association, 417(87): 178-83.

Hanousek, J., Palda, F. (2003). Why People Evade Taxes in the Czech and Slovak Republics: A Tale of Twins, in: Belev, B. (Ed.), The Informal Economy in the EU Accession Countries: Size, Scope, Trends and Challenges in the Process of EU Enlargement, Sofia: Center for the Study of Democracy, 139-74.

Hazans, M. (2011). Informal Workers across Europe: Evidence from 30 European Countries, IZA Discussion Paper No. 5871.

Hussmanns, R. (2004). Statistical Definition of Informal Employment: Guidelines Endorsed by the Seventeenth International Conference of Labour Statisticians (2003), Geneva: International Labour Office.

Immervoll, H. (2007). The OECD Tax-Benefit Model and Policy Database, in: Gupta, A., Harding, A. (Eds.), Modelling Our Future: Population Ageing, Health and Aged Care, International Symposia in Economic Theory and Econometrics, 16, Amsterdam: Elsevier, 503-6.

Immervoll, H., Pearson, M. (2009). A Good Time for Making Work Pay? Taking Stock of In-Work Benefits and Related Measures across the OECD, IZA Policy Paper No. 3.
International Labour Organization (ILO) (2003). General Report of the Seventeenth International Conference of Labour Statisticians, Geneva.
Koettl, J. (2009). The Role of Income Taxes and Social Protection in Providing Incentives for Informality. A First Glance at the Czech Republic, Hungary, Poland, and Slovakia, Background Paper prepared for World Bank, mimeo.
Koettl, J., Weber, M. (forthcoming). Disincentives for Formal Work in OECD and Eastern European Countries, Policy Research Working Paper Series, Washington, DC: World Bank.
Lawrance, E. C. (1991). Poverty and the Rate of Time Preference: Evidence from Panel Data, in: Journal of Political Economy, 99(1): 54-77.
Lehmann, H. (2010). Policies to Combat Informality and to Broaden the Tax Base: Lessons for Transition Countries, Background Paper prepared for World Bank, mimeo.
Levy, S. (2008). Good Intentions, Bad Outcomes: Social Policy, Informality, and Economic Growth in Mexico, Washington, DC: Brookings Institution Press.
Maloney, W. F. (1999). Does Informality Imply Segmentation in Urban Labor Markets? Evidence from Sectoral Transitions in Mexico, in: World Bank Economic Review, 13(2): 275-302.
Maloney, W. F. (2004). Informality Revisited, in: World Development, 32(7): 1159-78.
Organisation for Economic Development and Co-operation (OECD) (2004). Employment Outlook, Paris: OECD Publishing.
Organisation for Economic Development and Co-operation (OECD) (2011). Tax/Benefit Policies: Detailed Descriptions and Reforms since 2001, online database, http://www.oecd.org/document/29/0,3746,en_2649_34637_39618653_1_1_1_1,00.html.
Packard, T., Koettl, J., Montenegro, C. E. (2012). In From the Shadow: Integrating Europe's Informal Labor, Washington, DC: The World Bank.
Perotti, V., Sanchez Puerta, M. L. (2009). Personal Opinions about the Social Security System and Informal Employment: Evidence from Bulgaria, Social Protection Discussion Paper Series No. 0915, Washington, DC: The World Bank.
Perry, G., Maloney, W. F., Arias, O. S., Fajnzylber, P., Mason, A. D., Saavedra-Chanduvi, J. (2007). Informality: Exit and Exclusion, Washington, DC: The World Bank.
Saavedra, J., Chong, A. (1999). Structural Reform, Institutions and Earnings: Evidence from the Formal and Informal Sectors in Urban Peru, in: Journal of Development Studies, 35(4): 95-116.
Schneider, F., Enste, D. H. (2000). Shadow Economies: Size, Causes and Consequences, in: Journal of Economic Literature, 38(1): 77-114.
Schneider, F., Klinglmair, R. (2004). Shadow Economies around the World: What Do We Know?, IZA Discussion Paper No. 1043.
Terrell, K., Grindling, T. H. (2002). The Effect of Minimum Wages on the Formal and Informal Sector: Evidence from Costa Rica, Washington, DC: The World Bank.
Torgler, B. (2003). Tax Morale in Transition Countries, in: Post-Communist Economies, 15(3): 357-81.
Torgler, B., Schneider, F. (2009). The Impact of Tax Morale and Institutional Quality on the Shadow Economy, in: Journal of Economic Psychology, 30(2): 228-45.
World Bank (2011a). ECA Social Protection Database, Washington, DC: The World Bank.
World Bank (2011b). Enterprise Surveys 2009, Washington, DC: The World Bank.

Part II

Setting the Mandate of the Insurance Programs and Designing Redistributive Arrangements

7

Participation in Mandated and Voluntary Social Risk Management Arrangements: The Role and Limits of Financial Education and Other Interventions*

Robert Holzmann

7.1. Introduction: Background, Motivation, and Structure

Improving benefit coverage against key contingencies such as old age, sickness, and disability for the broad population is considered the ultimate challenge of social policy. The initial optimism that coverage increases would happen over time as benefit programs improved through benefit reforms, strengthened compliance, and increased income levels has since been replaced by a more realistic assessment: More and different instruments need to be considered to induce increased participation in voluntary marked-based and mandated social insurance schemes. General revenue-financed basic provisions can go some way, but if linked with earnings-related provisions may create issues of their own.

This chapter investigates the extent to which a higher level of literacy about financial affairs in general and social risk management

* *The chapter reflects only the view of the author and none of the institutions he is associated with. It has profited from comments received by the participants of the IZA-World Bank conference in Mexico in May 2011, the guidance provided by David A. Robalino, and highly valuable comments and suggestions from Markus Froelich. The author is solely responsible for any remaining errors and gaps.*

in particular would be conducive to such a coverage increase, and to what extent other substitute or complementary interventions (such as nudging) would be needed to increase coverage. Effective interventions would make individuals less inclined to evade mandated social insurance schemes and/or would strengthen voluntary participation in public or private sector programs (the latter could relax the mandate or rely on basic provisions only).

The ultimate goal behind enhanced financial literacy is to increase individuals' access and capability to use social risk management instruments in a welfare optimal manner. To accomplish this, government interventions are typically argued for three well known reasons:

(i) Actual or assumed market failure and/or redistributive objectives are a primary motivation for government involvement. Market failures in risk management emerge if the private financial sector is not able to develop and offer the required risk management instruments and institutions, such as financial savings vehicles to move resources across the life cycle, or annuities to insure against the uncertainty of death. The absence of such market-based instruments or perceived weaknesses in their supply motivates the government to offer the risk management instrument itself, with a specific design, or to regulate private sector providers to the same end. In turn, the assumption is that the more developed private (financial) sector provisions are, the less public provisions are needed.

Redistributive objectives in a functioning market-based risk management environment can, in principle, be easily addressed by transparent taxation and transfers (ideally in a lump sum manner) to minimize efficiency losses, but this is not often done. Furthermore, forced pooling of low and high risks for redistributive purposes in market-based arrangements may have no pooling equilibrium, suggesting a need for government provision and mandate. The theoretical alternative to separate the insurance, savings, and redistributive components under public or private provision but without mandate is likely to prove too challenging (and the issue is not dealt with in the remainder of this chapter).

(ii) Mandating the participation of workers, all employed or the total population, in social insurance schemes under public or private sector management and/or supply is primarily motivated by arguments of myopia; i.e., individuals have too short a planning horizon to make long-term provisions out of their own savings, even if appropriate risk management instruments are available. The lack of a long-term planning and action horizon can be attributed to many factors, ranging from a lack of information, awareness, and financial skills to a behavioral deficiency to outright psychological barriers for long-term planning and follow through. As a result, the scope of effective interventions also varies from simple improvement of knowledge and skills via financial education to continued mandates for subsets of the population. Which strategy would be most effective for overcoming myopia, and for whom, is still very much a work in progress and is the essence of this chapter.

Even if such myopia could be addressed, a secondary argument for government mandated participation is the self-defense by government against strategic behavior by individuals in case of the provision of minimum benefits as it reduces the incentives for own retirement saving. To reduce strategic behavior and hence the need for mandated coverage, modest basic benefits, strengthened eligibility conditions (say later retirement age), and better integration between basic and insurance benefits are essential.

(iii) Poverty reduction is a third main reason for government intervention. Minimum benefits are provided to alleviate the poverty issues of the lifelong poor who could never participate in earnings-related social insurance schemes even if they wanted to, or of those individuals who fall out of covered employment and end up with low benefit levels. In turn, the assumption is that reducing poverty during an individual's active life and addressing his lifetime risks proactively reduces the need for anti-poverty-oriented basic provisions.

Against this background of key motivations for government interventions and to investigate the role of financial education and other interventions in affecting the use of social risk management instruments, including participation in mandated social insurance programs, the chapter proceeds in three sections: Section 7.2 explores the role of information and capabilities for the use of private and public social risk management instruments. Section 7.3 outlines the progress made to date in defining what types of financial literacy/capabilities matter. Section 7.4 reviews the effectiveness of financial education as well as of alternative interventions to improve financial behavior, including addressing key contingencies. Section 7.5 offers conclusions.

7.2. The Role and Limits of Information/Capability to Foster Individual Self-Provision and Reduce the Need for Compulsion

This section explores how more information for and better capabilities of individuals are expected to foster individual self-provision with market-based social risk management instruments, thus reducing the need for mandatory provision with regard to the level and perhaps selectively also the range of government-provided instruments. To this end, the first part of the section investigates key reasons why individuals may choose not to participate in mandated and/or voluntary social insurance schemes; information/capabilities constraints are assumed to be one of the main reasons. The second part focuses on how non-participation decisions are likely influenced by the assumed informational context for individuals and the economy, with likely ambiguous results for participation when information/capabilities are improved.

7.2.1. Key Reasons for Non-Participation in Voluntary Market-Based and/or Mandated Social Risk Management Arrangements

There are many reasons why individuals may prefer not to participate in voluntary and market-based or mandated and government-provided/regulated social risk management arrangements. Under social risk management arrangements, we understand market-based, government-provided as well as informal (family- and community-based) instruments to address risks by pooling across individuals or time in an *ex ante* (through risk reduction or mitigation) or *ex post* (through risk coping) manner (see Holzmann and Joergensen 2001).

For ease of presentation, the many reasons for non-participation are next categorized around supply side issues (assuming that the demand is sufficiently well-defined) and demand side issues (assuming that the supply is sufficiently well-defined), with the latter addressing information, knowledge, and behavioral constraints. Most of these explanations are non-exclusive and may reinforce one another.

7.2.1.1. Supply Side Issues

Diverse supply side issues that reduce system participation exist for both voluntary market-based and mandated social insurance type provisions that can be government or private sector provided (under tight government regulation and supervision).

For the *voluntary use of market-based instruments,* it sounds self-evident that the supply of appropriate risks instruments needs to be available to address specific risks for which demand exists and is well-defined. Such supply, however, is a main constraint in most or all developing economies and is far from perfect in most or all developed economies. Instruments to address the main relevant risks in general, and the (social) risks according to the nine contingencies under ILO Convention 102 of 1952 in particular, are typically either not offered at all by markets, or only some instruments are offered, and then only late in economic development once the economy's financial sector is very well developed.[1]

Highly relevant risks for individuals in low and middle-income countries, where the majority of people still live in rural areas, include crop-related bad weather, animal disease, and natural catastrophes (such as strong winds, flooding, earthquake, and volcano eruptions). In such countries, the individual risks of personal health and disability take typically a lower priority, and even lower still are the main ILO contingencies regarding children, unemployment (after having been formally employed), and old age.

Market-based risk instruments for some of these key risks in developing economies are only gradually and selectively emerging (e.g., weather and earthquake insurance) and build on main public involvement. With respect to market-based instruments catering toward the ILO contingencies, some may never emerge or do so only for small and well defined subsets of the population. Because the underlying risks cannot be easily observed and/or the moral hazard is too high (such as for unemployment, maternity, disability, survivorship, and work injury), or because the public intervention aims to redistribute income across individuals (from rich to poor) and across the life cycle (such as for family benefits), private instruments are not likely to emerge.

Market-based instruments do exist for a very few contingencies (essentially private sector annuities for old age to address the uncertainty of death, or private sector health insurance to address catastrophic health risks) but even in highly developed countries, they operate mostly in a thin market; in low-income countries, they typically do not exist. Thin or non-existent markets can be due to: supply related reasons (e.g., no relevant information about mortality or morbidity risks is yet available); supply deficiencies (e.g., the developed risk management instruments are not attractive for a given low demand); or broader supply-demand issues. For example, the demand for old age annuities may become low or nil if there are more important (short-term) risks for which no risk management instruments exist (i.e., under incomplete financial markets; see Davidoff, Brown, and Diamond 2003).

In conclusion, market-based risk management instruments to address the key social (ILO) contingencies are in scarce supply around the world, and are essentially limited to individual savings accounts *cum* annuities and health care financing arrangements at best. In all countries, they require a well-defined demand from informed consumers to deliver the expected welfare economic results, and they also require appropriate regulation and supervision for efficient supply. In developing economies, such risk management instruments require for their introduction minimum enabling financial market conditions that have been specified and pilot tested for pension funds (see Rudolph and Rocha 2007; Holzmann, Feher, and von Gersdorff 2009). The required information/capability profile for an informed consumer of such risk management instruments remains a topic of dispute (discussed below).

A lack of market-based risk management instruments keeps individuals reliant on informal arrangements, such as extended family or community support, if available, or continued work, if feasible. The large-scale disintegration of such informal arrangements during industrialization and urbanization led governments to provide such instruments as public social insurance programs, so called because they mimic private sector insurance characteristics augmented by public features. The latter typically include pooling across different risk profiles linked with mandatory participation of specific groups or all employed, and redistributive and other politically determined features in financing and benefit design. This has a bearing on scheme participation, as discussed next.

Supply issues with social insurance schemes emerge essentially for two reasons – economic and political, or both. At times, high and low risk groups cannot be separated and individually priced for reasons of information or administration or political decisions. Having low- and high-risk groups in a joint risk pool with a common contribution rate can lead to adverse selection, as the lower risk individuals may leave the pool until only the higher risk individuals remain or no pool at all. Adverse selection can be addressed by mandating participation of all risk groups in the social insurance program (such as for unemployment), leading to redistribution from low- to high-risk groups, and thus rendering part of the contribution akin to a tax on the low risk groups and part of the benefits akin to a subsidy to the high-risk groups. The higher the tax component in the contribution rate, the stronger the incentives to avoid and evade it.

Politically motivated explicit and implicit redistribution within a social insurance scheme aggravated by political favoritism on both the contribution and benefit sides leads to badly designed programs. For example, in traditional defined benefit schemes, the redistribution has often been from low-income workers with a flat earnings profile to high-income workers with a steep earnings profile. Or a formally redistributive benefit design prescribes a very long waiting period to avoid opportunistic participation that low-income workers with a low contribution density could never aspire to achieve, turning their pension contribution into a full wage tax. Bad benefit design et al that eventually leads to sustainability issues is bound to reduce the trust of individuals in the program providers. While supply issues of bad design may be solved quickly with reforms, reestablishing trust takes much more time.

Under the described circumstances of supply deficiencies, non-participation by individuals may not be due to myopia. On the contrary, it may signal a very rational decision to turn from social insurance schemes toward other savings instruments, including housing and family reciprocity. In the blossoming literature on informality, many reasons are cited as to why individuals prefer to stay informal (or have no other choice as the employer does not or cannot make them formal), with most of them boiling down to the assessment that individuals consider participation in a formal economy, including in the social insurance scheme, a bad deal given their information set (see, for example, Perry et al. 2007; World Bank 2011).

In summary, both voluntary and market-based as well as mandated and social insurance provisions exhibit main supply-type deficiencies given an assumed well-defined demand for such instruments. The typical policy approach to deal with low coverage is to improve the design toward fewer distortions, higher credibility, and better adjustments to the preferences of individuals. Catering toward these ends has been the focus of many of the reforms during recent decades and includes the move toward funded or unfunded individual accounts, as they are claimed to offer these advantages and hence promise better take-up of voluntary private sector and/or mandated public sector provisions. Reforms since the early 1990s toward multi-pillar pension schemes have introduced further elements of individual choice (see Holzmann et al. 2005).

7.2.1.2. Demand Side Issues

The move toward increased choice in voluntary and mandated schemes has quickly raised the issue of whether individuals are able to make such choices. This question adds to longer standing issues about whether the information provided by private and public sector suppliers of social risk management instruments is adequate and if the individual's understanding of how the existing schemes operate is sufficient. Underlying all of this are the unanswered questions regarding the expected minimum and optimal information sets for and behavioral capability of individuals to use existing risk management instruments. But whatever the answers are, there is strong agreement that if system information and individual financial capability are not present, participation in market-based arrangements may not take place, and if it does, it may not be in the individual's best interest. Similar informational and other demand constraints also apply to mandated social insurance schemes, where it is not clear if information and capability improvements necessarily lead to more participation.

This sub-section discusses demand side issues in three areas that are likely to limit or distort individual demand for marked-based and publicly provided social risk management instruments, however well designed:

- Constraints due to products and systems information limitations
- Constraints due to knowledge, skills, and attitude limitations
- Constraints due to behavioral limitations

These constraints cascade on each other, meaning that even if the first and/or second are solved, behavioral constraints may be binding and lead to sub-optimal outcomes.

Constraints Due to Products and Systems Information Limitations

A first constraint emerges through private information by the supplier of the risk management instruments, be it a market-based provider or a publicly run social insurance scheme.

Market-based providers of risk management instruments have an interest in marketing their product but they can also hide a lot of important information critical to individuals' voluntary participation decisions as well as their selection among alternative providers and products. For example, private providers have an incentive to market their products to higher-income groups, particularly if the government enforces limits on administrative costs. Even when product information is provided, there are still incentives for the provider to do so in a way that hinders straightforward comparisons between competing products to reduce or eliminate competition. Public regulation can force public suppliers to provide minimum levels of product information and, perhaps, to offer a normalized "plain vanilla" product for easier comparison and choice. But even if the requested information is provided, it is not yet conceptually well established what it should best look like. As an example, consider a simple product such as individual accounts with private pension funds. What is the relevant performance indicator that would drive an individual's welfare optimal decision to participate or to choose among providers? The net rate of return and over what period? The risk-adjusted net rate of return? How are they estimated? Would a Sharp-ratio type indicator used for investment funds do justice for a product that should help optimize life-cycle choices? Whatever the outstanding answer, at the moment there is very limited comparability of even the most simple performance indicators of such pension funds savings and annuity products within and across countries (see Hinz et al 2010; Rocha et al 2011). Similar information limitations apply to private sector health care insurance.

In principle, the public provider(s) of social insurance schemes have a captive market, as individuals are mandated to participate if the legal conditions apply. This significantly reduces their incentives to market and explain the product. In various countries across income levels, this is seemingly still the case. However, the mostly unfunded nature of social insurance schemes and the system and demographic aging have increased incentives for such schemes to solicit potential contributors working in the informal economy.[2] Over recent decades, providers of social insurance schemes have started to use electronic media and postal sending to inform potential beneficiaries about the usefulness of the scheme and eligibility criteria, to provide expected benefits calculated for individual use or to offer normalized current service projections, and to inform about the financial status of the scheme. A prominent example is the "Orange Envelop" by the reformed Swedish social security scheme that attempts to improve understanding about the Non-Financial Defined Contribution (NDC) scheme and its related small funded component. Survey data suggest that everyone in Sweden knows about the Orange Envelop (albeit only 40 percent of citizens have read it), and self-reported system understanding increased, such that 44 percent of those interviewed claim to have a "good understanding." However, there is no indication about changes in behavior (Sunden 2013). Similar results also hold for the statements by the U.S. Social Security Administration that seemingly influence self-reported knowledge but not behavior (Mastrobuoni 2011). Yet the worth of this self-reported understanding still needs to be probed (in Sweden, the U.S., and elsewhere) and the reported percentage of "good understanding" has a lot of room for improvement. Additionally, there is still little (international) consensus about what system information should be provided, what empirical information is important (say on internal rate of return), and what information sticks through what means of communication. The overall consensus seems to be that such information does matter and that more needs to be done (see Atolin and Harison 2012).

In conclusion, for both market-based and government provided social risk management arrangements and instruments, there are many good arguments to offer (more and better) relevant system and product information. As both types of provider have an incentive to be selective in their information provision, the government has a role to play in specifying, regulating, and supervising the requested information set with appropriate institutions. These institutions likely lack knowledge of what matters for what outcome, however.

Constraints Due to Limitations in Knowledge, Skills, and Attitude

Assuming system and product information were provided in the right manner (to be defined), a binding constraint may still be an individual's lack of capability to use this information in a welfare optimal way. Doing so assumes an individual to be perfectly rational, with full information and all the ingredients to both make an optimal choice and to follow through with it: e.g., he has technical knowledge of social risk management products, the practical skills to undertake a life-cycle planning and product selection and to implement the decisions, and the willingness to prepare for an uncertain future and the risks at hand (i.e., to trade current for future consumption). All this should lead to optimal behavior and outcomes.

Much of the traditional thinking about financial literacy (as the level of achieved understanding) and financial education (as interventions to make the value chain happen) is based on the assumption of this sequential cognitive approach from awareness and knowledge via skills and attitudes to good behavior and outcomes. In its simplest form, the approach assumes that the binding constraint is always a gap between (i) the abstract technical knowledge appropriate for understanding the concept of life-cycle planning and analytically selecting between alternative (financial) instruments and (ii) the practical technical knowledge and attitude needed to translate these into action. The proposed approach to close this gap is learning, training, and information, via a well-structured education process delivered in diverse forms.

It seems evident that such a financial literacy/education approach is needed if individuals are to be motivated and able to voluntarily select their own social risk management instruments. The better the financial education and the higher the level of financial literacy in the population, the less need there is for mandated provisions. But to understand the net benefits of joining a mandated social insurance scheme, and to make good decisions about the individual contribution density and the timing of, say, retirement (i.e., one's formal labor supply), some level of financial literacy is also needed for mandated provisions. In some social insurance schemes, individuals also need to make more far-reaching decisions, such as the level of their contribution or the choice of pension fund (conservative, balanced, progressive), or the timing of shift between life-cycle funds.

But is this assumed cognitive process actually how good financial behavior and the use of social risk management are determined and/or best influenced? How much technical understanding does an individual need to plan for the future, and to decide on participation in voluntary or mandated pension or health schemes? How effective are the existing financial education programs at providing that understanding? These and further questions are dealt with in Sections 7.3 and 7.4. Before that, however, additional constraints are reviewed that may prevent (optimal) risk management behavior even if the first two sets of constraints are not binding.

Constraints Due to Behavioral Limitations

There are many indications that individuals often do not behave as classical utility maximizers even with full information and a complete set of risk management instruments, but are instead influenced by diverse behavioral limitations. This deviation can be explained by emotional, cognitive, and psychological factors. The notion of including psychological and other factors in the analysis of microeconomic decision making is not new but was (temporarily) sidelined during the almost absolute reign of neoclassical economics. It is now back with force within the exploding area of behavioral economics and the related area of behavioral finance. In general, behavioral economics does not substitute for neoclassical analysis but behavioral models typically integrate psychological insights into neoclassic economic theory.

For the purpose of this chapter – the effective use of social risk management instruments – behavioral limitations emerge prominently with respect to an individual's: level of understanding and appreciation of the need for long-term savings and risk management provisions; lack of follow through on such a savings plan even when the need is fully recognized; and capability to make good choices among alternative risk management instruments.

There are already plenty of identified potential explanations for such behavioral limitations in the literature and the list continues to grow. Some of the most relevant for long-term saving and decision deficiencies include:

- Hyperbolic discounting, which occurs when the discount rates for the near future are higher than those in the far future, resulting in time-inconsistent plans and decisions.
- Procrastination, when high-priority or important actions are replaced by tasks of lower priority, or when taking actions which bring one enjoyment defers more important tasks to a later time.
- *Status quo* bias, when individuals perceive the disadvantages of leaving a state to be greater than the advantages.
- Information/choice overload, which occurs when individuals are incapable/unwilling to make choices between alternatives when the number of alternatives is too large, or when individuals prefer no choice or to use the default option where available.
- Use of a heuristics approach, when individuals make decisions based on approximate rules of thumb rather than strict logic.

- Cognitive bias, which can lead to overconfidence in financial affairs (and sub-optimal individual decisions) or to social contagion of ideas and emotions that result in phenomena such as herding (at the aggregate level).

The policy responses to these limitations are only now emerging and include: the opportunistic use of these shortcomings for program design (such as *status quo* bias to select default options); more general thinking about nudging devices to achieve specific outcomes; and adjusting program designs to the shortcomings (for example, reducing the number of options to avoid decision blockage). These and more options are discussed in Section 7.2.

7.2.2. *Are More Information and Better Financial Education Always Beneficial to Higher Participation?*

The prior subsection showed that individuals' lack of information and financial capability is only one of three main constraints for more and better use of market-based risk management instruments and higher participation in mandated social insurance schemes. Supply constraints and other demand constraints due to behavioral deficiencies of individuals are of broadly equal importance. Each of these individual limitations can be a binding constraint that reinforces another. Consequently, policy actions to overcome these limitations need to be taken in parallel.

Hence the question that emerges is "Will more and better information for and greater financial capability by individuals unequivocally lead to higher instrument use and stronger participation?" The answer is "Not necessarily," and this subsection explains this answer in three parts, using the information level in the economy as an organizing principle. The results strengthen the argument that policy actions need to be taken in parallel to avoid a (temporary) worsening of the situation. The result should not be surprising, as in a second-best world, well-intended first-best interventions do not necessarily improve welfare outcomes.

7.2.2.1. In an (Almost) Full Information Economy with Utility Maximizing Individuals

For this first scenario, an almost full information economy is assumed, with the caveat that while individuals are assumed to be rational and utility maximizing, they nevertheless have gaps in their financial knowledge and skills that may impede them from making the optimal social risk management choice, or in this case, the right participation decision.

The benefit design exhibits features that exist in many real world social insurance schemes: A high level of redistribution within the Defined Benefit (DB) scheme from low- to high-risk groups, and from high-income and high-density contributors toward low-income and low-density contributors; that, in turn, requires a high vesting period to limit opportunistic behavior. Assumptions about implementation deficiencies in the form of a lack of transparency and credibility associated with the scheme and low capacity to enforce the mandate are also added.

With these assumptions, aggregate system participation will be somewhere in the middle – neither full coverage nor total absence of it. But what happens if the financial knowledge and skill level of individuals is increased, *ceteris paribus*? For low-income groups that benefit from the benefit design, there may be some additional increase in the already higher participation rate. For higher-income groups, the redistributive character of the scheme will become more transparent, leading to a further reduction in the participation rate. On a net basis, improved financial literacy and skills risk reducing overall system participation rather than increasing it.

7.2.2.2. In an Asymmetric Information Economy with Utility Maximizing Individuals

In the second scenario, the assumption of prevailing large pockets of asymmetric information in the economy serves to motivate major failures in the financial market (for example, lacking access to liquidity (loans) leads to high personal discount rates, and the many other risks and incomplete financial markets reduce, *inter alia*, the demand for old age annuity) and in the labor market (for example, via patchy formal employment).

In terms of the benefit design, such an economic situation is consistent with the broad provision of basic social benefits that create moral hazard effects with regard to system participation (a la Levy 2008). It is assumed again that individuals are fully rational and utility maximizing, but that they have major gaps in financial literacy and skills.

Given this setting, any improvement in financial literacy and skills should have little short-term effect on the functioning of financial and labor markets. However, such an improvement should increase the confidence level and capability of individuals to arrange for their own retirement benefits, as they can now better understand that they have a fallback position - the social pension - if things do not work out as expected. Again, improved financial literacy and skills risk reducing rather than increasing aggregate system participation.

7.2.2.3. In an Incomplete Information Economy with Rational/Bounded-Rational Individuals

The third scenario is consistent with major information/knowledge gaps on both the supply and demand sides. Supply side information/knowledge gaps may include broad ignorance about the working of the social insurance scheme and the level of future benefits, or about the working of the tax system and the interaction with the social insurance scheme, and thus the overall level of effective taxation. Demand side information/knowledge gaps may include how to make ends meet, or how to best address the many other risks individuals are confronted with.

In such an information setting, and presumably for both fully rational and bounded-rational individuals, an increase in the information/knowledge/skills/attitude set may increase or decrease aggregate system participation. The result is conjectured to depend crucially on the characteristics of the social insurance scheme: the more closely it accommodates individual needs, the greater the likelihood of participation, and vice versa.

The results in this sub-section are conjectured to broadly carry over to the use of market-based risk management instruments. That is, more information and better knowledge will not automatically translate into more and better use of the market-based instruments; perhaps to the contrary, depending on their proximity to individual needs, quality, and price.

7.3. The Role and Limits of Financial Literacy/Capability

The analysis in Section 7.2 assumed that more information, knowledge, and skills would eventually lead to enhanced use of market-based and government provided social risk management instruments, and assumed that there was a well-defined financial education intervention to make this happen. Section 7.3 briefly reviews these assumptions to shed some light (and water) on their validity. To that end, it first summarizes the areas where financial education is expected to increase knowledge, skills, and attitudes that ultimately lead to improved individual behavior. This is followed by a section that summarizes the state of the art practices for conceptualizing, defining, and measuring financial literacy/capabilities.

7.3.1. Main Content Domains of Financial Literacy/Capability to Improve the Use of Social Risk Management Instruments

The main areas assumed to be critical for improved use of risk management instruments by individuals to address the nine ILO social contingencies are:

(1) Understanding the diverse (social) risks (old age, disability, health, etc.) that confront individuals/families during their life cycle and having the capability for life-cycle planning.
(2) Understanding the diverse public and private social risk management instruments and having the financial capability to apply them, as appropriate, to address these risks over the life cycle.

The first area – the capability for life-cycle planning – asks individuals for awareness and understanding of social risks in a life-cycle context and capability planning in a consumption/saving and labor supply/retirement context. The second area – the capability to use social risk management instruments – asks for technical understanding of programs and products. These are higher-level decisions taken only occasionally during the life cycle (similar to housing and education decisions), but they need to be based on sound financial decisions in everyday life, such as on spending, budgeting, debt management, and credit card use. Thus, a third basic area of financial literacy/capability will need to exist to ensure financial room and cognitive and emotional attention to the high level concerns of risk management:

(3) Understanding the basic concepts of living within one's means, budgeting, and having the financial capability to understand and use basic financial products such as banking accounts, debt, and credit cards, as appropriate and available.

Each of these areas cascade, starting with the basic concept, and raise the question of how financial literacy/capability, if only at the basic level, is conceptualized and measured.

7.3.2. Conceptualizing and Measuring Financial Literacy/Capability

Financial literacy/capability is a booming business, as evidenced by increasing attention by policy-makers, financial sector participants, and the research community. Yet despite this attention, the area is still characterized by a high degree of uncertainty regarding how best to conceptualize, define, and measure this concept.

Good analytical and empirical answers are still outstanding for a number of questions, including:

- What are we primarily worried about and what matters? The lack of knowledge (literacy) and/or inappropriate behavior and outcomes?
- How are knowledge, behavior, and outcomes linked, and what are their drivers?
- What does this imply for measurement of what should be improved and for the effectiveness of interventions to do so?

In this section, some of these questions are addressed with a short presentation and discussion of polar views at the level of conceptualization and measurement that ultimately share the same challenges.

7.3.2.1. Conceptualizing Financial Literacy/Capability

Two polar views may be distinguished when conceptualizing financial literacy/capabilities: the normative/cognitive approach and the positive/agnostic approach. The first builds on sequential information and learning constraints but may not work; the second is focused on what matters but may not be fully able to explain why and how. Both approaches focus on the broader concept of financial capability for good financial behavior but with different emphasis.

The Normative/Cognitive Approach

This approach explicitly assumes that a lack of information and learning is the binding constraint for good behavior (and outcomes) and that the constraints need to and can be eliminated in a sequential and cognitive manner. It builds on knowledge and skills as the key determinants of traditional financial literacy components but also adds attitude and capability (see Figure 7.1). Actually, financial capability (at times called financial competence) is a summary description, as it refers to the ability to apply knowledge, skills, and attitude in a sustained manner to achieve the relevant financial behavior (and outcome).

This approach has financial knowledge (i.e., analytical understanding of financial concepts and products[3]) as the basic requirement that needs to be augmented by skills as the ability to apply knowledge in life to achieve financial literacy. This was the original concept and thought to be sufficient for good behavior and outcomes. However, it soon became clear that knowledge and skills are not sufficient to, say, save for rainy days – this also requires the attitude to do so. Even good attitude is not sufficient, as the behavior to follow through is also needed. But in this conceptualization, all of these steps are open to cognitive penetration and learning. One only needs to expose individuals to these concepts through financial education.

Figure 7.1

The Normative/Cognitive Approach

knowledge -> skills -> attitude -> behavior

knowledge:	cognitive understanding
skills:	ability to apply knowledge
attitude:	willingness to apply knowledge and skills
capability:	ability to apply knowledge, skills, and attitude in a sustained manner to achieved the relevant financial behavior (as output) and policy objectives (as outcome)

Source: Author, adapted from Kempson et al 2005.

With this conceptualization, an important move from financial literacy (with its focus on knowledge and skills) to capability (with its focus on behavior and results) took place, and both notions are now increasingly used interchangeably.[4] While the extension can be considered important progress, the focus on information and learning gaps (taken at face value) ignores at least two other main constraints to achieving good behavior:

- Constraints due to the enabling environment (e.g., restricted access to finance, lack of trust in financial institutions, etc.); and

- Constraints due to the behavior of individuals that is not amenable to change through learning (highlighted under behavioral economics/finance above).

Both these and likely other constraint areas will impact individual behavior compared to the counterfactual of their absence. Financial literacy/capability without these constraints thus becomes the idealistic benchmark under perfect (financial) markets and fully rational and utility maximizing individuals. The distance between constrained and unconstrained results could be measured and used for analysis.

However, this approach works only inasmuch as good financial behavior is largely driven by knowledge, skills, attitude, etc. If behavior is largely driven by psychology, peer effects, or other non-cognitive drivers, the approach fails.

The Positive/Agnostic Approach

This basic idea is to identify financial capability as financial behavior considered to matter for good outcomes. The assessment is not undertaken against an abstract benchmark but is instead based on the judgement of individuals (*vox populi*) and what they consider good outcomes and the good behavior that leads to those outcomes. This approach implicitly takes account of effective constraints (e.g., limited access to financial products), as they are part of the individual's judgment of what constitutes good behavior.

This approach to conceptualizing financial capability was spearheaded by work commissioned by the U.K. Financial Sector Authority (FSA) that first started in a different direction, around the notion of knowledge, skills, and attitudes (see Kempson et al 2005). Focus groups, however, made it clear that everyday people had a different notion of capability that they perceived in behavioral terms. Specifically, focus group members felt that financial capability had four discrete aspects (domains):

- **Managing money** (i.e., living within one's means and tracking one's expenditures);
- **Planning ahead** (i.e., coping with unexpected events and making provisions for the long term);

- **Making choices** (i.e., being aware of what options are available and being able to choose the most appropriate ones for an individual's circumstances); and
- **Getting help** (i.e., becoming self-reliant through information gathering and knowing where and when to turn for advice and help from a third party).

When probed, the focus groups agreed that knowledge, skills, and personality were relevant for each of these domains, but they did not have a clear view of the role and causality of these factors.

This outcome-driven conceptualization, relying on the *vox populi* to determine what matters, delivers a relative standard for both within and between countries. As the circumstances are likely to differ across income levels and between regions, the identified domains may differ, or at least their relative importance or content therein may. Application of the concept in other industrialized countries, however, has confirmed the approach and the four domains. For low and middle-income countries, individuals focus more on the first two domains.

7.3.2.2. Measuring Financial Literacy/Capability Across Time and Space

The two conceptualizations outlined above reflect very much the (implicit or explicit) basis on which surveys are undertaken to establish the baseline of financial capability in a country and to see how it compares with others and over time. The latter also serves as a measure of the effectiveness of national financial literacy/capability strategies, including financial education and other interventions.

Based on the two conceptualizations, two measurement approaches can be analytically distinguished: a normative approach and a positive approach. In reality and in implementation, both are typically combined. The **normative approach** to measuring financial capability defines inputs and outputs of how financially capable individuals should behave and takes them as the benchmark. Surveys then determine how the interviewed population (household heads, all adult household members) deviates from the benchmark and to what extent. Examples of normative questions include: knowledge questions about compound interest rates, inflation, and risk diversification; and attitude or behavior questions about planning and saving (see, e.g. Lusardi and Mitchell 2006). They reflect *ad hoc* assumptions or are derived from neoclassical models of choice or life-cycle planning. The results are used to establish a baseline and evaluate progress, and in analytical work to evaluate the extent to which the financial capability components – as measured - are correlated with outcome variables of interest.

The **positive approach** to measuring financial capability uses country-specific benchmarks derived from special-purpose focus groups. The benchmark establishes what is considered financially smart behavior in each country, using responses obtained from in-depth interviews; trial groups are then used to measure the deviation from this benchmark for each identified domain or sub-domain (e.g., living within one's means or budgeting; see FSA 2006, and World Bank 2012, for sample questions). Individual questions are scored and aggregated into a score per domain or sub-domain (e.g., living within one's means). Started in the U.K., this is the approach now also used in Ireland, Canada, and the U.S., and the questions used there have influenced more recent countries' surveys, as discussed next.

7.3.2.3. Measuring Financial Literacy/Capability Around the World

Over the last decade or so, a number of high and a few middle-income countries have undertaken surveys to establish their respective levels of financial literacy/capability. The surveys used different *ad hoc* methodologies, limiting comparability of the results, but overall they signal a low level financial competence worldwide.

Financed by the Trust Fund on Financial Literacy and Education established by the Government of the Russian Federation (RTF), both OECD and the World Bank have undertaken comprehensive work on financial surveys based on their comparative advantage (see Kempson 2011).

The OECD used its strong network of country representatives through the International Network for Financial Education (INFE) to identify and review twenty-six surveys in eighteen countries. From this synthesis, generic guidelines were produced on how to conduct a survey of financial capability, based on best practices to date, as well as a short questionnaire (nineteen questions) of topics commonly covered by existing surveys.[5]

The World Bank focused on developing survey instruments and manuals that would be appropriate for measuring the financial capability of low-income populations in low and middle-income countries (see Holzmann 2010; World Bank 2012). The selected conceptualization was the positive/agnostic approach developed in the U.K., with the first research question asking if the identified four domains would be replicated in low and middle-income environments, and in low-income groups. The results from pilots in twelve low and middle-income countries confirm the results for OECD economies for the domains of managing money and planning ahead, but give less importance on choice and help. The final questionnaire including manuals and a policy research report that summarizes the results and puts them into perspective will be publicly available on the RTF website.[6]

The parallel implementation of the OECD and World Bank survey approaches will allow for future testing and determination of what matters and for what kind of outcome – the normative and knowledge-based or the positive and agnostic focus. The results will also help to better assess what kind of financial literacy/capability approach is best suited to strengthen participation in voluntary and mandated social insurance schemes.

7.4. The Role and Limits of Financial Education and Other Interventions

Viewing financial knowledge and skills as basic drivers of financial literacy and capability is reflected in an enthusiasm for financial education as the key process to achieve better financial behavior and outcomes. The discussion about the conceptualization and measurement of financial literacy/capability in the prior section has already raised some issues associated with such a view, at least for some financial behaviors and outcomes. This calls for alternative interventions to steer the desired results in general and for social risk management-related events in particular. Section 7.4 first very briefly summarizes the empirical evidence on the effectiveness of financial education in general and in relation to social risk management. The second part offers a first glimpse on promising complementary or alternative interventions, with a focus on nudging and advocacy.

7.4.1. Does Financial Education Work in General and for Social Risk Management Use?

Ever since the topic of financial literacy gained momentum in the early 2000s, the topic of financial education has been the centerpiece of public and private interventions with the objective to increase of that was and is generally believed to be at too low, i.e., financial literacy (see OECD 2005). To strengthen the coordination of interventions across stakeholders, various countries have started to implement or plan national strategies for financial education that often also include consumer protection and financial inclusion activities.[7] A review of these strategies does not suggest a common approach or well-defined sets of education interventions. But common to all national strategies is the conviction that financial education interventions are needed and effective, starting with their inclusion in schooling systems' curricula, and ranging to hand-tailored education programs to enhance retirement income saving. Various developed and emerging economies have started to implement financial education in their schooling systems, with a wide range of focus, approaches, and sophistication. All use the cognitive approach and focus on the key dimensions of financial education: knowledge and understanding; skills and competences; and attitudes and values (see OECD 2011b).

But what has been the impact of such financial education programs? Overall, the result is quite sobering. The available meta studies on the effectiveness of financial education based on rigorous impact evaluation approaches suggest limited success, if any. All international reviews of the sparse evidence come to a similar conclusion, as stated by Atkinson (2008, p. 5): "...there is little in the way of robust evidence to show the overall effect of financial training."[8] This conclusion is valid across different types of interventions, from more academic training in schools to more *ad hoc* training at the workplace. They are also broadly echoed by the few rigorous evaluations in poorer countries, mostly undertaken around microfinance projects.

This lack of evidence is not proof that financial education has never worked and never will. But at the moment, there are few empirical leads to suggest which relevant elements should be strengthened with financial education of a specific type. There are emerging indications from individual country studies about possible effects that need to be substantiated by repetition in different contexts (country, income groups, gender, etc.) and stitched together into a consistent conceptualization/paradigm subject to its own testing. Very recent elements of such emerging indications (may) suggest: that teaching a rule of thumb for good financial decisions is more relevant than complex training (Drexler, Fisher, and Schoar 2010); that financial education may be effective to increase awareness of financial instruments and attitudes but does little to induce better performance, suggesting that cognitive constraints rather than lack of attention are a key barrier to improving financial knowledge (Carpena et al 2011); and that peer pressure plays a strong (and consistent) role in the savings decision (Kast, Meier, and Pomeranz 2012).

To the author's knowledge, no financial education interventions to increase participation in mandated social insurance schemes have ever been piloted (and evaluated). However, in the area of voluntary retirement savings, many financial education programs exist, at least in the Anglo-Saxon world, and some of them have been evaluated. The assessment of the effectiveness of such training interventions (retirement seminars, benefit fairs, etc.) for attitudes and actual retirement saving behavior still seems to be an act of faith.[9] It appears that focused training events at the workplace at the time of decision (a "teachable moment") to contribute to an employer-sponsored retirement scheme may have an impact at least on attitude and perhaps participation (signing up) but less so on follow-up saving. But too few interventions have ever been evaluated to draw overall conclusions about what works and what does not.

The overall empirical and conceptual uncertainty regarding the effects of financial education is largely grounded in the absence of rigorous impact evaluations for most financial education interventions in both developing and developed countries. The reasons for that lack are plenty and include: the failure to understand the advantages of rigorous M&E; the lack of an accessible toolkit to inform intervention financiers and implementers of the why and the how; and the high cost of impact evaluation (in addition to the intervention) that the financier/provider might not want to incur. Some claim that the low interest in rigorous evaluation by many financial education providers may also be strategic, as a negative assessment would threaten the future financing of the education intervention, many are which are provided by NGOs.

Against this background, the World Bank RTF established an M&E work program that consists of three interrelated components: (i) development of an impact evaluation toolkit for financial education and related capability enhancement interventions; (ii) financial support for impact evaluations for country-specific intervention projects; and (iii) financing for integrated impact evaluations of financial education projects. The ultimate objective is to develop an operational impact evaluation framework with a common results framework, a toolkit for quantitative and qualitative impact evaluation methods, and operational guidelines that can be used to assess the impact of financial education programs and related interventions in low and middle-income countries.[10]

7.4.2. *What are Promising Alternatives to Influence Behavior in General and for Social Risk Management Use?*

The lack of broad-based proof on the effectiveness of financial education, at least to improve critical parts of financial behavior (e.g., for the planning and execution of retirement income saving), may be systemic and never improved by a cognitive/education approach, at least for a large share of the population. The potential reasons for systemic failure of financial education interventions are numerous, but mostly center around the claim that financial behavior has much more to do with psychology than with (a lack of) financial education.

The psychology literature is full of examples of how psychology (i.e., emotion) influences (financial and other) behavior (Holden 2010), ranging: from early psychoanalysis theory (Sigmund Freud et al) that explicitly links childhood experiences with adult financial behavior; to psychosocial theory (Erik Erikson) that proposes different stages through which personality develops and also emphasizes the role of the primary caregiver; to learning theory/behaviorism (B. F. Skinner) that contends that once behavior is associated with a consequence, the likelihood of the action continuing changes; to cognitive theory (Jean Piaget) that proposes cognitive development stages needed to advance in stage-appropriate education; to the behavioral economics already alluded to in the previous section (e.g., Mullainathan and Thaler 2000). To explain some of the results and the observed deviation of individual behavior predicted by standard economic theory from observed individual behavior in real life, the many parallel and partly overlapping advances also include: neuroeconomics with research methods from neuroscience; experimental and behavioral economics; cognitive and social psychology (see Cramer, Loewenstein, and Prelec 2005; Loewenstein, Rick, and Cohen 2008); and other innovative approaches that attempt to explain the often as irrational perceived behavior of the poor due to the special psychological stress that poverty exerts (Mullainathan 2011). Traditionally, the poor have been the most difficult group to include under mandated and voluntary social insurance schemes.

While linking psychology (i.e., emotions) and economics (i.e., rational behavior) is in full swing with no dominating paradigm(s) yet emerging to guide interventions to improve financial behavior and outcomes, there are two promising domains under investigation and implementation: nudging and advocacy. The two may be characterized by polar opposite levels of confidence in cognitive learning. The following very briefly outlines each concept and a selected application for social risk management, in particular retirement income provisions.

7.4.2.1. Nudging

Nudging is a gentle pushing toward certain directions or decisions. Used as an intervention to overcome the behavioral weakness of an otherwise rational, teachable, and welfare maximizing individual, it consists of exploiting behavioral fallacies and biases to nudge individuals towards behavior and results that are considered superior. Hence, individuals are free to choose but the decision environment is framed to make some decisions and outcomes considered superior more likely. For this reason, the nudging approach has been coined "libertarian paternalism" by the authors of "Nudge: Improving Decisions about Health, Wealth, and Happiness" (Thaler and Sunstein 2009).

The biases, heuristics, and fallacies of individual behavior that are exploited include: anchoring (a cognitive bias wherein one relies too heavily on one trait or piece of information); availability heuristics (when people predict the frequency of an event based on how easily an example can be brought to mind); representativeness heuristics (where people judge the probability or frequency of a hypothesis by considering how much the hypothesis resembles available data); *status quo* bias (as defined earlier); and herd mentality (when people are heavily influenced by the actions of others, such as with peer pressure).

Nudging-inspired interventions proposed in the area of personal finance include:[11]

Nudges for better borrowing outcomes with official lenders such as commercial banks, credit card providers, and mortgage loan providers. Better credit choice architecture to overcome information asymmetries between borrower and lender is suggested to be achieved by streamlined information on rates and fees that allow for comparability across products and providers, and avoid information overload as well as excessive information requests. Under this libertarian paternalism, there is no need to regulate interest rates requested or fees charged for user services but there is a need to regulate disclosure practices on both (to apply the principle of Record, Evaluate, Compare Alternative Prices – RECAP). The informed consumer should be supported in his decisions but not restricted by government price and product regulation. Again, this assumes some level of financial capability towards which individuals can be educated (including product knowledge and where to turn for help).

Nudges for more savings, such as changing default options for tax-privileged and co-sponsored (employer or government) retirement savings plans to automatic enrollment, or simplifying the enrollment process in plans that require an active decision (such as offering a default option, or reducing the number of pension funds/ portfolios to choose from). As default options typically have low contribution rates and very conservative portfolios, leading to low rates of return, a further proposed nudge consists of scheduling future contribution increases at the time of annual wage increases (e.g., by 1 percentage point annually) until individuals either decide explicitly to stop the rate increase or it reaches the maximum tax deductible level (e.g., 15 percent). Both auto-enrollment and auto-escalation have proven highly successful in increasing program participation and contribution rates in the U.S. and abroad.

Nudges through better investment choice architecture for retirement savings, such as: the option for participants to select between conservative, balanced, and aggressive "lifestyle" portfolios; the offer of "life cycle" funds that move from aggressive toward conservative portfolios as individuals approach retirement; and the structuring of more complex choices for more sophisticated investors. For such choices that move away from single default options that risk being conservative, it is important to offer: independent advice from professionals; translation of abstract concepts into common terms; and some basic financial literacy to help individuals grasp the essence of diversification and instruments used.

To summarize, the nudging approach attempts to overcome identified behavioral issues of individuals, but is underpinned by the concept that individuals are capable of choosing well if the appropriate decision architecture, including nudges, is provided. This assumes that (most) individuals can be financially educated to make such choices and are able to achieve the needed knowledge, skills, and attitude to do so.

The basic assumption at the other end of the intervention scale is that most individuals cannot be educated to improve financial outcomes, especially those determined by intertemporal choices such as retirement income saving. This would call for influencing the emotions rather than the intellect of individuals (presented next). Of course, there are many possibilities for exploiting the grey shades between the two extremes.

7.4.2.2. Advocacy

Advocacy is defined as a systematic form of purposeful persuasion that attempts to influence the emotions, attitudes, opinions, and actions of specified target audiences for ideological, political, or commercial purposes through the controlled transmission of one-sided messages (which may or may not be factual) via leaflets, posters, or TV and radio broadcasts, and can also extend to any other medium.[12] Advocacy is generally an appeal to emotion, not intellect. It shares techniques with advertising and public relations, each of which can be thought of as advocacy that promotes views or shapes the perception of an organization, person, or brand. Advocacy as a generic term also includes propaganda. What sets propaganda apart from other forms of advocacy is the willingness of the propagandist to change people's understanding through deception and confusion rather than persuasion and cognitive understanding. The use of advocacy (or propaganda) as a special form of persuasion for the purposes of influencing financial behavior can be motivated by three conjectures: (i) it appeals directly to emotions and thus bypasses the cognitive route that may not work, or may be less efficient; (ii) it promises to be effective, as suggested by experience with public information campaigns of governments and NGOs intended to encourage or discourage certain forms of behavior (such as wearing seat belts, not smoking, not littering, and so forth); and (iii) through the use of modern media (radio and TV) and social media (YouTube, Twitter, etc.), it has the potential to reach very large audiences and be cost-effective.

There are two main avenues to promote specific financial behavior via advocacy-type interventions currently being piloted: social marketing and educational entertainment. Both are promising but their effectiveness for financial affairs is essentially untested. And while they have been applied to pass on some financial behavior messages, their application to social risk management, including participation in social insurance schemes, has been scarce.

Social marketing is the systematic application of marketing, along with other concepts and techniques, to achieve specific behavioral goals for a social good. Social marketing can be applied to promote merit goods, or to induce a society to avoid demerit goods and thus promote society's well-being as a whole. In many countries, applications include health (anti-smoking campaigns, safe sex), road safety (use seatbelts, anti-speeding), and environment (recycling, trash separation).

Social marketing theory and practice has progressed in several countries such as the U.S., Canada, Australia, New Zealand, and the U.K.; in the latter, a number of key government policy papers have adopted a strategic social marketing approach. In its simplest form, it offers key messages via posters, TV, and other media that aim to persuade a change in behavior. A variation of social marketing has emerged as a systematic way to foster more sustainable behavior (e.g., around energy conservation, environmental regulation, and recycling). Realizing that simply providing information is usually not sufficient to initiate behavior change, the Community-Based Social Marketing (CBSM) approach uses tools and findings from social psychology to discover the perceived barriers to behavior change and ways of overcoming these barriers (see McKenzie-Mohr 2011). Among the tools and techniques used by CBSM are focus groups and surveys (to discover barriers) and commitments, prompts, social norms, social diffusion, feedback, and incentives (to change behavior). The latter approach has many overlaps with nudging and the creation of a supportive choice architecture.

While the areas in which social marketing has mostly been applied appear appropriate and the claimed success stories convincing, the actual empirical evidence is sobering: The main claims that it works are derived by linking an intervention with a change in outcome (see the section on "Success Stories" at http://www.social-marketing.org). Very few interventions have undergone a rigorous impact evaluation, and those that have raise many doubts. The challenge of separating treatment and comparator groups is simply daunting, and the methodology to do so in a convincing manner is still a work in progress.

Meanwhile, social marketing has also reached out to influence financial behavior. In a study for the Consultative Group to Assist the

Poor (CGAP) that reviews over 100 case studies from 2009/10, Lee and Miller (2012) identify and present seven best practices where a social marketing approach was used to influence a financial behavior. The study identifies relevant behaviors, including those related to establishing a bank account, increasing savings, using credit wisely, avoiding over indebtedness, applying for micro finance loans, adopting new technologies, reducing chances of fraud, choosing the right insurance, reporting abuse, and shopping around and comparing offers. The potential target audiences of the reviewed social marketing interventions were broad, ranging from sex workers in India, to farmers in "self-help" groups in Kenya, to girls aged 10-18 in Mongolia, to the homeless in San Francisco, to households on tea estates in India. While the approaches and results of the identified best practices are interesting and promising, none of the over 100 case studies was subject to anything close to a rigorous impact evaluation.

To the author's knowledge, no systematic social marketing has been undertaken by governments, social security institutions, or NGOs to promote participation in mandated programs or government-supported voluntary schemes (such as the 401k in the U.S., the Riester pension in Germany, the KiwiSaver in New Zealand, or the new rural pension in China).[13] For mandated programs, there are both older and very recent examples of TV spots and other media tools used to persuade citizens that participation in these programs is useful.[14] Many government-sponsored programs have websites (or at least information pages). But no case comes to mind where social marketing instruments (as, say, for HIV/AIDS prevention) have been used to promote program participation, nor are there cases where their effectiveness been analyzed.

Educational entertainment, or edutainment, is a form of entertainment designed to educate as well as to amuse. The notion of merging education and amusement has existed for thousands of years in the form of parables and fables used to promote social change, and in the form of theater at least since ancient Greek or Chinese times. Modern forms of edutainment include television productions, film, museum exhibits, and computer software, which all use entertainment to attract and maintain an audience while incorporating deliberate educational content or messages.

Since the 1970s, various groups in the U.S., the U.K., and Latin America have used edutainment to address health and social issues such as substance abuse, immunization, teenage pregnancy, HIV/

AIDS, and cancer. More recently, the approach has gained traction in Sub-Saharan Africa, particularly in the form of popular TV series that have been spearheaded in Latin America (*telenovelas*) and the U.S. (soap operas). Packaging behavioral messages into popular TV series is considered attractive and effective due to both the entertainment effect and the star/peer effect. Having well-known TV series characters expressing views and behavior on desirable/undesirable behavior is considered very powerful. To be effective, convincing, and amusing, messages are woven into a general script rather than having the script developed around the messages. Producers of TV series in U.S. and Latin America are ready to do so upon request, and various foundations exist for their financing.

Given the promising ability of edutainment to push messages and promote socially desirable behavior, it is not surprising that this advocacy approach has reached the area of finance, with a few promising pilots under implementation. Some of them are supported by the World Bank-managed RTF a rigorous impact evaluation of financial behavior-oriented TV programs used in Sub-Saharan Africa. While edutainment interventions for health and other targeted behaviors are by now plenty, their effectiveness has not been well documented empirically (for a review, see Greer and Miller 2013). As with social marketing, it is very difficult to separate treatment and control groups associated with edutainment interventions, and to undertake unbiased assignments to each group. Work is underway to support the methodological development and to include useful results in the M&E toolkit for Financial Literacy and Education. If the edutainment approach does prove to be effective at affecting financial behavior, this will constitute major progress, as many individuals in low-middle and low-income countries could be reached at low cost.

To the author's knowledge, edutainment interventions have not yet been used to promote participation in either mandated or voluntary social risk management arrangements, but it is a promising avenue to complement or substitute for cognitive approaches to further enhance financial capabilities and achieve coverage outcomes.

7.5. Conclusions

The chapter asked a simple but important question: Can financial education or alternative interventions enhance financial literacy/capability and thus lead to better use of market-based as well as government-sponsored social risk management instruments? If so, this would have significant ramifications for the level of mandating and the scope of effective coverage against key risks. This review of the state of the art around this topic and further analyses provide rich, and at times unexpected, results, from which five key conclusions stand out, including a sketched policy framework:

(1) Enhancing financial literacy/capability alone may not lead to better use of social risk management instruments, as the outcome also depends on supply constraints (such as availability, quality, and credibility of risk management instruments) and other demand constraints (such as behavioral limitations). Consequently, enhanced financial literacy/capability alone may actually lead to lower use of the offered instruments (as individuals become more aware of their limitations) or to inappropriate use (as individuals become over-confident), especially if behavioral biases and fallacies exist. The second best environment calls for a coordinated and parallel policy approach on multiple fronts.

(2) The limitations on better use of social risk management instruments, however, may also be due to incomplete conceptualization of financial literacy/capability and how to enhance it. While there are a number of definitions of financial literacy/capability, there is continued conceptual uncertainty regarding how to best define and measure it, and its link to better financial outcomes. Another limitation is the financial education currently receiving a lot of attention and support from policy-makers, the financial industry, etc., across the world. Yet to date, there is limited empirical evidence that financial education enhances knowledge, skills, attitudes, and behavior (i.e., capabilities), or that these matter to improve outcomes. This calls for strengthened efforts for conceptualization and measurement of financial capability, and more rigorous monitoring and (impact) evaluation of financial education interventions across the globe.

(3) In addition to the cognitive role of financial education in improving behavioral outcomes, there are increasingly substantiated indications that much of financial behavior is driven more by emotion than intellect. A whole new branch of economics extends the neoclassical approach by identifying the behavioral limitations of the *homo economicus*. Applying the results of behavioral economics/finance to the design of interventions has given rise to the concept of libertarian paternalism, in which individuals are free to choose, but a well-

selected choice architecture nudges them to better outcomes. A more radical approach that further discounts the cognitive role relies solely on persuasion/advocacy, and social marketing and edutainment interventions already used reliably in health and road safety are now being piloted to determine if they are also effective at changing financial behavior.

(4) Only a few of these interventions have been applied to voluntary market-based social risk management instruments and close to none to mandated government-sponsored ones. The results from education-based interventions are few and sobering; there are some promising results for nudging-based interventions; and as of yet there are no social marketing/edutainment-based interventions in this area that in any case create a challenge for any rigorous (impact) evaluation.

(5) Against this background of conceptual uncertainty and empirical gaps, policy proposals to address mandating and coverage expansion are difficult to pronounce but not impossible. The results suggest that continuing the status quo and imposing the same mandate of risk management may not be the best way forward. Instead, governments should move on multiple fronts, including working on better access to and structure of risk management instruments, making individuals financially more capable, nudging individuals towards better behavior and outcomes, and marketing both with advocacy campaigns. But all this will need to happen under an overall results framework and rigorous evaluation: What you cannot measure you cannot manage.

Notes

1 The (minimum) benefits established under Convention 102 concern medical care, sickness benefit, unemployment benefit, old-age benefit, employment injury benefit, family benefit, maternity benefit, invalidity benefit, and survivor's benefit. See http://www.ilocarib.org.tt/projects/cariblex/conventions_14.shtml.

2 Interesting examples are mandated social insurance schemes that rely on private sector provisions, such as is frequently the case in Latin America and where fund associations have started recently to undertake joint information campaigns using modern media. See http://www.youtube.com/user/FIAPORG?feature=mhee, and http://www.youtube.com/watch?v=FefgSU6lBOc,http://www.facebook.com/pages/Federaci%C3%B3n-Internacional-de-Administradoras-de-Fondos-de-Pensiones-FIAP/193203747372960.

3 See, for example, the Wikipedia definition of financial literacy: "Financial literacy is the ability to understand finance. More specifically, it refers to the set of skills and knowledge that allows an individual to make informed and effective decisions through their understanding of finances."

4 For example, as of 2010. the OECD/INFE defines financial literacy "a combination of financial awareness, knowledge, skills, attitude and behaviours necessary to make sound financial decisions and ultimately achieve financial wellbeing" (OECD/INFE 2011c).

5 See http://www.oecd-ilibrary.org/docserver.

6 See the World Bank Russia Trust Fund website (http://www.finlitedu.org) for more information, including the pilot survey results, final questionnaire and manuals, and the knowledge management report (Holzmann, Mulaj and Periotti 2013).

7 As of autumn 2011, ten countries had implemented national strategies (Australia (2011), Brazil (2010), Czech Republic (2010), India (2006/2010), Ireland (2009), Malaysia (2003), Netherlands (2008), New Zealand (2008), Spain (2008), United Kingdom (2003)) and fifteen more countries had started to consider or were designing such a strategy (Canada, Colombia, Estonia, Indonesia, Latvia, Lebanon, Mexico, Peru, Poland, Portugal, Serbia, South Africa, Romania, Sweden, Turkey, United States). See OECD 2011a.

8 For other recent reviews on the effectiveness of financial education see Orton 2007; Atkinson 2008; Mundy 2009; O'Connell 2009 and Cole, Sampson and Zia 2011.

9 For critical quotes, see for example the references in Thaler and Sunstein 2009 (Chapter 6); for more optimistic assessments, see for example Lusardi and Mitchell 2006 and 2007a; b, and OECD 2005.

10 See Holzmann 2010 and the RTF website http://www.finlitedu.org.

11 See Thaler and Sunstein 2009, or www.nudges.org for more recent examples and references.

12 This definition for advocacy is an adjustment from a neutral definition on propaganda (see Nelson 1996). Propaganda has, however, nowadays in most languages (including English) a negative connotation, including the purposeful use of lies.

13 The public information campaigns for these programs are briefly described in the country papers of a forthcoming publication on Matching Defined Contribution schemes (see Holzmann et al. 2013).

14 For some kind of recent social marketing by the pension funds' associations in Mexico and Uruguay, see http://www.youtube.com/user/FIAPORG?feature=mhee.

References

Antolín, P., Harrison, D. (2012). Annual DC Pension Statements and the Communications Challenge, OECD Working Paper on Finance, Insurance and Private Pensions, No. 19.

Atkinson, A. (2008). Evidence of Impact: An Overview of Financial Education Evaluations, Consumer Research No. 68.

Carpena, F., Cole, S., Shapiro, J., Zia, B. (2011). Unpacking the Causal Chain of Financial Literacy, World Bank Policy Research Working Paper No. 5798.

Cole, S., Sampson, T., Zia, B. (2011). Prices or Knowledge? What Drives Demand for Financial Services in Emerging Markets?, in: The Journal of Finance, 66(6): 1933-67.

Camerer, C., Loewenstein, G., Prelec, D. (2005). Neuroeconomics: How Neuroscience Can Inform Economics, in: Journal of Economic Literature, 43(1): 9-64.

Davidoff, T., Brown, J., Diamond, P. (2003). Annuities and Individual Welfare, NBER Working Paper No. 9714.

Drexler, A., Fisher, G., Schoar, A. (2010). Keeping it Simple: Financial Literacy and Rules of Thumb, CEPR Discussion Paper No. DP7994.

Financial Service Authority (FSA) (2006). Financial Capability Baseline Survey: Methodological Report, Consumer Research 47a.

Greer, A., Miller, M. (2013, forthcoming). Entertainment Education and Financial Literacy, in: World Bank Research Observer.

Hinz, R., Rudolph, H., Antolin, P., Yermo, J. (2010). Evaluating the Performance of Pension Funds, Washington, DC: The World Bank.

Holden, K. (2010). Theories of Human Behavior and Emotions: What They Imply about Financial Behavior of Vulnerable Populations, Center for Financial Security Research Brief No. FLRC 10-4.

Holzmann, R., Jorgensen, S. (2001). Social Risk Management: A New Conceptual Framework for Social Protection, and Beyond, in: International Tax and Public Finance, 8(4): 529-56.

Holzmann, R., Hinz, R., von Gersdorff, H., Gill, I., Impavido, G., Musalem, A. R., Palacios, R., Robalino, D., Rutkowski, M., Schwarz, A., Sin, Y., Subbarao , K. (2005). Old-Age Income Support in the 21st Century: An International Perspective on Pension Systems and Reform, Washington, DC: The World Bank.

Holzmann, R., Feher, C., von Gersdorff, H. (2009). Were Financial Systems in CESE Countries Prepared for the Challenges of Multi-pillar Pension Reform?, in: Holzmann, R. (Ed.), Aging Population, Pension Funds, and Financial Markets: Regional Perspectives and Global Challenges for Central, Eastern, and Southern Europe. Washington, DC: The World Bank, 13-40.

Holzmann, R. (2010). Bringing Financial Literacy and Education to Low and Middle Income Countries: The Need to Review, Adjust, and Extend Current Wisdom, World Bank Social Protection Discussion Papers No. 1007.

Holzmann, R., Hinz, R., Tuesta, D., Takayama, N. (Eds.) (2013, forthcoming). Matching Defined Contributions (MDC) Schemes: Role and Limits to Increase Coverage in Low and Middle Income Countries.

Holzmann, R., Mulaj, F., Periotti, V. (2013). Financial Capability in Low- and Middle-Income Countries: Measurement and Evaluation. A Report on the World Bank's Research Program and The Knowledge From The Russia Financial Literacy And Education Trust Fund, Washington, DC: The World Bank.

Kast, P. S. Meier, Pomeranz, D. (2012). Under-Savers Anonymous Evidence on Self-Help Groups and Peer Pressure as a Savings Commitment Device, IZA Discussion Paper No. 6311.

Kempson, E., Collard, S., Moore, N. (2005). Measuring Financial Capability: An Exploratory Study, London: Financial Services Authority.

Kempson, E. (2011). Comparison of the World Bank and OECD (INFE) Surveys Developed under the Russian Trust Fund on Financial Literacy and Education, mimeo.

Lee, N. R., Miller, M. (2012). Influencing Positive Financial Behaviors: The Social Mar-

keting Solution, in: Journal of Social Marketing, 2(1): 70–86.
Levy, S. (2008). Good Intentions, Bad Outcomes: Social Policy, Informality and Economic Growth in Mexico, Washington, DC: Brookings Institution Press.
Loewenstein, G., Rick, S., Cohen, J. (2008). Neuroeconomics, in: Annual Review of Psychology, 59: 647-72.
Lusardi, A., Mitchell, O. S. (2006). Financial Literacy and Planning: Implications for Retirement Wellbeing, Pension Research Council Working Paper No. 1.
Lusardi, A., Mitchell, O. S. (2007a). Financial Literacy and Retirement Preparedness: Evidence and Implications for Financial Education, in: Business Economics, 42(1): 35-44.
Lusardi, A., Mitchell, O. S. (2007b). Baby Boomer Retirement Security: The Roles of Planning, Financial Literacy, and Housing Wealth, Journal of Monetary Economics, 54(1): 205-24.
Mastrobuoni, G. (2011). Do Social Security Statements Affect Knowledge and Behavior, Center for Retirement Research at Boston College, Brief 11-6.
McKenzie-Mohr, D. (2011). Fostering Sustainable Behavior: An Introduction to Community-Based Social Marketing, Gabriola Island: New Society Publishers.
Mullainathan, S. (2011). Lacea Lames 2011 - Sendhil Mullainathan, LACEA's Albert Hirschman Lecture, http://www.youtube.com/watch?v=xtfBj_iJz8Q&noredirect=1
Mullainathan, S., Thaler, R. H. (2000). Behavioral Economics, NBER Working Paper No.7948.
Mundy, S. (2009). Financial Education Programmes in Schools: Analysis of Selected Current Programmes and Literature – Draft Recommendations for Best Practices, in: OECD Journal: General Papers, 8(3): 53.
Nelson, R. A. (1996). A Chronology and Glossary of Propaganda in the United States, Westport, CT: Greenwood Press: 232-3.
O'Connell, A. (2009). Evaluating the Effectiveness of Financial Education Programmes, in: OECD Journal: 17(3): 9–51.
Orton, L. (2007). Financial Literacy: Lessons from International Experience, Canadian Policy Research Network - CPRN Research Report.
OECD (2005). OECD Publication Improving Financial Literacy: Analysis of Issues and Policies.
OECD (2011a). Financial Education Programmes in Schools Case Studies Report, Paris: OECD.
OECD (2011b). Report On National Strategies For Financial Education Revised Draft, Paris: OECD.
OECD/INFE (2011c). Financial Literacy Measurement Questions and Socio-Demographics, INFE(2010)3/REV3, Paris: OECD, mimeo.
Perry, G., Maloney, W. F., Arias, O. S., Fajnzylber, P., Mason, A. D., Saavedra-Chanduvi, J. (2007). Informality: Exit and Exclusion, Washington, DC: The World Bank.
Rocha, R., Vittas, D., Rudolph, H. (2011). Annuities and Other Retirement Products, Washington, DC: The World Bank.
Rudolph, H., Rocha, R. (2007). Financial Preconditions for Second Pillar, Washington, DC: The World Bank, mimeo.
Sunden, A. (2013). The Challenge of Reaching Participants with the Message of NDC, in: Holzmann, R., Palmer, E., Robalino, R. (Eds.), NDC Pension Schemes in a Changing Pension World, volume 2: Gender, Politics, and Financial Stability, Washington, DC: The World Bank, 257-72.
Thaler, R. H., Sunstein, C. R. (2009). Nudge: Improving Decisions about Health, Wealth, and Happiness, New York: Penguin Books.
World Bank (2011). Striving for Better Jobs: The Challenge of Informality in the Middle East and North Africa Region, Washington, DC: The World Bank.
World Bank (2012). Measuring Financial Capability and the Effectiveness of Financial Education, World Bank Trust Fund Supported by the Russian Federation, Washington, DC: The World Bank.

8

Labor Income and the Design of Default Portfolios in Mandatory Pension Systems: An Application to Chile*

Alfono R. Sánchez Martín
Sergi Jiménez Martín
David Robalino
Federico A. Todeschini

8.1. Introduction

The majority of countries, regardless of income, have implemented mandatory pension programs. One of the common justifications for these programs is that, left to their own devices, individuals would not save enough for retirement. This is either because they have inconsistent time preferences, because it is difficult to have the discipline to commit to a given savings plan, or simply because they lack the information and skills to make good investment decisions (see, for example, Benartzi and Thaler 2007). As a result, most governments have set up legislation that mandates individuals to join and contribute to public pension plans. Although there is a large heterogeneity in how these plans are designed and implemented, they always involve two critical choices: setting the targeted income replacement rate for a given retirement age and a given number of years of contributions;

* *We gratefully acknowledge the support from the World Bank and the Spanish Ministry of Education projects ECO2011-30323-C03-02, ECO2010-21706 and SEJ-6882/ECON.*

and defining how savings can be invested. In pure pay-as-you-go pension plans savings are mostly invested in pay-as-you-go assets (e.g., Brazil), in funded plans savings are invested in diversified portfolios of financial assets (e.g., Chile), whereas in "multi-pillar" systems savings are allocated to both types of assets (e.g., Sweden and Poland). In the case of financial assets, there are also restrictions regarding the types of securities that can be purchased and more and more countries are introducing default portfolios that change with age and to which most individual's stick.

An important policy question is how efficient are these choices. Having a single mandatory savings rate that applies to individuals with different characteristics already suggests that, for many, joining the public pension plan can be welfare decreasing (even after taking into account "myopia"), particularly if there are imperfections in financial markets that make it difficult for people to dissave. Making universal choices for the portfolio of pay-as-you-go and financial assets can further aggravate the problem and even provide incentives for evasion and informal work. Indeed, the optimal portfolio of assets depends not only on unobservable preferences, but also observable individual characteristics that are correlated with lifetime labor income.

In this chapter we consider these two problems in the case of Chile, paying special attention to asset allocations provided by default portfolios. Thus, we explore how current default portfolios differ from optimal portfolios and whether there is room to improve their design. Our results suggest that policymakers should consider different default portfolios for males and females with different education attainment and/or professional occupation. These observable characteristics are good predictors of the "riskiness" of the individual human capital (and its correlation with returns on assets) which, in turn, lead to large differences in the structure of the portfolio of assets. An important corollary is that the savings rate and the share of pay-as-you-go vs. financial assets could also be set as a function of observable individual characteristics. We argue that doing so could improve incentives to enroll and contribute among individuals who today are outside the system by choice either as informal wage employees or high-skilled self-employed (see Perry et al. 2007; Ribe et al. 2012).

Our analysis contributes to two strands of literature. It joins a growing body of research focusing on the impact of labor income on portfolio choice exemplified by, for example, Davis and Willen (2002), Campbell and Viceira (2002), Cocco, Gomes, and Mahenhout (2005), and Gomez, Kotlikoff, and Viceira (2008). Our analysis also links to research about the optimal design of defined contributions funded pension systems such as Bovenber et al. (2007) and Miles and Cerny (2006).

The main findings of our work, which display little sensitivity to the degree of individuals' risk aversion, can be summarized as follows:

(1) The labor income of the average wage earner in Chile (male, private sector, average education) exhibits a rather low degree of volatility and is largely uncorrelated with the returns of risky assets. Consequently, the optimal default portfolio in their retirement account should have a higher exposure to risky assets. The welfare gains from this change are appreciable and the implicit risk is very small, meaning that those who *ex post* suffer with the change could be easily compensated for their losses.

(2) For females and public-sector workers the conclusion is similar but weaker. The welfare gains are, on average, smaller and the number of the *ex post* losers is larger.

(3) Highly educated workers and employers have more volatile income profiles and higher correlation with aggregate stock returns. As a result, the optimal portfolio should be more "conservative" than that provided by the current legislation. This reallocation, however, would generate a large number of *ex post* "losers" (i.e., workers who experience a favorable combination of aggregate and idiosyncratic shocks and may, consequently, regret the prudence embedded in the *ex ante* optimal portfolio). The average gains are also smaller than in the benchmark case (the average wage earner). This then emphasizes the importance of combining default options with information to plan members about the tradeoffs involved when choosing among different portfolios.

The chapter is organized as follows. Our model of optimal life-cycle choices is explained in Section 8.2. The empirical procedures followed by its calibration to the Chilean case are the subject of Section 8.3. The simulation results are presented in Section 8.4. We finish with some conclusions and proposals for further research in Section 8.5. The more technical parts of the chapter are confined to a set of dedicated appendices.[1]

8.2. A Model of Life-Cycle Behavior

We model the "rational" consumption and portfolio allocation of individuals that operate in an uncertain environment. Rationality in this context means that people's preferences are represented by an additively separable utility function (taking absolute consumption as its argument) and that choices are made so as to maximize the expected discounted value of that lifetime utility. More precisely, individuals maximize:

$$U_{t0} = E_{t0}\left[\sum_{i=t0}^{T} \beta^{(i-t0)} S_i \frac{C_i^{1-\eta}}{1-\eta}\right]$$

where time is indexed by age, i, $t0$ is the age of entrance in the labor market, T is the maximum lifespan, β is a pure time discount factor, S_i is the probability of surviving to age i (conditional on surviving to $t0$), C_i is age-i consumption and η is the degree of relative risk aversion (assumed constant). Note that we omit the dependence on calendar time to ease notation.

Each year before retirement (assumed to take place at the exogenous age R), individuals receive labor income in the form of an exogenous and stochastic gross salary Y_i. As is standard, we decompose Y_i into the product of a permanent, P_i, and a transitory, Θ_i, component ($Y_i = P_i\Theta_i$).[2] The transitory income shock is lognormally distributed, with unitary mean and independent of the other sources of uncertainty in the model. The permanent labor income component is obtained as follows:

$$P_{i+1} = \Gamma_{i+1}\Psi_{i+1}P_i$$

where Ψ_i is a mean-one, lognormal shock to permanent income and the deterministic factor Γ_i reproduces the average growth rate of labor earnings at age i.[3] The log of the permanent component, then, is the sum of a persistent shock and a deterministic factor calibrated to reproduce the average profile of life-cycle earnings in the population (which is typically humped shape). The persistent shocks can be correlated with the stochastic return of risky assets in the economy described below (see, for example, Cocco et al. (2005) for a discussion of the use of this particular model of labor income in the literature of life-cycle consumption and portfolio choice).

We also take into account that the *disposable* labor income of the individual differs from the *gross* income due to the outflows derived from two compulsory government programs: the social contributions (to the individual retirement account, IRA, described in the next paragraph), and the general income taxes. For simplicity, the latter takes the form of a pair of constant tax rates, (τ and τ_R), applied, respectively to labor and capital income.

Throughout his life, our representative individual is enrolled with the Public Pension System,[4] which is *fully funded* and *defined contributions*. Each individual pays social contributions into his/her account before retirement, chooses the composition of the portfolio of assets in the account and collects the resulting pension benefit after retirement.[5] The compulsory contributions can be invested in two mutual funds: a riskless one that pays R_f with certainty, and a risky one with stochastic gross real return R. We assume R to take the form of independent lognormal shocks with mean $E[R]$ and variance $\sigma_R^{\ 2}$. We assume that the innovations to R can be correlated with the permanent component of labor income, denoting their covariance by ρ. The proportion of the portfolio allocated to risky assets at age i is represented by ω, and the value of the stock of assets accumulated in the IRA at the same age is represented by Π_i. The annual contribution rate, ς, is invariant during the life of the worker. Note that the accumulation of pension wealth depends on the particular realizations of the gross-income process of the individual *and* (whenever $\omega_i > 0$) on the sequence of aggregate returns of the risky asset:

$$\Pi_{i+1} = \left(R_f + \left(R_{i+1} - R_f\right)\omega_i\right)\Pi_i + \varsigma Y_{i+1}$$

The individual has a second source of liquid income in the principal and interest obtained from the stock of previously accumulated private savings A_{i-1}. *Cash-in-hand* or the total income available for consumption and savings at age i is represented by M_i. It evolves according to the simple budget constraint:

$$M_i = (1 - \tau_R)R_f A_{i-1} + (1 - \tau)\,(1 - \varsigma)Y_i$$

Note that, while M_i represents the funds available at the start of the period, A_i represents the end-of-period stock of assets (i.e., those remaining after the consumption decision have been made, $A_i = M_i -$

C_i). Private liquid savings are assumed to be held in deposit accounts that pay the riskless rate R_f. This strong assumption captures well the observed behaviour of a large part (but by no means all) of the targeted population of this study.

After retirement, the individual problem is substantially simplified. The pension wealth accrued in the IRA is converted into an individual pension benefit, B, according to the norms of the pension system (discussed in Section 8.1). The pension payment takes the form of a constant annuity, computed according to the average survival probabilities of the individual. For married men, the annuity is a joint annuity that provides the surviving widow with a certain percentage of the pension of the male worker. We thus model a deterministic flow of income during the retirement stage.[6]

In this work we do not let the individual take "short" or leveraged positions in any of the two available mutual funds (i.e. we impose $0 \leq \omega_i \leq 1$) and also prevent the individual from borrowing from future income at any age (i.e. the balance of the deposit account should always be positive $A_i \geq 0$). This is especially important after retirement to avoid the risk of dying with outstanding debts.

8.2.1. *Recursive Formulation of the Problem*

As usual in the life-cycle literature, the individual problem is too complex to be solved analytically and we must use recursive computational methods instead. Each period, the state of the individual under study is characterized by the vector $\{i, M, \Pi, P\}$. To solve the model we must express the consumption and portfolio choices as functions of that state vector: $C(i, M, \Pi, P)$, $\omega(i, M, \Pi, P)$. This is achieved by solving the Bellman equation of the problem:[7]

$$(1) \quad V_i(M, \Pi, P) = \max_{\{C,\, \omega\}} u(C) + \beta S_i E\left[V_{i+1}(M', \Pi', P')\right]$$

$$M' = (M - C)(1 - \tau_r)R_f + (1 - \varsigma)(1 - \tau)Y'$$

$$(2) \quad Y' = P'\Theta'$$

$$(3) \quad P' = \Gamma_{i+1}\Psi' P$$

$$(4) \quad \Pi' = \left(R_f + (R' - R_f)\omega\right)\Pi + \varsigma Y'$$

where future variables are denoted with a prime. A discussion of the first order conditions of the problem, the properties of the optimal behavioral rules and the numerical technique employed to solve the model (Carrol 2006 endogenous grid point algorithm) can be found in Appendix B.

8.3. Calibration of the Illustrative Examples

In this section we apply the theoretical life-cycle model of the previous section to the Chilean economy and pension system. The Chilean system of individual pension accounts is one of the most sophisticated in the world (see Appendix B for a description). Among its many features, the system provides its affiliates with age-varying defaults for their asset allocation (see Berstein et al. 2011b). These defaults are followed by almost 70% of the workers enrolled and are already conditional on individual characteristics (the gender of the affiliate). As discussed above, our aim is to explore the convenience of expanding the set of observable characteristics that are explicitly considered when designing default portfolios.

Table 8.1

Parameter Values Used in the Modeled Economic Environment

τ	Income & tax rate	0.22
ς	Contribution rate	0.1
R	Retirement age	65
B_m	Minimum Pension (% average labor income)	0.08
	Asset returns	
$R_f - 1$	Riskless rate (Multifondo E)	5.35
$E[R] - 1$	Mean return of risky assets (Multifondo A)	8.30
σ_R	Standard deviation of risky assets (Multifondo A)	0.209
	Preferences	
η	Risk aversion	5
β	Discount factor	0.98

Source: Own calculations.

We work with a stylized version of the public pension and tax systems and the set of assets available to transfer income across time and states of nature. All our representative individuals operate in the same environment and share a common set of mortality probabilities and preferences over life-cycle consumption and leisure (see Table 8.1 for a summary of the parameters defining institutions and preferences). They only differ in the properties of the stochastic process underlying the dynamics of their labor income. Differences in these processes are important enough to generate a large variation in the set of optimal individual decisions.

Survival probabilities are taken from the Human Mortality Database (2011) and correspond to the year 2000. For preferences, the parameters' values selected for our benchmark case are intended to result in standard life-cycle behaviors. The pure time discount factor, β, is set to reproduce the ratio of private assets to labor income at the age of 60, according to the 2006-wave of the EPS survey.[8] More specifically, we set to the value that generates a median A/Y at 60 close to the median of the private wealth-to-income ratio for workers with average education.[9] As indicated in the bottom rows of Table 8.1, the resulting individual is remarkably patient; he/she discounts the future at a 2% annual rate. The degree of risk aversion, η, was set to a value 5 which is common in simulation analysis of individual portfolio choice.[10] Such a degree of risk aversion is also quite close to values used in the macroeconomics literature (which, typically, assume a slightly higher degree of inter-temporal substitution). In Appendix B, Section C we explore the stability of our main findings to changes in this parameter value.

The characterization of the properties of the life-cycle labor income flows is a centerpiece of the calibration exercise. There is extensive evidence in the economic literature of large differences in the properties of labor income across different groups of individuals. The systematic exploration of the data has been done mainly for developed countries, but there is also a growing literature on developed economies.[11] These countries have, in general, less developed *formal* social protection networks, which can result in larger volatility of labor income and more intra-cohort heterogeneity. For Chile, there have been few systematic attempts to assess the differences in the labor income processes of different social groups. The analysis in Repetto and Huneeus (2005), based on the same ESI data as in our work, may be the most outstanding example.[12] In our analysis we use a broad definition of gross individual income, which includes wages, pensions, government benefits and income from individual business. We also do not limit ourselves to currently employed workers, reflecting in this way the volatility in income induced by unemployment spells. We undertake separate estimations according to three observable characteristics: education (disaggregated in three groups), gender, and type of work defined by sector of occupation (private vs. public) and type of labor relation (wage earners vs. employers or self-employed). We thus have a total of 24 different types of workers. In this section, however, we limit ourselves to only five "representative" cases.

We take as our benchmark a male of average education working in the private sector as a wage earner (see first row in Table 8.2). This is the type of worker most frequently observed in our sample.[13] The second profile is that of is a female counterpart of our benchmark case (referred as "Fml" as indicated in the second row of Table 8.2). The other three profiles involve a highly educated male employee referred as "HighE," the public sector *alter ego* of our benchmark named "Public," and a representative of employers identified as "Emp." We follow standard econometric procedures to estimate the statistical properties of labor income flows for all our representative cases.[14]

Table 8.2

Characterization of the Representative Agent by Gender, Education Type of Contract and Properties of Their Life-Cycle Labor-Income Processes

Short-name	Gender	Educ	Type	Avg	Tran	Perm	Cov
				$\bar{Y}$	$\sigma\theta$	$\sigma\psi$	ρ
Base	Male	Avrg	Wage earner	2.9	0.035	0.040	0.0
Fml	Female	Avrg	Wage earner	2.4	0.073	0.094	0.1
Public	Male	Avrg	Public sector	4.0	0.146	0.039	0.5
HighE	Male	High	Wage earner	9.0	0.077	0.155	0.3
Emp	Male	Avrg	Employer	7.1	0.264	0.051	0.75

Notes: Average, variance of the transitory and permanent components and covariance with the returns of the risky assets.
Source: Own calculations, based on data from Encuesta Suplementaria de Ingresos (ESI).

Figure 8.1

Average Labor Income by Age for Our Five Representative Individuals

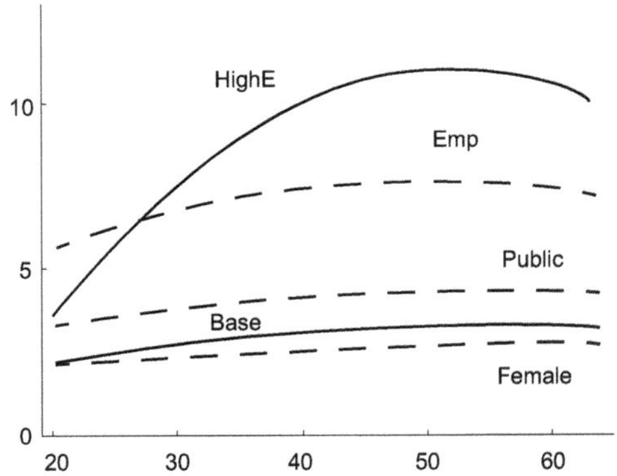

Source: Own calculations, based on ESI data.

Our key findings can be summarized as follows:

(1) The life-cycle profiles of labor income display standard dynamics (see Figure 8.1). All the profiles are "hump-shaped", showing raising incomes early in life that eventually flats out and ultimately declines. There are, however, strong differences in the curvature of the profiles. Highly educated workers have the steepest growing profile when entering the labor market, while all others display a more moderate growth rate. This growth rate becomes negative late in life for the highly educated (in the mid 50s) and somewhat earlier for the rest (typically in the mid forties), although the declines are very mild in most cases. Our female and public workers, in particular, have largely flat income profiles. Regarding average income levels the results are not surprising. Compensation is the highest for highly educated wage earners and employers, followed by public-sector workers, male wage earners with average education and, finally, female wage earners with average education.

(2) We find large differences in the estimated value of the permanent and transitory components of labor income. The permanent component, σ_Ψ, is lower in the case of the public-sector workers and higher in the case of wage earners with high education (see the second and third columns in Table 8.2). As discussed in the previous section and in Appendix B,

σ_ψ is expected to be a fundamental determinant of the individual portfolio choice. It is important to observe the much larger degree of volatility (both temporary and permanent) of females vs. males, and the fact that the large variability of the income of employers seems to be mostly transitory.[15]

(3) As expected, we find the labor income of employers to be strongly correlated with asset returns, which are themselves strongly procyclical (see rightmost column of Table 8.2 where assets refer to "Multifondo" A). Similarly, highly educated workers show a positive correlation, smaller than that of the employers but still larger than that of our base case (both male and female). Public employees have also a positive correlation, which is not surprising, but the level found (0.5) is larger than expected. As with the variance of the permanent component, standard theoretical results (see Appendix A) suggest a strong inverse relation between and the proportion of risky assets in the optimal portfolio, making it another critical component of the portfolio choice.

8.4. Results

This section discusses the results of the calculation of the optimal life-cycle behavior of our representative individuals.[16] We start by describing the optimal portfolio of male wage earners with an average education. Then, we quantify the welfare consequences of following the portfolio default provided by the current pension system rather than the optimal schedule. Finally, we look at the optimal portfolios of our other representative individuals.

8.4.1. *The Benchmark Individual*

Figures 8.2 and 8.3 illustrate the simulation results obtained for the benchmark individual introduced in Section 8.2: a wage earner with average education employed in the private sector. The panel on the left in Figure 8.2 displays the optimal consumption/savings behavior of the agent.

Figure 8.2

Simulation Results for the Benchmark Individual (Wage Earner of Average Education): Life-Cycle Income, Consumption and Savings

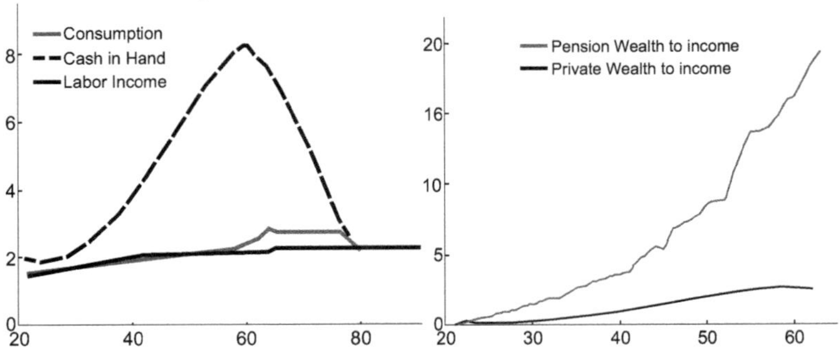

Nores: Median life-cycle consumption, labor income and cash-in-hand (left panel); median ratios of accumulated private and pension (IRA) wealth to income (right panel).
Source: Own calculations.

Figure 8.3

Benchmark Individual Simulation: Portfolio Choice and Distribution of Pension Replacement Rates

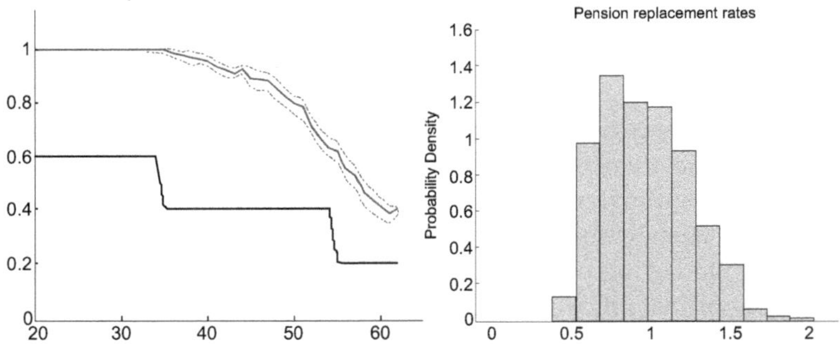

Notes: Left panel: median proportion of risky assets in the IRA account of the benchmark individual (gray continuous line), with bands corresponding to the 5% and 95% percentiles of the distribution of income shocks (gray dotted lines) versus the current institutional default in Chile (black continuous line). Right panel: simulated distribution of pension replacement rates – ratio of the pension benefit to labor income at the age of 64 – under the optimal portfolio rule.
Source: Own calculations.

We observe that consumption is close to income early in life and private assets accumulate at a very slow pace (see right panel). This is the usual response to the upward-sloping profile of net labor income: for precautionary reasons, workers build a relatively small buffer stock of assets very early in life, but their saving rates go subsequently down and stay low until the mid-forties. Serious voluntary savings only materialize in the twenty years immediately preceding retirement, with saving rates increasing progressively until they reach a maximum in the mid-fifties. By the time the worker reaches retirement age, he/she has accumulated around 4 years of net income in private liquid assets. The assets accumulated in the IRA are, at the same age, more than five times larger despite the smaller 10% mandate savings rate, which is the result of a higher compound average interest rate of return. This higher return stems from the inclusion of a large proportion of risky assets in the IRA (see left panel of Figure 8.3). Of course, these higher average returns only come as a compensation for the extra risk incurred, which is apparent in the simulated distribution of the level of the pension obtained upon retirement (see right panel of Figure 8.3). This pension ranges between less than 50% of pre-retirement earnings to 200%.[17] After retirement, individuals are assumed not to take portfolio decisions (all the liquid wealth stays in the deposit account), and run down their accumulated private assets quite rapidly. Eventually, late in their seventies or early in their eighties, they hit a borrowing constraint (they are not allowed to borrow from future pensions) and simply consume their pension benefit thereafter.

The optimal portfolio choice of our benchmark individual (see left panel of Figure 8.3) is characterized by a large share of risky assets early in life, followed by a progressive conversion into the safer bonds offered by Fund E. This decreasing life-cycle pattern of ω is consistent with well known principles of life-cycle portfolio choice when human capital is accounted for.[18] As workers get older, human capital constitutes a diminishing proportion of their total wealth. For our benchmark individual, human capital is an order of magnitude safer than risky assets, meaning that their implicit stock of private wealth tilts naturally towards riskier assets as the individual ages (i.e., the share of the risky asset in the total increases). It follows that, to keep a constant proportion of *total* wealth invested in risky assets, workers must progressively reduce the riskiness of their pension savings with age.

Figure 8.3 also displays the 5% and 95% quantiles of the simulated optimal portfolio choices. They illustrate the range of different outcomes that result from the accumulation of different income and return shocks throughout the working career of our representative individual. The dispersion increases with time, with very little heterogeneity at the onset of the professional life and a more distinctive widening of the upper and lower bounds in the ten years before retirement. Still, the decreasing pattern for ω is evident.

We find a higher proportion of risky asset in the optimal portfolio than in the default portfolio for the average worker.[19] Here we take as the "recommended" benchmark the default proposed by the Chilean authorities for the workers enrolled in the System of "Multifondos" (see Berstein et al. 2011a, p. 4). This benchmark prescribes Fund B as the default option for (male) workers of up to 35 years of age, Fund C for workers between 35 and 55 years, and Fund D for workers older than 56. Given the legal limitations on the assets composition of the different "Multifondos", we can estimate the proportion of risky assets in the pension portfolio by age. This share is plotted as the stepwise decreasing dashed-line in Figure 8.3, starting with a 60% share before the age of 35 and ending with just 20% after age 55. This legal default is appreciably more conservative than our optimal portfolio rule, meaning that there can be welfare gains from moving into riskier default portfolios.

8.4.2. *Welfare Analysis*

To assess the potential gains from a change in the asset allocation default, we compare the utility derived by our representative individuals when they follow the optimal portfolio rule and when they follow the default portfolio.[20] To focus exclusively on the differences stemming from the portfolio choice, we assume the same saving behavior in both cases (i.e. we apply the optimal saving rates to the simulation with the institutional default).

The relevant indicators are the pension replacement rate and the equivalent variation in life-cycle consumption (the standard welfare index used in this literature). For each individual in our simulation sample, the latter is defined as the increase in life-cycle consumption needed to keep the worker indifferent between the current default and the optimal portfolio rule (expressed as a percentage of consumption under the current default, and arranged in such a way that a positive value implies a welfare gain from adopting the optimal rule).[21]

The results for our reference individual are presented in Figure 8.4 and in the top row of Table 8.3. The optimal policy rule is more "aggressive", which naturally leads to larger (average) stocks of pension wealth and, consequently, higher replacement rates. The optimal share of risky assets is, on average, 84% throughout life, going down to 49% after age 55. On average, the accumulated wealth at the age of 65 amounts to almost 22-times current income under the optimal rule, versus around 19-times under the current default. This translates into an average replacement rate of almost 100% under the optimal system versus 87% under the current default. But averages are not enough to assess changes in welfare, given that higher returns come at the expense of additional risk. To check for this, the left panel of Figure 8.4 illustrates the estimated distribution of the replacement rates.[22] The picture is clear: there is some increase in risk, but it is definitely small. The shift in the density function is very close to a "first order stochastic dominance."

Figure 8.4

Optimal vs. Current Portfolio Rules: Pension and Welfare Distributions

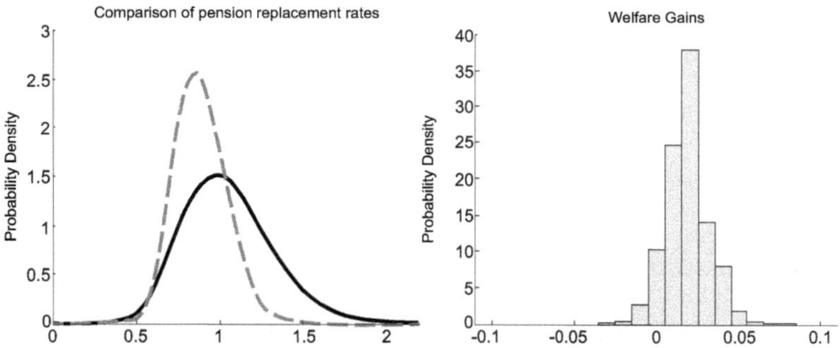

Notes: Left panel: distribution of the pension replacement rates obtained under the current portfolio default (gray, dashed line) versus those with the optimal portfolio rule (black, continuous line) for the benchmark individual; Right panel: Distribution of the welfare changes induced by the change in portfolio default for the benchmark individual.
Source: Own calculations.

The distribution of the formal welfare index (the equivalent variation in consumption) confirms the results obtained with the replacement rate (see right panel of Figure 8.4). On average, the welfare gain is 1.8%, the median gain is 1.7%, and the estimated proportion of welfare losers is 7.2%. The distribution is skewed, with maximum gains (95% quantile) close to 4.5% of annual equivalent consumption and maximum losses (5% quantile) of -0.6%. The order of magnitude of these figures is very close to those found in Cocco et al. (2005) for a similar experiment in the USA. Our interpretation of these results is that, in the absence of changes in the economic environment, a shift from the current default life-cycle portfolio to our proposed optimal portfolio should lead to an appreciable increase in welfare for a vast majority of male wage earners of average education. And, it should be possible to set up a mechanism to compensate the *ex post* losers and, therefore, guarantee an across the board increase in welfare.

Table 8.3

Simulation Results for Each Representative Agent

Name	Gender	Educ	Type	Repl. Rate	Welfare			
					Q5%	Median	Q95%	% losers
Base	Male	Avrg	Wage earner	1.01/0.87	–0,63	1,73	4,45	7,17
Fml	Female	Avrg	Wage earner	1.06/0.92	–1,6	1	6,8	20,7
Public	Male	Avrg	Public sector	1.08/0.93	–1,68	1,56	4,42	10,15
HighE	Male	High	Wage earner	0.93/0.87	–57,6	0,06	37,3	47,19
Emp	Male	Avrg	Employer	0.99/0.98	–42,5	0,34	4,04	42,4

Note: Pension replacement rates (under the optimal vs. current portfolio default) and selected statistics from the distribution of welfare changes induced by the substitution of the optimal for the current portfolio default.
Source: Own calculations.

8.4.3. *Simulation Results for Alternative Types of Individuals*

Shall we recommend the optimal portfolio found in the previous section as a new default for all affiliated workers? In this section we analyze the optimal portfolio choices of the other individual types. The results are reported in Table 8.3 and in Figures 8.5 to 8.8.

8.4.3.1. Female Wage Earners

Female wage earners differ from our base case essentially in that the life-cycle profile of their endowment of human capital is flatter, yields smaller income flows and, more importantly, the volatility of those flows is substantially higher.[23] Our simulation results (Figure 8.5) indicate that these differences do not add up to much in terms of changes in the optimal portfolio composition of their pension wealth. The extra income volatility results in a flatter distribution of the realized replacement rates (see left-bottom panel of Figure 8.5) but the optimal life-cycle portfolio choice is very similar: ω is slightly higher despite the higher volatility and the small positive correlation.[24] Overall, women expose themselves to a little more risk than men (87% vs. 84% on average), but follow an almost identical profile of progressive reductions in the riskiness of their IRAs with age. Individuals *ex post* profiles are, however, more disperse (the upper and lower bands in the graph are slightly more distant).

Figure 8.5

Simulation Results for a Female Wage Earner of Average Education

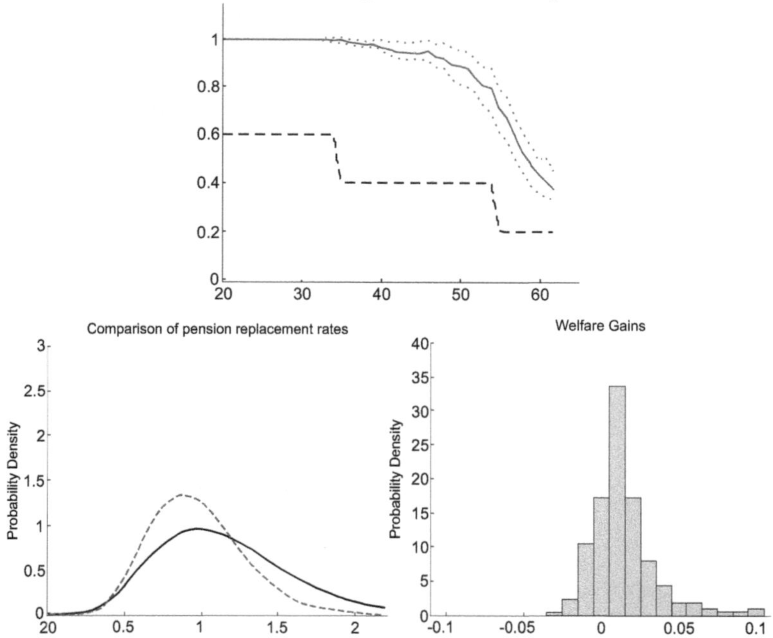

Notes: Top panel: median optimal portfolio choice (gray, continuous line) vs. current institutional default (black, dashed line); Left-bottom panel: distribution of the pension replacement rates obtained under the current portfolio default (black, dashed line) versus those with the optimal portfolio rule (gray, continuous line); Right-bottom panel: Distribution of the welfare changes induced by the change from the current portfolio default to the optimal.

Source: Own calculations.

For the welfare experiment we consider a slightly different benchmark than in the base case. Indeed, the Chilean legislation adjusts the default portfolio on the basis of gender – although the differences are small. Fund C is prescribed for workers between 35 and 50 years (vs. 55 for males) and Fund D for workers older than 51 years of age (vs.

56 for males). The results of the simulations are very similar (see second row of Table 8.3). Changing to the optimal portfolio rule is still welfare improving (1.4% gain on average and 1.0% median gain), but the extra risk of the change is bigger as 20.1% of workers, *ex post*, find themselves worse-off under the optimal rule. Their welfare losses are non-negligible with the 5% lower percentile of the distribution experiencing a 1.6% drop in life-cycle consumption. At the same time, the top 95% of the distribution experiences a 6.8% annual welfare gain. Given the size of the losses, it is no longer obvious that a compensating scheme can be constructed to guarantee uniform welfare gains.

Figure 8.6

Simulation Results for a Public Sector-Wage Earner of Average Education

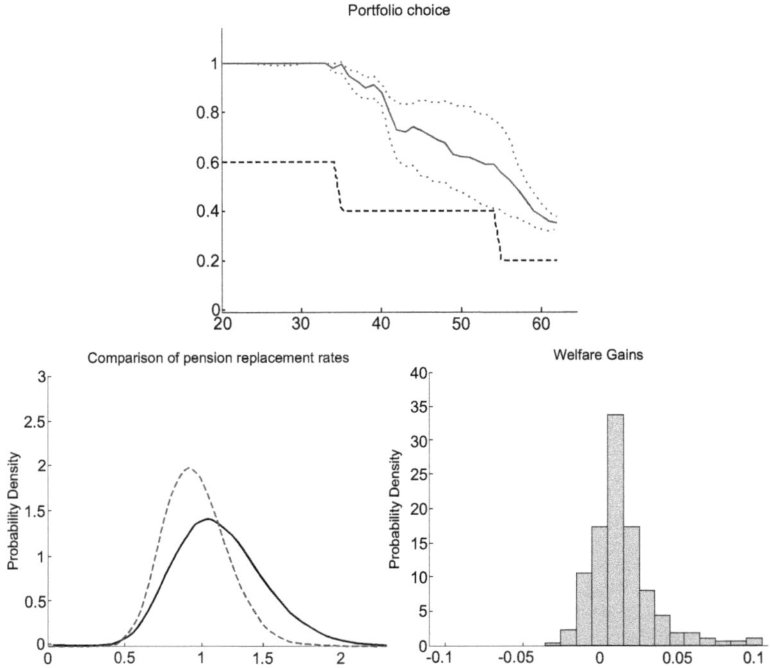

Notes: Top panel: median optimal portfolio choice (gray, continuous line) vs. current institutional default (black, dashed line); Left-bottom panel: distribution of the pension replacement rates obtained under the current portfolio default (gray, dashed line) versus those with the optimal portfolio rule (black, continuous line); Right-bottom panel: Distribution of the welfare changes induced by the change from the current portfolio default to the optimal.

Source: Own calculations.

8.4.3.2. Public Workers

Workers employed in the public sectors are also potential candidates for a different portfolio default. On the one hand, the stochastic properties of their labor income suggest the need for a more prudent portfolio composition: their income shocks display a higher permanent volatility and show an appreciable degree of synchronicity with the shocks on asset returns. But, on the other hand, they hold a substantially bigger stock of human capital, which can act as a cushion for unfavorable investment returns. In the end, our simulations (reported in the third row of Table 8.3 and in Figure 8.6) indicate that the first factor predominates, leading to a smaller average exposure to risky assets (78% versus 84% in the benchmark). Notwithstanding, the life-cycle profile of the optimal ω is very similar to that in the benchmark case. The main differences appear in later ages, as a result from a higher volatility of income (and a higher correlation with risky returns). Thus, there are important differences in the speed of risk reduction after the age of 40.

In terms of welfare, the results fall in between the base case and the case of females studied above. The average welfare results are positive (1.6% gain both in median and average annual consumption), but there is more risk than in the benchmark (10.1% of losers and a 1.7% loss for the 5% percentile).

Figure 8.7

Simulation Results for a Male Wage Earner of High Education

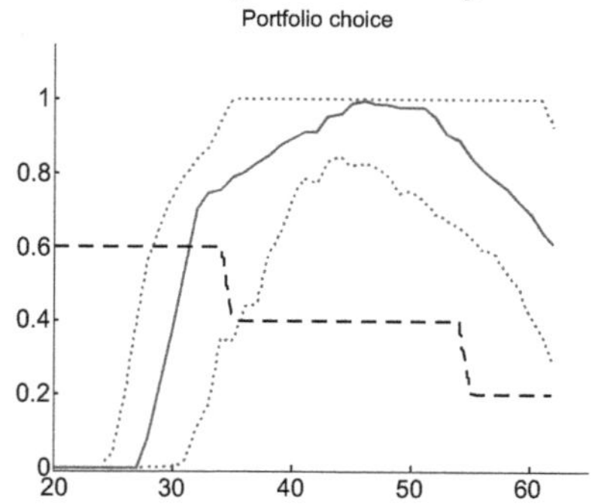

Figure 8.7 (continued)
Simulation Results for a Male Wage Earner of High Education

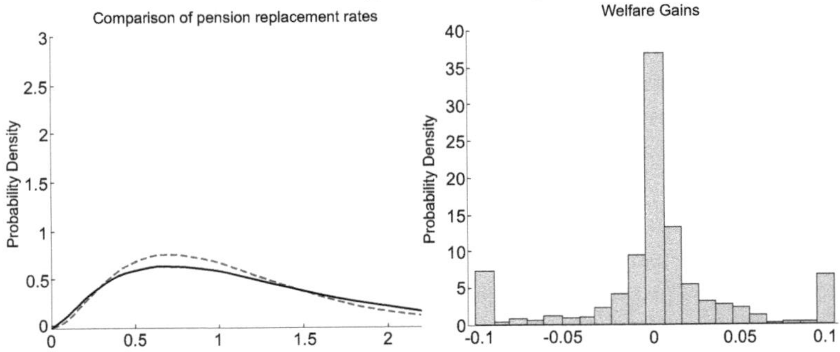

Notes: Top panel: median optimal portfolio choice (gray, continuous line) vs. current institutional default (black, dashed line); Left-bottom panel: distribution of the pension replacement rates obtained under the current portfolio default (gray, dashed line) versus those with the optimal portfolio rule (black, continuous line); Right-bottom panel: Distribution of the welfare changes induced by the change from the current portfolio default to the optimal.
Source: Own calculations.

8.4.3.3. High Education

Our simulations show large differences between the optimal and the default portfolio for male wage earners of high education (see fourth row of Table 8.3 and in Figure 8.7). This is not surprising, given how different these workers are with respect to our benchmark individual. The volatility of the permanent shocks is almost four times bigger and is correlated with shocks on aggregate returns. These two features clearly demand a more "conservative" portfolio allocation – although the allocation also depends on the relative proportion of human and financial wealth, and on the average age-profile of labor income (Figure 8.1). Overall, our simulations suggest much less exposure to the risky asset. The average proportion of stocks is only 64% and the optimal life-cycle profile is hump-shaped, indicating that individuals should only start investing in stocks after almost one decade of professional activity. Then ω goes progressively up reaching nearly full exposure in the mid-40s (the average weight between ages 35 and 55 is 92%). Afterwards, the share of risky assets is similar to that in the base case: a marked reduction that leaves the average between ages 56 and 64 at 75%. The visual comparison of the distributions of replacement rates obtained under the current default vs. the optimal portfolio helps to explain the essence of the results. In sharp contrast to the benchmark case, our "safety-first" optimal rule can deliver smaller final pensions in a significant number of cases (the probability mass is redistributed both to the right and to the left of the mode under the current default). The welfare gains of following our optimal portfolio are also smaller, with an average gain of 0.91% of annual consumption and a median gain only slightly positive (0.06%). Some people gain a great deal – the 95% percentile of the welfare distribution displays a staggering 37.7% increase in lifetime consumptions. But the losses in the opposite case (i.e., the potential gains that are missed due to the lower exposure to risk) are even higher at 57.6%. The proportion of individuals that do not benefit from the optimal portfolio (47.2%) is also much higher than in the base case. We can only conclude that the application of the optimal rule may generate a lot of *ex post* acrimony.

Figure 8.8

Simulation Results for an Employer of Average Education

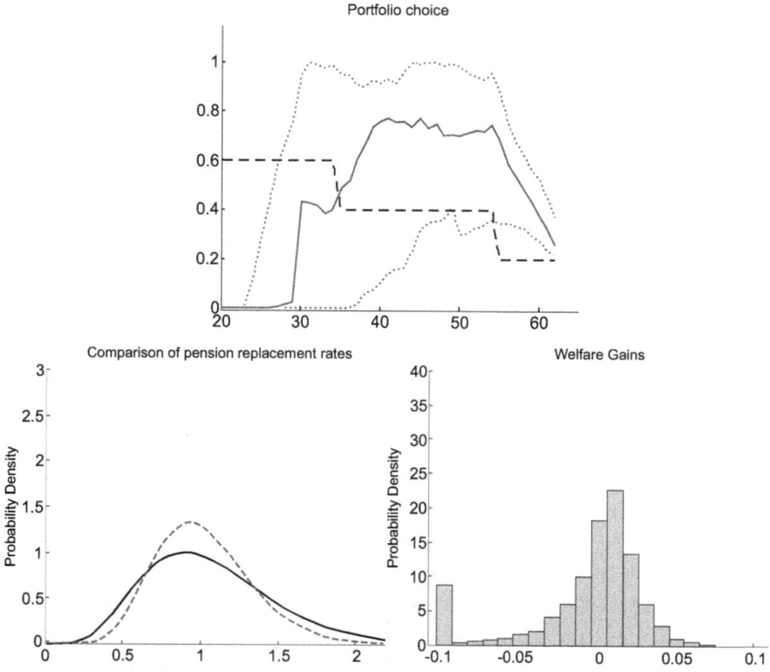

Notes: Top panel: median optimal portfolio choice (gray, continuous line) vs. current institutional default (black, dashed line); Left-bottom panel: distribution of the pension replacement rates obtained under the current portfolio default (gray, dashed line) versus those with the optimal portfolio rule (black, continuous line); Right-bottom panel: Distribution of the welfare changes induced by the change from the current portfolio default to the optimal.
Source: Own calculations.

8.4.3.4. Employers

We conclude our analysis with the exploration of the optimal default for Employers. As with highly educated workers, our *a priori* would have favored a very conservative portfolio, given the extremely high correlation between return shocks and their idiosyncratic income shocks. Only the relatively small volatility of their permanent income shocks would temper this conjecture. The simulated results (displayed in Figure 8.8 and in the bottom row of Table 8.3) clearly confirm our intuition. The optimal average exposure to risky assets is only 46% and, as with the highly educated workers, it is hump-shaped and concentrated in the age interval 35 to 50. Quantitatively, our optimal portfolio allocation is safer in this case, although there is a huge difference between the 5% and 95% band (see Figure 8.8). Overall, all the same issues discussed for highly educated workers reappear in this case. The shift towards more extreme replacement rates is more acute in this case (left-down panel of Figure 8.8). The median welfare gain is somewhat bigger, but still very small (0.34% increase in lifetime consumption). The proportion of losers is high (42.4%) and the welfare losses are also very substantial (the 5% percentile of the distribution of welfare changes by -42.5%). The maximum welfare gains derived from the extra protection against excessive risk taking are smaller in this case (slightly above 4%). The application of this rule would also result in *ex post* regrets.

8.5. Conclusions

Our research is a contribution to the analysis of optimal portfolios in mandatory pension systems. We show how the current default rules for portfolio allocation in Chile can be improved in an *ex ante* way by taking into account observable individual characteristics that affect labor income. Based on these observable characteristics, we develop a set of new rules for the life-cycle allocation of pension wealth that, on average, results in a higher *expected* welfare than that obtained by following the current defaults. Depending on the characteristics of the individual, our conditional rules can prescribe both higher exposure to risky assets (as in the case of male wage earners of average education) and lower exposure (as in the case of employers).

The policy implications are important. The results suggest that, beyond default portfolios for financial assets, governments should consider observable workers characteristics (age, gender, education, occupation) when defining the level of the contribution rate to the pension system, and the share allocated to pay-as-you-go vs. financial assets. We argue that doing so could not only increase welfare, but also improve incentives to enroll and contribute among individuals who today are outside the system by choice, either working as informal wage earners on self-employed.

At this stage, however, two important caveats should be remembered for the real-world applicability of our methods. First, it must be clearly understood that the optimal rules are a guarantee of improvement in only an *ex ante* way. It is always the case that, *ex post*, some individuals would have found themselves in a better situation under the current portfolio default. For instance, our optimal rule stipulates a less risky default portfolio for employers than the actual "one-size-fits-all" default allocation. This leads to welfare improvements for this group *on average*, but there are always combinations of idiosyncratic and aggregate shocks under which a more "aggressive" portfolio would have performed better. Our simulations indicate that the proportion of individuals that fall in this situation can be large for some type of workers. This, of course, does not invalidate our conclusions, but emphasizes the idea that further research on how to compensate *ex post* losers is needed.

A second, more technical, caveat results from how we construct the optimal portfolio rule. Note that we do not propose an automatic modification of the proportion invested in risky stocks with the age of the individual (as with, for example, the *Target-date-Funds* offered by default by US employers). Our optimal portfolio is a function, at each age, of the current realization of the stochastic labor income and of the current values of the stocks of accumulated private and pension wealth. With our rules, similar workers (in terms of age, education, gender and type of contract) get different advice for their portfolio choice depending on their present and past record of labor income shocks. In the real world, private wealth and the permanent component of income shocks can only be observed by the policy-maker approximately (e.g. within brackets and with measurement error). This would reduce the gains from the application of the optimal rule. Our results should, therefore, be taken as upper bounds on the gains that can be feasibly expected in a real world reform.

We conclude the analysis with some suggestions for improvements and future research. An important step forward to complete the current analysis (applied to some selected groups of workers) would be to develop a nationwide welfare evaluation of the outcome of our experiment. This can be done by taking a partition of our representative sample, evaluating the distribution of welfare gains for each group in the partition and aggregating the results (weighted by the population share of each group). A second promising line of research would focus on exploring feasible *ex post* compensation mechanisms for the workers that experience welfare losses from the change in the default rules. Improving the quality of the key empirical inputs (probably by incorporating more information from other databases) is another avenue for improving the robustness and relevance of the results of our experiments in the future.

Appendix A: The Details of the Model

A Labor Income, Asset Allocation and Portfolio Defaults

This section provides a rather informal review of the key principle underlying our calculations in this chapter: that differences in the properties of labor income would lead to different portfolio choices over the life cycle. We resort to well-known expressions of optimal portfolio choices to highlight the links between asset allocation and human capital.

It is very well established that the age of a person is an irrelevant factor for the portfolio choice of an investor who only possess financial wealth.[25] His/her asset allocation (summarized in the proportion of risky assets ω) will be identical to that of a short-term investor, known from the classical Markovitz mean/variance analysis:

$$\omega = \frac{E_t r_{t+1} - r^f_{t+1} + \frac{1}{2}\sigma^2}{\eta\sigma^2} \tag{1}$$

where we assume log-normal returns to the risky asset $r_{t+1} = Ln(1 + R_{t+1})$ and $r^f_{t+1} = Ln(1 + R^f_{t+1})$, constant variances and a constant degree of relative risk aversion, η, on the part of the investor. In this case, all investors should hold the same combination of risky assets, independently of age. This finding is, however, largely irrelevant for individual investors because human wealth is the most important form of wealth available during large parts of the individual life.[26] Actually, for a large majority of the population, it is *the only* form of wealth available early in life (the exception being people with large inheritances). If the stream of future labor income where riskless, the resulting portfolio choice is still quite straightforward. The optimal portfolio share of risky stocks on the individual's financial wealth should be:

$$\omega = \frac{E_t r_{t+1} - r^f_{t+1} + \frac{\sigma^2}{2}}{\eta\sigma^2}\left(1 + \frac{H_t}{A_t}\right) \tag{2}$$

with H_t standing for the value of the stock of human wealth and A_t representing the stock of financial wealth. The fundamental conclusion from a life-cycle perspective is that ω *should decline along* the working career of a typical individual (as H_t is progressively exhausted (in absolute terms) and also because of the drop in the relative weight of human vs. financial wealth derived from savings and the accumulation of retirement wealth. It is also evident from (2) that workers with different endowments of human capital may follow different portfolio rules along their life.

To complete the analysis we must acknowledge the uncertain nature of labor income.[27] We cannot get a closed-form expression in the most general case, but the basic intuitions can be derived in a two-period model with log-normal shocks to income and asset returns.[28] In this context the optimal risky assets weight is:

$$\omega = \left(\frac{1}{\phi}\,\frac{E_t r_{t+1} - r^f_{t+1} + \frac{\sigma^2}{2}}{\gamma\sigma^2}\right) + \left(1 - \frac{1}{\phi}\right)\frac{\sigma_y \rho}{\sigma} \tag{3}$$

where σ_y is the variance of the labor income shocks, ρ is the correlation with return shocks and ϕ is the elasticity of consumption with respect to financial wealth.[29] The first term is the usual solution for a short-run investor, now inversely weighted by the wealth-elasticity of consumption. The second component is an income hedging component. If $\rho < 0$ the risky asset offers a good hedge against negative income shocks, leading to a larger optimal allocation (and the opposite if the correlation is positive).

The properties of labor income are, then, of paramount important for asset allocation. As before, ω should systematically change with age according to how quickly human capital is exhausted. Furthermore, workers with very volatile labor incomes (large σ_y) and workers whose income is highly synchronized with the returns of the risky assets (large ρ) should have far more "conservative" portfolio allocation than otherwise.

B Life-Cycle Problem

This section provides a more detailed description of the formulation, theoretical solutions and numerical simulation of our model of rational life-cycle behavior.

B1 Bellman Equation (Active Worker)

The recursive version of the individual problem presented in section 8.1 has the key property that its associated value function is homogeneous with respect to the permanent component of labor income, P. As a result, a new equivalent problem with one less state variable can be formulated by expressing all variables as ratios to P. The recovery of the original variables from the transformed ones (denoted by lower case letters) is straightforward (eg. $M{=}mP$, $\Pi{=}\pi P$, and so on). Similarly, the original value function is obtained from the value function of the transformed problem, $v_i\,(m,\pi)$, after a direct transformation: $V(i,M,\Pi,P) = \Gamma^{1-\eta}\; v_i\;(m,\pi)$. The problem that is effectively solved with our numerical procedure is as follows:

$$v_i(m,\pi) = \max_{\{c,\omega\}} \{u(c) + \beta_{i+1}E_i[(\Gamma_{i+1}\Psi')^{1-\eta}v_{i+1}(m',\pi')]\}$$

$$a = m - c$$

$$m' = aR'_f + \varsigma\Theta'$$

$$R' = \frac{R^f + e'\omega}{\Gamma_{i+1}\Psi'}$$

$$R'_f = \frac{R^f}{\Gamma_{i+1}\Psi'}$$

where the discount factor $\beta_i = \beta S_i$ and we denote the excess return $e = R - R^f$. The expectation operator E reflects labor and returns uncertainty.

B2 *Theoretical Solutions*

Rational behavior is summarized in the first order conditions necessary conditions emerging from the problem above:

Optimal consumption at age i:

$$u'(c_i) = \beta_i E_i \left[\frac{R^f}{(\Gamma_{i+1}\Psi_{i+1})^\eta} \frac{dv_{i+1}}{dm} (m_{i+1}, \pi_{i+1}) \right]$$

which, applying a standard envelop theorem, leads to:

$$u'(c_i) = \beta_i R^f E_i \left[u'\left(\Gamma_{i+1}\Psi_{i+1} c^*_{i+1}(m_{i+1}, \pi_{i+1}) \right) \right]$$

where c^*_{i+1} is the optimal consumption function available from the immediately preceding iteration.

Optimal portfolio choice

$$0 = \beta_i E_i \left[\left(\frac{e_{i+1}}{(\Gamma_{i+1}\Psi_{i+1})^\eta} \right) \frac{dv_{i+1}}{d\pi} (m_{i+1}, \pi_{i+1}) \right]$$

where the derivative of the value function with respect to the IRA balance is also obtained via an envelop theorem:

$$\frac{dv_i}{d\pi}(m_i, \pi_i) = \beta_i E_i \left[\left(\frac{R^f + e_{i+1}\omega^*_{i+1}}{(\Gamma_{i+1}\Psi_{i+1})^\eta} \right) \frac{dv_{i+1}}{d\pi} (m_{i+1}, \pi_{i+1}) \right]$$

Note that, in order to solve this problem, the next-period functions ω^*_{i+1} and $\frac{dv_{i+1}}{d\pi}(m, \pi)$ should be available from a preceding iteration.

B3 *Numerical Solution Method*

The model is solved using the method of "endogenous grid point" developed by C. Carroll (see, for instance Carrol 2006). The method is a set of procedures for solving dynamic stochastic optimization problems intended to provide highly accurate solutions with large savings in the computational burden implied by more traditional techniques. Although the methods involves several choices (like the particular discrete approximation techniques used for numerical integration or the use of linear interpolation for the approximation of functions outside the solution grid), its key ingredient is the avoidance of root-finding algorithms in the solution of the first order conditions of the problem. This is achieved by solving the problem on an exogenous set of values for the end-of-period savings, rather than for the cash-on-hand (m) state variable. The values of m are recovered endogenously as a product of the solution method.

B4 Properties of the Solutions

Figure 8.9

Optimal Portfolio Choice as a Function of Cash in Hand for Three Level of Accumulated Pension Rights

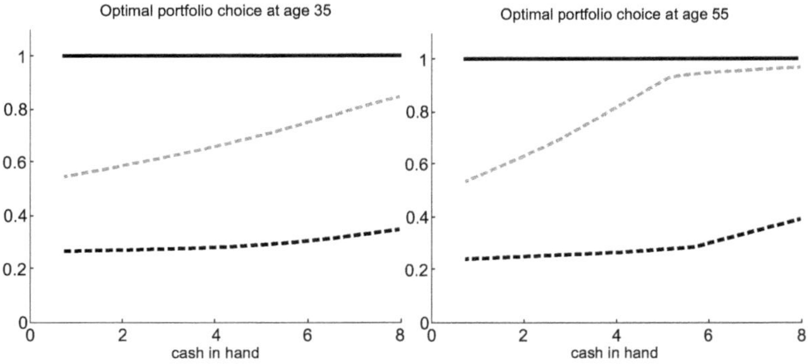

Note: Low (black continuous line); average (gray dotted line) and high (black dotted line).

Source: Own calculations.

Figure 8.10

Optimal Consumption Choice as a Function of Cash in Hand for Three Level of Accumulated Pension Rights

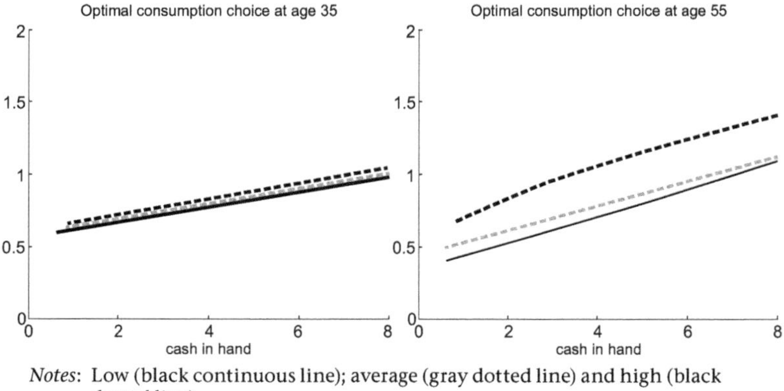

Notes: Low (black continuous line); average (gray dotted line) and high (black dotted line).

Source: Own calculations.

Figures 8.9 and 8.10 illustrate some of the basic properties of the optimal behavioral rules of our problem (for our benchmark calibration). The optimal portfolio choice as a function of the amount of liquid resources available (cash in hand) is illustrated in Figure 8.9 at two different ages and for three levels of accumulated pension wealth. The proportion of risky assets in the optimal portfolio is increasing in the size of liquid resources available (or constant if the individual is constraint at the corner with a 100% allocation to stocks). Ceteris-paribus, the exposure to risky assets tends to decrease with the size of accumulated pension assets and to be smaller later in life. Extremely risky portfolio choices are, therefore, optimal early in life or for workers with small pension assets (which means that only a small proportion of total wealth is at risk with those bets).

Figure 8.10 displays the optimal consumption decisions of our benchmark agent, arranged in a similar way as with portfolio choices. In accordance with the standard theory, our simulations uncover consumption functions that are, ceteris paribus, increasing in cash in hand and the level of pension wealth. Note how liquidity considerations are more important early in life (optimal consumption varies with cash in hand but is roughly constant with pension assets), while pension wealth takes a more prominent role as retirement approaches.

C *Sensitivity Analysis*

Our simulations assume specific values for some of the unobservable preference parameters of the model. To test the robustness of our findings, we have repeated the experiments under an alternative set of preference parameters. The results in the three most critical dimensions (degree of risk aversion, degree of time discounting of future events and intensity of the preference for leisure – revealed by an early retirement decision) are displayed in Table 8.4. To simplify the comparison, the table also reproduces the results for our benchmark simulation. It emerges that, although there are some appreciable numerical differences, the main findings of the chapter seem robust to the particular value assumed for these unobservable parameters.

Table 8.4
Sensitivity Analysis

Name	Gender	Educ	Type	Rep Rate	Welfare Avr	Q5%	Median	Q95%	% losers
				Base					
Base	Male	Avrg	Wage E	1.01/0.87	1,82	–0,63	1,73	4,45	7,17
HighE	Male	High	Wage E	0.93/0.87	0,91	–57,6	0,06	37,3	47,19
				Extreme risk aversion					
Base	Male	Avrg	Wage E	0.95/0.87	2,5	–0,58	1,17	14,4	12,1
HighE	Male	High	Wage E	0.79/0.87	1,2	–73,1	–0,11	7	72,5
				Impatient individuals					
Base	Male	Avrg	Wage E	0.99/0.87	0,11	–0,13	0,1	0,37	10,1
HighE	Male	High	Wage E	0.74/0.87	0,63	–1,9	–0,57	0,43	73,6
				Early Retirement					
Base	Male	Avrg	Wage E	0.91/0.79	2,52	–2,64	2,56	7,25	12,9
HighE	Male	High	Wage E	0.84/0.79	5,32	–59,1	0,14	151	45,8

Notes: Simulation results for the benchmark individual with high risk aversion ($\eta=8$), high discount factor ($\beta=0.9$) (welfare figures multiplied by 100) and early retirement at 60. As with Table 8.3, we reproduce the pension replacement rates (under the optimal vs. current portfolio default) and selected statistics from the distribution of welfare changes induced by the substitution of the optimal for the current portfolio default.
Source: Own calculations.

Appendix B: The Chilean Pension System

The public sector exerts a very large influence on individual savings decisions in Chile through the regulation of its pension system. Consequently, we pay special attention to reproduce the most fundamental features of this important public/private set of institutions. The core of the system is a set of privately managed individual accounts that operates under the *defined-contribution* principle (ie. participants bear the risk of poor performance of their retirement investments). The system is, however, strongly regulated by the public sector, who also provides a guaranteed minimum pension to all participants.[30] It follows a review of the main characteristics of the system (as they have been reproduced in our model of Section 8.2). A summary of the values selected for the most important parameters of the model is provided in Table 8.1.

A Retirement Accounts, Portfolio Choice, and Portfolio Defaults

The system is based on mandatory individual retirement accounts (IRAs) managed by private providers (Administradoras de Fondos de Pensiones, AFP). Registered individuals contribute 10% of their gross labor income to their retirement accounts and pay a 1.5% commission to the AFP for the management of the account.[31] They also pay a 1.5% contribution charge to finance the invalidity and survival's pensions provided by the system. Finally, individuals pay another 7% of their income to finance the health system, but we model that contribution as part of the general income tax.

Individuals can choose the proportion of risky assets in their retirement accounts. Since 2002 all AFP offer their affiliates a choice among five funds ("Multifondos") featuring clearly different asset compositions (i.e. risk/return profiles). The funds are identified by a capital letter and arranged according to their riskiness in a decreasing order: A's funds are mostly invested in variable-income while funds in E are invested almost entirely in fixed income products; Statistical information on the historical composition of each "Multifondo" can be found in page 15 of Berstein et al. (2011a).[32]

By default, workers are assigned a "Multifondo" (referred simply as a "Fund" in the text) conditional on age and gender. Fund B is selected for both men and women up to 35 years of age; Fund C is selected for men between 36 and 55 and for women between 36 and 50. Finally, Fund D is the default for men aged 56 and older and for women of 51 years of age or older. Effectively, these restrictions implement a life-cycle portfolio choice characterized by a decreasing proportion of risky assets (starting at 60% and ending at 20%, given the composition of Funds B/D). This pattern is similar to that provided by the "Target-date funds" or "life-cycle" funds normally offered by the private asset-management industry (see, for example, Bodie and Treussard (2007)). In Section 8.3 we discuss the convenience of adjusting these defaults according to other observable characteristics of the enrolled workers.

B Pension Benefits and Retirement Age

The legal retirement age is 65 for men (60 for women), although earlier retirement is possible for workers with large enough accrued pension assets. Actually, early retirement was the most popular option before the 2004 reform (see, for example, Estelle et al. (2005)). The conditions for early retirement, however, became considerably more restrictive after 2004 and we focus on the case of workers who retire at the age of 65 in our simulations (checking the robustness of our findings to this assumption in Appendix A, Section C, devoted to sensitivity analysis). Retirement from the labor force and the claim of the pension benefit are assumed to take place simultaneously at the legal retirement age.

The initial value of the individual pension benefit depends on the amount of funds contributed to the IRA during the life-cycle and the history of returns achieved (by the combination of Funds selected during the working ages). In reality, workers can withdraw their funds in three alternative ways: as programmed withdrawals, by conversion to a constant annuity or through a mixture of both mechanisms. The annuitization option is the most popular and we take it as our base case. In our model, we implement a simplified version of the pension formula used by insurance companies to determine the value of the annuity payout. Given a IRA balance at retirement of Π, the (age-dependent) old-age and survival pension $\overline{B_i}$ is set such that:

$$\Pi = E_R \left[\sum_{i=R}^{T} \left(\frac{1}{R^f} \right)^{i-R} \overline{B_i} \right]$$

where $E_R[.]$ stands for the expected value, at the age of retirement, of the sum in brackets, given a set of survival probabilities for husband and wife. For married men (or spouses with dependent children) $\overline{B}$ represents a joint annuity that secures 60% of the husband annuity, B, to the surviving widow (i.e, $\overline{B_i}$=$S_i B + (1 - S_i) S_i^f\ 0.6\ B$).[33]

C *Minimum and Maximum Pensions*

We reproduce the system of minimum pensions resulting after the 2008 overhaul of the preexisting safety nets. The most outstanding impact of the reform was a large increase in non-contributive pensions with the introduction of the Basic Solidarity Pension. In accordance with our focus on the behavior of affiliates to the AFP system, we model the details of the APS (*Aporte Previsional Solidario*) benefit, in particular the top up of the contributive pension of retirees age 65 or older to an annually legislated maximum (called PMAS).[34] The value of the PMAS benefit has seen successive increases as the new program was progressively phased in since 2008 (see AFP (2012)). In our simulations we calibrate to the value projected for 2011 (255.000

pesos or 8% of the average wage in 2008 according to the ESI data described below). We also model a maximum pension benefit, resulting from the existence of a legal ceiling on the amounts that can be paid into the retirement account. This upper constraint in the size of benefits is rarely binding in our simulations with representative cases.

D *Pension Assets Risk and Returns*

We simplify the real institutional structure of the system of Multifondos by assimilating the properties of the risky asset in our model to the historical performance of Fund A. Consequently, we calibrate $E[R]$ and σ_R^2 to the mean and variance of the annual real returns estimated from the monthly data available from *Superintendencia de Pensiones* (covering the period from the end of 2002 to the beginning of 2011).[35] In a similar fashion, the riskless rate of interest is assimilated to the return of Fund E. The resulting parameter values are displayed in Table 8.1.

The second leg of our representation of public institutions is the fiscal system. Here we really cut to the very basics of the system. We consider two constant tax rates: an 18% rate levied on capital income (inspired in the rate imposed on business profits) and a 25% rate applied to labor income (including the 7% contribution rate to the health system and the 1.5% collected for invalidity pensions). Social contributions are exempted on the tax base of the income tax.

Notes

1 Appendix A explores the link between labor income and portfolio choice, reviews the details of the life-cycle model and present a sensitivity analysis. Appendix 2 provides a brief overview of the Chilean pension system and its calibration for our numerical experiment.

2 We follow the notation in Carroll (2012).

3 Formally, we assume $Log\,\Theta{\sim}N(-\sigma_{\theta}^{2}/2,\sigma_{\theta}^{2})$ and $Log\,\Psi{\sim}N(-\sigma_{\Psi}^{2}/2,\sigma_{\Psi}^{2})$. These assumptions guarantee that $E(\Theta)=1$ and $E(\Psi)=1$, implying that the average growth rate of the process is set by Γ_{i}.

4 As mentioned in Section 8.1, we do not consider the (serious) issue of non participation in the pension system in this chapter.

5 Note that the individual is not allowed to withdraw funds from his/her pension account until retirement, even in presence of unfavorable labor income shocks. For simplicity, we assume that the claim of the pension and the retirement from the labor force take place at the same time.

6 Health shocks are a potential source of variability in (net) income at advanced ages, but we do not include them is this study. We also abstract from the existence of a bequest motive for saving in our representative individuals.

7 Our formulation has the advantage that the *value function* is homogeneous with respect to the permanent income P. As a result, the Bellman equation can be reformulated with all variables expressed as ratios to the current value of the permanent shock, P. This reduces the dimension of the problem, making the transformed problem significantly easier to solve. See Appendix B for more details.

8 The EPS (Encuesta de Protección Social) is a biannual longitudinal survey conducted by Universidad de Chile.

9 The median value of the ratio is approximately 3.7. The median private wealth (including liquid financial wealth, voluntary retirement savings and housing assets) is 12 million pesos; the average labor income is 3.2 millions.

10 See, for example, Campbell and Viceira (2002) and Gomez, Kotlikoff, and Viceira (2008). In Cocco, Gomes, and Mahenhout, the benchmark value is 10, but a simulation with our less extreme value is also provided.

11 See, for example, Davis and Willen (2002) for the USA. In this country, the PSID (Panel Study of Income Dynamics) has provided the foundations for a large number of life-cycle analysis like Storesletten, Telmer, and Yaron (2004) or Campbell et al. (2001) (or the references therein).

12 ESI (Encuesta Suplementaria de Ingresos) is a supplement to the annual Labor Survey organized by INE, the Chilean national statistics institute. It is a rotatory panel, with households staying in the sample for a maximum of 6 quarters. The sample is nationwide representative, with a sample size close to fifty thousand observations per annum. We use the information corresponding to years 2001 to 2009.

13 To guarantee an accurate estimation of the statistical properties of their labor income, we only work with type of workers that are well represented in our estimation sample.

14 The predicted component of life-cycle income is estimated by running regressions of the log of gross annual income on a quadratic polynomial. We use the residuals from these regressions to estimate the variance decomposition following the methodology in Carroll and Sanwick (1997). In summary, it proceeds in two steps: First, we compute the variance of the differences in incomes residuals separated d periods, $Var(\hat{y}_{t+d} - \hat{y}_{t})$. The permanent/transitory components are then subsequently recovered by using that $Var(\hat{y}_{t+d} - \hat{y}_{t}) = d\sigma_{P}^{2} + 2\sigma_{T^{-}2}$. The correlation of labor income shocks and stock returns is estimated following a very similar approach (see page 208 in Campbell and Viceira (2002)): we construct the excess returns of the risky asset by computing the average annual return enjoyed by "Multifondo" A in the interval 2000/2011 (obtained from the daily data provided

by Superintendencia de AFP). ρ is then obtained from an OLS regression of the annual cross-section averages on the constructed excess returns.

15 Exploring these rough stylized facts in more detail is an important aspect that we leave for future research.

16 In the simulation, we generate one particular time-series of the returns of the risky asset (following the stochastic process described in Section 8.8. This realization covers the entire professional life of each of the individuals of our simulation sample (a cohort of 500 *ex ante* identical individuals). We then simulate time series of permanent shocks for each of the individuals in our artificial sample, reflecting the (type-specific) correlations between permanent shocks and asset returns. Finally we generate independent life-cycle profiles of transitory income shocks for each of the individuals. We let workers react optimally to their specific shocks and store their resulting life-cycle paths of consumption, portfolio choices and stocks of private and public (IRA) wealth. This process is repeated 25 times in different aggregate scenarios (i.e. with different realizations of the common time-series of the returns of the risky asset). In what follows we report medians across individuals and across aggregate scenarios of the different statistics of interest (like optimal portfolios or welfare changes induced by policy changes).

17 To interpret these high replacement rates, recall that we are simulating workers that are permanently enrolled with the pension system.

18 They are reviewed in Section A of Appendix 1.

19 And, also higher that the proportion currently observed in the EPS data.

20 Berstein et al. (2011b) show that the institutional default weights have a very strong impact of the observed real-world behavior.

21 Formally, for each individual we compute the level of consumption that, if maintained constant throughout his/her life, results in the same expected utility level as that obtained in the simulation. These "certainty-equivalent" consumption levels are computed under the two portfolio rules considered (the current default and our optimal rule), resulting in the utility indexes $\overline{c_d}$ and $\overline{c_o}$ respectively. The welfare index is, simply, $\overline{c_o}/\overline{c_d} - 1$. See, for example, the appendix in Cocco et al. (2005) for a more complete description of this standard welfare metric.

22 We fit by maximum likelihood a gamma distribution to the simulated replacement rates. The plot displays the probability density functions of the resulting model.

23 Note that differences by gender in life expectancy are not reflected in this simulation.

24 This is slightly puzzling as the stock of human capital is, on average, also smaller and stronger precautionary savings should result in a smaller H/A ratio than their male counterparts. Note, however, that in this model the risky stock of wealth is confined to the retirement account, which is accumulated at a constant rate (leading to a smaller stock of "financial" wealth than males). Besides, note that the differences in the timing of the income flows (i.e. the slope of the life-cycle profile of income) also matters for the timing of the portfolio choice.

25 This is the classical result of Merton (1971), which assumes constant relative risk aversion and an environment characterized by constant investment opportunities.

26 The formula is still valid in a context of complete markets where investors can capitalize human wealth and hedge its risk (as shown in, again, Merton (1971)). This is obviously not the case in real world markets.

27 Due to both idiosyncratic and aggregate shocks, that can be permanent or transitory and that may be correlated with other sources of uncertainty.

28 See chapter 6 in Campbell and Viceira (2002) for a summary of the model and detail references.

29 The optimal consumption function is this context is

$$c_{t+1} = k + \phi\,(a_t + r_{t+1}) + (1-\phi)y_{t+1}$$

$$\phi = e^{\overline{a}_{t+1}-\overline{l}}/(1 + e^{\overline{a}_{t+1}-\overline{l}}) < 1$$

where a stands for private wealth, $\overline{y}$ is permanent income and $\overline{a}$ represent long term assets. To link (2) and (3) note that form the definition of ϕ it follows that

$$1/\phi = 1/(e^{\bar{a}_{t+1}-\bar{y}}) + 1 = e^{\bar{y}}/e^{\bar{a}_{t+1}} + 1 = E_t[H_{t+1}]/E_t[A_{t+1}] + 1$$

which in continuous time converges as $(\sigma_t \rightarrow 0)$ to $(1 + H_t/A_t)$.

30 The Chilean PAYG pension system was converted in 1981 into a "Fully Funded" (FF) system. It subsequently became a worldwide reference for funded (and private) pension systems. However, it can hardly be characterized as a pure FF pension system nowadays. After the 2008 reform the system is, in effect, a multi-pillar one, with a significant degree of protection to the eventuality of very low returns in private retirement accounts. This protection represents a contingent liability backed by the general tax revenue of the State (i.e., it implies the existence of a PAYG component on the system).

31 Commissions vary with the AFP chosen, but 1.5% is a representative figure.

32 "Multifondo" A can have up to 80% (and no less than 40%) of its assets invested in risky assets. These figures go down progressively along the sequence of "Multifondos", with fund E featuring a maximum 5% allocation to variable-income. Note also that affiliates can contribute to a maximum of 2 "Multifondos". This means that they can (approximately) implement any possible split between risky/riskless assets in their retirement accounts (e.g. by weighting "Multifondos" A and E in the correct proportions). This justifies our modeling of the portfolio choice, ω, as a continuous variable.

33 Insurance companies apply their own assumptions when setting the survival probabilities and discount factors in the annuity formula. Estelle et al. (2005) estimate the MWR (*money's worth ratio* or the ratio of the present expected value of the annuity streams to the initial payment) to vary (for men) between 91.6% and 98.1% in 1999 and between 95.8% and 99.3% in 2003. We model a prudent behavior by setting the MWR in our model to the smallest of those figures.

34 To qualify for the top-up, the claimant must be a resident in the country for 20 years and his/her family income must be below some specific threshold. We assume that these conditions are met by our simulated households.

35 The estimated values differ slightly according to the particular AFP considered, but the differences are very small and do not change the conclusions of our analysis in any relevant way.

References

AFP (2012). Aporte previsional solidario de vejez, APS-vejez, http://www.safp.cl/573/article-5786.html.

Benartzi, S., Thaler, R. H. (2007). Heuristics and Biases in Retirement Savings Behavior, in: Journal of Economic Perspectives, 21(3): 81–104.

Berstein, S., Fuertes, O., Torrealba, N. (2011a). Esquema de multifondos en chile, Documento de Trabajo 43.

Berstein, S., Fuertes, O., Torrealba, N. (2011b). La importancia de la opción por omisión en los sistemas de pensiones de cuentas individuales: Estrategias de inversión de ciclo de vida, Documento de Trabajo 44.

Bodie, Z., Treussard, J. (2007). Making Investment Choices as Simple as Possible but not Simpler, in: Financial Analysts Journal, 63(3): 42–7.

Bovenberg, L., Koijen, R., Nijman, T., Teulings, C. (2007). Saving and Investing over the Life Cycle and the Role of Collective Pension Funds, in: De Economist, 155: 347-415.

Campbell, J., Cocco, J., Gomes, F., Mahenhout, P. (2001). Investing Retirement Wealth: A Life-cycle Model, in: Campbell, J., Feldstein, M. (Eds.), Risk Aspects of Investment-based Social Security Reform, Cambridge, MA: NBER, 439-82.

Campbell, J., Viceira, L. (2002). Strategic Asset Allocation, Oxford: Oxford University Press.

Carroll, C. (2006). The Method of Endogenous Gridpoints for Solving Dynamic Stochastic Optimization Problems, in: Economics Letters, 91(3): 312–20.

Carroll, C. (2012). Solution Methods for Microeconomic Dynamic Stochastic Optimization Problems, http://www.econ2.jhu.edu/people/ccarroll/solvingmicrodsops.pdf.

Carroll, C., Samwick, A. (1997). The Nature of Precautionary Wealth, in: Journal of Monetary Economics, 40(1): 41–71.

Cocco, J., Gomes, F., Mahenhout, P. (2005). Consumption and Portfolio Choice along the Life Cycle, in: Review of Financial Studies, 18(2): 491–533.

Davis, S. J., Willen, P. (2002). Income Shocks, Asset Returns and Portfolio Choice, in: Mitchell, O. S., Bodie, Z., Hammond, P. B., Zeldes, S. (Eds.), Innovations in Retirement Financing, The Wharton School of the University of Pennsylvania: University of Pennsylvania Press, 20–49.

Estelle, J., Martínez, G., Iglesias, A. (2005). The Payout Stage in Chile: Who Annuitizes and Why?, Superintendencia de Pensiones Working Paper No. 14.

Gomez, F., Kotlikoff, L., Viceira, L. (2008). Optimal Life-cycle Inventing with Flexible Labor Supply: A Welfare Analysis of Life-cycle Funds, in: American Economic Review: Papers and Proceedings, 98(2): 297–303.

Human Mortality Database (2011), Technical report, www.mortality.org.

Merton, R. C. (1971). Optimum Consumption and Portfolio Rules in a Continuous-time Model, in: Journal of Economics Theory, 3(4): 373–413.

Miles, D., Cerny, A. (2006). Risk, Return and Portfolio Allocation under Alternative Pension Systems with Incomplete and Imperfect Financial Markets, in: The Economic Journal, 116(511): 529–57.

Repetto, A., Huneeus, C. (2005). The Dynamics of Earnings in Chile, in: Restrepo, J., Tokman, A., Loayza, N., Schmidt-Hebbel, K. (Eds.), Labor Markets and Institutions, volume 8 of Central Banking, Santiago de Chile: Central Bank of Chile, 383–410.

Storesletten, K., Telmer, C. I., Yaron, A. (2004). Consumption and Risk Sharing over the Life Cycle, in: Journal of Monetary Economics, 51(3): 609–33.

9

Assessing Redistribution within Social Insurance Systems: The Cases of Argentina, Brazil, Chile, Mexico, and Uruguay*

Alvaro Forteza

9.1. Introduction

The present chapter summarizes the main findings of five country-case studies conducted to analyze the impact of unemployment insurance and pension programs on the distribution of lifetime income in Latin America (Fajnzylber 2012; Forteza and Mussio 2012; Moncarz 2011; Zylberstajn 2011). Based on longitudinal data, we estimate econometric models of contributions to social security and labor income and run Monte Carlo simulations of expected lifetime labor income and net transfers to social security. Using these estimations we then compute indicators of distribution and redistribution of income. We find that some programs perform much redistribution, but the programs that redistribute more are not necessarily the ones that make the greater contribution to reducing inequality.

The pension programs covered in our project range from the fully PAYG-DB Argentinean and Brazilian to the individual accounts DC

* *This chapter summarizes the findings in five country-case studies conducted simultaneously using similar methodologies. The background papers are Fajnzylber (2012), Forteza and Mussio (2012), Moncarz (2011) and Zylberstajn (2011). The project was financed by the World Bank. We are grateful to David Robalino for proposing the initial idea and for his continuous support. The usual disclaimer applies.*

Chilean and Mexican programs, and also include the Uruguayan mixed program. Unemployment insurance is based on savings accounts and common pool schemes in Brazil and Chile and on common pool PAYG financing in Argentina and Uruguay. Hence, our sample allows for a comparison of the redistributive impact of different social security designs.

Previous studies show that densities of contribution are low and very heterogeneous in Argentina, Chile, and Uruguay (Forteza et al. 2009). We do not have similar longitudinal studies for Brazil and Mexico, but social security coverage of the labor force in these two countries suggests that contribution densities cannot be much higher in Brazil and Mexico than in the other three countries. Therefore, we are assessing social security redistribution in the presence of low density and highly fragmented histories of contributions, considering five social security programs with substantial differences.

In the next section we briefly describe the programs to be analyzed. In Section 9.3 we present the conceptual framework and discuss antecedents in the literature. We describe the data and methods in Sections 9.4 and 9.5. Section 9.6 contains the results and Section 9.7 concludes with some final remarks.

9.2. The Old-Age Pension and Unemployment Insurance Programs

In 1981, Chile pioneered a series of pension programs reforms that introduced mandatory individual savings accounts, phasing out the traditional PAYG-DB scheme. In the nineties, Mexico reformed its pension program along the same lines as Chile. Also in the mid nineties, Argentina and Uruguay introduced mandatory individual savings accounts, but without completely phasing out the PAYG-DB pillar. The result was a two pillar (or two tiers) mixed program. Brazil did a series of parametric reforms without introducing savings accounts in its pension program.

New reforms took place in the 2000s. The most radical of the new wave of reforms was the Argentinean abolition of the individual savings accounts. The current scheme is a partially funded DB program. Funds accumulated in the individual accounts were allocated to a collective pension fund. In 2008, Chile strengthened the redistributive component of its pension system, replacing the minimum pension and old-age assistance programs with a basic solidarity pension and a pension supplement. Also in 2008, Uruguay adjusted its program, loosening pension eligibility conditions.

We summarize in Table 9.1 the main parameters of these pension programs as they are today. These are the parameters used for the simulations in this study.

In addition, there is considerable variation in the design and scope of unemployment insurance programs in the set of countries included in this study. Argentina and Uruguay have traditional common pool PAYG programs, Brazil has parallel common pool and individual accounts programs, Chile has an integrated program that combines individual accounts with social insurance and Mexico does not have an explicit unemployment insurance program (Velásquez 2010).

The Argentinean program was enacted in 1992. It is financed out of employer contributions of 1.5% of wages on a PAYG common-pool basis and benefits are earnings related.[1] The first Brazilian unemployment program was founded in 1967 and consists of a compulsory contribution that employers have to deposit in an individual account, called FGTS (*Fundo de Garantia do Tempo de Servico*). A second program was enacted in 1986, incorporated in the Constitution in 1988 and implemented and expanded during the nineties. This program has common pool financing and earnings-related benefits (Barreto de Oliveira and Beltrão 2002). Chile introduced a new unemployment insurance scheme in 2002. This program combines self and social insurance: workers and employers contribute to individual savings accounts and the government and employers contribute to a common pool called the "solidarity fund." Mexico does not have an unemployment insurance program, save for the advanced age unemployment insurance scheme (*seguro de cesantía en edad avanzada*) that covers individuals aged 60 and above (Ochoa 2005). With antecedents dating to the early twentieth century, the current Uruguayan unemployment insurance program was enacted in 1981 and expanded in 2001 (Amarante and Bucheli 2008). It is a traditional common pool earnings related program.

9.3. Conceptual Framework

We assess redistribution within social insurance programs computing lifetime contributions and benefits. Our focus is on mostly con-

Table 9.1

Main Parameters in the Old-Age Pension Programs

Program	Contributions[a]	Qualifying conditions	Benefits
Argentina (PAYG-DB)	Employee: 11.00% Employer: 16.00%	Men: $age \geq 65$ & $los \geq 30$ Women: $age \geq 60$ & $los \geq 30$	PBU + "$Additional$" Minimum pension = 265 dollars (end of 2010) Where: $PBU = 125$ $dollars$ $(end$ of $2010)$ "$Additional$" $= 0.015 \times min(35, los) \times \bar{w}$
		$age \geq 70$ & $30 > los \geq 10$ (with at leat 5 years of contributions during the 8 years previous to retire)	$0.7 \times PBU$ + "$Additional$"
Brazil (PAYG-DB)	Employee: 8 to 11%. Employer: 20%.	a) "Length of service": Men: $los \geq 35$ Women: $los \geq 30$	$= \bar{w} *$ "$fator$ $previdenciario$" Note: the "*fator previdenciario*" is a decreasing function of life expectancy at retirement.
		b) "Advanced age": Men: $age \geq 65$ & $los \geq 15$ Women: $age \geq 60$ & $los \geq 15$	$= 0.7(1 + 0.01 los)\bar{w} \leq \bar{w}$
Chile (Individual accounts plus "solidarity" pillar)	Employee: 13.04% (10% individual account + 1.49% disability and insurance premium + 1.55% average administrative fee, as of April 2011) (Employers with more than 100 workers pay the 1.49% D&I premium)	Men: $age \geq 65$ Women: $age \geq 60$ or $annuity \geq 0.7\bar{w}$ & $annuity \geq 1.5 \times Min. Pen.$	Annuity + "solidarity complement" Note: "solidarity complement" is reduced with the level of the annuity and becomes zero if $annuity \geq PMAS$, where PMAS is the Maximum Pension with Solidarity Complement

Table 9.1 (continued)

Main Parameters in the Old-Age Pension Programs

Program	Contributions[a]	Qualifying conditions	Benefits
Mexico	Employee: 1.125% Employer: 5.15%	$age \geq 65$ & $los \geq 25$ or	$annuity \geq minpen$
(Individual accounts plus minimum pension and government flat contributions)	Government: 0.225% + flat contribution for each day of contribution (decreasing in the wage rate)	$annuity \geq 1.3\ minpen$	
Uruguay	Employee: 15%	$age \geq 60$ & $los \geq 30$	$rr \times \bar{w}$ With: $0.45 \leq rr \leq 0.825$
(Mixed program: (i) first tier: PAYG-DB; (ii) second tier: individual accounts)	Employer: 7.5%	$age \geq 70 - i$ & $los \geq 15 + 2i$ $i \epsilon \{0,1,2,3,4,5\}$	$rr \times \bar{w}$ With: $0.5 \leq rr \leq 0.65$
		$age \geq 65$ or $age \geq 60$ & $los \geq 30$	Annuity

Notes: age = age when pension is claimed, in years; los = length of service when pension is claimed, in years; $\overline{w}$ = average wage (wages included in this average vary considerably between programs);
$minpen$ = minimum pension.
[a] In most programs, contributions to old age, survivor and disability insurance (OASDI) cannot be separated into three distinct components. We report OASDI contributions in all cases. In Uruguay, contributions to old age pensions and unemployment insurance are bundled together.
Source: Author's elaboration based on Forteza and Ourens (2012).

tributory programs, but some non-contributory components cannot and should not be separated from the contributory ones. The Chilean solidarity supplement is an example of a well integrated non-contributory component in a mostly contributory program. The financing that governments often provide in PAYG programs is also a "non-contributory" component of social security. In some cases, this financing is incorporated in the design of the programs (for example, some points of the value-added tax are earmarked for social security in Uruguay), but in most cases governments just pay what is needed to keep social security programs working.

Social security programs are usually designed to redistribute income from the better to the worse off. Most benefit formulas include explicit redistributive components, such as minimum pensions and supplements to small pensions. Even individual accounts DC programs, which are based on the principle of actuarial neutrality, tend to incorporate non-actuarial redistributive ingredients.

But social security programs also redistribute income through less explicit mechanisms. First, high mortality rates may reduce the returns low-income workers get for their contributions in pension programs when unified mortality tables are used (Garrett 1995; Duggan et al. 1995; Beach and Davis 1998; Brown et al. 2009).[2]

Second, government transfers that contribute to finance social security in many countries favor the population that is covered by the programs, which in developing countries tends to be the better off (Rofman et al. 2008). But also these same groups are the ones that pay more taxes, so the net effect is not clear (Forteza and Rossi 2009). Ideally, we should trace the origin of the funds governments spend financing social security and include those taxes in the individuals' cash flows.

Third, low densities of contribution may leave many workers ineligible for benefits. Low-income workers have been shown to have particularly low densities of contribution (Forteza et al. 2009; Berstein et al. 2006). In this research project, we focused on this last channel, i.e. the redistribution stemming from the fact that low-income workers tend to have systematically shorter contribution histories. We will not assess the impact of different mortality rates and different coverage on implicit redistribution.

Social security redistribution is often assessed on an annual basis, analyzing taxes paid and benefits received by different groups of contributors. This type of analysis tends to show large transfers among groups which depend mostly on the ratio of beneficiaries to earners within each group. But most individuals transit from earning income and paying contributions to receiving pension benefits along their life cycle. Therefore, redistribution performed through social security can be better assessed adopting a lifetime perspective (Liebman 2001).

We run micro-simulations of lifetime income and social security contributions and benefits to assess redistribution, focusing on intra-generational redistribution: one cohort that lives with the current pension rules. It is worth noticing though that social security performs inter- as well as intra-generational redistribution and there is considerable evidence that inter-generational redistribution has been substantial, with early generations usually benefiting with high returns to contributions (Liebman 2001; Morató and Musto 2010).

The indicator used in this study to quantify transfers is the social security wealth, which is the net present value of the expected lifetime flows of contributions and benefits (Gruber and Wise 1999; 2004; Coile and Gruber 2001; Liebman 2001; Brown et al. 2009). Also, we assess the progressivity of the system by comparing the distribution of the expected pre- and post-social security lifetime income. Pre-social security lifetime income is the present value of income before contributions to social security and without benefits from social security. Post-social security income is the present value of lifetime income net of contributions to social security and including benefits from social security. The comparison is performed based on standard Lorenz and concentration curves, Gini indexes and an index of net redistributive effect.

We consider the individual as the unit of analysis, but it should be noticed that redistribution in the social security system may look very different at the family level. Gustman and Steinmeier (2001) show that, when analyzed at the individual level, the US social security looks very redistributive, favoring low-income workers, but it looks much less so at the family level (see also Lambert 1993, p 14). In the words of Brown et al. (2009): "...much of the apparent redistribution from Social Security occurs within, rather than between, households."

Two approaches can be identified in the literature that analyzes the impact of fiscal policies, namely non-behavioral microsimulations (Lambert 1993; Gruber and Wise 1999; 2004; Brown et al. 2009; Liebman 2001; Sutherland 2001) and intertemporal optimization models (Auerbach and Kotlikoff 1987; Huggett and Ventura 2000; Jimenez and Sanchez 2007; Forteza 2007). In our view, these two approaches are largely complementary. The optimization models have the obvious advantage of incorporating behavioral responses, so not only the direct effects of policies are considered, but also the indirect effects that go through behavioral changes. However, in order to keep things manageable, these theoretically ambitious models need to make highly stylized assumptions regarding not only individual preferences and constraints, but also social security programs. Given our goals, this is a serious drawback. We want to assess the lifetime implicit transfers in social security given the observed histories of contribution in Latin American countries. We are only beginning to characterize the very heterogeneous highly fragmented histories of contribution present in the region (Forteza et al. 2009) and quite far from having optimization models that can fit these patterns. Whether these histories of contribution are optimal responses to social security rules and various shocks is something we cannot answer yet. But given social security rules, it is pretty clear that these patterns of contribution seriously condition effective net transfers to social security. Non-behavioral micro-simulations are based on exogenously given work histories and geared to providing insights on the social security transfers that emerge from those histories. Thanks to their relative simplicity, non-behavioral models allow for a much more detailed specification of the policy rules and work histories than intertemporal optimization models. At the very least, we can expect to capture the first-order impact effects of social security on income distribution. The micro-simulation modeling can thus be seen as a first step in a more ambitious research program that incorporates behavioral responses at a more advanced phase.[3]

9.4. Data

We use two sources of data: administrative records from social security (Uruguay and Chile) and surveys (Argentina, Brazil, and Mexico). In what follows, we provide brief descriptions of the databases (for further details, see Fajnzylber 2012; Forteza and Mussio 2012; Moncarz 2011).

9.4.1. Argentinean Data

We used a household survey (the *Encuesta Permanente de Hogares* or EPH) for the period 1995-2003.[4] The EPH is carried out twice a year (May and October) covering only urban areas (around 61% of the country's total population, and 70% of the country's urban population). Each household included in the EPH, and all the individuals within it, is surveyed four consecutive times, with a replacement rate of 25% of the sample each survey. The EPH provides detailed information on the labor status, personal characteristics (age, gender, education, etc.) on each individual, as well as on characteristics of the household (number of members, living conditions, etc.).

9.4.2. Brazilian Data

The *Pesquisa Mensal de Emprego* (PME), or Monthly Employment Survey, is a monthly rotating panel of dwellers in six major metropolitan areas in Brazil (São Paulo, Rio de Janeiro, Belo Horizonte, Salvador, Porto Alegre, and Recife), compiled by IBGE. These six metropolitan areas cover approximately 25% of the country's population. The PME survey was redesigned in March, 2002. In this project, we worked with the survey waves carried out between March 2002 and August 2010.

The survey investigates schooling, labor force, demographic, and labor earnings characteristics of each resident aged 10 or more who live in the interviewed households. This results in approximately 100,000 individuals from 35,000 households every month.

9.4.3. Chilean Data

We have access to the *Base de Historias Previsionales de Afiliados Activos, Pensionados y Fallecidos* (Affiliates Pension Histories database, HPA), populated with individual contribution records from 1981 to 2009, for a sample of participants in the pension system.[5] The HPA includes the complete contribution history (in the pension system) for a sample of approximately 24,000 individuals, representative of the stock of affiliates of the system in July 2002.[6] In addition, the dataset also includes information on the recognition bonds held by the sampled individuals.

9.4.4. Mexican Data

The data source is a household survey carried out by the *Instituto Nacional de Estadística y Geografía de Mexico*, more specifically we use the *Encuesta Nacional de Empleo* (ENE). The ENE is a continuous quarterly national survey representative of the whole population. The unit of analysis of the ENE is the household, but with a specific questionnaire for each individual living in it, which allows control for personal characteristics. The replacement rate in the sample is 20% so each unit is surveyed during five consecutive quarters after which they are dropped from the survey. The period we work with runs from the third quarter of 2000 until the last quarter of 2004.[7]

9.4.5. Uruguayan Data

We used a random sample of the work history records of the main social security institution of Uruguay (BPS), collected in December 2004 by the Labor History Unit of the BPS (ATYR-BPS). Workers in the sample contributed at least one month between April 1996 and December 2004. The sample has close to 70,000 individuals.

This database provides detailed information about monthly contributions to social security, gender, age, and sector of activity.

9.5. Methods

The methodology is comprised of four steps. (i) Estimation and simulation of labor status and labor income models. (ii) Computation of social security contributions and pensions. (iii) Computation of pre- and post-social security lifetime income. (iv) Computation of income distribution measures.

9.5.1. Labor Income and Labor Status Models

We separately estimate models for labor income and working/contributing status. We model labor income to simulate strings of lifetime labor income, conditional on being working/contributing. We also model labor status, i.e. whether the individual is contributing or not, and simulate lifetime contributing status. Multiplying the simulated labor income and the contributing status, we generate the series of work histories on which we base our estimations of labor income distribution and social security redistribution.[8]

Notice that we are simulating the labor income that is declared to social security (according to administrative records or the surveys, depending on the country case). This is the relevant series for the computation of social security benefits, but it may be very different from total labor income in Latin American countries.

In the case of administrative data (Chile and Uruguay), we have a relatively large number of observations for each individual, but relatively poor socioeconomic information to characterize individuals.[9] We take advantage of the relatively long panel to estimate unobserved individual effects that capture much of the variance in the population. In the case of the survey data (Argentina, Brazil, and Mexico) we have shorter panels, but better socioeconomic characterizations. We could then explicitly model heterogeneity using education and related variables. The details depend much on data specificities that vary from country to country (for the details, see Fajnzylber 2012; Forteza and Mussio 2012; Moncarz 2011).

9.5.2. Computation of Social Security Contributions and Benefits

Once we had the simulated work histories, we computed social security contributions, unemployment benefits and pensions, according to the existing social security norms. This step involves programming the current social security rules. We considered both employee and employer contributions, as both eventually impact on net wages in the long run (Gruber 1999, p. 90; Brown et al. 2009, p. 13; Hamermesh and Rees 1993, p. 212).

We considered two social security programs, old age pensions and unemployment insurance. Old-age, survival and disability (OASDI) benefits are usually integrated in a single program. Unemployment insurance is often an independent program, but with important contributions from the government. In the case of Uruguay, contributions to social security finance both OASDI and unemployment insurance. Because of this, Forteza and Mussio (2012) modeled the two programs together. Regarding OASDI benefits, we focused on old age pensions, assuming the simulated individuals leave no survivors and suffer no disability.

Individuals are assumed to claim benefits as soon as they are eligible. In the cases of Argentina and Uruguay, a scenario in which vesting period conditions are not fully enforced was also simulated. In this alternative scenario, individuals who claim and receive pensions without having fulfilled the years of contribution legally required are assumed to receive minimum pensions. The aim of simulating this weak enforcement scenario is twofold. First, we want to assess the impact of vesting period conditions on social security progressiveness. Second, this scenario is a stylized representation of actual practices in two social security programs in which the testimony of witnesses to credit contributions is still common practice.

9.5.3. *Computation of Pre- and Post-Social Security Lifetime Income*

The expected pre-social security lifetime labor income is the present value of the expected simulated labor income:

$$\overline{W}(r) = \sum_{a=0}^{a=r-1} p(a)W(a)(1+\rho)^{-a}$$

Where r is age at retirement, $p(a)$ is the probability of worker's survival at age a, $W(a)$ is labor income at age a, and ρ is the discount rate.

We computed the lifetime social security wealth as an indicator of social security transfers. Social security wealth is the present value of expected net transfers to social security. It can be obtained as the sum of the discounted expected flow of old age pensions (PB) and unemployment benefits (UB), net of contributions (SSC).

$$SSW = PB + UB - SSC$$

$$PB = \sum_{a=r}^{a=max\ age} p\ (a)B(a,\ r)(1+\rho)^{-a}$$

$$UB = \sum_{a=0}^{a=r-1} p(a)UB(a)(1+\rho)^{-a}$$

$$SSC = \sum_{a=0}^{a=r-1} p(a)C(a)(1+\rho)^{-a}$$

Where $max\ age$ is maximum potential age, $B(a,\ r)$ is the amount of retirement benefits at age a conditional on retirement at age r, $UB(a)$ is the unemployment benefit collected at age a, and $C(a)$ is the amount of contribution to social security at age a.[10]

The formulas used in this study to compute social security wealth are adapted from the literature that studies incentives to retire (e.g. Blanchet and Pelé 1999, p. 132). Similar expressions are used in the literature that analyzes lifetime redistribution in social security (e.g. Liebman 2001).

Results are sensitive to the discount rate. Higher discount rates reduce social security wealth because benefits are mostly paid after contributions (particularly so in pensions). The progressivity of social security transfers measured through lifetime transfers is likely to be smaller the higher the discount rate, partly because of the social security wealth reduction it involves, but also because most social security programs perform redistribution through benefit rather than contribution formulas (Brown et al. 2009 make this point for the US public social security program). We used a discount rate of 3 percent per annum (ppa), but Forteza and Mussio (2012) and Moncarz (2011) performed sensitivity analysis for Uruguay and Argentina respectively. For the US case, Brown et al. (2009) use 2 and 4 ppa. Liebman (2001) uses the internal rate of return of the cohort he analyzes – 1.29 ppa – in order to focus only on intra-cohort redistribution.

Following our assumption of non-behavioral responses, we assume that social security does not impact on the age at retirement, so we used the same value of r to compute the pre- and post-social security labor income. The only departure from this assumption is in the weak enforcement scenario, in which all individuals retired at the minimum retirement age. Also, we assumed that the interruptions in labor history are exogenously given, independent of the unemployment insurance program.

9.5.4. *Computation of Income Distribution Indexes*

We first characterize the distribution of individuals (i) social security wealth and (ii) social security wealth to income ratios. These indicators provide a first assessment of how much redistribution is taking place within the social security system.

Second, we plot individual social security wealth versus pre-social security labor income. This is a first indicator of local progressiveness in social security redistribution. Liebman (2001) presents similar plots for the US.

Third, we compute the Lorenz curves of the expected pre-social security labor income and the associated concentration curves of the expected post-social security labor income (ranked by pre-social security income).

Fourth, we compute the Ginis of the pre- and post-social security labor income and 95% confidence intervals.

Finally, we compute the Reynolds-Smolensky-type index of net redistributive effect (Lambert 1993, p 256). This index assesses the redistributive impact of a program computing the area between the Lorenz pre-program income and the concentration post-program income. A positive (negative) value indicates that the program reduces (increases) inequality.

The Lorenz and concentration curves, the Gini coefficients and the Reynolds-Somelinsky index were estimated using DASP (Araar and Duclos 2009).

9.6. Results

Estimations of the econometric models used to project labor income and contributions are not presented in this chapter. Readers interested in these intermediate results should look at the background articles. The focus in this document is on the redistributive impact of the programs. To that we turn now.

We present in Table 9.2 some descriptive statistics of the simulated databases. Average expected lifetime income ranges from 64 thousand dollars in the Mexican to 223 thousand dollars in the Argentinean databases. In the five countries, the simulated databases exhibit much dispersion of income, which is crucial to effectively assess redistribution. There are some simulated individuals with very low income. The percentile one individual (P1) has almost no lifetime income in Brazil, partly due to small income when working but mostly due to very short histories of contribution. The other countries exhibit higher P1 incomes, but even in Argentina, which exhibits the highest P1 income, it is 4 thousand dollars. At the other end of the distribution, the percentile 99 individuals (P99) range from 260 thousand dollars in Mexico to more than 1,500 thousand dollars in Brazil. As expected, the distributions are skewed to the right, with median consistently lower than mean income.

Average social security wealth ranges from minus 27 thousand dollars in Argentina to 4.5 thousand dollars in Chile. Measured by the difference between percentiles 1 and 99 within each country, social security wealth exhibits more dispersion in Argentina, Brazil, and Uruguay than in Chile and Mexico. This is an expected result, since the Chilean and Mexican pensions programs are based on individual accounts, while the Argentinean and Brazilian programs are

PAYG-DB and the Uruguayan program is mixed, but with a large proportion of PAYG-DB. The Mexican social security system appears as almost actuarially neutral in these simulations. The Chilean system looks much less neutral: the P1 and P99 social security wealth are minus 3.3 and plus 9.4 thousand dollars, respectively.

Table 9.2

Pre-Social Security Lifetime Labor Income and Social Security Wealth (in Thousands of 2010 US Dollars)

		Mean	P1	Median	P99	Skewness
Argentina	Income	222.8	4.1	121.8	1460.2	5.5
	SSW	-27.6	-103.5	-16.1	-0.9	-1.4
	SSW/Income	-16%	-23%	-17%	-6%	0.3
Brazil	Income	143.3	0.0	48.1	1533.5	22.3
	SSW	-19.8	-258.2	-2.4	4.2	-23.4
	SSW/Income	6%	-30%	-6%	196%	3.2
Chile	Income	95.2	2.1	62.9	440.8	1.9
	SSW	4.5	-3.3	4.4	9.4	-0.3
	SSW/Income	28%	-1%	8%	331%	7.8
Mexico	Income	63.8	0.6	48.5	259.9	1.7
	SSW	0.0	0.0	0.0	0.6	6.2
	SSW/Income	0%	0%	0%	2%	6.7
Uruguay	Income	175.1	1.3	89.3	1211.4	20.1
	SSW	-3.6	-77.3	-0.2	17.1	-2.9
	SSW/Income	8%	-13%	-1%	147%	13.5

Source: Fajnzylber (2012), Forteza and Mussio (2012), Moncarz (2011) and Zylberstajn (2011).

Brazil is the country that exhibits the largest dispersion in social security wealth in our study. The P1 is as low as minus 258 thousand dollars. This large losses result from the lack of ceilings on employers' contributions combined with a maximum pension. Therefore, there is no lower bound on social security wealth, since the higher the wage, the higher the implicit tax (and the implicit redistribution). Argentina and Uruguay show much higher P1. Unlike in Brazil, because of the existence of ceilings on insured wages, total contributions cannot be higher than certain thresholds and social security wealth has a lower bound.

The distribution of social security wealth looks skewed to the left in Argentina, Brazil, Chile, and Uruguay and to the right in the Mexican system.

We also computed the expected social security wealth to lifetime income ratio for each simulated individual. This indicator exhibits much dispersion between and within countries. The average ratio ranges from –16 percent in Argentina to +28 percent in Chile. It is zero in Mexico, 6 percent in Brazil and 8 percent in Uruguay.[11]

The social security wealth to income ratio exhibits almost no dispersion in the simulated Mexican database. Therefore, according to these results, social security would not perform any significant redistribution in expected terms in Mexico. This is not surprising in an individual accounts program. Nevertheless, the other individual accounts program in our sample, Chile, exhibits much more dispersion. Sorting individuals by the social security wealth to lifetime income ratio, the P1 individual loses about 1 percent and the P99 individual gains 331 percent of their lifetime income in Chile. So, despite being based on individual accounts, the Chilean system seems to have enough departure from actuarial neutrality as to perform significant redistribution. The Argentinean program shows less dispersion in the ratio than other programs covered in our study, apart from Mexico. However, the fact that the P1 individual loses as much as 23 percent of his lifetime income through social security indicates that we cannot yet rule out significant redistribution from taking place within the Argentinean social security system. The Brazilian and Uruguayan programs show much more variation in the ratio, highlighting a potentially large redistribution.

Figure 9.1 plots social security wealth and pre-social security lifetime labor income. To facilitate comparisons, we limited the range of values in the figure from the minimum P1 to the maximum P99 in the set of countries. It should be noticed that in the case of Brazil individuals with income above P99 would have social security wealth smaller than the highly negative value observed in the figure. Instead, in the cases of Argentina and Uruguay, higher-income workers do not get more negative social security wealth, because as explained before they have already reached the lower bound.

The negative slope of the plots suggests that the PAYG Argentinean and Brazilian programs and the mixed Uruguayan program are progressive, while the flat plots of the individual accounts for Chilean and Mexican programs suggest much more neutrality. Actually, there is redistribution at the lower end of the distribution in the Chilean and Mexican programs, but when the scale of the graphs is unified to facilitate cross-country comparisons as we did in this figure, the plots of the individual accounts programs look flat compared to the plots of the PAYG and mixed programs.

Figure 9.1

Social Security Wealth and Lifetime Income

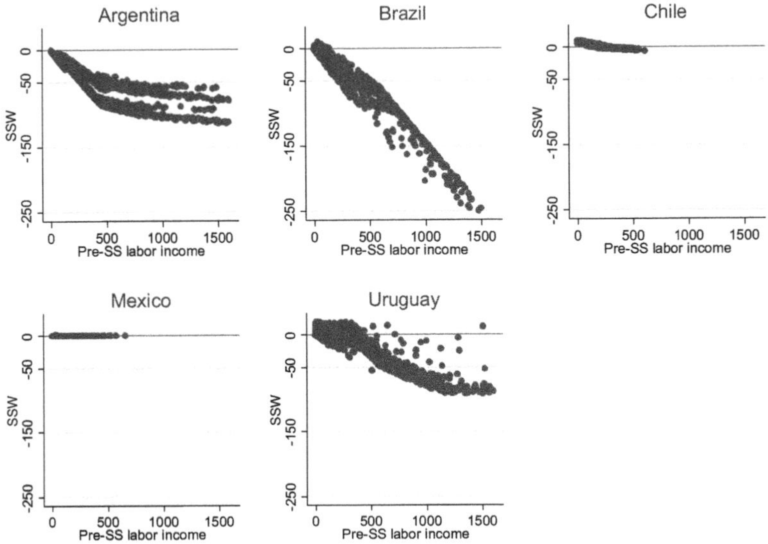

Source: Fajnzylber (2012), Forteza and Mussio (2012), Moncarz (2011) and Zylberstajn (2011).

Figure 9.1 also shows considerable variability of social security wealth for each level of lifetime labor income in Argentina, Brazil, and Uruguay. Therefore, there seems to be some redistribution that is not correlated to income levels in the PAYG and mixed programs covered in this study. Liebman (2001) reports a similar finding for the US.

These observations suggest that while the individual account programs perform less redistribution on average than the PAYG programs, they might be better targeted regarding redistribution. The net impact of the programs on the distribution of post-social security lifetime income is thus not *a priori* obvious.

Figure 9.2 presents the Lorenz curves of pre-social security labor income and the concentration curves of post-social security labor income. We do not observe large differences between the pre- and post-social security curves in these countries. Brazil and Chile are the only cases in which there seems to be an observable equalizing effect of social security.

Figure 9.2

Pre-Social Security Lifetime Labor Income Lorenz Curve and Post-Social Security Lifetime Income Concentration Curve

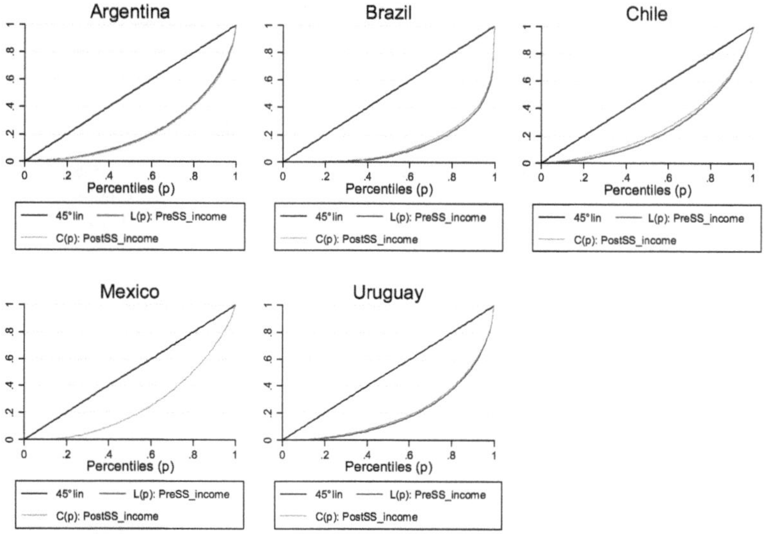

Source: Fajnzylber (2012), Forteza and Mussio (2012), Moncarz (2011) and Zylberstajn (2011).

The Gini coefficients of the simulated pre-social security lifetime labor income range from a minimum of 0.48 in Mexico to a maximum of 0.76 in Brazil (Table 9.3). According to this indicator, the distribution of the income measure considered in the present study is much more unequal than the distribution of current household per capita income reported to household surveys in Argentina, Brazil and Uruguay and more equal in Chile and Mexico.[12] Brazil is the most unequal in this group of countries according to both estimations, but the ranking regarding other countries differs considerably. We do not want to push the comparative perspective further, though, not only because the definition of income used in these studies is very different, but also because data sources used to compute lifetime income in the five countries covered in our project are also different (short panel surveys in Argentina, Brazil, and Mexico and administrative records in Chile and Uruguay). More research on the distribution of lifetime labor income declared to social security is needed. With this caveat in mind, we turn now to our estimations of the impact of social security on inequality.

Table 9.3

Gini Coefficients of Lifetime Labor Income Before and After Social Security

		Gini before SS	Gini after SS
Argentina	Estimate	0.5656	0.5798
	Lower confidence bound (95%)	0.5572	0.5707
	Upper confidence bound (95%)	0.5740	0.5888
Brazil	Estimate	0.7630	0.7435
	Lower confidence bound (95%)	0.7412	0.7214
	Upper confidence bound (95%)	0.7848	0.7655
Chile	Estimate	0.4991	0.4606
	Lower confidence bound (95%)	0.4902	0.4521
	Upper confidence bound (95%)	0.5081	0.4691
Mexico	Estimate	0.4787	0.4786
	Lower confidence bound (95%)	0.4728	0.4726
	Upper confidence bound (95%)	0.4847	0.4845
Uruguay	Estimate	0.6004	0.5822
	Lower confidence bound (95%)	0.5889	0.5701
	Upper confidence bound (95%)	0.6119	0.5943

Source: Fajnzylber (2012), Forteza and Mussio (2012), Moncarz (2011) and Zylberstajn (2011).

Table 9.4

Index of Redistribution (Reynolds-Smolensky Index of Effective Progression)

	Index	Standard Error
Argentina	–0.0139	0.00036
Brazil	0.0198	0.00028
Chile	0.0388	0.00079
México	0.0002	0.00001
Uruguay	0.0187	0.00045

Source: Fajnzylber (2012), Forteza and Mussio (2012), Moncarz (2011) and Zylberstajn (2011).

According to our estimations, Chile is the country in which social security causes the largest reduction in inequality (Tables 9.3 and 9.4). The point estimation of the Gini coefficient is reduced by almost 4 percentage points and the 95% confidence intervals do not overlap. The Reynolds-Smolenski index (RS) of effective progression is almost 4 percentage points and is significant at 1%. The second largest fall in the Gini coefficient due to social security in our study takes place in Brazil, where we see a 2 point fall, and the third in Uruguay, with a 1.8 point fall. The RS index is in the order of 2 percentage points and highly significant both in Brazil and Uruguay. Mexico shows almost no change in the Gini coefficients and the RS index is only 0.0002. Finally, Argentina shows a 1.3 point increase in the Gini coefficient due to social security, with a small overlap of the 95% confidence intervals. The RS index is -0.0139 and is significant at 1%.

The reduction in income inequality that the Chilean social security system performs is remarkable. It is a system based on mostly actuarially neutral individual savings accounts, and as such produces much less redistribution than the PAYG and mixed programs analyzed in Argentina, Brazil, and Uruguay. The difference between the P99 and P1 social security wealth is more than 90 thousand dollars in Argentina and Uruguay, and more than 260 thousand dollars in Brazil, but only 13 thousand dollars in Chile. And yet, the Chilean program is the one that shows the largest fall in income inequality in the countries studied. This result suggests that redistribution in the Chilean pension program is much better targeted than in the other four countries. The limited but well targeted redistribution in this social security system rests on the combination of a mostly actuarially neutral savings account and a relatively small but well targeted solidarity complement.

In addition, it is not surprising that the Mexican social security system does not impact on income distribution. Descriptive statistics of the social security wealth showed very small values, consistent with a mostly actuarially neutral program. Minimum pensions and government matching contributions represent departures from actuarial neutrality in the Mexican social security system, but the size of these deviations is not enough to significantly impact on income distribution.

The failure of the Argentinean and, to a lesser extent, the Uruguayan social security programs to reduce inequality represents a puzzle. Vesting period conditions might help explain the puzzle. In Argentina and Uruguay ordinary pensions can be claimed after thirty years of contribution, a condition that many contributors do not seem to be able to fulfill. Forteza et al. (2009) show that large segments of the population have a low probability of having contributed thirty or more years when they reach retirement ages, and this probability is particularly low among low-income individuals. In turn, Forteza and Ourens (2012) show that the implicit rate of return on contributions paid to these programs is very low when individuals have short contribution histories. Hence, low-income individuals might be getting a bad deal from social security because they have short histories of contribution (Table 9.5).

Table 9.5

Pre-Social Security Lifetime Labor Income and Social Security Wealth Under Weak Enforcement of Pension Eligibility Conditions (in Thousands of 2010 US Dollars)[a]

		Mean	P1	Median	P99
Argentina	Income	211,3	3,8	115,3	1389,2
	SSW	-26,5	-103,5	-18,3	6,6
	SSW/Income	-7%	-20%	-13%	146%
Uruguay	Income	173.8	0.8	87.8	1211.4
	SSW	-3.3	-80.1	0.8	11.1
	SSW/Income	34%	-9%	1%	505%

Note: [a] In this scenario, we dropped the vesting period conditions to access pensions. See text for the details.
Source: Forteza and Mussio (2012) and Moncarz (2011).

In order to test this hypothesis, Moncarz (2011) and Forteza and Mussio (2012) simulated an additional scenario in which the vesting period condition is not required in practice. In this "weak enforcement" scenario, the social security administration does not control whether individuals have contributed the required thirty years to get an ordinary pension at the minimum retirement age. The assumption is that everybody can claim an ordinary pension at that age. Individuals who did not contribute thirty or more years at that age receive the minimum pension. This scenario is not only useful to see whether vesting period conditions could be behind the redistributive puzzle, but also to get closer to actual practice in weak institutional environments in which the testimony of witnesses to credit periods of contribution to social security is still common practice. The results of this scenario are summarized in Tables 9.6 and 9.7 and Figure 9.3.

Table 9.6

Gini Coefficients of Lifetime Labor Income Before and After Social Security Under Weak Enforcement of Pension Eligibility Conditions[a]

		Gini before SS	Gini after SS
Argentina	Estimate	0.569	0.574
	Lower confidence bound (95%)	0.561	0.565
	Upper confidence bound (95%)	0.578	0.584
Uruguay	Estimate	0.606	0.58
	Lower confidence bound (95%)	0.594	0.568
	Upper confidence bound (95%)	0.617	0.592

Note: [a] In this scenario, we dropped the vesting period conditions to access pensions. See text for the details.
Source: Forteza and Mussio (2012) and Moncarz (2011).

Table 9.7

Index of Redistribution Under Weak Enforcement of Pension Eligibility Conditions (Reynolds-Smolensky Index of Effective Progression)[a]

	Index	Standard Error
Argentina	–0.0049	0.0005
Uruguay	0.0263	0.0006

Note: [a] In this scenario, we dropped the vesting period conditions to access pensions. See text for the details.
Source: Forteza and Mussio (2012) and Moncarz (2011).

Social security looks more progressive in the weak than in the strict enforcement scenario. In Uruguay, social security causes a 2.6 points fall in the Gini coefficient in the weak against 1.7 in the strict enforcement scenario. The RS is now 0.0263. An increase in the social security wealth of low-income individuals seems to be behind the improvement (Figure 9.3). In Argentina, social security still fails to reduce inequality in the weak enforcement scenario. The Gini coefficient does not increase as much as in the base case scenario, but post-social security income still exhibits higher Gini than pre-social security income and the RS index is negative and significant at the usual levels.

Figure 9.3

Social Security Wealth and Lifetime Income Under Weak Enforcement of Pension Eligibility Conditions

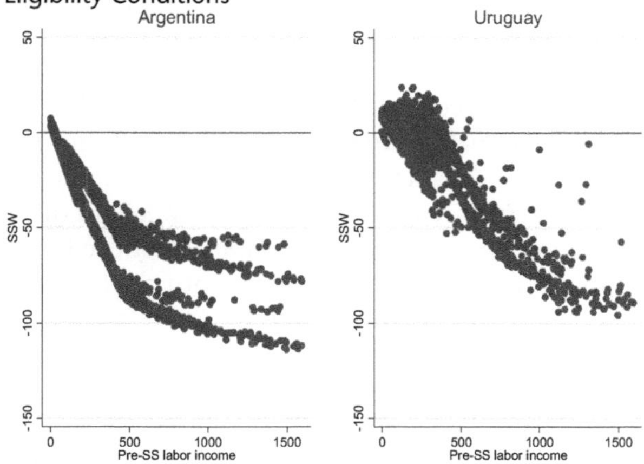

Source: Forteza and Mussio (2012) and Moncarz (2011).

Moncarz (2011) for Argentina and Forteza and Mussio (2012) for Uruguay run additional simulations with lower discount rates. Social security looks more redistributive when flows are discounted at lower interest rates, but the main results do not change qualitatively. In the case of Argentina, only in the scenario with weak enforcement and 1 percent interest rate (the lowest rate used) did social security significantly reduce inequality.

9.7. Concluding Remarks

The studies summarized in this document show that much redistribution is taking place through the social security systems in Argentina, Brazil, and Uruguay, very little in Mexico and something in between in Chile. Lifetime redistribution was measured by simulating histories of contribution and computing benefits and individual expected lifetime net transfers to social security (i.e. the individuals' social security wealth).

However, the net impact of social security on the distribution of income is not directly aligned to the size of total redistribution. Chile is the country in which the social security system makes the largest contribution to reducing inequality, despite of having the second smallest dispersion in social security wealth in our sample of countries. Fajnzylber (2012) reports an almost 4 points reduction in the Gini coefficient in Chile, as compared to about 2 points reduction in Brazil (Zylberstajn 2011) and Uruguay (Forteza and Mussio 2012), no changes in Mexico, and 1.3 points increase in Argentina (Moncarz, 2011).

The results summarized in this document suggest that the Chilean program has less but better targeted redistribution than the Argentinean, Brazilian and Uruguayan programs: with less total redistribution it performs a larger reduction in inequality. Key to this result is the "solidarity contribution" (*aporte solidario*) introduced in the 2008 reform. It provides a top up of low pensions, with no eligibility condition apart from belonging to the 60 percent lowest income.

The other four countries covered in this study impose vesting period conditions to access benefits. In the case of Mexico, individuals who do not comply with these conditions receive an actuarially fair pension, but lose right to receive any subsidy through minimum pensions. In the cases of Argentina, Brazil, and Uruguay, individuals who fail to comply with these conditions do not receive contributory pensions (at least not from the PAYG-DB pillar). These individuals experience losses from social security as they contributed and receive no benefits. To the extent that low-income individuals tend to have short histories of contribution, vesting period conditions cause regressive redistributions within social security.

Argentina, Brazil, Mexico, and Uruguay have minimum pensions geared to alleviating poverty and reducing inequality in old age. However, vesting period conditions undermine the effectiveness of this provision, as many low-income individuals have short histories of contribution and are not eligible for thebenefit.

No ceilings on contributions coupled with maximum pensions contribute to making the Brazilian program progressive, imposing a heavy burden on high-income individuals. This mechanism is not present in the other four countries in this study.

Notes

1 There is also a small unemployment insurance savings accounts program in Argentina for construction workers.
2 There is however contradicting evidence on the impact of differential mortality rates on social security progressiveness. Brown et al. (2009), for example, report very small effects on the measured progressivity of the US Social Security program of incorporating differential mortality rates by race and education.
3 An example of this strategy is the retirement research line followed by Jiménez and collaborators in the case of Spain (Boldrin et al. 1999; 2004; Jiménez and Sánchez 2007).
4 From the second half of 2003 the EPH suffered from an important methodological change that impede us to extend the period of analysis, also because the timing households are surveyed under the new EPH; this is less suitable for the purposes of the present study.
5 The sample was originally drawn as the basis for the Social Protection Survey, a panel instrument that carried out in 2002, 2004, and 2006 for a large fraction of the individuals in the sample. The Social Protection Survey was inspired by the American Health and Retirement Survey. For more information on the Chilean version, see www.proteccionsocial.cl.
6 Upon initial contribution, the individual is considered an "affiliate."
7 A new nationwide survey, the *Encuesta Nacional de Empleo y Ocupación* (ENOE) started in the first quarter of 2005. However, because of the information we require to carry out the analysis we work with the ENE.
8 Some of the methods used in this project are based on Forteza et al. (2009).
9 In the Chilean case, it would be possible to complement administrative records with information from the social protection survey (*Encuesta de Protección Social*) that provides valuable socio-economic information. However, to avoid problems stemming from imperfect matching of individuals in the two sources, we preferred not to use the social protection survey in this study.
10 In the Chilean case, pension benefits include the possibility of paying off the balance in the account of a worker who dies before retirement to her survivors, as a survivorship pension or inheritance.
11 Liebman (2001) computed the same indicator for the United States. Using a discount rate of 3 percent per annum - the same rate used in the present study - he finds the average ratio to be -6.6%.
12 CEDLAS and The World Bank (April 2011), for example, report Gini coefficients estimated on 2009 household per capita income of: 0.449 for Argentina, 0.537 for Brazil, 0.519 for Chile, 0.505 for Mexico and 0.44 for Uruguay. These indicators are not directly comparable to ours though. The Ginis reported in the present study refer to individual income as opposed to household per capita income, to labor as opposed to total income, to formal (in the sense of reported to social security) as opposed to formal plus informal income, and to simulated expected lifetime as opposed to reported current income. Also, in the case of Brazil, only private-sector workers are included.

References

Araar, A., Duclos, J.-Y. (2009). DASP: Distributive Analysis Stata Package, University of Labat, PEP, the World Bank, UNDP.

Amarante, V., Bucheli, M. (2008). Análisis del seguro de desempleo en Uruguay y discusión de propuestas para su modificación, Cuadernos del CLAEH, 31(1-2): 175-207.

Auerbach, A., Kotlikoff, L. (1987). Dynamic Fiscal Policies, Cambridge University Press.

Barreto de Oliveira, F., Iwakami Beltrão, K. (2002). The Brazilian Social Security System, in: International Social Security Review, 54(1): 101-12.
Beach, W., Davis, G. (1998). Social Security's Rate of Return, Center for Data Analysis Report No. 98-01.
Berstein, S., Larraín, G., Pino, F. (2006). Chilean Pension Reform: Coverage Facts and Policy Alternatives, in: Economía, 6(2): 227-79.
Blanchet, D., Louis-Paul P. (1999). Social Security and Retirement in France, in: Gruber, J., Wise, D. (Eds.), Social Security and Retirement around the World, Cambridge, MA: NBER, 101-33.
Boldrin, M., Jiménez-Martín, S., Peracchi, F. (1999). Social Security and Retirement in Spain, in: Gruber, J., Wise, D. (Eds.), Social Security and Retirement around the World, Cambrigde, MA: NBER, 305-53.
Boldrin, M., Jiménez-Martín, S., Peracchi, F. (2004). Micro-Modelling of Retirement Behavior in Spain, in: Gruber, J., Wise, D. A. (Eds.), Social Security Programs and Retirement around the World, Chicago, IL: University of Chicago Press, 499-578.
Brown, J. R., Coronado, J. L., Fullerton, D. (2009). Is Social Security Part of the Social Safety Net?, NBER Working Paper No. 15070.
CEDLAS, The World Bank (2011). Socio-Economic Database for Latin America and the Caribbean SEDLAC, http://sedlac.econo.unlp.edu.ar/eng/index.php.
Coile, C., Gruber, J. (2001). Social Security Incentives for Retirement, in: Wise, D. A. (Ed.), Themes in the Economics of Aging, Chicago and London: University of Chicago Press, 311-54.
Duggan, J., Gillingham, R., Greenlees, J. (1995). Progressive Returns to Social Security? An Answer from Social Security Records, US Department of the Treasury, Research Paper No. 9501.
Fajnzylber, E. (2012). Implicit Redistribution in the Chilean Social Insurance System, Working Paper, Universidad Alberto Ibáñez University, School of Government Working Paper No. 019.
Forteza, A. (2007). Efectos distributivos de la reforma de la seguridad social. El caso uruguayo, in: Latin American Journal of Economics, 44(129): 31-58.
Forteza, A., Apella, I., Fajnzylber, E., Grushka, C., Rossi, I., Sanroman, G. (2009). Work Histories and Pension Entitlements in Argentina, Chile and Uruguay, Superintendencia de Pensiones Working Paper No. 32.
Forteza, A., Mussio, I. (2012). Assessing Redistribution in the Uruguayan Social Security System, in: Journal of Income Distribution, 21(1): 65-87.
Forteza, A., Ourens, G. (2012). Redistribution, Insurance and Incentives to Work in Latin American Pension Programs, in: Journal of Pension Economics and Finance, 11: 337-64.
Forteza, A., Rossi, I. (2009). The Contribution of Government Transfer Programs to Inequality. A Net Benefit Approach, in: Journal of Applied Economics, 12: 55-67.
Garrett, D. (1995). The Effects of Differential Mortality Rates on the Progressivity of Social Security, in: Economic Inquiry, 33(3): 457-75.
Gustman, A. I., Steinmeier, T. L. (2001). How Effective is Redistribution under the Social Security Benefit Formula?, in: Journal of Public Economics, 82(1): 1-28.
Gruber, J., Wise, D. A. (Eds.) (1999). Social Security and Retirement around the World, Cambridge, MA: NBER.
Gruber, J. (1999). Social Security and Retirement in Canada, in: Gruber, J., Wise, D. A. (Eds.), Social Security and Retirement around the World, Cambridge, MA: NBER, 73-100.
Gruber, J., Wise, D. A. (Eds.) (2004). Social Security and Retirement Around the World. Microestimations, Chicago, IL and London: The University of Chicago Press.
Hamermesh, D. S., Rees, A. (1993). The Economics of Work and Pay, New York: Harper Collins College Publishers.
Huggett, M., Ventura, G. (2000). Sobre Los Efectos Distributivos De La Reforma De La Seguridad Social, in: Cuadernos Económicos de I.C.E., 64: 75-108.
Jiménez-Martín, S., Sánchez, A. R. (2007). An Evaluation of the Life Cycle Effects of Minimum Pensions on Retirement Behavior, in: Journal of Applied Econometrics,

22(5): 923-50.
Lambert, P. (1993). The Distribution and Redistribution of Income, Manchester: Manchester University Press.
Liebman, J. (2001). Redistribution in the Current US Social Security System, NBER Working Paper No. 8625.
Moncarz, P. (2011). Assessing Implicit Redistribution in the Argentinean and Mexican Social Security Systems, Universidad de Córdoba Working Paper, mimeo.
Morató, A. I., Musto, A. (2010). El impacto de la tasa de dependencia y de la antigüedad en los rendimientos de los regímenes jubilatorios, Facultad de Ciencias Económicas y de Administración, Montevideo: Universidad de la República.
Ochoa León, S. M. (2005). El seguro de desempleo en México y el mundo, Centro de Estudios Sociales y de Opinión Pública, Reporte Temático Núm. 3.
Rofman, R., Lucchetti, L., Ourens, G. (2008). Pension Systems in Latin America: Concepts and Measurements of Coverage, Social Protection Discussion Papers, Washington, DC.
Sutherland, H. (2001). Euromod: An Integrated European Benefit-Tax Model, in: Euromod Working Paper No. 9/01.
Velásquez, M. (2010). Seguros de desempleo y reformas recientes en América Latina, CEPAL Serie Macroeconomía del Desarrollo No. 99.
Zylberstajn, E. (2011). Assessing Implicit Redistribution in the Brazilian Social Security System, Working Paper, Fundação Getúlio Vargas, Brazil.

10

The Design of a Multi-Tier Contributory Pension System: The Distributional Impact of the 2008 Chilean Pension Reform*

Orazio Attanasio
Costas Meghir
Andres Otero

10.1. Introduction

Providing funding for consumption in old age takes many different forms, from simple saving by the individual, to tax-privileged savings, to public unfunded systems where the benefits are loosely related to the amount of contributions. Most systems, other than simple individual savings have a *de facto* redistributive role. Indeed many systems are designed with such redistribution in mind. The Chilean pension arrangements are a good example of a system designed to be in part funded and also to include a taxpayer-subsidized redistributive element offering a safety net for poorer individuals who either have not worked and saved enough over their working life or have worked in mainly informal jobs and have not contributed to the system.

* *We would like to thank the Chilean Ministry of Labor for access to some of the data used here. We are also thankful to Microdatos for help with the EPS data, and to numerous Chilean Government officials, especially in the Budget Office, for help and suggestions. Thanks also to Santiago Levy for some interesting discussions and comments.*

Before the early 1980s, public pensions in Chile were organized as a pay-as-you-go (PAYG) system characterized by a large degree of heterogeneity in terms of benefit and contribution rates, depending on the sector and industry of occupation. After a few attempts to simplify it and homogenize it, the entire system was reformed in 1981 when Chile instituted a mandatory defined contributions (DC hereafter) pension system. The Chilean example later became a model for the reform in public pensions in many countries that, since 1990, implemented a capitalization system, as a DC system is sometimes referred to. Countries that followed the Chilean example include Argentina (1994), Bolivia (1997), Colombia (1993), Costa Rica (1995), Dominican Republic (2003), El Salvador (1998), Mexico (1997), Panama (2008), Peru (1993), Uruguay (1996), Slovakia (2005).

The reasons and motivations of the early eighties reform were many. However, among the most important concerns were the high individual contribution rate of the previous defined benefit (DB) system, which varied between 16% and 23% depending on the sector of economic activity, and the low associated replacement rates. In the new system, every affiliate working with a labor contract was obliged to contribute to the system, starting with her first job, creating automatically an individual account which would accumulate her resources until retirement. These accounts were (and are) privately managed by regulated Pension Fund Administrators (PFAs hereafter) and accumulate returns each period depending on the financial investment choices made by the PFA. The PFAs face some signicant constraints on the type of investment they can undertake. The old PAYG system continued to work for individuals who had already accumulated some seniority and decided to stay in it. However, every worker was allowed to change to the new system until 1986. The exodus to the new system was massive and speedy. As of 1982 around 1,500,000 workers were contributing into the new system and just 500,000 stayed in the PAYG.

The new system was highly advertised during its implementation, offering a common low rate of contribution and promising higher future pensions. However, in practice, pensions have been lower than their initial expected value, generating relatively low replacement rates: 28% for women and 51% for men in 2005.[1] The main reason behind these *ex post* low average replacement rates seems to be the fact that many individuals do not contribute frequently enough to the system. After more than 25 years since its implementation, the low frequency of contributions appears as one of the main issues, which is particularly serious for groups with low (formal) labor market attachment, such as women. The system has reproduced and even accentuated labor market inequalities, reflecting the earning inequalities and the lack of contributions. The average frequency of contributions has been 42% for women and 61% for men. For women, 44% of the non contributed periods correspond to periods of inactivity.[2] This lower female labor attachment, together with lower female wages and longer female life expectancy have generated an important gender gap and much higher prevalence of poverty and hardship among female elderly.

In 2008, the Chilean government of President Bachelet implemented an important pension reform. The reform modified completely the first (redistributive) tier of the system introducing a non-contributory pension and a decreasing pension subsidy. At the same time, it introduced several elements aiming to compensate inequalities generated by the DC scheme and to encourage participation in the system. Some of the components of the reform, which we discuss in detail below, were designed explicitly to reduce the gender gap and improve the female labor market participation. The reform was not cheap: it costs annually around 1.1% of GDP,[3] being one the largest social reform in Chile in the last years.

The main goals of the reform were to reduce gender inequalities, prevent old-age poverty and guarantee a minimum and stable level of consumption upon retirement. The reform set up a more comprehensive system in which the redistributive and the mandatory tiers of the system are integrated with each other closing inequalities observed in the system. At the same time, the reform aims to promote participation into the system, in particular among groups whose attachment has been traditionally infrequent and/or irregular, such as women, the self-employed and young people, therefore reducing inequalities indirectly. For instance, the reform ensures some old-age income even to individuals who did save for retirement at all or saved too little to self-finance a minimum level of consumption.

The main aim of this chapter is to study the distributional impact of the 2008 Chilean pension reform on the accumulated pension wealth and pensions at retirement. To do so we use a representative sample of Chilean households and use it to predict their pension wealth and pensions under the new and the old system. Pension wealth and pensions depend on three things: the pension rules and legislation, individual earnings and contributory behaviour and other personal circumstances, such as children and marital status. We use the pension system's formulae and predictions of (formal) earning histories and other circumstances to compute the pre- and post-reform expected pension wealth at retirement and their associated pensions. Prediction of individual earning histories are obtained matching our survey data with administrative data sources and, therefore, incorporate a considerable amount of information. With those measures in hand we compare the distribution of pension wealth and pension before and after the reform. We focus in particular on differences across cohorts and gender. Our focus is justified by the fact that some elements of the reform were explicitly focused on women and young cohorts.

Our exercise is not without limitations and our results should be taken with some caution. Predicting future earnings and family histories is intrinsically difficult, although the use of individual histories, gained from administrative data makes us confident of the relevance of our predictions. Probably the main limitation is that we do not incorporate in our predictions of earnings and contributory behaviour any changes that might be caused by the reform. In this sense, our exercise should be interpreted as a first order approximation of future pensions and future pension changes induced by the reform, as it does not incorporate behavioural changes.

The reform has increased not only the self-financed pension wealth, due to the different mechanisms or subsidies received during the accumulation period, but also has importantly improved the final pension due to the first tier reform. For those workers retiring before 2015, the self-financed pension wealth and the final pension will increase on average by 0.6% and 15%, respectively. Even though the final pension changes have been positive for both genders, the female pension improvement has been 56% higher than the rise for men reducing importantly the gender inequalities. Overall, the reform has considerably reduced the inequality of future pensions and, therefore, in this dimension, has achieved its aim. In this chapter, we do not study explicitly the effect that the reform had on the incentives to participate into the formal labor market. That exercise is executed in Attanasio, Meghir, and Otero (2013).

The rest of this chapter is structured as follows: the next section describes the main elements of the Chilean pension system and explains the 2008 pension reform. Section 10.3 describes briefly the data used in our empirical strategy presented in Section 10.4. The main results are shown in Section 10.5, followed by the conclusion in Section 10.6.

10.2. The Chilean Pension System and Its Reform

Chile has been a pioneer in the design of a funded pension system, which, as we mentioned in the introduction, was introduced in the early 1980s. This system, however, underwent a major reform in 2008. In this section we give details both of the system as it stood on the eve of the reform and of the main changes introduced in 2008. We put particularly emphasis on the so-called "first tier" of the system, which plays a redistributive role.

10.2.1. The System in 2008

The Chilean pension system is referred to as a three tier system because its main Defined Contribution component (which is seen as the second tier) comes on top of a basic pension for the poor (the first tier) and complements private savings for wealthier individuals (the third tier). The second tier consists of a funded pension benefit, to be drawn at retirement from funds accumulated in an individual account during the working life of an individual up to retirement. Formal workers make compulsory monthly contributions of 10% of their pre-tax earnings, which are saved into such an individual account.[4] The individual account is created automatically once a worker enrolls in her/his first formal job and makes the first contribution. These savings are managed by a fund managing company (PFA), chosen by the worker from a list of approved providers. They invest the funds in the national and international financial market until the worker decides to retire.[5] PFAs charge a variable fee of 2%, which is used to cover the administration costs and finance a survivor and disability benefit pension through an insurance company. Workers can move their account, at any moment and without additional cost, from one PFA to another. Although the second tier is mandatory for employees, it is voluntary for the self-employed. As a result only a very small fraction of the self-employed, around 5%, contribute to the pension system every month. This in turn results in low pension benefits for this category.[6]

At the legal age of retirement,[7] 65 for men and 60 for women, individuals can withdraw from the labor force and start to receive a pension. Individuals can continue working and contributing to the system after the legal age of retirement. In this sense the legal age of retirement is defined as the minimum age under which individuals can start receiving their pensions. Retirees can choose mainly between two pension modalities, either a scheduled withdrawal scheme, which is paid until funds are depleted or an annuity scheme. Under the former, the accumulated resources are still managed by the PFAs and invested in the financial market during retirement. As for the latter, annuities are provided by insurance companies on payment of the individual capital.[8]

The level of the pension, therefore, depends primarily on the amount saved and contributed to the individual account during the life cycle and on the return to those savings. The former is mainly determined by the wage profile and the frequency of contributions observed during the life cycle. Thus, workers with low frequency of contributions, because of low attachment to the formal labor market, do not accumulate enough pension wealth, leading to low pensions. On the other hand, as contributions accrue returns over the life cycle, contributions made during the initial periods of the cycle bear more weight than those made in the periods near retirement. Consequently, individuals that do not participate in the pension system during the first part of their working life, such as women in their reproductive years, are more likely to end up with low pensions, replicating and possibly accentuating the inequalities observed in the labor market.

Before 2008, besides the mandatory second tier, the pension system also had a dual-component redistributive first tier consisting of a contributory minimum pension, Pension Minima Garantizada (PMG hereafter) and a means-tested welfare pension, Pension Asistencial (PASIS henceforth).

- To be eligible for the PMG, an individual had to contribute to the pension system's second tier for at least 240 months. Ind16:000ividuals who satisfied this number of contributions requirement and for whom the level of funds accumulated in the individual account could not generate a pension larger than the PMG, would receive the PMG. The PMG therefore constituted a floor for the pension for individuals who contributed at least 240 months. In 2008 the PMG was Ch$96,390 (US$184). While the PMG constituted an important insurance mechanism, individuals with low attachment to the formal labor market, such as women and the less skilled, would be less likely to contribute to qualify for the PMG as they might have not contributed for 240 months. According to Bernstein (2005), less than 37% of women and 67% of men would have pensions above PMG for the period 2020-5. However, 61% of the women who would not accumulate enough funds in the individual account to self-finance a pension higher than the PMG would also not satisfy the 240 months requirement needed for receiving it.

- Unlike the PMG, eligibility for the PASIS did not depend on contributions but was means tested. An individual had to satisfy certain conditions in terms of a "poverty indicator" to qualify for the PASIS and have no other pension entitlements. The PASIS was allocated according to a household level (rather than individual level) poverty indicator. The level that would qualify individuals for the PASIS was such that this pension would cover retirees belonging to the poorest quintile of households. Since 2006 the poverty indicator for allocating most of the Chilean welfare subsidies has been the FPS (Ficha de Protecion Social). This indicator, used for allocating the PASIS as well as the new welfare pensions implemented by the reform, is determined taking into account a complete set of socioeconomic household's characteristics such as permanent income, household size and its composition, health and years of education among others. In 2008 the PASIS was Ch$54,091 (US$103) a month, and was financed by the government out of general taxation. Its level, therefore, was substantially below the PMG.

Finally, the third system's tier comes on top of the compulsory DC component as a voluntary saving complement. Workers can save additional resources into their individual accounts in order to increase their self-financed pensions. Voluntary savings are excluded from taxable income.[9]

10.2.2. Description of the 2008 Reform

The 2008 reform modified and replaced completely the redistributive (first) tier of the pension system by introducing two new components: (i) a welfare pension (PBS hereafter), intended to alleviate poverty for those not entitled to a second pillar benefit; and (ii) a welfare pension complement (APS hereafter), intended to sustain consumption by topping-up the funded second tier pension. These two elements, which replace the PMG and the PASIS, modify the final pension and in particular the way the funds accumulated in the individual account relate to the final pension, especially for the left tail of the distribution of pension wealth.

In addition to the change in the first tier, the reform also introduced several elements aimed at fostering not only participation in the contributory and voluntary pillar, but also at encouraging continuity of contributions. These elements were targeted to groups with historically low attachment to the labor market, so as to encourage them to participate in the pension system and indirectly to reduce the pension inequalities. Women, young workers and the self-employed were the explicit target of these incentives.

For women, for each child they have, the reform introduced a subsidy to contributions to the pension system. The reform also introduced a pension saving compensation upon divorce in favour of the worst off member of the couple.[10] Young workers get a subsidy both to their wage, through the employer, and to their contributions. The reform allows the self-employed to be eligible for the benefits in the first tier and obliges them to participate in the pension system.[11] Lastly, the reform introduced new voluntary occupational saving plans and new tax exemption schemes in the third tier.

However, the most significant change introduced by the 2008 reform is the reform to the first tier system, which is obviously redistributive, through the new PBS and the APS. We now describe in detail these two components.

The PBS welfare pension was started on 1st July 2008 and intends to alleviate poverty among those not entitled to the second tier of the system. It is means tested using a poverty indicator FPS targeted to the 40% poorest of the population older than 65 years old. The coverage will be gradually increased each year until 2012 when it will have reached the poorest 60% of the elderly population. The PBS is a non-contributory pension set at Ch$60,000 for 2008 and increasing to Ch$75,000 from 2009. This new welfare pension could be understood as the minimum floor income that any older than 65 years old retiree, who belong to 60% poorest population, will receive. The reform eliminates the number of contributions as one of the eligibility conditions for getting a minimum pension.

The APS welfare pension complement, also starting on 1st July 2008, intends to sustain consumption by topping-up the funded second tier pensions between the PBS and a maximum funded pension, PMAS, which is increased gradually until it reaches the value of Ch$255,000 in 2012. The APS is decreasing in the self-funded pension and does not have, as the PBS but unlike the old PMG, a minimum contribution-periods condition. It is defined as $APS = (PBS$

$- \frac{PBS}{PMAS} * PB$), where PB is the sum of the funded second tier pension plus any received survivor pension and any pension received from the past PAYG system.

These two new welfare pensions come to replace the PMG and PASIS pensions described in Section 10.2.1, therefore changing completely the first tier of the system. The changes introduced by the reform are best illustrated graphically, which we do in Figure 10.1. Before the reform, retirees at the bottom of the distribution (of second tier pension benefits) could be divided into three groups: (i) those who received their funded pension (the 45 degree line in Figure 10.1); (ii) those who received the PMG, (which was the case if the funded second tier pension was lower than the PMG and the 240 months of contributions requirement was satisfied); (iii) those who received the PASIS pension (if the funded second tier pension is lower than PASIS and the retiree satisfies the means testing).

Figure 10.1

Pre- and Post-Reform First Tier

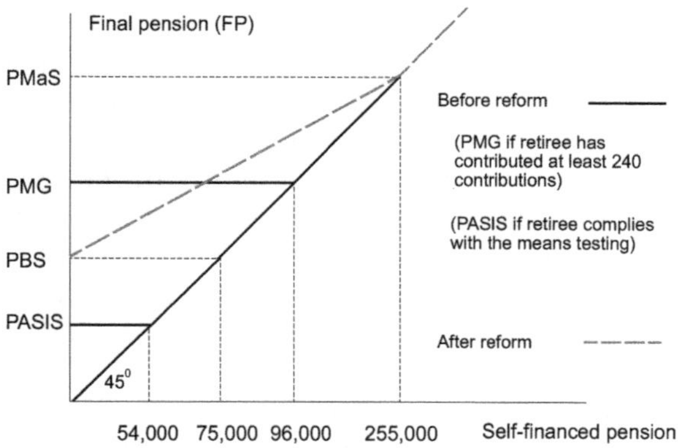

Source: Own calculation.

After the reform, the third group of retirees, receiving a PASIS before the reform, now gets a PBS, because of the weaker means testing criteria. The first group mentioned above (those receiving a pension lower than the PMG because they did not satisfy the contributory requirement) will receive a higher level of pension, as indicated by the gray line in Figure 10.1. Of those receiving the PMG before the reform, however, some will receive a higher and some a lower pension.[12] The latter group is constituted by those who satisfied the 240 months contribution requirement and had not enough entitlements in the second tier to self-finance a final pension of CH$75,000: under the new system, the PBS, while higher than their self-financed pension is below the PMG.

The new first tier modifies the final pension distribution and has important redistributive effects, whose quantication is the main objective of this chapter. However, the introduction of the PBS and PASIS also introduces different incentives to participate in the labor market affecting the inequality indirectly. Workers with low labor attachment, represented by group (i) and (iii) under the old system, now receive the PBS and the APS. This change reduces inequality in final pensions. On the other hand, the new post-reform pension changes the incentives to participate in the formal sector. These same two groups receive a higher pension for the same accumulated pension wealth. This wealth effect could deter contributions and participation in the formal sector. At the same time, for these groups, the reform reduces the accrual rate, that is, any extra Chilean peso saved is converted into a lower amount of extra pension. The pension benefits accruing due to work in this period are lower, reducing the incentives to contribute too. For other individuals, instead, such as those receiving the PMG before the reform, the change in the accrual rate (from zero to positive) should encourage participation. This additional features of the reform could change the final pension and affect the redistributive nature of the reform, as well as making the system much more expensive because people may rely on the more generous non-contributory system (see Attanasio, Meghir, and Otero 2013).

As mentioned above, in addition to the first tier, the 2008 reform also introduced a number of other elements. The main items were the following.

- A subsidy for every child ever born to the mother (implemented since 1st July 2009). Every woman older than 65 years old who is affiliated to the system receives a subsidy for contributions of 1.8 times the monthly minimum wage prevailing at the time of birth of every child.[13] Subsidies are deposited into the individuals accounts earning returns since the date of birth of the child until the date of retirement or from July 2009 until retirement in cases when children were born before this date. This specific component of the reform is designed to compensate women for their lower frequency of contributions due to their childbearing periods, reducing gender inequality in pensions.

- Around 2% percent of the individual mandatory monthly contribution is used for financing a survivor and disability insurance for each affiliate. Even though the risks of death and illness have been historically lower for women than men, the system did not recognize this fact charging a common premium rate. Since 1st July 2009 the reform introduced a mechanism which intends to recognize gender differences in longevity and disability risk. The premium rate for the survivor and disability insurance is determined by an auction mechanism where all PFAs bid for managing the insurance. PFAs could offer different rates for men and women recognizing the difference on their risks. Both groups will be charged with the higher offered rate but the difference will be incorporated in the women individual accounts as part of their contribution.
- Before 1st October 2008 survivor pensions were received just by wives, this has been changed by the reform incorporating a survivor pension benefit to the husband as well. On the other hand, the reform introduced a possible compensation upon divorce in favour of the worst off member of the couple. Compensation is determined by family courts as a fraction (up to half) of the accumulated resources of the best off member.

There are several other elements incorporated in the 2008 reform which we do not consider in our exercise. These components target different groups, such as young employees and the self-employed, start on different dates (some of them are not even active yet) and include some general modifications to the whole system, such as the elimination of the fixed fee charged by the PFAs and a new auction mechanism under which PFAs compete for administrating the funds of the new affiliates. A partial list of these components can be found in the Appendix C.

10.3. Data

In our study of the pension reform, we use two sources of data that complement each other: the Social Protection Survey (Encuesta de Protección Social, EPS) and the Pension System Administrative Records. The EPS is a nation-wide survey containing a rich set of information about a representative sample of Chilean households and their participation in the labor market and the social security system.[14] The first EPS was collected in 2002. Subsequent surveys were collected in 2004, 2006 and 2009. The first three surveys, therefore, were collected before the reform, while the last was collected a year after the reform. In addition, the EPS survey can be linked with a wide range of administrative files covering contribution and benefits patterns. These Pension System Administrative Records provide us with monthly earnings, contributions, fees paid and accumulated pension savings for all years since the beginning of the system until (including) 2009.[15]

We only use information about non-retired AFPs affiliates who are younger than 65 and older than 20 in all the EPS waves.[16]

As we explained before, the two new elements of the first tier are means tested and are targeted to the 60% poorest 65+ years old population. This target group is defined by the FPS poverty indicator (Ficha de Protection Social, FPS) we discussed above. In 2011 the FPS was changed and a new instrument, called Instrumento Tecnico de Focalizacion (ITF), was introduced for means testing.[17]In general terms both indicators are similar but they use different sources of data and weigh differently individuals within the household according to their age. To evaluate the redistributive elements of the pension reform we need to identify the individuals in the EPS that belong to the eligible group at retirement. As we do not have information about the FPS for all the EPS interviews, we use an estimation of the ITF score to allocate the welfare pensions. The ITF was computed using the all self-reported incomes in the survey. Although the EPS contains detailed information about different household income sources, which allows us to compute a precise measure for the ITF, the welfare pension allocation according to this indicator will probably differ from the one using the true ITF. Updating the results according the true ITF is in our future research agenda.

10.4. Methodology

The long-term and short-term effects of the reform are unlikely to be the same. The main reason to expect differences is that the impact of the reform depended on how advanced a cohort was in its life cycle. These differences arise both because of the provisos in the new law for individuals who already had some seniority and because older individuals have fewer years to adapt their accumulations to the new legislation. These effects are particularly important in the context of the 2008 reform, because it targets specifically certain groups, such as women in their fertility periods and young employees.

We compute the effects of the reform over the distributions of self-financed pension wealth and pension income, where the former is defined as the funds accumulated in the individual account without taking into account the capitalization of the welfare pension. We will then show how the reform changes these quantities differently for different cohorts and by gender. A key aspect of our methodology is the computation of expected (at a given point in time) self-financed pension wealth at retirement $E_t PW_{iR}$. In doing so, we need to estimate the future patterns of contributions to the pension system, the future wage profiles and various components of the pension system in place. The entire analysis is based on the assumption that individuals expect the system to be permanent. In this section, we briefly detail the estimation procedure we use. Details on its implementation can be found in Attanasio, Meghir, and Otero (2013).

10.4.1. Forecasting the Components Pensions and Pension Wealth

The main aim of this chapter is to estimate the extent of the immediate reduction in inequality in pensions and pension wealth induced by the 2008 reform (before accounting for any behavioral effects). The reform changes the distribution of future pension entitlements and pension wealth because it targets specific groups with the purpose of increasing their future entitlements and reducing old-age poverty. The groups that are explicitly targeted by the pension reform, either through the changes introduced to the first tier or through the additional components and subsidies are the poor, the young and the female.

To compute future pension entitlements before and after the reform we need to compute, for each individual in our sample the expected self-financed pension wealth at retirement, $E_t PW_{iR}$, and the expected pension, $E_t P_{iR}$. The reform changes the expected accumulated wealth through the different incentives attempting to increase the contributions to the system. It also changes final pensions, through the new first tier. The final pension wealth differs from the self-financed pension wealth because the latter only considers the pension that can be generated from the funds accumulated in the individual account, while the latter takes into account the first tier of the system.[18] Therefore, computing both E_tPW_{iR} and E_tP_{iR}, is useful to understand the mechanisms through which the reform achieves redistribution.

10.4.1.1. Wages and Labor Supply

The first element we need to forecast future pensions and pension wealth, is to forecast future earnings. Moreover, we need to know whether future earnings will be in the formal or informal sector. For this purpose, we use the EPS to construct a model that predicts participation to the formal and informal market. The model is made of two equations for participation (participation to the labor force and, conditional on participation there, participation to the formal sector) and two wage equations, one for wages in the formal sector and one for wages in the informal sector. In Attanasio, Meghir, and Otero (2013) we estimate such a model that allows us to construct predictions for formal earnings and participation taking into account the selection into the labor force and into the formal sector. Our model controls for age, gender, educational attainment, marital status, and the number of children, year of birth, and business cycle effects.

The details of the results can be found in Attanasio, Meghir, and Otero (2013). Here we notice that the estimated wage profiles, both in the formal and informal sector, fit with what is typically found in the literature: wages increase throughout the life cycle but at a decreasing rate, male workers earn higher wages than women and the more educated the employee is the higher is the wage. As for participation, the probability to participate in the formal sector is strongly related to the educational level of the individual: having a degree is one of the main variables explaining formality. As for participation to the labor market, women participate less in the labor market than men. Moreover, the gender difference is even larger when we consider married women and women with children.

The estimates in Attanasio, Meghir, and Otero (2013) allow for unobserved heterogeneity. The evidence in this respect indicate the existence of two groups within the population. The first group, around 30% of the population has lower preferences for the formal labor market while the second group, around 70% of the population, has higher preferences for working formally.

10.4.1.2. Child Subsidies

As the reformed system includes a subsidy for every child a woman has, we need to model how many children a woman will have during her life. We do this by estimating a simple discrete choice model for the probability of having a child in period t, conditional on having C children in $t-1$, age, education E and marital status M.

$$P(\Delta C_{it} = 1 \mid C_{it-1}, age_{it}, M_{it}, E_i) = \Phi(X_{it}\beta) \quad (1)$$

We estimate the equation (1) by maximum likelihood assuming random effects. The results are shown in Appendix A (Table 10.5). As it is expected, individuals who are married have a higher probability of having a child than those who are single and individuals who have more years of education have a lower probability of having a child. Using these estimations we forecasted for each individual the probability to have a child conditional on the set of used regressors. Figure 10.2a shows for each cohort the average forecasted probability of having a child at each age.

With these results on hand, we can then simulate fertility for a cohort of women born within a certain period. We assume that individuals expect the same number of children following the reform, that is, we assume that the reform does not affect fertility. We therefore generate, for each woman in our simulation, a complete fertility profile. We are then able to compute the subsidies that every women in a given cohort will receive at retirement for each child born to her. The two panels of Figure 10.2 below illustrate the results we obtain. In the top side panel, we plot, for each of the cohorts we consider, the probability of giving birth to a child at any given age. Figure 10.2b shows the average subsidy for each of the same four cohorts.

The subsidy for each child is equal to 1.8 times the minimum wage existing at the time of birth of the child.[19] Subsidies earn returns from the date of birth of the child until the date of retirement or from July 2009 until retirement in cases when children were born before this date. Despite lower fertility, younger cohorts get a higher level of pensions generated by subsidies, because their subsidies will earn returns during a longer period. The average child subsidy at retirement for the cohort born in the 60's will be Ch$4,729,981, which represents around 12% of the total expected (at year 2010) accumulated resources at retirement for those receiving the subsidy.[20]

Figure 10.2

Child Subsidy

a) Forecasted Probability to Have a Child (Women by Cohort)

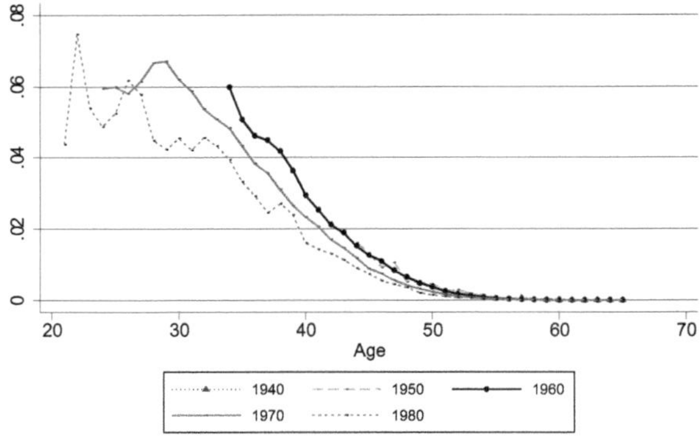

b) Child Subsidy Ch$ (1000) (Women by Cohort)

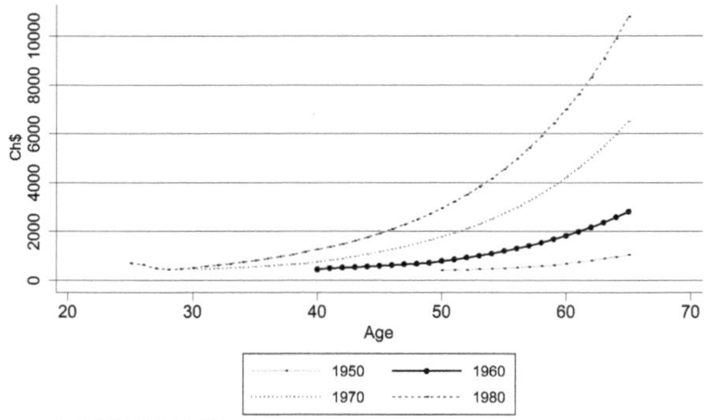

£=Ch$0.0012 (July 2010)

Source: Own calculation.

10.4.1.3. Compensation Upon Divorce

Expected benefits received as compensation upon divorce should be included in the expected pension wealth computations. To achieve this we compute the probability of divorce and the expected compensation amounts decided by family courts. We then impute to each individual period a forecasted expected compensation amount.

In the three last waves of EPS, we observe the individuals' marriage date and marital status. With this information, we estimate the probability of divorce using a proportional hazard model. The probability of divorce for individual i in period $j = \{[2004 - 6], [2006 - 9]\}$ is modeled as a function of a set of socioeconomic and demographic variables, which includes the age, sex, education E, number of children C, years of marriage YM and dummy variables controlling for cohort effects Dc. The hazard rate function, denoted by $h(j)$, or the instantaneous failure rate at time t could be written as:

$$(2)\quad h(j) = h_0(j)exp(\alpha_1 age_j + \alpha_2 sex + \alpha_3 E_j + \alpha_4 C_j + \alpha_5 YM_j + \alpha_6 Dc)$$

Table 10.7 in Appendix A has the results for the hazard ratios from a proportional Cox model estimation. The probability of divorce conditional on being married decreases with the age but increases with the number of years of marriage. The proportion of divorced individuals varies positively with the educational level. For example, for those who have finished a degree the probability of divorce is 36% higher than for those who have not finished primary school.

To be able to forecast the unconditional probability of divorce that a single individual will face in each future period, we need to estimate the probability to get married. The probability to get married is estimated using a proportional hazard model in the same way as the probability of divorce.[21]

The last two waves of the EPS contain information on partners' contribution patterns. Specifically, the surveys include two questions which allow us to figure out which individual within the couple could be considered as the worse off member upon divorce (see Appendix A, Section B for a detailed explanation). Combining this information with the unconditional probability of divorce, the affiliates' accumulated pension wealth at each period and assuming a compensation fraction equal to 30% of the partner pension wealth, we impute, for each affiliate, an expected compensation in case of divorce. As with child subsidies, we assume that the reform does not change the expected probability of divorce. Individuals compute their expectations about the probability of being married without taking into account the incentives introduced by the reform. This simplifies enormously our computations and avoids us dealing, through an additional model, with the potential effects of the reform on marital status.

Figure 10.3 displays the distribution of simulated compensation upon divorce by gender. The simulated average divorce compensation upon divorce is around 12% of the total accumulated resources at retirement for those receiving it. However, just 8% of the retirees will receive this compensation.[22]

Figure 10.3
Divorce Compensation upon Divorce Ch$

Source: Own calculation.

10.4.1.4. Survivor Pension

Before 2008, only wives had the right to receive a survivor pension. However, the reform introduced a survivor pension for the husband in case his wife passes away. When workers choose the annuity modality as a pension, upon retirement, they exchange with an insurance company their accumulated resources for a fixed pension. In this bargaining process the insurance company takes into account the risk of death of the pensioner's partner. On the other hand, when retirees choose a scheduled withdrawal scheme pension this is computed considering any survivor who potentially would continue receiving the pension. Thus, it is plausible to expect a decrease in the female pension values as either the expected cost for the insurance companies has risen or the schedule withdrawal is determined taking into account a longer period of payment. To assess the impact of this new element on the final pensions we simulated scheduled withdrawals for women considering both scenarios, i.e. financing a survivor pension and not.

10.4.1.5. Disability Insurance

Men and women pay the same premium rate for a compulsory disability insurance before the reform. Around 2% of the monthly contributions were used to finance the insurance. An auction mechanism was incorporated with the reform, in which all the PFAs must bid a gender dependent premium rate. The difference between the male and female premium rates is transferred each period into the woman's individual accounts earning returns upon retirement. We are assuming that the observed average premium rate difference will be equal to 0.002 in any future period (Reyes 2009). Figure 10.4 shows the simulated average disability insurance subsidy by cohorts. Younger cohorts will get a higher subsidy because they will receive the monthly subsidy during more periods earning at the same time the associated returns until retirement. The average disability insurance subsidy is around 0.3% of the total pension wealth.

Figure 10.4

Disability Insurance Subsidy Ch$ (Women by Cohort)

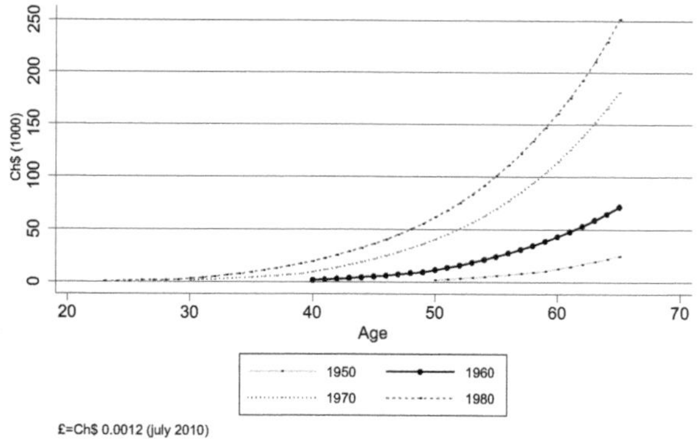

Source: Own calculation.

10.4.2. Forecasting Individual Pensions and Pension Wealth

Having assessed the value of all subsidies and having incorporated all mechanisms introduced by the reform and listed in Section 10.2, we computed both the expected accumulated pension wealth and accrual rate at retirement for periods $t = \{2002, \ldots, 2009\}$.[23] In these computations, we use the administrative records, which contain disaggregated information about the accumulated pension wealth for all years previous to 2005, and the EPS, which has information about contributions between 2005 and 2009. Future contributions were simulated using the predicted wages and frequency of contributions obtained from our estimated system explained in Section 10.4.1. The next section describes the results we obtain in terms of accrual rates and expected pension wealth at retirement.

10.5. Results

Although the main focus of this chapter and of this session is the impacts of the 2008 reform on the distribution of pension wealth and pension entitlements, we start with some results on the impact of the reform on accrual rates and average pension wealth and pensions. These changes obviously have an impact on the incentive to contribute to the pension system and to participate into the formal sector.

10.5.1. Accrual Rates and Average Pension Wealth

The changes introduced to the welfare pensions, such as the replacement of PMG and PASIS with the PBS and the APS change substantially accrual rates. As is clear from Figure 10.1, different individuals experience different changes to accrual rates. For instance, an individual who was receiving the PMG before the reform, goes from a zero accrual rate over a large region of her contributions, to a positive accrual rate, represented by the slope of the gray line in the left hand side of 255,000. On the other hand, an individual who was on the 45 degree line to the left of 255,000 (for instance a wife of a relatively well off husband – who therefore did not qualify for PASIS – and with relatively low attachment to the labor market – so that she had less than 240 months of contribution) would now receive the PBS supplement and have the accrual rate relative to the post-reform situation. Needless to say, these changes to accrual rates are also accompanied by changes to the level of pensions and pension wealth.

In the two panels of Figure 10.5, we plot, over time average accrual rates for different cohorts. In Figure 10.5a, we plot the accrual rates for women, while in Figure 10.5b, the accrual rates for men. The graphs show that the reform has a strong effect on accrual rates for the youngest cohorts considered.

Figure 10.5

Expected Accrual Rate

a) Accrual Rate – Reform in 2008 (Women)

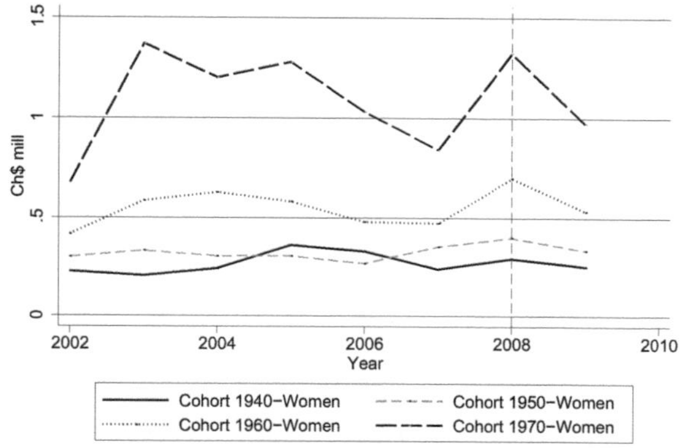

b) Accrual Rate – Reform in 2008 (Men)

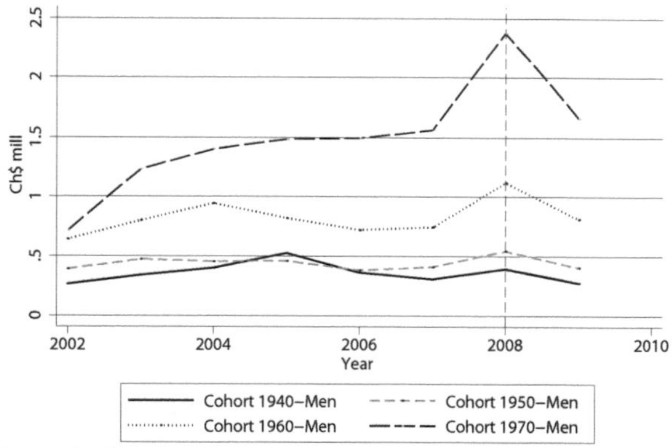

Source: Own calculation.

Figure 10.6 shows, considering all the elements of the reform listed in Section 10.2 (including the first tier reform), the expected (at year *t*) average pension wealth at retirement by gender and cohort. The effects of the pension reform are large. In particular, we see that pension wealth increases for all groups. However, for the youngest groups and for women the increase is particularly large. Given the nature of the changes implemented these results are not very surprising. However, the sizes are remarkable: for women born in the 1970s (1960s), the pension reform implies an increase of pension wealth by 85% (75%). For men belonging to the same cohorts the same increase is 36% (23%).

Figure 10.6

Expected Pension Wealth

a) Expected Pension Wealth for Women

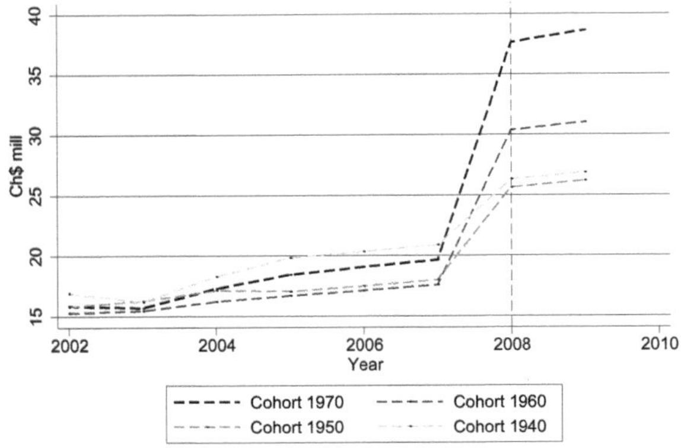

b) Expected Pension Wealth for Men

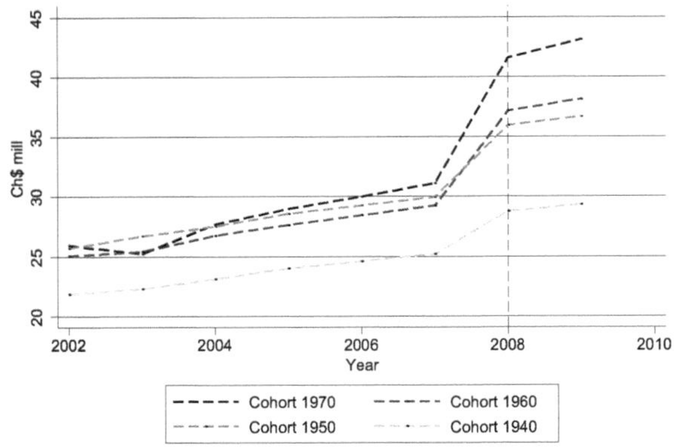

Source: Own calculation.

There are mainly two factors that explain average pension wealth changes in 2008. First, the pension reform itself. However, the reform is not the only aggregate event that affected the value of accumulated savings: the financial crisis that happened around the same time (see Hurd and Rohwedder 2010) has a direct effect on the value of the individual accounts. The pension system's funds lost on average around 15% of their value.[24] It should be stressed, however, that the impact of the financial crisis can be different across workers as individual portfolios can be invested differently. Workers can invest their accumulated resources in funds with different combinations of risk and return. When workers do not express a preference, the funds are invested in a default option. Such default options differ, in terms of risk composition, by age. An implication of this policy and of the fact that nearly 70% of workers opt for the default option (Berstein et al. 2011) is that there are important cohort effects on the impact of the financial crisis on pension wealth. These impacts of the financial crisis (both in terms of averages and in terms of distribution) have to be kept in mind when interpreting the results we present.

10.5.2. *Changes in the Accumulated Pension Wealth Before and After the Reform*

In Figure 10.7, we show some evidence on the changes in the self-financed pension wealth accumulated in the individual accounts before and after the reform. Any observed change after the reform will be due to the new mechanism and subsidies other than the changes to the first tier. The graphs display the frequency distribution for the self-financed pension wealth for women belonging to the 1940 and 1960 cohorts. Taking into account that older workers, at the moment of the reform, do not have many years to take advantage of the subsidies, such as the return for every born child or the disability insurance compensation, the change for this cohort should be smaller than the one for those workers belonging to the 1960 cohort.[25]

Figure 10.7

Pension Wealth Changes

a) Pension Wealth Distribution (Women Cohort 1940)

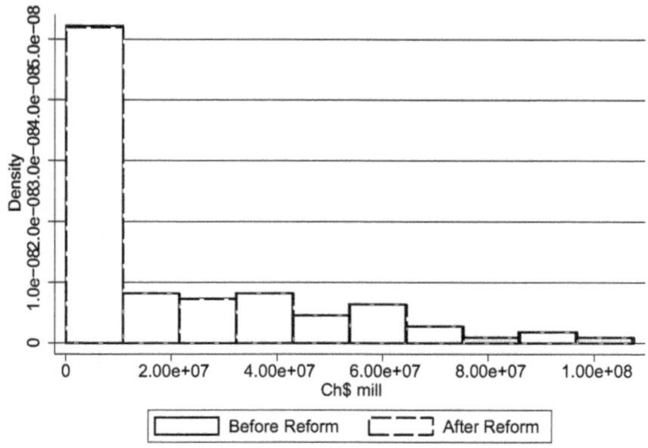

b) Pension Wealth Distribution (Women Cohort 1960)

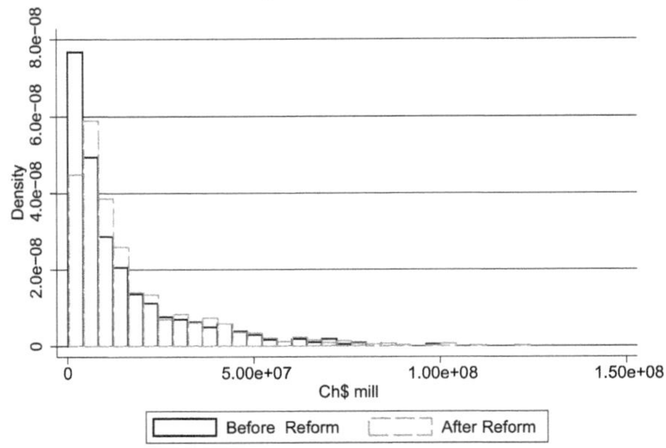

Source: Own calculation.

The average predicted self-financed pension wealth change for employees born in the 60s is Ch$1,020,413 which is almost 8 times larger than the change for the ones born in the 40s and represents an average increment of 4% of the PW before the reform.

10.5.3. Changes in the Distribution of Pensions Resulting from the Reform

The subsidies introduced by the reform changed the accumulated resources and through it the self-financed pension. Additionally, conditional to a particular self-financed pension wealth, the changes introduced to the first tier of the system modified the final pension distribution. These pension and pension wealth changes are different for different population groups. For example, as some elements of the reform are just affecting younger workers, the change in final pension will be probably larger for this group. In the two panels of Figure 10.8, we plot the distribution of pension amounts, measured in Ch$1000, before and after the reform for female[26] workers belonging to the cohorts born in the 40s and the 60s. The first group is composed of workers who are retiring between 2005 and 2015.[27] This is the first group of employees retiring under the post-reform system. The 1960 cohort, composed of employees who will retire around 2025-35, is the first group that will retire having contributed all their working life to the DC system. We observe that for both groups the final pension will increase importantly after the reform. The average female pension change is Ch$29,748 for those workers belonging to 1940 cohort and Ch$69,231 for those belonging to the 1960 cohort, representing an increment of 25% and 69% of the final pension before the reform, respectively.

Figure 10.8

Pension Distribution by Cohort

a) Pension Distribution (Women Cohort 1940)

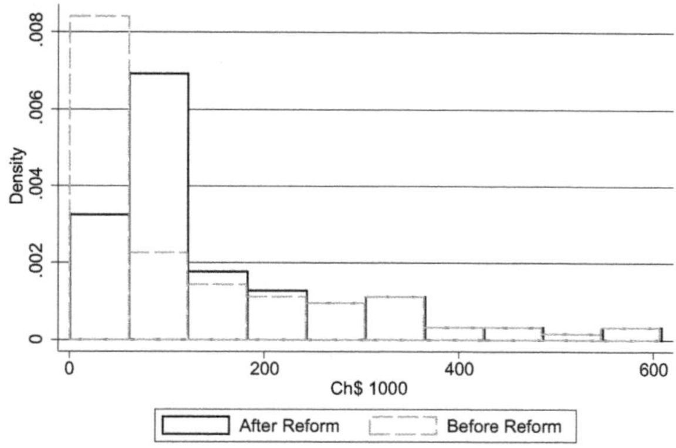

b) Pension Distribution (Women Cohort 1960)

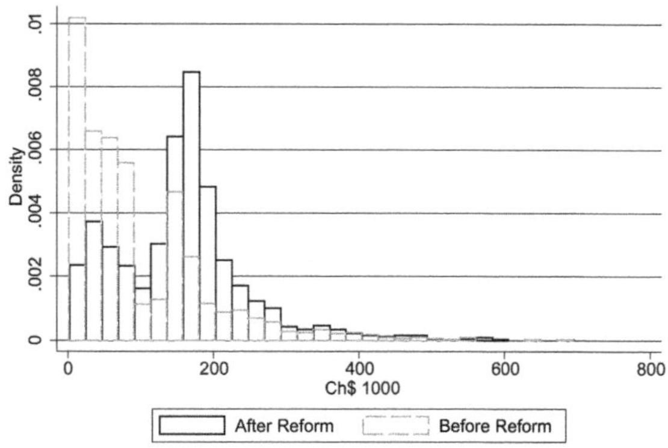

Source: Own calculation.

The most impressive change, however, is the shift in the distribution. The left tail of both distributions is substantially reduced and the middle of the distribution is increased. In Section 10.5.5 below we show how these shifts are reflected in changes in different measures of inequality.

As long as the first tier reform affects particularly workers with low self-financed pensions, because they will qualify for the new welfare pension subsidies (APS), the change in the final pension should be larger for them. In the two panels of Figure 10.9, we graph pension distribution for workers without formal education or incomplete primary school, and for those who got a college degree, respectively.[28] Although the reform shifts the distribution for both groups, it is clearly much more important for the groups with lower education, who are much more directly affected by the changes in the first tier. While the graph refers to the 1940 cohort, a similar story holds for other cohorts.

Figure 10.9

Pension Distribution by Education

a) Pension Distribution – Non Education (Women Cohort 1940)

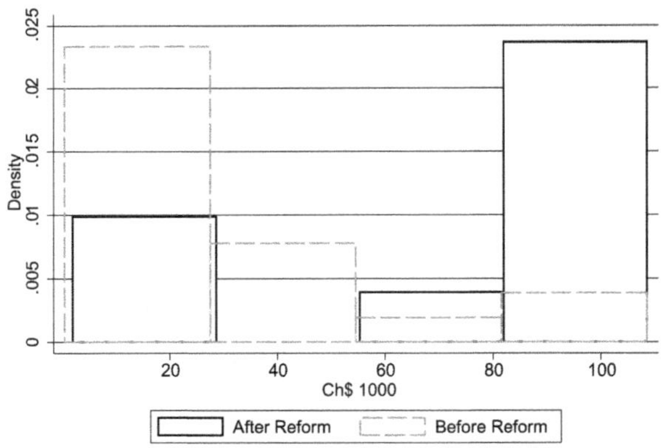

b) Pension Distribution – College (Women Cohort 1940)

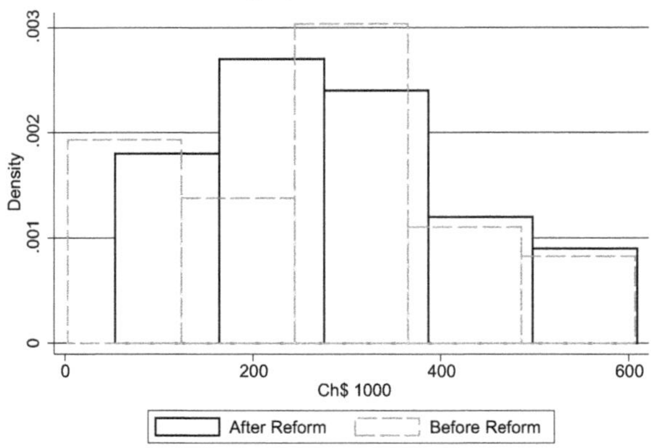

Source: Own calculation.

10.5.4. *Changes in the Distribution of the Pension Difference Between Men and Women*

As some of the subsidies were specifically targeted to women, we can expect larger shifts for the distribution of women final pensions than for that of men pensions. This hypothesis is strongly supported by comparing the two panels of Figure 10.10, that plot, for the 1940 cohort, the distribution of pensions before and after the reform for men and women. Although the final pensions increase in both cases, the change in the distribution is much larger for female pensions, reducing substantially the gap between them. The gender pension difference for workers belonging to the 1940 cohort is Ch$23,254 and Ch$14,073 before and after the reform, respectively. Graphs for the 1960 cohort are in Appendix A, Figures 10.15. The gender pension difference for workers belonging to the 1960 cohort is Ch$81,120 and Ch$57,379 before and after the reform, respectively.

Figure 10.10

Pension Distribution by Cohort

a) Pension Before Reform (Cohort 1940)

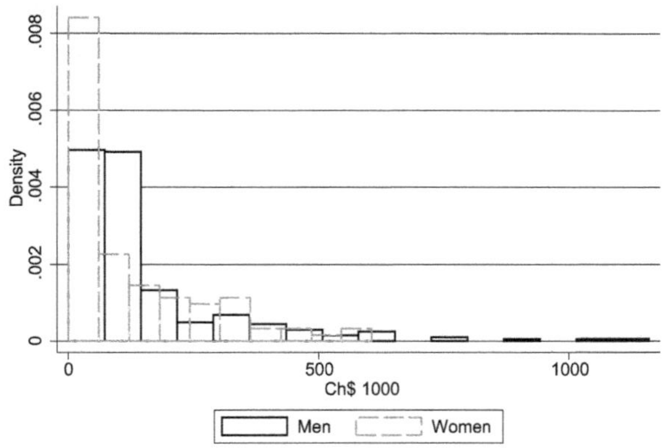

b) Pension After Reform (Cohort 1940)

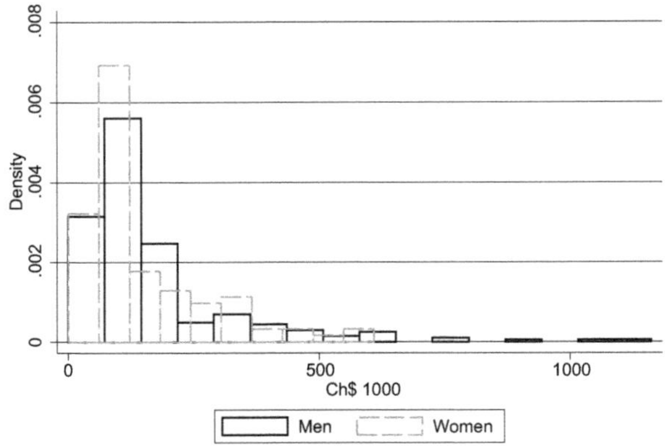

Source: Own calculation.

The two panels of Figure 10.11, show the estimated frequency distribution for the pension changes induced by the reform, considering two different cohorts. In Figures 10.15 of Appendix A, we report the frequency distribution for pension changes by educational level. The final pension increases importantly for both cohorts. However, the increase is clearly larger for those workers belonging to the 1960 cohort. In both cases the increase in female pensions is larger than that for males, closing gender inequalities. The average change for the female pension is Ch$77,977, which is 70% larger than the average male change. The average male pension change is Ch$15,148 and Ch$35,263 for those workers belonging to the 1940 and 1960 cohort, respectively.

Figure 10.11

Pension Change Distribution by Cohort

a) Pension Change Distribution (Cohort 1940)

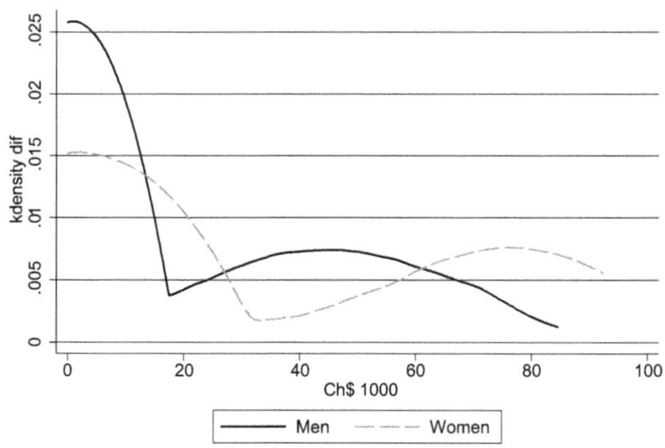

b) Pension Change Distribution (Cohort 1960)

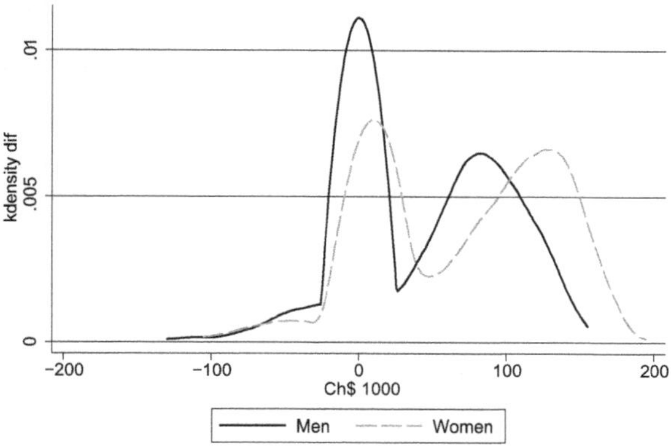

Source: Own calculation.

10.5.5. *Changes in Pensions and Pension Wealth Inequality*

Having looked at changes in the distribution of pension and pension wealth, we now focus on specific measures of inequality that complement the graphical analysis we have provided so far. In particular, for both pension and pension wealth, and for both men and women, we report the level of the Gini coefficient, the standard deviation of logs as well as ratios of different quantiles of the distribution. We start, in Tables 10.1 and 10.2, with some figures for the distribution of accumulated pension wealth. As we mentioned above, this does not take into account the first tier and the redistributive role that it plays and focuses only on the predicted amount in the individual accounts upon retirement. In each table, we report two panels, one for women and one for men and, in each panel, figures for different cohorts and for the total.

A simple look at Table 10.1 and 10.2 confirms what was already evident from the analysis of the distribution graphs: the changes in the means in Figure 10.6 hide much more complex changes in the distribution. The general picture is that, even neglecting the effect of Tier 1 and the redistributive role it plays, the reform reduces the amount of inequality in accumulated pension wealth for women. The overall Gini coefficient for women is reduced from 0.53 to 0.49. The standard deviation of logs from 1.21 to 1.04. The reduction in inequality is particularly marked for the youngest cohorts.

Table 10.1

Inequality Measures Final Pension Wealth (Before (BR) and After (AR) Reform)

	St.deviation BR	St.deviation AR	Gini Coeff. BR	Gini Coeff. AR
Women				
Cohort 1940	1.94	1.72	0.60	0.60
Cohort 1950	1.47	1.28	0.62	0.59
Cohort 1960	1.19	1.01	0.56	0.51
Cohort 1970	1.05	0.85	0.49	0.43
Cohort 1980	0.86	0.76	0.43	0.38
Total	1.21	1.04	0.53	0.49
Men				
Cohort 1940	1.20	1.20	0.53	0.53
Cohort 1950	1.11	1.11	0.50	0.50
Cohort 1960	0.98	0.98	0.46	0.46
Cohort 1970	0.82	0.82	0.40	0.40
Cohort 1980	0.71	0.71	0.36	0.36
Total	0.95	0.95	0.44	0.44

Note: Pension wealth is the total accumulated saving into the individuals accounts.
Source: Own calculation.

Table 10.2

Inequality Measures Final Pension Wealth (Before (BR) and After (AR) Reform)

	P90/P10 BR	P90/P10 AR	P90/P50 BR	P90/P50 AR	P75/P25 BR	P75/P25 AR	P50/P10 BR	P50/P10 AR
Women								
Cohort 1940	5.28	4.60	1.90	1.87	2.91	2.78	3.38	2.72
Cohort 1950	3.90	3.38	1.82	1.74	2.12	1.82	2.08	1.64
Cohort 1960	3.17	2.66	1.58	1.42	1.81	1.45	1.59	1.24
Cohort 1970	2.77	2.20	1.21	1.07	1.52	1.18	1.56	1.13
Cohort 1980	2.32	1.91	1.01	0.90	1.18	0.97	1.32	1.01
Total	3.12	2.65	1.39	1.24	1.73	1.44	1.73	1.41
Men								
Cohort 1940	3.12	3.12	1.41	1.41	1.23	1.23	1.71	1.71
Cohort 1950	2.83	2.84	1.24	1.24	1.31	1.31	1.60	1.60
Cohort 1960	2.55	2.55	1.08	1.09	1.26	1.25	1.46	1.46
Cohort 1970	2.09	2.10	0.90	0.90	1.06	1.06	1.20	1.20
Cohort 1980	1.81	1.82	0.80	0.80	0.94	0.94	1.01	1.01
Total	2.38	2.38	1.01	1.01	1.19	1.20	1.37	1.37

Note: Pension wealth is the total accumulated savings into the individuals accounts.
Source: Own calculation.

For men, instead, there are virtually no changes in inequality in accumulated pension wealth. These results are explained by the fact that the changes in accumulated wealth induced by the reform are mainly driven by the child subsidies, the divorce regulations and the other elements we discussed. It is remarkable that they not only reduce the inequality between men and women (as is clear comparing the means in Figure 10.6) but also inequality among women.

The general story that emerges from Table 10.1 is confirmed in Table 10.2, where we report the ratios of different percentiles. Once again, only the ratios of women change with the reform. We notice that the largest reductions seem to occur in the left tail of the distribution. For instance, for the whole sample of women, the ratio between the 90th and 50th percentile goes from 1.39 to 1.24, while the ratio between the 50th and 10th percentile goes from 1.73 to 1.41. Once again the largest reductions in inequality occur for the youngest cohorts.

In Tables 10.3 and 10.4, we report the inequality measures and ratio of percentiles for predicted pensions. As mentioned above, the main reason these tables differ from Tables 10.1 and 10.2 is that they reflect the redistributive role played by the first tier and the social pensions, before and after the reform. First, as to be expected, the inequality measures in Table 10.3 are considerably lower than those in Table 10.1. Moreover, the reduction is more pronounced after the reform than before. For instance, if we compare the Gini coefficient for women in Table 10.1 and Table 10.3 it goes from 0.53 for pension wealth to 0.49 for pension entitlements before the reform. The same figures after the reform are 0.49 and 0.38: the first tier after the reform implies an 11 point reduction in the Gini coefficient when going from pension wealth to pension. Before the reform the same reduction was only 4 points.

Table 10.3

Inequality Measures Final Pension (Before (BR) and After (AR) Reform)

	St.deviation BR	St.deviation AR	Gini Coeff. BR	Gini Coeff. AR
Women				
Cohort 1940	1.83	1.50	0.57	0.50
Cohort 1950	1.40	1.18	0.59	0.48
Cohort 1960	1.09	0.91	0.52	0.37
Cohort 1970	0.94	0.78	0.45	0.32
Cohort 1980	0.75	0.76	0.39	0.31
Total	1.11	0.95	0.49	0.38
Men				
Cohort 1940	1.12	1.07	0.51	0.48
Cohort 1950	1.02	0.90	0.48	0.42
Cohort 1960	0.89	0.79	0.44	0.36
Cohort 1970	0.78	0.71	0.39	0.33
Cohort 1980	0.67	0.65	0.34	0.30
Total	0.88	0.80	0.42	0.36

Source: Own calculation.

Table 10.4

Inequality Measures Final Pension (Before (BR) and After (AR) Reform)

	P90/P10 BR	P90/P10 AR	P90/P50 BR	P90/P50 AR	P75/P25 BR	P75/P25 AR	P50/P10 BR	P50/P10 AR
Women								
Cohort 1940	5.15	3.97	1.81	1.24	2.40	1.51	3.34	2.73
Cohort 1950	3.67	3.00	1.55	0.89	1.84	1.43	2.12	2.11
Cohort 1960	2.96	2.31	1.35	0.63	1.55	1.05	1.62	1.67
Cohort 1970	2.47	1.88	1.19	0.52	1.18	0.93	1.29	1.36
Cohort 1980	1.97	1.84	0.99	0.42	0.88	0.99	0.98	1.42
Total	2.87	2.30	1.25	0.70	1.43	1.13	1.62	1.60
Men								
Cohort 1940	2.87	2.69	1.28	1.21	1.16	1.06	1.60	1.49
Cohort 1950	2.51	2.13	1.21	1.02	1.28	0.82	1.30	1.12
Cohort 1960	2.23	1.93	1.03	0.79	1.22	0.72	1.19	1.14
Cohort 1970	1.91	1.76	0.89	0.64	0.99	0.72	1.02	1.12
Cohort 1980	1.70	1.61	0.77	0.55	0.84	0.74	0.93	1.05
Total	2.14	1.92	0.96	0.77	1.13	0.86	1.18	1.15

Source: Own calculation.

The second thing to notice is that, while in Tables 10.1 and 10.2 there are no effects on men, now the more aggressive (and more expensive) first tier implies a reduction in inequality for men as well as women. For instance, the overall Gini for men ranges from 0.42 to 0.36, while that for women is reduced from 0.49 to 0.38.

The final element to notice, is that in Table 10.4, the changes in the left tail of the distribution of pensions are somewhat surprising. In particular, we notice that the ratio between the 50th and 10th percentile distribution of pensions for some cohorts increases (rather than decrease) for some cohorts, especially in the case of the younger cohort of women. This somewhat surprising result is probably explained by the complexity of the reform and by the fact that the 10th percentile of pension values increases moderately after the reform while the 50th percentile pension value increase greatly, explaining most of the change.

10.5.6. Changes in Poverty Levels Before and After the Reform for Elderly People, in Particular, for Elderly Women

Between 1990 to 2006 the fraction of the Chilean population below the poverty line decreased gradually from 39% to 14%. This reduction has also been important among the elderly population, changing from 21% to 8%, for those older than 60 years old.[29] One of the objectives of the reform was the reduction of the prevalence of poverty among pensioners. Therefore another interesting aspect of the distribution of pensions before and after the reform we might want to consider is the prevalence of poverty at retirement.

The two panels of Figure 10.12 and 10.13 show, for different groups, the cumulative distribution of expected pensions at retirement before and after the reform. Using the poverty line set by the government at Ch$64,000 in 2009,[30] we show the fraction of retirees who are below the poverty line, assuming that they do not have any other income source. The poverty levels usually reported by the Chilean Government are computed considering per capita household income, which includes all household earnings, pensions and all different types of governmental transfers and subsidies. In what follows we only look at individual pensions. Our results are therefore not directly comparable with the Government poverty statistics. However, the point that we want to make here is to show how the reform changes the left tail of the distribution of pensions. We choose as the cut off point at which we look the level that defines poverty in the absence of other incomes.

The reform reduces the fraction of women with a pension below the poverty line by 32% (from 53% to 21%) and 36% (from 56% to 20%) for the 1940 and 1960 cohort, respectively. This effect differs by educational level and is particularly relevant for low education groups. For example, for women without complete primary education, the prevalence of (expected) pensions below the poverty line goes from over 90% to just over 40%.

Figure 10.12

Poverty Level Changes by Cohort

a) Expected Pension 2009 (Women Cohort 1940)

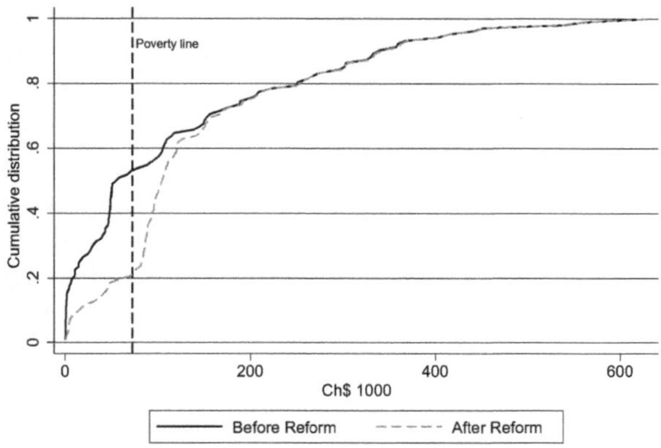

b) Expected Pension 2009 (Women Cohort 1960)

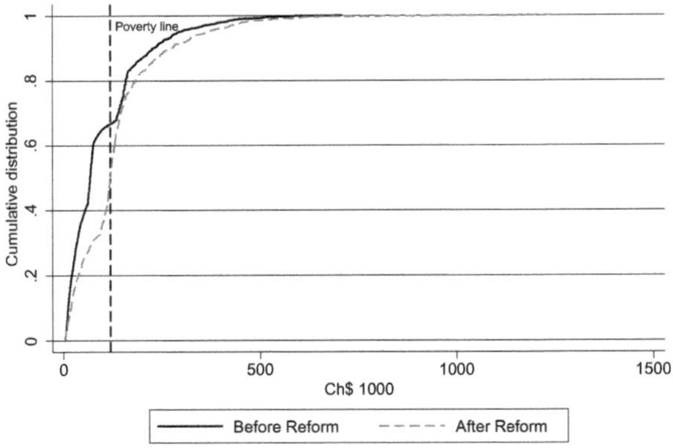

Source: Own calculation.

Finally, it is important to note that, by changing the present discounted value of future benefits and how participation into the labor market affects future pension rights, the reform will change current and future labor supply as well as the participation into the formal labor market. In Attanasio, Meghir, and Otero (2013), we look at the impact of the reform on the propensity to work in the formal labor market. Here, instead we have focused on the immediate impact of the reform on inequality. The exercise we perform in Attanasio, Meghir, and Otero (2013) is important because, from a theoretical point of view, the reform has an ambiguous effect on participation to the formal labor market. Most individuals will experience both income and substitution effects as a consequence of the reform. The former will typically decrease the propensity to participate to the formal labor market, while the latter can go both ways, depending on whether, for a specific individual, the rate of conversion of participation into future pension benefits (the accrual rate) increases or decreases, that is where in Figure 10.1 each individual is located. In Attanasio, Meghir, and Otero (2013) we find that, empirically, income and substitution effects work in a way consistent with the theory. When aggregating the different impacts, we find that the overall effect on the probability to contribute to pension system is negative as a result of the reform, reducing the participation in the formal labor market around 4.1% for those workers older than 40 years old. The results differ by gender and age. The reform reduces the probability of being formal by 3.2% and 2.8% for women and men between 56 and 65 years old, respectively. As the reform has reduced the probability to contribute to the pension system we can expect a lower increment in the final pension due to the reform. In our exercise here, we do not consider these impacts on behavior and therefore will overestimate the inequality gap reduction due to the reform.

Figure 10.13

Poverty Level Changes by Education

a) Expected Pension 2009 (Women Non Education)

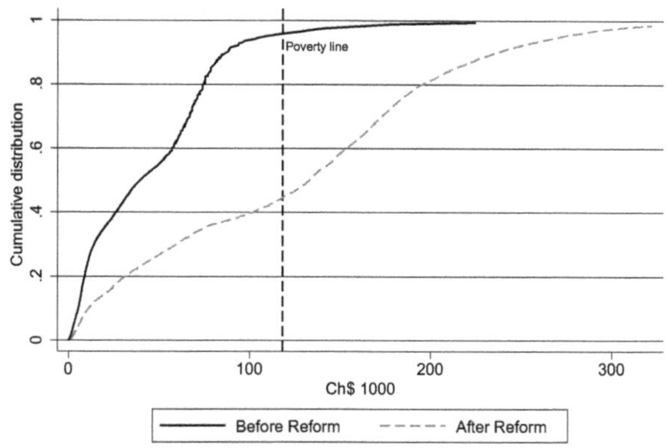

b) Expected Pension 2009 – Women Primary

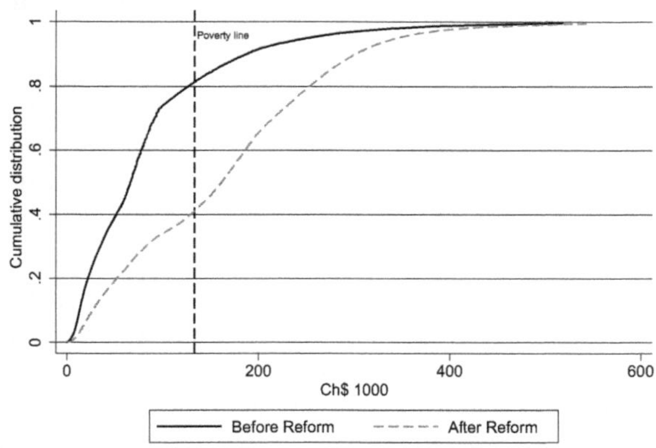

Source: Own calculation.

10.6. Conclusions

The 2008 reform was devised to increase the amount accumulated in individual pension accounts for certain targeted groups (such as the young, women and the self-employed) and to reduce the number of individuals with very low pensions at retirement. These objectives were achieved through a number of subsidies and various other mechanisms and through a radical change in the first tier of the system, which provides social pensions. The immediate impact of the reform has been very different for different groups in the population.

For those workers retiring before 2015, the self-financed pension wealth and the final pension have increased, on average, by 0.6% and 15%, respectively. Although the final pension changes have been positive for both genders, the female pension improvement has been 56% higher than the rise for men, reducing importantly gender inequalities. Moreover, the pension reform has substantially reduced inequality in pensions and pension wealth, even within groups. The reduction in inequality in pensions is particularly visible and, albeit larger for women, is present for both genders.

The changes in expected pension at retirement and the expected accrual rate for each period also changed the incentive to participate in the system and, indirectly, to the formal labor market. There is possibly a trade-off in terms of pension wealth improvements and formal labor market participation that the new subsidies and welfare pensions have raised. The larger pensions due to the reform could potentially change the incentives to work formally, through a direct negative income effect, explained by the changes in the pensions, and an indirect substitution effect explained by the changes in the accrual rate. As these changes are different for different groups of the population they will affect the final pension distribution. This trade-off raises the issue of the optimal subsidies and welfare pensions. In Attanasio, Meghir, and Otero (2013), we look at the impact of the reform on the propensity to work in the formal labor market. Here, instead we have focused on the immediate impact of the reform on inequality. From this point of view the reform has reduced inequalities (between groups and genders and within groups) substantially. It has also substantially changed the incentives to accumulate, increasing them for some groups and decreasing them for others. The impact of these important changes is the subject of our other paper (Attanasio, Meghir, and Otero 2013).

Appendix A: Tables

A Children Profiles

Table 10.5

Estimates the Probability to Have a Child (Probit RE)

Variables	Delta Child=1
Sex (1=Men)	–0.027
	(3.40)**
Age	0.119
	(42.96)**
Age 2	–0.002
	(59.95)**
Year	–0.004
	(4.00)**
Primary (1=Yes)	–0.048
	(4.74)**
Secondary (1=Yes)	–0.085
	(7.01)**
Degree (1=Yes)	–0.154
	(11.65)**
Married (1=Yes)	0.814
	(92.18)**
Number of Children	–0.103
	(27.15)**
Cohort 1940 (1=Yes)	–0.042
	(2.19)*
Cohort 1950 (1=Yes)	–0.097
	(3.72)**
Cohort 1960 (1=Yes)	–0.151
	(4.44)**
Cohort 1970 (1=Yes)	–0.251
	(5.84)**
Cohort 1980 (1=Yes)	–0.314
	(5.89)**
Constant	4.618
	(2.50)*
Observations	645413
Number Individuals	19874

Notes: z statistics in parentheses.
* significant at 5%; ** significant at 1%.
Source: Own calculation.

B Divorce Profiles

Table 10.6

Hazard Ratios from Cox Proportional Model Estimates for the Probability of Marriage

Variables	Married=1
Age	0.956
	(2.10)*
Age 2	1.001
	(2.28)*
Dummy Cohabiting (Yes=1)	2.76
	(11.44)**
Number of Children	1.115
	(4.07)**
Delta Children 2004-6	1.231
	(−1.85)
Delta Children 2006-9	1.695
	(4.79)**
Primary (1=Yes)	1.265
	(2.24)*
Secondary (1=Yes)	1.44
	(3.01)**
Degree (1=Yes)	1.49
	(3.08)**
Observations	6759

Notes: z statistics in parentheses.
* significant at 5%; ** significant at 1%.
Source: Own calculation.

Table 10.7

Hazard Ratios from Cox Proportional Model Estimates for the Probability of Divorce

Variables	Divorce=1
Age	0.868
	(3.66)**
Age 2	1.001
	(2.45)*
Years as married	1.036
	(2.85)**
Total number of children	1.297
	(2.73)**
Children with other couples	0.708
	(3.39)**
Primary (1=Yes)	1.042
	(−0.28)
Secondary (1=Yes)	1.071
	(−0.41)
Degree (1=Yes)	1.356
	(−1.71)
Observations	10513

Notes: z statistics in parentheses.
* significant at 5%; ** significant at 1%.
Source: Own calculation.

Using the information provided by the two following questions in the EPS we computed an indicator in order to determine who could be considered as the worse off member, in terms of the pension system participation, during the marriage. We basically recorded the answers creating an indicator between 0 and 1 in the following way:

1. Did your partner work frequently during the relationship? a) Most of the time = 1; b) Almost half of the time = 0.5; c) For a little time = 0.25; d) Did not work at all = 0.
2. How frequently did your partner make contributions when she/he was working? a) All the time (monthly) = 1; b) Over half the time = 0.75; c) Half the time = 0.5; d) Under half the time = 0.25; e) Occasionally contributed = 0.

With the product of these two new recorded variables we created, for each at least once married interviewed, the worse/better indicator, which is shown by gender in the figure below. The higher the indicator the higher the partner's frequency of contributions reported by the individual. For all future periods and for all single individuals we imputed the indicator using age, education, and gender groups. Finally, combining this indicator with the individual's frequency of contributions we imputed an individual as the worst off member (the best off member) upon divorce in case the worst/better off indicator is above 0.8 (below 0.2) and her frequency of contribution is below 0.8 (above 0.2).

C *Outcomes of Interest*

Figure 10.14

Changes in the Distribution of Pensions Resulting from the Reform

a) Pension Distribution (Men Cohort 1940)

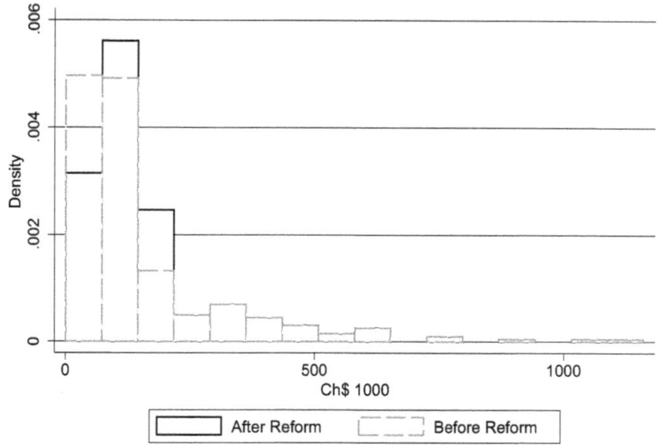

b) Pension Distribution (Men Cohort 1960)

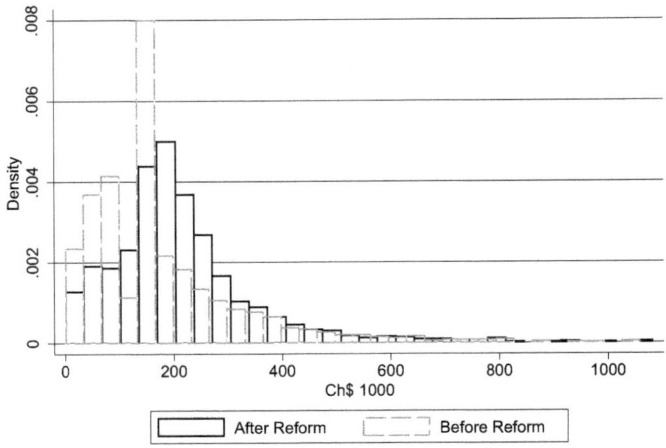

c) Pension Distribution – Primary (Women Cohort 1940)

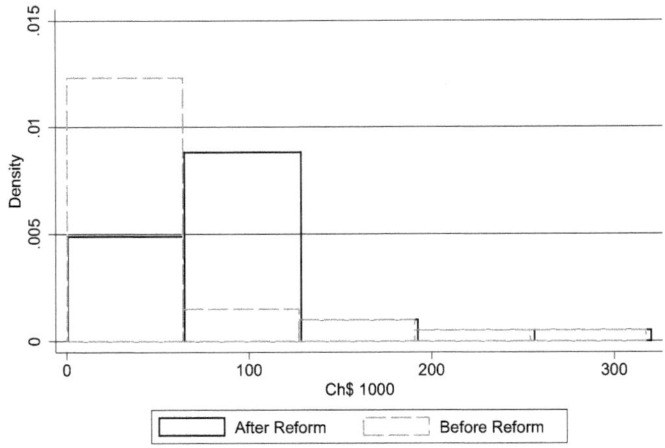

d) Pension Distribution – Secondary (Women Cohort 1940)

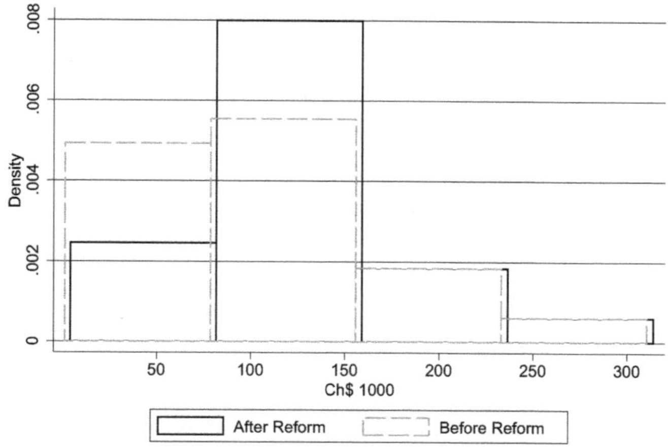

e) Pension Distribution – Non Education (Women Cohort 1960)

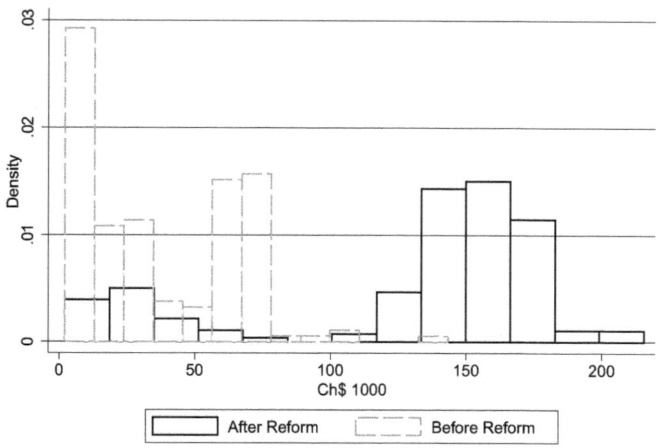

f) Pension Distribution – College (Women Cohort 1960)

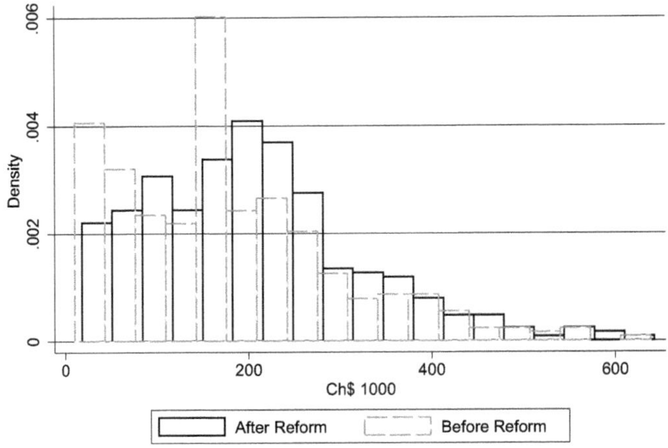

g) Pension Distribution – Primary (Women Cohort 1960)

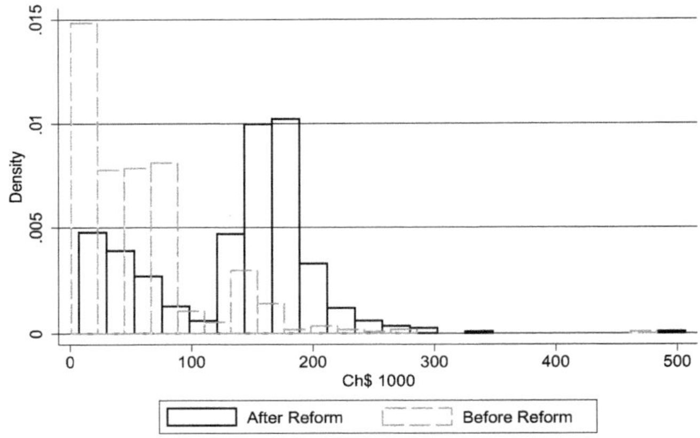

h) Pension Distribution – Secondary (Women Cohort 1960)

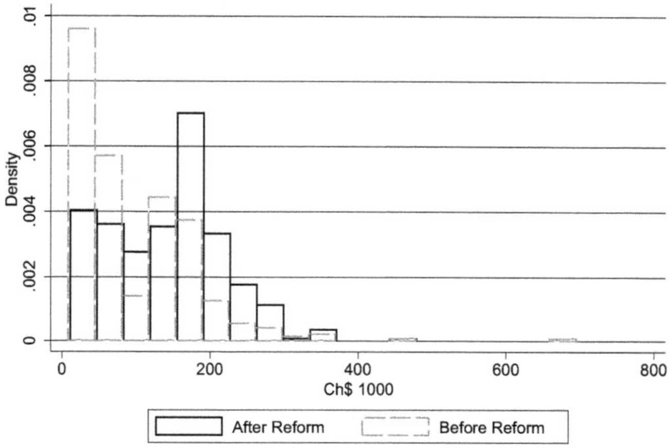

Source: Own calculation.

Figure 10.15

Changes in the Distribution of the Pension Differences Between Men and Women

a) Pension Before Reform (Cohort 1960)

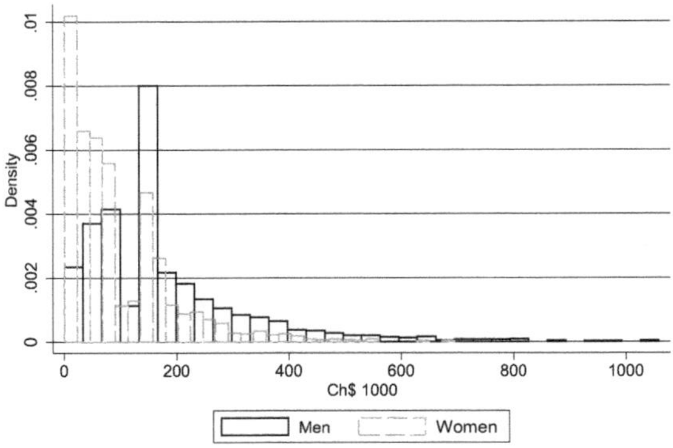

b) Pension After Reform (Cohort 1960)

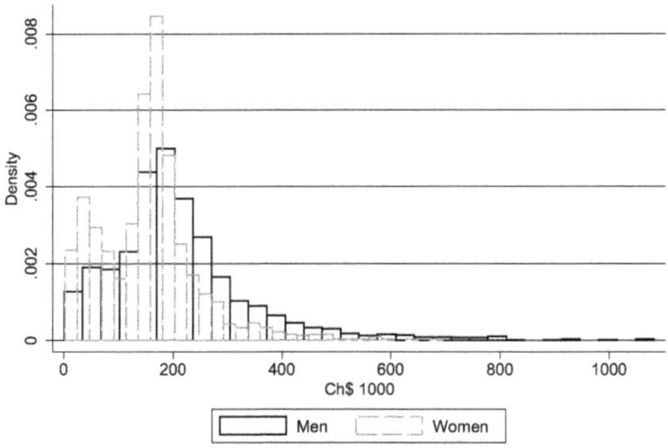

c) Pension Change Distribution (Non Education)

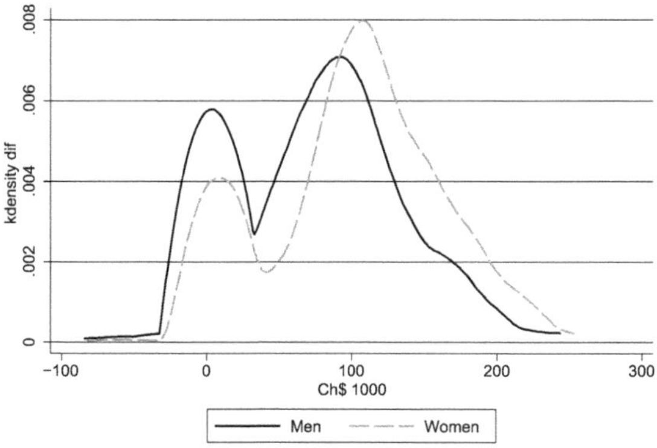

d) Pension Change Distribution (Primary)

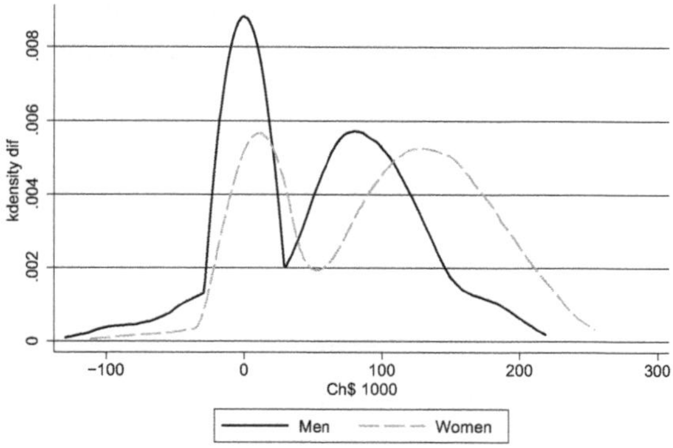

e) Pension Change Distribution (Secondary)

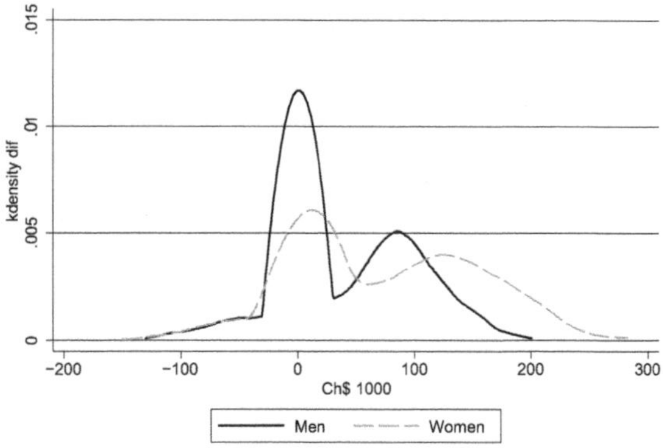

f) Pension Change Distribution (College)

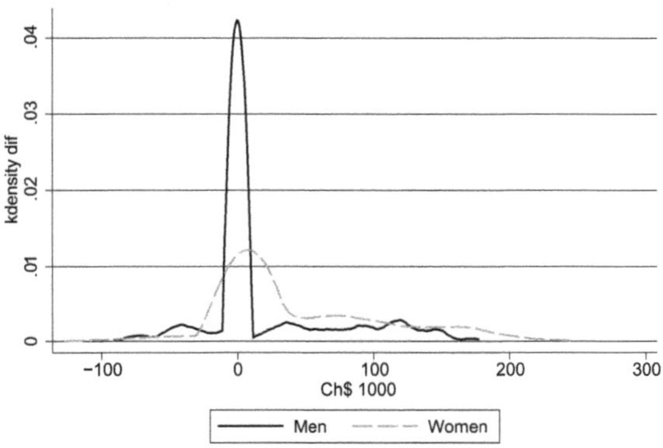

Source: Own calculation.

Figure 10.16

Changes in Accumulated Pension Wealth Before and After the Reform

a) PW Distribution – Non Education (Women Cohort 1940)

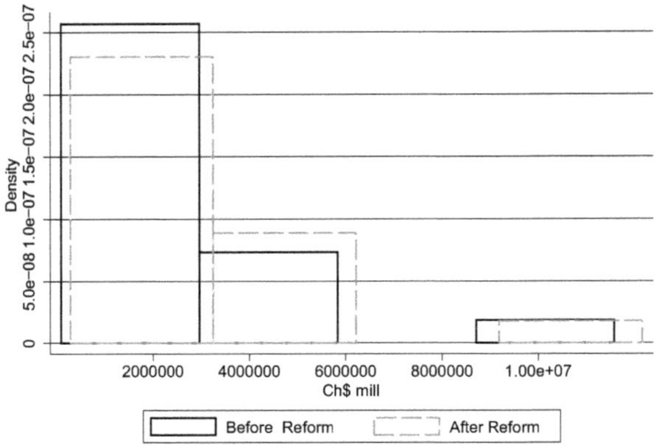

b) PW Distribution – Primary (Women Cohort 1940)

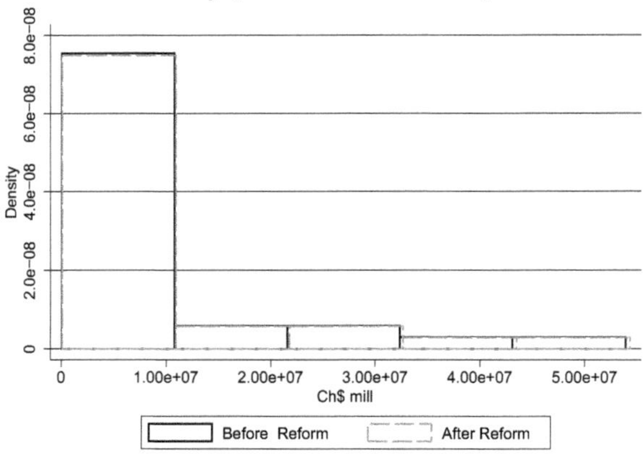

c) PW Distribution – Secondary (Women Cohort 1940)

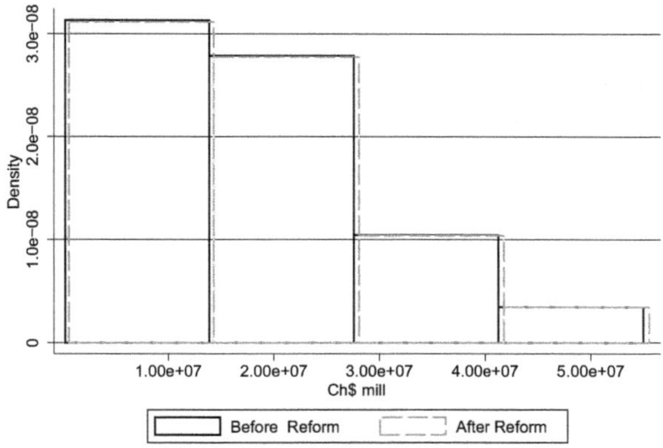

d) PW Distribution – College (Women Cohort 1940)

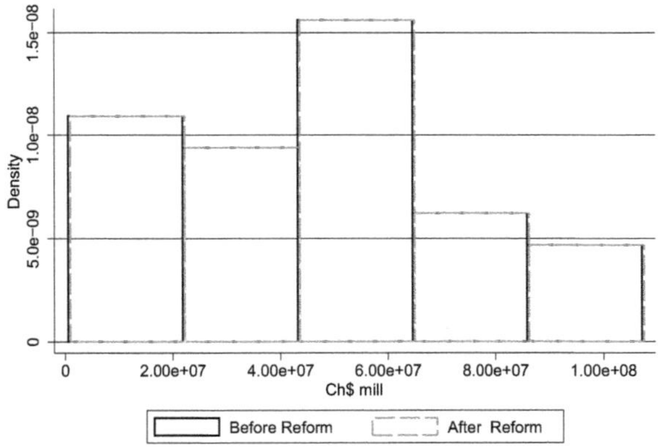

Source: Own calculation.

Figure 10.17

Changes in Poverty Levels Before and After the Reform for Elderly People, in Particular, for Elderly Women

a) Expected Pension 2009 (Women Secondary)

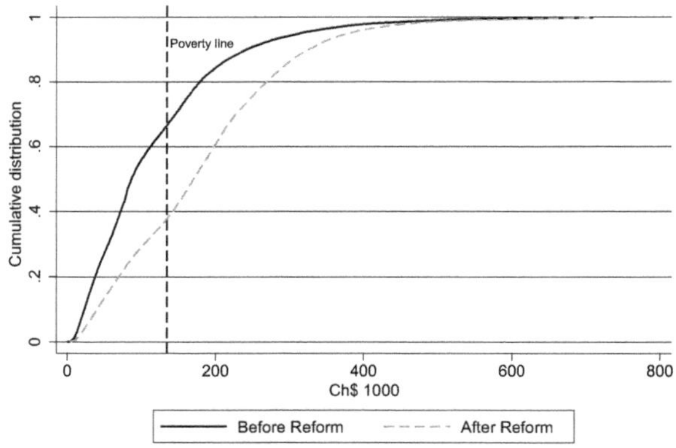

b) Expected Pension 2009 (Women College)

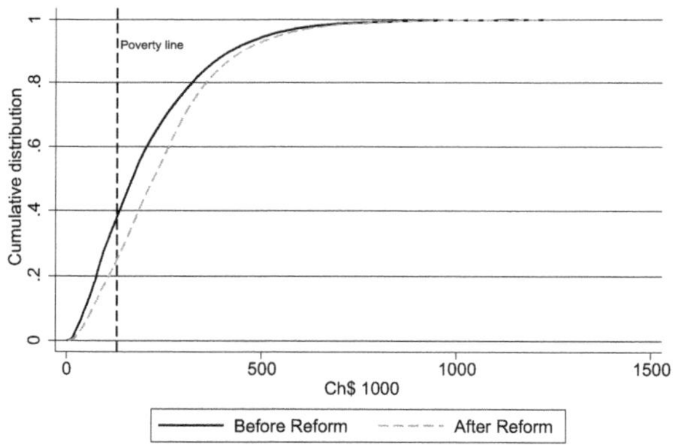

Source: Own calculation.

Appendix B: Assumptions

1. Sample. Not retired AFP (No INP) workers between 20 and 65 years old.
2. Retirement age: We are assuming that all individuals will retire at 65 years old. No early retirement.
3. Interest rate: We assume different interest rates by age according the default multi-funds structure, where Fund B return

= 11%, Fund C return = 9% and Fund D return = 7%. We observe if workers have chosen a fund in the year 2009, in these cases we assume that individuals hold the same fund between 2006-9.

4. Recognition bond return = 4.5% Individuals that contributed in the old PAYG system (pre-80s) will receive at retirement a bond (RB) recognizing those contributions. We are assuming a return of 4.5% for that bond. For individuals that have not claimed the RB, and then its value is not observed in the administrative record, we are assuming average values by age, education, and gender groups.
5. Discount factor = 0.98.
6. PMG/PASIS/PBS and PMAS values. For the welfare pensions before (PMG and PASIS) and after (PBS) the reform we are using the following Ch$ values: PASIS = 44,186; PMG = 96,391; PBS = 7,500; PMAS = 70,000 at 2008, 120,000 at 2009, 150,000 at 2010, 200,000 at 2011 and 255,000 at 2012 onwards.
7. PBS and PMAs growth = 2% and PMG and PASIS growths at 3% annually.
8. Disability premium rate difference between men and women = 0.2%
9. Partner's pension wealth fraction as compensation upon divorce = 30%
10. Minimum wage: Value of Ch$1,650,000 at 2009 and assuming a rate of growth of 3%
11. Total contribution rate = 12%
12. Cap contributions: 64 UF (Ch$20,319). UF is indexed on inflation.
13. Pensions: All retirees are buying a phased withdrawal at retirement.

Appendix C: Other Components Introduced by the Reform

- Self-employed contributions. From the 1st of January 2012, the self-employed are incorporated gradually into the mandatory system. They will be eligible for the first tier benefits, but they must contribute annually according to 80% of their gross earnings.[31]
- Subsidy for young people's contributions. From the 1st of July

2011, employees between 18 and 35 years old who earn a salary below 1.5 times the minimum wage receive a subsidy for all their first 24 contributions. The subsidy will be equal to 5% of the minimum wage at the period in which the contribution is done. This subsidy is deposited into their individual accounts as part of their pension wealth. Considering that this new element and the previous one will start to be effective since 2011 and 2012 respectively, we do not expect a current effect on the labor market due to them.

- Subsidy for hiring young people. From the 1st of October 2008, employers receive a monthly subsidy when they hire young workers between 18 and 35 years old. As in the previous case, the subsidy is equal to 5% of the minimum wage and workers must be doing any of their first 24 contributions and earning a salary lower than 1.5 times the minimum wage at that point in time.[32]
- Subsidy for voluntary contributions. From the 1st of October 2008, the third tier of the system is subsided for workers who choose the new tax form introduced for voluntary savings. In this case, employees pay taxes for the amount saved at the moment of doing them and pay taxes for the earned returns at retirement. Before the reform, voluntary savings were excluded from taxable income and all taxes were paid at retirement. Those workers choosing the first tax scheme option will receive a subsidy equal to 15% of all the saved amount.[33] On September 2010 the number of voluntary contributions operating with this new tax regime was 7% of the total voluntary number of contributions.[34]
- Occupational voluntary saving plans. From the 1st of October 2008, employers are allowed to set up collective voluntary saving plans for their employees in which they can define joint contributions. Employers have tax incentives for contributing in their employees accounts, as those contributions are considered as company's expenditures and thus do not pay taxes. Employees will not only get the subsidy given by the employer but also can get all the available benefits for voluntary savings described above. Even though this element has been operating since 2008, the number of collective voluntary saving plans has been minor according the regulator information. Therefore, we do not expect any important effect on the labor mar-

ket due to this element.

- Fixed fee elimination. From the 1st of October 2008, the PFA fixed fees, charged before the reform for managing the individual accounts, are abolished.
- New affiliates auction. From the 1st of October 2008, new affiliates to the system are allocated to the winning PFA of an auction for the new affiliates portfolio. Affiliates can choose another PFA after 24 months of the original auction. This new mechanism aims to generate more competition in the system reducing the charged fees.

Appendix D: Computing Pension Entitlements

The present value[35] of the expected accumulated pension upon retirement in periods $t = \{2002, \ldots, 2009\}$ is computed as

$$(3) \qquad E_t(PW_{iR}) = \sum_{j=0}^{t}(cont_{ij}) \prod_{j}^{t}(1 + r_j) + E_t \left[\sum_{j=0}^{t}(cont_{ij}) \prod_{k=t+1}^{R}(1 + r_k) + \sum_{j=t+1}^{R}(con_{ij}) \prod_{j}^{R}(1 + r_j) \right] + NE_{ij} + RB_{iR}$$

The first sum is the total observed[36] accumulated pension until period t. The elements following the expectation incorporate the unobserved future returns earn for the contributions done before t and all the future contributions and their own returns until retirement R. NE_{ij} captures the new elements introduced by the reform, such as the child subsidy and compensation upon divorce forecasted, $cont_{ij}$ is the annual contribution described below, r is the interest rate earned by the accumulated resources[37] and RB_{iR} is the recognition bond created for capturing any old contributions to the PAYG system.[38]

$$cont_{ij} = \phi w_{ij} \times (\imath[W^F]\imath[W^E]) + \phi 0.8 w_{ij} \times (\imath[W^F]\imath[W^{SE}])$$

Where $\imath$ is an indicator function taking the value of 1 if the expression in the brackets is true and W^F, W^E, W^{SE} take the value of 1 if individual i is a formal worker, employee and self-employed,[39] respectively.

$$(4) \qquad NE_{ij} = \lambda_i \times CA_{td} \prod_{j=td}^{R} (1 + r_j)\imath[Woff] \; - \lambda_i \times \sum_{j=0}^{td} (cont_{ij})$$

$$\prod_{j}^{R} (1 + r_j)\imath[Boff] \; + \sum_{nc=1}^{Tc} [1.8MW_{tb(nc)}] \prod_{j=tb(nc)}^{R} (1 + r_j)\imath[WO];$$

$$0 < \lambda_i < 0.5$$

The first two terms in equation (4) are the compensations upon divorce introduced by the reform. Family courts will determine if one of the member must be compensated receiving a fraction λ_i of the partner's accumulated resources, CA_{td}, when divorce happens at period $j = td$.[40] $Woff(Boff)$ takes the value of 1 if individual i is considered by the court as the worst (better) off member. The final summation includes all the subsidies received for each child. Where MW is the minimum wage at period tb,[41] Tc is the total number of children, $tb(nc)$[42] is the period in which child number nc was born and WO takes the value of 1 if individual i is a woman. Finally using the total expected accumulated self-financed pension wealth we compute pensions according the following formulas in the post-reform scenario.

$$(5) \qquad P_{iR} = \begin{cases} PBS & \text{if } \frac{E_t PW_{iR}}{12 \times CNU_{iR}} = PBS \\ & \text{and } i \in 60\% \text{ poorest} \\ \frac{E_t PW_{iR}}{12 \times CNU_{iR}} + (PBS - \frac{PBS}{PMaS} \times PB_{iR}) & \\ & \text{if } 0 < \frac{E_t PW_{iR}}{12 \times CNU_{iR}} \leq PMaS \\ & \text{and } i \in 60\% \text{ poorest} \\ \frac{E_t PW_{iR}}{12 \times CNU_{iR}} & \text{if } PMaS < \frac{E_t PW_{iR}}{12 \times CNU_{iR}} \\ & \text{or } i \in 40\% \text{ richest} \end{cases}$$

Where PBS is the new non-contributory welfare pension, $PMaS$ is an upper limit pension[43] such as affiliates receive a pension complement defined as $APS = (PBS - \frac{PBS}{PMaS} \times PB_{iR})$, PB_{iR} is the sum of the self-financed pension plus any received survivor pension and any pension received from the past PAYG system and CNU_{iR} is a factor that incorporate the individual's life expectancy.[44]

Pre-reform pensions are computed similarly but considering the cases when retirees receive either a PMG or the PASIS at retirement. Thus, retirees self-finance annuities according the accumulated wealth under the non-reform scenario, receive a PMG if the annuity is below the value of the minimum pension at retirement and the 240 months of contributions requirement is satisfied and receive a PASIS if the the self-financed pension is lower than this value and the means tested requirement is satisfied.[45]

Notes

1 Final report, 2006 Pension Reform Commission. See Marcel (2006).
2 Final report, 2006 Pension Reform Commission. See Marcel (2006).
3 According to forecasts by the Chilean Pension Regulator, Superintendencia de Pensiones (SPE), and the Budget Office, Direccion de Presupuesto (DIPRES). See Marcel (2006).
4 Accumulated savings are tax free during the working life. However, pensions pay income taxes.
5 Since October 2002, workers can choose among 5 funds with different combinations of risk and return. When workers do not choose any fund, their savings are invested in a default fund defined by age. The PFAs' investments are regulated in terms of the possible set of financial instrument to be chosen and on the proportion of foreign investments done.
6 Final report, 2006 Pension Reform Commission. See Marcel (2006).
7 Early retirement is allowed if the worker can finance a pension larger or equal to 150% of the Minimum Pension, described below, and 70% of the last 10 years average wages.
8 By 2005, more than 60% of retirees chose the annuity scheme. See Mitchell and Ruiz (2009).
9 For monthly amounts below $Ch 1,050,000 (US$ 2,000).
10 Women will also have to provide pension funds to leave a survivor pension benefit to her husband.
11 From 2012 to 2014 self-employed participate voluntarily in the system, but they have to explicitly opt out to avoid participation. From 2015 participation is compulsory and contributions will be done over 80% of gross earnings.
12 Workers older then 50 years old in 2008 will receive the higher pension, either the PMG or the post-reform pension.
13 In 2009, it was equivalent to Ch$286,200.
14 See Arenas et al. (2006) for a complete description about the aims and the relevance of the EPS.
15 We do not observe the accumulated pension savings for the periods between 2006 and 2009. However, we computed them using the observed monthly earning and making some specific and educated assumptions about the investment returns. In doing so we assumed returns according the multi-funds default scheme introduced in 2002. Having the Administrative Records information containing the accumulated pension saving for all years previous (including) to 2009 allow us to reduce the amount of assumptions, increasing the efficiency of our estimation. For example, observing the complete pension wealth history give us information about the heterogeneous returns obtained by each affiliate.
16 As we mentioned earlier, it is possible to continue working after the legal age of retirement. However, we are not considering those individuals who continued working after 65 and, for simplicity, in some of the computations we perform we will assume that all employees retire at the age of 65 in the post-reform scenario.
17 Detailed information about this new indicator, including its formula, can be found in Decreto Supremo N. 2, and Resolucion N. 155 and N. 164. Superintendencia de Pensiones (SPE), Ministry of Work.
18 Workers who did not have enough self-saved pension wealth to self-finance a pension above the PBS, but satisfy the means tested requirements such as they obtain a PBS, have implicitly a pension wealth equivalent to the one to self-finance a PBS.
19 In 2009, it was equivalent to Ch$ 286200. We assumed an annual rate of growth of 3%.
20 Including all the elements introduced by the reform detailed in section 2.
21 The results are shown in the Appendix A (Table 10.6).
22 The simulations show that older cohorts will be less affected for this part of the reform. Just 2% of the retirees belonging to the 1940 cohort will receive this compensation.

23 A detailed description of the formulas used to compute the accumulated pension wealth and pension is in the Appendix, section D.

24 Centro de Estadisticas de la Superintendencia de Pensiones. Rentabilidad Real de los Fondos de Pensiones 2008. Superintendencia de Pensiones, Chile. See http://www.safp.cl/safpstats/stats/.

25 Section A.4.3 has figures with the frequency of the self-financed pension wealth by educational levels.

26 The same graphs for men (Figure 10.14) are in the Appendix A.

27 We are just considering those who have not retired in 2009 yet.

28 The pension distribution for workers with primary and secondary level of education are in the Appendix A, Section A.C.

29 Serie Analisis de Resultados de la Encuesta de Caracterizacion Socioeconomica Nacional (CASEN 2006). Ministerio de Planicacion, Chile.

30 CASEN 2009. We assume a rate of growth for the poverty line of 3%, in line with expected inflation. Although the growth in the poverty line between 2006 and 2009 was 19%, it stayed around the same real value before 2009.

31 From 2012 to 2014 a default-voluntary participation is introduced, where workers have to explicitly decide not to participate in the system. For the years 2012 and 2013 contributions will be done considering the 32% and 56% of annual salary, respectively. After 2015 the participation is compulsory and contributions are done over the 80% of annual salary from 2014 onwards.

32 Two additional programs, Subsidio al Empleo Juvenil and Jovenes Bicentenario, which focused on the young workers (18-24 years old) were implemented around the same time of the reform implementation. The benefits have been larger than those proposed by the reform.

33 With a maximum of Ch$221,178 at 2009. This value will be updated each year according to inflation.

34 Superintendencia de Pensiones de Chile.

35 To make the things simpler we are not writing the discount factor, which is assumed to be equal to 0.98, in the following formulas.

36 Observed by the employees, but not necessarily by the econometrician. We observed the real accumulated resources just for periods previous to 2005.

37 Historical returns of the system have been higher than 10% since its beginning, see Superintendencia de Pensiones. We will assume future returns equal to 7%.

38 We observe the RB value for those affiliates who have claimed it. However, for affiliates who have not claimed the recognition bond, we assume their values according to groups defined by education, age and cohorts groups.

39 Self-employed workers will be incorporated gradually to the system since 2012. Thus, we are not incorporating these workers in the analysis.

40 Compensation upon divorce is for divorces after 2008 only.

41 We are assuming a rate of growth of 3% for the minimum wage in all future periods.

42 For children born before the reform the bond receives return since 2008.

43 The PBS pension are readjusted annually according inflation. We are assuming a annual rate of growth of 3%.

44 As the pension formulas show, we are computing pensions as phased withdrawals. All the computations were done using stata codes provided by the Chilean pension regulator, Superintendencia de Pensiones. See Pino (2005).

$$\frac{1}{CNU_{iR}} = \frac{l_x \frac{1}{(1+r)^x}}{\sum_x^{110} l_x \frac{1}{(1+x)^x}} - \frac{11}{24}$$

Where $l_x = l_{x-1}(1 - q_{i,x-1,R-1})$ is the number of people alive at the age x in period R, $(1 - q_{i,x-1,R-1})$ is the probability to die at age $x - 1$ in period $R - 1$ and r is the relevant interest rate used to compute phased withdrawals (Norma 79, Ministerio del Trabajo y Planicacion Social de Chile), which is assumed equal to 4.5%. If retiree has potential survivors the final retiree's CNU is the sum of survivors' CNU and his own CNU. We use mortality tables defined in RV-2009. As the insurance companies must finance retiree's funerals, they discount a mortuary fee from the original accumulated resources. Even though we are considering a mortuary fee in our computations we are not explicitly writing it in the formulas just for simplicity.

45 PASIS is allocated according a poverty indicator and it has been usually given to retirees belonging to the first quantile.

References

Marcel, M. (2006). El derecho a una vida digna en la vejez. Hacia un contrato social con la prevision de Chile, http://www.consejoreformaprevisional.cl/view/presentacion.asp.

Ministerio de Planicacion, Chile (2006). Serie Analisis de Resultados de la Encuesta de Caracterizacion Socioeconomica Nacional.

Arenas de Mesa, A., Behrman, J., Bravo, D. (2004). Characteristics and Determinants of the Density of Contributions in a Private Social Security System, Michigan Retirement Research Center Working Paper No. 2004-077.

Arenas de Mesa, A., Behrman, J., Bravo, D., Mitchell, O., Todd, P. (2006). The Chilean Pension Reform Turns 25: Lessons From the Social Protection Survey, NBER Working Paper No. 12401.

Athey, S., Imbens, G. (2007). Discrete Choice Models with Multiple Unobserved Choice Characteristics, in: International Economic Review, 48(4): 1159-92.

Attanasio, O., A. Brugiavini (2003). Social Security and Household Saving, in: The Quaterly Journal of Economics, 118(3): 1075-119.

Attanasio, O., Meghir, C., Otero, A. (2013). Pensions, Work and Informality: The Impact of the 2008 Chilean Pension Reform, UCL Department of Economics Working Paper.

Attanasio, O., Rohwedder, S. (2003). Pension Wealth and Household Saving: Evidence from Pension Reforms in the United Kingdom, in: The American Economic Review, 93(5): 1499-521.

Berstein, S., Castaneda, P., Fajnzylber, E., Reyes, G. (2009). Chile 2008: A Second Generation Pension Reform: Superintendence of Pensions.

Berstein, S., Fuentes, O., Torrealba, N. (2011). Esquema de Multifondos en Chile, Documento de Trabajo No 43.

Berstein, S., Larrain, G., Pino, F. (2005). Cobertura, Densidades y Pensiones en Chile: Proyecciones a 20 Anos Plazo, Documento de Trabajo No. 12.

Blundell, R., Duncan, A., Meghir, C. (1998). Estimating Labor Supply Responses Using Tax Reforms, in: Econometrica, 66(4): 827-62.

Heckman, J., Singer, B. (1984). A Method for Minimizing the Impact of Distributional Assumptions in Econometrics Models for Duration Data; in: Econometrica, 52(2): 271-320.

Hurd, M., Rohwedder, S. (2010). Effects of the Financial Crisis and Great Recession on American Households, NBER Working Paper No. 16407.

Krueger, A., Pischke, J.-S. (1992). The Effect of Social Security on Labor Supply: A Cohort Analysis of the Notch Generation, in: Journal of Labour Economics, 10(4): 421-37.

Laird, N. (1978). Nonparametric Maximum Likelihood Estimation of a Mixing Distribution, in: Journal of the American Statistical Association, 73(364): 805-11, 1978.

Lindsay, B. (1983). The Geometry of Mixture Likelihood, in: Annals of Statistics, 11(1): 86-94.

Magnac, T. (1991). Segmented or Competitive Labour Market, in: Econometrica, 59(1): 165-87.

Mitchell, O., Ruiz, J. (2009). Pension Payouts in Chile: Past, Present, and Future Prospects, PARC Working Paper No. WPS09-02.

Packard,T. (2007). Do Workers in Chile Choose Informal Employment? A Dynamic Analysis of Sector Choice, World Bank Policy Research Working Paper No. 4232.

Pino, F. (2009). Retiro Programado y Nuevas Tablas de Mortalidad, Nota Tecnica No 1.

Reyes, G. (2009). Diseno de Mercado para la provision de seguridad social: El caso del Seguro de Invalidez y Sobrevivencia en Chile, Documento de Trabajo No. 30.

11

Should Cash Transfers Be Confined to the Poor? Implications for Poverty and Inequality in Latin America*

Pablo Acosta
Phillippe Leite
Jamele Rigolini

11.1. Introduction

Cash transfer programs have become the centerpiece of many Latin American countries' social protection agenda. They have become popular not only as short term instruments to help the poor cope with economic shocks, but also as longer-term poverty alleviation programs supporting minimum consumption levels and promoting the accumulation of human capital.

Yet, while several evaluations have demonstrated the impact of cash transfers on poverty reduction and human development outcomes, they do absorb an important share of governments' budgets (Grosh et al. 2008; Fiszbein and Schady 2009; World Bank-IEG 2011). Most countries in the Latin America and Caribbean (LAC) region count with conditional cash transfer programs (CCTs) targeted to poor households with children that account for budgets up to 0.6 percent of GDP (Table 11.1). Some countries in the region (fewer than those with CCTs) also provide cash

* *We would like to dedicate this chapter to Gozalo Llorente, who unexpectedly left us during its writing. We would like to thank Gonzalo and Alinne Veiga for excellent research assistance. We also thank helpful comments from Margaret Grosh, Ruslan Yemtsov, and Javier Baez. The findings, interpretations, and conclusions expressed in this chapter are entirely those of the authors.*

transfers to the elderly, many of them on a universal (i.e. categorical) basis, that requires an even more sizeable share of public budget – up to 1.3 percent of GDP (Table 11.2). These programs can account, in a country like Brazil, for up to 1.7 percent of GDP, and for the average in the region, between 1 and 2 percent of GDP (Grosh et al. 2008).

Resource constraints and ethical considerations have led to a heated debate on the scope and coverage of cash transfers. Few doubt the neciessity of providing benefits to people falling within demonstrable categories of vulnerable groups, such as children, the elderly or the disabled, though there is still an open debate on how children and the elderly compete as the primary group to focus social assistance.[1] But there is less consensus on whether transfers should be given to all people within these categories (i.e. be "categorical"), or if they should be restricted to poor people within categories of beneficiaries (i.e. be "poverty targeted"). While poverty targeted transfers are more cost effective because limited resources are distributed among fewer beneficiaries, they remain more complex and costly to administer. And even the most sophisticated targeting systems miss some of the poor, and may have difficulties to adapt to entry and exit to and from poverty because registers of beneficiaries cannot be updated frequently.

It is therefore not always obvious that poverty-targeted social assistance programs are the best approach to alleviate poverty. At the heart, the optimal design relates to societal preferences for redistribution and taxation (Mkandawire 2005), as well as tolerance to exclusion errors or deviating from a "rights" approach. But the choice of design can also be informed by technical considerations, such as looking at the accuracy and cost effectiveness of different targeting mechanisms, which is the focus of this chapter.

This chapter simulates impacts of categorical and poverty targeted cash transfers on poverty and inequality in 13 Latin American countries: Argentina, Bolivia, Brazil, Chile, Colombia, Costa Rica, the Dominican Republic, Ecuador, Guatemala, Mexico, Nicaragua, Panama, and Peru. The simulations focus on two programs that tend to be the most widespread in the region: transfers to children up to five years of age, and to elderly people that are older than 65.

While, by their nature, poverty targeted transfers always deliver a higher poverty impact, both the incidence of poverty and the depth of the poverty gap appear to be important factors affecting the relative effectiveness of categorical vs. poverty targeted transfers. The comparison of transfers to children and the elderly also supports the

Table 11.1

Conditional Cash Transfers in Latin America and the Caribbean

Country	Program	Target Population	Amount (monthly US$)	Number of Beneficiaries (latest available)	Cost (% of GDP)
Argentina	Programa Familias	Household Heads, Pregnant Females, Children <19	40-80 per child	500,000 households	
Bolivia	Juancito Pinto	Public school children up to grade 6	2 per child	500,000 households	
Brazil	Bolsa Familia	Poor and extreme poor households	30 per household + 7 per child	11,100,000 households	0.36
Chile	Chile Solidario	Extreme poor households (means-tested)	14 per child	256,000 households	0.08
Colombia	Familias en Accion	Extreme poor households with children <7 (health), and with children <17 (education)	Education: 8-33 per child; Health: 28 per household	1,700,000 households	0.20
Dominican Republic	Solidaridad	Poor and extreme poor households with children <17	29 per household	461,000 households	
Ecuador	Bono de Desarrollo Humano	Households in first 2 income quintiles with children <17	15 per household	1,060,000 households	0.60
El Salvador	Comunidades Solidarias Rurales	Extreme poor households with children <16 in 100 rural municipalities	Education: 15 per household; Health: 15 per household	100,000 households	

Table 11.1 (continued)
Conditional Cash Transfers in Latin America and the Caribbean

Country	Program	Target Population	Amount (monthly US$)	Number of Beneficiaries (latest available)	Cost (% of GDP)
Guatemala	Mi Familia Progresa	Extreme poor households with children <16 in 130 municipalities	Education: 20 per household; Health: 20 per household	250,000 households	0.20
Honduras	Programa de Asignacion Familiar	Poor households with children 6-12 years old up tp grade 4	Education: 5 per household; Health: 4 per household	240,000 households	
Jamaica	Program of Advancement through Health and Education	Poor households (means-tested) until they graduate from secondary school	100 per child	100,000 households	
Mexico	Oportunidades	Extreme poor households (means-tested)	Education: 12-23 per household; Health: 17 per household	5,000,000 households	0.40
Panama	Red de Oportunidades	Extreme poor households (means-tested)	50 per household	70,000 households	
Paraguay	PROPAIS II	Extreme poor households with children <15 in rural areas	120 per household	5,800 households	0.08
Peru	Juntos	Poor households with children <15	33 per household	454.000 households	0.11

Source: Based on Fiszbein and Schady (2009).

Table 11.2

Non-Contributory Social Pensions in Latin America and the Caribbean

Country	Program	Target Population	Transfer (monthly US$)	Number of Beneficiaries (latest available)	Cost (% of GDP)
Argentina	Pensiones No Contributivas Asistenciales por Vejez	65+ without contributory pension and in poverty	151.5	65,900	
Bolivia	Renta Dignidad (former Bonosol)	60+ universal	22-29	782,660	1.30
Brazil	Rural Pension	65+ in rural areas	342	800,000	
Chile	Pension Basica Solidaria	65+ in 3 lowest quintiles of income distribution	150	407,000	0.50
Costa Rica	Regimen No Contributivo	65+ in poverty	135	53,492	0.24
Ecuador	Pension Asistencial	65+ without contributory pension	35	502,828	

Table 11.2 (continued)

Non-Contributory Social Pensions in Latin America and the Caribbean

Country	Program	Target Population	Transfer (monthly US$)	Number of Beneficiaries (latest available)	Cost (% of GDP)
El Salvador	Pension Basica Universal	70+ in severe extreme poor municipalities	50	19,534	
	70 y mas	70+ in selected municipalities, universal	28.5	2,000,000	
Mexico	Oportunidades Adulto Mayor	70+ in households receiving CCTs (Oportunidades)	22.7	80,000	
	Pension Alimentaria	70+ in Mexico DF, universal	63.2	470,000	
Peru	Gratitud	75+ without contributory pension and in poverty	36		0.03
Trinidad and Tobago	Senior Citizen Pension	65+ income means-tested	189-472	73,110	1.30
Uruguay	Beneficio No Contributivo	70+ Income means-tested	240	31,577	

Source: Murrugarra (2011).

view that choosing categories of beneficiaries carefully is almost as important as targeting the poor for achieving a high poverty impact. Overall, the findings suggest that in the Latin American context targeting assistance to the poor tends to deliver higher poverty impacts. There are nonetheless circumstances under which categorical targeting confined to geographical regions may be a valid option to consider. This is particularly the case in low-income countries with widespread pockets of poverty.

The chapter proceeds as follows. The next section summarizes trends in social assistance and the ongoing debate on categorical vs. targeted social transfers. Section 11.3 discusses the methodology used in the simulations. Section 11.4 presents the simulation results for the 13 Latin American countries. Section 11.5 concludes.

11.2. The Cash and Targeting Revolutions

All over the developing world, and particularly in Latin America, social protection programs are moving from universal in-kind benefits and subsidies, to targeted cash transfers. The rationale behind the silent revolutions towards cash lies in higher welfare impacts (cash can support households' needs beyond food), economic efficiency (e.g., avoidance of dead-weight losses and distortions from subsidies), transparency and accountability, and simplification of the administrative procedures in service delivery (Grosh et al. 2008). While cash transfers are far from being a panacea and should be designed in the context of a broader social assistance strategy that takes into account the local context and political economy, they undoubtedly improved in many countries both beneficiaries' welfare and the cost effectiveness of social assistance programs.

With the expansion of cash transfers, a debate has however arisen on the extent to which assistance should be provided to all people falling within demonstrable vulnerable categories (such as the children, the elderly or the disabled), or only to the poor within these categories. Is it optimal, and, equally important, is it ethically correct to handpick beneficiaries within categories?

From an ethical perspective, many advocate that social assistance programs should favor horizontal equity and that any person falling into a category that tends to be vulnerable should have the right to receive assistance (ILO-UN Social Protection Floor initiative 2010). This universal view of social assistance is strengthened by three potential drawbacks of confining assistance only to poor beneficiaries within each category. First, poverty targeting may generate behavioral distortions and induce informality. For instance, poverty targeted pensions and health insurance programs financed out of general taxation that coexist with contributory ones may generate incentives to remain in the informal labor market and thus avoid contributing to the system (Levy 2008). Poverty targeted cash transfers may also discourage labor force participation. Second, there is no targeting system that can perfectly identify vulnerable individuals within a given category. Even the most sophisticated targeting mechanisms miss some of the poor (exclusion error), and include some wealthier individuals (inclusion error). The question there is up to which point a society is ready to exclude some of the poor from assistance because of efficiency considerations. Finally, potential stigmas related to poverty targeting may also affect participation of the most vulnerable (Grosh et al. 2008). Leite (2011) finds, for instance, that in Tanzania some of the elderly from rural poor villages did declare having 3 meals a day to avoid the stigma of being perceived as poor.

The extent to which these drawbacks represent a strong argument against targeting still remains an open discussion. When the benefits of social assistance programs do not become disproportionate, existing studies find that labor market distortions from poverty targeted Conditional Cash Transfers remain moderate (Parker and Skoufias 2000; Skoufias and Di Maro 2009; Fiszbein and Schady 2009; World Bank-IEG 2011), although for social pensions evidence suggests that there may be a small impact on formal labor market participation (Attanasio et al. 2011). And while exclusion errors may still be considerable, many categorical programs also miss some of the poor – though in lower proportions – because of information failures and high participation costs in remote areas (Barrientos 2009; Sluchynsky 2008).

The categorical approach is also challenged by the reality of hard budget constraints and political economy considerations. Countries have limited resources to fight poverty and promote equity. Broad social assistance policies in developing countries already cost on average 2 percent of GDP (Weigand and Grosh 2008; Grosh et al. 2008), though wide disparities subsist across countries.[2] And even if some countries may have the fiscal space to expand further coverage, this can be politically costly. In general, policy discussions tend to center on how to improve the programs' impact within the existing resources.

In addition to ethical and political economy considerations, there are also technical arguments both in favor and against targeting. The main advantage of poverty targeting is to increase the amount that can be transferred to each beneficiary for a given budget, which maximizes the poverty impact of transfers. For instance, Grosh and Leite (2008) analyze cash transfers for the elderly in four countries – Yemen, Niger, Panama, and Kyrgyzstan. They find that, despite exclusion errors, poverty targeted social pensions are much more cost-effective per dollar spent, and, for a fixed budget, convey a higher poverty impact. On the other hand, however, targeting is costly. Caldes et al. (2006) and Grosh et al. (2008) find that administrative costs of poverty targeted conditional cash transfers (including the cost of collecting the data needed to construct a proxy means test and periodical reclassification of beneficiaries) tend to be around 10 percent of the program's budget. In some extreme cases it can absorb up to 30 percent of it, which can seriously affect the ability to provide larger transfers. Unless targeting really delivers strong differences in impact, categorical transfers should thus be considered as a valid option.

In sum, the optimal design of programs and the extent to which they target accurately depends very much on local conditions (Coady et al. 2004; Grosh et al. 2008). In designing a cash transfers program, one must have a clear idea of the incidence of poverty among the target population and political economy considerations in favor and against poverty targeting. How many people are poor or at risk of poverty? How many belong to the target population group? Where do they live? What are their characteristics? What are the causes of their poverty and vulnerability? And also, which system would be subject to less local capture? Is there enough capacity to support an effective and transparent targeting system? Only thereafter a clear assessment on whether and how to target can be performed.

This chapter abstains from ethical considerations, and aims at contributing to the technical debate. The objective is to understand, by means of simulations, gains from poverty targeting in Latin America with respect to simpler categorical targeting. In doing so, it also provides some guidance on circumstances under which targeting may bring more benefits. It does not provide, however, a definitive answer for three reasons. First, because simulations are done for 13 countries only – too few to conduct a statistical meta analysis. Second, because the simulations do not consider behavioral changes of beneficiaries that could alter labor market decisions and poverty status. Third, and more importantly, because there is no clear-cut answer to the question, which depends very much on budget, societal preferences and political economy considerations.

11.3. Data and Methodology

In what follows, we look first at the impact on poverty and inequality of poverty-targeted and categorical cash transfers to children up to five years of age. We then repeat the exercise for social pensions to elderly people of age 65 and higher, and conclude by comparing the two. Our workhorse simulation consists of a hypothetical cash transfer program that transfers an amount equal to 0.5 percent of GDP to a reference group (i.e. children or the elderly). The amount was chosen to strike a balance between large CCT programs such as *Oportunidades* or *Bolsa Familia* that transfer around 0.3-0.4 percent of GDP, and more costly social pensions programs that in some countries transfer up to or even more than one percentage point of GDP. In choosing a common metric, we will be better able to compare the poverty impact of both types of programs.

The simulations run as follows. For the targeted variant, we consider all households that meet the categorical criteria, and that have a gross income below US$2.5 a day in per capita terms (an international widely used poverty line). In the literature, this group is referred to as the extreme poor. In 2010 the extreme poor consisted on average of 15 percent of the Latin America population (World Bank 2010), and is the main beneficiary of social assistance programs. To estimate the size of the transfer, we then allocate 0.5 percent of GDP in equal shares to all beneficiaries (if there are 2 beneficiaries in one household, we give twice the transfer). To allow comparisons across countries, all simulations are done in 2005 PPP US Dollars. For the categorical variant, we repeat the same exercise but consider all households meeting the categorical criteria regardless of their poverty status. Having allocated the funds, we re-calculate for both variants households' poverty status.

Our estimations are based on several assumptions. First, we assume there are no behavioral changes, in particular that the program has no impact on labor market decisions and poverty status. The current evidence suggests that labor market distortions of cash transfer programs remain moderate, and we do not expect results to change dramatically if behavioral responses were considered. Second, the impact of a national program can change substantially by urban and rural areas, and hence in a robustness exercise we discuss the impacts by geographical areas separately. Finally, the basic simulations neglect considerations related to the effectiveness of targeting, and assume that our hypothetical program is able to perfectly target the poor. To address this issue, we also discuss a simulation where we assume that targeting has 15 percent higher administrative costs than categorical transfers (so that the targeted program only distributes 0.425 percent of GDP), and that exclusion errors lead to missing 30 percent of the (randomly selected) poor, who do not receive the transfer.

Observe, also, that we look at the poverty and inequality impact of programs that are in addition to the ones that are already implemented. Ideally, it would be preferable to first subtract from households' incomes all transfers that they already received, and subsequently add our transfers from the hypothetical program. In doing so, it would be possible to provide an idea on the extent to which the coverage of current programs could be improved to enhance cost effectiveness. Unfortunately, we only have limited and imperfect data about the amounts transferred to households in each country survey. We chose therefore not to explore that avenue.

The simulations are based on household surveys from 13 Latin American countries that have been collected and harmonized as part of the Socio-Economic Database for Latin America and the Caribbean (SEDLAC), a partnership between the Center for Distributive, Labor and Social Studies (CEDLAS) and The World Bank. The list of countries and surveys used is shown in Annex 1. The analysis uses the income aggregates provided in SEDLAC, which, where available, add to labor income revenues from pensions, rents from capital and benefits, and other transfers. We convert all incomes in 2005 USD PPP.

11.4. Results

11.4.1. Children

We begin by looking at the poverty and inequality impact of targeted and categorical cash transfers programs to families with children up to 5 years of age (Figures 11.1 to 11.3). Several features emerge. First, we can observe a relationship between income per capita, and the effectiveness of the program in reducing poverty under both the targeted and untargeted modality. The same program (if implemented ideally) is more than twenty times more effective in reducing poverty rates in Argentina than in Nicaragua under both modalities, and eight times more effective in reducing the poverty gap. Without even considering implementation issues, it is thus far easier to achieve a poverty impact in wealthier countries than in poorer ones. Two main reasons stand out: transfers remain higher in wealthier countries because of larger budgets available, making it easier to lift people above US$2.5 a day: 0.5 percent of GDP corresponds to an average of 715 US$ per capita (in PPP terms) in 2008 in Argentina, but only to 134 US$ per capita in Nicaragua. In addition, wealthier countries also display lower poverty rates and a lower proportion of children in the population, and therefore, under the targeted modality, a higher budget is distributed among fewer beneficiaries.

Figure 11.1

Changes in Extreme Poverty Rates – Children

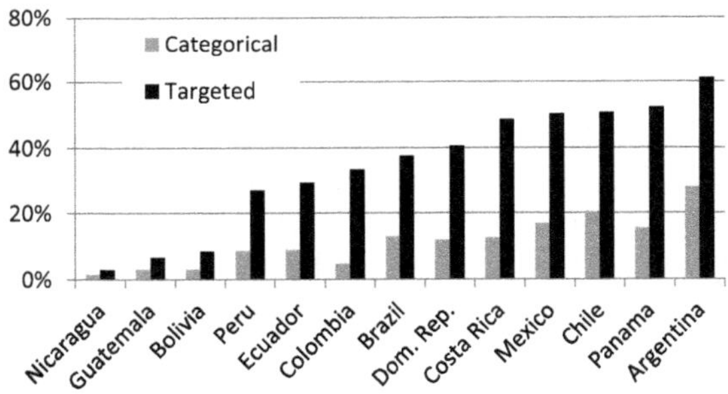

Source: Own calculations based on SEDLAC databases.

Figure 11.2

Changes in Poverty Gap – Children

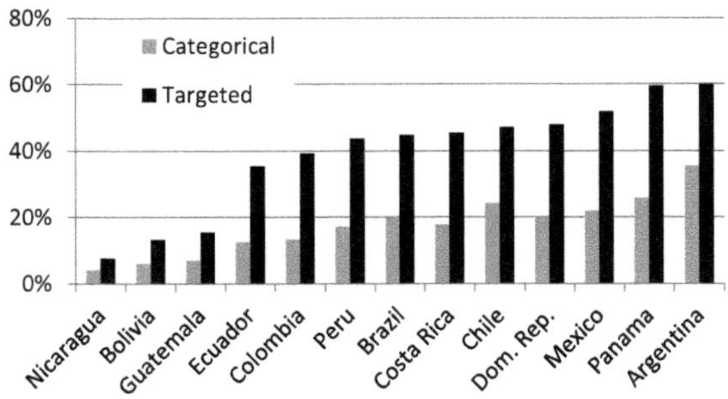

Source: Own calculations based on SEDLAC databases.

Figure 11.3

Changes in the Gini Coefficient – Children

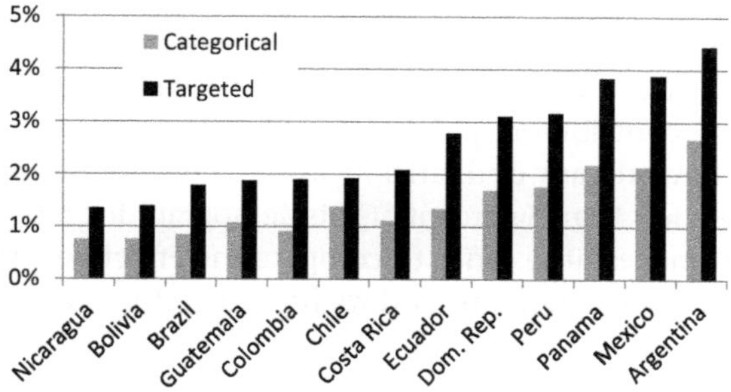

Source: Own calculations based on SEDLAC databases.

Second, targeted programs are, on average, 3.2 times more effective in reducing poverty rates (and 2.3 more effective in reducing the poverty gap) than categorical programs. There is, however, considerable variation across countries: in Nicaragua, a perfectly targeted program would only be 2 times more effective in reducing poverty rates than a categorical one, while in Colombia (the other extreme) this ratio jumps to 7.1. These differences are not explained by income levels alone: effectiveness in Nicaragua and Argentina, two countries with very different income levels, is for instance very similar. Rather, differences in impact depend on a more complex combination of factors, such as how widespread are pockets of poverty with people far off the poverty line. In Colombia, not only is poverty more widespread, but the poverty gap is twice as much as in Argentina. That implies the need of higher transfer levels to the poor to lift them out of poverty, hence a categorical transfer, which dilutes available resources among more beneficiaries, remains less effective.

Targeted programs are also much more effective in reducing income inequality. On average, in our sample, a categorical transfer of 0.5 percent of GDP to children reduces the Gini coefficient by 1.4 percent, against 2.6 percent for a targeted program. However, in contrast to poverty, there is little connection between the initial level of inequality, and the higher effectiveness of targeted programs as opposed to categorical ones.

11.4.2. *Elderly*

Next, we turn attention to social pensions given to beneficiaries of age 65 and older (Figures 11.4 to 11.6). Observe that some countries in the sample have already in place large and widespread contributory and non-contributory pensions systems (Argentina, Brazil, and Chile) that have already dramatically lowered poverty among the elderly to reach less than 5 percent of this demographic group. In these countries, it makes little sense to compare the effectiveness of categorical vs. targeted programs, and we have therefore excluded them from the analysis.

Figure 11.4

Changes in Extreme Poverty Rates – Elderly

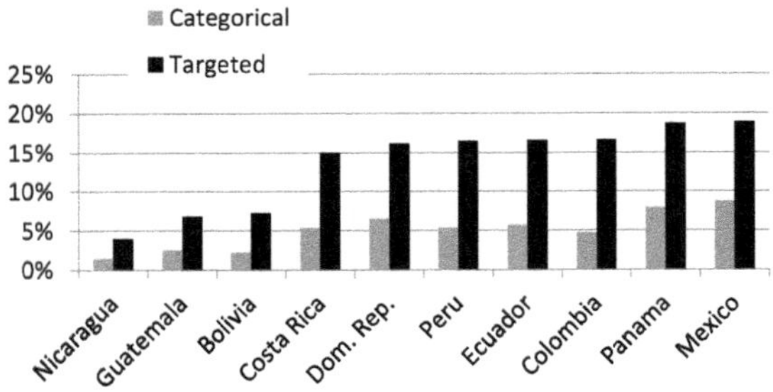

Source: Own calculations based on SEDLAC databases.

Figure 11.5

Changes in Poverty Gap – Elderly

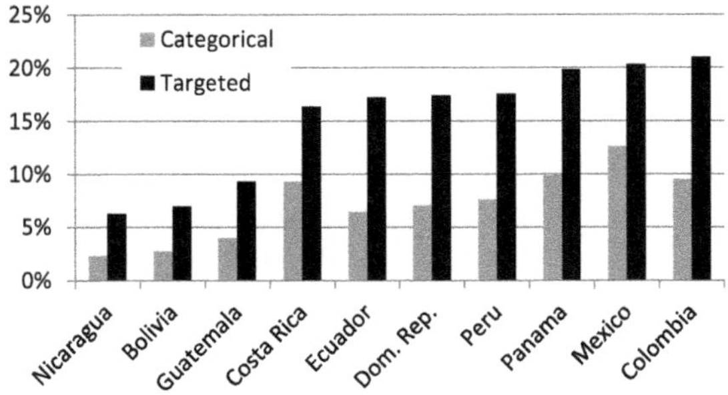

Source: Own calculations based on SEDLAC databases.

Figure 11.6
Changes in the Gini Coefficient – Elderly

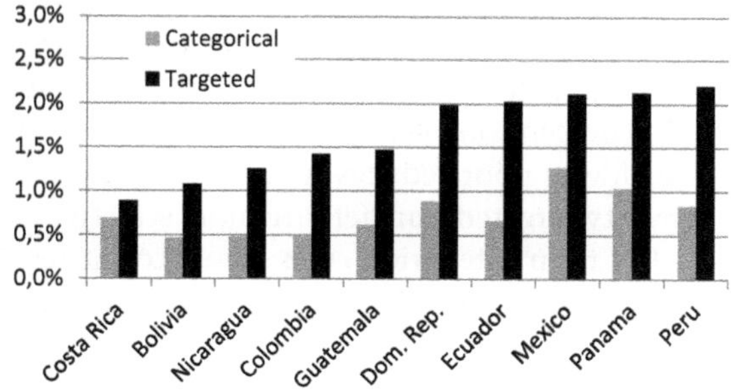

Source: Own calculations based on SEDLAC databases.

The first, striking contrast with respect to transfers to children is that in all countries (with the exception of Nicaragua, and under some circumstances Guatemala), both targeted and categorical transfers to the elderly have a significantly lower impact on poverty than an equivalent program for children. The difference in poverty impact is large: on average, categorical transfers to children are 1.6 times more effective in reducing poverty than categorical transfers of equal budget to the elderly, and targeted transfers twice more effective. The reasons are straightforward: poverty rates among the elderly are, on average, lower than for children; and poorer families have more children, but not more elderly people. The simulations also suggest that the common belief that cash transfers to the elderly can reduce poverty substantially by trickling down to all family members has limited validity: with fewer elderly than children living in poor households, for the trickledown effect to be effective money should be transferred across family members living in different households, a much less likely event.

There is nevertheless considerable variation across countries in the poverty impact of transfers to the elderly. The maximum reduction in poverty rates (close to 20 percent) is achieved, as expected, in countries with high poverty incidence among the elderly, such as Mexico and Colombia. Effectiveness of a targeted program as opposed to a categorical one also varies substantially across countries, being 0.7 times higher in Nicaragua, to 1 in Guatemala, to 2 in Colombia and 3.2 times in Costa Rica, and 2.8 percent on average across countries. Similar conclusions apply for the reduction in poverty gaps (poverty targeted transfers are on average 2.3 more effective in reducing poverty gaps than categorical ones).

In addition to lower impacts on poverty, transfers to the elderly have also a lower impact on inequality than transfers to children. While, on average, targeted transfers to poor children reduce income inequality by 2.6 percent on average, the same amount of resources targeted to the elderly poor reduces income inequality by 1.7 percent. Again, poverty targeted transfers are more effective in reducing income inequality than categorical ones across countries (2.3 times more on average), though the difference is less pronounced in Costa Rica and Mexico.

11.4.3. Cost-Effectiveness of Categorical vs. Targeted Programs

The previous section deals with the extent to which, for a given budget, targeted programs are more effective in reducing poverty and inequality. But the reverse question is also of interest: how much would it cost to achieve the same poverty impact of a targeted program using a categorical one? To address this question, we proceed as follows. For a categorical program to achieve the same poverty impact than a targeted one, it must transfer the same amount of resources but to all beneficiaries – not simply poor ones. With this simple rule in mind, we look at the cost-effectiveness of categorical vs. targeted cash transfers, which is summarized in Figure 11.7.

In all countries under consideration, a targeted cash transfer can achieve the same poverty impact as a categorical one using 2 to 13 times less resources. The large difference in costs suggests that in most countries some form of targeting, even if costlier and far from perfect, can lead to large efficiency gains and allow for more generous transfers to the poor. Efficiency gains show, however, strong heterogeneity across countries, with poorer countries demonstrating lower gains than wealthier ones, from around 2 in Nicaragua, Bolivia and Guatemala to around 7 in Argentina and Costa Rica, to 13 in Chile. In all cases, the cost-effectiveness of targeted interventions is even greater for transfers to the elderly than for children. The heterogeneity seems to have a direct link to the fact that wealthier countries have fewer poor people, and therefore, for a given overall budget, they can transfer a significantly larger amount of resources to a narrower set of people under targeted programs.

Figure 11.7

Cost-Effectiveness of Targeting

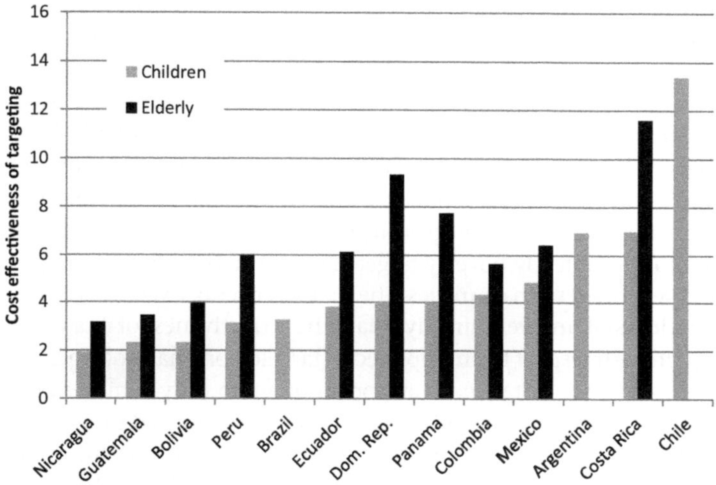

Source: Own calculations based on SEDLAC databases.

The heterogeneity in efficiency gains also suggests that targeting methods should vary by country. For instance, in low-income countries with widespread poverty, implementing a sophisticated proxy means test (PMT) may lead to high costs and strong implementation challenges without being necessarily much more effective than simpler targeting based on categorical and geographic exclusion restrictions. In contrast, in wealthier countries, unless pockets of poverty show a strong geographical concentration, implementing a more sophisticated targeting mechanism (such as proxy-means or means-tested mechanisms) could lead to large efficiency gains. In these countries, a stronger implementation capacity could also better resolve some of the technical implementation challenges that lead to exclusion errors.

11.4.4. Imperfect Targeting and Administrative Costs

These basic simulations miss an important feature. Actual poverty targeting, means or proxy-means tested, is costly and far from being perfect. As a robustness exercise, we therefore simulate the impact of an "imperfect" poverty-targeted program to children. To do so, we presume that the targeted program spends 15 percent more than the categorical program in administrative costs (so that 15 percent less resources are being transferred to the beneficiaries), and that exclusion errors lead to missing 30 percent of the extremely poor (randomly selected among potential beneficiaries). For comparison purposes, we also explore the possibility that categorical targeting is also subject to a degree of imperfectness, missing 10 percent of the poor.[3] These assumptions are in line with what is suggested by targeting evaluations of transfer programs in the region (Fiszbein and Schady 2009).

Figure 11.8 presents the poverty impacts of the various variants. In all countries, the imperfectly targeted program continues to deliver a better poverty impact than the categorical programs. The impact remains in fact closer to the perfectly poverty targeted program, than to the categorical ones. Nevertheless, in countries where differences between targeted and categorical systems were already small, the attractiveness of a categorical program with respect to an imperfectly targeted one has now increased: in Nicaragua, for instance, a categorical program only achieves almost the same poverty reduction than an imperfectly targeted program that costs the same – but does not "miss" 30 percent of the extreme poor. In contrast, in wealthier and more unequal countries, such as Colombia, the need to transfer higher amounts to a smaller pool of poor beneficiaries makes an imperfectly targeted system still an attractive option.

Figure 11.8

Imperfect Targeting and Administrative Costs (Children Only)

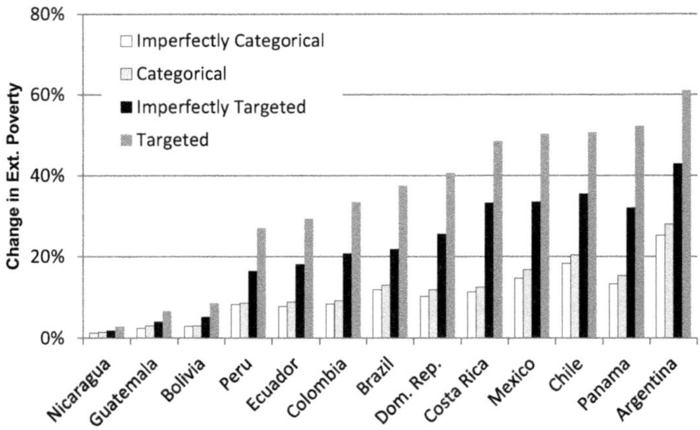

Note: Only kids between 0 and 5 years old.
The Imperfectly Categorical skips 10% of the poor population.
The Imperfectly Targeted has 15% of the budget in administrative costs and then skips 30% of the recipients (those below 2.5 USD a day).

Source: Own calculations based on SEDLAC databases.

11.4.5. *Relative Targeting*

Some countries do not target beneficiaries using an absolute poverty line, but a relative one, in which case transfers are targeted to people below a certain percentile, rather than those below a particular income threshold. Accordingly, we simulate the poverty impact of a program that targets the poorest income quintile, and compare the results with a program that targets the population below 2.5 US$ per day.

Figure 11.9

Relative Targeting (Children Only)

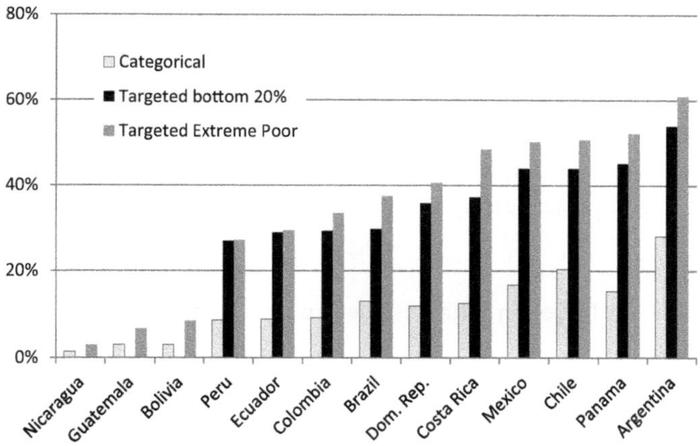

Notes: Plans for kids only, using kids with age between 0 and 5 years old. Targeting those in the bottom 20% of the income distribution.
Source: Own calculations based on SEDLAC databases.

The poverty impact of targeting the poorest quintile varies dramatically according to the poverty headcount and gap of each country (Figure 11.9). In Peru and Ecuador, where extreme poverty incidence among children is close to 20 percent, the two approaches are equivalent. In cases where poverty incidence is lower than 20 percent, a relative targeting would still reach all poor, but will dilute the average transfer due to the inclusion of non-poor beneficiaries. The resulting lower average transfer would imply that some of the poor will not be able to be lifted out of poverty. The lowest poverty impact in targeting the poorest quintile is however in countries with widespread pockets of poverty exceeding 20 percent, and in countries that have large poverty gaps, such as Nicaragua, Guatemala, and Bolivia. In these cases, targeting the bottom quintile misses the beneficiaries who remain close to the poverty line, hence the transfers lift very few (or no) beneficiaries out of poverty. At the same time, however, the transfers reach more generously the poorest beneficiaries that remain far from the poverty line. It is not possible to assess, from a welfare perspective, which modality delivers higher welfare. The exercise shows, however, that changing the targeting modality can significantly affect the profile of beneficiaries, and hence how to target should be at the center of the discussion when discussing a program's objectives.

11.4.6. Alternative Age Groups

All simulations assume that the targeted beneficiaries are children up to 5 years old, and elderly who are 65 years old or more. This section investigates whether slightly changing the eligibility age profiles can affect the poverty impact of the program. It is to be expected that the poverty impact will be affected only if the poor are concentrated in specific age or profile groups.

Figure 11.10

Poverty Impact Targeting Different Age Groups (Children Only)

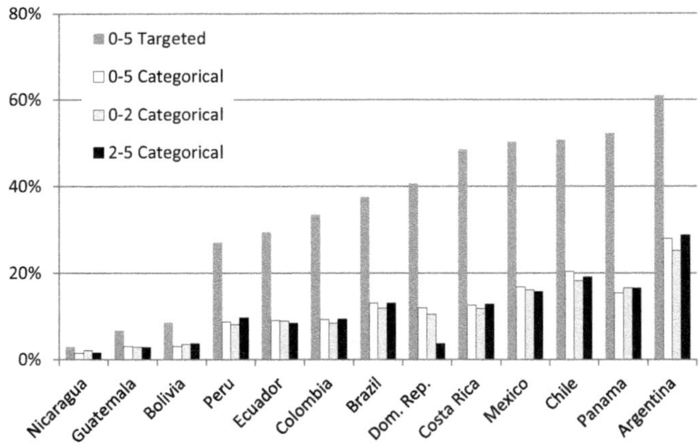

Note: Robustness Check. Plans for kids only. Targeting those below 2.5 US$ a day. Here we compare different age brackets for the kids.
Source: Own calculations based on SEDLAC databases.

Figure 11.10 explores alternative age group definitions for children (it considers children 0 to 2 and 2 to 5 separately), to check if the poverty impact changes significantly by narrowing the age groups. With the exception of the Dominican Republic, the age group under consideration for a categorical transfer does not seem to significantly alter the results. This suggests that, overall, the distribution of income across age groups of children is such that providing higher transfers to a narrower group delivers a similar poverty impact than delivering lower transfers to a wider group. In all cases, the poverty impact under categorical targeting remains lower than under the targeted modality.

11.4.7. Geographic Targeting

The poverty impacts of targeted vs. categorical programs may also vary geographically, for instance between urban and rural areas. Figures 11.11 and 11.12 present the differential poverty impact of a national program in urban and rural areas that transfers equal amounts to beneficiaries in both regions. Overall, despite the poverty incidence being on average three times higher in rural areas, there appears to be surprisingly little differences in program's impact between rural and urban areas. In fact, a few results may appear counter intuitive at first sight, and we discuss them next.

Figure 11.11

Impact on Urban Areas (Children Only)

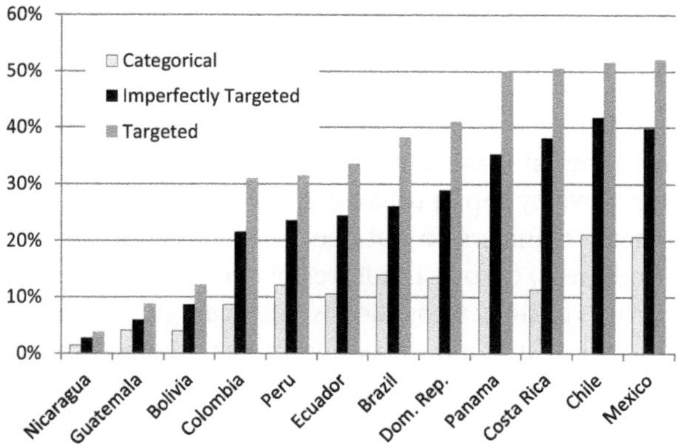

Source: Own calculations based on SEDLAC databases.

Figure 11.12
Impact on Rural Areas (Children Only)

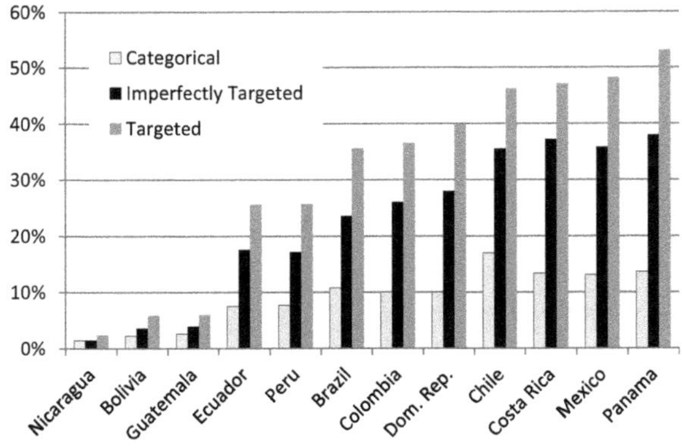

Source: Own calculations based on SEDLAC databases.

In many countries, both categorical and targeted transfers achieve a greater poverty reduction in urban than in rural areas. This is because, independently of poverty incidence levels, the poverty gap is smaller in urban areas (poverty gaps in rural areas are on average 3.5 times higher), hence, equal amounts transferred to beneficiaries achieve greater poverty reduction in urban areas. However, aside from Bolivia where the same targeted program achieves twice as much poverty reduction in urban than in rural areas, differences in poverty impact remain fairly modest, from 1.6 times in Nicaragua to 0.9 times in Colombia. This suggests that, on average, benefits ought not to differ much between urban and rural areas, though they could be slightly higher in rural areas.

The lower poverty gap in urban areas also provides an explanation of why targeted transfers do not necessarily perform better in urban than in rural areas, despite the lower poverty incidence. In fact, the picture remains quite heterogeneous. In Nicaragua, where two thirds of the population in rural areas live in extreme poverty (against a quarter in urban areas), targeting performs much better in urban than in rural areas: in urban areas, it achieves 2.7 times higher poverty reduction than a categorical program, as opposed to only 1.7 times in rural areas. But in Panama, on the opposite side of the spectrum, poverty targeting performs way better in rural areas. This is because the poverty gap in urban areas remains so small (2.3 against 12 in rural areas), that even a "diluted" categorical transfer would achieve massive poverty reduction. In contrast, targeted transfers in rural areas perform way better because they allow to transfer higher resources to the poor, and hence to overcome the higher poverty gap more easily.

11.5. Conclusions

From a theoretical perspective, targeting social assistance to the poor always improves the programs' poverty impact since, for a given budget, targeted programs transfer more resources to fewer beneficiaries. However, the extent to which these gains are substantial enough to overcome some of the drawbacks related to targeting remains an empirical question. The findings suggest that the incidence of poverty is key, but not the only factor affecting the relative effectiveness of targeted vs. categorical transfers. The rural-urban analysis strengthens the view that the relative effectiveness depends on a variety of factors, in particular the depth of the poverty gap: if it is relatively low, the difference in poverty impact of categorical vs. targeted transfers may not be that large.

The comparison of programs for children and the elderly also supports the view that choosing the beneficiaries carefully is almost as important as targeting to achieve poverty reduction. The simulations show that because, overall, there are less elderly than children who are poor, for given resources social assistance programs to the elderly achieve a lower poverty impact - even if they are poverty targeted. This does not necessarily call for phasing out social pensions, but for a rebalancing of the budget of social assistance programs towards the largest vulnerable groups.

Overall, the findings support the view that in the Latin American context targeting assistance to the poor tends to deliver higher poverty impacts. There are nonetheless circumstances under which simpler schemes, such as categorical cash transfers for vulnerable groups that are geographically confined to regions with strong pockets of poverty, may be a valid option to consider as an alternative to means tested or proxy means tested programs. This is particularly the case in low-income countries with widespread pockets of poverty.

We would like to conclude with a note of caution. To achieve comparability across countries, the simulations abstained from looking at country specific factors that ought to be considered in the design of effective social assistance programs. Among these are more precise identifications of vulnerable groups and of geographic differences. The results should thus be taken as they are – a suggestive cross country comparison with no ambition to provide guidance for specific countries, which ought to include more country specific factors.

Appendix

Table 11.3

Surveys Used in the Analysis

Country	Year	Survey	Observations (Households)
Argentina	2009	Encuesta Permanente de Hogares Continua	27,842
Bolivia	2007	Encuesta de Hogares	4,148
Brazil	2009	Pesquisa Nacional por Amostra de Domicilios	129,333
Chile	2009	Encuesta de Caracterización Socioeconómica Nacional	71,460
Colombia	2009	Gran Encuesta Integrada de Hogares	112,102
Costa Rica	2009	Encuesta de Hogares de Propósitos Múltiples	13,244
Ecuador	2009	Encuesta de Empleo y Subempleo y Desempleo	19,435
Guatemala	2006	Encuesta Nacional de Condiciones de Vida	13,686
México	2008	Encuesta Nacional de Ingresos y Gastos de los Hogares	29,468
Nicaragua	2005	Encuesta Nacional de Hogares sobre Medición de Nivel de Vida	6,884
Panamá	2009	Encuesta Continua de Hogares	13,386
Perú	2009	Encuesta Nacional de Hogares-Condiciones de Vida y Pobreza	21,753
Dominican Republic	2009	Encuesta Nacional de Fuerza de Trabajo	8,281

Notes

1 Some argue that political lobbying tends to favor the elderly ("the elderly can vote, the children cannot": Preston 1984). Even in countries with well-developed social assistance schemes with a family accompaniment approach like Brazil and Chile, public spending per older is significantly higher than public spending per child (Turra et al. 2011).

2 Programs focused on the elderly poor range for instance from 0.1 percent of GDP in the Seychelles to 10.6 percent of GDP in Ethiopia. See Schwarz (2003), and Kakwani and Subbarao (2005).

3 To keep the budget at 0.5 percent of GDP, under the categorical variant of the simulation we distribute all the resources of the program to the remaining 90 percent of the population.

References

Attanasio, O., Meghir, C., Otero, A. (2011). Formal Labor Market and Pension Wealth: Evaluating the 2008 Chilean Pension Reform, mimeo.

Barrientos, A. (2009). Social Pensions in Low-income Countries, in: Holzmann, R., Robalino, D., Takayama, N. (Eds.), Closing the Coverage Gap: The Role of Social Pensions and Other Retirement Income Transfers, Washington, DC: The World Bank, 73-84.

Caldes, N., Coady, D., Maluccio, J. (2006). The Cost of Poverty Alleviation Transfer Programs: A Comparative Analysis of Three Programs in Latin America, in: World Development, 34(5): 818-37.

Coady, D., Grosh, M., Hoddinott, J. (2004). Targeting of Transfers in Developing Countries: Review of Lessons and Experience, Washington, DC: The World Bank.

Fiszbein, A., Schady, N. (2009). Conditional Cash Transfers: Reducing Present and Future Poverty, World Bank Policy Research Report.

Grosh, M., del Ninno, C., Tesliuc, E., Ouerghi, A. (2008). For Protection and Promotion: the Design and Implementation of Effective Safety Nets, Washington, DC: The World Bank.

Grosh, M., Leite, P. G. (2009). Defining Eligibility for Social Pensions: A View from a Social Assistance Perspective, in: Holzmann, R., Robalino, D., Takayama, N. (Eds.), Closing the Coverage Gap: The Role of Social Pensions and Other Retirement Income Transfers, Washington, DC: The World Bank, 161-86.

International Labor Organization (ILO) (2010). ILO-UN Social Protection Floor Initiative.

Kakwani, N., Subbarao, K. (2005). Ageing and Poverty in Africa and the Role of Social Pensions, World Bank Social Protection Discussion Paper No. 0521.

Kakwani, N., Veras Soares, F., Son, H. (2005). Conditional Cash Transfers in African Countries, UNDP International Poverty Center Working Paper No. 9.

Leite, P. G. (2011). Improving Cost-effectiveness of Targeting in Tanzania: The CB-CCT Program, mimeo.

Levy, S. (2008). Good Intentions, Bad Outcomes: Social Policy, Informality and Economic Growth in Mexico, Washington, DC: Brookings Institution Press.

Mkandawire, T. (2005). Targeting and Universalism in Poverty Reduction, UNRISD Social Policy and Development Programme Paper No. 23.

Murrugarra, E. (2011). Aging, Poverty and Social Protection in Colombia: Evidence and Policy Options, mimeo.

Parker, S., Skoufias, E. (2000). The Impact of PROGRESA on Work, Leisure and Time Allocation, Final report at International Food Policy Research Institute.

Preston, S. (1984). Children and the Elderly: Divergent Paths for America's Dependents, in: Demography, 21(4): 435-57.

Sluchynsky, O. (2009). Administration of Social Pension Programs, in: Holzmann, R., Robalino, D., Takayama, N. (Eds.), Closing the Coverage Gap: The Role of Social Pensions and Other Retirement Income Transfers, Washington, DC: The World Bank, 203-14.

Skoufias, E., Di Maro, V. (2009). Conditional Cash Transfers, Adult Work Incentives, and Poverty, in: Journal of Development Studies, 44(7), 935-60.

Schwartz, A. M. (2003). Old Age Security and Social Pensions, Social Protection Department, Washington, DC: The World Bank.

Turra, C., Holz, M., Cotlear, D. (2011). Who Benefits from Public Transfers? Incidence across Income Groups and across Generations in Brazil and Chile, in: Cotlear, D. (Ed.), Population Aging: Is Latin America Ready?, Washington, DC: The World Bank, 211-31.

UNICEF (2010). Progress for Children: Achieving the MDGs with Equity (No. 9), UNICEF.

Weigand, C., Grosh, M. (2008). Levels and Patterns of Safety Net Spending in Developing and Transition Countries, World Bank Social Protection Discussion Paper No. 0817.

World Bank (2010). Did Latin America Learn to Shield the Poor from Economic Shocks?, LAC Poverty and Labor Brief, Washington, DC: The World Bank.

World Bank - IEG (Independent Evaluation Group) (2011). Evidence and Lessons Learned from Impact Evaluations on Social Safety Nets, Washington, DC: The World Bank.

Part III

Financing Social Insurance Programs

12

Labor Market Institutions and Informality in Transition and Latin American Countries*

Hartmut Lehmann
Alexander Muravyev

12.1. Introduction

Informality and informal employment pose a major challenge to policy makers in all parts of the world. In this chapter we focus on informality in the transition countries of Central and Eastern Europe and the Commonwealth of Independent States as well as in Latin America.[1] While it is difficult to precisely estimate the size of these phenomena, there can be no doubt that in these areas of the world a large part of economic activity is not registered or only partially registered and that many workers enter employment relationships that provide only partial or no protection against unemployment, illness and old age (see, e.g., Slonimczyk 2012; Lehmann and Pignatti 2007 regarding transition countries and Perry et al. 2007 regarding Latin America).

There exists a large and growing literature that discusses the reasons why employers and employees are unwilling or unable to work in the formal economy.[2] The empirical part of this literature provides evidence on the determinants of informality and informal employ-

* *We are grateful to David Robalino for encouraging us to write this paper. We are very grateful to Viviana Mora for carefully assembling the LAC data and to Sebastian Lebig and Florian Plum for collecting and processing the transition economies data. Financial support by the Volkswagen Foundation within the project "The political economy of labor market reform in transition countries: A comparative perspective" is also gratefully acknowledged.*

ment looking, for the most part, at individual countries or, when providing a cross-country analysis, focusing at one determinant. In contrast, this chapter is to our knowledge the first that uses panel data covering many countries in order to analyze the impact of a *set of determinants* on informality. We, however, restrict our analysis to the impact of labor market institutions on informality. In particular, using a hand-collected macro-level data set of labor market institutions, we pursue the question whether employment protection legislation (EPL), the tax-wedge, the unemployment benefit level, unemployment benefit duration and union density affect the size of the informal economy in the ECA and LAC regions. The chapter is interesting for its broad geographic coverage and because of the nature of the data since, having panel data at our disposal, we can avoid some of the pitfalls apparent in much of the empirical literature that is limited to OLS estimation.

Informality and informal employment are not only of academic interest, they are actually an important policy issue. There exist equity and efficiency considerations that point to a strong need to vigorously pursue policies that increase the shares of formal economic activity and employment.

It is certainly inequitable if part of the workforce and some firms do not pay their taxes since this implies that those who are formal, whether workers or entrepreneurs, have to bear a disproportionate burden in the financing of public goods that are also of benefit to those being economically active without registration. If the informal part of the economy becomes more substantial this can also mean that governments have to raise taxes and contributions on the formal part and thus have to increase the costs of being formal, which in the final analysis can result in even more informality and a reduced tax base. Furthermore, often workers in informal jobs are severely exploited and are working under conditions that can be hazardous to their health.

Turning to efficiency, most economists maintain that employment in the formal sector is associated with a greater use of physical capital that requires human capital acquisition on the part of the employed workers, while the informally employed often work with little or no physical capital. Since physical and human capital are very important ingredients of growth, an economy with a relatively large formal sector will, *ceteris paribus*, grow at a more rapid pace than an economy with a smaller formal sector. In the medium run, policies combating informality and informal employment are thus vital for raising income and welfare of low and middle-income countries.

These equity and efficiency considerations clearly point to the importance of policies that formalize informal activities. However, the literature on informality provides us with competing paradigms that point to a very complex picture. We need to keep this complexity in mind if we want to discuss policies meant to enhance the emergence of firms and workers from the informal sector and informal employment relationships into regularized economic activity and into regular jobs. The existence of the informal segment of the labor market alongside the formal sector and the reasons posited for its existence have given rise to several paradigms in the literature. One key question in the labor market literature for developing countries is whether informal employment or self-employment reflects voluntary choice or is involuntary due to segmentation in the labor market (Guasch 1999).

The traditional dualistic view, going back to Harris and Todaro (1970), sees the informal segment as the inferior sector, the option of last resort. Due to barriers to entry, minimum wages, unions, or other sources of segmentation, formal jobs are rationed. Workers in the informal sector are crowded out from the formal sector involuntarily, their wage being less than that in the formal sector.[3] For example, an increase in the statutory wage in the formal sector will reduce formal employment but lead to a lower informal wage and higher informal employment. During a recession informal employment and output expands because formal employment is reduced, while the informal labor market clears. In this view labor market segmentation between formality and informality is the defining feature of the labor market.

In contrast, in a competitive labor market one would expect workers to be able to move freely between occupations, and for wages (broadly interpreted) to equalize accordingly. In this view the formal and informal labor markets are not segmented, but integrated. Voluntary choice regarding jobs and particular attributes of these jobs, such as flexible hours, working as a self-employed and being one's own boss as a micro-entrepreneur, and not valuing social security benefits, can be the reasons for remaining in or moving to the informal sector (Maloney 1999, 2004; Cunningham and Maloney 2001). Here, contrary to the segmentation case, formal and informal employment are not necessarily negatively correlated over the business cycle.

Segmentation and integration of the formal and informal labor markets are two very polar views regarding the interaction of formality and informality. However, as mooted by Fields (1990), it is possible, given the heterogeneity of the informal labor market that these features co-exist in the same labor market. Fields subdivides the informal sector of the labor market into two categories: an "easy-entry" informal sector, which constitutes the involuntary segment, and an "upper-tier" informal sector, where barriers of entry persist and in which participation is voluntary. Hence, the labor market is divided into the formal sector, a "disadvantaged" subsistence-level informal sector and the "small firm" and micro-entrepreneur informal sector.

The macro evidence presented in this chapter is not meant to lead to a confirmation or rejection of the above sketched paradigms. Instead it tries to identify channels through which informal activities and informal employment are affected in general. Thus far such an exercise has not been undertaken in the literature because of a lack of appropriate data. Anticipating our findings, we establish that in most fixed effects (FE) specifications a more regulated labor market increases the size of the informal economy. In some specifications a larger tax-wedge also increases the size of informal economic activities. These two results, dominating our empirical evidence, are in line with the literature, which identifies labor market regulation and the tax-wedge as important drivers of informality. The other three labor market institutions have little or no predictive power in our regressions.

The rest of the chapter has the following structure. The next section discusses definitions of informality, which helps us to better understand the dependent variable in our empirical work. In Section 12.3, we sketch those policies that have an impact on the tax-wedge and regulation and thus on informality. This is followed by a section that looks at tax policies, with a focus on the question whether these policies were instrumental in formalizing informal activities that existed in the formal economy. Section 12.5 is the empirical core of the chapter, describing the data, the methodology and the main findings of our macroeconometric estimations. A final section gives some policy conclusions.

12.2. Using a Broad Definition of Informality

The definition of informality and the informal sector poses a challenge in itself due to its very nature of not being easily observable (Kanbur 2009; Schneider and Enste 2000; Mead and Morrisson 1996). A broad definition defines the informal economy as including "unreported income from the production of legal goods and services, either from monetary or barter transactions, hence all economic activities that would generally be taxable were they reported to the tax authorities" (Schneider and Enste 2000, pp. 78-9).[4] It is this broad definition that we employ in our macroeconometric analysis in this chapter, since informality with this very general definition encompass activities that *totally* or *partially* sidestep the taxing authorities. In other words, this definition looks at activities that are 100% informal, but also at informal activities within the formal economy.

However, we could use a more restricted definition of informality, where a dichotomous situation is analyzed in the labor market, i.e. a situation where workers are either formally or informally employed. This viewpoint essentially restricts itself to the labor market and income generating activities of waged workers or the self-employed with earnings. Even with this restricted view, informality in the labor market is difficult to pin down and can be characterized according to several dimensions, depending on data availability, the legal system present and the nature of the labor market.

There are two reasons why we use the broader definition of informality in our empirical analysis. First, labor market institutions might not only be associated with a dichotomous labor market but might also influence informal activities in the formal sector. Second, the only data on informality available for the ECA and the LAC regions are the data provided by Schneider, Buehn, and Montenegro (2010). This source uses the above cited broad definition of informality and gives estimates for 162 countries, including Eastern European, Central Asian, and Latin American countries over the years 1999 to 2007.

12.3. The Impact of Policies to Lower Labor Costs and to Reduce Regulation

The literature identifies the tax-wedge and labor market regulation as potential channels that affect formal employment, unemployment and informal employment. In what follows we therefore discuss how lowering labor costs and decreasing the extent of regulation might increase formal employment and thus reduce unemployment as well as the size of informal activities. In economies where income support for the unemployed is weak or does not exist, unemployment is not always an option for those without a formal job. Consequently, expansion of formal employment translates, at least partially, into a reduction of informal activities. We start off with some simple theoretical predictions and then present some of the salient empirical evidence on the nexus of taxes and regulation and formal employment.

12.3.1. A Partial Equilibrium Model of Lowering Labor Costs to Employers

Extending Katz (1998), we provide a simple graphical exposition of the effects of lowering labor costs on employment and wages in Figures 12.1a–c. These effects of lowering labor costs, which are conceptually equivalent to providing wage subsidies to employers, are only clear-cut in the polar cases when labor supply is perfectly elastic or perfectly inelastic as Figures 12.1a and 12.1b demonstrate. Lowering labor costs implies a rightward shift of the labor demand curve from $L^d(w)$ to $L^d(w[1 - s])$. When labor supply is perfectly elastic this translates into an employment expansion of $(L_1 - L_0)$. For example, we could have a pool of unemployed low-skilled workers or low-skilled workers in informal jobs. If this pool of the unemployed/informal workers is large or if in addition w_0 is a statutory minimum wage, firms can expand employment without having to raise the wage. In a second scenario where we assume a perfectly inelastic labor supply the lower labor costs are “passed through” to workers in their entirety leading to a wage hike of $(w_1 - w_0)$ and no additional jobs. Most realistic is the scenario between the two polar cases shown in Figure 12.1c where the comparative statics take place in a relatively elastic portion of the labor supply curve. Now we get both an increase in employment and in wages. The relative magnitudes of the effects of lowering labor costs on employment and wages are determined by the labor demand and supply elasticities. For a given labor demand elasticity, the employment effect will be larger, the larger the elasticity of effective labor supply, while the wage effect is inversely related to the elasticity of effective labor supply.

Discussion of the empirical evidence on the elasticity parameters leads Katz (1998) to conclude that low-skilled workers have a higher elasticity of effective labor supply than skilled workers. The elasticity of labor demand for low-skilled workers also seems to be larger in absolute value for low-skilled workers. Thus, subsidizing jobs for low-skilled workers via direct subsidies or via reducing social security contributions might give larger employment effects than subsidizing jobs for workers of all skill levels. Of course, in the presence of large structural unemployment and/or a minimum wage the employment effects would be particularly large. There are, however, at least two problems with direct targeted subsidies. Employers might not know about these subsidies, and targeting low-skilled workers might stigmatize them in the eyes of employers. Of course, when we talk about lowering labor costs via a reduction of social security contributions in particular at the lower end of the wage distribution, these two problems are not present.

12.3.2. Empirical Evidence on the Effects of Lowering Labor Costs to Employers

We report on policies that have attempted to encourage formal job creation through decreasing the tax-wedge by direct cutting of labor costs or via job or wage subsidies to firms. Since rigorous evaluation studies of such policies are hard to come by we cover a variety of country types in this summary.

There are some special pitfalls in the evaluation of wage or job subsidies or of a decrease of labor costs. If these treatments are general, i.e. applying to all firms and workers, it is basically impossible to find a contemporaneous control group, and panel data needed to be used to contrast the average outcome of the treated at the time of the treatment with the average outcome of the treated before the time of the treatment. Even when wage or job subsidies are targeted, e.g. at all low-skilled workers, we have the same difficulties in constructing a counterfactual.

The study by Betcherman, Daysal, and Pagés (2010), which evaluates regionally targeted subsidies in Turkey, is able to establish convincing counterfactuals because they exploit the design of the subsidies and the timing of their introduction in a very apt way. In addition, they match regions as controls that have similar pre-treatment trends of several outcome variables as the treated regions. They thus take account of the point that conditioning on the pre-treatment history and on observables reduces selection biases significantly as e.g. shown in Heckman et al. (1997) in connection with active labor market policies. The careful construction of counterfactuals by Betcherman et al. produces highly credible results. We, therefore, discuss their study in some detail.

The subsidies in Turkey are targeted at low-income regions, where the negative characteristics of the Turkish labor market are especially prominent: low job creation, low employment and participation rates, and a large share of informal workers. The analyzed subsidies directed at firms and legislated through Law 5084 (2004) and Law 5350 (2005) and containing (i) reductions in employers' social security contributions; (ii) credits on income taxes on wages; (iii) subsidies on electricity consumption; and (iv) land subsidies were conceived to boost formal job creation and employment. The subsidies are targeted at regions with a specified relatively low average per capita income and are of the marginal type, i.e. the subsidies are paid on additional formally employed workers. One of the main differences in the design of the two subsidy schemes consists in the size threshold beyond which a subsidy can be given. Law 5084 foresees a threshold of only 10 employees while Law 5350 raises it to 30 employees.

The authors analyze the following outcome variables: formal employment levels and growth, number of establishments and earnings. Their findings point to differences in employment levels between treated and non-treated regions amounting to roughly 14% (Law 5350) and 8% (Law 5084). In terms of employment growth these differences amount to 1.8% points and 1% point per month, respectively. These results thus show large effects regarding the expansion of formal employment. Turning to the number of establishments, the results are more tenuous since only subsidies emanating from Law 5084 show significant positive effects which are robust to the chosen control group and specification. Subsidies connected to Law 5350 seem to work only at the intensive margin since virtually all specifications show no increase in the number of establishments relative to non-treated regions. Using average real earnings at the regional level, the authors essentially find no "pass through" of earnings, a result that would point to a scenario where the effect of subsidies works through the employment channel only (Figure 12.1a).

In a complementary study of the Turkish labor market, Papps (2007) investigates the effects of changes in labor costs on employment at the lower and upper ends of the wage distribution, taking advantage of a quasi-natural experiment. This experiment arises because the contribution base of social security contributions for employers and the minimum wage changed in July 2004. By constructing a treatment variable that consists in the difference of total labor costs over two periods for any gross wage under the assumption that a worker holds on to his/her job in both periods, Papps can establish a causal effect of increases in total labor costs on employment. The precise outcome variables are overall employment and employment in registered jobs and are estimated for workers around the minimum wage thus ensuring homogeneity of unobservables for the treated and the controls. The author uses an individual panel for the year 2004 and a pseudo-panel (synthetic panel) for the years 2002 through 2005.

The results with the individual panel show small but significant effects of raising labor costs: a 1 percentage point rise in total labor costs lowers the probability of being employed by 0.64 percentage points for those previously employed. At the mean this implies that an increase of 1% of labor costs lowers the probability of being employed by 0.2%. When the treatment variable is restricted to those who had previously registered jobs, an increase of 1% of labor costs lowers the probability of being employed by roughly 0.1% at the mean. The evidence for a shift from formal to informal employment is, however, inconclusive when the individual panel is used. With the synthetic panel the results are economically more significant: raising labor costs by 1% point lowers employment by roughly 1.1%. If only those are treated who had previously a registered job, this effect is 1% point. It is also noteworthy that the synthetic panel results show a shift from formal to informal employment by roughly 2% points when labor costs rise by 1% point. Finally, since treatment might affect demographic groups to different degrees,[5] Papps documents different treatment levels by gender, residential status (urban-rural), age group, and education. Women tend to have higher disemployment rates than men and also tend to shift more frequently from formal to informal employment. The same pattern holds for workers under 30 years of age. In contrast, urban and rural dwellers show divergent behavior in response to a rise in labor costs, since urban workers exit employment, while workers in rural regions, where informal jobs are especially abundant, predominantly shift from formal to informal jobs.

One way to get at the effect of lowering labor costs at the individual level is to produce estimates of labor demand elasticities and of the pass through to wages of decreases in labor costs. This approach is chosen by Taymaz (2006) who estimates constant output labor demand elasticities for the Turkish manufacturing and construction sectors with a dynamic labor demand equation and a wage equation with an employer's social security contributions variable included as a determinant of wages. The coefficient on the social security contributions variable is taken as an estimate of the pass through. Using a GMM-System estimator, Taymaz estimates labor demand elasticities that are between -0.41 and -0.64 and are thus at the higher end of the elasticities found in developed market economies (Hamermesh 1993). Since he also finds relatively fast adjustment speeds in international perspective, his overall results seem to imply that the Turkish labor market is very responsive to changes in labor costs. However, these changes do not necessarily translate into large changes in employment since Taymaz' estimates of the pass through imply that about 70% of a 1% point fall in social security contributions translate into higher wages for workers. So, if we assume an average labor demand elasticity of -0.5 a 1% point lowering of social security contributions will only result in an expansion of employment amounting to 0.15%. Particularly important in our context is the fact that for low-wage workers (with wages just slightly below the minimum wage), the pass through estimates are much smaller than for the average worker. So, again we find that targeting workers at the low end of the wage distribution might expand employment most. The note of World Bank (2005a) also emphasizes this point for the EU8 countries.

An important study on the pass through of lowering payroll taxes is Jonathan Gruber's (1997) paper. He takes advantage of a quasi-natural experiment in Chile where at the beginning of the 1980s pension provision was privatized resulting in a dramatic fall of social security contributions paid by employers. Consequently, the change in the payroll tax was clearly exogeneous, making it possible to establish a causal link between the lowering of the payroll tax and changes in wages. To understand Gruber's contribution it is useful to reproduce some of his equations. Labor demand and labor supply are given by the following two equations:

$$D = D(w(1 + t_f), \quad (1)$$

$$S = S(w(1 - at_e) + qwt_f), \quad (2)$$

where w = pretax wage; t_f = payroll tax rate on firm; and t_e = payroll tax rate on workers. Particularly interesting are the parameters a

and q. The parameter a is the fraction by which workers discount their payroll tax payments relative to cash income, while q is the extent to which workers value employer payments relative to cash income. In the case when workers value the social benefits financed by taxation at their full tax cost, $a = 0$ and $q = 1$. In other words, workers do not consider their own contributions as a cost to be subtracted from their wage since they consider these payments being returned to them as benefits 100% in the future. By the same token, when workers think that employer contributions will be transformed into benefits for them 100% in the future, they will treat employer contributions as cash income. The equilibrium solution of this model becomes:

(3) $$\frac{\frac{dw}{w}}{dt_f} = \frac{h_s q - h_d}{h_d - h_s(1 - at_e)},$$

where h_s and h_d are the supply and demand elasticities. It is easy to show that the right hand side of equation (10) becomes -1 under three conditions:

- Labor supply is perfectly inelastic;
- Labor demand is infinitely elastic;
- There is a complete linkage of benefits and taxes ($a = 0$ and $q = 1$).

When $\frac{\frac{dw}{w}}{dt_f} = -1$, this implies, of course, that the lower payroll tax rate is fully shifted into higher wages, i.e. there is no effect on employment at all. Let us look closer at the third condition, when $a = 0$ and $q = 1$. Assume that the payroll tax is exclusively used to pay benefits to the workers for whom employers pay this tax. Then, when taxes on labor paid by the employer fall by a certain amount workers perceive this fall as translating in its entirety into a fall of their future benefits. They thus will want to be paid a higher wage that fully compensates for this fall in benefits.

Figure 12.1c demonstrates a large albeit not perfect shifting into higher wages of a fall in labor cost (let us say that the government wants to subsidize employment by lowering the payroll tax). The upward shift in the labor supply curve from $L^s(w)$ to $L^s(w)'$ demonstrates that the same number of workers working *ex ante* are only willing to work *ex post* if the wage is raised substantially since they interpret the fall in payroll taxes as eating into their future benefits. Hence, the wage increase is now much larger, $(w_1' - w_0)$ compared to $(w_1 - w_0)$, and employment expansion is more modest ($L_1' - L_0$ and not $L_1 - L_0$). Undertaking a very careful empirical analysis Gruber finds very robust results: lowering payroll taxes does not cause any increase in employment since his regression results imply full shifting of lower taxes into higher wages. These results hold for both white-collar and blue-collar employees.

Figure 12.1

Lowering the Tax-Wedge to the Employer (Employer Subsidies) – Partial Equilibrium Effects

a) Labor Supply Infinitely Elastic

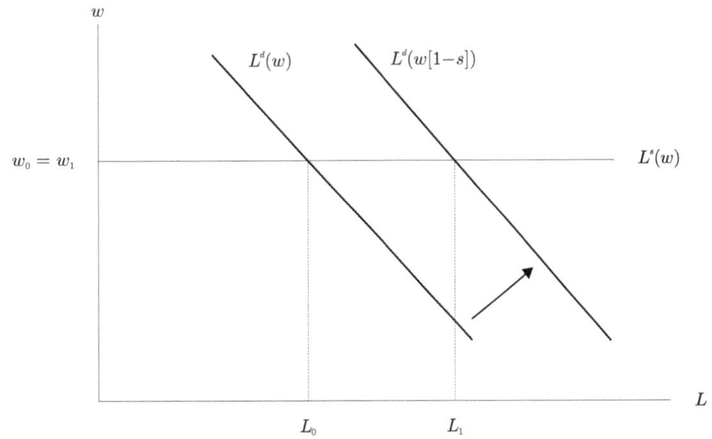

b) Labor Supply Perfectly Inelastic

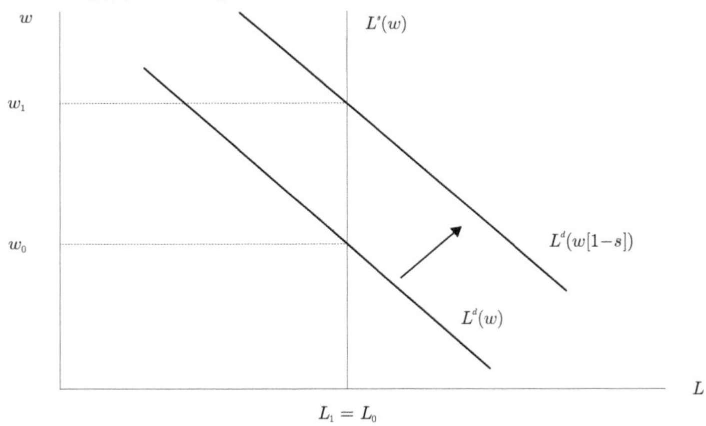

c) Labor Supply Has Positive Elasticity But Is Not Perfectly Elastic

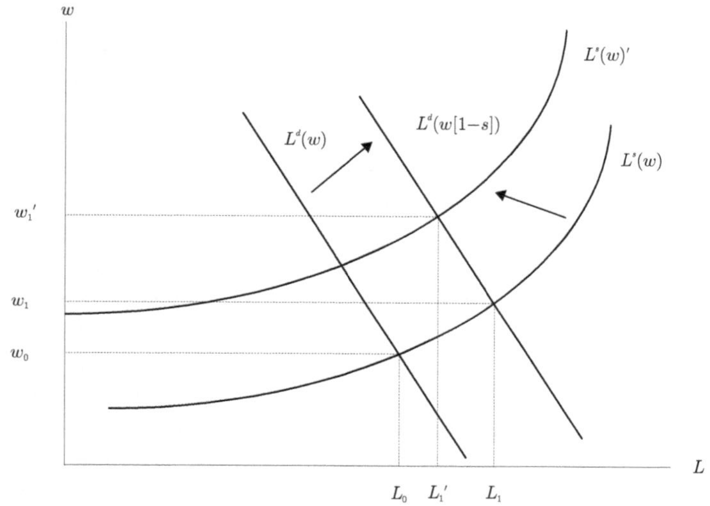

12.3.3. Labor Supply Effects of Lowering the Tax-Wedge

We now turn to policies which *predominantly* entail tax incentives on the supply side, focusing first on certain parts of the labor market reforms in Germany ("Hartz reforms"), which were enacted at the beginning of the century and further developed and fine-tuned in 2003. The parts that interest us here relate to the labor legislation that encourages the increase or the formalization of jobs in the low-wage sector, i.e. legislation regarding "mini-jobs" and "midi-jobs."

In the case of mini-jobs, the revised law of 2003 foresees that employees who earn up to 400€ per month (mini-jobs) do not have to pay any income tax nor social security contributions, while the employer pays an overall contribution of 25%, above all for pension and health insurance. For mini-jobs in households the employer only pays an overall contribution of 12%. The previously existing limit of 15 hours per week has been abolished. It is noteworthy that employees who in a regular first job pay social security contributions in full are allowed to hold a second mini-job where the same conditions hold as for those workers who only hold a mini-job. In other words, the additional income from the secondary job is not counted in the calculation of social security contributions in connection with the primary job. The revised law of 2003 also reduces transaction costs for employers by having one institution selected for the whole country to which the contributions have to be paid ("Bundesknappschaft"). An important point about mini-jobs in Germany is the fact that potential claimants of mini-job status are very well informed about the rules and regulations of the law.

The revised law also stipulates that workers in the low-wage sector who earn between 400.01€ and 800€ (midi-jobs) face a sliding scale of social security payments, i.e. subsidies of the employee's social security contributions declining with earnings are set in place. Before the revision of the law the full amount of social security contributions and taxes had to be paid by the employee once monthly earnings exceeded the mini-job threshold of 325€ (the threshold of mini-jobs before the revision). As a consequence some workers fell into the "social security trap" since a very unfavorable ratio of net to gross wages materialized above the threshold leading to strong incentives to keep earnings below 325€ and thus to less hours worked than actually desired by employer and employees. The revised law thus clearly wanted to encourage employment in the middle and higher segments of the low-wage sector. In the context of our chapter it is also important to stress that one motive for the revised labor market legislation was, of course, the formalization of above all informal secondary jobs or of informal primary jobs in the middle and high segments of the low-wage sector. Another declared aim of the legislation was to have mini- and midi-jobs as a bridge to regular employment with earnings above 800€.

It is uncontroversial that the revised law on mini-jobs has boosted formal employment in the bottom part of the low-wage sector. While the available estimates are based on data with some limitations, Fertig and Kluve (2006) find an increase of 1.8 million mini-jobs between April 2003 and June 2004, which they attribute nearly in its entirety to the new labor market legislation. They also establish that men have increased their share of the formal mini-jobs, which can be explained by a large rise in the incidence of secondary mini-jobs which are predominantly held by men. Ernste and Schneider (2006) state that due to the revised law of 2003, the number of formal mini-jobbers increased from 4.1 to 7.3 million between the spring of 2003 and the beginning of 2006. So, their reading of the data is that having legislation that gives the right incentives to formalize jobs held at the low end of the wage distribution can result in formalization on a large scale. Eichhorst et al. (2012) find a large increase of mini-jobs that are secondary jobs from 1,437,627 in 2003 to 2,492,559 in 2011, while the number of mini-jobs that provide the only employment for workers rises modestly from 4,554,180 in 2003 to 4,894,322 in 2011. This also points to the formalization effect of the legislation of formerly informal jobs.

The employment effects of midi-jobs are a lot more modest. Fertig and Kluve (2006) establish that about 38% of those in the earnings range between 400.01€ and 800€ take up the scheme. A large number of potential participants are not aware of the scheme or do not understand the benefits arising from participation. Being able to estimate the levels of jobs in the earnings range in the absence of the scheme (counterfactual scenario) and in its presence, the authors take the difference of the two scenarios as the causal impact of the scheme on employment levels in the stipulated earnings range. They find this impact to amount to roughly 25,000 additional employment relationships per quarter. Behind this overall effect is hidden a large heterogeneity with respect to gender, age groups and skill levels. Female workers are strongly overrepresented in midi-jobs. Low-skilled workers between 25 and 39 years of age have a substantially higher likelihood to work in this segment of the low-wage sector as have young workers with medium skills. Relative to the counterfactual scenario, older workers with high skills show a slight increase in taking up the scheme.

One important concern of the analysis discussed by Fertig and Kluve (2006) and by Eichhorst et al. (2012) is the bridging function of mini- and midi-jobs. Both studies find that mini-jobs hardly ever end in jobs that require full payment of social security contributions and taxes, while there is a substantial increase in such employment relationships for workers who previously held midi-jobs. Particularly worrisome is the fact that firms in Germany since the inception of the "Hartz reforms" seem to have substituted regular full-time formal jobs with part-time mini-jobs on a large scale (Eichhorst et al. 2012).

A related important study that analyzes the disincentives to formalize jobs at the lower end of the wage distribution is the study by Koettl and Weber (2012, and Chapter 6 in this volume). The authors investigate the role of labor taxation and social benefit design on the disincentives for formal work. They propose a new synthetic measure, the formalization tax rate, which takes into account not only the costs due to additional taxes one has to pay by engaging in the formal economy but also the losses from benefit withdrawal due to formalization. Focusing on some of the European New Member States, they find that the disincentives for formal work as measured by the formalization tax rate are especially high for low-wage earners and that the higher the disincentives the higher is the incidence of informal employment. Their analysis also suggests that existing measures such as the tax-wedge may not be sufficient in capturing disincentives for formal work.

12.3.4. Labor Market Regulation and Informality

Employment protection is at the center of labor market regulation. We can understand employment protection as restrictions imposed on firms that prevent them from using labor freely (Addison and Teixeira 2001). A purely neoclassical view of the world invoking "Chatelier's Principle" would thus claim that employment protection *a fortiori* must result in the inefficient use of labor by firms. On the other hand, employment protection, which comes about through national legislation, collective bargaining or judicial process, is put in place to protect workers from undue pressures on the part of employers and to guarantee them reasonable employment and income stability. What interests economists is, of course, how employment protection affects the overall levels of employment and unemployment in the medium run and whether the speed of employment adjustment is affected by employment protection. Since economic theory is ambiguous about these outcomes there has been a large empirical literature trying to answer these questions (for a survey see Addison and Teixeira 2001).

The empirical literature has established that the employment of prime-age male workers is not affected by employment protection. This very robust finding can have implications for the issue of informality and employment protection, since younger and older workers show a greater incidence of informal employment. In other words, very restrictive employment protection might encourage informal employment of these latter groups of workers. Consequently loosening employment protection stipulations for some type of employment might decrease informal employment for these workers. For example, in Spain a major labor market reform in the 1980s abolished severance pay for temporary work and allowed several renewals of temporary jobs. The result of this reform according to Aguirregabiria and Alonso-Borrego (2009) was an overall increase in employment, which was exclusively driven by a rise of temporary employment contracts. So, one can moot that the loosening of regulations for temporary employment decreased informal employment to some degree. However, one also needs to keep in mind that this increase in overall employment was not associated with a rise in labor productivity and in earnings for firms. A counterfactual exercise by these authors that simulated a loosening of employment protection of permanent jobs showed a more substantial increase in overall employment and in labor productivity. The example of Spain also shows that changing regulations regarding the core of the workforce is politically difficult to implement and indicative of the situation that in OECD countries reforms of employment protection are predominantly focused on employment of the contingent type. As already mentioned, loosening the regulation of contingent employment relationships might, on the other hand, contribute to the formalization of many informal jobs.

The empirical literature dealing directly with the impact of loosening labor market regulation in general and employment protection in particular on informal employment or informality has not produced robust and thus credible results. The work done under the aegis of the Institute of the German Economy has produced an overall index of regulation and an index of labor market regulation for most of the OECD countries (Enste and Hardege 2007). The overall index has five components: regulation in product, capital and labor markets, regulation in education and innovation as well a good governance index taking into account the quality of institutions within which the economy operates. The authors make the salient point that any economy needs regulation implemented by public institutions; what matters, though, is that regulatory legislation does not create strong incentives to avoid this regulation. With the help of macro data Ernste and Hardege perform simple beta regressions in order to show the influence of various factors and of the overall regulation index on the size of the informal economy. They demonstrate that even if one controls for general tax burden, tax ethics, per capita income and the unemployment rate, the overall regulation index remains highly significant and has a large positive beta coefficient (0.351). They repeat the same exercise with the regulation index for the labor market as an explanatory variable and get very similar results, i.e. a significant beta coefficient of 0.221. Since these beta regressions are based on OLS regressions with two averaged data points, these regressions show correlations rather than causal effects running form regulation to the size of the informal economy. Nevertheless, these regression results are interesting in that they state that OECD countries with high regulation *ceteris paribus* have a larger informal economy. Consequently reducing the strictness of overall regulation and of regulation in the labor market should diminish the size of the informal economy.

Studies, which are econometrically rigorous and use firm or household micro data, have investigated regulation and employment protection and informality with a special focus on developing countries, in particular Latin America. These studies, summarized in Kucera and Roncolato (2008), show contradictory results, with some analyses suggesting a positive relationship between labor market regulation and employment protection and the level of informal employment, other studies a negative relationship and some studies no relationship at all. So the jury is still out on whether labor market regulation affects informal activities in the LAC region.

12.4. Taxation and Informality within the Formal Sector

In many countries undeclared work by dependent employees or by the self-employed who do operate in the formal economy is a widespread phenomenon (see, e.g., Brookmann et al. 2010; Sabirianova Peter 2009). In this section, we summarize empirical studies that have analyzed the effect of a flat tax reform on the informal economy.

The paper "Myth and Reality of Flat Tax Reform: Micro Estimates of Tax Evasion Response and Welfare Effects in Russia" by Gorodnichenko, Martinez-Vazquez, and Sabiarianova Peter (2009) uses the flat tax reform in Russia to establish the effect with respect to tax evasion and the productivity effect of the Russian tax reform that imposed a flat tax of 13 percent on all levels of income as of 2001. The authors employ state-of-the-art methods to derive measures of tax evasion and to get convincing empirical estimates of the above mentioned effects. The authors use various measures of the consumption-income gap to get at the level of tax evasion in Russia and show very convincingly that these large positive gaps cannot be attributed to dis-saving. In multivariate regressions they demonstrate that the factors driving these gaps are the same factors that are established when tax evasion is directly tackled in "Taxpayer Compliance Measurement Program" studies. Hence the consumption-income gap in Russia can be taken as a good proxy for tax evasion.

Using the household panel of the Russian Longitudinal Monitoring Survey (RLMS) the authors then proceed to establish the "treatment effect" of the tax reform with respect to tax evasion using difference-in-differences and regression discontinuity approaches. Households whose incomes even before the reform were taxed by 13 percent belong to the control group while households whose tax rates were higher before the reform belong to the treated group. Essentially subtracting the difference of the consumption-income before and after the reform of the treated from the difference of the control group establishes the effect of the reform on tax evasion as long as confounding (endogeneity) problems are minimized. The authors minimize these problems by using the post-reform income to identify the control and treatment groups. Going through several estimation methods and many robustness checks the authors establish a large treatment effect of the tax reform in Russia with respect to tax evasion as they find that income grows by roughly 11 percent more than consumption.

The chapter also undertakes welfare analysis by asking the question whether lower tax rates give a supply side boost to the economy. The authors show that in the presence of large tax evasion the positive effects of tax reform might be overstated by conventional approaches. Their consumption based approach shows that the productivity effect of tax reform is small relative to the tax evasion effect, i.e. they show that an increase in income following tax reform is not predominantly driven by an increase in labor supply or other supply side factors but is driven by an increase in tax compliance. In other words pre-reform undeclared, i.e. informal activities are formalized by Russian workers.

The paper by Slonimczyk (2012) directly investigates the impact of the Russian tax reform on informal activities, using the Russian Longitudinal Monitoring Survey, covering the period 1998-2009 and taking advantage of a special supplement on informality fielded in 2009. Slonimczyk takes advantage of the fact that some workers are not affected by the reform, i.e. that their pre-reform tax rate was 13 percent or less, while other workers experience a strong reduction in their tax rate from 21 or 31 percent to 13 percent. This latter group comprises the treated, the former group the controls. Taking various manifestations of informality as the dependent variable he then analyzes whether there is a difference in the change of informality pre- and post-reform among the two groups, i.e. he estimates the difference-in-differences (DID) in the labor market outcomes of interest, performing OLS, fixed effects regressions as well as using a semi-parametric matching DID estimator.

The study finds that the tax reform reduced significantly the incidence of informal employment. The largest reduction is observed on the prevalence of informal irregular activities and for the individuals in the top income brackets who benefited the most from the reform.

Sabirianova Peter (2009) gets qualitatively similar results when estimating the introduction of a flat tax regime on the size of the informal economy, employing a panel data set of 170 countries that spans 25 years. She finds that imposing a flat tax reduces informal activities especially at the top of the income distribution. However this effect only works in the first year after the introduction but vanishes in the long run. The author also establishes that in countries with poor institutions tax cuts do not produce any discernible impact.

12.5. Empirical Analysis with Macro Data

12.5.1. Data Sources and Descriptive Statistics

12.5.1.1. Data Sources

Our analysis is based on data from several principal sources. The first source is a database of the IZA Program Area 'Labor markets in emerging and transition economies', which is a new hand-collected dataset that provides essential information about the evolution of labor markets in the countries of Central and Eastern Europe and Central Asia. It includes 27 countries of the region and spans 4 years, 1995, 1999, 2003, and 2007. The database contains four key variables characterizing labor market outcomes and six key variables describing labour market institutions. The latter include employment protection legislation (OECD version II), expenditures on active labor market programs, tax-wedge, unemployment benefit size (measured as average benefit to average wage), unemployment benefit duration, and union density. There are 71 observations with complete data on these 10 variables, corresponding to 23 countries. Details about the variables included in the database are shown in the Appendix.

The second source is new data on labor market institutions in Latin American countries provided by the World Bank. This database contains the same institutional variables as the mentioned IZA database except for expenditures on active labor market policies, which are omitted for data availability reasons. We thus have variables characterizing employment protection legislation (OECD version II), the tax-wedge, unemployment benefit size and duration, as well as union density. This information is available for 25 countries and 3 years, namely 1999, 2003 and 2007. The only notable difference with regard to the IZA dataset is in measuring unemployment benefit size. Due to information constraints, for Latin American countries it is measured as the replacement ratio during the third month in unemployment. Further details on this source are available from the authors upon request.

The third building block is data on the size of the informal economy taken from the paper by Schneider, Buehn, and Montenegro (2010). This source provides estimates for 162 countries, including Central and Eastern European, Central Asian, and Latin American countries over 1999 to 2007. This is a unique dataset providing comparable estimates for most countries of the world based on the MIMIC estimation method.

Finally, we have added some key macroeconomic variables from the World Bank database (http://data.worldbank.org/), such as employment to population ratio, GDP growth rate, and inflation. These variables are commonly used in macro-labor regressions for various robustness checks.

12.5.1.2. Descriptive Statistics

Descriptive statistics for the key variables used in subsequent analysis are shown in Table 12.1. Panel A of Table 12.1 provides information for the pooled sample of transition economies and Latin American countries, and Panels B and C describe the two sub-samples separately.

As can be seen from the data in Table 12.1, the size of the informal economy (variable INFORMAL) is quite large in the countries sampled (about 38%), and does not differ much across the two subsamples (37% in transition economies and 39% in Latin America). These numbers are considerably higher than in the OECD or EU (see Schneider et al. 2010). Importantly, the variables measuring labor market institutions and policies are, in general, at lower levels than in mature market economies, especially of Western Europe. For the entire sample, the EPL appears to be relatively flexible, at the level of 1.56 (variable EPL). This is much less than in the OECD or EU, where EPL exceeds 2.0. The tax-wedge (variable TAX) is non-negligible, although still less than in mature market economies. Unemployment benefit (variable BENEFIT) is rather small, and its duration is just 7 months (variable BNFT_DUR), on average. Again, this is much less than in most high-income countries, especially of Western Europe.

Union density (variable DENSITY) is at the level of 32%, which is considerable.

Table 12.1

Descriptive Statistics

Panel A: Full Sample

Variable	Obs	Mean	Std. Dev.	Min	Max
INFORMAL	138	37.99	11.57	16.8	68.3
EPL	146	1.56	1.03	0	3.6
TAX	138	39.51	9.14	8.22	77.45
BENEFIT	132	20.53	19.32	0	80
BNFT_DUR	129	7.39	6.36	0	24
DENSITY	102	32.18	22.31	1.3	94
GDP_GR	159	4.56	4.53	−11.2	20.8
INFL_CH	141	0.77	7.71	−20.25	31.56
EMP-POP-RAT	154	55.19	7.04	31.5	69.5

Panel B: Transition Countries

Variable	Obs	Mean	Std. Dev.	Min	Max
INFORMAL	70	36.86	11.42	16.8	68.3
EPL	71	2.37	0.55	0.38	3.6
TAX	76	38.43	5.75	23	53.2
BENEFIT	74	24.9	11.39	0	60
BNFT_DUR	74	11.02	5.46	0	24
DENSITY	69	40.79	20.78	13.17	94
GDP_GR	84	5.57	4.79	−11.2	20.8
INFL_CH	73	0.87	9.21	−20.25	31.56
EMP-POP-RAT	79	51.43	6.83	31.5	65

Panel C: Latin American Countries

Variable	Obs	Mean	Std. Dev.	Min	Max
INFORMAL	68	39.16	11.7	18.5	67.7
EPL	75	0.79	0.75	0	3.1
TAX	62	40.82	11.99	8.22	77.45
BENEFIT	58	14.96	25.2	0	80
BNFT_DUR	55	2.5	3.64	0	12
DENSITY	33	14.19	12.65	1.3	63.1
GDP_GR	75	3.43	3.95	−10.89	13.2
INFL_CH	68	0.66	5.74	−12.42	29.42
EMP-POP-RAT	75	59.15	4.74	49.1	69.5

Notes: INFORMAL is the dependent variable in the analysis; measures the size of the informal economy according to Schneider et al. (2010). Key independent variables: EPL measures stringency of employment protection legislation, TAX is the tax-wedge on labor, BENEFIT is the size of unemployment benefits, BNFT_DUR is the duration of unemployment benefits, and DENSITY is union density. Control variables: GDP_GR is GDP growth between time t−1 and t, INFL_CH is change in inflation betwee time t−1 and t, and EMP-POP-RAT stands for employment-to-population ratio.

The picture becomes more nuanced when we look at the two subsamples separately. In particular, the two groups of countries appear to be similar with respect to only one institutional variable, namely the tax-wedge. As regards other variables measuring labor market institutions and policies, there are notable differences between transition economies and Latin American countries. In particular, EPL, benefit size and duration, as well as union density all appear to be much higher in the former group of countries as compared with the latter group. As these variables are usually associated with better protection of workers, we conclude that labor market institutions seem to be more labor-friendly in transition countries as compared with Latin American countries.[6]

Table 12.2 shows pairwise correlation coefficients between the key variables. Again, we present information for the pooled sample (Panel A) and the two regional sub-samples (Panels B and C). Statistical significance (at the 5% level) of the correlation coefficients is marked by an asterisk. As can be seen from raw correlations in Panel A, the informal economy is negatively and statistically significantly correlated with all institutional variables save union density, where the correlation is positive and statistically significant. Some of these correlations appear to be rather counter-intuitive, for example, the negative correlation between the tax-wedge and informal economy. This suggests the importance of more sophisticated techniques of analysis aimed at netting out the effect of confounding factors and establishing causal links between the variables of interest.

Table 12.2

Raw Correlations

Panel A: Full Sample

	INFORMAL	EPL	TAX	BENEFIT	BNFT_DUR	DENSITY
INFORMAL	1					
EPL	−0.23*	1				
TAX	−0.25*	0.14	1			
BENEFIT	−0.22*	0.18*	0.14	1		
BNFT_DUR	−0.34*	0.58*	0.13	0.51*	1	
DENSITY	0.26*	0.43*	−0.30*	0.27*	0.37*	1
GDP_GR	−0.03	0.17*	−0.12	−0.16	−0.02	−0.08
INFL_CH	0.18*	−0.04	−0.11	−0.05	−0.01	0.1
EMP-POP-RAT	0.31*	−0.53*	−0.17*	−0.27*	−0.60*	−0.38*

Panel B: Transition Countries

	INFORMAL	EPL	TAX	BENEFIT	BNFT_DUR	DENSITY
INFORMAL	1					
EPL	−0.04	1				
TAX	−0.47*	0.25*	1			
BENEFIT	−0.32*	0.17	0.27*	1		
BNFT_DUR	−0.24	0.22	0.27*	0.52*	1	
DENSITY	0.55*	0.18	−0.35*	−0.06	−0.03	1
GDP_GR	0.07	−0.05	−0.34*	−0.14	−0.23*	−0.2
INFL_CH	0.26*	0.05	−0.11	−0.13	0	0.17
EMP-POP-RAT	0.21	−0.41*	−0.18	−0.26*	−0.28*	−0.11

Panel C: Latin American Countries

	INFORMAL	EPL	TAX	BENEFIT	BNFT_DUR	DENSITY
INFORMAL	1					
EPL	−0.21	1				
TAX	−0.2	0.38*	1			
BENEFIT	−0.16	−0.09	0.21	1		
BNFT_DUR	−0.49*	0.05	0.57*	0.62*	1	
DENSITY	−0.13	−0.01	0.35*	0.56*	0.49*	1
GDP_GR	−0.13	0.02	0.05	−0.33*	−0.33*	−0.19
INFL_CH	0.07	−0.05	−0.16	−0.02	−0.24	−0.22
EMP-POP-RAT	0.47*	0.04	−0.50*	−0.14	−0.51*	−0.25

Note: Asterisks denote statistical significance at the 5% level.

Panels B and C show some differences in raw correlations between the informal economy and labor market institutions across the two sub-samples. In both sub-samples, the correlation of the informal economy with EPL is negative, but statistically insignificant. In transition countries, the size of the informal economy is negatively correlated with the tax-wedge and benefit size, and positively correlated with union density. For Latin American countries, the only statistically significant correlation is with unemployment benefit duration (negatively signed).

12.5.2. *Methodology*

Our analysis of the link between the size of the informal economy on the one hand and labor market institutions and policies on the other hand draws heavily on the standard macro-regressions proposed in the seminal study by Nickell (1997). In that study, labor market outcome variables are related in a panel regression framework to a set of variables measuring institutions and policies, as well as by the change in inflation. We proceed in an essentially similar fashion by considering, in the baseline specification, five variables characterizing institutions and policies.

We note that our results do not necessarily have a causal interpretation as both institutions and policies may be shaped by labor market outcomes, for example, via the mechanism of elections (Blanchard 2006). Nevertheless, we try to address endogeneity (at least some of its sources) by controlling for omitted factors (including unobserved characteristics of countries) using random- or fixed-effects specifications of our regression model. These are necessary as the paucity of the degrees of freedom does not allow inclusion of many potentially relevant explanatory variables. The baseline (pooled OLS) regression equation can then be written in the following way:

$$(4) \quad INFORMAL_{it} = \alpha + \beta_1 EPL_{it} + \beta_2 TAX_{it} + \beta_3 BENEFIT_{it} + \beta_4 BNFT\_DUR_{it} + \beta_5 DENSITY_{it} + \varepsilon_{it}$$

where index i denotes countries and index t denotes time, $t \in \{1999, 2003, 2007\}$, $INFORMAL$ stands for the size of the informal economy as measured in Schneider et al. (2010), EPL measures the strictness of employment protection legislation, TAX is the tax-wedge on labor, $BENEFIT$ stands for the average unemployment benefit replacement rate, $BNFT\_DUR$ stands for the maximum duration of unemployment benefits, $DENSITY$ measures union density, and ε is a white noise disturbance. We then proceed by adding country and time effects.[7] Because macro-trends in the two regions may be very different, we allow for different time trends in transition and Latin American countries. We then consider additional macro controls: change in inflation and cumulative growth of GDP in the years before labor market outcomes are measured. Last but not least, we estimate the regressions separately for each region, transition economies and LAC countries.

As can be seen from the specification of equation (4), one substantial difference from the study by Nickell (1997) and subsequent studies (e.g., Lehmann and Muravyev 2012) is that we do not employ variables measuring expenditures on active labor market policies. This is both due to data constraints as well as the absence of a clear theoretical link between informality and active labor market programs.[8] In addition, we do not include variables measuring union coverage rates and bargaining type – again, mostly for data reasons, but also due to the difficulties in interpreting these variables in less developed countries.[9] We, however, believe that we capture the essential aspects of wage setting with our union density variable since it is regarded as the most important of the related factors (Eichhorst, Feil and Braun 2008).

12.5.3. Empirical Results

We start with the results of estimating the baseline regressions using three alternative specifications: OLS, random-effects (RE), and fixed-effects (FE). Table 12.3 shows the results. The regression in Column 1 is estimated using OLS. In addition to key explanatory variables, we add a dummy for Latin American countries in order to account for potential differences between the two sub-samples. The results suggest a negative and statistically significant effect of the tax-wedge on the informal economy and a positive effect of union density. There is also a negative (albeit marginally statistically insignificant) coefficient on EPL, suggesting, if taken at face value, that stricter employment protection is associated with less informality. We have serious doubts regarding these results. In particular, the first result implying that increasing taxes reduces informality is especially counterintuitive in the light of the theoretical considerations and the discussed empirical evidence on the effects of changing the tax-wedge. We therefore explore, in Columns 2 and 3, whether it may be endogenous, e.g. driven by omission of important factors at the country level.

Table 12.3

Comparing Different Estimation Methods: OLS, RE, and FE Results

Dependent var: INFORMAL	(1) OLS	(2) RE	(3) FE
EPL	−2.638	0.396	1.375*
	(1.943)	(0.856)	(0.717)
TAX	−0.675***	0.056	0.136**
	(0.174)	(0.066)	(0.063)
BENEFIT	−0.027	−0.080*	−0.087
	(0.064)	(0.047)	(0.056)
BNFT_DUR	−0.323	−0.253*	−0.104
	(0.272)	(0.130)	(0.114)
DENSITY	0.176***	0.058	0.044
	(0.063)	(0.037)	(0.037)
LAC	6.499	0.666	
	(6.180)	(4.748)	
INTERCEPT	64.703***	34.988***	28.317***
	(9.816)	(5.853)	(3.426)
R^2	0.41	0.11[a]	0.24[b]
N	85	85	85
Diagnostics			
Breusch&Pagan chi2(1)		35.15	
Prob>chi2		(0.000)	
Hausman chi2(5)			22.68
Prob>chi2			(0.000)

Notes: Cluster robust standard errors (clustering on countries) are reported in parentheses. Asterisks denote significance levels: * for 10%, ** for 5%, and *** for 1%.

[a] overall R2.

[b] within R2.

Column 2 shows the results obtained using the random-effects estimator. Interestingly, the coefficients on both EPL and tax-wedge change signs (to positive), but remain statistically insignificant. The coefficient on union density loses statistical significance. Instead, we observe negative and statistically significant (at the 10% level) coefficients on unemployment benefit size and duration. This implies, *ce-*

teris paribus, that more generous unemployment benefit schemes are associated with lower informality.

Next, Column 3 shows the results from the fixed-effects estimation. The picture is now very different to what we have seen in Columns 1 and 2. In particular, both EPL and tax-wedge are now positively and statistically significantly associated with informality. In other words, stricter employment protection as well as a higher tax-wedge on labor increases the size of the informal economy. The coefficients on the other variables are statistically insignificant, although the corresponding t-statistics are usually greater than unity in absolute value. Note that the coefficient on the dummy for LAC countries cannot be estimated in this specification as the respective effect is now subsumed in country fixed-effects.

Beneath the main estimation results in Column 2 and 3 we report standard diagnostic tests, namely the Breusch and Pagan test for random effects and the Hausman test. Both are rejected at conventional significance levels. The rejection of the first test suggests the importance of unobserved time-invariant effects at the country level (and thus, inferiority of the OLS specification), the rejection of the latter implies inconsistency of the random effects (and, of course, OLS) estimator. Therefore, the fixed-effects estimator appears to be the only one which can potentially deliver consistent estimates of the effect of labor market institutions on the size of the informal economy. In what follows we therefore rely on this estimator and skip OLS and random-effects specifications altogether.[10]

In Table 12.4 we expand the analysis presented in Table 12.3 by adding time effects (which are supposed to control for general macro-trends) and testing the importance of missing observations as well as of differences in measuring unemployment benefit size between the two groups of countries. For comparison purposes, Column 1 reproduces the FE specification from Table 12.3, which is now our baseline specification. Column 2 of Table 12.4 shows the results when the baseline specification is augmented with time effects (assumed common for both regions). Here and later in the analysis the base year is 1999. The coefficients on the time dummies, therefore, can be interpreted as showing the dynamics of informality net of the effect of the institutional variables. In particular, the regression in Column 2 suggests a monotonic decline in informality in the sampled countries between 1999 and 2007. Regarding the key variables of interest, the coefficients on both EPL and TAX lose statistical significance.

Instead, we observe a negative and statistically significant coefficient on BENEFIT suggesting that informality decreases with more generous unemployment benefits (higher replacement ratios). The regression in Column 3 differentiates between the macro trends in transition and LAC countries. The results suggest that these trends were not the same in the two regions of the world: while there seems to have been a steady decrease in informality in transition countries, informality appears to have peaked in LAC countries in 2003. However, the coefficients on the main variables of interest are barely affected by this change in specification.

Table 12.4

Comparing Different Models

Dependent var: INFORMAL	(1) FE	(2) FE	(3) FE	(4) FE	(5) FE
EPL	1.375*	0.609	0.506	0.418	0.464
	(0.717)	(0.404)	(0.410)	(0.428)	(0.442)
TAX	0.136**	−0.002	0.008	−0.039	0.008
	0.063	(0.035)	(0.031)	(0.031)	(0.031)
BENEFIT	−0.087	−0.066*	−0.070*	−0.061	−0.086
	(0.056)	(0.037)	(0.038)	(0.042)	(0.057)
BNFT_DUR	−0.104	−0.049	−0.052	−0.076	−0.053
	(0.114)	(0.064)	(0.066)	(0.065)	(0.070)
DENSITY	0.044	0.009	0.008		0.007
	(0.037)	(0.016)	(0.015)		(0.015)
YEAR 2003		−1.191***	−1.537***	−1.646***	−1.606***
		(0.227)	(0.238)	(0.2869	(0.305)
YEAR 2007		−3.457***	−3.657***	−3.852***	−3.709***
		(0.361)	(0.449)	(0.476)	(0.494)
LAC*YEAR 2003			1.301***	1.622***	1.404***
			(0.473)	(0.500)	(0.512)
LAC*YEAR 2007			0.775	0.474	0.773
			(0.765)	(0.625)	(0.764)
BENEFIT*LAC					0.038
					(0.062)
INTERCEPT	28.317***	37.433***	37.338***	41.006***	37.641***
	(3.426)	(2.018)	(1.911)	(1.741)	(2.093)
R^2	0.24	0.81	0.83	0.80	0.83
N	85	85	85	105	85

Notes: Regression with country fixed-effects. Cluster robust standard errors (clustering on countries) are reported in parentheses. Asterisks denote significance levels: * for 10%, ** for 5%, and *** for 1%.

In Column 4, while controlling for a differential macro-trend in the two regions, we drop the density variable from the regression. The rational is the presence of too many missing observations for this specific variable in LAC region (see Table 12.1, Panel C). The results are not very different from the previous specifications. The negative coefficient on BENEFIT loses statistical significance; all the other institutional variables are insignificant, too.

Finally, in Column 5 we bring back union density, but now differentiate between benefits size in transition and LAC countries (because they are measured somewhat differently). This robustness check brings no visible changes to the previously reported results.

Table 12.5

Robustness Checks With Different Additional Controls

Dependent var: INFORMAL	(1) FE	(2) FE	(3) FE	(4) FE	(5) FE	(6) FE
EPL	1.095	0.38	1.505**	0.706***	1.181**	0.545**
	(0.817)	(0.454)	(0.583)	(0.241)	(0.472)	(0.232)
TAX	0.123*	0.004	0.085*	–0.015	0.099*	–0.030
	(0.062)	(0.029)	(0.048)	(0.020)	(0.055)	(0.035)
BENEFIT	–0.074	–0.071*	–0.064	–0.060**	–0.043	–0.046**
	(0.057)	(0.038)	(0.044)	(0.022)	(0.043)	(0.021)
BNFT_DUR	–0.128	–0.062	–0.152*	–0.088*	–0.085	–0.079*
	(0.105)	(0.062)	(0.077)	(0.046)	(0.065)	(0.046)
DENSITY	0.042	0.007	0.024	0.000	0.022	0.001
	(0.039)	(0.015)	(0.027)	(0.012)	(0.027)	(0.013)
YEAR 2003		–1.669***		–1.325***		–1.117***
		(0.219)		(0.246)		(0.250)
YEAR 2007		–3.663***		–3.131***		–2.928***
		(0.447)		(0.292)		(0.346)
LAC*YEAR 2003		1.430***		0.495		0.030
		(0.479)		(0.420)		(0.482)
LAC*YEAR 2007		0.976		0.259		–0.216
		(0.802)		(0.563)		(0.797)
EMP-POP-RAT	–0.224*	–0.062				
	(0.113)	(0.064)				
GDP_GR			–0.119***	–0.070***	–0.167***	–0.094***
			(0.041)	(0.017)	(0.023)	(0.022)
INFL_CH					–0.003	0.002
					(0.005)	(0.003)
INTERCEPT	41.233***	41.133***	31.962***	38.841***	32.085***	40.126***
	(7.072)	(3.569)	(2.826)	(1.428)	(2.662)	(1.968)
R^2	0.31	0.83	0.52	0.90	0.67	0.92
N	85	85	85	85	77	77

Notes: Regression with country fixed-effects. Cluster robust standard errors (clustering on countries) are reported in parentheses. Asterisks denote significance levels: * for 10%, ** for 5%, and *** for 1%.

The regressions reported in Table 12.5 introduce several additional control variables: employment to population ratio (variable EMP-POP-RAT, the data are taken from the WB open sources), GDP growth in period $t-1$ (variable GDP_GR), and change in inflation in year t relative to year $t-1$ (variable INFL_CH).[11] There are two baseline specifications to which these extra controls are added – the regression without any time effects (Column 3, Table 12.3) and the regression with differential trends (Column 3, Table 12.4). Overall, the results in Table 12.5 suggest the high importance of lagged GDP growth for informality, with higher growth rates associated with a decrease in informal economic activity. Employment-to-population ratio matters in some specifications while change in inflation has little relevance – at least in our regressions – for informality. Looking at the coefficients on the institutional variables, one may note that four out of five of them are statistically significant, at least in some specifications. The only consistently insignificant institutional variable is union density, DENSITY. The coefficients on the other variables have the expected signs. In particular, higher EPL as well as a higher tax-wedge are associated with an increase in informality. Unemployment benefit size and duration, are in contrast, negatively related to informal economic activity.

Table 12.6

Comparing Results for the Two Regions

Dependent var: INFORMAL	(1) TEs	(2) LAC	(3) TEs	(4) LAC
	FE	FE	FE	FE
EPL	0.259	0.823	1.237***	−2.862
	(0.436)	(0.918)	(0.416)	(3.083)
TAX	0.079	−0.068	0.053	−0.033
	(0.063)	(0.044)	(0.064)	(0.094)
BENEFIT	−0.086	−0.033	0.004	−0.048
	(0.051)	(0.021)	(0.046)	(0.064)
BNFT_DUR	−0.054	0.079	−0.066	−1.091***
	(0.058)	(0.151)	(0.062)	(0.258)
DENSITY	0.027		0.031	
	(0.018)		(0.029)	
YEAR 2003	−1.413***	−0.147		
	(0.271)	(0.427)		
YEAR 2007	−3.374***	−3.494***		
	(0.532)	(0.414)		
GDP_GR			−0.173***	−0.328***
			(0.033)	(0.052)
INFL_CH			−0.004	−0.155**
			(0.004)	(0.054)
INTERCEPT	34.458***	42.799***	31.192***	50.060***
	(3.392)	(2.542)	(2.609)	(5.298)
R^2	0.85	0.81	0.76	0.71
N	58	46	55	39

Notes: Regression with country fixed-effects. Cluster robust standard errors (clustering on countries) are reported in parentheses. Asterisks denote significance levels: * for 10%, ** for 5%, and *** for 1%.

In Table 12.6 we analyze the effects of labor market institutions on informal economic activity separately for two regions, transition and LAC countries. Odd columns show the results for transition economies and even columns for LAC countries. In regressions with LAC countries we have to exclude union density from the list of regressors for otherwise the number observations drops below 30, which makes the results unreliable. The paucity of the degrees of freedom in the two sub-samples makes most of the coefficients statistically insignificant. However, some of the results from the previously reported tables survive. In particular, the regression in Column 3 confirms the importance of EPL in transition economies and the regression in Column 4 confirms the importance of unemployment benefit duration in LAC countries.

From both research and policy perspectives it may be important to characterize the estimated effects quantitatively, as is usual, in terms of elasticities. Below we provide such an assessment for several institutional variables based on the results in Table 12.5. Note that since the models estimated are linear, the elasticities will differ for different values of the independent variables. We follow the common approach and evaluate them at the sample means. Assuming the coefficient on EPL equal to 0.9 (the rough average in the regressions where this coefficient is statistically significant) and given the sample average for EPL at the level of 1.56 and the sample average for INFORMAL at 38, the elasticity of EPL with respect to the informal economy turns out to be about 0.04. In other words, reducing EPL by 1% will result in a decrease of informality by 0.04%. Similarly, if we assume the coefficient on the tax-wedge variable equal to 0.1 and take the sample average for INFORMAL (38) and TAX (39.5), the elasticity of the tax-wedge with respect to informal economic activities (evaluated at the sample mean) is close to 0.1. In other words, decreasing the tax-wedge by 1% leads to a drop in informality by 0.1%. For the unemployment benefit, the sample mean is 20.5, and the coefficients – when statistically significant – average -0.06. These numbers suggest the elasticity of unemployment benefit with respect to informal economic activities to be about -0.03. In other words, raising unemployment benefit by 1% will result in the decrease of informality by a mere 0.03%.

12.6. Conclusions

Using unique hand-collected country level data on labor market institutions in transition and Latin American countries this chapter provides some first estimates on the impact of EPL, the tax-wedge, benefit levels and duration as well as union density on informality in these two regions of the world. Our results suggest that mainly two labor market institutions matter for informality, confirming the main findings of the literature, which identifies taxes and labor market regulation as important determinants of the size of the informal economy.

Our quantitative assessments show that the tax-wedge produces the highest positive elasticity. Hence, lowering the tax-wedge might be one of the important policy instruments in combating informality. The positive impact of EPL on informality, on the other hand, while significant is very small.

Our analysis also strongly suggests that cross-country studies of determinants of informality should be based on panel data which allow controlling for unobserved country effects. The results from our OLS specifications (where unobserved country effects are not controlled for) turn out to be dramatically different from what we obtain in the fixed-effects regressions.

Appendix – IZA-World Bank Panel Data Base

The data used in the analysis is a combination of the database of the IZA Program Area “Labor markets in emerging and transition economies” and data on LAC countries provided by the World Bank. The first database is a new hand-collected dataset that provides essential information about the evolution of labor markets in the countries of Central and Eastern Europe and Central Asia. It includes 27 countries of the region and spans 14 years, 1995-2007 (data are collected every 4 years). The database contains 4 variables characterizing labor market outcomes, among them the employment to population ratio for workers aged between 15 and 59, and 6 variables describing labor market institutions and policies. There are 71 observations with complete data on these 10 variables, corresponding to 23 countries. The database of the World Bank provides information on essentially the same characteristics (except for expenditures on active labor market policies) for 25 countries from LAC region in 1999, 2003, and 2007. The details about the variables proxying for labor market institutions and polices are presented in what follows.

A *Labor Market Institutions and Policies in Transition Countries:*

- Employment protection legislation (EPL) index is based on version 2 of the OECD (2004) indicator and is a weighted average of 18 cardinal summary indicators of EPL strictness which can be gathered in three main areas: (i) employment protection of regular workers against individual dismissal; (ii) specific requirements for collective dismissals; (iii) regulation of temporary forms of employment.
- Active labor market policies (ALMP) – expenditures on active measures of labor market policies and public employment services as per cent of the country's GDP. Note: this variable is not available for LAC countries.
- Tax-wedge on labor (TAX) is defined as the difference between the salary costs of a single "average worker" to their employer and the amount of net income ("take-home-pay") that the worker receives. The taxes included are personal income taxes, compulsory social security contributions paid by both employees and employers, as well as payroll taxes for the few countries that have them; no consumption taxes are included.
- Union density (DENSITY) measures trade union density based on surveys, wherever possible. Where such data were not available, trade union membership and density were calculated using administrative data adjusted for non-active and self-employed members.[12]
- Average unemployment benefit (BENEFIT) – the average benefit as a percentage of the average wage. This deviates from the estimates typically used by the OECD because OECD replacement rates are not very meaningful in the transition countries due to the caps on the size of the benefit in many countries.[13] For LAC countries, the variable is defined as the replacement ratio during the third month in unemployment.
- Maximum duration of unemployment benefits (BNFT_DUR) – defined as the period for which a person aged 40 years who has been employed for 22 years prior to unemployment receives unemployment benefits, wherever possible.

Notes

1 Employing World Bank nomenclature our geographic coverage extends to the ECA and LAC regions.
2 For a succinct summary of these reasons, see Chapter 6 in this volume.
3 In this school of thought, formal sector jobs not only command higher wages but also provide fringe benefits that are absent with informal sector jobs.
4 This definition excludes unpaid activities such as home production and illicit activities such as drug smuggling. A distinction between licit, illicit, legal and illegal is made in the economic sociology literature definition of informality (Portes and Haller 2005; Portes and Schauffler 1993).
5 For evidence on this point with respect to ALMP see Kluve, Lehmann, and Schmidt (2008).
6 A caveat is due. There may be further aspects of the institutional environment that are not properly reflected in the variables presented. These include, for example, law enforcement, eligibility rules for unemployment benefits, and bargaining and coverage patterns. We nevertheless believe that the consistent pattern appearing in the five key variables available justifies our general conclusion concerning the two regions.
7 As many of the previous studies, we do not apply logarithmic transformation to the dependent variables in the model.
8 When we estimated the determinants of the size of the informal economy separately for transition countries and included ALMP expenditures (available only for this group of countries), this variable had no predictive power in any of the specifications. These results are available upon request.
9 For example, how would one interpret data on bargaining in a country where trade unions with high membership rates are effectively controlled by the government? It is therefore no surprise that the World Bank did not provide statistics on the coverage rates and bargaining type in the CIS countries (World Bank 2005b).
10 The diagnostic tests reject OLS and random-effects estimation methods also in the other specifications that we consider below.
11 We have also experimented with longer lags. They have worse predictive power while the main coefficients of interest stay similar to those reported in the paper.
12 A caveat concerning the quality of the union density data is due. There is a measurement problem in at least some of the selected countries. The World Bank notes, for instance, that "Armenia provides an example of the difficulty of interpreting union density figures in the CIS, with 75 percent union density by official estimates, but 80 percent of workers claiming to 'have nothing in common' with trade unions, and half of those claiming to be totally uninformed about unions." For that reason the World Bank (2005b) did not provide any statistics on the coverage rates in the CIS countries. Whenever possible we therefore examined alternative estimates of unionization, especially in the CIS countries.
13 In most countries of the region, the size of the unemployment benefit is related to past earnings. The rate may be as high as 100% (like in Croatia at the end of the 1990s and in Ukraine in the mid-2000s). The problem is that there is an upper cap on the size of the benefit, which often implies, de facto, a flat rate benefit. For example, in the early 2000s the benefit replacement rate in Croatia was 100% of average salary in the last three months of employment, but the maximum was restricted to 900 Kn. Compared to the average wage of 3600 Kn, the amount is far less than the 100% replacement rate. Similarly, the unemployed in Russia can get 75% of their average wage in the last three months of employment, but there is a cap of 4900 RUR (or 110 Euro) as of mid-2009. Relative to the average wage in the economy (17441 RUR as of 1st quarter 2009), the unemployment benefit is very low. The minimum benefit is almost negligible, amounting to 850 RUR only. It is essential that the minimum and maximum amounts of unemployment benefits are not established by a law, but are subject to government discretion.

References

Addison, J. T., Teixeira, P. (2001). The Economics of Employment Protection, IZA Discussion Paper No. 381.

Aguirregabiria, V., Alonso-Borrego, C. (2009). Labor Contracts and Flexibility: Evidence from Labor Market Reform in Spain, Working Paper 09-18, Economic Series (11).

Betcherman, G., Daysal, N. M., Pages, C. (2010). Do Employment Subsidies Work? Evidence from Regionally Targeted Subsidies in Turkey, in: Labour Economics, 17(4).

Blanchard, O. (2006). European Unemployment: The Evolution of Facts and Ideas, in: Economic Policy, 21(45): 5-59.

Boockmann, B., Rincke, J. (2005). Wirksamkeit der Bekämpfung der Schwarzarbeit durch die "Finanzkontrolle Schwarzarbeit"(The Efficacy of Fighting Undeclared Work through "Finanzkontrolle Schwarzarbeit"), ZEW, Mannheim.

Boockmann, B., Döhrn, R., Groneck, M., Verbeek, H. (2010). Abschätzung des Ausmaßes der Schwarzarbeit (The Estimation of the Extent of Undeclared Work), Tübingen and Essen.

Cunningham, W. V., Maloney, W. F. (2001). Heterogeneity among Mexico's Microenterprises: An application of Factor and Cluster Analysis, in: Economic Development and Cultural Change, 50(1): 131-56.

Eichhorst, W., Feil, M., Braun, C. (2008). What Have We Learned? Assessing Labor Market Institutions and Indicators, IZA Discussion Papers No. 3470.

Eichhorst, W., Hinz, T., Marx, P., Peichl, A., Pestel, N., Siegloch, S., Thode, E., Tobsch, V.(2012). Gerinfuegige Beschaeftigung: Situation und Optionen (in German), IZA Research Report No. 47.

Enste, D., Hardege, S. (2007). Regulierung und Schattenwirtschaft, in: IW-Trends, 34(1).

Enste, D., Schneider, F. (2006). Welchen Umfang haben Schattenwirtschaft und Schwarzarbeit? Ein Versuch zur Lösung des Rätsels, in: Zeitschrift für Wirtschaftspolitik, 86(3).

Fertig, F., Kluve, J. (2006). Alternative Beschäftigungsformen in Deutschland: Effekte der Neuregelung von Zeitarbeit, Minijobs und Midijobs, in: Vierteljahreshefte zur Wirtschaftsforschung, 75(3): 97-117.

Fields, G. S. (1990). Labour Market Modelling and the Urban Informal Sector: Theory and Evidence, in: Thurnham, D., Salomé, B., Schwarz, A. (Eds.), The Informal Sector Revisited, Paris: OECD.

Fields, G.S. (2007). Modeling Labor Market Policy in Developing Countries: A Selective Review of the Literature and Needs for the Future, World Bank Policy Research Working Paper No. 4362.

Gasparini, L., Tornarolli, L. (2007). Labor Informality in Latin America and the Caribbean: Patterns and Trends from Household Survey Microdata, CEDLAS Working Paper No. 46.

Gorodnichenko, Y., Martinez-Vazquez, J., Sabiarianova Peter, K. (2009). Myth and Reality of Flat Tax Reform: Micro Estimates of Tax Evasion Response and Welfare Effects in Russia, in: Journal of Political Economy, 117(3): 504-54.

Gruber, J. (1997). The Incidence of Payroll Taxation: Evidence from Chile, in: Journal of Labor Economics, 15(3): 72-101.

Guasch, J. L. (1999). Labor Market Reforms and Job Creation: The Unfinished Agenda in Latin America and the Caribbean Countries, Washington, DC: The World Bank.

Harris, J. R., Todaro, M. P. (1970). Migration, Unemployment and Development: A Two Sector Analysis, in: American Economic Review, 60(1): 126-42.

Kanbur, R. (2009). Conceptualizing Informality: Regulation and Enforcement, Unpublished Working Paper.

Katz, L. F. (1998). Wage Subsidies for the Disadvantaged, in: Freeman, R. B., Gottschalk, P. (Eds.), Generating Jobs: How to Increase Demand for Less-Skilled Workers, New York: Russell Sage Foundation.

Kluve, J., Lehmann, H., Schmidt, C. M. (2008). Disentangling Treatment Effects of Active Labor Market Policies: The Role of Labor Force Status Sequences, in: Labour Economics, 15(6): 1270-95.

Koettl, J., Weber, M. (2012). Does Formal Work Pay? The Role of Labor Taxation and Social Benefit Design in the New EU Member States, in: Research in Labor Economics, 34: 167-204 [Chapter 6 in this volume].
Kucera, D., Roncolato, L. (2008). Informal Employment: Two Contested Policy Issues, in: International Labour Review, 147(4): 321-48.
Lehmann, H., Muravyev, A. (2012). Labour Market Institutions and Labour Market Performance: What Can We Learn from Transition Countries?, in: Economics of Transition, 20(2): 235-69.
Lehmann, H., Pignatti, N. (2007). Informal Employment and Labor Market Segmentation in Transition Economies: Evidence from Ukraine, IZA Discussion Paper No. 3269.
Maloney, W. F. (1999). Does Informality Imply Segmentation in Urban Labor Markets? Evidence from Sectoral Transitions in Mexico, in: World Bank Economic Review, 13(2): 275-302.
Maloney, W. F. (2004). Informality Revisited, in: World Development, 32(7): 1159-78.
Mead, D. C., Morrison, C. (1996). The Informal Sector Elephant, in: World Development, 24(10): 1611-9.
Nickell, S. (1997). Unemployment and Labor Market Rigidities: Europe versus North America, in: Journal of Economic Perspectives, 11(3): 55-74.
Organization for Economic Cooperation and Development (2008). Employment Outlook, Paris: OECD.
Papps, K. L. (2007). The Effect of Social Security Taxes and Minimum Wages on Employment Growth in Turkey, Background Paper for the World Bank, Oxford.
Perry, G., Maloney, W. F., Arias, O. S., Fajnzylber, P., Mason, A. D., Saavedra-Chanduvi, J. (2007). Informality: Exit and Exclusion, Washington, DC: The World Bank.
Portes, A., Haller, W. (2005). The Informal Economy, in: Smelser, N. J., Swedberg, R. (Eds), The Handbook of Economic Sociology, Princeton and Oxford: Princeton University Press, 403-26.
Portes, A., Schauffler, R. (1993). Competing Perspectives on the Latin American Informal Sector, in: Population and Development Review, 19(1): 33-60.
Saavedra, J., Chong, A. (1999). Structural Reform, Institutions and Earnings: Evidence from the Formal and Informal Sectors in Urban Peru, in: Journal of Development Studies, 35(4): 95-116.
Sabiarianova Peter, K. (2009). Income Tax Flattening: Does it Help to Reduce the Shadow Economy?, IZA Discussion Paper No. 4223.
Schneider, F., Buehn, A., Montenegro, C. E. (2010). Shadow Economies all over the World: New Estimates for 162 Countries from 1999 to 2007, unprocessed.
Schneider, F., Enste, D. H. (2000). Shadow Economies: Size, Causes and Consequences, in: Journal of Economic Literature, 38(1): 77-114.
Slonimczyk, F. (2012). The Effect of Taxation on Informal Employment: Evidence from the Russian Flat Tax Reform, in: Research in Labor Economics, 34: 55-100.
Taymaz, E. (2006). Labor Demand in Turkey, Background Paper for the World Bank, unprocessed.
World Bank (2005a). Labor Taxes and Employment in the EU-8, Quarterly Economic Report EU-8, Washington, DC.

13

Financing Social Expenditures in Developing Countries: Payroll or Value-Added Taxes?

Richard Bird
Michael Smart

13.1. Introduction

At present social insurance (SI) systems in most Latin American countries are financed primarily through taxes on labor, including both payroll taxes that finance contributory SI regimes and other taxes on wages and labor income that finance a broader array of social programs. Payroll taxes that are explicitly linked to social insurance programs are levied at rates ranging from a low of about 8 percent in Mexico to a high of about 45 percent in Colombia. By definition, these taxes are applied only to the formal sector of the economy. Similarly, many of the benefits from the social programs financed by these taxes may be claimed only by those who are or have been employed in the formal sector and have therefore contributed to funding the programs, although there is often no tight connection between taxes paid and benefits received.[1] Issues related both to contributory schemes (and the extent to which they are regarded by workers as benefit taxes) and to voluntary arrangements are discussed elsewhere. In the present chapter, we focus primarily on the efficiency of payroll taxes (PRT) compared to value-added taxes (VAT) as a means of financing social programs in countries with important informal sectors.

Increasingly, some countries (e.g. Colombia) are both providing some benefits from the social protection system on a more universal basis and supplementing contributory finance to some extent from general revenues. This expansion of social protection regimes in Latin America raises closely related questions with respect to the link between taxes paid and benefits received and the effects of the labor tax burden on employment and productivity. As social insurance expands beyond its original contributory basis, a key question is whether it should continue to be financed primarily or exclusively through payroll and other taxes on labor, or whether efficiency and equity would be enhanced by shifting reliance to general revenues of government – and potentially to other tax bases, of which the value-added tax is the most obvious candidate. To answer such questions, it is important to compare the effects of such finance with the alternative of increasing either the rate or coverage (or both) of existing payroll taxes.

To set the stage for such analysis, this chapter begins with a brief overview of both the current SI financing arrangements and the general tax systems in a number of major Latin American countries. In most countries, SI is financed to a considerable extent by dedicated payroll taxes, most of which are imposed on employers rather than on employees. Despite these dedicated revenues, most SI systems are far from self-financing and a substantial fraction of general revenues also ends up financing SI systems. Nonetheless, the very limited coverage of SI regimes has increasingly led countries to devote still more general revenue to expanded social protection (SP) systems. In most countries the marginal source of general revenue is usually the VAT, which is often both the largest and one of the most elastic revenue sources available.

In considering possible alternative financing arrangements for SI, one important issue is to assess how the current system compares to such alternatives in terms of such standard criteria as economic incidence, equity, and efficiency. In particular, in view of the marked and persistent importance of the informal sector in most Latin American countries, it is critical to understand the likely effect of alternative SI financing on the relative growth of employment in the formal and informal sectors as well as the possible consequences of increasing (or reducing) informality on the pattern and level of economic growth.[2]

Levy (2008) and others have argued that current SI payroll tax systems, together with non-contributory benefit programs available to workers in the informal sector, constitute a subsidy to the informal sector which suppresses development of the formal sector and results in productivity losses. To remove this bias, Levy has proposed financing SI from the VAT instead of through contributory payroll taxes. These proposals have been controversial. Several authors, most notably Emran and Stiglitz (2005), have criticized VATs for encouraging tax evasion and the informal economy in developing countries.[3] The notion that increased reliance on VAT may be a solution to informality may thus appear surprising. Sorting out these differences is key to understanding the effect of SI financing on productivity. These issues are explored to some extent with respect to VAT, for example, in such studies as de Paula and Scheinkman (2008; 2009) on Brazil, Pomeranz (2010) on Chile, and, with respect to both VAT and payroll taxes by Anton and Hernandez (2010) on Mexico. What is more, and of considerable concern to governments, if the two taxes have different bases that may grow at different rates and are subject to evasion to different degrees, alternative forms of SI financing may have important revenue implications.

At first, the comparison between payroll and value-added taxation seems complex, since the legal and economic basis of the taxes is so different. Payroll taxes are levied on producers; while the legal incidence of VAT is also on producers, it is commonly viewed as a tax on consumption rather than production. As a tax on domestic production, the payroll tax is a tax on an origin basis, whereas almost all VATs are levied on a destination basis, zero-rating exports and fully taxing imports for domestic consumption. The two taxes may in principle have different effects on the development of the tradable and non-tradable sectors and on the pattern and level of economic growth. Finally, the different base and the invoice-and-credit structure of the VAT mean that the incentives for tax evasion and distortions to formal-sector production are potentially quite different than for payroll taxes. Some recent research (e.g. Anton and Henandez, 2010) has made progress in elucidating certain aspects of this comparison, but some of the fundamental economic issues may remain obscure.

For this reason, in Section 13.4 of this chapter we construct a simple formal model of the effects of labor and value-added taxes, contrasting in particular their incidence on wages, their implications for government revenue and for equity, and their effects on the informal economy.

The starting point of our model is a fundamental equivalence result: in a closed economy, and in the absence of informality, a consumption-based VAT is equivalent to a payroll tax plus a tax on the existing capital stock of firms and on other rents. In other words, in this idealized framework, the two taxes have identical effects on labor markets, but the VAT raises additional revenues over a transition period from taxing quasi-rents to installed capital.

Thus far, the results of the model are standard: VAT is a more efficient tax than payroll taxation in the model because its base is broader than the payroll tax base. One implication is that VAT raises the same revenues at a lower tax rate than the payroll tax. However, the story becomes more complicated when we consider informality. In the model, we suppose that firms and workers may move between the formal sector (subject to VAT and payroll taxes) and the informal sector (not subject directly to either tax). The base of VAT is broader than payroll taxes to the extent that VAT taxes rents (and quasi-rents) of formal-sector firms. Therefore, incentives to enter the informal sector are greater under VAT than under a payroll tax at the same statutory rate. In spite of this tradeoff between revenues and efficiency of the tax, we show that there exists a revenue-neutral reform from payroll taxation to VAT that increases national output and welfare in the model.

However, the analysis differs when various real world complications are considered. For example, under (destination-based) VATs, exports are zero-rated and imported goods are subject to taxation. This changes the efficiency effects of the two taxes, and may change the incentives for informality, to the extent that formal-sector firms are more or less involved in the export sector of the economy. Effects may also differ if, for example, markets are very imperfect and the infra-marginal rents taxed by VAT are relatively large, if capital is relatively more mobile than labor (or vice versa) between the formal and informal sectors and the elasticity of substitution for capital and labor is different in the two sectors, or if VAT is more regressive than the payroll tax and the existing income distribution is very unequal. However, although these factors may be important to differing extents in different countries, on the whole the critical factors are (1) the size of the factor market distortions created by the tax-wedges (e.g. the labor share in the VAT base) and (2) the relevant elasticities in the formal and informal markets.

13.2. Financing SI in Latin America

Over the last few years, issues related to social protection (SP) – a term encompassing both social insurance (SI) and social assistance (SA) – have come to the forefront of policy discussion in Latin America, with the UN, the World Bank, the Inter-American Development Bank, the IMF, the OECD, and many others contributing numerous reports and research papers to the growing pile of documentation related to this topic.[4] Several different concerns underlie the marked recent expansion of policy discussion in this area.

13.2.1. Current Concerns

Many Latin American countries introduced traditional compulsory social insurance schemes financed by payroll taxes decades ago. As Mesa-Lago (2008) notes, some countries such as Argentina, Brazil, and Chile introduced limited pension plans even before World War II; others including Colombia, Mexico, and Peru followed in the 1950s; late comers, like most of the Central American countries, followed in the 1960s and 1970s. The coverage and benefits of these schemes varies considerably from country to country (Social Security Administration 2010). In all cases, however, as Table 13.1 shows, the social insurance system is financed, to varying extents, through payroll taxes ("contributions"). On average, the level of these payroll tax rates is 23%, although with wide variation from country to country from a low of 8% in Mexico to a high of 45% in Colombia.

The literature offers several reasons for being concerned with the efficacy of the SI systems now existing in Latin America. One obvious reason is, as shown in Table 13.2, simply because almost none of the SI systems in Latin America are "self-financing." On average, less than 40% of social security outlays are financed by contributory finance, with the result that close to 20% of general tax revenues in effect finance SI spending. As shown in Table 13.2, there are of course wide differences from country to country, with the SI financing deficit being particularly large in Argentina and Brazil. These differences reflect both the differing scope and age of the SI systems in different countries and the reforms undertaken in a number of countries in recent years, both in response to fiscal pressure and as part of the effort to expand coverage in the face of continuing high levels of both inequality and informality (see Table 13.3).[5] Major reforms have taken place in Chile and Argentina – originally in the early 1990s and more recently in the last few years (Rofman, Fajnzlyber, and Herrera 2010) as well as in Colombia (Clavijo 2009) and to some extent in Bolivia, Mexico and Peru (Kritzer, Kay, and Sinha 2011).[6]

Table 13.1

Contribution Rates for Social Security and VAT Rates, Selected Countries, 2009 (percent)

Country	(1) Insured person	(2) Employer	(3) Share Levied on Employer	(4) Total Payroll Taxes	(5) "Labor Tax TTR"	(6) Standard VAT Rate
Argentina	17	23	58	40	29.4	21
Bolivia	10	10	50	20	15.5	13
Brazil	8	21	72	29	41.3	37
Chile	18	3	14	21	3.8	19
Colombia	8	37	82	45	33.9	16
Costa Rica	9	17	63	27	29.3	13
Dominican Republic	6	14	70	20	17.8	16
Ecuador	9	10	53	19	13.7	12
Salvador	9	12	57	21	17.2	13
Guatemala	5	9	64	14	14.3	16
Honduras	4	7	64	11	10.7	12
Mexico	1	7	88	8	26.7	16
Nicaragua	6	15	68	22	19.2	15
Panama	8	12	60	20	22.6	7
Paraguay	9	14	61	23	18.6	10
Peru	10	10	50	20	11.0	18
Uruguay	18	12	40	30	15.6	22
Venezuela	4	14	78	18	18.1	12
Average	9	14	61	23	21.6	16

Sources and notes: Columns (1) - (4) rounded from data in Social Security Administration (2010); may not add to total; column (3) is the ratio of column (2) to column (4). Column (5), the " labor tax TTR" is employers' payroll taxes as percent of commercial profits calculated for a hypothetical firm as estimated in World Bank (2011). Column (6) is based on KPMG (2010); different contributions are included for different countries in many cases; similarly, while the VAT rate in most countries is the standard rate applying to most transactions, in Brazil the figure shown is only an approximation to the average rate, given the different state rates and the different bases of the various federal and state taxes. Averages are unweighted.

An additional reason for SI reform has been the desire to expand the present limited coverage of SI schemes in most countries of the region. A more important attack on the problem of the very limited access to such SI-linked services as pensions and health, however, has been the rapid expansion in a number of countries of various forms of direct social assistance (SA), such as non-contributory SI schemes ("social pensions") and conditional cash transfers (CCTs). In principle, SI and SA are quite different, with the former directed at consumption-smoothing and the latter at income redistribution but, as Ferreira and Robalino (2010) note, this distinction is so often blurred in practice that it has become common in Latin America to lump SI and SA together under the label Social Protection (SP). We focus here on such non-contributory SI reforms as funding pensions, either universal or means-tested, out of general revenues and health insurance schemes targeted to the poor (Holzmann, Robalino, and Takayama 2009). Some recent studies (Ortiz and Cummins 2011) suggest that these schemes have already brought about noticeable improvements in terms of both poverty reduction and inequality in some countries in the region.

Table 13.2

Taxes and Social Security Spending 2008, as percent of GDP, Selected Countries

Country	(1) Taxes	(2) VAT	(3) Income Taxes	(4) Share of Income Taxes from CIT (%)	(5) Social Security Contributions	(6) Social Security Spending	(7) Share of SS funded by Payroll Levies (%)	(8) Share of General Tax Revenue Needed to Fund SS (%)
Argentina	18.1	3.8	2.8	67**	4.2	9.5*	44	38
Bolivia	20.8	10.0	4.0	95	1.8	4.4*	41	14
Brazil	24.0	4.9	7.9	52	7.7	13.4	58	34
Chile	19.9	8.9	7.2	90	1.4	6.4	22	8
Colombia	15.5	5.7	5.1	—	2.0	7.1	28	35
Costa Rica	15.6	6.0	4.4	84	0.3	5.6	5	9
Dom. Rep.	15.0	4.7	3.7	46	0.0	1.3*	0	—
Ecuador	16.0	5.2	4.3	74**	3.9	2.4*	—	—
El Salvador	14.6	6.6	4.5	59**	1.6	0.0*	—	—
Guatemala	11.5	5.5	3.3	85**	0.2	1.1	18	7
Honduras	16.2	6.2	5.0	70**	1.2	0.3*	—	—
Mexico	9.8	3.8	5.2	52**	1.6	3.7	—	—
Nicaragua	22.1	7.4	5.8	61	4.1	—	—	—
Panama	16.5	2.3	4.7	43	5.7	6.0*	95	3
Paraguay	13.0	6.1	2.1	100	1.2	2.9	41	14
Peru	17.2	6.1	6.7	78	1.8	3.2	56	9
Uruguay	24.2	8.6	4.7	56	6.4	11.0	58	25
Venezuela	14.3	4.7	6.9	45	0.8	4.6*	18	28
Average	18.5	5.5	3.6	68.0	2.6	4.9	37	19

Sources and notes: Columns (1)-(6): calculated from data in CEPALSTAT data base available at www.eclac.cl. Central government only (note that in Brazil an additional 8% of GDP is collected by subnational VAT). Taxes include social security contributions. Social security spending data in column (6) for countries marked by asterisk from Ferreira and Robalino (2010); it is not always for same year. Similarly, CIT share in column (4) for countries marked with double asterisk from Jimenez, Gomez Sabaini, and Podesta (2010) is for varying years in the early 2000s; in many countries some income tax revenues are not allocated either to corporations or persons. Column (7) is calculated from data in columns (5) and (6); since not all these numbers are from same source, these figures are only very rough estimates in some cases. Column (8) is calculated as the ratio of the share of SS not funded by contributions. These figures are calculated as column (7) divided by the difference between column (1) and column (5); again, for the reasons just noted, the results are at best only a rough approximation. Averages (for countries for which values are shown) are unweighted.

Table 13.3

Some Economic Characteristics, Selected Countries

Country	(1) GDP Per capita ($US)	(2) Gini coefficient	(3) Poverty Headcount	(4) Social Security Coverage (% of unemployed)	(5) Informal Economy (% of GDP)	(6) Inputed VAT Base (% GDP)	(7) Inputed PRT Base (% GDP)
Argentina	8,593	50.4	14.2	56.0	32.9	18	11
Bolivia	3,402	61.7	43.5	14.5	—	76	9
Brazil	8,010	58.8	27.4	47.8	28.4	35	46
Chile	10,810	55.2	9.1	64.9	32.1	47	6
Colombia	6,521	57.2	37.8	26.0	43.5	36	4
Costa Rica	8,096	45.8	14.7	65.3	—	46	1
Dominican Republic	5,925	51.0	15.8	44.7	44.8	29	0
Ecuador	5,879	56.0	46.8	32.3	50.7	43	20
El Salvador	5,350	51.9	29.7	32.9	36.4	51	8
Guatemala	4,011	54.2	34.6	17.8	42.3	34	1
Honduras	2,969	54.5	41.8	—	—	52	11
Mexico	11,905	53.8	20.2	55.1	28.2	24	20
Nicaragua	2.132	50.2	47.5	18.3	64.4	49	19
Panama	8,070	56.5	28.6	53.8	44.4	33	28
Paraguay	3,715	56.2	27.5	13.5	68.2	61	5
Peru	5,637	48.9	25.6	13.0	38.1	34	9
Uruguay	7,942	43.0	3.3	63.8	36.2	39	21
Venezuela	8,689	44.0	30.6	61.5	43.0	39	4
Average	6,536	52.7	27.7	40.1	42.2	41	12

Sources and notes: Columns (1)-(3) for early 2000s from Ferreira and Robalino (2010). Column (4) from Economic Commission for Latin America (2006) for social security coverage (based on survey data for different years in early 2000s, and defined somewhat differently in various countries but usually proportion paying some SI contributions; for Argentina, Ecuador, and Uruguay figure is for urban areas only); the coverage figure for Colombia is based on Clavijo (2009). Column (5) estimates (for early 2000s) from Vuletin (2008). Columns (6)-(7) are rough estimates of the actual tax bases reached by these taxes; the figures are calculated simply by dividing the revenue figures in columns (2) and (5) of Table 13.2 by the rates in columns (6) and (4), respectively, of Table 13.1. Averages, for countries for which values are shown, are unweighted.

While clearly motivated primarily by the basic distributional considerations suggested by the inequality and poverty measures shown in Table 13.3, these programs have also responded in part to the increasing perception that the basic SI system was deeply flawed, given its limited coverage of only the formal sector, the marked evasion even within that sector, and the fact that transfers are regressive in that they do not go to the poor. In short, as a detailed study of social transfers in eight countries concluded, the system is in general both "grossly inefficient and regressive" (Lindert, Skoufias, and Shapiro 2006: 44).[7]

This result is not altered by the fact that to a considerable extent (see Table 13.2) such transfers were in fact funded not by SI contributions but by general revenues because in most countries the tax system is too limited and – largely owing to the very limited role of the personal income tax (Bird and Zolt 2005) – insufficiently progressive to effect any noticeable degree of redistribution (Goni, Lopez, and Seven 2008).[8] Not only are tax burdens in the region relatively low but, unsurprisingly in light of the dependence of most economies on commodities, revenues have demonstrated high volatility in recent years (Fricke and Sussmith 2011).[9]

13.2.2. Economic Aspects of Payroll Taxation

In short, there are macroeconomic and distributional problems with the design and financing of SP programs in Latin America. What is more, the recent expansion of such programs has accentuated concerns about the possibly undesirable economic effects on labor markets, productivity and growth of both sides of the SI equation – payroll tax (PRT) finance on one hand and subsidized transfers on the other – particularly in economies with large informal sectors. Observations along such lines as the remark by Goni, Lopez, and Seven (2008, p. 23) that "payroll taxes encourage informality and ultimately tend to detract from the revenue-raising ability of the overall tax system" are common in the literature.[10] Indeed, such arguments are simply an extension of the standard view of the disincentive effects of the "labor tax-wedge." This wedge is often defined to include "direct" taxes on labor, notably the personal income tax on labor income and payroll taxes. It is probably more appropriate to include consumption taxes also, since presumably workers respond to changes in net real wages (OECD 2007). However, few empirical studies do so. Levy (2008) took this long-standing argument about the disincentive effect of PRT on employees further by arguing (particularly with respect to Mexico) that not only did wage taxes imposed on formal-sector workers encourage informality but that the recent expansion of the subsidized provision of social services to informal-sector workers reinforced the resulting disincentives to economic growth and productivity.[11] His proposed solution was essentially to replace payroll tax financing of social transfers by general revenue financing and in particular (at least in the case of Mexico) the VAT.

Of course, Levy (2008) was by no means the first to propose general revenue financing of SI or even the first to propose that the source of such finance should be the VAT. New Zealand, for example, has always financed all of its extensive social transfers from general revenues, as for the most part has Australia. Indeed, many countries finance first-pillar old age pensions (usually income-tested) from general revenues even when they also have contributory financing of earnings-related pensions. Even countries with long-established PRT financed SI schemes have recently considered shifting some of the fiscal burden to general taxes, and in particular the VAT, both because of concerns about unemployment and for macroeconomic reasons. For example, a "social VAT" – that is, an additional VAT rate earmarked to finance social purposes – was seriously discussed in France recently (Besson 2007) and a somewhat similar proposal was made for the Czech Republic (Dalsgaard 2008).[12]

13.2.2.1. Statutory Incidence

As Table 13.1 shows, every country imposes part of the tax on employees and part on employers; however, with the exceptions of Chile and Venezuela, in most countries most payroll taxes (on average, 61%) are imposed on employers. This split financing of SI contributions may not be economically significant in the sense that all taxes on wages are likely borne by workers in the long run, but some evidence suggests that it may be considered relevant in some respects by both employers and employees.[13] More recently, there has also been some discussion in the US of the possibly beneficial effects on employment of reducing payroll taxes, although perhaps unsurprisingly in the present US context there appears to have been little or no consideration of making up the revenue loss through increases in other taxes. Interestingly, the Congressional Budget Office suggested that the most effective – in terms of increasing employment – way to cut SI taxes would be to reduce the employer's portion.[14] Presumably on somewhat similar reasoning, as part of its "Paying Tax" report on the investment climate in different countries, World Bank (2011) separates out the so-called "Labor TTR" shown in Table 13.1, which is more or less the employer's share of SI contribution as a share of commercial profits (for a hypothetical firm), as if only that part of the tax influenced business decisions. However, the arguments offered in support of this position are neither very explicit nor particularly strong.[15]

13.2.2.2. Payroll Taxes as Benefit Taxes

Similarly, the argument sometimes found in the SP literature that social security "contributions" are not really taxes because they finance benefits received by the contributors is weak in general. In contrast, the exclusion of most informal workers from the scope of PRT means that, even with the ceilings imposed on the wage bases subject to such taxes, they are almost certainly progressive whether measured against income or consumption.[16]

In any case, the Levy (2008) proposal clearly touched a nerve not only in Mexico but in other countries in the region in part because it not only suggested a way to finance expanded SP – a distributionally desirable objective – but it would also reduce the damaging effect on productivity and growth of the current PRT based SI financing structure. Such "double dividends" are always attractive to both analysts and politicians. In the present chapter, however, we concentrate on the "cake" – the economic effect – rather than the "frosting" – the distributional effect, in part because the evidence in support of the former is much stronger and less country-specific.[17]

13.2.2.3. Informality

PRT has detrimental economic effects in Latin America not only because it constitutes a major component of the labor tax-wedge as usually defined but in particular because it encourages informality, and informal firms are not only in general small but also less productive than equally-sized formal firms (Pagés 2010). As La Porta and Shleifer (2008) argue, on the whole the evidence appears to support this negative view of the economic effects of increasing informality. Informal firms to a considerable extent appear to self-select into the informal sector, with those at the lower end of the underlying distribution of firm productivity (entrepreneurial or managerial ability) joining the informal sector (de Paula and Scheinkman 2008). Once there, although they gain by being able to dodge taxes, they find it more costly and difficult to secure capital as Feltenstein and Shamloo (2011), developing some aspects of the argument in Gordon and Li (2009), have recently argued. Informal-sector firms are hence likely to do little investment in either physical or human capital, thus dragging aggregate productivity performance and the development of the economy's growth potential down (Arias et al. 2010).[18]

13.3. The Choice of Tax Base

13.3.1. Payroll Taxes and VAT: The Policy Landscape

At the other end of the world from the US both economically and geographically, some of the same arguments discussed in Ainsworth

(2011) have come up in a recent proposal in New Caledonia to replace PRT financing of social transfers by VAT – in effect, the French "social VAT" revived in the south Pacific. Although both the factual and analytical setting in a recent analysis of this proposal by Lagadec and Ris (2010) are very different to that prevailing in Latin America, notably in the omission of any discussion of the informal sector, in many ways this chapter comes closer to dealing with the specific issues we analyze here than anything else in the literature, so one way to introduce the simple model set out in the next section may be simply to review the Lagadec and Ris (2010) analysis and raise some questions about it.

First, Lagadec and Ris (2010) consider, much as in the French case mentioned earlier, two possible disadvantages of VAT substitution – the presumed greater regressivity of VAT and the possible inflationary effect. Neither of these arguments appears to be a major issue in the case of most Latin American countries. Although, as Smart and Bird (2009) and other studies have shown, VATs are indeed usually passed forward to consumers, there is little or no evidence, in either developed or developing countries of any significant effect on general price levels.[19]

On the other hand, assuming full forward-shifting, VATs in most Latin American countries are indeed mildly regressive in terms of income, although they are mildly progressive when measured against consumption (Barreix, Bes, and Roca 2010). Moreover, the exclusion of most informal workers from the scope of PRT means that, even with the ceilings imposed on the wage bases subject to such taxes, they are almost certainly regressive whether measured against income or consumption (although social security contributions seem only rarely to be included in incidence analysis, perhaps in the belief – mistaken in most Latin American countries – that they are matched in some meaningful sense by SI benefits). Although only a limited amount can be said about such issues in general analytical terms, empirical analysis of VAT-to-payroll tax substitution in the setting of any particular country should presumably pay close attention to these politically important distributional questions, while recognizing that the distributional outcomes shown in such analyses, no matter how data-intensive or analytically sophisticated, often reflect as much or more the assumptions made as the reality being examined.[20]

Lagadec and Ris (2010) go on to suggest that substituting VAT for PRT financing of SI will have three major advantages. First, it will expand the revenue base. Second, it will increase employment by lowering labor costs. And third, it will remove the trade distortion arising from the fact that PRT affects export but not import prices. However, no formal analysis supporting these arguments is offered; instead, the chapter provides a simulation of the effects under a particular set of assumptions. We discuss these three advantages of VAT over PRT briefly below and more formally in the next section.

To begin with, as a glance at the two right-hand columns of Table 13.3 may suggest, the first of these points – the expanded revenue base under VAT seems perhaps too obvious to be worth discussion. In fact, however, while the point is basically correct, the issue is considerably more subtle than such simple numerical manipulation suggests. For example, some evidence suggests, in line with conventional wisdom (Bird and Gendron 2007) that VAT is relatively easier to enforce effectively than "single point" taxes like PRT (e.g. de Paula and Scheinkman 2009; Pomeranz 2010). Some aspects of this differential enforcement in economies with informal sectors have recently been explored in both theoretical and empirical terms. For example, Boadway and Sato (2009) responding in part to a critique of VAT's effects in an economy with an informal sector by Emran and Stiglitz (2005) and building on Keen (2008), show that since enforcement can affect the size of the informal sector, the case for relying on VAT, which is easier to enforce in the informal sector, is stronger. With respect to the specific case of Mexico, Leal (2010) argues that fully effective VAT enforcement would expand output by as much as 17% while Anton and Hernandez (2010), using a different model, similarly suggest that an expanded tax base would be one likely outcome from a PRT-VAT substitution.

Finally, although this point does not so far seem to have received much consideration in the Latin American discussion, attention should also be paid to the "trade" effect of a VAT-PRT substitution, the third of the positive effects postulated by Lagadec and Ris (2010). As Cardi and Restout (2010), like others, have noted, shifting all or some of the tax burden from labor to consumption in a neoclassical open economy model will produce heterogeneous sectoral responses operating largely through firm entry – responses which may be amplified by the increased labor elasticity resulting from the tax shift. However, their model does not have an informal sector. The simple model presented in the next section builds a simple framework which – without delving too deeply into "the world of the second best" in which most developing countries exist – analyzes such a tax substitution in an open economy with an endogenously determined informal sector and differential tax enforcement.

13.3.2. A Conceptual Framework

To summarize the foregoing discussion, the proposals of Levy (2008) and the actual experience with policy reform in several countries suggest that a key question is whether SI is better financed through (contributory or non-contributory) payroll taxes, or through a broader tax base like VAT. At first, the choice between labor taxes and VAT seems rather stark, since the legal base and structure of the taxes is so different. The previous economics literature has however posited simple general equilibrium models of the economy that elucidate the similarities and differences of the two taxes. In brief, the key issues are:

(1) Value-added versus payroll base: In a pure consumption VAT, essentially all purchases are taxable, but taxable purchasers (businesses) receive credits for taxes paid on material inputs and capital goods purchased. The residual base of the value-added tax is therefore labor costs of production (payroll) plus the returns to other primary factors of production *in excess of the normal return to capital employed in production*. Of these, one may highlight in particular rents to land, quasi-rents to old capital, and supranormal profits. As such, the base of an ideal VAT is broader than that of the payroll tax. A revenue-neutral shift from payroll tax to VAT therefore typically permits a reduction in the statutory tax rate, and it may have different distributional implications.

(2) Destination versus origin: Viewed in this way, both taxes are taxes on domestic production, rather than consumption. But most VATs apply zero-rating to exported commodities, and fully tax imports. As such, a VAT is typically a destination-based tax on domestic consumption, whereas a PRT is an origin-based tax on domestic production. This distinction is often held in policy circles to favor the VAT as an enhancement to "international competitiveness". But this difference is less important than it appears, since a switch from origin to destination bases will in principle generally result in changes in exchange rates or domestic wage costs that render the two bases nearly equivalent (e.g., Lockwood, de Meza and Myles 1994).

(3) Incentives for informality: Levy (2008) emphasized that existing SI systems entail a distortionary tax on formal-sector employment that implicitly favor (less productive) informal-sector firms. In contrast, Emran and Stiglitz (2005), and others, showed that VAT similarly favored informality. Clearly, both taxes (or any taxes, for that matter) create incentives for tax evasion, informality, and other economic distortions, but the nature and magnitude of these incentives differ under VAT and PRT by virtue of their different legal and economic structures. Comparing the two taxes in this dimension requires more detailed analysis.

Despite the importance of the issue, there is yet little direct empirical evidence on the real world effects of VAT on informality in the developing world. Keen and Lockwood (2010) study the effects of VAT adoption on the overall efficiency of the tax system, as measured by the ratio of tax revenues to GDP, and find that, while VAT reforms are generally revenue-neutral, adoption by low-income countries is associated with a small decline in revenue. As the authors recognize, this association may reflect other changes coincident with VAT adoption rather than the effects of induced informality; however, the result is suggestive. Desai and Hines (2005) examine the impact of the VAT on international trade in a cross-section of countries, finding that existence of VAT is associated with lower openness to trade, particularly for low and middleincome countries. In interesting recent work using Brazilian business microdata, De Paula and Sheinkman find that informal businesses are more likely to have informal suppliers and customers, a result that is consistent with the VAT chain effect on tax evasion. Pomeranz (2010) examines field experiments in Chile that show how VAT noncompliance behaviour cascades through the supply chain. To date the differential effects of VAT and other tax bases on informality have not been explored in the data.

These considerations suggest that the differences between labor taxation and VAT are subtle. Sorting out the differences requires a formal economic model. In the next section, we analyze the effects of a switch from a payroll tax to VAT on real wages, productivity, trade, and the distribution of income in a simple general equilibrium model of a small open economy. Our model includes a (simple) model of the incentives each tax creates for firms in the formal and informal sectors, and it leads to clear implications about the distributional and efficiency effects of a reform from payroll taxation to VAT.

13.4. A Formal Model

In a small open economy, a homogeneous consumption good is produced using labor as the sole productive input. There is a large population of potential entrepreneurs in the economy, each of whom chooses whether to enter the market or not and, if they enter, whether to operate in the formal or informal sector. Each firm is endowed with potential productivity θ. The density of θ in the population of potential entrepreneurs is $f(\theta)$. The scale of firms is fixed, but it differs between the informal and formal sectors of the economy. If a firm operates in the formal sector, it hires 1 unit of labor and so produces θ units of output. If it operates in the informal sector, however, a firm hires only $(1 - s)$ unit of labor and produces $\theta(1 - s)$ units of output, where the scale advantage s may be regarded as reflecting the greater capital intensity typically observed among firms in the formal sector. Firms in the two sectors also differ in their ability to evade taxes, to which we return below.

The representative worker supplies labor and consumes output to maximize utility $U(c, l)$ subject to the budget constraint $qc = wl$, where q is the consumer price of output and w the net wage received. Let

$$L(w/q) = \text{argmax } U(lw/q, l)$$

be labor supply as a function of the net real wage w/q. Because of taxes, producer prices of the consumption good and of labor may differ from prices faced by the worker; let p denote the producer price of output, and x the net-of-tax price of labor. The consumption good can be imported as well as produced. The world (border) price is fixed at p^*.

We compare two tax systems: a payroll tax at rate τ_p and a value-added tax at rate τ_v. Under the payroll tax, labor used in domestic production is taxed, so that the gross-of-tax wage paid by firms is $x = (1 + \tau_p)w$. Under the value-added tax, domestic production and imports of the consumption good are taxed, so that the domestic consumer price is $q = (1 + \tau_v)p$. Government revenues are used to finance purchase of a public good whose consumption enters additively into workers' utility, and which is therefore suppressed from the model for simplicity. Profits of entrepreneurs, defined below, are likewise consumed through purchases of the consumption good. Because the economy is a small open economy, demands adjust to ensure a balance-of-trade equilibrium; that is, purchases of the consumption good by workers, entrepreneurs, and government are equal to domestic production plus imports at any real wage in the model.

13.4.1. Tax Incidence Without Informality

To set ideas, start with the case that all firms that operate will operate in the formal sector. Let the producer price of output be p. Profit of an entrepreneur of productivity type θ is

$$\pi(\theta) = \theta p - x$$

if the firm operates, and zero otherwise. Firms therefore operate if $\pi(\theta) \geq 0$ or

$$\theta \geq \theta^* = \frac{x}{p}$$

Let the proportion of firms with productivity above any threshold z be

$$G(z) = \int_z^\infty f(\theta)d\theta$$

Thus $G(\theta^*)$ represents both the mass of firms that operates in the economy, and also the demand for labor, given the real wage paid by firms. Given the tax system (τ_p, τ_v), the wage paid in the domestic market adjusts to clear the labor market, so that

$$G(x/p) = L(w/q)$$

The labor market clearing condition, together with the pricing equations

$$x = (1 + \tau_p)w$$

$$q = (1 + \tau_v)p$$

characterize the equilibrium in the economy.

13.4.1.1. Equal Tax Rate Comparisons

Our first results concern the incidence of VAT and payroll taxes at some common rate $\tau_p = \tau_v = \tau$ in the absence of an informal sector.

Recall that under the payroll tax the gross wage paid by firms is $x = (1 + \tau)w$. Since there is no tax on imports or on domestically produced consumption, $q = p = p^*$: domestic consumer and producer prices of the consumption good equal the exogenous world price. The equilibrium wage with a payroll tax $\overline{w}_p$ therefore solves

$$G\left(\frac{(1+\tau)\overline{w}_p}{p^*}\right) = L\left(\frac{\overline{w}_p}{p^*}\right) \tag{1}$$

Under VAT at rate τ, there is no direct tax on wages so that $x = w$, but the tax raises the consumer price to $q = (1 + \tau)p$. Since VAT applies equally to domestic and imported consumption goods, $p = p^*$. The equilibrium wage under VAT $\overline{w}_v$ therefore solves

$$G\left(\frac{\overline{w}_v}{p^*}\right) = L\left(\frac{\overline{w}_v}{(1+\tau)p^*}\right) \tag{2}$$

It is immediately obvious from comparing these two expressions that $\overline{w}_v = (1 + \tau)\overline{w}_p$. Thus we have:

Result 1 **–** *In the absence of an informal sector, at equal tax rates $\tau_p = \tau_v$, a switch from payroll taxation to value-added taxation leaves the real wage paid by firms and received by workers unchanged. Consequently, the tax reform is neutral for labor supply, domestic production, and net imports.*

Although the payroll tax is an origin-based tax on domestic production, whereas the value-added tax is a destination-based tax on domestic consumption, a switch from payroll to value-added taxation causes the real exchange rate to appreciate, leaving trade unaffected. In this model, such a tax reform is neutral for international trade, domestic production, and labor supply.

However, the two taxes are not equivalent in terms of government revenue. Revenue under the payroll tax is

$$R_p = \tau\overline{w}_p \int_{\theta^*} f(\theta)d\theta$$

whereas under the VAT it is

$$R_v = \tau p^* \int_{\theta^*} \theta f(\theta)d\theta$$

The difference in revenues is

$$R_v - R_p = \tau \int_{\theta^*} \pi(\theta)f(\theta)d\theta$$

Since $\pi(\theta) > 0$ for all $\theta > \theta^*$ we have:

Result 2 **–** *At equal tax rates $\tau_p = \tau_v$, tax revenue is strictly higher under the value-added tax than under the payroll tax.*

This highlights the fact that a value-added tax is equivalent to a payroll tax plus a tax on excess profits of taxable firms. Since in this model profits are consumed by domestic entrepreneurs, the difference in the two tax bases may be regarded as either profits or entrepreneurial consumption - which are exempted under a payroll tax. Thus while the incidence of the two taxes on wages is the same in the absence of an informal sector, the value-added tax is more progressive because it taxes entrepreneurial consumption. In this model, the two taxes have identical economic effects. But since the base of VAT is broader, an equal-revenue shift from payroll taxation to VAT would permit a reduction in the statutory tax rate, which in turn would induce a rise in the real wage, and in domestic production and consumption. In this sense, VAT is both more progressive *and* more productive than a payroll tax in a model without informality.

In a richer model, profits of firms may comprise both pure profits to entrepreneurial fixed factors of production and also quasi-rents to "old" capital installed at the time the value-added tax is introduced. Under a consumption-VAT expenditures on capital goods are deductible from the tax base. While we abstract from capital for simplicity in this model, it should be recognized that revenues even from a strict consumption-VAT exceed that of a payroll tax over a (long) transition period, because the value-added base includes returns to old capital.

13.4.2. The Informal Sector

We now add the informal sector to the model. Given prices, each entrepreneur of type θ now decides whether to produce in the formal sector, in the informal sector, or to exit the market. All firms in the formal sector are fully taxable under both the payroll tax and the VAT. Whereas previously we define profits $\pi(\theta)$ at producer prices $(p,\ x)$, it turns out to be more convenient to measure profits at after-tax prices $(q,\ w)$. Accordingly, we define the value-added tax rate on a tax-inclusive basis as

$$T_v = \frac{\tau_v}{1 + \tau_v}$$

so that the producer price under VAT is $p^* = p = (1 - T_v)q$. Profits in the formal sector are then

$$\pi(\theta) = (1 - T_v)q\theta - (1 + \tau_p)w$$

If the firm operates in the informal sector, it suffers the scale penalty s, but it also evades taxes. We assume that an informal firm may evade all payroll and value-added taxes, and therefore receive q for each unit of output sold while paying w for each unit of labor hired, in contrast to the corresponding prices $(p,\ x)$ faced by formal-sector firms. Accordingly, profits in the informal sector are

$$\tilde{\pi}(\theta) = (1 - s)q\theta - (1 - s)w$$

Under these assumptions, the difference in profits in the formal and informal sectors is

$$\pi(\theta) - \tilde{\pi}(\theta) = (s - T_v)q\theta - (s + \tau_p)w \tag{3}$$

Then an entrepreneur θ operates in the formal sector if $\pi(\theta) \geq \tilde{\pi}(\theta) \geq 0$, and operates in the informal sector if $\tilde{\pi}(\theta) \geq 0 \geq \pi(\theta)$. Otherwise, the entrepreneur chooses not to produce. Assume that

$$T_v < s$$

so that the scale disadvantage of informal-sector firms exceeds the value-added tax disadvantage of formal-sector firms. Then the profit differential in (3) is increasing in productivity θ, and an entrepreneur of productivity θ chooses:

$$\left.\begin{array}{l}\text{the formal sector}\\ \text{the informal sector}\\ \text{no production}\end{array}\right\} \text{ if } \left\{\begin{array}{l}\theta \geq \frac{s + \tau_p}{s - T_v}\frac{w}{q} = \hat{\theta}\\ \tilde{\theta} = \frac{w}{q} \leq \theta \leq \hat{\theta}\\ \theta < \tilde{\theta}\end{array}\right.$$

Thus:

Result 3 **–** *The most productive firms operate in the formal sector. Some firms of intermediate productivity operate in the informal sector whenever the payroll tax or VAT rate is positive, while the least productive firms exit the market.*

Our goal is to analyze how the two tax systems affect equilibrium real wages and production in the economy; i.e. the incidence and efficiency of taxes. To simplify notation, let

$$A(\tau_p,\ T_v) = \frac{s + \tau_p}{s - T_v}$$

denote the effect of taxes on the threshold productivity level of formal-sector firms; thus $\hat{\theta} = Aw/q$. It follows from (4) that the equilibrium mass (number) of formal-sector producers is

$$N^f = G(\hat{\theta}) = G(Aw/q)$$

and of informal-sector producers is

$$N^i = G(\tilde{\theta}) - G(\hat{\theta}) = G(w/q) - G(Aw/q)$$

Given the real net wage w/q and the scale disadvantage s, the aggregate demand for labor by domestic producers is

$$L^d(w/q) = (1 - s)[G(w/q) - G(Aw/q)] + G(aw/q) = G(w/q) + sG(Aw/q)$$

Combining these expressions, we can solve for the equilibrium real net wage $\overline{w}/q$ that clears the labor market under any tax system (τ_p, T_v), i.e.

$$G(\overline{w}/q) + sG[A(\tau_p, T_v)(\overline{w}/q)] = L(\overline{w}/q) \quad (5)$$

This condition, together with the pricing condition $p = (1 - T_v)q$, fully characterizes the equilibium real wage for any payroll or value-added tax system.

13.4.2.1.Comparing Tax Systems

We now turn to the comparison between a payroll tax at rate $\tau_p - \tau$ and a VAT at the equivalent tax inclusive rate $T_v = \tau/(1 + \tau)$.

It is evident from (5) that the incidence of the two taxes on equilibrium wages depends only on the tax term $A(\tau_p, T_v)$, which determines the threshold productivity at which firms operate in the formal or informal sectors of the economy - and thus determines the size of the economic distortion caused by the tax system. We define

$$A_p(\tau) = A(\tau, 0) = \frac{s + \tau}{s}$$

as the tax distortion under the payroll tax, and

$$A_v(\tau) = A(0, \tau/(1 + \tau)) = \frac{s}{s - \tau/(1 + \tau)}$$

as the corresponding tax distortion under the value-added tax. The labor market equilibrium conditions under the two taxes are then

$$G(\overline{w}_p/q_p) + sG[A_p(\tau)(\overline{w}_p/q_p)] = L(\overline{w}_p/q_p) \quad (6)$$

under the payroll tax, and

$$G(\overline{w}_v/q_v) + sG[A_v(\tau)(\overline{w}_v/q_v)] = L(\overline{w}_v/q_v) \quad (7)$$

under the value-added tax, where it is understood that the consumer price is $q_p = p^*$ under the payroll tax, and $q_v = (1 + \tau)p^*$ under the value-added tax.

It may be easily verified that

$$A_p(\tau) < A_v(\tau) \text{ for all } \tau > 0$$

Since G is decreasing in its argument and labor supply L is increasing in the real wage, it follows from (6)–(7) that

$$\frac{\overline{w}_p}{q_p} > \frac{\overline{w}_v}{q_v} \text{ for all } \tau > 0$$

Furthermore, since the residual supply of labor to the formal sector

$$L^r(w/q) = L(w/q) - (1 - s)\ G(w/q) = s^{-1}[L(w/q) - G(w/q)]$$

is increasing in the net real wage w/q, and the supply of and demand for labor in the formal sector must be equal in equilibrium, it follows that

$$N_p^f = G[A_p(\tau)(\overline{w}_p/q_p)] > G[A_v(\tau)(\overline{w}/q_v)] = N_v^f$$

Collecting these results:

Result 4 - *Compared to a payroll tax at rate τ, in the presence of informality a value-added tax at rate τ results in:*

- *a lower real net wage paid to workers;*
- *a smaller formal sector and a larger informal production sector.*

Aggregate domestic production may be either smaller or larger under the payroll tax, depending on the magnitude of the scale disadvantage of informal producers.

The result is illustrated in Figure 13.1, which depicts the residual labor supply function of the formal sector L^r and the labor demand functions of the formal sector under the two tax systems. Since $A_p < A_v$, the formal-sector demand for labor under the payroll tax exceeds that of the equivalent value-added tax at all real wage rates, implying that the real wage rate and the size of the formal sector is larger under the payroll tax. The reason is that the value-added tax is imposed on entrepreneurial profit as well as on payroll, which creates an additional incentive for firms to move to the informal sector under the VAT compared to the payroll tax.

Figure 13.1

Wages and the Formal Sector Under Alternative Tax Bases

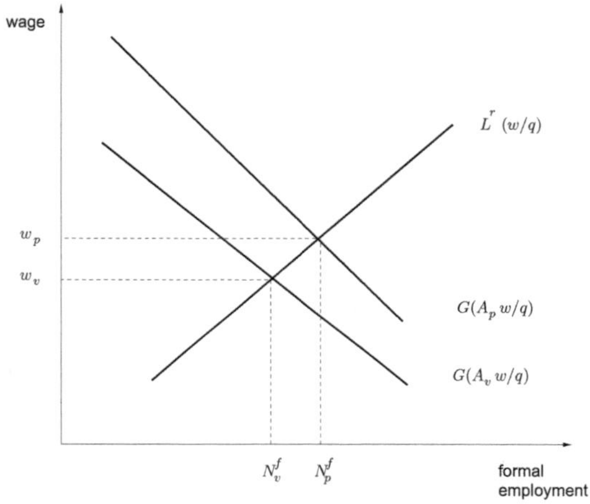

While the VAT is in this sense more distortionary than the payroll tax, the revenue comparisons of Result 2 still hold without change in the presence of an informal sector, implying that the VAT raises more revenue than the payroll tax at the same tax rate. This highlights the tradeoff between the greater reach of the VAT and the associated greater incentives for informality, consistent with the issues emphasized by Emran and Stiglitz (2005).

13.4.2.2. Is VAT More Efficient Than Payroll Taxation?

A more useful comparison is therefore between a payroll tax at rate τ and a value-added tax at a tax-inclusive rate T^* that yields the same economic effects. Observe from (6)-(7) that the market clearing real wage is the same under the two tax systems if and only if

$$\frac{s}{s - T^*} = s + \tau s$$

or

$$T^* = \frac{s\tau}{s + \tau} \tag{8}$$

When a payroll tax at rate τ is replaced by a VAT at tax-inclusive rate T^*, the real wage is unchanged, and so is the size of the formal sector $N^f = G(Aw/q)$ and of the informal sector $N^i = G(w/q) - G(Aw/q)$.

Revenue under the two tax systems is

$$R_v = T^* q \int_{\hat{\theta}} \theta f(\theta) d\theta$$

and

$$R_p = \tau w \int_{\hat{\theta}} f(\theta) d\theta$$

The ratio of tax revenues is therefore

$$\begin{aligned} \frac{R_v}{R_p} &= \frac{T^*}{\tau} \frac{q}{w} E(\theta|\theta > \hat{\theta}\,) \\ &= \frac{s}{s+\tau} \frac{q}{w} E(\theta|\theta > \hat{\theta}\,) \\ &= E(\theta|\theta > \hat{\theta}\,)/\hat{\theta} \end{aligned}$$

In the above derivation, the first equality shows that the comparison of tax revenues under equivalent payroll tax and VAT systems depends on the average profitability of labor in the formal sector. This is as expected, since the VAT is levied on value added in the formal sector, whereas the payroll tax is on wages in the formal sector. The second equality follows from the definition (8) of the equivalent VAT rate T^*, and the third from the definition (4) of the marginally profitable firm in the formal sector $\hat{\theta}$. Since $E(\theta|\theta > \hat{\theta}\,) \geq \hat{\theta}$ for any distribution of productivities, it follows that $R_v \geq R_p$, with strict inequality whenever the distribution has positive mass above the threshold $\hat{\theta}$.

Thus we have:[21]

Result 5 **–** *For any payroll tax rate* τ*, there exists a value-added tax rate* T^* *that results in:*

- *the same real wage paid to labor,*
- *the same level of production in the formal and informal sectors, but*
- *higher tax revenues paid to government.*

Our analysis highlights the tradeoff between higher revenues from taxing profit under the VAT, but correspondingly greater incentives for firms to switch to the informal sector. It turns out that this tradeoff is unambiguous. Beginning from a payroll tax at rate τ, there exists a lower value-added tax rate T^* at which the taxes paid by the marginal formal-sector firm are unchanged from the payroll tax equilibrium, so that the size of the formal and informal sectors is unchanged as well. Since the value-added tax levies higher taxes on the pure profit of inframarginal formal-sector firms than the payroll tax, aggregate tax revenue is unambiguously higher under the VAT than the payroll tax with equivalent economic effects.

The magnitude of the welfare gains from VAT finance depends on the distribution of productivities in the population of formal-sector firms, which drives the magnitude of inframarginal rents that are partially captured through VAT. To illustrate, suppose that productivity follows the Pareto distribution with parameter $k > 0$ above a lower bound $\theta = 1$. Then the density function is

$$f(\theta) = k\theta^{-k-1} \qquad \theta > 1$$

The complement of the cumulative distribution function is

$$G(\theta) = \theta^{-k} \qquad \theta > \theta_0$$

The average productivity of formal-sector firms is

$$E(\theta|\theta > \hat{\theta}) = \frac{k\hat{\theta}}{k-1}$$

The ratio of tax revenues under VAT and payroll taxation is

$$R_v/R_p = \frac{k}{k-1} = E\theta$$

Thus, in the Pareto case, the revenue advantage of value-added taxation is proportional to the average productivity in the population of firms in the economy.

13.4.3. Discussion

Our goal in this section has been to present a simple yet precise framework, of special relevance to economies where the potential for tax evasion may be high, in which the effects of labor and value-added taxes may be compared. Our analysis of tax incidence shows that the differences between the two tax bases are smaller than they may first appear. While a payroll tax is an origin-based tax on production and the VAT a destination-based tax on consumption, this difference has no real effects in our model, because taxable commodities are traded internationally, and real wages adjust to offset the effects of the two taxes on "competitiveness." A more complete theory would incorporate taxes on non-tradable as well as tradable goods, which would admit some differences in the effect of the two taxes on external trade, but previous research has shown these differences to be small in any case.

In our model, a more important difference is that the base of the VAT is broader, encompassing entrepreneurial profit and, over a long transition period, quasi-rents to "old" capital investments, as well as labor costs. The broader base of the VAT permits the same revenue to be raised at a lower statutory tax rate, implying a lower excess burden of taxation. It is also apt to be more equitable, in the sense that a shift from labor taxation to VAT shifts real income from entrepreneurs to workers.

These considerations become more complex when incentives for informality are considered. At first blush, it seems clear that, despite its positive effect on revenues, a move from payroll taxation to VAT will also move production to the informal sector, because of the additional tax on profitable formal-sector firms under VAT. In spite of this tradeoff between revenues and efficiency of the tax, we show that there exists a revenue-neutral reform from payroll taxation to VAT that increases national output and welfare in the model. Since most entrepreneurial profits are inframarginal, adoption of a VAT permits a lower statutory tax rate to be levied than under payroll taxation, so that incentives for informality can be controlled, and higher tax revenues are generated in a less costly way.

Our model thus generates clear empirical predictions: in the model, a revenue-neutral move from payroll taxation to VAT generates less informality, higher wages, and an improvement in the balance of trade. There is as yet no direct evidence on the real world effects of such reforms in the developing world, but the results from cross-country studies are informative. Keen and Lockwood (2010) suggest that if VAT is more efficient than the taxes it replaces, then tax revenues should rise as a percentage of GDP following introduction of VAT. In fact, there is generally no association between VAT adoption and revenues, except in very low-income countries, where there is a small decline. Desai and Hines (2005) examine the impact of the VAT on international trade in a cross-section of countries, finding that existence of VAT is associated with lower openness to trade, particularly for low and middle-income countries. While this evidence is far from conclusive, it is not inconsistent with the predictions of the model.

In order to focus on essentials, a number of simplifying assumptions are being made. We have assumed that both VAT and payroll taxes may be fully evaded by firms in the informal sector. If there were differences in the ability of firms to evade the two taxes, our results would change in obvious ways. In particular, an often-cited advantage of VAT is that it is levied on a refundable basis on material inputs to production, which means that even tax-evading firms pay some tax, to the extent that it is embedded in their own input costs. This reduces the incentives for VAT evasion in a way that has no parallel for payroll taxes. We abstract from this issue. Second, we assume that there is no tax enforcement, so that the expected penalty for evasion is zero. Incorporating enforcement would not change our qualitative results, as long as the enforcement technology is the same for the two taxes. In principle, VAT has enforcement advantages over payroll taxation, because invoices may be checked. Although there is some evidence supporting this conclusion, the importance of this difference in practice is largely an open question.

A useful extension would be to consider the effects of VAT taxes on intermediate inputs. The conventional story is that incentives for tax evasion are weaker under an invoice-and-credit VAT than other taxes, because the "VAT chain effect" creates incentives for registered traders to do business with other registered traders. Consistent with this, De Paula and Sheinkman (2009) find that informal businesses are more likely to have informal suppliers and customers, a result that is consistent with the VAT chain effect on tax evasion.

13.5. Concluding Remarks

It is a long way from the simple model of Section 13.4 to the complex world of tax-financed social insurance in Latin America described earlier in this chapter. The issues emphasized in the model are nonetheless at the core of the debate over practical policy concerns, and they should inform the quantitative research over policy options for Latin America. On the whole, the results derived from the model provide some support for the concern Levy (2008) and others have expressed about extending payroll tax finance of social insurance, and of broader social protection programs, in countries with significant informal sectors. The issue is far from a simple one, and close examination of the specific context is obviously required in every country. Nevertheless, our analysis highlights a number of key factors that favor incremental financing of social insurance through a broad-based tax like VAT in Latin America in place of expansion of the payroll tax.

Notes

1 Details of country programs may be found in Social Security Administration 2010 (available at http://www.ssa.gov/policy/docs/progdesc/ssptw/2008-2009/americas/index.html).
2 This has been the subject of considerable work by the World Bank – see, for instance, Perry et al. (2003) – as well as in country studies such as Arias et al. (2010) and Hanson (2010).
3 See Keen (2008) for an alternative approach stressing the extent to which VAT may actually tax rather than favour the informal sector.
4 For a sampling, see e.g. Economic Commission on Latin America (2006), Mesa-Lago (2008), Riber, Robalino, and Walker (2010), IMF (2010), and Da Costa et al. (2011).
5 As Mesa-Lago (2008) notes, for example, Argentina, Brazil, Chile Costa Rica, and Uruguay led the way in developing SI systems, while Paraguay, Nicaragua, Honduras, Guatemala, El Salvador, and the Dominican Republic are late-comers.
6 As Kritzer, Kay and Sinha (2011) discuss in detail, much of this reform activity has taken the form (to look only at pensions) of moving away to varying degrees from the traditional SI model of mandatory contributory financing through a central public agency of defined benefit pensions to models that, again to varying extents, introduce more voluntary components in either the level or allocation of contributions and move to what is in effect a defined contribution pension system. We shall not discuss such schemes further here, however.
7 The same point is made by Goñi, López and Sevén (2008).
8 Similar conclusions emerge from the various country studies presented in Barreix, Roca, and Villela (2007) and the recent summary appraisal by Jimenez, Gomez Sabaini, and Podesta (2010).
9 As Fricke and Sussmith (2011) show, for the region as a whole, although with considerable variation from country to country, the long-run elasticity of income taxes is greater than for VAT. However, since much of the higher elasticity is associated with the CIT, the most important income tax in most countries, income tax revenues are also considerably more volatile than VAT revenues. On the other hand, in Argentina, Mexico, and Peru, VAT is more elastic than social security contributions (PRT) while in Brazil the two are equally elastic; only in Chile and Ecuador is PRT more elastic than VAT.
10 See, for example, Perry et al. (2003).
11 This theme was subsequently picked up to a considerable extent in studies by international agencies such as Pagés (2010) and Riber, Robalino, and Walker (2010).
12 For the most part, the analysis of the social VAT proposal in Besson (2007) as well as such other contributions as Maarek (2008) took the form of simulations (including some CGE analysis) that focused on the possible macroeconomic effects of this substitution on the balance of payments and inflation, although some attention was also paid to short-run effects on employment.
13 Studies of payroll tax incidence in Latin American countries have yielded varying results, but as a rule suggest some shifting: see e.g. Cruces, Galiani, and Kidyba (2010), Kugler and Kugler (2009), and Heckman and Pages (2004)
14 For a summary of the recent US discussion, see Ainsworth (2011).
15 Ainsworth (2011), though he presents no formal analysis, does a good job of criticizing this reasoning. Interestingly, he also notes that cutting PRT is in many ways identical to cutting VAT and draws on some European experiments with VAT cuts to encourage employment to argue that probably the most effective approach would be to target PRT cuts only to unemployed persons who enter employment.
16 Social security contributions seem only rarely to be included in incidence analysis, perhaps in the belief – mistaken in most Latin American countries – that they are matched in some meaningful sense by SI benefits. The tendency in most countries to impose most SI taxes on employers rather than employees (see Table 13.1)

presumably reflects the view of politicians that voters are likely to be most aware of the direct impact of the latter on their net wages. Of course, while this may be largely true within the short-run horizon within which most political decisions are made, it is much less likely to be relevant in a long-run economic perspective. For these reasons, we assume in this chapter, as in most of the economic literature, both that SI contributions can meaningfully be considered simply as a tax - the PRT - and that the incidence and effects of PRT are similar regardless of whether the tax is legally imposed on employer or employee.

17 Even in the case of Mexico, Arias et al. (2010, p. 48) conclude that, while labor taxation has led to greater informality and informality has definitely reduced productivity growth in Mexico, there is "... little evidence that the introduction of social programs targeted towards informal workers has played a major role in promoting informality."

18 While the evidence on these links is still far from complete, utilizing a model of Hsieh and Klenow (2009), Camacho and Conover (2010), although not focusing on informality, find some evidence in Colombia that productivity was reduced by policy changes that raised the costs to employers of formal-sector labor and increased by changes that reduced such costs.

19 For a Mexican study, see Pagan, Soydemir, and Tijerino-Guajardo (2001).

20 For a good example, see the recent incidence study by Barriex, Roca, and Villela (2007).

21 It may easily be verified that $T^* < s$ for all τ, as required for Result 3.

References

Ainsworth, R. T. (2011). Will Cutting the Payroll Tax Increase Jobs in the U.S.? (Empirical Evidence from the EU VAT), in: Tax Notes International, 61(8): 581-90.

Antón, A., Hernández, F. (2010). VAT Collection and Social Security Contributions under Tax Evasion: Is there a Link?, Documento de Trabajo 480.

Arias, J., Azuara, O., Bernal, P., Heckman, J. J., Villarreal, C. (2010). Policies to Promote Growth and Economic Efficiency in Mexico, IZA Discussion Paper No. 4740.

Barreix, A., Roca, J., Villela, L. (2007). Fiscal Policy and Equity: Estimation of the Progressivity and Redistributive Capacity of Taxes and Social Public Expenditures in the Andean Countries, INTAL-INT Working Paper No. 33.

Barreix, A., Bés, M., Roca, J. (2010). El IVA Personalizado: Aumentando la recaudación y compensando a los más pobres, Inter-American Development Bank, Washington, DC.

Besson, E. (2007). TVA Sociale, Secrétariat d'État, Chargé de la Prospective et de l'Évaluation des Politiques Publiques, Paris.

Bird, R. M., Gendron, P.-P. (2007). The VAT in Developing and Transitional Countries, Cambridge, MA: Cambridge University Press.

Bird, R. M., Zolt, E. M. (2005). Redistribution via Taxation: The Limited Role of the Personal Income Tax in Developing Countries, in: UCLA Law Review, 52(6): 1627-95.

Boadway, R., Sato, M. (2009). Optimal Tax Design and Enforcement with an Informal Sector, in: American Economic Journal: Economic Policy, 1(1): 1-27.

Camacho, A., Conover, E. (2010). Misallocation and Productivity in Colombia's Manufacturing Industries, IDB Working Paper Series No. IDB-WP-123.

Cardi, O., Restout, R. (2010). Sectoral Effects of Tax Reforms in an Open Economy, UCL Discussion Paper No. 2010-45.

Clavijo, S. (2009). Social Security Reforms in Colombia: Striking Demographic and Fiscal Balances, IMF Working Paper No. 09/58.

Cruces, G., Galiani, S., Kidyba, S. (2010). Payroll Taxes, Wages and Employment: Identification through Policy Changes, in: Labor Economics, 17(4): 743-9.

Da Costa, R., de Laiglesia, J. R., Martínez, E., Melguizo, Á. (2011). The Economy of the Possible: Pensions and Informality in Latin America, OECD Development Centre

Working Paper No. 295.
Dalsgaard, T. (2008). Tax and Welfare Reforms in the Czech Republic: Structural Implications and Challenges, IMF Working Paper No. 08/52.
de Paula, Á., Scheinkman, J. A. (2008). The Informal Sector. Third version, PIER Working Paper No. 08-018.
de Paula, Á., Scheinkman, J. A. (2009). Value Added Taxes, Chain Effects and Informality. Second version, PIER Working Paper No. 09-041.
Desai, M. A., Hines, J. R. Jr. (2005). Value Added Taxes and International Trade: The Evidence, University of Michigan Working Paper.
Economic Commission for Latin America and the Caribbean (2006). Shaping the Future of Social Protection: Access, Financing and Solidarity, Santiago: United Nations.
Emran, M. S., Stiglitz, J. E. (2005). On Selective Indirect Tax Reform in Developing Countries, in: Journal of Public Economics, 89(4): 599-623.
Feltenstein, A., Shamloo, M. (2011). Tax Reform, the Informal Economy, and Bank Financing of Capital Formation, Andrew Young School of Policy Studies Research Paper Series No. 11-25 .
Ferreira, F. H.G., Robalino, D. (2010). Social Protection in Latin America: Achievements and Limitations, World Bank Policy Research Working Paper No. 5305.
Fricke, H., Süssmuth, B. (2011). Growth and Volatility of Tax Revenues in Latin America, CESifo Working Paper No. 3312.
Goñi, E., López, J. H., Sevén, L. (2008). Fiscal Redistribution and Income Inequality in Latin America, World Bank Policy Research Working Paper No. 4487.
Gordon, R. H., Li, W. (2009). Tax Structures in Developing Countries: Many Puzzles and a Possible Explanation, in: Journal of Public Economics, 93(7-8): 855-66.
Hanson, G. H. (2010). Why Isn't Mexico Rich?, in: Journal of Economic Literature, 58(4): 987-1004.
Heckman, J., Pagés, C. (2004). Introduction, in: Heckman, J., Pagés, C. (Eds.), Law and Employment: Lessons from Latin America and the Caribbean, Chicago, IL: University of Chicago Press/NBER, 1-108.
Holzmann, R., Robalino, D., Takayama, N. (Eds.), Closing the Coverage Gap: The Role of Social Pensions and Other Retirement Income Transfers, Washington, DC: The World Bank.
Hsieh, C.-T., Klenow, P. J. (2009). Misallocation and Manufacturing TFP in China and India, in: Quarterly Journal of Economics, 124(4): 1403–48.
International Monetary Fund (2010). Macro-Fiscal Implications of Health Care Reform in Advanced and Emerging Countries, IMF Policy Paper.
Jimenez, J. P., Sabaini, J. C. G., Podesta, A. (2010). Tax Gap and Equity in Latin America and the Caribbean, Fiscal Studies No. 16.
Keen, M. (2008). VAT, Tariffs and Withholding: Border Taxes and Informality in Developing Countries, in: Journal of Public Economics, 92(10-11): 1892-906.
Keen, M., Lockwood, B. (2010). The Value Added Tax: Its Causes and Consequences, in: Journal of Development Economics, 92(2): 138–51.
KPMG (2010). Latin America Indirect Tax Guide, Toronto: KPMG International.
Kritzer, B. E., Kay, S. J., Sinha, T. (2011). Next Generation of Individual Account Pension Reforms in Latin America, in: Social Security Bulletin, 71(1): 35-78.
Kugler, A., Kugler, M. (2009). Labor Market Effects of Payroll Taxes in Developing Countries: Evidence from Colombia, in: Economic Development and Cultural Change, 57(2): 335-58.
Lagadec, G., Ris, C. (2010). Reform of Indirect Taxation and VA-based Employers' Contributions: New Caledonia on its Way to a Social VAT?, in: Pacific Economic Bulletin, 25(3): 215-31.
La Porta, R., Shleifer, A. (2008). The Unofficial Economy and Economic Development, in: Brookings Papers on Economic Activity, 39(2): 275-364.
Leal Ordóñez, J. C. (2010). Informal Sector, Productivity and Tax Collection, Mexico City, Centro de Investigación y Docencia Económicas.
Levy, S. (2008). Good Intentions, Bad Outcomes: Social Policy, Informality and Economic Growth in Mexico, Washington, DC: Brookings Institution Press.

Lindert, K., Skoufias, E. and Shapiro, J. (2006). Redistributing Income to the Poor and the Rich: Public Transfers in Latin America and the Caribbean, World Bank Social Protection Discussion Paper No. 0605.
Lockwood, B., de Meza, D., Myles, G. D. (1994). When are Origin and Destination Regimes Equivalent?, International Tax and Public Finance 1(1): 5-24.
Maarek, G. (2008). La réforme du financement de la protection social, essais comparatifs entre la "TVA Sociale" et la "TVA Emploi", Nice: EDHEC Business School.
Mesa-Lago, C. (2008). Social Insurance (Pensions and Health), Labor Markets and Coverage in Latin America, UN Social Policy and Development Programme Paper No. 36.
OECD (2007). OECD Employment Outlook 2007, Paris: OECD.
Ortiz, I., Cummins, M. (2011). Global Inequality: Beyond the Bottom Billion, UNICEF Social and Economic Policy Working Paper.
Pagan, J. A., Soydemir, G., Tijerina-Guajardo, J. A. (2001). The Evolution of VAT Rates and Government Tax Revenue in Mexico, in: Contemporary Economic Policy, 19(4): 424-33.
Pagés, C. (Ed.) (2010). The Age of Productivity: Transforming Economies from the Bottom Up, Washington, DC: Inter-American Development Bank.
Perry, G., Maloney, W. F., Arias, O. S., Fajnzylber, P., Mason, A. D., Saavedra-Chanduvi, J. (2007). Informality: Exit and Exclusion, Washington, DC: The World Bank.
Pomeranz, D. (2010). No Taxation Without Information: Deterrence and Self-enforcement in the Value Added Tax, Harvard Business School Working Paper, No. 13-057.
Riber, H., Robalino, D. A., Walker, I. (2010). Achieving Effective Social Protection for all in Latin America and the Caribbean, Washington, DC: The World Bank.
Rofman, R., Fajnzlyber, E., Herrera, G. (2010). Reforming the Pension Reforms: Argentina and Chile, in: Cepal Review 101: 83-106.
Smart, M., Bird, R. M. (2009). The Economic Incidence of Replacing a Retail Sales Tax by a Value-added Tax: Evidence from Canadian Experience, in: Canadian Public Policy, 35(1): 85-97.
Social Security Administration (2010). Social Security Programs Throughout the World: The Americas 2009, Washington, DC.
Vuletin, G. (2008). Measuring the Informal Economy in Latin America and the Caribbean, IMF Working Paper No. 08/102.
World Bank (2011). Paying Taxes 2010, Washington, DC: The World Bank.

14

Financing Universal Social Security in Mexico*

Arturo Antón
Fausto Hernández

14.1. Introduction

A contributory social insurance system (the so called "Bismarck" model of social insurance, henceforth CSI) has been in place in most Latin American countries since the early part of the 20th century. As well known, this program was implemented with the objective of providing workers and their families with protection against health shocks, poverty in old age and other risks. Even though this system is now several decades old, there is still a large number of workers in Latin America not covered against such risks. For example, Gasparini and Tornarolli (2009) estimate that on average about 56% of workers in the region are not enrolled in a contributory social insurance scheme. This has led to characterize this situation as the "truncated welfare state" (Fiszbein 2005; Perry et al. 2007).

In an attempt to at least partially revert this situation, over the last years a non-contributory social insurance (NCSI) system has been built in parallel by several governments in the region. However, this dual social insurance scheme may yield undesirable outcomes over time as the non-contributory system may incentive informality and erode the tax base (Levy 2008).[1] Given this policy dilemma, is it pos-

* *The authors express their gratitude for financial support from the Inter-American Development Bank (IDB). We also thank David Kaplan and participants of the 6th IZA/World Bank Conference "Employment and Development" for helpful comments. Errors are solely our responsibility.*

sible to think about an alternative situation, where the State provides insurance to all workers without simultaneously promoting informality? That is, can the State provide a non-contributive universal social security scheme?

This chapter claims that such an alternative is possible and financially viable. In particular, we consider the proposal by Levy (2008) whereby a universal social insurance (USI) scheme is guaranteed to all workers, regardless of formality status. This proposal aims at abolishing the current CSI system and financing social insurance through value-added taxes instead (henceforth, the *social security reform*). We argue that this is a major reform as it breaks down the duality present in social insurance policy in Mexico and other Latin American countries. In this sense, this proposal would in fact put an end to both informality and the truncated welfare state problem, in the sense that all workers would be covered by the same regulations with regard to social insurance.

To evaluate Levy's proposal, we construct a static, general equilibrium model with tax evasion.[2] The model is calibrated for the Mexican economy, as this country is characterized by a large informal sector, high rates of tax evasion, and a knotty tax system, including differentiated rates on value-added taxes.[3] Taking into account the existence of differentiated VAT rates, the model is simulated to study whether a uniform VAT rate of 16 percent yields the necessary resources to finance USI. The advantage of having a model is to understand how the change in relative prices resulting from the social security reform affects firms' decisions in a tax evasion framework. It is also useful to identify other parallel benefits of this reform that include, among others, a potential increase in workers' real wage. Finally, the model allows us to examine how the government fiscal balance would be affected by this reform.

After calculating the costs of implementing USI from Mexican data, the simulation suggests that the social security reform with a uniform VAT rate of 16 percent is financially viable at least in a static way. This is true even after taking into account a direct income transfer to the poorest households to compensate them for the VAT increase on those goods not currently taxed. The model also suggests that real wages in the formal sector might rise by 15 percent, as a result of the large increase in labor demand due to the elimination of CSI. In parallel, we acknowledge that the pressure on public finances as a result of the social security reform may increase over time, given the natural changes in the demographic structure of the population. For this reason, a policy warning is that additional sources of financing the scheme might need to be considered over the medium term.

This chapter is organized as follows. Section 14.2 briefly compares the current social insurance and tax policy in Mexico against USI's proposal. Section 14.3 presents the model. Section 14.4 compares the model to Mexican data. Section 14.5 presents a preliminary estimation of the effects of USI on government's budget balance, wages and the labor market. Section 14.6 concludes with some remarks.

14.2. Current Social Insurance and Tax Policy vs. USI

14.2.1. Current Social Insurance vs. USI

Social insurance policy in Mexico may be characterized by a dual scheme (Levy 2008). On the one hand, there is a social security structure for formal workers providing health, work-risk, and life an disability insurance; day care for workers' children; a contributive retirement pension system; and housing loans (see Table 14.1). In order to get access to these benefits, a contributory scheme applies while being and remaining in formality. To the extent that these benefits are not fully valued by workers, contributions to social insurance constitute a "pure" tax on salaried labor.

On the other, social insurance benefits are offered to both non-salaried (i.e., self-employed and workers in family firms) and salaried informal workers financed by general revenues.[4] These benefits include health services provided by Federal and State governments (through *Seguro Popular,* a joint federal and state program); subsidies for housing; day care; and pensions provided by *Oportunidades* and some State programs (Distrito Federal, Estado de México, and Michoacán). These benefits constitute in fact a subsidy to informal workers as they are based on a non-contributive scheme. As of today, informal workers are not covered from life, disability and work risks (see Table 14.1).

Despite the access of informal workers to health insurance, currently there are important differences in the array of services provided to formal and informal workers and their families in Mexico. In particular, health services available to informal workers are limited in scope, as compared to those provided to formal workers. For example, *Seguro Popular* covers a package of mostly primary and secondary health care services, including preventive, outpatient, inpatient, emergency, and a restricted (but gradually increasing) list of surgical interventions. In contrast, formal workers are provided with a wide coverage of health services, including tertiary care services.

Table 14.1

Social Insurance: Status quo vs. USI

Coverage	Status quo		USI
	Formal	Informal	
Health insurance	Wide coverage	Basic coverage	Wide coverage
Life and disability insurance	Yes	No	Yes
Work-risk insurance	Yes	No	Contributory system only for salaried workers
Pensions	All workers	All *Oportunidades* affiliates and the elderly in some Mexican states	All workers
Day care	Yes	Yes	No
Housing	Yes	Yes	No

Source: Authors' elaboration based on Antón, Hernández, and Levy (2012)

The coexistence of these two mutually exclusive programs clearly incentivizes firms to hire salaried informal workers in order to avoid paying for CSI. If a firm perceives that the probability of being detected by the authority evading CSI payments is small, it will be less costly for the firm to hire a worker with no CSI coverage at all. This is especially true for small firms as it is more plausible for them to go undetected by the authorities in such illegal practice. Hence this dual scheme not only incentivizes informality but it also incentivizes firms to keep small in size, with potentially adverse effects on productivity and fiscal revenues.

Under the social security reform proposed here, a universal health, life, and disability insurance along with a retirement pension is provided *equally* to all workers regardless of formality status. The proposal contemplates a wide coverage of health services, similar to those currently available to formal workers. It also guarantees both a life and disability insurance and a retirement pension not currently available to all informal workers (see Table 14.1). Work-risk insurance is contemplated for salaried workers only, financed through a firm's specific, wage-based contributory rate (see Antón, Hernández, and Levy 2012 for details). In contrast, USI does not consider day care and housing coverage as they are not perceived as essential risks for which all workers need to be protected (see Levy 2008 for a discussion).

Under USI, social security contributions (other than work-risk insurance) are thus eliminated in order to minimize distortions in the labor market and the perverse incentives under the current status quo.

14.2.2. Current Tax Policy vs. USI

Mexico's tax system is complex. Like many countries, revenue collection is very centralized as the most important taxes (corporate income, value added, foreign trade and most excise taxes) are levied and collected by the federal government (approximately, 96% of total tax revenue). The structure, however, is highly knotty as there are plenty of special treatments in both corporate/personal income and value-added taxes. With respect to VAT, the current rate is 16 percent. However, there are several special treatments: food and medicines are zero-taxed while other goods and services are tax-exempted (see Table 14.2). Furthermore, VAT rates at border zones are different from the rest of the country, currently set at 11 percent.

Table 14.2 also presents the current structure of SI taxes and subsidies in Mexico. CSI taxes are estimated at 38% of formal worker's wage rate on average (Antón, Hernández, and Levy 2012). Out of this tax, the government subsidizes approximately 16 percent. On the other hand, subsidies to informal workers are gradually increasing over time. In 2008, they are estimated at 5,650 Mexican pesos per informal worker, which represent approximately 7% of the informal wage rate on average.

These features of the tax system combined with a set of other factors, like the existence of high levels of illegality (à la de Paula and Scheinkman 2010); a deficient rule of law (Laporta et al. 1999; World Bank Doing Business 2010); a low quality of public expenditures (Scott 2010, for social expenditures; World Bank IPER 2005, for public infrastructure); and an inefficient tax collection authority in the presence of some corruption (see mandatory public evaluations at www.sat.gob.mx for different taxes), have induced high levels of tax evasion. In the particular case of value-added taxes, it is estimated that VAT revenue would be close to 6.1% of GDP under full compliance, given the current tax rates. Instead, observed revenues were 3.77% of GDP in 2008 (Antón and Hernández 2010). As for CSI taxes, it is estimated that about two thirds of the total labor force engaged in market activities in Mexico do not pay social security contributions (Levy 2008; Antón, Hernández, and Levy 2012).

Table 14.2

Value-Added and SI Taxes and Subsidies: Status quo vs. USI

Tax/subsidy	Status quo	USI
Value-added	A 16% VAT rate on non-border states; a 11% VAT rate on border states. A zero VAT rate on food and medicines. Education, cultural activities, private medical expenses, some financial services, and books and magazines are tax-exempted	A uniform VAT rate of 16% on all goods and services
Tax on formal workers	An average 38% tax rate on formal workers' wage must be paid by law. The government subsidizes approximately 16% out of this tax	Zero
Subsidy to informal workers	Approximately $5,650 pesos per year per informal worker in 2008	Zero

Source: Antón, Hernández, and Levy (2012).

Under USI, social security contributions (other than work-risk insurance) and subsidies to informal workers are eliminated in order to minimize the distortions in the labor market mentioned earlier. To finance social security, a uniform VAT rate on all goods and services is proposed. Such proposal is a major break down with respect to the status quo. It has the advantage of eliminating distortions in after-tax relative prices across the different sectors in the economy. It may also reduce substantially many loopholes and elusion strategies currently in place. However, a major concern is the negative impact that a uniform VAT rate could have on the poorest households, as a proportionately larger share of their income is spent on food and medicines. For this reason, a direct income transfer to the two lowest-income deciles of the population is contemplated as part of the costs of the proposal, as explained below.

Arguably, the social security reform proposed here brings substantial changes in both social and tax policies. It does not only provide social insurance for all workers (a legitimate social policy goal for its own sake) but in addition eliminates several relative price distortions currently in place in both labor and goods markets. There are other potentially advantages of this reform, such as an increase in real wages and a smaller size of the self-employed sector, which typically goes undetected to the tax authorities and is arguably less productive. To prove this point, we rely on a general equilibrium model that helps to understand why this may be the case.

14.3. The Model

This section briefly presents the structure of the model used in this chapter to evaluate the effects of the social security reform on variables such as the government's fiscal balance and real wages, among others. The interested reader is referred to Antón, Hernández, and Levy (2012) for further details.

The model is a static, neoclassical general equilibrium model of a small open economy with government. There are three sectors: an intermediate, a final, and a self-employed sector, with firms behaving in a competitive fashion.[5] Goods produced in these sectors are tradable so their prices are exogenously given, as well as labor and capital endowments. GDP is endogenously determined after aggregating all firms' value-added.

The government may impose three different taxes on firms: value-added taxes (τ_{vat}), income taxes (τ_{ct}), and social security contributions (τ_n). However, firms have an incentive to evade taxes. The probability of being detected in such practice by the authority is directly proportional to firm's size, so a relatively large firm faces a higher probability of detection relative to smaller firms. Thus a relatively large firm will evade less so that its rate of tax compliance will also be higher. In contrast, the self-employed sector is able to evade all taxes as the size of such firms is typically small; thus this sector does not pay taxes at all.

Intermediate goods are produced with two inputs: labor L and capital K, which is distributed exogenously across firms. There are two types of intermediate goods (indexed by $z = i,j$) that differ in the technology level A_z, the distribution of capital K_z and the value-added tax rate $\tau_{vat,z}$ they face by law. In particular, the VAT rate in sector i, $\tau_{vat,i}$, is set to zero whereas in sector j it is positive. Conveniently, intermediate sectors i and j are labeled as the "non-taxed" and "taxed" sectors, respectively.

Intermediate good firms demand salaried labor, and they choose whether to hire workers with social security benefits (formal) or not (informal). If firms hire formal workers, they must pay the formal wage w_f plus CSI taxes for the amount $\tau_n w_f$. If government subsidizes a share η of CSI, the unit cost of a legally hired salaried worker is just $[1 + (1 - \eta)\tau_n]w_f$. In contrast, if firms hire informal workers they pay the informal wage w_{nf}. However, firms may be discovered by the authority in such practice with probability $\lambda_{ssc,z}$. If discovered, firms must pay the amount θ, which includes all unpaid social security contributions times a penalty. Hence, the expected unit cost of a illegally hired salaried worker is $w_{nf} + \lambda_{ssc,z}\theta$. To the extent that the probability of being detected evading CSI taxes is less than one, it will be optimal for firms to demand a mix of formal and informal workers.

The problem for a profit-maximizing firm of size K_z is to choose total labor demand $L_z(K_z)$ and salaried informal workers $L_{nf,z}(K_z)$.[6] For the first case, the demand function is given by

$$(1) \qquad L_z K_z = \left(\frac{(1 - \tau_{vat,z}\xi_{vat,z}(K_z))\alpha A_z p_z}{[1 + (1 - \eta)\tau_n]w_f} \right)^{1/(1-\alpha)} K_z, \qquad \text{for } z = i,j.$$

In expression (1), α is the labor elasticity of income, p_z is the exogenous price of the intermediate good z, and $\xi_{vat,z}(K_z)$ is the (size dependent) firm's VAT rate of compliance.[7] Thus $\tau_{vat,z}\xi_{vat,z}(K_z)$ represents the *effective* VAT rate faced by a firm of size K_z. From (1), it may be noticed that both value-added taxes and social security contributions negatively affect labor demand.

Standard optimality conditions also yield a demand function for salaried informal labor $L_{nf,z}(K_z)$ given by the following expression:

$$(2) \qquad L_{nf,z}(K_z) = \left\{ \left[\frac{[1 + (1 - \eta)\tau_n]w_f - w_{nf}}{3\theta\hat{\lambda}_{ssc}} \right] \left(\frac{1}{K_z^v} \right) \right\}^{1/2}.$$

Here, $\hat{\lambda}_{ssc} > 0$ and $v > 0$ are parameters related to the firm's probability of being detected evading CSI taxes. Either a higher value for these parameters or a higher payment θ translates into a lower demand for informal labor. Notice also that $L_{nf,z}(K_z)$ is an increasing function of the wage gap $[1 + (1 - \eta)\tau_n]w_f - w_{nf}$. Functional forms (1) and (2) imply that the fraction of informal salaried workers relative to total labor, $L_{nf,z}(K_z)/L_z(K_z)$, decreases as the firm's capital size is larger.

In the final good sector, perfectly competitive firms simply aggregate intermediate goods i and j according to a CES production function. Thus labor is not required to produce the final good. However, firms must pay value-added and income taxes. As in the intermediate sector, these firms have an incentive to evade these taxes. It is assumed that the rates of tax compliance in the final sector are a weighted average of the tax compliance rates in the intermediate sector.[8]

In the model, the self-employed sector comprises self-employed workers and workers in family firms with non-salaried contractual relations. Here, labor L_{ae} is the only input for producing goods, and the cost of labor is simply the informal wage rate w_{nf}. Firms maximize profits in the usual fashion, so that optimal labor demand is inversely related to the wage rate w_{nf}.

Regardless of status, workers value social insurance services provided by the government. Following Levy (2008), let $\{\beta_f, \beta_{nf}\}$ denote respectively the parameters indicating how formal and informal workers value such services, with $0 \leq \beta_f, \beta_{nf} \leq 1$. Accordingly, the indirect utility of a formal worker, U_f, may be written as $U_f = w_f(1 + \beta_f \tau_n)$. Similarly, the utility of an informal worker is just $U_{nf} = w_{nf} + \beta_{nf} T_{nf}$, where T_{nf} denotes social insurance spending per informal worker.

Some studies on labor markets suggest a large mobility between formal and informal employment (see Maloney 1999; 2004; Gong, Soest and Villagomez 2004; Navarro and Schrimpf 2004; Calderon 2000; 2006). This evidence suggests that workers are indifferent to the wages they can earn in either sector, once the valuation of social insurance services is included. From the above discussion, this implies a relationship between w_f and w_{nf} of the form

$$(3) \qquad w_{nf} = (1 + \beta_f \tau_n) w_f - \beta_{nf} T_{nf}.$$

Let $\overline{L}$ represents total labor endowment and L_z total labor demand in the intermediate sector $z = i, j$. Thus it must be the case that $\overline{L} = L_i + L_j + L_{ae}$. This resource condition along with expression (3) solve for equilibrium wages w_f^* and w_{nf}^*. In the model, real wages are defined by w_f^*/P and w_{nf}^*/P, where P is the (endogenously determined) consumer's price index.

Finally, it remains to specify the government's fiscal balance. In the model, there are four revenue sources and three spending sources. Revenue sources arise from value-added taxes (R_{vat}), social security contributions (R_{ssc}), income taxes (R_{ct}), and other sources $\overline{R}$.[9] Here, the first three sources are endogenously determined. On the other hand, spending sources are divided into exogenous spending ($\overline{G}$) and endogenous subsidies to CSI (G_{ss}) and NCSI (G_{sp}) programs. These subsidies are proportional to the number of formal and informal workers, respectively.

Let FB denote the government's fiscal balance. Thus

$$(4) \qquad FB = (R_{vat} + R_{ssc} + R_{ct} + \overline{R}) - (\overline{G} + G_{ss} + G_{sp}),$$

where a "bar" over a variable denotes that it is exogenous.

It turns out that labor demand equation (1) has direct implications on government revenue in (4), as labor is directly linked to intermediate firm's value-added. For example, an increase in the CSI tax τ_n lowers labor demand and thus value-added for intermediate good firms. It also decreases profits for those firms with a relatively large capital size, as these firms cannot avoid being undetected by the tax authorities.[10] These two effects naturally erode the tax base for both value-added and income taxes. Given that formal labor is now more costly than informal labor, informality increases. This explains the negative relationship between informality and government revenue out of value-added and income sources. Notice that a similar effect is obtained if government subsidies to formal labor, η, decrease.

A larger subsidy T_{nf} to informal labor works in a similar fashion. From the arbitrage condition (3), the informal wage w_{nf} must decrease for a given formal wage w_f. This effect increases the demand for non-salaried, self-employed workers and thus the relative size of informal workers. Again, the increase in informality erodes government revenue.

Two issues deserve a further comment. First, from equation (1) it is clear that an increase in the value-added tax $\tau_{vat,z}$ has a negative effect on labor demand. This effect is greater for larger firms in the intermediate sector z, as they face higher effective VAT rates. In fact, labor optimally reallocates from larger to smaller firms so the net effect is an increase in informal labor. Hence, implementing a positive VAT rate in the "non-taxed" sector and simultaneously eliminating CSI taxes (as it is the case under USI) in principle have an ambiguous effect on informality. However, the exercises below illustrate that the net effect on formal labor is positive as the self-employed sector contracts sharply under USI.

Second, the model endogenously yields a zero salaried informal labor under USI. To see this point, notice that the arbitrage condition (3) implies that formal and informal wages must be equal, as USI eliminates both taxes and subsidies on labor ($\tau_n = T_{nf} = \eta = 0$). The equalization of wages thus implies a zero wage gap, so that salaried informal labor must be zero (see equation 2). Simultaneously, labor demand for a firm of size K_z must increase as CSI taxes are eliminated (see equation 1). For a given labor supply, the wage rate must increase in equilibrium. The exercises below suggest that such increase is relatively large under USI.

14.4. Taking the Model to the Data

To discuss the social security reform at the light of the previous section, the model is calibrated to replicate relevant features of Mexican data. In particular, the model aims at reproducing the government's fiscal balance in 2008 as well as other characteristics of the economy. We do not report here how parameters are calibrated. The interested reader is referred to Anton, Hernández, and Levy (2012) for details. Instead, we present the model's fitness for the variables of interest.

Table 14.3 compares the macroeconomic and fiscal accounts of the model with those in the data. The exogenous components of expenditures and revenues are the only elements in the table that are set equal to those in the data; the remaining entries are endogenously obtained in the model. As it may be seen, these accounts are replicated remarkably well, including the government's fiscal deficit of 192.5 thousand of million pesos.

Table 14.3

Macroeconomic and Fiscal Accounts

	Observed		Calibrated	
	Pesos[a]	% GDP	Pesos[a]	% GDP
GDP	12,110.50		12,146.00	
Public Expenditures				
Social insurance for informal workers	151.5	1.25	151	1.24
Social insurance for formal workers	63.7	0.52	62.2	0.51
Other exogenous	2,679.50	22.1	2,679.50	22
Public Revenues				
Value-added tax	457.2	3.77	457.9	3.76
Income tax	393	3.24	392.4	3.23
Other exogenous	1,852.00	15.29	1,852.00	15.24
Fiscal balance[b]	–192.5	–1.58	–190.4	–1.56

Notes: [a] Thousands of millions of 2008 pesos.
[b] Negative is deficit.
Source: National Institute of Statistics and Geography (INEGI) and Cuenta de la Hacienda Pública Federal, Ministry of Finance (SHCP), 2008.

The social insurance accounts from data and the model are presented in Table 14.4. Here, social insurance is divided into private (i.e., firms and workers) and government contributions. Expenditures on contributory social insurance are classified into four major items: IMSS (the public institute in Mexico providing health services to formal workers), retirement pensions (Afores), housing (Infonavit), and state taxes. Expenditures on non-contributory social insurance are divided into health, pensions, housing, and day care. It may be observed that health is by far the item with the largest expenditure share under both insurance systems, followed by pensions. Remarkably, the model closely replicates the data for all items.

Table 14.4

Social Insurance Accounts

	Observed		Calibrated	
	Firms and workers	Government	Firms and workers	Government
	A. Contributory social insurance			
IMSS				
Health	109.3	44.3	111.9	43.2
Disability	21	1.9	21.5	1.9
Work-risk	16.8	0	17.2	0
Day care	8.4	0	8.6	0
Afores				
Retirement	54.9	17.5	55.4	17.1
Infonavit				
Housing	43.4	0	44	0
State taxes	25.7	0	26.4	0
	B. Non-contributory social insurance			
Health	0	131	0	130.6
Pensions	0	9.5	0	9.5
Housing	0	9.2	0	9.1
Day care	0	1.7	0	1.7

Note: Figures in thousands of million pesos.
Source: Own calculations based on IMSS, National Commission for the Pension System (Consar), Infonavit annual reports, and Cuenta de la Hacienda Pública Federal 2008 (SHCP).

Table 14.5 presents employment data according to different criteria. Part A divides total labor force into non-taxed, taxed, and self-employed sectors. Here, the model is able to closely match the data for all items. Part B presents data according to formality status. The model replicates informal, non-salaried labor well but over-estimates salaried informal labor by about 440,000 workers (at the expense of formal workers). This number represents about 6 percent of total salaried informal workers. The third part shows data by firm size, according to the Economic Census 2009. The model follows the data at the tails of each distribution, but fails slightly to replicate the middle of the distribution in the taxed sector.

Table 14.5

Composition of Employment

	Observed		Calibrated	
A. By sector				
Non-taxed sector	5.28		5.24	
Taxed sector	14.84		14.86	
Self-employed sector	18.91		18.93	
Total	39.03		39.03	
B. By formality status				
Formal	12.76		12.29	
Informal	26.27		26.73	
Salaried	7.36		7.8	
Non-salaried	18.91		18.93	
C. By firm size				
	Non-taxed sector		Taxed sector	
	Observed	Calibrated	Observed	Calibrated
1-5 employees	2.53	2.39	4.24	3.86
6-20 employees	0.7	0.67	2.31	1.89
21-50 employees	0.44	0.49	1.27	1.71
50-100 employees	0.34	0.4	0.97	1.71
101+ employees	1.27	1.29	6.05	5.69

Note: Numbers are millions of workers.
Source: Economic Census 2009, INEGI; National Survey of Occupation and Employment, INEGI; and IMSS.

VAT revenue as a percentage of GDP under alternative scenarios is presented in Table 14.6. For that purpose, the model is calibrated to closely replicate a revenue rate of 3.77 percent observed in the data. If full compliance in value-added taxes is assumed, the model yields a revenue rate of 6.12 percent. Remarkably, this number is close to the estimate of 6.08 percent reported by Antón and Hernández (2010) based on National Accounts data. The model also predicts that VAT revenue would amount to 6.2 percent of GDP if a uniform rate of 15 percent is implemented, assuming no change in government's enforcement efforts. This number increases to 10.6 percent under the hypothetical case of full compliance, which is close to the 10.7 percent estimated from National Accounts by Antón and Hernández (2010).

Given that the model replicates the data quite well along several dimensions, now it may be used to evaluate the impact of current social policy on labor markets and fiscal accounts. For that purpose, we take as a benchmark a hypothetical situation with no social insurance. Then labor taxes and subsidies are added each at a time, according to the values observed in the data in order to account for its marginal impact on the variables of interest.

Tabke 14.6

VAT Revenue (% of GDP)

	Observed or calculated from National Accounts	Model
$\tau_i^{VAT} = 0, \tau_j^{VAT} = 0.15$		
Under current enforcement	3.77[a]	3.76
Assuming full compliance	6.08[b]	6.12
$\tau_i^{VAT} = 0.15, \tau_j^{VAT} = 0.15$		
Under current enforcement	N.O.	6.2
Assuming full compliance	10.7[b]	10.6

Notes: [a] Observed.
[b] Calculated from National Accounts by Antón and Hernández (2010).
N.O. Not observable.
Source: National Accounts, INEGI, and Antón, Hernández and Levy (2012).

Table 14.7 presents the results of such exercise. Column 2 is the benchmark scenario, which represents the no social insurance (SI) case, namely $\tau_n = \eta = T_{nf} = 0$. Column 3 introduces CSI at the observed rate of 38 percent in the data. Column 4 adds government subsidies at the current rate (η, implying a subsidy per worker of 5,062 pesos) to the scenario in column 3. Finally, column 5 considers the status quo in 2008, which includes the scenario in column 4 plus NCSI for the amount of 5,650 pesos per worker.

Several observations are worth to point out from Table 14.7. First, real wages are higher with no social insurance. Second, firms shift most of CSI taxes to formal workers in terms of a lower wage. Hence, social insurance is mostly changing the composition of workers' consumption (less disposable income and more social benefits), rather than re-distributing income from firms to workers. Third, the tax on salaried labor and the subsidy to informal labor induce firms to evade. The tax base contracts and VAT and income tax (IT) revenues fall. Finally, subsidies to CSI increase formal employment, expand the tax base and raise VAT and IT revenues; whereas subsidies to NCSI do the opposite.

The results from Table 14.7 are also useful to evaluate the effect of NCSI on formal labor. As the government introduces subsidies to informal workers (columns 4 to 5), formal employment in the model falls by 1.36 million workers, namely from 13.65 to 12.29 million. This effect takes into account all the spending on this type of programs, which amount to 1.24% of GDP.

Table 14.7

Impact of Social Security on Variables of Interest

	No SI	Only CSI	Subsidies to CSI	Status quo: Subsidized CSI + NCSI
Wages and utility[a]				
Formal wage	1.00	0.79	0.81	0.83
Informal wage	1.00	0.88	0.9	0.88
Worker's utility	1.00	0.88	0.9	0.93
Employment[b]				
Formal salaried	26.04	12.65	13.65	12.29
Informal salaried	0	7.68	7.97	7.8
Self-employment	12.99	18.7	17.41	18.93
Fiscal[c]				
Subsidies to CSI	0	0	67.3	62.2
Subsidies to NCSI	0	0	0	151.1
VAT revenues	496.7	459.5	468.2	457.9
IT revenues	399	392.4	393.8	392.4
Net fiscal impact[d]	—	(-)43.8	(-)101.0	(-) 258.7

Notes: [a] Index; [b] millions of workers; [c] thousands of millions of pesos;
[d] Calculated as the net fiscal cost vs. the no social insurance situation.

To the best of our knowledge, there is no econometric evidence measuring the impact *of each* NCSI program on formal labor in Mexico. However, there is some evidence out of *Seguro Popular*, a program gradually implemented in Mexico since 2002. In 2008, *Seguro Popular* represented about 25% of total spending on NCSI programs. If we proportionally assume that one fourth of the previous 1.36 million workers that transit from formality to informality can be explained by the introduction of *Seguro Popular*, such program would imply a fall in formality of about 340,000 workers. Remarkably, this number is not too far from the estimate reported by Bosch and Campos-Vázquez (2010). These authors estimate that *Seguro Popular* since its inception has increased informality by around 300,000 workers.[11]

14.5. Is the New Scheme Financially Sound?

Now it is time to discuss financing issues of the social security reform under alternative scenarios based on the model's structure and Mexican data. This section details the cost of such scheme and analyzes whether a uniform VAT rate generates enough revenue to finance the proposal. Here, it is important to pinpoint that the following calculations are made using data for the year 2008. Hence the analysis ignores dynamic features (i.e., demographic and epidemiological aspects), which are left for future calculations.

Table 14.8 contains the necessary data to calculate the cost of universal social insurance for the year 2008. Note that all calculations are based on the economically active population (EAP) at the end of 2008 and that we are excluding bureaucracy.

Table 14.8

Target Population

Number of IMSS affiliates, December 2008[a]	13,774,185
Economically Active Population, December 2008[b]	41,064,469
Not affiliated to IMSS, 2008	27,290,284
Daily Minimum Wage, 2008[c]	52.59
Population 65 years old or older, December 2008[b]	1,803,207

Sources: [a] IMSS; [b] Own calculation based on National Population Council (CONAPO) and Economic Census, 2009; total labor force (45,894,469 workers) excluding bureaucracy (4,830,000 workers); [c] National Commission of Minimum Wages (Consamin).

The first step is to estimate the universal health and life and disability insurance. Here, all members of the economically active population would have access to exactly the same services any formal worker has today. Table 14.9 presents the corresponding estimations for 2008. As it may be noted, the cost per IMSS affiliate reaches $11,512 pesos. Applying this number to all EAP would yield a cost of $472.7 thousand of million pesos.

Table 14.9

Universal Health and Life and Disability Insurance for 2008

Type of insurance	Current annual expenditure	Annual expenditure per IMSS affiliate	Total expenditure on EAP[a]
Health	147,232,680	10.689	438,938,109
Illness and maternity	142,604,280		
Family practice	4,628,400		
Life and disability	11,342,000	0.823	33,796,058
TOTAL	158,574,680	11.512	472,734,167

Note: [a] Annual expenditure per IMSS affiliate times the economically active population (EAP) excluding bureaucracy.
Figures in thousands of pesos. Health expenditures take into account that approximately 16 cents of every peso are in fact diverted to pay the pension liabilities of IMSS's already retired workers. See IMSS (2005).
Source: Own calculations.

The second step is to calculate the cost of the universal pension system. In particular, we calculate two alternative pension schemes. The first one ("Alternative A") is a pension scheme where the federal government is the sole contributor, as in Levy (2008). Here, the government makes an individual contribution equivalent to 8.5 percent of a two-minimum wage worker's annual earnings. The second alternative is a non-contributive scheme consisting of a guaranteed contribution equivalent to the earnings of a two-minimum wage worker per year ("Alternative B"). Estimations are presented in Table 14.10. Clearly, the first one is more expensive (in total terms) in the short-run whereas the second alternative is more expensive only in the long-run.

Table 14.10

Costs of Alternative Pension Systems for 2008

Retirement pension	Number of retirees	Annual expenditure per head	Total expenditure
Levy's proposal	*N.A.*	3.218	132,166,321
Two minimum wages	1,803,207	37.865	68,278,072

Note: N.A.: Not applicable.
Total expenditure under Levy's proposal is annual expenditure per head times economically active population. Total expenditure under the two-minimum wage proposal is number of retirees times annual expenditure per head. Figures in thousands of pesos.
Source: Own calculations.

We are now in a position of calculating the whole cost of the proposal. Table 14.11 presents the total cost under both alternatives. Levy's proposal has a cost around 4.99% of GDP, while the second has a lower cost, equivalent to 4.47% of GDP.

Table 14.11

Total Cost of Universal Social Insurance for 2008

Alternative A: Universal Health and Pension System	
Universal Health System (IMSS-like)	472,734,167
Levy's Universal Pension System	132,166,321
Total cost	*604,900,488*
Total cost (% of GDP)	*4.99*
Alternative B: Universal Health and Pension System	
Universal Health System (IMSS-like)	472,734,167
Universal Pension System (two minimum wages)	68,278,072
Total cost	*541,012,239*
Total cost (% of GDP)	*4.47*

Note: Figures in thousands of pesos.
Source: Own calculations.

Table 14.12

How much is already spent? (2008, in thousands of pesos)

Non-contributory social insurance programs	
Imss Oportunidades	6,370,722
Health Funds transferred to states	48,480,421
States' health expenditures	24,715,075
Popular Health Insurance	36,250,635
Fonhapo	2,342,231
Habitat	1,887,399
CONAVI	4,984,370
National Child Care Program	1,711,029
Federal Transfers to National Health Institutes	12,416,613
First Generation Program	1,699,724
Elderly Program (older than 70)	9,536,677
Federal contributions to Social Security	
Work Risk Insurance	5,523,793
Childcare and other social benefits	2,541,856
Health	29,639,302
Family Practice	303,071
Life and Disability Insurance	7,737,976
Sub total	196,140,900
Pensions (government contribution to pensions)	17,539,500
Total	213,680,400

Source: Cuenta de la Hacienda Pública Federal 2008; IMSS (estado de resultados).

To make an appropriate assessment of the costs of universal social insurance, it is necessary to take into account what the federal government currently spends on health, life and disability insurance, and pensions. Table 14.12 presents the corresponding data. All items sum up to 213.68 thousand of million pesos, or 1.76 percent of GDP.

Using Tables 14.11 and 14.12 we get Table 14.13, which yields the amount needed for the reform on social insurance. Clearly, we would need extra revenues equivalent to 3.23 and 2.71 percent of GDP under alternatives A and B, respectively.

Table 14.13

Amount Needed to Implement USI in 2008

	Alternative A	Alternative B
Total cost of Universal Health and Pension System	604,900,488	541,012,239
Current Federal Government expenditure	213,680,401	213,680,401
Amount needed	391,220,087	327,331,838
Amount needed in % GDP	3.23	2.71

Note: Figures in thousands of pesos.
Source: Own calculations

The final issue is whether a generalization of VAT rates generates the extra revenue needed. For that purpose, the model is simulated assuming a uniform VAT rate of 16 percent ($\tau_{vat,i} = \tau_{vat,j} = 0.16$) and zero labor income taxes and subsidies ($\tau_n = T_{nf} = \eta = 0$). This parametrization is consistent with the social security reform proposed. The extra revenue out of value-added taxes is reported in Table 14.14. For convenience, the table also presents the costs of the reform.

Table 14.14

Estimated Fiscal Balance under USI (% of GDP)

	Alternative A	Alternative B
Total cost	4.99	4.47
Already spent	1.76	1.76
Amount needed	3.23	2.71
Extra revenue at 16% VAT rate	3.42	3.42
Compensations to the poor	0.24	0.24
Balance	–0.05	0.47

Source: Own calculations.

A major concern is the negative impact that a uniform VAT rate may have on poor households, as now food and medicines would be taxed. The proposal in Antón, Hernández and Levy (2012) contemplates a direct income transfer to the two poorest deciles in the population. To estimate the cost of such transfer, we take data from the income-expenditure survey in 2008 that indicates that about 6.9% of total private consumption goes to the first two deciles of the income distribution. The model suggests that a uniform VAT rate of 16% would subtract 418.4 thousand of million pesos from all households. These numbers imply that about 28.8 (=0.069*418.4) thousand of million pesos are taken away from the poorest households. This is exactly the amount that would be transferred to the poor in order to compensate them for the VAT increase.

Table 14.14 reports the cost of this transfer program to the poor in terms of GDP. Clearly, after taking into account all the costs the reform is financially viable under both alternatives. Here, we need to emphasize that these calculations are made only for the year 2008 and thus do not include dynamic issues, like changes in demographics and its associated epidemiological costs.

Finally, the effect of the social security reform on employment and wages is presented in Table 14.15. The second column displays the corresponding numbers from the calibrated model. Here, the formal sector's real wage is normalized to one under the benchmark. The third column illustrates the effect of a fiscal reform that keeps the current social security system in place. Notice that a uniform VAT rate of 16% increases informal employment (at the expense of formal employment) and decreases the real wage as the higher VAT rate partially translates to the consumer's price index.

Table 14.15

Social Security Reform and the Labor Market

	Calibrated	VAT reform under CSI and NCSI	VAT reform under USI
Legal salaried employment	12.29	11.66	25.61
Illegal salaried employment	7.8	7.94	0
Self-employment	18.93	19.42	13.41
Real wage index in formal sector	1.00	0.97	1.15

Notes: Employment is in million of workers. CSI: contributory social insurance; NCSI: non-contributory social insurance; USI: universal social insurance.
Source: Own calculations.

However, if the same VAT reform is implemented along with the USI scheme proposed here, the results would be reverted. In particular, formal employment might be roughly twice as large as under the benchmark and the real wage might increase by 15 percent, as CSI taxes are eliminated. Hence, the incentives to evade value-added taxes in the intermediate sector are more than offset by lower labor costs, and demand for salaried workers expands despite the higher VAT rate.

Remarkably, the social security reform brings a major correction in the relative prices between salaried versus non-salaried labor, and between the relative price of legal versus illegal salaried labor. This explains the substantial increase of formal salaried workers at the expense of self-employed workers in Table 14.15.[12]

More detailed work needs to be carried out, but the central message suggested by the model is unequivocal: it is feasible to implement a fiscal reform that increases VAT rates uniformly to 16%, and at the same time to provide all workers with social insurance. Such reform would increase real wages and maintain fiscal balance, even assuming no additional enforcement efforts by the tax authorities.

14.6. Conclusions

This chapter builds on Levy's (2008) proposal for a universal social security scheme. In particular, we estimate the hypothetical cost of such scheme for 2008 as well as the extra revenues generated after imposing a uniform VAT rate of 16 percent. The results suggest that the USI scheme is financially viable, even after taking into account a compensatory transfer to poor households as a result of the VAT increase. In addition, real wages in the formal sector might increase by 15 percent as a result of USI. This number should be interpreted as an upper bound estimate, given that the model assumes an inelastic labor supply.

These calculations are based on a static general equilibrium model, which takes into account the change in firms' behavior in a tax evasion framework. We acknowledge, however, that demographics and epidemiological issues should be taken into consideration, an aspect that we leave for the future research agenda.

Notes

1. We follow Kanbur (2009) and define formality with respect to "a" regulation. In this chapter we focus on social insurance, so the relevant regulation in this case is coverage of social security. Hence a worker is labeled as formal if she is enrolled in a contributory social insurance scheme according to law; otherwise, the worker is classified as informal.
2. In this chapter, we only present a sketch of this model. For details, see Antón, Hernández, and Levy (2012).
3. As of 2011, value-added taxes in Mexico apply to some goods and services at a rate of 16 percent. VAT is excluded from goods such as food and medicines, among many others.
4. In Mexico, salaried informal workers are illegal in the sense that CSI contributions must be paid by law but are evaded. In contrast, non-salaried informal workers are legal in the sense that they are not forced by law to comply with CSI taxes.
5. As this is a model for profit maximizing firms, government employees, and people engaged in religious activities are excluded from the analysis.
6. Naturally, salaried formal workers $L_{f,z}(K_z)$ are defined as the residual $L_{f,z}(K_z) = L_z(K_z) - L_{nf,z}(K_z)$ with the restriction $L_z(K_z) \geq L_{nf,z}(K_z)$.
7. The rate of compliance is defined as the ratio of the amount of taxes effectively paid by the firm over the amount of taxes that should be paid under full compliance of the law.
8. By this way, the intermediate-final good structure in the model gives place to a transmission mechanism of tax evasion between sectors, as in de Paula and Scheinkman (2010).
9. In Mexico, "other" income sources mostly refer to oil revenues.
10. In contrast, profits for small firms increase as they are able to substitute informal for formal labor, given the small probability of being detected by the tax authority.
11. There is a debate in the literature on whether *Seguro Popular* yields negative and significant effects on informality. For a review, see Duval and Smith (2011).
12. From the arbitrage condition (3), the informal wage rate also increases under USI's equilibrium. This brings down labor demand in the self-employed sector.

References

Antón, A., Hernández, F. (2010). VAT Collection and Social Security Contributions under Tax Evasion: Is There a Link?, Working Paper No. 480, Department of Economics, CIDE.

Antón, A., Hernández, F., Levy, S. (2012). The End of Informality in Mexico? Fiscal Reform for Universal Social Insurance, Washington, DC: Inter-American Development Bank.

Bosch, M., Campos-Vázquez, R. (2010). The Trade-offs of Social Assistance Programs in the Labor Market: The Case of "Seguro Popular" Program in Mexico, Serie documentos de trabajo del Centro de Estudios Económicos Working Paper No. 12.

Calderon-Madrid, A. (2006). Mobility of Workers between Formal and Informal Job Status: An Empirical Assessment of Earnings Variations and Exit Hazards in Mexico's Urban Labor Market, mimeo.

Calderon-Madrid, A. (2000). Job Stability and Labor Mobility in Urban Mexico: A Study Based on Duration Models and Transition Analysis, Inter-American Development Bank Research Network Working Paper No. R-419.

de Paula, A., Sheinkman, J. A. (2010). Value Added Taxes, Chain Effects and Informality, in: American Economic Journal: Macroeconomics, 2(4): 195-221.

Duval, R., Smith, R. (2011). Informality and Seguro Popular under Segmented Labor

Markets, mimeo.
Fiszbein, A. (2005). Beyond Truncated Welfare States: Quo Vadis Latin America?, Washington, DC: The World Bank, mimeo.
Gasparini, L., Tornarolli, L. (2009). Labor Informality in Latin America and the Caribbean: Pattern and Trends from Household Survey Microdata, in: Revista Desarrollo y Sociedad, 63: 13–80.
Gong, X., Soest, A., Villagomez, E. (2004). Mobility in the Urban Labor Market: A Panel Data Analysis for Mexico, in: Economic Development and Cultural Change, 53(1): 1-36.
Instituto Mexicano del Seguro Social (2005). Informe al Ejecutivo Federal y al Congreso de la Unión sobre la Situación Financiera y los Riesgos del IMSS 2004-2005.
Kanbur, R. (2009). Conceptualising Informality: Regulation and Enforcement, V.V. Giri Memorial Lecture, in: Indian Journal of Labour Economics, 52(1): 33-42 (an earlier version is available as IZA Discussion Paper No. 4186).
La Porta, R., López de Silanes, F., Shleifer, A., Vishny, R. W. (1998). Law and Finance, in: Journal of Political Economy, 106(6): 1113-55.
Levy, S. (2008). Good Intentions, Bad Outcomes: Social Policy, Informality and Economic Growth in Mexico, Washington, DC: Brookings Institution Press.
Maloney, W. (2004). Informality Revisited, in: World Development, 32(7): 1159-78.
Maloney, W. (1999). Does Informality Imply Segmentation in Urban Labor Markets? Evidence from Sectoral Transitions in Mexico, in: World Bank Economic Review, 13(2): 275-302.
Navarro, S., Schrimpf, P. (2004). The Importance of Being Formal: Testing for Segmentation in the Mexican Labor Market, mimeo.
Perry, G., Maloney, W. F., Arias, O. S., Fajnzylber, P., Mason, A. D., Saavedra-Chanduvi, J. (2007). Informality: Exit and Exclusion, Washington, DC: The World Bank.
Scott, J. (2010). The Failure of the Mexican Revolution, Mexico-City: CIDE, mimeo.
World Bank (2010). Doing Business Report 2010, Washington, DC: The World Bank.
World Bank (2005). Mexico: Infrastructure Public Expenditure Review, Washington, DC: The World Bank.

15

Alternative Ways of Pricing and Financing Social Insurance*

Robert Gillingham
Alain Jousten

15.1. Introduction

Social insurance systems vary widely in terms of coverage of workers and risks, financing sources and the structure and generosity of benefits. Latin America - the focus of this book - is no exception, with rather large differences in the design of national social insurance that are at least partially linked to differing paradigms regarding the role of social insurance. With respect to pensions, for instance, Chile has led the way toward privately managed, fully funded individual retirement accounts, while its neighbor Argentina recently abandoned its experimentation with such accounts and reverted to a more traditional defined-benefit scheme. Contribution/tax rates for old age, survivors and disability insurance range from 3 percent of wages in Honduras to 28 percent in Brazil (Table 15.1). For all social insurance programs combined, the contribution/tax rate ranges from 10.5 percent in Honduras to 44.8 percent in Colombia.

The predominant source of financing for social insurance comes from "deductions" from payrolls. These deductions are typically categorized as either "taxes" or "contributions," but - as discussed below - they share the characteristics of both. The confusion created by

* *The authors would like to thank the participants of the 6th IZA/World Bank Conference: Employment and Development (Mexico City 2011) and the editors of this book for helpful comments and suggestions.*

Table 15.1

Statutory Social Insurance Contribution/Tax Rates

	Old age, disability & survivors[a]			Other social insurance programs[b]			All social insurance programs		
Country	Employee	Employer	Total	Employee	Employer	Total	Employee	Employer	Total
Argentina	11.0	10.2	21.2	6.0	12.5	18.5	17.0	22.7	39.7
Bolivia	10.0	0.0	10.0	0.0	10.0	10.0	10.0	10.0	20.0
Brazil	8.0	20.0	28.0	0.0	1.0	1.0	8.0	21.0	29.0
Chile	10.0	0.0	10.0	7.6	3.4	11.0	17.6	3.4	21.0
Colombia	3.9	11.6	15.5	4.0	25.1	29.1	7.9	36.8	44.6
Costa Rica	3.7	8.2	11.8	5.5	9.3	14.8	9.2	17.4	26.6
Ecuador	6.6	3.1	9.7	2.0	7.3	9.3	8.6	10.4	19.0
El Salvador	6.3	4.1	10.3	3.0	7.5	10.5	9.3	11.6	20.8
Guatamala	1.8	3.7	5.5	3.0	5.0	8.0	4.8	8.7	13.5
Guyana	5.2	7.8	13.0	0.0	0.0	0.0	5.2	7.8	13.0
Honduras	1.0	2.0	3.0	2.5	5.0	7.5	3.5	7.0	10.5
Mexico	1.1	5.2	6.3	1.3	6.4	7.6	2.4	11.5	13.9
Nicaragua	4.0	6.0	10.0	2.5	9.0	11.5	6.5	15.0	21.5
Panama	7.5	3.5	11.0	0.5	8.3	8.8	8.0	11.8	19.8
Paraguay	9.0	14.0	23.0	0.0	0.0	0.0	9.0	14.0	23.0
Peru	10.0	0.0	10.0	0.0	9.6	9.6	10.0	9.6	19.6
Uruguay	15.0	7.5	22.5	3.0	5.0	8.0	18.0	12.5	30.5
Venezuela	4.0	11.0	15.0	0.5	2.8	3.3	4.5	13.8	18.3
Average	6.6	6.5	13.1	2.3	7.1	9.4	8.9	13.6	22.5
Minimum	1.0	0.0	3.0	0.0	0.0	0.0	2.4	3.4	10.5
Maximum	15.0	20.0	28.0	7.6	25.1	29.1	18.0	36.8	44.6

Source: US Social Security Administration (2011) and IMSS (2011).

Notes: [a] In some countries, the rate covers additonal programs.

[b] Includes Old Age, Disability and Survivors; Sickness and Maternity; Work Injury; Unenmployment and Family Allowances. In some countries, the rate might not cover all of these programs.

the use of the term "payroll taxes" further reinforces this confusion. Any analysis of how best to finance social insurance must thus start from an analysis of social insurance pricing: a decomposition of the insurance component (the true contribution) from the pure tax component (the true tax). Only then can an informed discussion about reforming financing mechanisms proceed. Such a discussion is indeed important for Latin America, where there is increasing urgency to develop a financing method that promotes efficiency in both the labor market and in the tax system.

Pricing clearly matters and can be a driver for reform. For example, the high degree of labor market informality in Latin America has often been attributed - at least in part - to the use of payroll levies to finance social insurance. Informality, in turn, has been identified as a drag on growth in the region (Perry et al. 2010). Levy (2010) has suggested the abandonment of payroll taxes as a mechanism for financing many categories of social insurance, arguing that universal benefits financed with consumption taxes will reduce the size of the informal sector and promote efficiency. Such arguments implicitly rely on the idea that social insurance acts like a pure tax and is thus not neutral with respect to individual decision making.

The purpose of this chapter is to identify and analyze the factors that determine the true tax rates inherent in the payroll financing of social insurance. Section 15.2 will start with a short description of the social insurance and tax systems in Latin America. Section 15.3 will lay out a framework for analyzing the inefficiencies created by the current structure of social insurance and social assistance programs and their current financing mechanisms. Section 15.4 will identify options for reforming the current programs to reduce inefficiency and discuss the option of eliminating contribution financing and transforming social insurance into a pure tax-and-transfer system. Section 15.5 will discuss the impact on informality.

15.2. Current Social Insurance and Tax Structures

15.2.1. Social Insurance Financing

As noted above, social insurance programs in Latin America vary widely (Table 15.1). For pensions, several countries have followed Chile in setting up funded individual accounts. These countries vary, however, in the manner in which they treat the unfunded legacy costs of the systems they replaced. Moreover, the unfunded liabilities for these legacy costs also vary widely. The pension contribution/tax rates need not be adequate to cover future benefit costs, especially without adjustment of retirement ages or benefit structures. Many other countries have maintained or reinstated pay-as-you-go, defined-benefit systems. Many of these systems also face serious financial problems, with cash flow deficits either already in place or forecast for the relatively near future.

Although most countries in Latin America have relatively low old-age (over 64) dependency ratios (Table 15.3 in Appendix A), these ratios are all projected to increase by a factor of three over the next forty years, as the impact of higher life expectancy and lower fertility kicks in. This will increase the financial pressure on the systems, with revenues shrinking and payouts increasing. This financial pressure can be absorbed in three ways. First, the government could dedicate an ever-increasing share of general tax revenues to plug the budgetary holes of the pension system to absorb the shortfall of revenues over expenditures – likely neither a viable nor desirable strategy. Second, structural cuts in the level and growth of benefits could help restore pension system finances. Finally, contributions and earmarked taxes could be progressively increased by either increasing rates or broadening the bases on which they are levied, adding to the concerns about their impact on informality in particular and efficiency in general.

Holzmann et al. (2004) estimated the unfunded pension liabilities for a number of the countries in Latin America. They focus on the cost that would be incurred if the system were shut down and all pension claims accrued to date were honoured. Depending on the maturity and sustainability of the system, the estimates could – under reasonable parameter assumptions – be greater than the infinite-horizon, open-group liabilities that are arguably more appropriate for pay-as-you-go pension systems. However, even taking that into account, as well as the fact that some reforms have taken place in recent years, the unfunded liabilities are quite formidable. They range from 40 percent of GDP for Peru to 330 percent of GDP for Brazil (using a 4 percent discount rate, the authors' central scenario).

The statutory contribution/tax rates also vary widely. These rates are an interesting, though imperfect indicator of the size of the social insurance system. Ideally, they should be adjusted for several factors, such as possible caps and floors in terms of taxable income, differences in population coverage that lead to differences in inherent risk characteristics of the covered populations and the system's deviation from pure budgetary balance.

The variation in statutory rates is even more pronounced for all other (non-pension) social insurance programs, ranging from zero contributions for several countries to 29.1 percent for Colombia. For instance, in Colombia, the payroll contribution/tax rate for sickness and maternity benefits (including both medical services and income replacement) is 16.5 percent. In Mexico, for a roughly comparable level of services, there is a lump sum contribution of 20.4 percent of the minimum wage (levied on employers) plus a combined employer/employee contribution rate of 2.45 percent of wages for those earning more than three times the minimum wage in Mexico City, and an even lower rate for those below this threshold. For medical services and any other part of the benefit package that does not vary with wages, any contributions or taxes beyond those, if any, that are required for benefit eligibility are economically speaking pure taxes.

In summary, the social contribution/tax rates vary widely across countries. Moreover, based on available evidence, today's tax/contribution rates are unlikely to be sufficient to meet future liabilities – even in those cases where they currently do allow social insurance budgets to break even. This latter fact makes a careful analysis of the funding and pricing of social insurance imperative, since additional funding requirements have the potential to significantly exacerbate the inefficiencies resulting from the current funding mechanisms.

15.2.2. Income Taxes and VAT

The contribution/tax rates for social insurance must be placed in the context of the other taxes in the economy. In particular, the VAT is often viewed as a substitute for payroll contributions/taxes for financing social insurance. At the same time, income taxes on wages earned in the informal sector can have a similar impact on incentives to operate informally as they also increase the labor tax-wedge. Table 15.2 presents some indicators with respect to the VAT and income tax.

Table 15.2

VAT and Income Tax Indicators

	VAT indicators				
	Standard rate	Revenue productivity ratio[a]	Revenue as share of GDP	Registration threshold (US$)	Income tax top rate
Argentina	21.0	48.0	7.2	37,655	35.0
Belize	10.0	88.2	7.4	37,500	
Bolivia	13.0	51.1	6.4		
Brazil	20.5	51.1	8.3		27.5
Chile	19.0	60.5	7.4	441,501	40.0
Colombia	16.0	43.1	5.5	36,921	33.0
Costa Rica	13.0	52.3	5.4	121,943	15.0
Ecuador	12.0	59.1	5.4		35.0
El Salvador	13.0	51.7	7.0	50,000	
Guatemala	12.0	46.8	5.4	7,059	31.0
Guyana	16.0			49,000	
Honduras	12.0	8.1	0.8	9,493	
Mexico	16.0	32.6	4.2	147,275	30.0
Nicaragua	15.0	51.7	7.3		
Panama	7.0	39.4	1.6	36,000	25.0
Paraguay	10.0	63.1	5.4	3,581	10.0
Peru	19.0	46.3		75,000	30.0
Uruguay	22.0	54.2	10.7	18,500	25.0
Venezuela	12.0	78.2	6.4		34.0
Average	14.7	51.4	6.0	76,531	28.5
Minimum	7.0	8.1	0.8	3,581	10.0
Maximum	22.0	88.2	10.7	441,501	40.0

Note: [a] Revenue productivity = Total VAT revenue as percentage of consumption, divided by the VAT standard rate.

Source: IMF VAT data base, KPMG (2011).

VAT – The standard VAT rate – that is, the rate applied in the absence of a particular preference for a good or service – ranges from 5 to 22 percent.[1] Many countries apply preferential lower rates on specific goods and services. While motivations for these preferential regimes vary, they generally encompass a mix of social goals – to reflect the different consumption patterns of and ease the burden on low-income households – and efficiency goals – that argue, for instance, for lower rates on goods and services that are labor-intensive or close substitutes for those produced in the informal sector. Comparable arguments are sometimes advanced for exempting some goods and services or some producers altogether from VAT. While the general impression might be that any reduction in VAT, be it by means of reduced rates or exemptions, will necessarily lead to lower tax burdens and thus losses in tax revenues, this is not necessarily so. Actually, it is easy to show that this only holds true if the special treatment is strictly reserved to the last link of the value creation chain; any exemption in the intermediate goods sector might have effects of unexpected sign and magnitude as the VAT loses its neutrality and can cause cascading of taxes. The mechanics are simple. Consider an intermediate goods producer whose sales are exempted. Since his output is *exempted* from the VAT, rather than *zero-rated*, he is ineligible for refunds on VAT paid to suppliers. He cannot claim back VAT paid on his purchases – this VAT thus accrues to the government. If his (VAT-subjected) customer sells the good on to a final consumer (e.g., after further processing), he charges VAT on the full amount as he will not be able to deduct the VAT that had already been paid by the exempt supplier and thus applies the VAT to the total sales price without any credit for upstream VAT paid. Thus, de facto on part of the transaction, VAT was levied twice, contrary to the structure of a VAT.

The revenue productivity ratio is defined as the actual revenue collected as a percentage of the revenue that would be collected if total consumption were fully taxed at the standard rate. Empirically, the average ratio turns out to be roughly 50 percent across a wide range of countries – meaning that only one-half of the theoretically potential revenue is realized (Figure 15.1). In other words, the effective VAT rate on total consumption is roughly one-half of the standard VAT rate. Efficiency is high in Belize, likely because most consumer goods are imported. The VAT is relatively easy to collect on imports, and thus compliance with VAT rules is high. The efficiency levels in Latin America are not unusual by global standards. As Table 15.2 demonstrates, revenue productivity ratios are low on average in the African region, and high on average in the Asia and Pacific region (in fact, the revenue productivity ratio in Fiji exceeds 100). In particular, the revenue productivity ratio in Latin America is only slightly lower than the ratio of 53.8 in the entire OECD.

Beyond rate differences, exemptions and simple compliance issues, other determinants matter, such as the threshold below which firms do not need to register with the VAT authorities or collect the VAT on their sales. The threshold is designed to improve administrative efficiency and reduce the burden on small firms. The exclusion of small and medium-sized enterprises (SME) from the VAT net by means of a registration threshold is fundamentally just a special case of VAT exemption. Any excluded SME that charges services or goods to a VAT-subjected customer can give rise to VAT-cascading. To minimize these cascading effects, and to improve incentives for SME to leave informality, numerous tax systems allow voluntary registration. This means that the taxpayers below the threshold have an option to register for and comply with VAT voluntarily. Table 15.2 provides VAT registration thresholds in Latin America expressed in annual USD turnover. However, if they sell to anyone other than final consumers, they "break" the VAT chain, and allow some *cascading* of the VAT if the firm to which they sell is above the VAT threshold. That is, the exempt firm will charge no VAT, but still pass on the VAT it has already paid to its customers. As with other tax and contribution parameters the threshold varies widely across the countries for which we have data.[2]

Figure 15.1

VAT Revenue Productivity Ratios

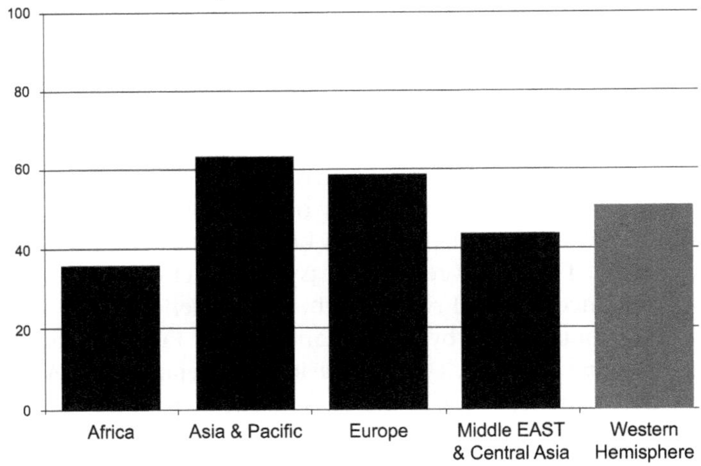

Source: IMF VAT data base.

Income tax – The final column of Table 15.2 details the top income tax rate for most of the Latin American countries. With the exception of Costa Rica and Peru, which appear to have essentially a flat tax, the top marginal rate in all of the countries for which we have data is at least 25 percent and ranges up to 40 percent. This is important, since income taxes will also provide an incentive for workers and firms to organize in the informal sector. As noted above, the true social insurance tax component is not the statutory rate, but rather the difference between the statutory rate and the true contribution rate that a worker would be willing to pay to receive the promised benefits. Consequently, a given statutory income tax rate will, in general, provide a stronger incentive for informality than a contribution/tax rate of the same level.

15.3. Problems with Payroll Financing of Social Insurance

15.3.1. Background

In analyzing the financing of social insurance, it is instructive to start with an analysis of private insurance. According to *Wikipedia*, "in law and economics, [private] insurance is a form of risk management primarily used to hedge against the risk of a contingent, uncertain loss. Insurance is defined as the equitable transfer of the risk of a loss, from one entity to another, in exchange for payment." Note the importance of the word "equitable" in this definition. The implication is that both the insurer and the insured are willing to shift risk in exchange for the specified payment. Certainly the analysis of private insurance markets is complex. The complexities arise from asymmetric information, leading to phenomena such as moral hazard and risk selection. These factors typically require a significant regulatory role to make certain that neither party can manipulate private insurance contracts. However, the underlying market principle still applies. A willing buyer and a willing seller agree to the transfer of risk in exchange for compensation.

An additional level of complexity is added when we add the word "social" to "insurance." The term "social insurance" is subject to a variety of denotations and connotations. For the purposes of this chapter, we follow the Actuarial Standards Board (1998, p. 1) in defining a social insurance plan as a government-sponsored program with all of the following characteristics:

- The program, including benefits and financing method, is prescribed by statute.
- The program provides for explicit accountability of benefit payments and income, usually in the form of a trust fund.
- The program is financed by contributions (e.g., taxes or premiums) from or on behalf of participants, which in some programs are supplemented by government income from other sources.

Investment income on program assets may also be used to finance the program.
- The program is universally (or almost universally) compulsory for a defined population, or the contribution is set at such a subsidized level that the vast majority of the population eligible to participate actually participate.

As defined above, social insurance shares many characteristics with private insurance. However, one key difference is that social insurance focuses on achieving social goals – for instance, breadth of population coverage or adequacy of benefits – and consequently focuses less on the balance of costs and benefits on an individual level, as in a private insurance contract. Pursuit of such “social” goals does not, however, mean that the entire population will benefit from adequate or sustainable benefits; sometimes only privileged subgroups, such as civil servants, will benefit from special and often costly social insurance schemes. Another difference with private insurance is that a social insurance program need not rely solely on (appropriately regulated) market forces to achieve its objectives. The problem, however, is that when social insurance programs use compulsion or subsidization to elicit participation, they risk distorting the behavior of program participants, reducing the efficiency of labor and product markets and crowding out pre-existing or potentially competitive private insurance.

15.3.2. Sources of Social Insurance Pricing Problems

As the previous section emphasizes, to the extent that a social insurance program can emulate a private insurance program – that is, that the worker would be willing to pay the required contribution rate in exchange for the program’s benefits – even if the program were not mandatory, the contribution would provide no incentive for informality. The “pure tax” component of a social insurance contribution is equal to the difference between the contribution and the amount the worker would pay without coercion to participate in the program. Even if the pure tax is zero, the social insurance contribution could distort individual behavior or create disincentives for work under certain conditions. For instance, individuals may want to retire earlier in the presence of retirement saving or stay longer on benefits if unemployment insurance is not tightly monitored or time-constrained.[3] Similarly, as in any life cycle problem, liquidity constraints might hamper an individual’s freedom of choice.

One reason why a mandatory pension scheme may be warranted is that workers may be short-sighted or time-inconsistent and, without coercion, will not save enough – or as much as they will later wish they had saved – for retirement. That said, the requirement that it is mandatory is prima facie evidence that the worker is unwilling to pay the full contribution. In this case, the mandatory aspect is welfare enhancing, but time inconsistency on the part of the worker – especially a young worker – may cause her to perceive the contribution as a tax.

The remainder of this section will discuss other reasons why a worker would not be willing to pay the required contribution – what we call "pricing problems" – with a special focus on the link between contributions and benefits. If the benefit from a social insurance program does not vary across workers, a contribution that varies with wages is a pure tax, at least on the margin. This problem is most obvious in the case of health insurance. The social health insurance "policy" is typically the same for all workers. Consequently, the marginal contribution/tax provides no benefit for the worker. If a worker has a private option for health insurance, all workers for whom the contribution is less than the premium in the private market would prefer to pay the contribution rather than buy in the private market – they are subsidized – but the marginal contribution is still a tax. In the absence of a private-market option, all workers for whom the contribution is less than their reservation price for the policy would be willing to pay.

A more perverse example – which occurs in private markets as well – is when the social insurance program includes a benefit that is of value to only a subset of the participants. For instance, maternity benefits – both medical and income-replacement – are of much greater value to workers who are of child-bearing age and want to have a family. When a social insurance program requires a benefit of this type, it creates a cross-subsidy, taxing some workers and subsidizing others. The problem can be even more complicated if both spouses are forced to buy maternity insurance. The second policy is redundant and a pure tax.

15.3.2.1. Inadequate Rate of Return

A special case of an insufficient tie between contributions and benefits occurs when the implicit rate of return on contributions is perceived by the worker to be too low. (For the moment, we consider only the direct link between contributions and benefits, although, as discussed below, policy interactions can affect the net rate of return on contributions.) This problem applies only to social insurance schemes within which benefits are tied to contributions - most notably pay-as-you-go pension schemes. As noted above, for social insurance programs with no link between contributions and benefits - such as health care - at least the marginal rate of return on contributions is zero.

The steady-state, sustainable rate of return in pay-as-you-go pension systems is the rate of growth of contributions. Under reasonable assumptions, this, in turn, is roughly equal to the rate of growth of GDP. In developed countries, where populations are shrinking and productivity growth is on the order of 1 to 2 percent, GDP will grow quite slowly. In South America, the population between 20 and 60 is expected to grow at an annual rate of only 0.3 percent between now and 2050. Even if these economies converge with the developed economies, the rate of growth of GDP is not likely to be high over the extended future. Moreover, additional adjustments in contributions and benefits will have to be made to account for increasing longevity (the population 65 and over in South America is projected to grow at an annual rate of 3.2 percent over the same period).

As a result of these demographic and macroeconomic trends, participants may well perceive the sustainable rate of return in pay-as-you-go pension systems as too low, reducing the contribution they would be willing to pay if the system were not mandatory. Funding can partially address this problem. However, funding generates problems of its own. For example, administrative charges in funded, individual account plans can be high, especially when many of the accounts are small, reducing the net returns in these accounts. While collective or group capitalization may help address this administrative cost issue, it creates new possibilities for cross-subsidization between individuals of the same or different generations and hence generates new behavioral distortions. As discussed below, funding of public pension schemes can augment returns, but incur transition costs, raise equity issues and create governance and principle-agent problems.

15.3.2.2. Conflicts with Social Assistance Programs

At the most abstract level, social insurance programs may suffer from moral hazard. Workers may believe that if they do not participate in social insurance, the government will still provide assistance in the event that they cannot afford to pay for needed benefits - including health care and income in old age - on their own. This type of conflict becomes more tangible when we consider the types of conflicts that exist now. A minimum pension, for instance, may not affect the marginal rate of return on pension contributions for higher-income individuals, but it will affect the average rate of return, making participation less attractive. The same minimum pension might however generate undesirable effects on the margin, reducing the incentives for individuals to work and save (see, e.g., Sefton et al. 2008). The same issue applies to social insurance for health care. Will society come to the aid of someone who needs medical care even if that person chooses to operate in the informal sector and not make social insurance contributions?

15.4. How Can Pricing Issues Be Addressed?

There are a number of steps that can be taken to mitigate the pricing problems that turn social insurance contributions into social insurance taxes. Most of these steps are standard suggestions for entitlement reform, but they have not been widely adopted, even in many developed countries. They are not, however, devoid of unintended consequences.

15.4.1. Tie Benefits More Closely to Contributions

For pay-as-you-go pension schemes, this can be done in several ways. For defined-benefit plans, the entire history of contributions - appropriately indexed - can be used to calculate the initial pension (see Appendix A for a description of the important dimensions of social insurance programs and definitions of important terms). This will reward all contributions at the system's rate of return, although this rate of return will differ, in general from financial market returns. To render the system financially sustainable in the long term, such a reform must be combined with a careful specification of replacement-rate accruals.

A second option is to implement notional defined-contribution (NDC) accounts within a pay-as-you-go system. This approach allows a pay-as-you-go scheme to emulate an individual retirement account pension system with adjustments to benefits endogenously occurring as contributions and the sustainable rate of return change. It has been implemented in a number of European countries (for instance, Sweden, Latvia, and Poland). Some implementation problems have been encountered, however. For instance, in Latvia, the interest paid on NDC accounts reflected (very high) short-term rates of growth in the wage bill rather than the long-run sustainable pay-as-you-go rate of return. This created overly optimistic expectations about likely rates of return and perceptions of unfairness relative to those already retired. Instead of addressing the fact that the rate actually paid was too high, the government supplemented pension payments to existing pensioners. The combination created serious fiscal problems in the wake of the financial crisis.

A third, and comparable alternative is to rely on a pay-as-you-go point system with endogenous adjustments to contributions and/or benefits (for instance, in Germany and France). In a point system, each worker collects annual earnings points in the proportion of his contributions to the average contribution during that year. All years of work and all extra contributions are thus rewarded in both an NDC and a point system, with the key difference being one with respect to the adjustment mechanism. While for NDC the adjustment occurs fully (and in a specific way) through the benefit side, adjustments in point systems can be more varied.

What these three approaches share is a more explicit link between contributions and benefits. However, the selection of the rate of return is crucial. Tying benefits more closely to contributions is clearly a step in the right direction, but it does not address the problem of low rates of return – actual or perceived – caused by (slowing) productivity growth and (less favorable) demographics and labor supply.

Old age, survivors, and disability schemes are analogous to "whole life" insurance policies. Participants save during their working years to provide income in retirement. At the same time, they receive several types of insurance to protect them against the risks of early death, disability, or longevity. Other social insurance programs are more analogous to "term life" or "property and casualty" insurance. The contribution protects the participant against the occurrence of certain risks on an ongoing basis, with no saving component. When the benefit is unrelated or only loosely related to wages, it is more difficult to tie benefits to contributions without requiring significant cross subsidies or social assistance. One can conceive of a social insurance program for medical care in which the maximum contribution is capped at the implicit premium for the health insurance policy. The question would then become how to address the needs of low-wage workers. Alternatively, the cap on wages subject to contributions could be set at a higher level to reduce the funding gap. This would create a relatively narrow wage band in which marginal taxes are high. Current plans that are largely uncapped, as for instance in numerous continental European countries and the United States, create massive cross-subsidies and marginal disincentives, as noted above.

15.4.2. Increase the Rate of Return on Pension Saving

The rate of return has important implications both at the aggregate and the individual level. We discuss both in turn.

In a pay-as-you-go pension system, the maximum sustainable rate of return is potentially quite low, especially as a country becomes more developed and fertility rates fall. In an ideal world without risk or with an exogenously given risk profile, whenever the actual rate of return on contributions is below the sustainable rate, there is room to increase it. However, setting it higher than a sustainable rate is problematic. Some social insurance systems, including in the United States, issue government bonds to social insurance trust funds when cash flow is positive. However, this is equivalent to using the cash surpluses as sources of financing, rather than net revenue.

Another alternative is to increase the degree of funding in social insurance programs. This creates transition costs; paying them requires fiscal discipline. Funding – and, in particular, diversification into riskier assets – is a mixed blessing, however. It can increase the rate of return in defined-benefit schemes, and the defined-benefit structure allows the rate of return to be smoothed across cohorts. However, it also creates a cross-subsidy from "lucky" cohorts, for whom the current rate of return would have been higher than average, to "unlucky" cohorts, for whom current rates of return would have been lower than average. In defined-contribution schemes, funding increases the average *expected* rate of return for most countries, because historical rates of return in diversified financial portfolios have been significantly higher than the projected pay-as-you-go rate of return. However, individual accounts provide much less risk sharing across cohorts (Appendix C).

Funding of public, defined-benefit schemes does not suffer from the same equity issue, but creates a different set of problems revolving primarily around governance. Prefunding pension plans can result in a substantial accumulation of assets. Currently, funded pension plans in the OECD, where most of the major systems are pay-as-you-go, hold a weighted average of 72 percent of GDP in financial assets. The vast proportion of these assets is privately held. If public pension schemes were funded, they would hold a much higher quantity of financial assets, begging several questions. What would happen if the public pension scheme owned a significant proportion of the marketable securities of private, domestic corporations? Is this socialism through the back door? Should the government owners of these assets vote their shares? If not, what are the implications of concentrating control among a subset of the owners of the corporations?

Although financial rates of return have in the eighties and nineties outperformed the pay-as-you-go rate of return, the situation is currently less clear-cut. Rates of return in financial markets have been historically low over the past 12 years, thus starting their fall well before the onset of the financial crisis of 2007. According to the OECD (2011), the real return on funded pension schemes averaged -1.4 percent per year from 2007 to 2010. This performance was largely driven by the financial crisis. However, rates of return have been depressed for over a decade (Appendix C). The real rate of return on the S & P 500 stock index averaged -1.9 percent from December 1999 through December 2011. This performance was even worse than that experienced in the Great Depression and the stagnation in equity markets during the 1970s. Whether real rates of return on equities will rebound to their long-run average – roughly 6 percent per year – is an open question that will have important implications for equity financing of pension saving.

At the individual level, the issue of the low perceived rate of return in pay-as-you-go pension systems can lead to substantial incentive and efficiency issues. For example, people might under-invest in annuity protection – that is, minimize their participation in annuity-based, pay-as-you-go schemes and shift into pure savings products with higher perceived or expected rates of return. This can leave them more exposed to both market and longevity risks. One option is to subsidize pensions products. This can take the form of the well-known tax incentives for pension savings, but also more controversial direct budget subsidies to the pay-as-you-go public pension system – such as, for example, in Belgium. The latter technique makes the system look like a hybrid between the two extremes of pure social insurance and pure social assistance (tax and transfer). While such a system might not be desirable from a macro point of view because of the risk that budgetary costs spiral out of control, it has the potential to correct incentive issues at the individual level.

15.4.3. Coordinate Social Insurance with Social Assistance

This step would require carefully structuring social assistance – minimum and universal pensions, health care requirements, etc. – to reduce its attractiveness as an alternative to social insurance. In other words, benefits would have to be low, eligibility requirements strict and targeting narrow. This approach increases the likelihood of "errors of exclusion" – denying benefits to someone who should have qualified with complete information – at the same time that it reduces "errors of inclusion."

Several countries have opted to go in the opposite direction in recent years. For example, the recently passed pension law in Egypt includes a universal old age pension equal to 18 percent of the economy-wide average wage. This greatly reduces the incentive for a worker – especially a relatively low-wage worker – to participate in the earnings-related pension system. The universal pension is slowly phased out, decreasing its negative impact, but it still provides support to beneficiaries with pensions greater than 54 percent of the average wage. Similarly, the recent pension reforms in Chile implemented a "solidarity pillar" that provides a universal minimum benefit and a solidarity top-up payment to workers who have not earned a sufficient pension under the individual account system. These operate in a similar fashion to the Egyptian plan, with a 37.5 percent tax rate on a worker's earned pension until the solidarity pillar is clawed back.[4]

15.4.4. Make Social Insurance a "Menu"

One other approach would be to make social insurance a menu of options – as could be justified as a protection against the uncertain length of a working life.[5] Workers could choose the combination that maximizes the value of social insurance to them. The problem with this approach is that it invites adverse selection and moral hazard. Workers choose the options with the highest net value, and the net value of individual components will vary across workers. No matter what price is set, the only workers who will choose an option are those with an expected gain. This in turn reduces cash flow. Setting higher prices simply changes the proportion of workers who select the option, but does not eliminate adverse selection. A real world example is the use of average "actuarial" adjustments for early retirement. Given asymmetric information, workers have more information about their life expectancy than the plan sponsors. Faced with a common adjustment factor for the whole population, workers with low life expectancy choose early retirement, while workers with high life expectancy do the opposite. Similarly, effectively allowing early retirement through unemployment insurance (as most notably in Belgium or France) or disability insurance (the best known example has historically been the Netherlands), there is also potential for moral hazard as people have little or even no incentive at all to keep on working or to reintegrate the labor market. Consequently, allowing workers to freely pick and choose from a large menu of options is likely to exacerbate financial stress. Reform simulations have shown that some of the most promising effects on system finances are associated with changes to the key eligibility ages – and thus limitations to the menu of choices (see, e.g., Gruber and Wise 2004).

15.4.5. Summary

In sum, a number of steps can be taken to reduce the difference between what a worker would be willing to pay for social insurance and the mandatory contribution. Of course subsidies can increase the incentive to participate, but only at significant fiscal cost. Social insurance cannot be priced as accurately as private insurance. It embodies social goals that conflict with private goals. Some pricing imprecision is necessary to achieve these social goals.

15.5. Implications for Informality

Some analysts – for instance, Levy (2010) – blame imprecise pricing of social insurance for high and increasing informality. Levy argues that society provides different types of social protection to workers in the formal and informal sectors, and that this dichotomy creates perverse incentives and has significant implications for investment and growth. There are two components to the argument. The first relates to the differences in social protection and their implications for informality. The second relates to the implications of informality for investment and growth. The arguments are carefully laid out and provide a foundation for a lot of additional work that is beyond the scope of this chapter. Rather, the rest of this section will discuss one aspect of the Levy framework: to what extent is the social insurance/social assistance framework in a country responsible for the degree of informality?

Figure 15.2 displays the degree of formality – defined as the active contributors to a pension scheme as a percent of the working-age population – by region. Latin America and the Caribbean are in the middle of the distribution, but still well above the worldwide average. As with every other region except North Africa, the number of pensioners as a percent of the population over 64 is higher than the degree of formality in the labor market. This occurs for several reasons, including the fact that workers need not contribute in every year to qualify for a pension and many current pensioners collect survivor benefits.

Figure 15.2

Social Insurance Coverage of Workers and the Elderly, 2000-2005

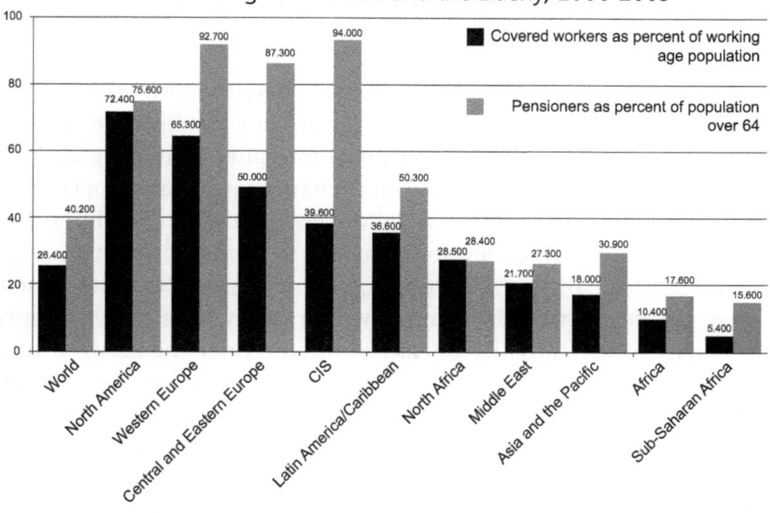

Source: ILO (2010).

The social insurance coverage for Latin American countries is displayed in Figure 15.3. All of the Central American countries except Belize and Costa Rica have low levels of formality. South American countries have higher levels of formality on average, although Colombia, Ecuador, Paraguay and Peru are relatively low.

Figure 15.3

Social Insurance Coverage

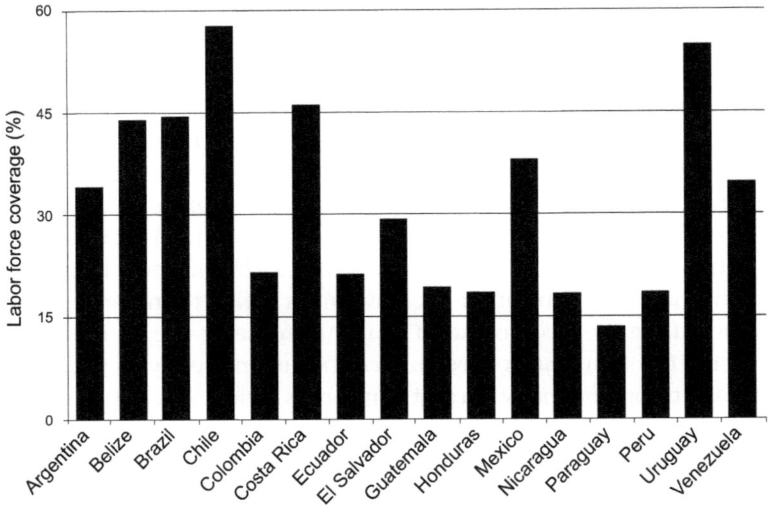

Source: ILO (2010).

Figure 15.2 implies that the relationship between formality and degree of development is very strong, just as Levy would argue. In fact, the correlation between the measure of formality used in Figure 15.2 and GDP per capita is 0.71 using an exchange rate measure of GDP or 0.70 for a PPP measure. The correlation, however, does not address the issue of causality. Does development lead to greater formality or vice versa? If informality retards growth, as Levy suggests, then it is much more pernicious than if it simply withers away with development. This part of the causality puzzle, however, is not the focus of this chapter. Rather, the question at hand is if social insurance schemes financed from payroll taxes and contributions cause informality.

A model of informality is beyond the scope of this chapter. The likely determinants of informality are complex, including not only the mechanisms for financing social insurance but its coverage, contribution rates, other taxes and regulations that can be evaded through informality, the will and capacity to enforce formality and cultural influences that can vary significantly across countries. The degree to which a restructuring of the pricing and financing of social insurance can mitigate informality is still an open question.

15.6. Implications for Financing Social Insurance

Even if payroll taxes and contributions do not cause informality, they can still be inefficient in achieving their program goals. Sections 15.3 and 15.4 discussed sources of inefficiency and possible mitigating steps. But would a greater reliance on consumption taxes be a more efficient way to finance social insurance. The VAT and other consumption taxes are pure taxes; there is no quid pro quo. It is impractical to try to apply a Ramsey rule to consumption taxes and set rates inversely proportional to demand elasticities. Even if it were practical, such a policy would have adverse equity implications, with higher rates on necessities that have a higher weight in the market baskets of lower-income households. Most countries in the region already go the opposite direction and give preferential rates to at least some necessities, reducing the revenue productivity ratio.

There are two ways to increase revenue from the VAT: increase the rate or increase the revenue productivity ratio. Both will have similar effects:

- Since they increase the effective rate of taxation, they will both change the relative price of consumption of market goods relative to leisure. The prevailing evidence is that this will have an impact on willingness to work, primarily on the extensive margin. Potential workers will be less willing to enter the labor force.
- Both will also have an impact on the excess burden of the VAT since the excess burden of a tax increases with the square of the effective tax rate. The efficiency of the VAT as a source of revenue will likely go down though the opposite may happen in some circumstances.[6]

As the VAT rate is lower than the social insurance contribution/tax rate in almost all of the countries in the region, reducing the contribution rate and increasing the VAT rate might seem like a good tradeoff given the above. However, any attempt to recoup all of the revenue collected through social insurance contributions would require a very large increase in the VAT. Moreover, as noted, the statutory social insurance rate is not the true tax rate. There is a quid pro quo for these contributions/taxes. Finally, if social insurance is dismantled and replaced with VAT-financed universal social benefits, should the VAT be increased even more to replace all labor taxes? This, again, would require significant rate increases and a change in the distributional incidence of taxes. If other labor taxes are left in place, will the perceived problems with respect to informality be solved?

There are several steps that could be taken before shifting all social insurance funding to the VAT and substituting flat universal benefits for the current array of benefits:

- Scale back and redesign current social insurance programs to reduce the tax component of contribution rates. This could involve some of the steps discussed in Section 15.4. Careful targeting and design of social assistance programs to minimize their conflicts with social insurance can help reduce the tax component of social insurance.
- Redesign will be most difficult where benefits have no obvious reason to vary with wages, such as in health care. In these cases, careful consideration of the government role will be needed to determine if the social objective is to have a universal, government-provided social insurance scheme or whether the goal could be narrowed to addressing the special needs of the poor (and – for health care – the very sick, for whom private markets may not provide an alternative). When a program is structured as a tax and transfer scheme, alternative financing mechanisms might be preferable to payroll contributions.
- In this context, consider the role that the government should play in the social insurance program. Should it be a provider, a source of financing or a regulator?

Appendix A: Defining the Structure of a Social Insurance Program

A Policy Dimensions

Typically, social insurance programs are characterized across two dimensions. The dimensions are easiest to understand in the case of a pension scheme.

- **Defined-contribution vs. defined-benefit** – Under a defined-contribution plan, a participant's access to benefits is related directly to the contributions she has paid into the system. In a defined-contribution pension system, workers build up either explicit or implicit retirement accounts that fund retirement. The benefit is determined by (1) the level and timing of contributions, (2) the rate of return on the retirement accounts and (3) the form in which benefits are realized, including annuitization, programmed withdrawals and lump-sum distribution. The relationship between contributions and benefits is transparent, which may improve compliance incentives. In a defined-benefit system, benefits are determined by a legislated or regulatory rule. In a defined-benefit pension scheme, benefits are typically determined

Table 15.3

Demographic and Macroeconomic Indicators

		Dependency rates		Life expectancy		Staturory pension age		GDP per capita	
	Population	Over 64	Under 15	Males	Females	Males	Females	Exch rate	PPP
Argentina	40.7	16.6	38.6	72.5	80.0	65	60	7,728	14,524
Belize	0.31	6.7	56.3	75.5	79.5	65	65	4,114	7,838
Bolivia	10.0	8.1	60.1	65.0	69.4	65	65	1,708	4,451
Brazil	195.4	10.2	37.7	69.9	77.2	65	60	10,453	8,360
Chile	17.1	13.4	32.6	76.2	82.3	65	60	14,289	9,485
Colombia	46.3	8.5	43.9	70.4	77.7	60	55	9,192	5,154
Costa Rica	4.6	9.5	37.1	77.1	82.0	62	60	10,795	6,488
Ecuador	13.8	10.7	48.8	72.9	78.9	60	60	7,573	3,570
El Salvador	6.2	11.9	51.6	67.5	77.0	60	55	7,355	3,623
Guatemala	14.4	8.1	76.9	67.9	75.0	60	60	4,832	2,689
Guyana	0.76	9.6	45.0	66.2	71.9	60	60	6,678	2,629
Honduras	7.6	7.3	62.5	70.7	75.6	65	60	4,340	1,892
Mexico	110.6	10.1	42.6	74.9	79.7	65	65	13,681	8,203

Table 15.3 (continued)

Demographic and Macroeconomic Indicators

	Population	Dependency rates		Life expectancy		Staturory pension age		GDP per capita	
		Over 64	Under 15	Males	Females	Males	Females	Exch rate	PPP
Nicaragua	5.8	7.6	56.6	71.5	77.8	60	60	2,924	1,082
Panama	3.5	10.4	45.0	73.8	79.1	62	57	11,798	6,951
Paraguay	6.5	8.5	54.7	70.7	74.9	60	60	4,560	2,265
Peru	29.5	9.4	46.6	71.6	76.9	60	60	8,626	4,363
Uruguay	3.4	21.9	35.3	73.7	80.7	60	60	13,101	9,364
Venezuela	29.0	8.6	45.5	71.8	77.7	60	55	12,184	11,383
Average	28.7	10.4	48.3	71.6	77.5	62	60	8,207	6,017
Minimum	0.31	6.7	32.6	65.0	69.4	60	55	1,708	1,082
Maximum	195.4	21.9	76.9	77.1	82.3	65	65	14,289	14,524

Source: US Social Security Administration (2011), US Census Bureau and IMF databases.

by multiplying a replacement rate by a pension base. The replacement rate is typically an accrual factor times years of service, and the pension base is a function of a worker's earnings history. Since this type of system often ignores the time path of contributions in calculating the replacement rate and the pension base, the tie between benefits and contributions can be quite loose.

- **Funded** vs. **pay-as-you-go** – In a funded system, the contributions of each cohort are invested to ultimately support the benefits that cohort will receive – that is, each cohort finances it own future benefits. In contrast, under a pay-as-you-go system, the contributions of each cohort are used to finance the benefits of earlier cohorts – that is, each cohort must rely on the contributions of subsequent cohorts for its benefits.

Although these dimensions are usually applied to pension schemes, they are relevant to a broad array of social insurance programs, including unemployment, disability, and health insurance plans. The choice of a characteristic along one dimension need not imply a particular choice along the other. Neither is the choice of a characteristic stark. Social insurance schemes can mix funding with pay-as-you-go financing. Moreover, the link between contributions and benefits can be quite strong, even in a defined-benefit system. These dimensions represent continuous rather than discrete choices, and Appendix B provides an example that clarifies this point in the context of defined-benefit and defined-contribution pension plans.

Both of the above dimensions relate to the behavioral incentives implicit in social insurance programs. In the extreme, a funded, defined-contribution pension plan is a retirement saving account. With a retirement saving account, a worker saves for retirement and, once that milestone is reached, can choose among alternative ways to disburse the balance of the account, including by purchasing an annuity. All aspects of the saving behavior are voluntary and involve arms-length transactions between the saver and financial service providers. The only difference between the retirement saving account and a funded, defined-contribution scheme is that the worker may be required to save a certain percentage of her income, and some ways of distributing the benefits – for instance, as a lump sum, might be proscribed. On the other hand, if the government imposes a payroll tax to pay for a defined-benefit health insurance plan that does not vary across workers, there is no relationship between the level of "contributions" and the level of benefit.

These examples suggest that another dimension is needed to define the structure of a social insurance program and its effect on behavioral incentives:

- **"Individual-pricing" vs. "tax-and-transfer"** – The funded, defined-contribution pension plan described above is an example of what we would call an "individual-pricing" social insurance program. Despite the fact that full freedom of choice might be curtailed, the choices available allow the participant to internalize the *individual* costs and benefits of alternative choices. Without any curtailment of choices, the participant would choose the plan that maximizes her welfare. With constraints on choices, the participant chooses a constrained maximum. The implicit "tax" or "subsidy" under individual pricing is the amount the participant is required to pay for her choice minus what she would be willing to pay without compulsion. With a "tax-and-transfer" social insurance program, the participant receives the benefit as long as she meets certain eligibility criteria. Once these criteria are met, any funding mechanism – even if it is ear-marked for the social insurance program – becomes a pure (marginal) tax. The participant receives nothing in return.

It is impossible to analyze the implications of a social insurance program for labor market efficiency or the efficiency of the tax system just by determining where the system falls on the defined-contribution/defined-benefit and funded/pay-as-you-go dimensions. A more detailed analysis is needed to evaluate (1) the extent to which a program imposes individual-specific costs on a program participant; (2) how much participants value the benefits provided by the program; and (3) the size of any implicit or explicit tax or subsidy on program participants. Only when this has been done is it possible to assess the impact of the taxes or subsidies on the labor market, the efficiency of the tax system and the fiscal stance of the government. This, in turn, will inform decisions on how to fund each social insurance program.

Appendix B: (Notional) Defined-Contribution vs. Defined-Benefit Systems

To see how the distinction between defined-contribution and defined-benefit schemes in pay-as-you-go plans is nebulous, it is useful to compare the notional defined-contribution (NDC) system of Sweden with the defined-benefit (DB) scheme in the United States. Although the Swedish pension system is categorized as "NDC" and the US system is categorized as "DB," the approaches are more similar than they appear. The Swedish system records and cumulates *contributions*, indexing the contributions by an internal rate of return that depends on the rate of growth of the contribution base and age-related wage and mortality patterns. The US system cumulates wages, indexing the wages by the rate of growth of the economy-wide average wage. If we hold the contribution/tax rate constant, the two are conceptually equivalent, but use a different rate of return. The US "average indexed monthly earnings" ($AIME$) can be rewritten as a notional account multiplied by a constant factor:

$$AIME = \sum_{i=1}^{35} W_i \prod_{j=1}^{35} (1 + r_j) = \frac{1}{35c} \sum_{i=1}^{35} c_i \prod_{j=i}^{35} (1 + r_j) = \frac{1}{35c} NDC,$$

where W_i and C_i are the wage and contributions in period i, r_j is the wage indexation factor in period j, c is the constant contribution/tax rate, and wages are averaged over the highest 35 years.

Neither the Swedish nor the US system gives participants access to the "accounts" they have accumulated. The Swedish system multiplies the value of the notional account by an annuity factor to get an initial benefit, and the US system multiplies the $AIME$ by a wage-based replacement rate (equivalent to multiplying the implicit NDC by an annuity factor equal to the replacement rate divided by $35c$). Both systems "redistribute" from high-mortality to low-mortality participants. The US system also redistributes from high-wage to low-wage participants. Each superimposes a mechanism to control benefits when financial sustainability is either threatened (Sweden) or breached (United States). The point of this comparison is to suggest that any system that imposes a close tie between contributions and benefits is implicitly an NDC system. The Swedish system differs most significantly from the US system in its automatic balancing mechanism, which does not rely on a cataclysmic event. The key question is whether an NDC system will face severe political hurdles if and when the internal rate of return in a particular country falls significantly below the rate of return in financial markets or the replacement rates from NDC accounts falls so far below the replacement rates prior to the introduction of an NDC system.

Appendix C: Financial Market Rates of Return

A Intercohort Risk Sharing

To evaluate the implications of individual retirement saving accounts on intercohort variation in benefits, we simulate the performance of individual accounts over the past 48 years. We assumed that workers made regular investments of $1,000 (in real terms) in an S&P 500 indexed fund over a 40-year working life. The only variable is the S&P rate of return, which is allowed to follow its historical path. The results of the simulation are displayed in Figure 15.4, where the horizontal axis displays the year in which the worker retires.

Figure 15.4

Variation in Performance of Individual Retirement Accounts

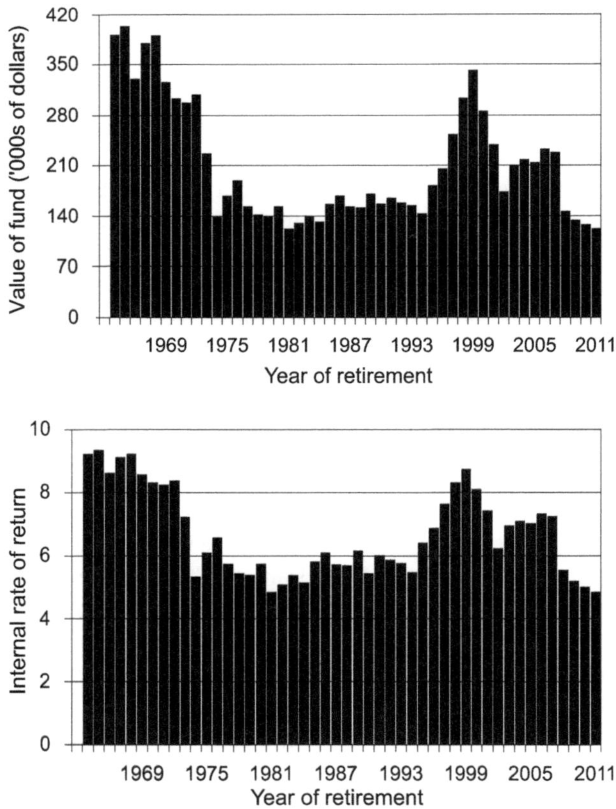

As Figure 15.4 demonstrates, there is a huge amount of inter-cohort variation. The value of the accounts vary from $121 thousand to $402 thousand. The real internal rates of return (IRRs) earned on the deposits (the single rate that yields the same account total) show similar variation, ranging from 4.8 to 9.3 percent per year. It is interesting to note, however, that the minimum IRR, which applied to those retiring at the end of 2011, is still higher than the pay-as-you-go rate for mature economies despite the meltdown in the S&P 500 over the past 12 years. In other words, even though the individual accounts produce "lucky" and "unlucky" cohorts, they still provide a reasonable rate of return even for unlucky cohorts.

B How Persistent is the Current Downturn in Equity Markets Likely to Be?

A key long-term concern for the efficacy of funding in increasing the rate of return to pension saving is whether the current downturn in equity markets is part of a structural break in the dynamics of economic growth and financial market returns. A relatively short drop in financial markets would have limited and specific effects, primarily for households that are either in or near retirement. On the other hand, a longer structural break would have serious consequences for the size and adequacy of retirement saving. The current market conditions are roughly similar to two previous periods in the 20th century, during the Great Depression and the 1970s (Figure 15.5). During the Great Depression, the value of an investment in the S&P 500 portfolio (assuming reinvestment of dividends) fell by almost 60 percent in three years. It recovered in year 8 only to fluctuate above and below its initial value until well into World War II. A similar investment at the end of 1968 never reached a similar low point, but it remained below its original value for 12 of the next 14 years. More recently, an investment at the end of 1999 lost 20 percent of its real value between December 199 and December 2011. Moreover, its value at this point is below the value of the investments in the earlier periods after the same number of years. The market recovered after the two previous stagnant periods. The question is if and how quickly it will recover now.

Figure 15.5

Real S&P 500 Total Return Index for Three Extended Market Slowdowns

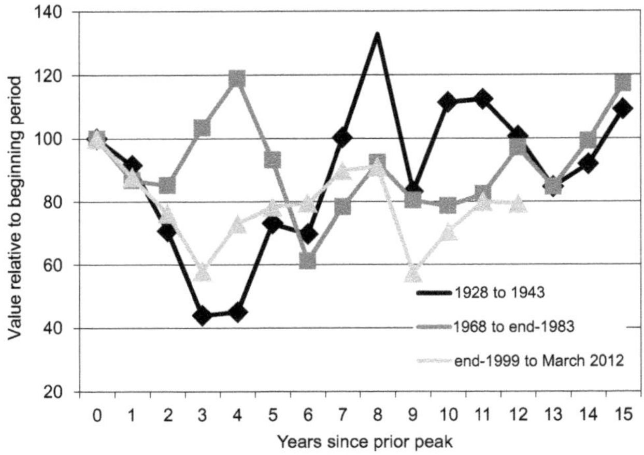

Notes

1 Notice that VAT rates can vary geographically within a country. In Brazil, for example, state VAT rates that are levied in addition to the federal rate vary from 7 to 25 percent.
2 Notice that VAT thresholds should be seen as an endogenous parameter, with thresholds likely higher for countries with less formalized business sectors, and likely lower for more formal economies, such as Chile.
3 For example, even if a pension system is fairly priced on average, it can still be non-neutral with respect to the early retirement decision. Similar considerations apply to unemployment and disability insurance. See, e.g., Gruber and Wise (2004) and Wise (2012) for a detailed discussion of incentive effects for a set of 12 developed countries.
4 See Fajnzylber (2010) for a discussion of the incentive effects.
5 See Diamond and Mirrlees (1986) for a theoretical framework.
6 For example, such an (unexpected) decrease in excess burden could occur if goods and services that are complementary to leisure are subjected to VAT as a result of a base-broadening exercise. See Corlett and Hague (1953).

References

Actuarial Standards Board (1998). Social Insurance, Actuarial Standard of Practice No. 32 (Document No. 062).

Corlett, W. J., Hague, D. C. (1953). Complementarity and the Excess Burden of Taxation, in: Review of Economic Studies, 21(1): 21–30.

Diamond, P., Mirrlees, J. (1986). Payroll-Tax Financed Social Insurance with Variable Retirement, in: Scandinavian Journal of Economics, 88(1): 25-50.

Fajnzylber, E. (2010). Incentives Under the New Pension Solidarity Pillar in Chile, mimeo.

Gillingham, R. (2003). Note on Pension Reform Objectives, mimeo.

Gruber, J., Wise, D. (Eds.) (2004). Social Security Programs and Retirement around the World: Micro Estimation, Chicago, IL, and London: University of Chicago Press and NBER.

Holzmann, R., Palacios, R., Zviniene, A. (2004). Implicit Pension Debt: Issues, Measurement and Scope in International Perspective, Bank Social Protection Discussion Paper No. 0403.

Instituto Mexicano del Seguro Social (IMSS) (2011). Informe al Ejecutivo Federal y al Congreso de la Unión Sobre la Situación Financiera y los Riesgos del Instituto Mexicano del Seguro Social, 2010-2011.

International Labor Organization (ILO) (2010). World Social Security Report 2010-2011, Geneva: ILO.

International Monetary Fund (IMF). VAT Data Base.

International Monetary Fund (IMF). World Economic Outlook Data Base.

KPMG (2011). KPMG's Individual Income Tax and Social Security Rate Survey.

Levy, S. (2008). Good Intentions, Bad Outcomes: Social Policy, Informality, and Economic Growth in Mexico, Washington, DC: The Brookings Institution.

Perry, G., Maloney, W. F., Arias, O. S., Fajnzylber, P., Mason, A. D., Saavedra-Chanduvi, J. (2007). Informality: Exit and Exclusion, Washington, DC: The World Bank.

Riber, H., Robalino, D. A., Walker, I. (2010). Achieving Effective Social Protection for all in Latin America and the Caribbean, Washington, DC: The World Bank.

US Census Bureau. International Data Base.

US Social Security Administration (2010). Social Security Programs Throughout the World: The Americas 2009, Washington, DC.

Wise, D. (Ed.) (2012). Social Security and Retirement around the World: Historical Trends in Mortality and Health, Employment, and Disability Insurance Participation and Reforms, Cambridge, MA: NBER.
World Bank (2005b). Enhancing Job Opportunities: Eastern Europe and the Former Soviet Union, Washington, DC.

Notes on Editors and Authors

Pablo A. Acosta joined the World Bank in 2008 where he works as a Senior Economist in the Social Protection and Labor Department, Latin America and the Caribbean Region. He received his Ph.D. in Economics at the University of Illinois at Urbana-Champaign in 2006. Acosta also holds a BA degree in Economics from the University of Buenos Aires (Argentina), and an MA degree in Economics from the National University of La Plata (Argentina). Prior to his position at the World Bank, he worked at the Andean Development Corporation (CAF, Venezuela), at the Ministry of Economy in Argentina, and the Foundation for Latin American Economic Research (FIEL, Argentina). His main areas of interest are labor social protection economics, migration, and international trade. In particular, he has studied extensively the impact of international remittances on migrant sending countries, at both macro and micro levels. He has also published work in the area of internal labor markets, and poverty and inequality analysis. Acosta has been a member of the IZA Research Fellow network since 2011.

Arturo Antón is Assistant Professor of Economics at the Centro de Investigación y Docencia Económicas (CIDE), Mexico. Before joining CIDE, he was a Senior Research Economist at the Central Bank of Mexico. His research interests are related to macroeconomics, business cycles, fiscal policy, and informal markets. He has published more than 10 academic articles and book chapters. He is a member of Mexico's National Research System and has been a consultant for international organizations such as The World Bank, the Inter-American Development Bank and the Economic Commission for Latin America and the Caribbean. Anton received his Ph.D. in Economics from Cornell University.

Orazio Attanasio is one of the Directors of the ESRC Centre for the Microeconomic Analysis of Public Policy and co-directs the Centre for the Evaluation of Development Policies (EDePo@IFS). He is a Professor at University College London, a Research Associate at the National Bureau of Economic Research (NBER), a Senior Fellow at the Bureau for Research and Economic Analysis of Development and a Research Fellow at the Centre for Economic and Policy Research. In 2001 he was elected Fellow of the Econometric Society and in 2004 Fellow of the British Academy. After getting a Ph.D. at the London School of Economics, Orazio taught at Stanford University and the University of Bologna. He was also a National Fellow at the Hoover Institution at Stanford and visiting professor at the University of Chicago. He was Managing Editor of the Review of Economic Studies and he is now one of the editors of the Journal of the European Economic Association. His current research interest focusses mainly on development economics, household consumption and saving behaviour, risk sharing and inequality.

Marcelo Bérgolo is a Research Assistant at the Instituto de Economía at the Universidad de la República (Montevideo, Uruguay) and doctoral candidate in Economics at the Universidad Nacional de La Plata. He is also a researcher at the Uruguayan' National Innovation and Research Agency (ANII), and associate researcher of the Center for Distributive, Labor and Social Studies (CEDLAS), Argentina. His main research areas are labor market policies, social protection in Latin America and Caribbean, and impact evaluation.

Richard M. Bird is Professor Emeritus at the Rotman School of Management, Senior Fellow of the Institute for Municipal Governance and Finance at the Munk School of Global Affairs, Distinguished Visiting Professor at the Andrew Young School of Public Policy in Atlanta, and Adjunct Professor at the Australian School of Taxation and Business Law in Sydney. He has lectured and published a number of books and many articles on tax and public finance issues, with special emphasis on the fiscal problems of developing countries. He is also a member of the Central Advisory Group of the International Centre for Tax and Development at the Institute for Development Studies. Bird spent several years with the Fiscal Affairs Department of the International Monetary Fund and frequently served as a consultant to the World Bank and other national and international organizations.

Mariano Bosch is a senior specialist at the Labor Markets and Social Security Unit of the Inter-American Development Bank (IDB). Since joining the IDB in 2011, he has been leading research projects in the area of labor markets, pensions and welfare policies. Prior to joining the Bank, he worked as a consultant for the World Bank and as an assistant professor at the University of Alicante in Spain. He has published articles in the area of labor markets and development in refereed journals such as American Journal: Applied Economics, Journal of Development Economics, World Bank Economic Review and Labor Economics. He has a Ph.D. in Economics from the London School of Economics.

Guillermo Cruces is the Deputy Director of the Center for Distributive, Labor and Social Studies (CEDLAS) at the Universidad Nacional de La Plata, Argentina (UNLP). He is also a researcher at Argentina's National Scientific and Technical Research Council (CONICET). His research is focused on labor economics, distributional analysis and social protection policies in Latin America and the Caribbean. He has worked previously for the UK's Department for Work and Pensions and for the Development Studies Division of the UN's Economic Commission for Latin America and the Caribbean. He has also been a researcher at STICERD, London School of Economics and Political Science, where he obtained an M.Sc. and a Ph.D. in Economics. He joined IZA as a Research Fellow in 2010.

M. Belén Cobacho is Senior Lecturer at the Universidad Politécnica de Cartagena (Spain), where she got her Ph.D. in Economics. Belén is a research associate to the Health Economics and Public Policies Research Group at Universidad Politécnica de Cartagena. Her main research areas and publications are related to Health Economics and Public Policies Assessment. She has published work in the area of health economics, inequality, discrimination and labor markets.

Alvaro Forteza is Full Professor of Economics at the Universidad de la República, Uruguay. His main research areas are social security and political economy. He received his Ph.D. in economics from Gothenburg University, Sweden, in 1996. He has been a consultant to the World Bank, the Inter-American Development Bank, the Economic Commission for Latin America and the Caribbean and International Labor Organization. He has published in several economic journals, including Journal of Macroeconomics, European Journal of Political Economy, Journal of Applied Economics, and Journal of Pension Economics and Finance.

Markus Frölich is Full Professor of Econometrics at the University of Mannheim and former Program Director of the IZA/World Bank research area "Employment and Development." His main research areas are labor market policies, unemployment, social protection, microfinance and econometric policy evaluation in Africa and Asia. He received his Ph.D. in economics from the University of St. Gallen in 2002. He is Associate Editor of IZA World of Labor, the IZA Journal of Labor & Development, the Journal of Business and Economic Statistics (JBES) and Co-Editor of Labour Economics. He has published in leading economic journals such as the Economic Journal, Journal of American Statistical Association, Journal of Econometrics, Journal of Royal Statistical Society, Journal of Applied Econometrics, Review of Economics and Statistics, among others.

Robert Gillingham has broad experience in the formulation and implementation of economic and fiscal policy at the domestic and international level. He has held high-level positions in the International Monetary Fund (IMF) and the United States Department of the Treasury. He also has broad expertise in economic measurement, with many years of experience in the United States Bureau of Labor Statistics. Since the end of 2009, he has been an economic consultant on topics ranging from tax and expenditure policy to addressing the fiscal challenges of aging populations. Recent clients include the International Monetary Fund, the World Bank, the OECD, the UK Department for International Development, the Caribbean Regional Technical Assistance Center and the Mercatus Center at George Mason University. He is also serving on an expert panel on the design of household expenditure surveys for the National Academy of Sciences.

Fausto Hernández Trillo is a Professor of Economics at the Centro de Investigación y Docencia Económicas (CIDE), in Mexico City, where he previously has served as the dean of the Economics Division. He has worked as an economist at the Mexican Stock Exchange, and has been Assistant General Director of Budget for the Mexican Federal Government. He has served as a regular consultant to the World Bank, the International Monetary Fund, the Interamerican Development Bank, and the governments of Mexico and Guatemala. Likewise has served as a consultant to the private sector and was a member of the Board of Directors of IXE, Financial Group in Mexico.

His research and teaching interests are in the area of international finance and public finance with a special focus on exchange rates, public debt management, credit ratings, finance of Subnational Governments and tax reform. Among others, he has published in the Journal of Empirical Finance, Journal of Development Economics, Review of Development Economics, World Development, Economía (LACEA journal) and Journal of Applied Economics. He is currently the editor of El Trimestre Economico, the oldest Spanish-speaking academic journal in the field.

Robert Holzmann directs the RH Institute for Economic Policy Analyses (Vienna), holds the chair of Old Age Financial Protection at the University of Malaya (Kuala Lumpur), is honorary professor at the Centre of Excellence in Population Ageing Research, University of New South Wales (Sydney) and Research Fellow at IZA and CESifo, and researches, teaches and consults internationally on pensions, financial literacy/capability, labor and migration issues. Before his return to Austria he was the Research Director of the Labor Mobility Program (Marseille Center for Mediterranean Integration) and Senior Advisor of the Financial Literacy & Education Program (Russia Trust Fund) of the World Bank. From 1997 to 2009 he was Sector Director and Head of the Social Protection & Labor Department leading, inter alia, the strategic and conceptual work on pensions and labor at the World Bank. Before joining the Bank he was professor of economics and the director to the European Institute at the University of Saarland, Germany (1992-97), and before professor of economics at the University of Vienna, Austria. As principal administrator at the OECD (1985-87), he wrote a comprehensive report on public pension reform in industrialized countries. As senior economist at the IMF (1988-1990), he was heavily involved in fiscal and social security issues during the initial transition from plan to market in Central and Eastern Europe.

Sergi Jiménez-Martin is an Associate Professor at the Universitat Pompeu Fabra. He is the Director of the Barcelona Microeconometrics Summer School (BMiSS, Barcelona GSE), and of the Chair LaCaixa-FEDEA Economía de la Salud y Hábitos de Vida at FEDEA. He is also the Scientific Coordinator of the evaluation of Social Sciences calls at AGAUR (Generalitat de Catalunya), and Member of the Scientific Board of Cuadernos Económicos de ICE.

Alain Jousten is Professor of Economics at HEC – University of Liège since 1999 and a Visiting Professor at Maastricht University since 2005. He is a co-director of CREPP and a co-founder of the Tax Institute, both at the University of Liège. He holds a Ph.D. in Economics from the Massachusetts Institute of Technology. His research centers on public economics and the economics of aging. He is interested in questions relating to the viability of pension systems, as well as the incentive issues created by them. Jousten has extensive experience in policy advice – both in a national and international setting. In 2006-2008, he served as a resident tax policy expert for the International Monetary Fund (IMF) in Washington DC. Jousten is a Research Fellow with IZA in Bonn, Netspar in Tilburg, and is a member of the panel of experts of the Fiscal Affairs Department of the IMF. He regularly acts as a referee for journals such as the Journal of Public Economics, the Journal of Public Economic Theory, and the IZA Journal of European Labor Studies. He previously held positions at the IMF, the Center for Operations Research and Econometrics in Louvain-la-Neuve, the Department of Economics at ULB in Brussels, and the Université des Sciences Sociales in Toulouse.

David S. Kaplan is a Senior Labor Market Specialist in the Labor Markets and Social Security Unit of the Inter-American Development Bank (IDB). Prior to joining the IDB in 2010, he worked as a research economist at the US Bureau of Labor Statistics; as an assistant professor of economics at the Instituto Tecnológico Autónomo de México; and as a private sector development specialist at the World Bank. He is an expert in labor markets in developing countries, particularly in the areas of labor regulations and social insurance. Kaplan has published research articles in journals such as the Journal of Economic Perspectives, the Journal of Development Economics, the Journal of Public Economics, and the Review of Economics and Statistics. He received a Ph.D. in economics from Cornell University in 1998 and has been a member of the IZA Research Fellow network since 2012.

Johannes Koettl is a Senior Economist at the Human Development Department of the World Bank's Europe and Central Asia unit. He has been working on issues related to labor markets, migration, health, and social protection at the World Bank since 2004. Previously he completed an M.A. in International Relations at Johns Hopkins University's School of Advanced International Studies and a Ph.D. in Economics at the University of Vienna and the Institute for Advanced

Studies (IHS) Vienna. His current work focuses on long-term care for the elderly, informal employment, and the social protection for international migrants. Koettl has been an IZA Research Fellow since 2011.

Hartmut Lehmann is Professor of Economic Policy in the department of economics at the University of Bologna and Program Director of the IZA research area "Labor Markets in Emerging and Transition Countries." He is a Research Professor at DIW Berlin, a WDI Fellow, a consultant to the World Bank and the OECD, and has been a consultant to UNDP. Lehmann was president of the Association of Comparative Economic Studies for the year 2013. Among his recent publications are articles in the Journal of Comparative Economics, Journal of Health Economics, Economics of Transition, Labour Economics, Research in Labor Economics, Journal for Labour Market Research and European Economic Review.

Phillippe Leite is an Economist at the World Bank's "Human Development Network – Social Protection and Labor (HDNSP)" Safety Nets & Transfers focus area. Before joining the network, he worked for the Development Research Group of the World Bank on determinants of poverty and inequality, poverty maps methodology, evaluation and design of social safety-nets programs to poor families, and micro-econometric simulation models. He holds a B.A. and M.Sc. in statistics (sampling and modeling) from ENCE/Brazil, M.Sc. in Economics from École des Hautes Études en Sciences Sociales (Paris) and is finishing his Ph.D. in economics from École d'Économie de Paris.

Santiago Levy has been Vice President for Sector and Knowledge of the Inter-American Development Bank (IDB) since 2008. From 2007 to 2008 he served as General Manager and Chief Economist for the IDB Research Department. From 1994 to 2000, Levy served as the Deputy Minister at the Ministry of Finance and Public Credit of Mexico, becoming the main architect of the renowned social program Progresa-Oportunidades that benefits the poor. Previous positions include President of the Federal Competition Commission and Director of the Economic Deregulation Program at the Ministry of Trade and Industrial Promotion. He is the author of more than 75 articles, monographs and book chapters on such diverse subjects as poverty reduction, competitiveness, foreign exchange policy, export imbalances, pricing, microeconomics and energy. His paper "Poverty in Mexico" won the 1992 National Research Prize in Economics awarded by the Bank of Mexico. He joined IZA as a Research Fellow in 2011.

David N. Margolis is a Research Director in economics with France's Centre National de la Recherche Scientifique (CNRS), assigned to the Centre d'Economie de la Sorbonne at the Université Paris 1 Panthéon-Sorbonne. From 2009 to 2012 he was on loan to the World Bank's Social Protection and Labor Department. Since 2001 he serves as an IZA Research Fellow. Margolis obtained his Ph.D. in Economics from Cornell University in 1993, and taught at the Université de Montréal before moving to France. His research interests include the econometrics of matched employer-employee data, labor market insertion of youth and welfare recipients, and integrating industrial organization with labor economics, often approached from a perspective that compares equilibrium outcomes across different countries.

Costas Meghir is Douglas A. Warner III Professor of Economics at the Department of Economics, Yale University, an International Research Fellow of the IFS, Fellow of the British Academy, Fellow of the Econometric Society and Research Associate of the NBER. He joined the IZA Research Fellow network in 1999. Meghir completed his Ph.D. at the University of Manchester in 1985. He was awarded the Frisch Medal by the Econometric Society in 2000. His research interests include Labor Economics and Public Finance with special emphasis on labor supply, wage determination, family economics and the economics of education, and development economics, with emphasis on informality and on early childhood development in poor communities. Recent work includes research on the impact of microfinance, on developing policies for early childhood stimulation and on understanding the effects of informality.

Alexander Muravyev joined IZA as a Research Associate in 2008 and is Deputy Program Director for "Labor Markets in Emerging and Transition Countries." Previously he worked as a Research Associate at the Department of International Economics of the German Institute for Economic Research (DIW Berlin), as lecturer at the School of Management, St. Petersburg State University and economist at the Russian-European Centre for Economic Policy in Moscow. He received his Ph.D. in Economics from European University Institute (Florence) in 2007 after completing his studies at St. Petersburg State University and at Stockholm University. His main research interests are in labor economics, economics of transition and applied microeconometrics.

Lucas Navarro is an Assistant Professor in Economics at ILADES-Universidad Alberto Hurtado. Prior to coming to Santiago, he held a full-time position at Queen Mary, University of London (2005-2008) and a part-time position at NYU London (2007-2008). His areas of interest are Labor Economics, Applied Macroeconomics and Development Economics. His research has been published in Economic Journal, Economic Letters, CEPAL Review and other Latin American journals. Navarro has a Ph.D. in Economics from Georgetown University.

Andres Otero is finishing his Ph.D. in economics at University College London. Affiliated with IZA since 2013, his fields of interest are applied microeconomics, labor economics and development economics. He works in structural econometrics, solving life cycle models in order to evaluate policy reforms and to understand how labor market incentives work. His current research is focused on the role of pension incentives in the creation of informal labor markets, inequality reduction and poverty alleviation. His short-term research agenda is threefold: to model structurally beliefs and subjective expectations about retirement in order to understand how they affect household labor market choices, to model retirees' withdrawal pension choices to estimate the effect of different pension modalities on the labor market participation and eventually to continue studying the differences between structural models and reduced form approaches.

Carmen Pagés is the Chief of the Labor Markets and Social Security Unit of the Inter-American Development Bank (IDB). Previously, she was a principal research economist at the IDB's Research Department and led key publications such as "The Age of Productivity: Transforming Economies from the Bottom Up," "Law and Employment: Lessons from Latin America and the Caribbean" (jointly with Nobel Laureate J. Heckman), "Good Jobs Wanted: Labor Markets in Latin America and the Caribbean," and "Job Creation in Latin America and the Caribbean: Recent Trends and Policy Challenges" (jointly with S. Scarpetta and G. Pierre). She has published extensively in leading academic and policy journals in the areas of labor markets and social security. Prior to joining the IDB, she was a senior labor economist at the World Bank from 2004 to 2006. She holds a M.A. degree in economics from the Universidad Autónoma de Barcelona and a Ph.D. in economics from Boston University. Pagés acts as an IZA Research Fellow since 2005.

Jamele Rigolini is a Senior Economist in the World Bank Chief Economist Office for Latin America and the Caribbean. His research interests include social protection, labor markets, institutions, and economic growth policies. Prior to joining the World Bank he was an Assistant Professor of Economics at the University of Warwick, where he taught classes on development economics and economic growth. He also worked for the Inter-American Development Bank, McKinsey & Co, and the International Union for the Conservation of Nature. Jamele Rigolini graduated in Physics from the Swiss Federal Institute of Technology (ETH) in Zürich, and holds a Ph.D. in Economics from New York University. Being an IZA Research Fellow since 2011, he has published in leading economics and development journals including the Journal of Public Economics, the Journal of Development Economics, and World Development.

David Robalino is the Manager Jobs Group and Lead Economist of the World Bank and the Co-Director of the IZA research area on "Employment and Development". Since joining the World Bank he has been working on issues related to social security, labor markets, and fiscal policy. Robalino has published on issues related to macroeconomics and labor markets, social insurance and pensions, health financing, the economics of HIV/AIDS, and the economics of climate change. More recently he has been working on issues related to the design of unemployment benefits systems in middle income countries, the extension of social insurance programs to the informal sector, and the integration of social protection and education/training policies to improve labor market outcomes. Prior to joining the Bank Robalino was a researcher at the RAND Corporation where he was involved in research on health, population and labor, and climate change. He also served on the Presidential Committee for Social Security Reform in Ecuador.

Alfono R. Sánchez Martín is Associate Professor at the Department of Economics of Universidad Pablo de Olavide (Sevilla, Spain). He has worked as a Research Fellow at the Bank of Spain, as a Marie

Curie Fellow at Imperial College London and as an external lecturer at IE University. He has also been an external consultant of the World Bank. His research is focused on life cycle behavior, pension economics and applied macroeconomics. He has published in academic journals such as the Journal of Applied Econometrics, Journal of Economics Dynamics and Control, Labour Economics and Fiscal Studies. He holds a Ph.D. in Economics from Universidad Carlos III de Madrid.

Michael Smart is Professor of Economics at the University of Toronto with a special research focus on public economics and micoeconomics theory. His various publications have been published in journals such as American Economic Review, Journal of Public Economics and International Tax and Public Finance. He served as Associate and Co-Editor of various journals. In 1999 he received the John C. Polanyi Prize in Economics from the Council of Ontario Universities for his outstanding early career research achievement.

Federico A. Todeschini has been Visiting Professor of Economic Analysis at the University of Alicante and a researcher at the Argentinian Fundacion Para La Integracion Federal (FUNIF). He has authored and co-authored several articles and working papers focusing on aspects of health economics, labor economics and finance. He advised govermental institutions in Argentina and served as a consultant to the Inter-American Development Bank (IDB). Todeschine received Ph.D. in Economics from the University Pompeu Fabra (2010), a Master in Economics from the University of San Andrés (2002) and his BA in Economics from the National University of Rosario (2002).

Michael Weber is an Economist with the "Human Development Network – Social Protection and Labor (HDNSP)" Labor Markets focus area where he heads the "Labor Regulation and Social Insurance" cluster. He has worked on the topics of unemployment insurance, employment services, labor regulation, school-to-work transition and youth employment. Prior to joining the World Bank in 2008, Weber worked at a joint research organization of the three main Universities of Vienna on research topics at the intersection between economics and computational statistics. He holds a Ph.D. in Social and Economic Sciences, a Master's in Economics as well as a Master's in International Business Administration from the Vienna University of Economics and Business Administration.

Index

A

B

F

I

J

L

M

R

S

T

U

V

W